FAME

BY CHANCE

*An A-Z of places that
became famous (or infamous)
by a twist of fate*

Donough O'Brien

FOREWORD BY

Peter Ackroyd

Art Directors: Tony Eckersley, Prue Fox,
Rosemary Gooding, Clare Sutton and Donough O'Brien

Additional contributors: Edmond O'Brien, Lucy Lerner,
John Akeroyd, Clare Sutton, Murrough O'Brien,
Jessica Whittaker, John Blake, Guy Whittaker, Robin Rhoderick-Jones and Liz O'Brien

Editors: Liz Cowley and Auriol Griffith-Jones

BENE FACTUM PUBLISHING

PUBLISHED IN 2003 by

Bene Factum Publishing Ltd
PO Box 33, Honiton, Devon EX14 9YD
Tel: +44 (0) 1404 831080 Fax: +44 (0) 1404 831090

ISBN   1-903071-05-4

Printed in The United Kingdom

CONTENTS

ACKNOWLEDGEMENTS

Innumerable people and organisations have helped to make this book possible, to verify these stories and to fill the pages with photographs, paintings and illustrations. Let us try to thank you. Please forgive us if we have left anyone out.

The Duke of Abercorn
Acol Bridge Club
Christopher Ailsby
The Hon. Brian Alexander
Earl Alexander of Tunis
Alexandra Palace Television Society
Brigadier Giles Allen
Marie-Claire Baroness von Alvensleben
Anne Frank House
Augusta National Golf Club
Bath Tourism Bureau
Battle Museum
Bayreuther Festspiele
Berchtesgaden National Park
Bite Communications
John Blake
Bletchley Park
David Blumlein
Bournville Village Trust
Michael Boyle
Broekema Advertising bv
Frank Brusca
Brooklands Museum Trust
Buck's Club
Bureau National Interprofessionel du Cognac

Capp Enterprises Inc
Cavalry and Guards Club
Cavern City Tours
Tony and Sylvia Chesterman
Colonial National Historical Park
Major General Patrick Cordingley
Madhu Chibber
Julian Chichester
Civic Museum of Cremona
Bryan Coode
Henry Dallal
Dendrology Society
Viscount Dupplin
The Eden Project
Edison National Historic Site
Antony Edwards
Edwards Air Force Base
Empire State Building
Elvis Presley Enterprises Inc
Serhan Ergezer
Eton College
Flatford Mill Museum
Fleet Air Arm Museum
Ford Motor Company
Giverny.org
Reg Green
Petra Guemmer
Colonel Tom Hall
Hamburg Chamber of Commerce
Henley Royal Regatta
Historic Charleston Foundation
Historic Pullman Foundation
Richard Holmes
Stephen Howarth
Indianapolis Motor Speedway

Irish Guards
The Jamestown Foundation
Sir John Keegan
Leavenworth Chamber of Commerce
Levi Strauss & Co
The Earl of Lichfield
The Linnean Society of London
Air Vice Marshal Robin Lees
Phil Liggett
Procter Lippincott
Danny Litani
Joerg Lofink
Louisiana State Museum
Sir Ian Lowson, Bt
Robert McAlpine Ltd
Sir William McAlpine Bt
Finbarr McCabe
Laurence McDonnell
Terry Marshall
Martin Luther King National Historic Site
Martin Van Buren National Historic Site
Moët & Chandon
Sir Stirling Moss
Mount St. Helens National Volcanic Monument
Museum of the Jewish Community of Venice
The Mustique Company
National Civil Rights Museum
National Historic Route 66 Federation
National Maritime Museum
Neanderthal Museum
Neiman Marcus
New York Historical Society
Nokia Corporate Communications
Nome Tourist Information
Nord-Ostsee-Kanal
Fionn O'Brien
O'Brien Trust
Ulick O'Connor
Marta Palfalvi
Maj (Retd) Iain Park-Weir
Chapman Pincher
Plant Talk magazine
Henry Poole & Co
Mary Pottorff
Air Commodore HA Probert
Gian Quasar
The RAF Changi Association
Raffles Hotel
Royal Aeronautical Society
Royal Air Force Club
Royal Botanic Gardens, Kew
Royal Military Academy Sandhurst
Royal Observatory Greenwich
Royal Yacht Squadron
Thomas Ryan
Asheesh Sangamneheri
The Savoy Hotel
Lt Col AJ Scott
David Sheffield
The Sherlock Holmes Museum
The Sixth Floor Museum at Dealey Plaza
Society for the Realisation of the Monument to the Children's Casualties of War
Chris Spring
Spring O'Brien Inc
The Staffordshire Regiment
Statue of Liberty National Monument & Ellis Island
Hugh Synge
Stowe School
Tolpuddle Martyrs Museum
J. Walter Thompson
John Urquhart
US National Park Service: (Alcatraz Island, Andersonville, Appomattox Court House, Fort Sumter, Harpers Ferry, Springfield Armory)
The Whitechapel Bell Foundry
General Chuck Yeager Inc

PICTURE CREDITS

Where possible picture credits have been given on the appropriate page, next to individual images. However where this is impractical, additional credits are acknowledged below. Every effort has been made to acknowledge all sources. If any pictures have, in error, not been credited, please contact the publisher.

CORBIS
4, 6 bottom left, 12 top left, 12 bottom right, 15 centre right, 15 bottom right, 17, 21, 24 bottom left, 32 top, 32 bottom left, 38 top left, 40 top left, 43 bottom right, 46 top left, 46 bottom left, 47 top right, 50 bottom left, 51 bottom right, 53 top right, 55 bottom right, 60, 61 top right, 61 bottom right, 64, 65 top right, 67 top right, 71 centre right, 74 top left, 77 centre right, 79, 85 bottom right, 86 top left, 95 top right, 96 bottom left, 102

top left, 105 bottom right, 106 top right, 107 bottom right, 109, 113 bottom right, 113 centre, 115, 120, 121 top right, 121 bottom right, 123, 124, 125, 127, 129, 132, 133, 136 bottom left, 137, 141, 145 top right, 147, 151 bottom right, 152 centre left, 152 bottom right, 153, 154 centre right, 155 bottom right, 156 centre left, 157 top right, 157 centre right, 166 bottom left, 166 centre right, 168, 174, 178 top, 178 bottom left, 182, 185 top right, 187 top right, 192 bottom left, 195 top right, 198 bottom right, 202 top left, 208 top right, 208 bottom left, 209, 210, 212, 213, 216, 217, 226 top left, 227 top right, 233, 240, 241 bottom, 244 top left, 251 bottom right, 254, 255 top right, 257, 260 top left, 260 centre left, 261 top right, 261 bottom right, 266 bottom left, 267 top right, 267 bottom right, 269, 273 top right, 275, 276 centre left, 280 bottom left, 281 bottom right, 285 top right, 285 bottom right, 287 bottom right, 289 bottom right, 293 bottom right, 295, 309 top right, 309 bottom right, 311 top right, 311 centre right, 313 bottom right, 314 centre left, 315 centre right, 316 bottom left, 317, 320, 327, 332, 337 top right, 337 bottom right, 338 centre left, 340 bottom left, 344 top left, 345 top right, 346 top left, 348, 349 top right and centre right, 350 top, 350 bottom left, 351 top right, 352 top, left & right and centre left, 352 bottom left, 353 bottom right, 355 centre right, 358, 359, 360, 362, 363, 366 bottom left, 367 top right, 367 centre right, 371, 372 bottom left, 374, 375, 376, 377 centre, 377 right, top, centre, bottom, 379, 380, 382 top left, 382 bottom left, 383, top right, 384, 386 bottom left, 387 top right, 388 centre left, 389 bottom right, 391 top right, 391 bottom right, 392 centre left, 394 centre left, 395 centre right, 395 bottom right, 398, 403, 404.

GETTY IMAGES
7, 59, 188 top left, 189, 190 244 bottom left, 266 top left, 277 bottom right.

HULTON ARCHIVE
9, 19 top right, 25, 29 top right, 30 bottom left, 31, 83 bottom right, 92 centre left, 104 top left, 126 centre, 139 centre left, 148, 170 top left, 192 top left,

200 top left, 204, 225 top left, 227 top right, 227 centre right, 232, 235 top right, 238, 283 top right, 283 bottom right, 289 top right, 292 bottom left, 296, 297, 300 bottom, 302 top left, 325 centre right, 334, 343, 373, 385 centre right (top), 399 top right.

POPPERFOTO
82, 104 bottom right, 246 top left, 390.

PRESS ASSOCIATION
51 top right, 158 top left, 158 centre, 228, 248 top left, 281 top right, 341, 400 left and right.

ROHR PRODUCTIONS
26, 30 top left, 246 bottom left.

DRAWINGS
BY MICHAEL GRIMSDALE
1 bottom right, 5 bottom right, 11, 14 bottom left, 20, 29 bottom right, 36 top left, 38 bottom left, 41, 45 bottom right, 48, 58 top left, 66 top left, 87 bottom right (bottom), 98 top left, 98 centre left, 108 centre left, 116 bottom left, 117 bottom right, 131 top right, 160, 165 centre left, 184, 203, 215, 220, 230 bottom left, 258 centre top, 272, 276 top left, 299, 333 top right, 339, 346 centre left, 387 bottom right.

MAPS
BY RHODA & ROBERT BURNS
Bermuda Triangle, 49 bottom left, Chisholm Trail, 90, Great Hedge, 170 bottom right, San Serriffe, 319, Silk Road, 330.

Other photographs by Tony Eckersley, Donough O'Brien, Hugh Synge and Marie-Claire Baroness von Alvensleben

AUTHOR'S NOTE

This book was born in an Irish pub. On holiday in Dublin, my wife Liz and I had just visited Clontarf, where Brian Boru had defeated the Danes a thousand years ago, and then looked at the General Post Office, scene of the Easter Rising in 1916. Over a drink later, we began to think about the places all over the world that only became famous because something dramatic had happened there; battles, disasters, artistic centres, even mythical places.

I have a strong suspicion that Liz wishes she had never become so enthused, because the research, writing, picture research and art direction about so many places has been a huge and even obsessive task. My younger son, Edmond was even heard to say to friends that his father had been *'faming at the mouth again'*.

I also have a confession to make. I did not write all 380 of the stories, only 305 of them. Let me thank my contributors, Edmond O'Brien, Lucy Lerner, John Akeroyd, Clare Sutton, Murrough O'Brien, Guy Whittaker, Jessica Whittaker, John Blake, Barry Palin and Liz O'Brien, who also acted as a critical editor and was a very patient wife.

We realise that this is a book to be dipped into and that readers will have their own special interests. So we have usually added to each story a list in red of places of a similar nature.

Many people have kindly helped us to make the stories as accurate as possible. If there are still some factual mistakes the Publisher would like to hear about them so that changes can be included in future foreign editions. We would also value ideas for further places which our readers feel are worthy of 'Fame by Chance'.

FOREWORD
by Peter Ackroyd

The sense of place is one of the most important in human consciousness. I call it the territorial imperative by means of which a certain area or neighbourhood exerts a formidable influence upon the lives and activities of those who inhabit it. Most religions harbour a sense of sacred place which, in many instances, is part of the landscape and of the earth itself. Other cultures have seized upon some spot as the seed or origin, and reverenced it accordingly.

Yet I do not remember reading an anthology of places that became famous quite by chance, whether that chance arrived in the form of a sudden disaster, a murder, a food, even a strange breed of dog. This book contains many such stories of fortuitous association, fascinating and surprising in equal measure.

I was not surprised by the origins of Big Ben, Bedlam, Harley Street, Downing Street and Savile Row, but I still learned, for example, about Abbey Road's musical heritage, and about Hampstead's Acol Road which gave millions of bridge players their conventions. Some of the narratives have a more serious import, such as those concerned with the taming of malaria, the vital significance of salt, the horrors of genocide and secret murder, the effects of terrorism and the fatal changes in warfare. Yet there are also more amusing, and possibly more surprising histories. Here the reader will discover the real location of the first hamburger, how Tin Pan Alley created pop music, who picked up the first rugby ball, why Fray Bentos was named after a monk, how Kitty Hawk was not the site of the Wright Brothers' famous flight and why Botany Bay never actually saw a convict.

The author has also examined how our 'conventional villains' have made places famous by chance: Hitler, Stalin, Eichmann, Genghis Khan, Dracula, Al Capone, Milosevic, and Osama bin Laden. At the same time, the decisions of some of our traditional 'heroes' are scrutinised – in certain cases controversially – Churchill, Wellington, Clive of India, Mountbatten, Jack Kennedy, Martin Luther King, Charles Darwin and Elvis Presley, as well as 'false' heroes like George Custer and J. Edgar Hoover.

I am convinced that the power and significance of place will come to be recognised as a serious topic for research and theoretical disquisition. This book is an unusual and compendious addition to the literature of famous topographies.

PETER ACKROYD

Writer and poet Peter Ackroyd is the author of *The Great Fire of London*, *The Last Testament of Oscar Wilde*, *Hawksmoor*, *Chatterton*, *Dickens*, *T.S. Eliot, a life*, *The Life of Thomas More*, *London: the Biography* and *Albion, the origins of the English imagination*.

ABBEY ROAD
England

Year after year, people travel from all over the world to be photographed walking across a humble pedestrian crossing in North London. Why? To emulate the Beatles on the cover of their last and most successful album, *Abbey Road.* It is, therefore, most fortunate that the Beatles decided against their first choice of title, *Mount Everest,* named after the brand of cigarettes that their sound engineer happened to be smoking. On the whole, it is easier to stroll across a 'zebra' crossing than to

ABBEY ROAD NW8
CITY OF WESTMINSTER

climb a 29,000 ft mountain in Tibet.

For the rest of the world, Abbey Road was on the map forever. For the musical world it always had been. The footpath from Lisson Grove to Kilburn Abbey had become a fashionable road by the 1870s, and Number 3 was a smart nine-bedroom residence. It was this house that was purchased by The Gramophone Company in 1929 and extended to become the greatest recording studio in the world. Two years later, coinciding with the merger of The Gramophone and Columbia companies to become EMI, the studio was opened by the composer Sir Edward Elgar. He was the first of many giants of music to play and record here. Classical legends like Menuhin, Pablo Casals, Sir Thomas Beecham, André Previn and Elizabeth Schwarzkopf were to follow, along with jazz greats like Fats Waller, Johnny Dankworth and Ella Fitzgerald. In 1944,

Glenn Miller made his last recordings there with Dinah Shore before his tragic air crash. And then there were the comedy stars like Noël Coward, Morecambe and Wise and Peter Sellers, dancers like Fred Astaire, and creators of musicals like Tim Rice and Andrew Lloyd-Webber, all of whom performed at Abbey Road.

But most people would now connect Abbey Road with the explosion of pop music, a culture which relaxed the formal dress code at the studio and removed the staff's long white coats that had once momentarily foxed Winston Churchill into thinking he had entered a hospital! Not only did the Beatles virtually make it their home. The list of other stars is endless, as is the string of No. 1 hits that emanated from this address. Tommy Steele, Cliff Richard, Connie Francis, Cilla Black, Manfred Mann, The Seekers, Gene Vincent, Stevie Wonder, Pink Floyd, Elton John; all of them and many more added to the Abbey Road legend.

Paul McCartney loved the place so much that he not only used it for his post-Beatles group 'Wings' – and especially their hit *Mull of Kintyre* – he actually reproduced 'Studio Number Two' at his home in 1977, a replica with exact and uncanny detail.

And year in, year out, the fans keep trooping across the most famous pedestrian crossing in the world.

See: Brazil, Carnegie Hall, Cavern, Mull of Kintyre, Tin Pan Alley

Ringo   *George*   *Paul*   *John*

1

Disasters always seem more terrible when children are the innocent victims of the folly, crimes or neglect of their elders. So it was with Aberfan. At 9:15 am on Friday 21st October 1966, on the last day before half-term, the infant children at Pantglas Junior School in this little Welsh village, one of dozens of close-knit coal mining communities in the Welsh valleys, had just returned to their classes after singing the hymn 'All Things Bright and Beautiful'.

Suddenly, they looked up from their books as a mysterious and deafening sound came closer and closer. Hidden by the fog, one of the huge Merthyr Vale Colliery waste tips that loomed over the valley, Number Seven, was sliding down towards the village. Watched helplessly and with total horror by the tip workers, the mountain of slurry – 'in great black waves, making a noise like a jet plane' – first demolished a terrace of trim little cottages, smothering their inhabitants. Roaring over the railway embankment at fifty miles an hour and loaded with boulders, railway trucks, trams and trees, the thirty foot high wall of wet and suffocating slurry then hit the waiting school, filling the classrooms with a substance 'like black toothpaste'. A horrible silence fell. Desperately, the people of Aberfan began to claw at the muck to save their trapped children. The miners quickly came back up out of the pit to find their women, blackened by mud, digging with bleeding bare hands. Strong men – fathers, miners, firemen and police – many of them weeping, dug all day. Parents pushed forward, desperate for news of their children, but no-one was brought out alive after 11 o'clock.

Right: A policeman carries out one of the small bodies

144 had died. 116 were children aged between 7 and 10 – half the school. Five of their teachers perished, and the most poignant discovery was the Deputy Head Master, found dead with his arms around the little bodies of five children.

Soon, the terrible grief turned to anger. It emerged that Tip Number Seven had been built on a stream, contrary to the National

MELVIN PARRY COURTESY OF THE WESTERN MAIL AND ECHO

Coal Board's own directives. For three years, the water had quietly saturated and undermined the mountain of waste. The tip had started to slide, sometimes 10 feet at a time, and on the very morning of the disaster the anxious Charge Hand had ordered all tipping to be stopped. Too late.

During angry scenes with the Coroner, parents demanded that he should declare that the children had been 'buried alive by the Coal Board'. *The Court of Inquiry declared that the Coal Board was* 'guilty, not of wickedness, but of ignorance, ineptitude and failure of communications'. It was not the last example. When the Coal Board at last removed the seven tips, they had the nerve to send the bill for £150,000 to the voluntary Aberfan Disaster Fund. It took until 1997 for the bereaved to get their money back.

DAILY POST LIVERPOOL

Whole generation of children buried as Aberfan slag tip hits village school

200 FEARED LOST UNDER MAN-MADE MOUNTAIN

Premier flies to disaster area

MY KID BROTHER IS DOWN THERE...

Councillor gave a warning in 1964

ACOL ROAD
England

In every corner of the globe, people play card games. The origin of cards is slightly obscure, but thought to have been invented in China around the 8th or 9th century. They then spread through the Islamic world, before being imported into Europe during the Crusades. Some games are international, like Poker, Canasta, Rummy and Solitaire. Some are specific to countries, like Belotte in France, Scopa in Italy and Skat in Germany.

Among the many games that were created was Whist, invented in England, probably in the early 16th century. It became very popular in the 18th and 19th centuries, spreading around the world. In the late 19th century, probably in Turkey, somebody had the idea of putting a *dummy* (or non-playing hand) on the table, and Bridge was born. The new game spread back into England in the 1890s, when a new feature was added: the auction. This early version of the game, Auction Bridge, introduced the bidding, where each side competed to choose the *trump suit*. Auction Bridge was refined by the American Harold Vanderbilt, who introduced a more sophisticated method of scoring, and improved the rules for the Auction. Out of this grew the modern game of Contract Bridge which quickly became more popular than Auction Bridge.

Bridge is a highly mental game, which helps to develop mind skills and memory. It has the advantage that it can be very competitive when played at national or international level, yet also can be played in a more social atmosphere. One of the most recognised international players is the Egyptian movie star Omar Sharif.

In Britain, Bridge rivals angling and golf as a participant hobby. It has millions of players, most of whom play by the 'Acol System'. This system of bidding is now standard in British tournament play and widely used in other parts of the world. There are Acol Bridge clubs from Chicago to Cyprus, but few Bridge players even know why they use the word 'Acol.'

Omar Sharif

The origin comes from the bidding system created by a group of players that included Maurice Harrison-Gray, Iain Macleod (later to be Conservative Chancellor of the Exchequer), John Marx, Terence Reese and S J Simon. Many of the ideas broke away from the early writings of the American Ely Culbertson. And the reason that it was called Acol was because it was first devised in 1934 in the small North London bridge club in leafy Acol Road, off the Abbey Road in Hampstead. By 1936 it dominated Bridge.

IAIN MACLEOD M.P.

BRIDGE IS AN EASY GAME

describes the Acol system which is now played by nearly all the leading players in Great Britain

The first book to explain the Acol system was written in 1952 by Iain Macleod, already a Member of Parliament. Everyone thought that he would be a future Prime Minister but he died prematurely.

Left: Acol Road off the Abbey Road in Hampstead

There is still an Acol Bridge Club, which is now in nearby West End Lane. It is something of a magnet for Bridge players, with a thriving Bridge school. Some enthusiastic overseas visitors are known to call the Acol Bridge Club 'almost as soon as they get off the plane'.

See: Abbey Road, Aintree, Ascot, Brooklands, Cowes, St Andrews, Wimbledon

After the assassination of Julius Caesar, two men appeared to have delivered Rome from its seemingly endless period of civil war. They had both been close to Julius Caesar; Octavian, his great nephew, and Mark Antony, his good friend. They pursued Brutus and Cassius, Julius Caesar's killers, and avenged his death at the battle of Philippi in 42 B.C. The Roman world was carved up between Antony, Octavian, and the nonentity Lepidus. Loosely speaking, Octavian controlled the west and Antony the east.

But the sufferings of the Roman people were far from over. The world would once again be turned upside-down, this time not by the murder of a dictator, but by a love affair, one of the most famous and destructive in history. Antony, during his command in the east, fell for the Queen of Egypt Cleopatra. As William Shakespeare put it: *The triple pillar of the world transformed into a strumpet's fool'*.

Cleopatra was famed for her powers over men. She had in the past won the heart of Julius Caesar, mothering his child, Caesarion. Her actual beauty was questionable and there was plainly something more, as Shakespeare has Enobarbus describe:
'Age cannot wither her, not custom stale Her infinite variety. Other women cloy The appetites they feed, but she makes hungry Where most she satisfies; for vilest things Become themselves in her'.

More attractive than her physical charms was her intelligence. She spoke nine languages and was also a trained mathematician. Some have seen the relationship as political; Cleopatra providing Antony with ships and men. However, his dedication to her, even when the relationship was politically

In 1963 Elizabeth Taylor portrayed a more beautiful Cleopatra than was probably the case.

The film Cleopatra went horribly overbudget. The director Joseph Mankiewicz was heard to say:

'I am not biting my fingernails. I'm biting my knuckles. I finished the fingernails months ago'.

disastrous, reveals the truth. He really was, as Dryden would say, prepared to throw it away *'all for love'*.

The reaction to the affair back in Rome was one of outrage, especially due to their debauched lifestyle, which Octavian's propaganda machine did much to highlight: *'too besotted with lust and drink to think either of his friends or of his enemies'*.

Conflicts between the two previous allies escalated. Even the attempted reconciliation at the Treaty of Brundisium, including the political marriage of Antony to Octavian's sister, Octavia, was not enough to prevent the inevitable. The world was, as it were, 'not big enough for the both of them'. Antony broke the final taboo, not only by marrying Cleopatra despite being wed to Octavia, but also by celebrating in Alexandria a 'triumph', one of the most sacred of Roman military processions. Seizing his opportunity, Octavian brushed aside Lepidus, who had always been closer to Antony, and put the final nail in the coffin of Antony's public image by reading his will publicly. It stated that he wished to be buried in Egypt, even if he died in Rome. Patriotic Romans were appalled, and their loyalty clearly lay with Octavian, who later wrote: *'The whole of Italy of its own free will swore allegiance to me and demanded me as the leader in the war in which I was victorious at Actium'*.

Events came to a head in open conflict. Attempting to return to the safety of Egypt, Antony and Cleopatra were cornered, low on supplies, at the naval battle at Actium, Akri, in north-west Greece. The battle was, in fact, fairly bloodless, as Antony's men defected to what was obviously the winning side. Antony and Cleopatra fled, but pursued relentlessly by Octavian and denied any chance of a peaceful settlement, the two lovers killed themselves.

For his love, Antony had lost the support of the Roman people, and thrown away his share in the known world. Octavian became its undisputed ruler. Though he constitutionalised his position, (and brought the Senate into government once more, being granted the name Augustus – 'venerable' – for doing so), he now had control of the world. Augustus, by his victory at Actium, had destroyed the Roman Republic, and created the Roman Empire.

See: Armageddon, Delphi, Elba, Ibiza, Lesbos, Olympos, Pompeii, Rubicon, Venice

ACTOR'S STUDIO
New York, USA

It was probably the rising young star, Marlon Brando, who first drew the world's attention to 'The Method'. This was a technique used by the Actor's Studio, on Broadway at 46th Street, New York, in the heart of the theatre district. The studio was not a school but a workshop for professional actors – founded by Elia Kazan, Cheryl Crawford and Robert Lewis in 1947. Under the direction of Lee Strasberg, it became a major centre for US acting, a 'laboratory', where trained actors could work, free from the pressures of a production.

Lee Strasberg had been inspired by the Russian Stanislavsky's system – particularly with the part concerned with the actor's *'work on himself'*. 'The Method' stresses inner motivation and psychological truth.

Throughout the forties and fifties it was *the* place to study and be discovered. The most talented actors, directors, and playwrights in America vied for attention in classes that often included celebrities like Noël Coward, Laurence Olivier, Joan Crawford, and members of the Kabuki and Moscow Art theatre companies.

In addition to Brando, other famous products of the Actor's Studio were Ann Bancroft, Jane Fonda, Joanne Woodward, Geraldine Page, Jack Lemmon, Montgomery Clift and Paul Newman, who later became President of the Board of Directors, with Al Pacino as one of the artistic co-directors.

Perhaps a less likely visitor to the Studio was Marilyn Monroe who, in 1960, described how she used to go on Tuesdays and Fridays, as well as attending Lee Strasberg's private classes.

'I think Lee changed my life more than any other human being. That's why I love to go to the Actor's Studio whenever I'm in New York. My one desire is to do my best, the best I can from the moment the camera starts until it stops. That moment I want to be perfect, as perfect as I can make it'.

Sadly, Marilyn Monroe ended up far from perfect, very insecure, dependent on drugs and, as a result, sometimes horribly un-punctual, and a real strain on the rest of the production team.

Susan Strasberg went on to be Marilyn's mentor, on the one hand blamed for many of her excesses, while in fact desperately trying to keep her on the straight and narrow. Laurence Olivier, the finest actor of his generation, had the misfortune to be cast opposite Monroe in *The Prince and the Showgirl*, which she produced and therefore controlled, and he ended up hating both her and 'The Method'.

But all in all, the influence of the Actor's Studio was a significant contribution to the art of acting.

See: Big Apple, Broadway, Dallas, Desire, Texas School

Marilyn Monroe, famous Studio pupil

AGINCOURT
France

How slowly some lessons sink in, however painful those lessons may be. Three times did France, with five times the population, suffer defeat at the hands of the English during the Hundred Years War, a conflict which lasted from 1337 to 1443 and which covered the reigns of no less than five English and five French kings.

It may have been snobbery, with the French knights in expensive armour only willing to test their chivalry against their peers, their social equals on the English side. Nobody else mattered, least of all the archers, to them an ancillary force of social inferiors. Tragically, they had entirely missed the point.

The longbow was a formidable weapon, carefully carved from a stave of yew, its heartwood compressing and its sapwood tensing. An experienced archer could fire fifteen steel-tipped arrows a minute capable of penetrating armour at 350 yards. The 150 lb draw required great strength, and yeoman archers were required to train regularly (the brand new sport of golf was banned as a distraction from archery practice!) A disciplined body of English archers could fill the sky with lethal arrows.

The French chronicler Froissart had recorded the deadly effect at Crécy in 1346. *'And ever still, the Englishmen shot where they saw the thickest press. The sharp arrows pierced the knights and the horses, and many fell, both horse and man. And when they were down they could not rise again, the press was so thick that one overthrew another'.*

Many of France's finest nobleman had been killed at Crécy, with tiny English losses. Only ten years later, Poitiers had been much the same.

Decades had passed and now King Henry V of England with 6,000 men, many weakened by disease, was facing more than 25,000 Frenchmen near the little village of Agincourt near Calais. 5,000 of the English were archers.

It is not as if the French did not understand the threat. They had modified their armour and had even learned to cut off the index and middle fingers of English prisoners, preventing them from using a bow. The English archers would raise these fingers to show that they were still free and able to fight, hence the mocking two-finger salute that persists to this day.

But somehow the French proceeded with an over-confident plan of attack. Squeezed in a narrowing valley between two woods, their massed dismounted men-at-arms were the first to receive the English arrow storm, which had the intended effect of goading the French cavalry into charging. Under a shower of 40,000 arrows, most of these never even reached the lines of sharpened stakes protecting the archers. Maddened and wounded horses smashed back through the waiting men-at-arms. These then advanced, but were so densely pressed they could hardly raise their weapons. And all the time the deadly arrows struck. Bodies piled on bodies.

When the confusion was at its worst, the archers laid down their bows, waded into the floundering charge, and attacked the French, many lying helpless in the mud, with swords, axes, and even the mallets they used for hammering stakes into the ground. The French army collapsed into total chaos, retreat and surrender.

With the controversial slaughter of many of the French prisoners, once again a whole generation of French

Fame by chance. Henry could have chosen a dozen other places for the battle.

Laurence Olivier at Agincourt in the stirring film 'Henry V', which revived Britain's morale during World War II

6

aristocracy was wiped out, souring relations with France for years. Killed were the French commander, Charles D'Albert, and 500 members of France's noble elite, along with 5,000 other French knights. The English lost less than 200 men.

Not for three centuries, with the advent of the machine-gun, would a weapon be capable of destroying its enemies so easily, however brave. Indeed in the years after Agincourt, English commanders frustrated with the low hitting power, range and rate of fire of the flint-lock musket, tried to bring back the longbow. Too late. Nobody knew how to use them any more.

See: Bayonne, Somme

AINTREE
England

In 1839, seventeen riders took part in the first 'Grand Liverpool Steeplechase' at Aintree. They galloped four miles across open countryside, jumping banks, hedges and three brooks.

Nobody may remember the name of the winner, but the name of one loser is recorded forever.

One of Britain's best-known riders, Captain Martin Becher, was in the lead when he was thrown by his mount 'Conrad' into the brook, where he sheltered from the other horses thundering over his head. He later coolly remarked, *'I had not realised how dreadful water tastes without whisky in it'.*

By 1847, the name of the race was changed to 'The Grand National', and its popularity grew – as did its reputation – as a race that steadily removed horses by attrition.

Aintree's Becher's Brook has earned an especially notorious reputation, not because it is the tallest jump, but because the horse lands six foot nine inches lower than where it takes off. This is tricky enough the first time round, but really difficult on the second circuit when horses and riders are exhausted.

The race is one of the most popular events in Britain's sporting calendar and, because so many horses fail to finish, millions of people place bets who would never normally be seen anywhere near a betting shop. With thirty fences to cross, the chances of things going wrong are very high, and only seven favourites and four joint favourites have won in the last century. In 1928, out of 42 starters only two horses crossed the finishing line, the surprising and surprised *'Tipperary Tim'*, was the 100-1 winner.

The horses that do well in the Grand National tend to be mature and experienced – nine year olds have won 34 times. Two horses stand out; *'Manifesto'*, which raced eight times and won in 1897 and 1899, and *'Red Rum'*, which won in 1973, 1974 and 1977, coming second in 1975 and 1976.

In 1989, Becher's Brook was modified to make it slightly less dangerous, but it is still feared by jockeys, and is still the most famous jump of the most famous race in the world.

See: Ascot, Brooklands, Cowes, Henley

THE ALAMO
Texas, USA

'God and Texas – Victory or Death'.

In some ways, Colonel William Travis achieved both victory and death at the Alamo.

For most Americans, the battle of the Alamo was a simple case of a few very brave Texans making a last stand against overwhelming Mexican odds.

As with much of history, it is rather more complicated than that.

The dusty little fort that so transfixed Texas, America and the world had started life as a Franciscan mission, San Antonio de Valero, and later became known as 'El Alamo', the Spanish word for cottonwood. To understand why so dramatic a battle occurred here, one must first understand the history of Texas and the two men who created it, Stephen Austin and Sam Houston. It was Stephen Austin's father, Moses, who conceived the idea of helping the Spanish to populate the province of Texas with the *'right kind of Americans, steady, responsible, law-abiding farmers'.* As an impresario, he promised to provide 300 families who would become Spanish citizens, and at least pretend to be Roman Catholic.

Moses duly died, and young Stephen swore to continue his mission. With enormous difficulty he established his 'Colony', only to hear the disastrous news, for him, that the Mexicans had risen against the Spanish and he would have to re-negotiate with the new revolutionary masters in Mexico City.

He struggled for eleven months to create a colonisation law as political power kept shifting, but he succeeded and returned to his colony just in time to stop it dissolving.

Soon things improved, with corn and more importantly, cotton, thriving on the rich soil. But there were danger signs. Other, less responsible and more speculative impresarios were given licences by the Mexicans. The original 'Old Three Hundred' were joined by 16,000 Americans by 1830 – three times the local Mexican population. Worse were a number of very rough and turbulent people that Austin had promised to keep out – the *'Leatherstockings'*, some on the run, 'GTT' (*'Gone to Texas'*). And these were impatient of Austin's sensible and conciliatory approach to the Mexicans.

Sam Houston had lived with the mysterious Cherokee Indians as a child, been a successful soldier, and at 34 Governor of Tennessee until a failed marriage. He had also survived as a politician after publicly beating a fellow Congressman. Passionate about Texas, he was to play a crucial role in the coming months.

Back in Mexico City, things had deteriorated. The vain and ambitious General Antonio López de Santa Anna had grabbed dictatorial powers, and the visiting Austin was imprisoned. He implored the Texans not to react, and to maintain peace. But the Texans

intercepted messages revealing that Santa Anna planned to attack, and the 'Texas Revolution' began, with a first tiny victory by William Travis. What is more, Stephen Austin soon returned from prison a changed man, exclaiming, 'Santa Anna is a base, unprincipled, bloody monster. War is our only recourse.'

For the Texans, several successful battles culminated in the humiliating surrender at San Antonio of Santa Anna's brother-in-law, General Cós, with 1,100 men. Only Houston seemed to understand the likely reprisals for such a victory. He knew that the invasion would come straight up the 'Camino Real' and through the Alamo, which he ordered blown up and abandoned, so that the Americans could use their long rifles and mobility in open country. But it was not to be. His friend, Jim Bowie (famous for the Bowie Knife) did nothing to implement Houston's strict orders to evacuate, and stayed where he was. Then Travis rode into the fort and took command of the regulars, and soon the legendary hunter and Congressman Davy Crockett added his Tennessee sharpshooters to the tiny garrison.

And so it was that 183 Texans faced 5,400 Mexicans.

For 13 days the fort was bombarded by artillery, with Travis's heroic messages reaching a disorganised, helpless Texas and the outside world. The guns moved ever closer and, finally, to the sinister music of the *Degüello*, signalling 'no quarter', the final assault by thousands of Mexican troops began. In 90 minutes, despite their individual

Davy Crockett and the last moments of hand-to-hand fighting

bravery, all the Texans were dead. A widow, her baby and a servant rode into Houston's camp, and he had to rally his dispirited forces. Santa Anna resumed his advance. At Joliad, he murdered 352 Texans who had surrendered, stacking and burning their bodies like cordwood, and marched on. But the over-confident and self-styled 'Napoleon of the West' foolishly split his forces, and was beaten by Sam Houston and an infuriated army of Texans shouting 'Remember the Alamo' at the battle of San Jacinto.

In 1846, when Texas opted to become a state, war broke out and Santa Anna was again defeated. And, in 1848, the United States, perhaps cynically, went on to gain California, Arizona, Nevada, New Mexico and Colorado.

Some might say that's how the West was really won.

See: Camerone, Chisholm Trail, Dallas, Los Alamos, OK Corral, Texas School Book Depository, Waco

ALBERT SQUARE
England

Radio and television 'soap operas' started in America, so named because the earliest ones were aimed at housewives and were sponsored by the detergent companies.

It is curious and amusing to contrast some soap operas from America and Britain. *Dallas* and *Dynasty* were full of glamorous, beautiful, wonderfully dressed and impossibly rich people. *Coronation Street* and *Eastenders* are full of very ordinary, working class and rather

unglamorous people, who happen to be much more human and believable. So it may be no coincidence that the British shows are still going strong, long after their US counterparts have become nostalgic memories.

Granada's *Coronation Street* started in December 1960, in black and white of course, and amazingly went out live for quite a time. Twenty six years later, the BBC launched *Eastenders*. 'Albert Square', as part of the fictitious 'Borough

Above: 'The Queen Vic' pub is the centre of life in Albert Square.

Below right: Steve McFadden and Barbara Windsor as Phil and Peggy Mitchell

of Walford, E20', comprises one of the biggest television sets in the world. The BBC's top designer, Keith Harris, spent weeks in the real East End of London to help him recreate its unique atmosphere at Elstree Studios in Hertfordshire. In May 1984, the site was cleared and the building of 'Walford' started, based on a cardboard model. Roads and pavements were laid, and steel frames held up the fronts and sides of buildings that were soon to be familiar to millions of viewers. Scrapyards were raided to buy up authentic window frames and doors, while many of the finished buildings were 'distressed' and weathered to make them grittily realistic. Over the years, the shops and businesses in the famous set have changed hands as often as in a real High Street. A chip shop, video store, bistro, nightclub and pizza parlour have all come and gone and sometimes returned again.

We are often reminded that Eastenders is a soap, because other places in London, or indeed the rest of Britain, are hardly ever mentioned. If the *Eastenders* do ever venture beyond the confines of Walford, invariably, it is to go 'Up West' (for a night out or to go shopping) or to Southend or Manchester (on a more permanent basis).

The main source of action in The Square is the only pub that anyone ever visits, 'The Queen Vic'. This venue sees more entertainment than a circus and a funfair put together. Buy half a pint and often get a free punch-up with it. It is here that 'Dirty Den' and gin-swilling wife Angie were the first landlord and landlady, and where, when they moved on, daughter Sharon took over. One of the most memorable scenes was when Sharon's taped confession that she had slept with husband Grant Mitchell's brother, Phil, was played to the shocked ears of the entire residents of Walford – and to Grant himself. Needless to say, there were a few choice words spoken, and some violence on Grant's part. It wasn't the first time 'The Queen Vic' had seen a showdown like that, and undoubtedly, it won't be the last.

Albert Square has seen almost all of the dramas that affect everyday life; more pregnancies, affairs and weddings than bacon butties served in the caff, accidents, divorces, abortions, deaths, murders, homosexuality, robberies and many misunderstandings. Sensitively tackled and informative story lines have included

AIDS, rape, breast cancer, child abuse and teenage pregnancy. Naturally, the characters always have a special way of dealing with their tragedies, with a nice cup of tea, or a pint of beer at 'The Vic'. (Americans have commented about our soaps that 'it is amazing how everyone is always sitting around consuming fluid').

Watched by over fifteen million viewers in Britain and millions more overseas, Albert Square has become a comforting, familiar and very real place. One wonders how many fans wander round the real East End trying to find it.

ALCATRAZ
California, USA

Of all the fearsome prisons in the American penitentiary system, surely the most evocative must be 'Alcatraz'. For 80 years, until 1933, the rocky island in the middle of San Francisco Bay had been used by the U.S. Army as a fortress and then as a military prison, earning its name 'The Rock'. In 1934, the Federal Government decided to open a maximum-security, minimum-privilege prison to deal with the most incorrigible inmates in the prison system, and to show the public that it was serious about stopping the rampant and highly publicised crime wave of the 1920s and 1930s.

There are many myths surrounding 'The Rock'. The first is that it was only for famous criminals. While some of the most notorious – like Al Capone, George 'Machine-Gun' Kelly', Alvin Carpis and 'Doc' Barker – did serve in Alcatraz, the fact is that most of the prisoners were actually not high profile gangsters, but simply those who refused to conform to the normal rules in other prisons. Many were also considered to be violent or dangerous, or were major escape risks. Thus, Alcatraz became a dumping ground for the prison system. If a man did not conform in another institution, he was sent to Alcatraz, where the highly structured, monotonous day to day routine was designed to teach him to follow the regulations. There, he had four rights – food, clothing, shelter and medical care. Everything else was regarded *as a privilege that had to be earned.'*

When a prisoner behaved, Alcatraz was probably no tougher than many other places; in fact some inmates considered it one of the safest institutions. However, persistent bad behaviour could be punished with time in D-Block, officially known as 'The Treatment Unit', where 24 hour lock-down was the norm. Worse was the 'Special Treatment Unit' or 'The Hole', a steel cell-sized 'box' where a prisoner was deprived of human contact and even light.

After a prisoner appeared to be of no further threat, and was following the rules – often about 7 years – he was then transferred back to another prison to finish his sentence.

There are many other beliefs about Alcatraz that are untrue. Robert Stroud, the so-called 'Bird Man of Alcatraz' – portrayed by a kindly Burt Lancaster in the film – never had any birds at Alcatraz and was far from kindly, although he had written two bird books about canaries while he was at Leavenworth. While here, Stroud did not help his case when prison officers discovered that some equipment he had requested for his 'bird studies' was being used to make an alcohol still.

Another myth is that one of the reasons that it was so difficult to escape from Alcatraz was the man-eating sharks in San Francisco Bay. In fact, the small bottom-feeding sharks were not the danger. The main problem was the very cold water and the strong current.

Another film, *Escape from Alcatraz,* starring Clint Eastwood, records possibly the only successful escape from the island in 1962. Three prisoners enlarged the air vents at the back of their cells, and created false pieces of wall to cover it up. They left realistic dummy heads, complete with human hair, in their beds and succeeded in crawling through vent holes into a works corridor, from which they reached the roof. They then climbed down a drainpipe on the outside of the cellhouse and made their way to the water. Some of their life vests and letters and photographs were found, but no sign of the men. Their escape is still an open case with the FBI and US Marshals.

All other escapes resulted in recapture or death of the prisoners. The most violent attempt, in May 1946, was called the 'Alcatraz Blastout' when six prisoners obtained guns. It culminated in the death of one prison officer with 18 more injured. The US Marines had to be

Al Capone, probably the prison's most famous inmate

Isolated in San Francisco Bay, all supplies, including water, came by boat.

called in to end the battle.

One very famous inmate did manage to leave 'The Rock', but with little to show for it. Al Capone, after seven years as a model prisoner, one day was seen staggering in the canteen. He was diagnosed with syphilis. By the time he was released in 1939, Jake 'Greasy Thumb' Guzik, the famous gang accountant, described him as '*nutty as a fruit-cake*'.

In 1963, Alcatraz was closed after twenty-nine years. This had nothing to do with the escapes, or with a successful law

case brought by a mistreated prisoner, but all to do with the cost of running the place. It cost three times as much as any other US prison – mainly because its very isolation meant that everything had to be brought out by boat. It did not even have fresh water, and nearly a million gallons had to be brought in every week.

Alcatraz's dramatic position and history has meant that it continues to be a mecca for the movie industry, with Lee Marvin in *Point Blank* and Sean Connery and Nicholas Cage in the appropriately named *The Rock* being filmed there.

See: Andersonville, Devil's Island, Las Vegas, North Clark Street, Reading Gaol, Robben Island, Spandau

ALDERMASTON
England

As soon as atomic weapons were used, their new and appalling power created opposition all over the world, with motives ranging from humanitarian, religious and muddled to the sometimes nefarious.

In Britain, in 1951, the first buildings were erected on a former World War II airfield for what was to become the Atomic Weapons Establishment. On this 880-acre site, staff have ever since researched, developed and manufactured atomic weapons, and then dismantled and disposed of them when they were no longer needed.

Britain's anti-nuclear movement began to target Aldermaston. In February 1958

the Campaign for Nuclear Disarmament was founded, passionately led by the Member of Parliament and future Labour leader, Michael Foot, the philosopher Bertrand Russell and the author J.B. Priestley.

Only two months later the first 'Aldermaston March' took place, walking the 50 miles from London to the gates of the research complex. Led by the cheerful music of jazz bands, the marchers were mostly young, but with many earnest older people and little children.

This pilgrimage took place for many years, and almost like Ascot, Henley and Wimbledon, was a colourful and eccentric fixture in the British calendar, later over-shadowed by the siege of Greenham Common - a protest against cruise missiles. Arguably, none of these demonstrations had the slightest effect on British nuclear policy.

See: Bikini, Chernobyl, Greenham Common, Hiroshima, Los Alamos, Three Mile Island

ALEXANDRA PALACE
England

Its name might imply a huge and magnificent edifice somewhere in Imperial Russia, but Alexandra Palace is actually in North London, near Muswell Hill. It was built in 1873 as an exhibition building, featuring Europe's largest hall. Never very successful as an exhibition centre, its offices and high altitude gave it its real claim to fame. It was the studio from which the world's first regular television programmes were transmitted in November 1936.

The world had been racing to make television practical ever since 1925, when a long-haired Scot, John Logie Baird, transmitted his first pictures between two rooms in London's Soho with his complicated, mechanical 'Televisor'. In 1932, RCA, with its 'iconoscope' (cathode ray tube), had successfully demonstrated an all-electronic system. The Germans were not far behind, and 150,000 of them watched the 1936 Berlin Olympics in twenty-eight *Fernsehenstuben* – public viewing theatres.

But it was the British Broadcasting Corporation which, on November 2nd 1936, launched the first regular television service. You had to be wealthy to watch, because television sets cost £150 (£7,500 at today's prices). The first afternoon featured an opening ceremony, followed by Chinese jugglers and two American comics called 'Buck and Bubbles' with a song and dance routine. The initial service, while regular, only operated at 3pm for an hour, and then again between 9pm and 10pm. Soon, however, programmes like 'Picture Page', a magazine programme hosted by Joan Miller with a regular feature of demonstrating the steps of the latest dance crazes, were broadcasting to about a thousand viewers. Programme presenters were expected to speak the 'King's English' and, as a result, many had the most amazing, strangulated upper-class accents. This was, after all, the era in which invisible newsreaders at the BBC's radio studios still always wore dinner jackets.

When the war intervened, Alexandra Palace stopped broadcasting and became a vital part of electronic warfare. It came under the control of the Air Ministry in 1942 and was blacked out, its formerly bustling studios empty and its dressing rooms deserted.

In 1945, 'Ally Pally' was released from military use, and on 7th June 1946, the BBC resumed television where it had left off. Soon a new generation of viewers would see on their screens the Alexandra Palace transmission tower with the circling words 'BBC Television News & Newsreel'. The other slogan the BBC used was *'Nation shall speak peace unto nation'*, a pious and somewhat optimistic thought.

By 1980, BBC television had largely moved to West London, and in July a fire broke out which destroyed 60 per cent of the Palace and sent two million square feet of glass crashing to the ground.

After huge efforts, it has been restored with exhibition and banqueting halls and an ice rink – but sadly no television studios.

See: Ambridge, Albert Square, Bull & Finch, Coronation Street, Peyton Place, Ramsay Street, Truth or Consequences

An early fashion show on pre-war television

Partly renovated after a disastrous fire, the transmission tower remains a symbol of its pioneering role.

ALMA UNDERPASS
France

A nondescript concrete underpass near the banks of the Seine in Paris was the scene of probably the most famous and highly publicised car crash in the world.

On a warm summer night on Sunday 31st August 1997, a black Mercedes 600 travelling at perhaps 80 miles an hour, entered the tunnel pursued by a batch of motorcycles. There was a tremendous crash followed by several thuds, and then just the sound of a car horn. The Mercedes contained the most famous woman in the world, Princess Diana, her new boyfriend Dodi Al Fayed, her bodyguard Trevor Rees Jones and driver Henri Paul. Dodi and Henri Paul were dead, Trevor Rees Jones remained in hospital for months and the Princess of Wales died at 4 a.m. in the Pitie Salpêtrière Hospital.

The affair of The Princess of Wales and Dodi, the playboy son of the colourful and controversial owner of Harrods, Mohammed Al Fayed, had driven the world's media into even more of a 'Diana frenzy' than they normally displayed.

On the road from the airport where they had arrived from their holiday in Sardinia, the couple's car was buzzed by motorcycles with dozens of paparazzi photographers, and their driver was dazzled by the camera flashes. The motorcycles, and even cars containing paparazzi, drove extremely dangerously and the Princess became intensely anxious.

Therefore, that night, when they were again mobbed by paparazzi whilst visiting Dodi's apartment, the Princess, although used to photographers, began to become highly disturbed and frightened, and Dodi became increasingly angry about them.

There has been unconfirmed speculation that Dodi intended to propose marriage to the Princess that evening, so the presence of the photographers

Right: The underpass with its deadly pillars

must have been doubly irritating. They could not even have their planned dinner at Chez Benoit because of the attentions of the photographic mob, and instead were forced to retreat to the L'Espardon Restaurant in Dodi's father's Ritz Hotel.

To return to the apartment without too much trouble, a decoy plan was devised. The two regular vehicles would go from the front of the Ritz, while a third car, the Mercedes with another chauffeur, would leave from the rear. Henri Paul

was pulled in at the last minute to be the driver, and the car set off. The decoy plan failed. They were soon spotted and, once again, an unwanted escort of paparazzi followed the car. It was to escape the photographers that the Mercedes was travelling so fast, but as the car rounded the bend at the entrance to the Alma Underpass, the driver lost control, smashing into a concrete pillar and somersaulting in the tunnel. Several of the photographers were arrested at the scene, and held under suspicion of causing the crash and breaking French law by taking photographs – instead of going to the aid of the wounded Princess and her bodyguard.

It was later revealed by a post-mortem on the driver that Henri Paul's blood contained a high level of alcohol and that he was on medication; this could have contributed to his lack of judgement.

Princess Diana's funeral was one of the most dramatic ceremonies in history, and was broadcast all over the world. The very fact that she was the most photographed woman in the world meant that an enormous number of people knew her – or thought they did.

As time passes, opinions vary about Diana. Prime Minister Tony Blair had said, 'She was the People's Princess.' Maureen Dowd in the *New York Times* called her the 'Queen of Surfaces' and Julie Burchill in *The Guardian* summed up her tragic mixed-up life thus: *'Now at last this sad glittering century has an image worthy of it: a wandering, wondering girl, a silly Sloane turned secular saint, coming home in her coffin to RAF Northolt like the good soldier she was'.*

If you visit the Alma Underpass now, you will see little to mark the scene – cars flash past the scarcely-dented pillar that killed Diana. Above the underpass is a monument, but it is nothing to do with her. It is a replica of the Statue of Liberty's torch, installed in 1986, marking the centenary of the Statue's erection in 1886. Rather sadly, it is covered with a few rather tatty cards and flowers as tributes to the Princess. It is hardly a fitting dedication to an icon who through her charity work had earned her title *'Queen of Hearts'.*

See: Beckingham Palace, Bedloe's Island

The monument above the underpass. The golden flame has nothing to do with Diana's tragedy: it records the 100th Anniversary of The Statue of Liberty.

AMBASSADOR HOTEL KITCHEN
California, USA

Four years after President Jack Kennedy's assassination, some of the magic freshness and hope of 'Camelot' had revived and, in June 1968, another Kennedy seemed to be on the way to the White House. With much of his older brother's charisma, Robert Kennedy's campaign was going well when he gave his speech celebrating his California primary victory (over Senator Eugene McCarthy) at his campaign headquarters in the Ambassador Hotel.

The hotel was certainly no stranger to celebrities. Opened in 1921 on Wilshire Boulevard, the Ambassador with its legendary night club, *The Coconut Grove,* soon became famous – mostly as a haunt for the film industry. Long-term residents included Howard Hughes, Jean Harlow, John Barrymore and Gloria Swanson. Joan Crawford, Carole Lombard and Loretta Young were discovered when dancing at the Grove and Bing Crosby started singing there. Even the artificial palm trees were left over from the set of Rudolph Valentino's *The Sheik.* British royalty and every US President had stayed there. It was an obvious choice for a political celebration.

On that evening, Bobby Kennedy, to avoid the crush of his jubilant supporters, was led by his bodyguards on a short cut through the hotel's kitchen and pantry. There, in a crowd of cheering well-wishers, RFK was approached and suddenly shot by Palestinian-born Sirhan Sirhan, who was wrestled to the ground by Kennedy's bodyguards, including the famous athletic stars Rosey Grier and Rafer Johnson. Eight bystanders were injured – and Robert Kennedy died in minutes – surrounded by his distraught supporters.

Coming just two months after Martin Luther King's death, conspiracy theories still abound. The initial FBI report which was released only after Kennedy's enemy J. Edgar Hoover died, indicated that twelve or more bullets were fired. Sirhan's gun could fire just eight. What *is* certain is that the disaster in that kitchen almost certainly stopped a second Kennedy presidency, and doomed the Democrats who were thrown into disarray. There were horrific riots and fierce street battles between Mayor 'Boss' Daley's police and anti-Vietnam war protestors at that year's Chicago's Democratic convention, and Republican Richard Nixon beat Hubert Humphrey in a victory nearly as close as was his defeat by Jack Kennedy four years before.

Now owned by Donald Trump, the Ambassador Hotel still stands, closed to guests but earning its keep as an expensive party venue,

Above: Robert Kennedy

Below: Sirhan Sirhan is led away after the shooting

See: Bay of Pigs, Dallas, Lorraine Motel, Montgomery, Texas School Book Depository

and returning to its roots as a movie location. Glimpses of its fabulous but anonymous interior can be seen in *Forrest Gump, Pretty Woman, Murder She Wrote, Fear and Loathing in Las Vegas* and about 200 other productions.

But it is a few horrible moments in the pantry which will mean we will remember the Ambassador Hotel.

AMBRIDGE
England

With a population at the last census of just over four hundred, Ambridge lies in the heart of Borsetshire, six miles south of the county town of Borchester and half-way between the city of Felpersham and the nearest railway at Hollerton Junction on the main Paddington-Hereford line. There is a church (St. Stephen's), a pub (The Bull), a post-office with a shop, and a country house hotel (Grey Gables). Cricket is played each summer on the village green outside The Bull, but sadly the village policeman has gone and the doctor's practice has closed down. A further sign of rural decline is that St.

Stephen's has to share a vicar with neighbouring parishes. Ambridge is the home of the Archers.

The Archer family has lived at Brookfield Farm in Ambridge for at least four generations – first as tenants and then owners. The present incumbent is David, grandson of Dan and Doris, the occupiers when we first heard about the family. Other members of the family still on the land are David's cousin Tony at the organically-run Bridge Farm and Jennifer, Tony's sister, who is married to Brian Aldridge at the estate–sized Home Farm. These days Brookfield, at around 500 acres, having previously been a dairy farm for years, concentrates mainly on producing Hereford beef for a specialist market.

All of them and their charming village are, of course, entirely fictitious, much as their many legions of fans would like them to be real. As a radio drama *The Archers* is not only one of the best-loved, it is one of the longest-running in the world. But it had what we might now feel to be a curious origin. In 1950, five years after the war, Britain still had food rationing, in marked contrast to most of the rest of the war's participants. A BBC producer, Godfrey Baseley, who had worked on agricultural broadcasts, conceived the programme as something that would help farmers with their productivity, thus cutting down on imported food and easing rationing. During Whit Week the first five, fifteen minute pilot episodes were broadcast by BBC Midlands Home Service. People liked what they heard, so six months later it was beamed to the rest of the United Kingdom. Little did Godfrey Baseley or anyone else then realise that it would still be a favourite fifty years and more than 13,000 episodes later.

In 1955, the year in which Philip Archer's wife Grace was killed in a stable fire, the audience peaked at a staggering 20 million. The competition from television made inroads thereafter, but the listenership still runs at over 7 million, divided almost equally between those who tune in every evening (Sunday to Friday inclusive) and those who catch up with the omnibus edition on Sunday mornings. Programmes are recorded about a month in advance, but topicality is ensured by including subjects of real rural interest such as the Foot and Mouth crisis, and even by the ability to insert short scenes on the day an important real-life event takes place.

To boost the NSPCC's centenary appeal in 1994 for example, both Princess Margaret and the Duke of Westminster appeared live at 'a Grey Gables fund-raising function.'

The tum-ti-tum-ti-tum-ti-tum, tum-ti-tum-ti-tum-tum signature tune, *'Barwick Green'* is surely one of the most recognisable in the world, and those who believe that it is strange that so many townies still listen to an essentially countryside programme have perhaps under-estimated the fascination that rural England still holds for us all.

But perhaps it is no more strange than viewers who cannot get enough, through soap operas, of a terraced street near Manchester or a square in the East End of London, let alone a suburban street in Melbourne.

See: Albert Square, Coronation Street, Dallas Peyton Place, Ramsay Street, Truth or Consequences

AMRITSAR
India

For centuries the Sikhs have been one of the most independent, religious and uncompromising people of India. They are also one of the most warlike, a strength appreciated by the British, who regard them as some of their finest soldiers.

Founded in 1577 by the guru Ram Das as the holy city of the Sikhs, Amritsar has been in the news for tragic reasons too often. On 13th April 1919, under British rule, after rioting against new British security laws had grown out of hand, the police asked for military support from Lahore. General Dyer arrived, and ordered his troops to open fire on the demonstration. Several hundred in the crowd were shot, trampled to death or died trying to escape down a well, including many women and children. Unsurprisingly, this massacre did little for the long-term prospects for British rule over the huge subcontinent.

When the British did eventually leave in October 1947, the tensions between Moslems and Hindus forced the partition of India, and Amritsar was the site of several of the worst sectarian massacres. In one, a train full of Moslem refugees on its way to the safety of Pakistan was attacked by Sikh soldiers and a Sikh mob. In spite of the heroic action of the lone British officer commanding the escort, who machine-gunned the mob until his ammunition gave out and he was killed, 1,200 men, women and children were hacked and stabbed to death in a three-hour orgy of killing. 600 survivors, many wounded, reached safety after hiding under the bodies of their fellow passengers, only emerging when their attackers grew tired of killing.

In 1984, the warrior sect of the Sikhs once again burst into the headlines.

Demanding their own independent state of Khalistan, a fanatical and heavily armed group of militants took over the Golden Temple of Amritsar, the very holiest of Sikh shrines, under whose gold and copper dome is kept Adi Granth, the sacred book.

Always a staunch defender of Indian unity, the Prime Minister, Mrs Indira Gandhi, was forced to take action and order an assault. The battle against the well-prepared defenders proved unexpectedly fierce, and over 100 soldiers and 712 extremists died while some of the sacred buildings were

The Golden Temple

damaged. For what they regarded as a desecration, Mrs Gandhi incurred the hatred of many Sikhs. Three months later, walking in her garden, she was gunned down by her three bodyguards. They were all Sikhs.

See: Bhopal, Deolali, Dum Dum, Jodhpur

ANDERSONVILLE
Georgia, USA

Prisoners, who had died of neglect, were buried side by side in long trenches.

In November 1864, in the closing months of the American Civil War, the soldiers of a company of General Sherman's Federal troops on their 'March through Georgia', were eating their evening meal when a band of gaunt and starving men tottered into their camp.

The strangers had escaped from the Confederate prison camp at Andersonville, and their pathetic condition was but a foretaste of what was to be found there.

Designed to hold 10,000 Federal prisoners, by August 1864 it 'housed' 33,000 – making it statistically the fifth largest city in the Confederacy. Although the camp was surrounded by timber, its ill-tempered Commandant, Swiss-born Henry Wirz, forbade the building of proper shelters, so most prisoners lived in holes in the ground with scraps of tent and tree branches for cover.

Such conditions, coupled with a pitiful diet and little medical support, ensured that almost 13,000 men died there, to be buried in trenches. On just one day, a prisoner died every eleven minutes.

A Southern woman, who was allowed to climb a tower to look at the camp, said: *'I am afraid God will suffer some terrible retribution to fall upon us for letting such things happen. If the Yankees should ever come to south west Georgia and go to Anderson and see the graves there, God have mercy on the land'.*

The Yankees did indeed come, and stared with horror at the camp (although, in fairness, some of the Union camps were little better). Commandant Wirz was duly executed in November 1865.

See: Alcatraz, Andrassy, Bastille, Dachau, Devil's Island, Landsberg, Robben Island, Reading Gaol, Spandau

ANDRASSY, 60
Hungary

Andrassy, 60, in its modern role as a tourist attraction

'Be careful or you'll go to Andrassy, 60 and never come out'.

For Hungarians, the very mention of one building in Budapest used to inspire a particular chill. It was like Russians muttering about the NKVD's Lubyanka prison, or akin to Germans whispering about the Gestapo's Prinz Albrechtstrasse. Andrassy Street, number 60 was the feared headquarters, prison and interrogation centre in Budapest, of the Allamvedelmi Osztaly (AVO), Hungary's secret police and their uniformed colleagues, the AVH.

The Second World War had hardly been pleasant for the Hungarians. Forced reluctantly to fight along-side the Germans, they had lost thousands on the Russian Front, their Jews had been deported from the ghettos in Pest and the capital had been subjected to a 4 month brutal, hand-to-hand battle between the Russians and the Germans, ending in the tunnels and caves of the hill of Buda.

After their 'liberation' by the Russians, the Hungarians in 1945 voted for democracy, with the Small Farmers Party getting fifty seven per cent of the vote and the Communists only seventeen per cent. But behind Stalin's Iron Curtain, cosy Small Farmers parties were not to be.

The Red Army still occupied Hungary and the Communists wanted complete control of the Government, so they created the AVO (Allamvedelmi Osztaly), which served as the Communists' secret police. It was controlled by Soviet advisors, and Gabor Peter was named Director. Peter was a Jewish tailor and former NKVD agent. He began a series of Stalinesque purges to cut away the support for the Small Farmers Party. The AVO arrested the most outspoken critics of the Communists, accusing them of '*Fascist coercion*' and of '*wartime collaboration with the Fascists*'. Thousands of loyal

Communists were also dragged into Peter's office at Andrassy, 60 and tortured and killed.

It was Hungary which first attempted to loosen the Soviet grip on Eastern Europe. On 23rd October 1956, students from the universities took to the streets, and a quarter of a million people from Budapest joined them. In order to read a proclamation via Radio Budapest, a crowd gathered at the station's downtown studio around 9 p.m. that evening. The AVH, the AVO's uniformed colleagues guarding the studio, lost patience, shot into the crowd and killed several protesters. The infuriated crowd acquired guns and hand grenades, attacked the studio building and took bloody revenge on the remaining AVH guards. The shooting was heard on the radio across the country until the crying announcer could not continue the programme, the transmission ending with classical music. In the next few hours, the protesters gathered weapons from sympathisers in the Hungarian army and police. Revenge against the AVO and the AVH was brutal and public, with their bodies lined up outside a sacked Andrassy, 60.

But the Hungarian uprising was a short-lived triumph. Within days the Soviets invaded, with Prime Minister Imre Nagy abducted and killed, and General Pal Maleter murdered while negotiating with the Russian Army, whose tanks rolled into Budapest and snuffed out freedom.

There would be other false dawns on the way to throwing off Soviet dominance. The Prague Spring of 1968 ended the same way as Budapest. But in Poland in 1989, Lech Walesa, leader of the Gdansk shipyard strike, at last succeeded in cracking the Soviet monolith. Then, quite suddenly, the Berlin Wall was down – after which puppet governments were to fall like dominoes.

Andrassy, 60 is in the middle of one of Budapest's longest and most fashionable avenues, now full of shops and restaurants. It has been restored and painted a sinister grey, with the word 'TERROR' on a controversial roof extension, and is a popular tourist attraction.

Without such a reminder, and with Budapest, Prague and Berlin now popular for tourist weekends, it is hard to imagine an Eastern Europe full of Andrassy Prisons.

See: Alcatraz, Andersonville, Bastille, Dachau, Devil's Island, Landsberg, Robben Island, Reading Gaol, Spandau

A Hungarian girl freedom fighter with captured sub-machine gun.

ANGORA
Turkey

It is not often that the capital city of a major country becomes famous not because of its achievements, but because of a goat. But that is the case of Ankara, once known as Angora.

The Angora goat has for thousands of years provided the long and lustrous fibre from which mohair (*mukhayyar* in Arabic) is made. Soft angora boleros and sweaters have long been a popular female fashion item, as are pashminas now.

Ankara, now the administrative centre of Turkey, has always been less famous than the great metropolis of Istanbul – the legendary former Constantinople and Byzantium – once arguably the focal point of the civilised world.

The city has another curious claim to fame. The hillsides around the city are covered in somewhat ramshackle houses with no paved roads. These are called 'overnight houses'. Built on government land, they are knocked down only when the land is needed, often with great drama with their 'owners' threatening to throw themselves from the roof tops.

See: Bazaar, Bikini, Carnaby Street, Duffel, Dum Dum, Jodhpur, Nimes

THE ANNEXE OF ANNE FRANK
The Netherlands

The Frank family was caught out twice. As Jews in an increasingly hostile Nazi Germany, they had realised the danger in time, unlike so many of their German Jewish friends, who had assumed that being loyal Germans would protect them. Indeed, the Frank brothers had all fought in the German army in the First World War, Otto Frank rising to the rank of Lieutenant. But Otto saw the Nazi warning signs, and realised that much more than his job and his comfortable apartment could soon be in jeopardy. He moved his family to the perceived safety of Amsterdam in the fond belief that Holland's neutrality would not be violated.

However, by May 1940, Holland was indeed invaded and soon the destructive Nazi machine began to close the net on its 140,000 Jews. When his eldest daughter, Margot, was ordered to report to a labour camp, Otto again acted with foresight and next morning moved his family into a carefully prepared secret 'Achterhuis' (house at the back) at his company's office at 263 Prinsengracht. They were joined by his business partner and his family and another Jewish friend, making eight in all.

For 25 months the refugees shared the 6 rooms of the secret annexe in a monotonous routine, which included long periods of no noise or movement when the warehouse below was being used. Only the radio, the BBC and the company workers who brought them food told them of the outside world. These helpers also told them of the steady removal of their fellow Jews to an unknown fate.

Anne Frank, Otto's lively and imaginative second daughter, decided to keep a diary of her two years of strange and unnatural incarceration. In March 1944, a call-up on the radio for ordinary citizens to provide their diaries for historical collection, prompted her to re-write it as if to 'Kitty', an imaginary friend she could never have.

In October 1943, aged only 14, she wrote: *I wander from room to room, climb up and down the stairs and feel like a songbird whose wings have been ripped off and who keeps hurling itself against the bars of its dark cage*.

On August 4th 1944, with the Allies tantalisingly close and approaching from France and Belgium, the prisoners' worst fears came true. The Gestapo and Dutch collaborators broke through into the annexe. The group was first sent to a transition camp, Westerbork in the north-east of the Netherlands, then on to Auschwitz and from there some went to other camps. Otto Frank survived, and dared to hope that his family might have done the same. But, searching the women's section of the camp, he found that his wife had died just before liberation, and that his daughters had been moved to Bergen-Belsen. Two months before the war ended, Margot and then Anne had perished from typhus.

Miep Gies, one of the family's helpers, found Anne's diary on the floor after their arrest. She kept it, planning to return it to Anne. On hearing that she had died, Miep gave the diary to Otto who published it in 1947, under the name *Het Achterhuis*, that Anne had chosen. It so moved the world that it ran into dozens of languages and millions of copies. Seldom can the poignant memories of a little suite of rooms have achieved such posthumous fame.

See: Lidice, Oradour, Dachau, Getto, Katyn Wood, Masada, Nuremberg, Reichstag, Spandau

'ANTHRAX ISLAND'
Scotland

In 1942, the sheep on Gruinard Island were herded into wooden frames, and a bomb was detonated in their midst. It was a scientific test, conducted in the expectation that the Germans were planning a biological, or chemical assault. It contained *Anthrax*, one of the most deadly bacteria known to man. Three days later the sheep started to die, and the island had its name changed forever. It was now 'Anthrax Island'.

Gruinard Island lies off the rugged coast of the western Scottish Highlands in Gruinard Bay, between Ullapool and Gairloch. It covers 520 acres and is half a mile from the mainland. It was an apparently insignificant place that was to become uninhabitable for decades.

The island was coated in a bacterium that has a 95 per cent mortality rate, even when medical care is given. Experts think that 100kg of anthrax sprayed on to a major city would kill three million people. In humans, anthrax can be contracted by skin contact, ingestion, and inhalation. Death takes approximately seven days from symptoms which include internal bleeding, blood poisoning, and even meningitis.

The report of the experiment on the island was that such a weapon could be used to render cities uninhabitable *'for generations'*.

For the next 48 years, red signs on the island's shores warned of a deadly danger that its picturesque nature belied. It was not until 1990 that Junior Defence Minister, Michael Neubert, made the journey from the mainland, walked on to the island, and symbolically removed the red warning signs, declaring the island *'safe'*. It had taken a lot of effort. In 1986, a company was paid £500,000 to drench the island with 280 tons of formaldehyde mixed into 2000 tons of seawater.

However, the good news was not met with the enthusiasm that the Government hoped for. Archaeologist Dr Brian Moffat informed the *Glasgow Herald* that he was unconvinced of the island's safety. Given that he had discovered buried anthrax spores that had survived hundreds of years, Dr Moffat said he, for one, *'would not go walking on Gruinard!'*

One need not be a Doctor of Archaeology to agree with him.

Anthrax occurs naturally, and it was once not uncommon for those working with animals to become infected. It had even been dubbed *'woolsorter's disease'*. More recently, following the atrocities of September the 11th 2001 in America, anthrax was to hit the headlines. As letters packed with the spores started arriving in US Government offices and workers died, it seemed like the second wave of terrorist attack could be underway. However, it is now widely believed to have been the work of a lone, home-grown lunatic, with the added worry that the type of anthrax used in the attacks could only have originated in an American military laboratory.

More recently, an Arab sailor died in a Brazil hotel room. He had foolishly opened the suitcase that he had been bribed to deliver to Canada - almost certainly an attempted Al Qaeda attempted attack on America as a revenge for the war on Iraq.

Gruinard Island, through the eagerness of wartime scientists under pressure to deliver, was given a name and a history that have scarred it forever.

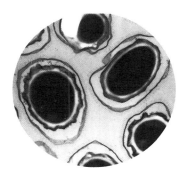

Deadly anthrax bacteria

See: Aldermaston, Bhopal, Bikini, Chernobyl, Ebola, Greenham Common, Hiroshima, Lassa, Three Mile Island, World Trade Center

APPOMATTOX COURT HOUSE
Virginia, USA

Just as wars have to start somewhere, they also have to end somewhere. In April 1865, Robert E. Lee's army, on its last legs, found itself near a village called Appomattox Court House. The Confederate army was outnumbered by two to one, and had just lost four precious train-loads of supplies – and had little to eat. When the soldiers bravely attacked the next morning, they soon faced an advancing 'solid wall of blue' and realised that the end had come. Just before noon on Sunday 9th April, Lee dispatched a letter to the Federal Commander in Chief, General Grant, requesting a suspension of hostilities. Lee also sent Colonel Charles Marshall to find a suitable building where he could surrender his army. The first civilian he met, Wilmer McLean, had moved to the area for business reasons and as he liked to tell people to 'escape the war' because the first major battle, Bull Run, had been fought near his previous house. He reluctantly offered his front parlour.

The meeting between Grant and Lee was characterised by dignity, and almost comradeship. Indeed, Grant discussed serving together in the Mexican War for so long that Lee had to remind him of the purpose for the meeting. The terms of the surrender were very generous, with officers and men allowed to return home as paroled prisoners of war. Grant ordered 25,000 rations to be delivered at once to the hungry Confederates.

Lee, on his famous horse 'Traveller,' rode back to his camp, his head sunk low on his breast with depression. But as he approached his camp and braced himself to greet his men, they began to cheer. Strong men, including the officers, wept like children. Lee turned and addressed his men, 'Boys, I have done the best I could for you. Go home now, and if you make as good citizens as you have soldiers, you will do well, and I shall always be proud of you. Goodbye, and God bless you all'. He turned again, and went into his tent.

See: Andersonville, Arlington, Fort Sumter, Gettysburg, Hampton Roads, Harpers Ferry, Little Big Horn, West Point

General Ulysses. S. Grant (right) watches Robert. E. Lee sign the surrender document

TOM LOVELL / NATIONAL GEOGRAPHIC IMAGE COLLECTION

Traditionally, it is held that Mount Ararat in eastern Turkey is where Noah's Ark came to rest, after the great flood described in Genesis, the first book of the Old Testament.

According to the Bible, God had become so disenchanted by the foibles of the human race that he resolved to destroy mankind by a flood that would cover the world. He judged that Noah and his family were alone in qualifying for salvation, and instructed him to build a wooden ark, bringing aboard two representatives of all the animal species so that they could propagate when the flood had subsided.

Genesis chapter 6, verses 14-16, describes in detail the specifications required for the Ark. It was to be made of 'gopher wood' and sealed with bitumen. The size was to be three hundred cubits long, fifty cubits wide and thirty cubits high. It was to have a window around the top, a door in the side and have three levels within.

A cubit is measured as the distance between an adult's elbow and tip of a finger, and most Hebrew scholars agree that this would be no less than 18 inches. This means that the length of the Ark would have been at least 450 feet, its width 75 feet and its height 45 feet, making it similar in proportion to modern ocean liners. In addition, its length-to-width ratio of six to one would have provided excellent stability in stormy conditions, and shipbuilding engineers agree that such a vessel would have been extraordinarily unlikely to capsize.

It is said that it took Noah 120 years to build the Ark, although the Bible does not say whether he did this alone or together with hired help. During that time he valiantly tried to warn everyone else of the impending disaster, urging them to repent of their sins. Clearly, they ignored his advice because, in the event, the only humans to be saved were Noah and his family, along with all the animals.

How many animals there were, and whether the Ark was large enough to hold them has prompted considerable academic debate. It has been suggested by scholars that although there are over one million species of animals in the world, most of them live in the sea, so it would not have been necessary to bring them all on to the Ark, and ducks, geese and other water birds could presumably have hung on for a while. The number of land-dwelling species has been

estimated at anywhere between 2,000 and 35,000 (depending on whether all sub-species are included; i.e. every different breed of dog or just one breed, and whether extinct species were included). In any case, supporters of the Ark as historical fact point out that the size of the Ark would have enabled it to hold up to 50,000 species. They claim that, from the dimensions given, the available floor space would have been over 100,000 square feet and the total cubic volume over one and a half million cubic feet (equivalent to the capacity of 569 railway cars).

The design and practicality of the Ark itself is, however, the least of the questions we should debate. How did Noah get the animals into the ark? It is

Did the ark have height restrictions? Scholars have debated for centuries whether Noah's Ark is fact or fiction.

one thing to take in domestic animals like cows and sheep. But two White Rhinos? Two Black Mambas? Two Polar Bears? Even then, careful separation between certain species would have been required. Cats and mice, spiders and flies? Who was feeding them all? With what? How much space was devoted to food supplies?

The story of the Ark may at least be part myth, but there are certainly similar stories of catastrophic floods during the period in other religions, particularly in the Babylonian 'Gilgamesh Epic', and in Roman and Greek mythology. There is

also plenty of evidence of animal bones being found in caves now very high up in various mountains to which they appear to have been forced by rising water.

As for the Ark, the US Air Force, in 1949, first discovered an 'anomaly' two thousand feet from the summit of Mount Ararat, since confirmed by spy satellites. It is a rectangle measuring 600 feet long, submerged in a glacier. Nobody has yet been able to reach it. When they do, the mystery of the Ark may be solved once and for all.

See: Tower of Babel, Gethsemane, Masada, Olympos

THE BRIDGE AT ARLES
France

The town of Arles, in the heart of Provence, was the thriving southern centre of Roman Gaul, as its magnificent arena, now used for bullfighting, still attests. Religious scholars will know of the Council of Arles in 314 AD, convened by Emperor Constantine I to deal with the now obscure problem of the 'Schism of the Donatists' in North Africa.

But most of us will have looked at Arles, whether we know it or not, through the eyes of the brilliant but troubled artist, Vincent van Gogh.

Son of a pastor, he had tried his hand at teaching (in Isleworth and Ramsgate), but then devoted

The Langlois Bridge near Arles painted by Vincent van Gogh and recently rebuilt.

himself to religion as an itinerant preacher in the Belgian coal mining town of Le Borinage. When he started painting, he portrayed dark, haunting scenes of peasant poverty at his father's new parish, at Nuenen. In Paris, supported by his devoted art dealer brother Théo, he made friends with Paul Gauguin, Toulouse Lautrec and Seurat, and his palette lightened under the influence of these Impressionists and Post-Impressionists.

In February 1888, he left Paris and arrived alone and poor in Arles, seeking the intense colours and the blazing sun of Provence. Instead, he found an Arles unusually cold. Indeed, his first painting was *Landscape with Snow*. But the sun returned and soon he was producing what was to amount to no less than 189 paintings at Arles, now recognised as some of the best and most valuable works of art in the world.

Some were portraits, some still-life scenes, but many were of the local landscape – including the distinctive bridges, a subject to which he returned several times. He wrote to Vincent, *'I cannot help it if my pictures do not sell. Nevertheless, the time will come when people will see that they are worth more than the price of the paint'.*

Van Gogh wanted to found a colony of artists at Arles, and, above all, he wanted his friend Gauguin to visit him. In the event, it was not so much a disappointment as a disaster. When Gauguin arrived in October, at first all went well, with the pair out painting together in Vincent's beloved country-side. But the weather deteriorated in December and they were cooped up in the Yellow House for days, leading to violent arguments. Finally, came the famous incident of van Gogh cutting off part of his ear, which he presented to the women of the local brothel before collapsing. Gauguin telegraphed Théo and left for Paris, never to meet van Gogh again.

Vincent struggled through the winter, slowly recovering physically and mentally, and by February 1889 he had painted his *Sunflowers*. But the local citizens had become so alarmed by his behaviour that they signed a petition to

the Mayor and the police and, in May, he committed himself to the asylum at nearby San Rémy de Provence. Tragically, he was on the inevitable road to the maniacal *Cornfield with Crows* and his suicidal shot.

Never appreciated in his lifetime, poor and depressed, Vincent van Gogh has left Arles and the world with a legacy of wonderful, passionate paintings for which we should be forever grateful.

See: Barbizon, Flatford, Giverny, Moulin Rouge

Vincent's bedroom at the asylum at San Rémy.

ARLINGTON
Virginia, USA

When the American Civil War started on the 12th April 1861 with the shelling of Fort Sumter, President Abraham Lincoln turned to the most promising officer in the United States Army, Robert E. Lee. Lee was a proud American citizen, and feared what a war would bring. *'I can anticipate no greater calamity for the country than the dissolution of the Union. It would be an accumulation of all the evils we complain of, and I am willing to sacrifice everything but honour for its preservation'.* But honour intervened, because the day after he was offered supreme command, his native state, Virginia, voted to secede from the Union. Sadly, Lee decided to go with his state, saying to a friend, 'I cannot raise my hand against my birthplace, my home, my children.' Lee went south to command the Confederate Army of Northern Virginia, and left his beautiful home in Arlington. Previously owned by George Washington Parke Custis, the adopted grandson of George Washington, it had held many of Washington's memorabilia from the Revolutionary War. Mary, Custis's daughter, had married Robert E. Lee. But it is not for these reasons that the house and its land is famous.

By 1864, the military cemeteries in the north were full and the Quartermaster General, Montgomery Meigs, was ordered to find a new site. Meigs had once served under Lee, but had developed a great hatred for Southerners who fought against the Union. So he chose Lee's lawn at Arlington for the new army cemetery. He ordered that the Union dead be laid as close as possible to the front door so that no one could ever live in the house again – an order that was initially disobeyed. Arlington became the National Cemetery and Meigs also built, in the centre of what had been Mrs Lee's rose garden, the Tomb of the Unknown Dead, filled with the bones of 1,100 soldiers.

Many of America's greatest men have been buried at Arlington, including the assassinated Commander in Chief, President John F. Kennedy, and his brother Robert.

Major General MC Meigs, who took Robert E. Lee's garden and made it into a cemetery

See: Andersonville, Appomattox Court House, Fort Sumter, Gettysburg, Hampton Roads, Harpers Ferry, Little Big Horn, West Point

ARMAGEDDON
Israel

'And he gathered them together into a place called in the Hebrew tongue, Armageddon'. (Revelations 16:16)

We tend to use 'Armageddon' to describe some final, cataclysmic event like a colossal battle or the destruction of earth by a meteor. It is not surprising, considering the history of the real Armageddon

Har Megiddo – The Mountain of Megiddo in Hebrew, is near Nazareth in Israel, and lies in the Jezreel valley – which was a classic invasion route and one of the most strategic locations in the

See: Ararat, Tower of Babel, Gethsemane, Masada, Olympos

world, controlling the *Via Maris* (The Way of the Sea). As a result, it was the site of no less than 34 battles from 2350 BC to 1973. The armies included Egyptians,

Canaanites, Israelites, Midianites, Amalekites, Philistines, Hasmonaeans, Greeks, Romans, Muslims, Crusaders, Mamlukes, Mongols, French, Ottomans, British, Australians, Germans, Arabs and Israelis.

The roll call of the commanders is no less impressive. Thutmose III, Deborah and Barak, Sisera, Gideon, Saul and Jonathan, Shishak, Jehu, Joram, Jezebel, Josiah, Antiochus, Ptolemy, Vespasian, Saladin, Napoleon, and Allenby. Alexander the Great was there too, but his enemy sensibly surrendered.

There have been other places which have seen more than one battle, for example, Sedan, Bull Run and Ypres, but this little area, only 20 miles long and seven miles wide, takes the prize for being the most fought-over area in history. So many times, indeed, that it was even possible for Britain's General Allenby to copy in 1918 the tactics used there by Pharaoh Thutmose III, 3,400 years earlier.

After all this continuous mayhem, it is not surprising that St John the Divine, in the Bible's book of Revelations, should regard Armageddon as the perfect spot for the final future battle between good and evil.

ARNHEM BRIDGE
The Netherlands

The tanks of the 2nd Battalion Irish Guards were beginning their advance to 'The Island', the narrow road raised above the Dutch fields between Nijmegen and the bridge at Arnhem. Suddenly, there was a clang, and a Sherman tank's sprocket wheel came flying over the trees. *'I knew we were in big trouble',* said a young officer as eight more tanks exploded. It was not just the Irish Guards that were in trouble. So was the whole British Army.

The Guards Armoured Division was trying to play its part in Field Marshal Bernard Montgomery's 'Operation Market Garden', a bold attempt to punch a corridor into Germany's industrial heartland and *'win the war in forty four'.* It was to link up with American, British and

eventually Polish airborne troops dropped by parachute and glider near the bridges at Nijmegen, Eindhoven and Arnhem. The first two bridges on the corridor were captured. But Arnhem was to prove to be *'a bridge too far'.*

The disaster that unfolded reflected strange anomalies with the way Montgomery usually behaved, because he was normally extremely cautious and meticulous in his planning and very careful of his men's lives.

The Irish Guards' problems were only part of it. The Dutch had long ago concluded that the narrow, exposed, elevated road would be a deathtrap for tanks, and so it proved to be, with rows of burning vehicles blocking the road, predictable victims of the German lethal

88 mm and 75 mm anti-tank guns, and even of infantry with *Panzerfaust* rockets.

But this was nothing compared to the almost criminal rejection of intelligence reports that had revealed that Britain's 1st Airborne Division was about to land right among two crack SS Panzer Divisions, resting there by chance. Dutch resistance confirmed it, and a Spitfire photographed the waiting camouflaged tanks. But the Intelligence Officer who tried to point all this out was sent on sick leave to ensure his silence – perhaps because so many airborne operations had been cancelled and the airborne troops were thirsting to get on with it. Arnhem then proved to be a catastrophe. The lightly-armed airborne troops in Arnhem fought against tanks for eight days with incredible bravery. The - glider-borne 2nd South Staffords was the only battalion to win two Victoria Crosses in one battle during World War II. But, short of ammunition and supplies, all the troops at Arnhem, were forced either to surrender or to escape by night back across to Rhine. Out of 10,000 men, only 2,163 made it to safety.

Why did it happen? Almost certainly everyone was blindly following the will of Montgomery. And Montgomery was an egotistical and complex man.

After the war, Montgomery was asked to list the three greatest Generals in History. Without hesitation, he named Alexander the Great, Napoleon and himself. And he was not joking.

Years later at Wellington School, he read the lesson *'and God said unto the Israelites, and I have to say I agree with him'*. Believing absolutely in his high opinion of himself, he resented the growing American dominance – and especially that other egotist, US General George Patton, whom he had never forgiven for getting to Palermo in Sicily ahead of him. He also denigrated General Eisenhower, now his boss, as a *'hopeless amateur'* as a hands-on commander. So he was determined to

spite the Americans and pull off his own British victory, and was prepared to abandon all the cautious, in-depth planning and attention to detail that usually served him so well.

It was a great tragedy, because he was probably right to opt for a single, powerful push into Germany. If he had been less complex a personality and had got on rather better with his own side, he

might just have pulled it off and won the war in 1944. The Russians might not have reached Berlin first and there might have been no Iron Curtain and no Cold War. If...

Above: The bridge, with the wreckage of a German attack.

Below: With his men dead or wounded, Sergeant Baskeyfield of the South Staffords died fighting tanks alone, for which he won a posthumous VC.

See: Anne Frank's Annexe, Biggin Hill, Dakota, Dien Bien Phu, Dunkirk, Oradour

ASCOT
England

Queen Anne deserves thanks from many people. The last Tudor, she should certainly have been owed a debt of gratitude by her husband Prince George of Denmark in trying to produce an heir.

She bore him seventeen children. Tragically, sixteen died as infants and one, a son, was only to reach the age of twelve. Her reign gave us the superb style of houses, furniture and silver that bears her

HENRY DALLAL

Royal Ascot: old traditions and new influences. HM The Queen with Prince Philip, The Aga Khan, Ivana Trump and Sheik Mohammed Al Maktoum

MCvA

See: Aintree, Brooklands, Buck's Club, Champagne, Cowes, Eton, Farnborough, Indianapolis, Lord's, Savile Row, Wimbledon

name. The world of horses and racing can thank her for riding out one day from Windsor Castle, and chancing upon a piece of wasteland called East Cote. She decided that it was ideal *'for horses to gallop at full stretch.'* Royal Ascot was born.

The first race, for 'Her Majesty's Plate', held on August 11th 1711, was very different from today's racing, with three separate heats of four miles. No wonder the seven riders raced English Hunters – real stamina was needed.

Until 1945, Ascot shared a tradition with another racecourse, Indianapolis, because the racing only took place during the Royal Meeting, much as motor-racing at Indianapolis confined itself to the week of the 'Indy 500'. Now Ascot has 25 days of racing a year. But for the world, the five days of 'Royal Ascot' in the third week of June are the ones that matter.

In the nineteenth century, Royal Ascot became an essential centrepiece of the highly social 'English Season', with Queen Charlotte's Ball and the debutantes being presented to the Monarch and then indulging in their own season of parties and 'coming out' balls, complete with eligible young men, known as 'Debs' Delights'. 'The Season' continued with 'The Trooping the Colour', celebrating the Queen's official

birthday, the Henley Regatta, the Wimbledon Tennis Championships, Cowes Week and the Eton – Harrow cricket match. It only ended when 'everyone' in this elite social circle went north in August for the grouse shooting.

Twenty eight million television viewers in seventy countries now follow the racing at Royal Ascot, and as a social event, just as significant is the 'people watching'. Over the five days, 120,000 bottles of champagne are drunk, and 6,000 lobsters and over four tons of strawberries are eaten. But it is the fashion which attracts the headlines, especially in the Royal Enclosure, with its strict dress code of grey or black morning dress for men and, for ladies *'formal day dress with hats to cover the crown of the head'*. With heavy competition to look great and attract attention, it is not surprising that the stunning hats on 'Ladies Day', are star attractions. It is the one day that 'anyone who is anyone' must attend, and which drives the newspapers to paroxysms of frothy delight.

In addition to the long list of prestigious corporate sponsors vying to be associated with the event, Royal Ascot has made itself into a luxury brand in its own right, marketing its own champagne in the UK, golfware in America and, curiously, home furnishings in France. The march of progress. One can't help but wonder what Queen Anne would make of it all.

HENRY DALLAL

ASSISI
Italy

A ssisi was an unlikely birthplace for a saint such as Francesco di Pietro Bernadone – St Francis. He even said himself that it *'has the worst reputation in the world as the home of every kind of rogue and scoundrel'.*

Born of a rich, though not aristocratic,

family, he was originally christened Giovanni in 1182 after John the Baptist (by his mother), and renamed Francesco, 'Frenchman', by his father (who had been away in France at the time of his birth).

Despite an extravagant and frivolous

early life, Francis was always tortured by the sight of misery, especially when all about him was wealth – his own, that of his family and, above all, that of the church. A chance meeting with a leper finally convinced him that his destiny lay not with his bourgeois, worldly family, but with those who wandered, listless and hopeless, beyond society's furthest bounds.

He founded a new order of friars, one that would live in poverty like Christ, and whose mission was not to eradicate penury but to sanctify it. This ideal proved illusory as the number of friars swelled – to 5,000 in ten years – and the order was forced to acquire possessions in order to pursue its ministry. He finally gave up authority of the Franciscan Order, readily returning to being simply another brother.

Usually depicted surrounded by birds, animals and flowers, it is his love of nature that really defines St Francis – stories of his sermons to birds and rapport with wild animals abound. He was not, however, quite the happy-go-lucky preacher that children are told

about. His views on austerity were considered harsh and radical by the Catholic Church, and he also nursed a burning desire to convert infidels which led him on several risky and fruitless journeys abroad. His frailty was exacerbated in 1224 when he received the stigmata, causing him increasing suffering from then until his death, an account of which is preserved at Assisi.

The body cannot have been heavy. Though still alive, Francis was so wasted by illness, incompetent surgery and long penance, that his frame must have seemed to its six bearers as light as a sack of brushwood. He, and they, had little time to complete his last journey to his home town of Assisi, to save him from the grasp of Siena, which had vowed that he should die there, thus sanctifying a state for which he felt little fondness. By luck and doggedness, he and his companions reached Assisi, where he died on 4th October 1226 – a date now commemorated as the Feast of St Francis, and named after the most loved and revered Saint in the Catholic tradition.

See: Bethlehem, Fatima, Lourdes

THE MRS ASTOR'S BALLROOM
New York, USA

For decades, there was only one street worth living in for the rich in New York City. From its opening in 1826, Fifth Avenue had attracted New York's wealthiest and most elegant citizens; the Fricks, the Pulitzers, the Carnegies, The Harrimans, the Goulds, the Rockefellers and the Astors.

Their ever more magnificent houses had marched up from Washington Square, and no house was more important than 350 Fifth Avenue, that of Caroline Schermerhorn Astor. Having married one of the richest men in the world, William B. Astor, whose family wealth came originally from fur trading and rack renting, she determined to dominate the social scene. In spite of her stout figure and bulbous nose, she succeeded and described herself as *The* Mrs Astor. Indeed, such was her success that New York 'Society' was deemed to be made up of only those called the 'Four Hundred' who could be accommodated in her Fifth Avenue

ballroom. In an atmosphere of appalling snobbery and bigotry (no Catholics, no Jews) she and her Svengali-like adviser Ward McAllister were also determined also to keep out anybody who was even fractionally behind in the race for social acceptance. It was the Vanderbilts, the even more *nouveau* and more *riche* railroad millionaires, who especially needed to be kept out of Mrs Astor's 'Society' and McAllister's 'Social Register'.

William Henry Vanderbilt, the New York Central's railroad baron famous for his brutal phrase 'The Public be Damned', had moved into a magnificent house, filled with a superb art collection. Nearby, Alva, the ambitious wife of his second son, built the finest house in New York, at 660 Fifth Avenue, and planned its first ball in 1883, the most expensive party ever given, with 1,000 guests including the

Caroline Schermerhorn Astor dominated New York 'Society'

former President, Ulysses S. Grant. 'Society' and the press waited with baited breath.

In one of the planned *Star Quadrilles* of 'approved' young ladies was young Carrie Astor. Alva Vanderbilt, after the girls had been practising for weeks, suddenly told Carrie she was 'not welcome because your mother has never called on me'. The desperate Carrie bullied her mother into paying a formal visit to Alva. The Vanderbilts had made it into 'Society'.

ASWAN HIGH DAM
Egypt

The Nile, the longest river in the world, gave Egypt its ancient prosperity, creating a ribbon of fertile green to the sea. Without it, there would

have been no wealth, no Pharaohs, no pyramids and no legend of Cleopatra. Every year for centuries it flooded, depositing millions of tons of silt to create excellent agricultural land along its banks and in its Delta, the food basket of the Roman Empire.

In 1902 a dam was created at Aswan on the Sudan border to tame the uncontrolled flooding, but in 1952 the new Revolutionary Council decided to build a new High Dam four miles upstream. The plans for this great undertaking were to have unforeseen effects.

The Governments of Britain and America had initially promised to finance the new dam, due to cost one billion dollars. In the event, they pulled out. So, one month after Britain had handed over its military bases in the Canal Zone, Egypt's President Gamel Nasser decided on a radical move, nationalising the Suez Canal in July 1956 to use its revenues to finance the dam. 'We shall industrialise Egypt and compete with the West. We are marching from strength to strength'. With memories of pre-war appeasement, Britain's Prime Minister Sir Anthony Eden was almost hysterical in his belief that Nasser was a latter-day Hitler; 'A man with Colonel Nasser's record cannot be allowed to have his thumb on our windpipe'.

After weeks of fruitless negotiations brokered by the United Nations and America, a plan to use force was secretly hatched between Britain and France (co-owners of the Canal) and Egypt's enemy, Israel. Laborious military preparations took months (compared with the 72 hours that it took the Falklands Taskforce to sail) and the politically-dominated plans were flawed. At the end of October, Israel attacked Egypt. After bombing raids, the British and French then invaded to *'separate them'*. The Russians threatened with force (probably not atomic but conventional) but the Americans, furious at being left in the dark by the old allies, did something more practical – refusing to support Britain and its plummeting currency. Despite complete military success, the French and British were forced to withdraw in humiliation, as was a broken Eden – from public life.

Winston Churchill, Eden's old mentor, was privately asked in November if he would have attacked Egypt. 'I would never have dared, and if I had dared, I would never have dared stop'.

The Aswan High Dam was indeed completed, partly with help from the Soviet Union. Built with enough material to create 17 Great Pyramids, the water from Lake Nasser irrigates the Nile Valley and provides half of Egypt's electricity.

However, there are problems. The one million tons of fertiliser which farmers are now forced to use are no substitute for the 40 million tons of nutrient-rich silt that used to be deposited each year. The Nile Delta is eroding, fields are suffering from salinity and parasitic diseases are on the increase.

But, in spite of these problems, most Egyptians would say that the dam that started a war is, on balance, a good thing.

Anthony Eden tries to reassure Great Britain.

ATLANTIS
Atlantic Ocean ?

Most people have vaguely heard of Atlantis. The question is, did it ever exist? It was the Greek philosopher Plato, who first described in two of his 'dialogues', the existence of a vast island continent in the Atlantic off Spain. It had an advanced civilisation, and military power which dominated Europe and Africa. But whether through the anger of the Gods – or more prosaic physical reasons like volcanic explosions or undersea earthquakes – it had sunk without trace in 9,600 BC. Plato had heard the story from Egyptians passed down from father to son.

In spite of the efforts of numerous researchers, and even occultists, to locate the 'Lost Continent', it is perhaps more likely that it has been muddled with the very real explosion of Thera or Santorini in 1520 BC. Thera was a thriving commercial centre for the Minoan civilisation in the centre of the Mediterranean. Increasing earth tremors and minor eruptions gave enough warning for the Therans to flee their island. When it finally exploded, it would have been heard 1,800 miles away. The eruption was four times as powerful as Krakatoa and covered the remaining island in 98ft of ash, and everything else 430 miles downwind. The final tidal waves may have also destroyed the civilisation of Crete. Atlantis may never have existed outside the Mediterranean but it sounds more promising then Thera or Santorini!

See: Krakatoa, Mount St Helens, Pompeii

AUGUSTA
Georgia, USA

The world of sport can boast only a few places that have been created by the enthusiastic whim of one individual. Augusta, home of the US Masters golf tournament, is certainly one of them.

In 1930, Bobby Jones had just won all four of the great golf tournaments, the Open and Amateur Championships of both Britain and the United States. So, just 28, he decided to retire and build a dream golf course of his own where he could play with his close friends. Together with Clifford Jones, a New York financier, he looked at Augusta, near Atlanta, Georgia, with its excellent climate – and found a property called Fruitlands Nursery.

The rolling land was already beautiful and, with the advantage of the many trees and shrubs left behind from its nursery days, had the potential to be one of the most dramatic and lovely courses in the world. The Scottish designer, Dr Alister MacKenzie, then made sure Jones's dream was achieved.

As soon as the course was finished, Bobby Jones invited a first group of amateurs and professionals to come and play at Augusta, and the now famous U.S. Masters was born.

Horton Smith, winner in 1934, was the first Masters Champion, a title much prized by later legendary winners like Ben Hogan, Sam Snead, Gary Player, Arnold Palmer, Jack Nicklaus, Seve Ballesteros, Bernard Langer, Nick Faldo and Tiger Woods.

The Masters, held in April, tees off the season of the four great international 'major' tournaments, and for a brief few days its beauty and style are shared with millions of television viewers around the world. But for the rest of the year, it maintains the character that Bobby Jones had envisaged; a small exclusive club, closed, quite often, for the regular and constant improvements that make Augusta what it is – perhaps second only to the Old Course at St Andrews – the most famous golf course in the world.

Arriving at its old colonial club house, reached by an avenue of magnolia trees, and playing its sweeping fairways and perfect greens surrounded by shrubs ablaze with colour, will have to remain an impossible dream for most of the world's golfers.

Bobby Jones retired at 28 to build the superb Augusta golf course.

See: Brooklands, Cresta Run, Hillsborough, Le Mans, Lord's, Indianapolis, St. Andrews, Tour de France, Wembley, Wimbledon

AYERS ROCK
Australia

If you ask people to name a famous rock, most would probably opt for Gibraltar, the key strategic gateway to the Mediterranean. But there is another rock, which is now famous because of its extraordinary shape and beauty. Over 1,100 feet high and two miles long, Ayers Rock rises out of the desert near Alice Springs like a red island, which it indeed was seventy million years ago.

It is the largest monolith in the world and its strange and changing colour, caused by the rusting in its arkose sandstone, have made it one of the most talked – about and photographed natural features, especially at sunset when its colour is at its most dramatic red-orange hue.

The Aborigines call it *'Uluru'*, and it has played an important part in their spiritual life and legends for thousands of years. Their rock paintings cover its caves.

The first European to find the Rock was William Christie Gosse in 1873, who kindly named it after Sir Henry Ayers, then Chief Secretary and later Premier of South Australia – no doubt a worthy but not particularly interesting public servant. A perfect case of undeserved fame by chance!

See: Botany Bay, Mt. Everest

THE TOWER OF BABEL
Babylonia

'The Tower of Babel' by Pieter Breugel

The Bible (Genesis 11: 1-9) describes how, after the Flood in the land of Shinrar, the Babylonians decided to 'make a name for themselves' by building a great city and a tower 'with its top in the heavens'. It records that God was so alarmed by this that he disrupted the construction by confusing the language of the workers so that they could not longer work together, whereupon they were scattered across the earth speaking their own languages.

The remains of great Babylonian circular towers called *'ziggurats'* have indeed been found in the area by archaeologists and, north of the Marduk temple, is one called Bab-ilu (Gate of God) or Babel in Hebrew.

Thus, if you have a tendency to talk too fast or incoherently, you are said to be 'babbling'.

See: Ararat, Gethsemane, Masada, Olympos

BAEL NA BLATH
Ireland

In a little valley called Bael na Blath, the 'pass of the flowers', an ambush took place that was to alter Ireland forever. Michael Collins, 'the Big Fella', was killed.

Michael Collins is regarded as one of the most attractive, charismatic and tragic figures in Irish history – some have said the greatest since Brian Boru. He was a complex character, a mixture of infectious, warm enthusiasm and ice-cold calculation. He knew Britain and the British, having worked at financial institutions in London. And it was there that he joined the Irish Republican Brotherhood, quickly becoming the IRB's Treasurer of London and the South East, through his tireless energy, financial and organisational skills. The IRB would provide his power base in the years to come.

In May 1914, after years of negotiation, the Home Rule Bill for Ireland had passed the House of Commons. But within weeks, the out-break of the Great War would fatally ensure its postponement. Resistance to Home Rule by Ulster's Protestants had not gone away and they had even been importing guns from Germany to fight the British, if necessary. The Irish Volunteers saw no reason why they should not follow suit.

In January 1916, under threat of conscription into the British Army and hearing of clandestine activity in Ireland, Collins set sail for Dublin in time for the doomed Easter Rising. Collins was one of the survivors of the battle of the General Post Office, and was captured. The British did not recognise him and he escaped the firing squad, soon to become their most formidable enemy. Released from prison in England, he returned to Ireland to start his war.

It was the threat of extending conscription to Ireland that once again was hardening resistance against Britain, coupled with restrictions on Irish language and sports.

When the Great War ended, Sinn Fein MPs, (those not in English jails) set up their own Parliament, Dáil Eireann. On the day of its first sitting, the first shots of the Anglo-Irish War were being fired, far away in Tipperary.

Collins masterminded the brilliant escape of his colleague Eamon de Valera from Lincoln Jail, who then decided to go to America to raise support. In his absence, Collins then began a sophisticated intelligence war, with spies

Michael Collins

in Dublin Castle, where he even had the nerve to spend the night himself sifting through the British files. He also recruited the 'Squad', hand-picked trained assassins, who began the killing of informers and the more brutal policemen.

1920 was a year of terror, with killings and counter-killings, and the introduction of British volunteers to fight in Ireland, dubbed the *'Black and Tans'*, and the more effective ex-officer *'Auxiliaries'*. Murder and atrocity escalated. By the end of the year, 50,000 troops and 15,000 policemen were in conflict with 15,000 Volunteers.

Michael Collins, still an unknown and invisible figure to the British, coolly cycled round Dublin and plotted his next moves. The bleakest moment of the war was 'Bloody Sunday', when Collin's 'Squad' tracked down and wiped out the newly-arrived 'Cairo Gang' of British intelligence officers. The authorities reacted by shooting 14 dead at the Croke Park football stadium, with many more wounded. They did not drive on to the pitch and machine-gun from an armoured car, as depicted in the otherwise excellent film *Collins*.

De Valera returned from America in time for the first peace feelers and a truce. He was plainly jealous of Collins, snarling as he arrived, 'We'll see who's the Big Fella'. But when he first went to London, he pointedly excluded Collins from his group of negotiators.

When the real negotiations began, however, de Valera refused to go, and sent Collins, trapping him into signing a Treaty that partitioned Ireland. Britain's Lord Birkenhead said to Collins, 'I may have signed my political death warrant tonight.' Michael Collins replied prophetically, 'I may have signed my actual death warrant.'

De Valera duly rejected the Treaty, and the Irish split, and a Civil War erupted. To avoid the return of the British, Collins was, ironically, even forced to borrow field guns from them to shell his anti-Treaty former comrades holed up in the Four Courts. The tragic Civil War lasted eleven months, and killed more Irish than the war with Britain ever did.

And so it was that the Irish Free State's Commander in Chief, Michael Collins, feeling confident and at home in his native West Cork, was ambushed by a group of IRA men at Bael na Blath, the 'valley of flowers'. But he was over-confident. He had been warned of the possible ambush and, when attacked, grabbed a rifle, shouting 'Let's fight, boys'.

Rashly, standing up away from the cover of his armoured car, he was hit, in the failing light, by a last parting shot from a former British Army marksman, Sonny O'Neil.

His death caused an outpouring of grief which has never been seen before or since in Ireland. The sense of loss was shared by friends and foes alike, Irish and British. Had he lived, Ireland might have been a different place under Michael Collins than under the colder, more fanatic Eamon de Valera.

Who knows?

Ireland's tragic Civil War killed more Irishmen than the British ever did

See: Ballingarry, The Bogside, River Boyne, General Post Office

221b BAKER STREET
England

Of course, there never was a real 221b Baker Street, because there never was a real Sherlock Holmes or a real Dr Watson to live there. They were both products of the prolific imagination of Sir Arthur Conan Doyle.

Born in Edinburgh, Arthur was one of ten children, and some of his brothers also distinguished themselves. James wrote *The Chronicles of England,* Henry managed the Irish National Gallery, and Richard, the artist, was most famous for his cover of *Punch.*

Whilst Arthur studied medicine at Edinburgh University, two of his tutors caught his literary eye. The bearded Professor Rutherford would later be transformed into Professor Challenger in the dinosaur-filled *Lost World.* Dr Joseph Bell's medical deductive powers were to be assigned to his future master

Sherlock Holmes is the most filmed character in history. Seventy-five actors have played him in 220 films.

detective, Sherlock Holmes.

Even as he practised medicine, the first Sherlock Holmes novel appeared, *A Study in Scarlet*, netting Arthur a mere £25, followed by the highly successful non-Holmes historical novel, *Micah Clarke.*

The Strand Magazine published the next two Sherlock Holmes novels but, almost at once, Conan Doyle was worried about his creation and already wondering how to stop the Holmes success; writing to his mother, *'I think of slaying Holmes and winding him up for good and all. He takes my mind from better things'.* (Later he chose the Reichenbach Falls in Switzerland as the scene for the fatal struggle with Professor Moriarty).

In spite of his varied mass of world class writing, his medical career, his

34

sporting skills, his work on behalf of the underdog, his knighthood and his being Deputy Lieutenant of Surrey, Conan Doyle never succeeded in detaching himself from Sherlock Holmes. He produced no less than 56 Holmes stories, and 221b Baker Street became one of the most famous addresses in the world – albeit entirely fictitious.

So it is a good thing that admirers of the famous detective do not have to be satisfied with a plaque on the wall of the Abbey National Building Society, the modern occupier of the theoretical site. Just up the road, a house in Baker Street has been created to reproduce exactly

the 221b we read about. There, you can find in every detail the study that Holmes and Watson shared, their bedrooms and that of Mrs Hudson, their landlady. It really was a lodging house between 1860 and 1934 – which adds to the whole air of authenticity. It is worth a visit.

Sherlock Holmes' study, lovingly reproduced in every detail

BALACLAVA
Crimea

Half a league, half a league
Half a league onward
All in the valley of Death
Rode the six hundred

The ill-fated 'Charge of the Light Brigade' near the little Black Sea port of Balaclava was just one example of the extraordinary level of British incompetence during the Crimean War.

The British and French had come to the aid of Turkey in 1854 to help her resist Russia's expansionist moves against the weakened Ottoman Empire. As with so many wars, it was never meant to last long but limited to a short, sharp 'lesson'.

Lord Tennyson's stirring poem ensures that most people have heard of the charge, and the series of misunderstandings that sent Lord Cardigan's Brigade of light cavalry up the wrong valley and towards the wrong guns:
Cannon to right of them
Cannon to left of them
Cannon in front of them
Volleyed and thundered.

The disaster might be put down to Lord Raglan's different viewpoint from a hill, and his vague orders, or Lord Lucan's hatred of his brother-in-law, the brave but headstrong Lord Cardigan, whose career was dogged by scandal and disgrace. Like many rich aristocratic British

officers, Cardigan had repeatedly bought his commissions and had even outfitted his Regiment at his own expense, a man whom *The Times* had once called *'the plague-spot of the British Army'*. It could even have been the impetuosity of the bearer of the final order, Captain Nolan, pointing wildly in the wrong direction and shouting, 'There is your enemy! There are your guns!'

The end result was a tragedy that destroyed a Brigade, spoiled the earlier successes of that same day of the Heavy Brigade and the Highlanders, and prolonged the war into a ghastly winter. *'C'est magnifique, mais ce n'est pas la guerre'.* ('Magnificent, but it is not war') said a

The Charge of the Light Brigade by C E Stewart

COURTESY OF THE CAVALRY AND GUARDS CLUB

French observer, and in many ways he was right. Britain was not ready for war.

Many people know of the efforts of Britain's Florence Nightingale, known as the 'Lady of the Lamp', because of her nightly care of the wounded and her attempts to bring some order to the chaotic and neglected medical system. What was really disgraceful was the suffering of men and animals through sheer stupidity, cruel inaction and lack of initiative. Twelve thousand greatcoats had arrived in Balaclava, but only three thousand were issued because of a regulation that

'troops should only be issued with greatcoats every three years.' British soldiers were reduced to stripping their Turkish allies' bodies of their boots, so pitiful were the British ones. The horses suffered horribly. Cardigan, so fiercely proud of his Regiment and Brigade, sat on his yacht continuing his quarrels with Lucan while his horses starved to death or died of exposure. What price glory?

It is little wonder that the Army began to change, and that three items of clothing remain with us today – the *Raglan Sleeve,* the sweater we call a *Cardigan,* and a woollen protective headpiece, now publicly worn by protesters or the Irish Republican Army, the *Balaclava Helmet.*

*See: Gettysburg,
Little Bighorn, Waterloo*

> *'You have a starving population, an absentee aristocracy, an alien church, and, in addition, the weakest executive in the world. That is the Irish Question.'*
> Benjamin Disraeli

William Smith O'Brien M.P.

BALLINGARRY
Ireland

In 1845, Ireland had a population of eight million, compared with England, Wales and Scotland with sixteen million. Such a huge number of people could only be sustained by the potato, 'the lazy crop', which could be left in the ground while the men went to work at other jobs, and could be grown in little plots of land. No less than three million were dependent on this one source of food.

Then a sudden and devastating disaster struck, *Phytophthora infestans,* the potato blight, which overnight could turn healthy potatoes into black, evil-smelling, rotting mush. It reduced the 1845 crop by one third; next year it was worse, with three quarters lost. The removal of a staple food, rich in vitamins, caused immediate starvation and worse – diseases like typhus, scurvy and dysentery. Millions died. These disasters were quickly followed by mass immigration to escape; to England, the United States, Canada and Australia. The 'Famine Ships' sat in north American harbours with their hapless passengers dying on board, or in quarantine stations in sight of freedom. Soon they were called 'Coffin Ships'.

By 1848, Ireland had lost one quarter of its people. Weakened by deprivation and disease, Ireland was in despair. With three colleagues, William Smith O'Brien hatched the ill-fated 'Young Ireland Revolt' against British rule, to be fought

under the French Revolution-inspired tricolor of green, white and orange, now Ireland's flag. O'Brien, (the author's great, great uncle), was a somewhat unlikely candidate for an Irish revolutionary, with his traditional background of an education at Harrow and Cambridge. What is more, he was a Protestant.

From all over Ireland, O'Brien was promised, rather over-optimistically, 5,000 'fully armed men'. Thoroughly alarmed, another Irishman, the aged Duke of Wellington, urged the sending of 10,000 troops from England.

In humiliating reality, the rebels mustered only 32 'fully armed men' and another 20 'prepared to throw stones'. On July 29th 1848, this trusty band managed to intercept a troop of mounted constabulary who retreated into a stone cottage near the village of Ballingarry, owned by a widow, Mrs McCormack. *'The Battle of Widow McCormack's Cabbage Garden'* was interrupted by the furious widow returning home to find her house under fire and her children trapped inside. Fiercely, she ordered all the combatants to cease-fire and go home, and this they did, rather shamefacedly. William Smith O'Brien was arrested by a suspicious guard at Thurles railway station – surely the only time that railway staff have arrested a man for High Treason.

He and the other three ringleaders were found guilty, and were among the last people to be sentenced to 'hanging, drawing and quartering.' The young Queen Victoria was horrified to find out what this entailed, and insisted that the sentence be reduced to transportation to Australia. Smith O'Brien refused this clemency, demanding death or a Royal Pardon. A special Act, called the 'Transportation for Treason Act' of 1849, was passed – just to be rid of him and his companions.

In the event, the way he handled his exile had a far greater political effect than the original abortive revolt. In Van Diemen's Land (now Tasmania), O'Brien, as an MP and probably the best-connected felon ever to be transported, became the natural focus of the anti-transportation movement. Curiously, this was Australian-led. Previously transported folk, now respectable with families, wanted to prevent the arrival every few weeks of ships carrying disreputable people. These, normally released after a fortnight, often went back to the bad old ways for which they were sentenced in

the first place. One notable robber gang used to avoid identification by leaving victims tied to trees and incoherently drunk.

Smith O'Brien's three companions eventually escaped to America where one, Thomas Meagher, had a distinguished career as a Union General in the Civil War, leading the Irish Brigade in brutal, sometimes suicidal battles like Cold Harbor (where he saved the day 'fighting in his shirtsleeves'), Malvern Hill, Antietam and Fredericksburg.

More poignant still were the losses suffered by Meagher's Young Ireland convict friend, John Mitchel, who had tragically espoused the Confederacy and edited Jefferson Davis's newspaper. Of his three sons, Willy died at 'Pickett's Charge' at Gettysburg, and John, who had fired the first shells at Fort Sumter in 1861, was killed in command there by one of the very last.

See: Bogside, River Boyne, Falls Road, Fort Sumter, Gettysburg, General Post Office

The plaque at Thurles station recording William Smith O'Brien's arrest for High Treason by a railway guard

BARBIZON
France

The Forest of Fontainebleau is a magical place, with deep glades, magnificent trees and curious huge grey elephantine rocks left behind from some pre-historic age. It is not surprising that it should have been an inspiration to landscape painters. The name of one little village on the north west edge of the forest was to resound around the world, and the 'Barbizon' school of painting was to have a huge influence, particularly on the Impressionists.

The first well-known artist to arrive at Barbizon was Théodore Rousseau in 1846, followed three years later by Jean François Millet.

Both had been inspired by John Constable's superbly evocative portrayals of the English countryside when his work was shown in France. But in fact the forest, so close to Paris, had been attracting artists for years. Among painters inspired to paint from nature were Bruandet, Michel, de Valenciennes,

Berthu and his pupils Michallon, Cognet and Corot. These days it is amazing to think that Rousseau and Millet were shocking to the art world with the sheer realism of their paintings, especially Millet with his portrayal of peasant life.

After a while, the paintings of the Barbizon School began to sell quite well thanks to the growth of art dealers, and especially those of Paul Durand-Ruel, who bought 70 paintings by Rousseau in 1866.

FRANCOIS WHETTNALL

The bizarre elephantine rocks of the Forest of Fontainebleau

'Mansion Through The Trees and Lake' by Corot

The reputation of the stars of the Barbizon School, Rousseau, Millet and Corot would, however, soon be rather overshadowed by the movement they helped to inspire, 'Impressionism'. The Salon des Refusés, organised by Napoleon III to bypass the stifling influence of the official Salon, and the first Impressionist exhibition in 1874, brought on to the world stage artists who were initially mocked. Indeed, 'Impressionist' was used by a raft of contemporary art critics as a term of abuse for the likes of Edouard Manet, Claude Monet, Camille Pissaro and Auguste Renoir. However, one writer, who realised their purpose, described them, *'They are impressionists in that they render not a landscape but the sensation produced by a landscape'*.

The dealer, Durand-Ruel, bought the work of the Impressionists, but they sold much more slowly than the Barbizon painters, and his stock of 23 Manets, purchased in 1871 for 35,000 francs, remained unsold for a long time. It would be years before the art world could not get enough of them.

Artists still come to Barbizon and its magical forest to paint. No wonder the official tourist website is simply called: *Barbizon, village of painters*.

See: Bridge at Arles, Flatford, Giverny, Moulin Rouge, Sistine Chapel, Vinci

THE BASTILLE
France

Every year on 14th July, the French nation celebrates its most important national holiday, Bastille Day. It marks the real beginning of the French Revolution, the first decisive moment when the Bourbon monarchy of Louis XVI was publicly challenged by the people, exasperated by the feudal and corrupt regime.

'The Bastille' was the fortress of St Antoine, built in 1370 as part of the fortifications of Paris, guarding one of the gates to the city against the English.

More significantly, for two centuries it was a grim state prison and a symbol of arbitrary royal power created by the despotic Cardinal Richelieu. The Bastille had housed many of the victims of the 'lettres de cachet', which allowed imprisonment without trial.

However, its reputation as portrayed in Dickens' *'A Tale of Two Cities'*, as a place of chained prisoners in rat-infested dungeons, is now disputed. Prisoners apparently lived in surprising luxury, playing host to their aristocratic visitors, with whom they strolled through the gardens.

The Paris mob stormed the Bastille on 14th July 1789, killing 100 guards, old veterans invalided out of the army, and the Governor, whose head was paraded around town. Primarily an arms raid, as a rescue mission it was something of an anti-climax. The massive building then housed only seven prisoners, and none were political detainees. Four of them were forgers, the Comte de Solages was in for sexual offences, and the remaining two were lunatics, one a 'Major Whyte', an Irishman convinced he was Julius Caesar! The notorious Marquis de Sade, ending 5 years imprisonment for 'gross indecency', missed being 'liberated' by one week.

But the torch of revolution was lit, and the King's authority fatally damaged. Four years later, the deposed monarch faced the guillotine as 'Citizen Capet', as did so many members of the *ancien régime*. Europe was plunged into 17 years of war and turmoil caused by the man who benefited most from the fall of the Bastille, Napoleon Bonaparte.

See: Alcatraz, Andersonville, Andrassy, Changi, Dachau, Devil's Island, Getto, Great Hedge of India, Gulag, Landsberg, Reading Gaol, Robben Island, Spandau

BATH
England

The names of some places have come to describe what they are. Health springs, for instance, were called 'Spas', after a town in Belgium. But, sometimes it is the other way round. Bath, in Avon, is named quite literally after a bath.

According to legend, it was Bladud,

The Roman baths of Aquae Sulis

son of Celtic King Lud, who discovered the healing baths in about 825 BC. Suffering from leprosy, he was exiled to Swainswick on the outskirts of today's Bath. He noticed his pigs curing themselves of scurvy by rolling in the hot mud oozing from the ground, tried it himself and was cured of his ailment.

When he became King, he built a temple on the site. The Celtic Dubunni tribe built five hill forts to protect the hot spring, which was soon regarded as an entrance to the underworld. The Romans appropriated both the baths and the Celtic goddess Sul, creating a temple to Sulis Minerva, with the hot healing waters attracting pilgrims to *'Aquae Sulis'* (Waters of the Sun) from all over the Empire.

After the Romans left in 400, Bath continued to be important. King Arthur defeated the Saxons at nearby Badon Hill in 518, but at Dyrham they turned the tide in 577. The hated William Rufus razed the city for rebellion in 1088. Slowly, wool and cloth rebuilt the town's prosperity, while all the time visitors came for the therapeutic powers of Bath's hot waters, although the great 16th century traveller, John Leland, thought that their smell *'rikketh like a*

seething potte'.

In 1727, a bronze head of the goddess Minerva was discovered while a huge trench was being dug to lay sewers, and sixty years later, a solid Roman pavement was found 20 feet below ground. The Roman baths that the Saxons had destroyed gradually began their restoration.

Three men contributed to Bath's transformation in the 18th century. Richard 'Beau' Nash used his money from gambling and Queen Anne's visit as a launch pad to make Bath into the social rival of London. Nash earned his nickname by dressing the part of *'King of Bath'* in a black wig, driving the streets in a chariot drawn by six horses, his postillions blowing French horns. Former postmaster and millionaire Ralph Allen cut the huge golden blocks of Bath stone from his quarries, and architects John Wood, and later his son, used the stone to create the elegant glories of Queen Square, the Parades, the Circus and the curved terrace of the Royal Crescent.

Soon the Georgian city was filled with the great people of the era, Horace Walpole, Dr Johnson, James Boswell and Thomas Gainsborough and the future Prime Minister William Pitt became its Member of Parliament.

Bath's fame was enhanced by its appearance in the literary works of Smollett, Sheridan and Jane Austen, who wrote in *Northanger Abbey*, 'Oh! Who can be tired of Bath?'

Bath's name now lives on in a profusion of products: The Bath Oliver biscuit, Bath Buns, Bath stone and the invalid Bath Chair. And, of course, in superb arcitechture and a useful piece of plumbing.

See Spa, Vichy

The magnificent Royal Crescent

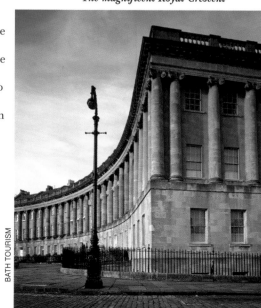

THE BAUHAUS
Germany

There were several times in the 1930s when Germany's loss was the world's gain. When Berlin's police loaded students from the Bauhaus into trucks in 1933, it marked just another exodus of talent from Nazi Germany.

The Bauhaus (the house of building) was set up by the architect Walter Gropius in 1919, with the revolutionary concept of combining architecture with a practical knowledge of craftsmanship.

Students took a six month course in carpentry, metalwork, pottery, stained glass, weaving, graphics, typography and stagecraft.

Its teachers included artists Paul Klee and Wassily Kandinsky. In its product design, the Bauhaus stressed the need for producing for the masses, not the élite, and geared its products like tubular steel chairs and reading lamps to mass production.

In 1930, Gropius's successor, Hannes Meyer, was ousted because of his alleged left-wing views. Ludwig Mies van der Rohe, who took over, tried to keep in with the Nazis by making rules for students, instructing them '*not to stay late in the canteen, avoid political discussions, make no noise and go out well-dressed to the town*' – hardly student behaviour even then.

It did no good. This was the year the Nazis were eliminating Germany's creative genius. Jewish musicians like Schoenberg were dismissed from the Prussian Academy of Art, as were the conductors Erich Kleiber and Otto Klemperer of the Berlin State Opera, and Fritz Busch, conductor of the Dresden Opera.

But anyone could be a victim of the Nazi's narrow view of what was suitable '*Kultur.*' After all, Herman Goering said, 'When I hear the word culture I release the safety catch of my Browning.'

The 'unsuitable' music of Paul Hindemith, who was not Jewish, was banned from the radio. Toscanini refused to conduct at Bayreuth in protest at Nazi treatment of artists.

Under the same kind of pressure Bertolt Brecht and Kurt Weill, whose musical play *The Three-penny Opera* had run since 1928 in Berlin, had left, as had playwright, Ernst Toller and film director Fritz Lang, to whom Propaganda Minister, Goebbels offered a post at UFA film studios. 'My mother had Jewish parents', said a reluctant Lang. 'We'll decide who's Jewish', said Goebbels. Lang left that very night for Paris. The greatest name in German letters, Thomas Mann, was exiled in Switzerland. His novelist brother Heinrich and Arnold and Stefan Zweig were on the list of many banned authors whose works were removed from public libraries and burned. Also banned was Erich Maria Remarque's anti-war book *All Quiet on the Western Front.*

On April 11th 1933, the Gestapo closed the Bauhaus, and its famous teachers left the country and were soon spreading its influence in art, graphics, furniture design and architecture across the world, especially in the United States. Walter Gropius became Chairman of the Harvard School of Architecture, and designed the MetLife building spanning New York's Park Avenue. László Moholy-Nagy founded the New Bauhaus (later the Institute of Design) in Chicago, and Mies van der Rohe became head of architecture at the Illinois Institute of Technology and designed the Seagram Building.

Seventy years on, Bauhaus products are still selling all over the world. Probably only art students know why.

Walter Gropius

Above: The Bauhaus building in Germany, the spiritual birthplace of a whole generation of influential artists.

Below right: New York's Met Life building, designed by Gropius.
PHOTO: MICHAEL BURCZYK

See: Barbizon, Bazaar, Carnaby Street, Harlem, Menlo Park Motown, Savile Row, Storyville, Tin Pan Alley

THE BAY OF PIGS
Cuba

In the darkness of the night on April 16th 1961, 1,500 armed men waded ashore at two beaches in a bay on Cuba's south west coast, called 'Bahia de los Cóchinos'. It was the climax of one of the most incompetent and arguably immoral foreign policy actions in which the United States has ever become involved.

As a way of explaining how on earth the 'Bay of Pigs' came about, it is important to remember that, by the end of the fifties, America had become obsessed with 'Communism.' The vicious and unrestrained anti-Communist witch hunts by Senator Joe McCarthy and his un-American Activities Committee had only just ended, J. Edgar Hoover was devoting an inordinate amount of FBI time to domestic Communism, and the Central Intelligence Agency was certainly not going to be outdone in such paranoia.

Imagine the horror of the United States and its Government when, in 1959, Communist Fidel Castro overthrew the corrupt Mafia-linked Batista regime in Cuba. While the Mafia and its casinos were rightly kicked out of Cuba, Communism was now on America's doorstep, just 90 miles away.

With the approval of President Eisenhower, in 1960 the CIA started to plan to discredit Castro. Ludicrous schemes included spraying LSD into a TV studio, or making Castro's beard fall out. More seriously, the CIA was working with the Mafia on actual, if hardly more credible, murder plots.

During the Presidential campaign of 1960, young Senator John Kennedy cynically and repeatedly accused Eisenhower of 'not doing enough about Cuba', knowing perfectly well that the Republican administration of Eisenhower and Nixon was indeed hatching a coup against Castro, but could not reveal it.

Eisenhower had approved a CIA plan and a budget in March 1961 to attack and overthrow Castro, using US-trained and armed Cuban exiles. When Kennedy was elected, he endorsed the plan, except that he fatally changed the landing place from the more suitable town of Trinidad, and made it a risky night-time assault.

Not surprisingly, there was honourable and justified opposition to the whole idea by many Administration and other politicians. On March 29th, Senator Fulbright wrote to Kennedy '*to give this activity even covert support is of a piece with the hypocrisy and cynicism for which the United States is constantly denouncing the Soviet Union in the United Nations and elsewhere. This point will not be lost on the rest of the world – nor on our own consciences.*'

Kennedy and his team, buoyed up by infectious optimism and over-confidence in their own luck, ignored such opposition and gave the go-ahead.

Everything went wrong. Bombing raids by poorly disguised American B-26s failed to destroy the Cuban airforce, which immediately sank two vital ships. The Cuban people did not rise to join the invaders. The Cubans were well organised and competent, and Castro displayed calm and impressive leadership.

Adlai Stevenson, the US Ambassador to the United Nations, was embarrassed

Some Cubans, subjected to decades of Castro's five hour speeches, may have wished that the Bay of Pigs invasion had succeeded.

and furious to discover that he had been duped by his President, and that Kennedy had been referring to him as *'my official liar'*. After four American pilots had been killed in limited and desperate last minute air strikes, Kennedy pulled off the air cover, finally dooming the operation after 3 days. The last radio message from Brigade 2506 said, *'We have nothing left to fight with. How can you people do this to us, our people, our country?'* A good question.

Two hundred of the invaders were killed and 1,197 captured, later to be ransomed privately for food and medicine worth $53 million.

While publicly taking responsibility, Kennedy made the CIA scapegoats. As he said to Richard Bissell, the main planner of the Bay of Pigs, 'If this were the British parliamentary Government, I would resign and you, being a civil servant would remain. But in our Government, you and Dulles have to go and I have to remain'.

Neither the Kennedys nor the CIA had learned their lessons well enough. The Kennedys, with their exaggerated competitiveness, their feeling that they had lost a round in a game, authorised *'Operation Mongoose'* , a whole series of new, illegal and sometimes ridiculous attempts by the CIA to 'eliminate' Castro. These included poison pens, exploding cigars and contaminated wet

suits. Moreover, the Kennedys became further involved in the unholy alliance with the Mafia, and one of the tasks of Jack Kennedy's mistress, Judith Exner, was the very dangerous one of asking her other boyfriend, Sam Giancana (the head of the Mafia) for help over Cuba.

More importantly for the rest of the world, the Bay of Pigs fiasco also led to Soviet Premier Nikita Khrushchev embarking on the equally reckless and ill-conceived idea of placing missiles in Cuba. The result was a 'Missile Crisis', which very nearly brought the world to nuclear war. Cuba also destroyed Khrushchev. The Soviet Praesidium dismissed him a year later quoting his *'harebrained scheming, hasty conclusions, rash decisions and his actions based on wishful thinking'*.

The bitterness of the Bay of Pigs failure, together with feelings of multiple betrayal, also ensured that when John Kennedy was assassinated in Dallas two years later, the long list of candidates for suspicion included pro-Castro Cubans, anti-Castro Cubans, the CIA and the Mafia.

As Dean Acheson commented to Arthur Schlesinger, *'In view of the fact that God limited the intelligence of man, it seems unfair that he did not also limit his stupidity'*.

See: Aldermaston, Ambassador Hotel, Arlington, Chappaquiddick, Dallas, Greenham Common, Havana, Texas School Book Depository

BAYONNE
France

In Bayonne in the French Pyrenees, a group of 17th century Basque musketeers found themselves surrounded by Spanish cavalry. Without the twenty foot pikes that the infantry then used to keep cavalry at bay, one of the soldiers stuck his short knife down his musket barrel, as he

had learned to do hunting boars. His comrades quickly copied him, and they survived – against all odds. The ridge where they fought became known as *'La Bayonette.'*

Soldiers from Bayonne led the fashion to create 'bayonettes' as a protection against cavalry. Soon, the 'plug' bayonet

which blocked the muzzle was replaced by the 'socket' bayonet which enabled the weapon still to be fired, although recharging the muzzle with a long sharp knife attached could certainly be hazardous.

'The bul-let is a crazy thing. Only the bayonet knows where it is going', said a Russian General. Unfortunately, by 1860, the bullet knew exactly where it was going and firepower devastated infantry assaults long before the bayonet could be used. At both Fredericksburg and Gettysburg, 7,000 men died in twenty minutes. At the final assault of Port Arthur, the Japanese lost 60,000. In the First World War whole

regiments disappeared as they walked steadily towards enemy machine guns with bayonets bravely fixed.

However, that is not to say the bayonet was useless and never used again. In close quarter fighting it was essential, as at Rorke's Drift, where it gave British soldiers a worthy counter to the dreaded Zulu stabbing *assegai*. Indeed, it became a tool of infantrymen all over the world, to be used when appropriate. 'Fix bayonets!' is a universal and chilling order.

One nation that espoused the bayonet fanatically was Japan. The weapon perfectly fitted the Japanese code of Bushido and the Samurai tradition, and was the soldiers' version of their officers' Samurai swords. They practiced bayonet drill constantly, even on campaigns. Horrifyingly, they used humans for practice, as with innocent civilians at the 'Rape of Nanking' and with their Allied prisoners after the fall of Bataan and Singapore. But, once again, flushed with early victories, they forgot the lessons of history and believed in the weapon too

The bayonet charge, the final, savage encounter

much. '*A good bayonet charge is an adequate response to most military problems*'. But, when their enemies were steady, resourceful, and had firepower on their side, innumerable 'Banzai' charges were stopped in their tracks with appalling Japanese losses.

It is strange that even in today's hi-tech military world, there is no soldier anywhere that, in the last resort, does not rely on that knife which the quick-witted musketeer of Bayonne decided to jam down his muzzle.

See: Changi, Corregidor, Gettysburg, Kohima, Kwai, Rorke's Drift, Somme, Waterloo

BAYREUTH
Germany

While it was already an important city and a centre of the arts, Bayreuth was only made really famous because one man chose to settle there.

As a composer, Richard Wagner had enjoyed what we would now call a 'chequered' career. In Paris, where he had spent time in a debtor's prison, productions of *Tannhäuser* were fiascos, in Vienna the artists were unequal to the complexity of *Tristan* and, in spite of the comparative success of *The Mastersingers of Nürnberg,* his excessive spending had forced him to leave Vienna to avoid imprisonment for debt – again.

At 51, he appeared to be in real trouble. But his capacity for making friends, and his obvious genius, saved him. The eccentric Ludwig II, aged only 18 and a great supporter of Wagner, ascended the throne of Bavaria and invited him to put his poem *The Ring* to music in Munich.

For six years his other works were successfully performed in Munich, with

Tristan and *The Mastersingers* being conducted by the great Hans von Bülow. But plans for a new theatre and music school in Munich were wrecked by Wagner's lifestyle, as he ran once more into debt and egotistically interfered in politics. His image in Munich was further dented when he became the lover of Cosima – his mentor Franz Liszt's daughter and the wife of von Bülow – who bore him three children before they were able to marry. Wagner moved on in a hurry and was set up by his friend the King in Triebschen on Lake Lucerne in Switzerland.

At last *The Ring*, Wagner's masterwork, was completed. But he broke his agreement with the King to perform it first in Munich, dreaming that a new site and purpose-built theatre were necessary. Then he found Bayreuth. Once again the

Richard Wagner

The Festspielhaus at Bayreuth

his wife Cosima took over the management of the Bayreuth Festivals. Later his son Siegfried carried on, and now his grandsons, Wolfgang and Wieland, have taken over.

It is rather like Duke Ellington's family still running jazz festivals at the Cotton Club after 125 years.

There was, and still is, a shadow over Bayreuth and Wagner, created by the way Adolf Hitler espoused the composer and his work. The dictator was obsessed with Wagner, turning the Bayreuth festivals into major Nazi events. He purchased some of the original scores from the Wagner family, and indeed, died with two of them in the Berlin bunker.

Wagner's work is not to everyone's taste. Rossini once said, *'Wagner has lovely moments, but awful quarters of an hour'*.

But he is the only musician to have created and maintained the fame of a town.

See: Abbey Road, Carnegie Hall, Cotton Club, Glastonbury, Ibiza, Motown, Nuremberg, Storyville, Woodstock

ever-patient Ludwig supported him, giving him his Bayreuth house 'Wahnfried', ('Peace from Illusion') and providing much of the funds for the new Festspeilhaus. *The Ring* was a triumph, first performed in August 1876. Performances at Bayreuth have continued ever since as, after his death,

BAZAAR
England

Mary Quant

In 1957, a young designer in London called Mary Quant opened a boutique, *Bazaar,* at 130 King's Road, with her husband and partner who used its basement for his restaurant. She was just in time to become one of the great fashion influences of the 'Swinging Sixties.'

With quite a conventional training at Art School (in hat design), Mary Quant realised the power of youth, and turned radical. Fashion-conscious teenagers no longer wished to dress like their mothers. She started designing clothes reminiscent of little girls at dancing class – short pleated skirts, white anklets and black patent ankle-strap shoes, perfect for the new style of models like 'Twiggy.' Her skirts grew shorter and shorter, becoming the

'miniskirt' that first shocked and then entranced the world. At one stage, miniskirts needed so little material that they qualified as children's clothes and escaped British sales tax.

With dozens of imitators, and other original designers, King's Road was soon lined with shops and boutiques and became a fashion mecca for 'swinging Londoners', and indeed the world.

Many of the changes during the Sixties, including those in fashion, began as a mostly urban, and especially London phenomenon. Some young people were nervous of shocking their parents, who often still controlled the purse strings. One newspaper photographed conventionally dressed young people arriving from Croydon or Southend, slipping into the Sloane Square lavatories to change, then strolling up and down the King's Road dressed 'outrageously' until evening, when they changed back into 'civilian clothes' to face their parents in the suburbs.

Within a few years Mary Quant's style and influence had spread worldwide, and she was selling and mass-producing clothes and cosmetics for Europe and the United States on a multi-million dollar scale. Like her fellow innovators and dollar-earners, The Beatles, she earned an MBE from the Queen. Seldom has one small shop had such a huge effect.

See: Abbey Road. Bikini, Carnaby Street, Cavern Club, Savile Row, Sibylla's

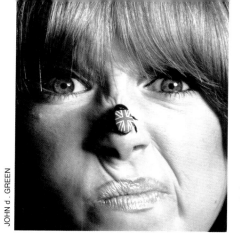

JOHN d . GREEN

From a time when Britain ruled the culture waves. Patti Boyd, model and wife of Beatle George Harrison, on the cover of the best-selling 'Birds of Britain' book, celebrating the country's pretty and enterprising young women.

'BECKINGHAM PALACE'
England

No, not Buckingham Palace, and not the home of Britain's first family. But, arguably, that of the next one.

A mention of Britain's most famous celebrity couple at the time of writing, and you know instantly it is Victoria 'Posh Spice' and her footballer husband, David Beckham. They are perhaps the most publicised couple of the last four years, even more so than Madonna who is truly the 'queen of pop.'

It is quite ironic that the Beckhams are so protective of their privacy, but exploit themselves through a slick publicity machine to tabloids and magazines all over the world. A prime example of this exploitative nature was a website that was launched in July 2001, dubbed 'Beckingham Palace' (a joke that suggests the Beckhams are, indeed, the next Royal Family). The 'Royal' theme was carried throughout the site, featuring a tour of the mock-Georgian £3 million mansion in Hertfordshire. The cartoon image of the inside of the house even used a distinct royal purple hue, and visitors could also see 'the Royal Bathroom', with matching gold monographed cisterns and showers as well as two identical toilets – questionably in opposite taste to that of the genuine Royals. Amusing, some might say, although tacky and distasteful to a million others. Sadly, the website was changed in 2003 to *'coincide with the next phase of Victoria Beckham's career'*.

It was, however, all convenient publicity to promote Victoria's new single and album, which could be heard on the jukebox in the website.

'Beckingham Palace' even gleaned a mention on the national UK news.

Although not as extravagant as another British singer, Elton John, the Beckhams could surely run a close second with their exuberant spending. At their wedding reception at an Irish castle, they sat on red and gold thrones, now permanently installed in their real mansion which, after a £3 million refit, boasts a gym, recording studio, three gazebos and Versailles-style fountains. Their eldest son, Brooklyn, is fortunate to have a nursery which has a £20,000 ceiling scattered with fibre optic stars, and a frieze portraying his parents as Cinderella and Prince Charming. One wonders if this will be appreciated by the youngster in a few years time.

There were reports in the tabloids in February 2001 that the Beckhams were planning to spend £300,000 on their garden alone. They ordered 25,000 daffodil bulbs, 15,000 hyacinths, 4,000 crocuses, 2,500 snowdrops, 2,000 cyclamen and 1,125 fritillaria. Surely this could rival Kew Garden?

But maybe they are having second thoughts about the 'Royal' aspects of their life. Victoria has mused: *'I don't know if I'll really be calling the house Beckingham Palace. It makes me laugh, but there's a lot of cynical people who say 'who does she think she is?'* You don't have to be too cynical to ask the same question.

Victoria and David Beckham - Britain's second 'First Family?'

See: Old Trafford

BEDLAM
England

It was the rather unpleasant English desire to go and stare at the insane that has given us the word 'Bedlam.'

Founded as a refuge for the poor in 1247, by 1377 the Priory of St Mary of Bethlehem in London's Bishopsgate had added a hospital and was admitting the mentally ill. In the 16th century the Priory was dissolved, but the hospital continued as an asylum for the insane. It was known as the Bethlehem Royal Hospital and in 1675 moved to a new site in Moorgate. The care for the 'lunatics' in this place was both primitive and brutal and the public's fascination with the insane led to the asylum charging 2 pence for visitors to come and stare – or jeer at the unfortunate inmates, a practice which continued into the early 19th century. The visitors often caused the patients to become disruptive and noisy, creating chaos and disorder, and gradually the word Bethlehem became shortened to 'Bedlam' and was used to denote madness. Bedlam was also a place for assignations, and *The London Spy* in 1698 commented *'All I can say for Bedlam is thus; it is an almshouse for madmen, a showing room for harlots, a sure market for lechers, a dry walk for loiterers'*. In 1815 the asylum moved yet again under the same name when a new building was constructed for it near Lambeth Road, a building which is today home to the Imperial War Museum. But almost two centuries after spectators were finally banned from the hospital, the word 'bedlam' is still applied worldwide to any scene of commotion and uproar.

BEDLOE'S ISLAND
New York, USA

Fame by chance is often thrust upon a place. Sometimes it is then snatched away. This is what happened to Isaack Bedloo, a merchant who acquired Great Oyster Island in New York Harbour in the 1660s. The City bought it in 1758 and Bedloe's Island, as it was then called, was then ceded to the Federal Government, who built Fort Wood there to protect New York during the War of 1812. But it acquired its real fame when the Statue of Liberty arrived.

The Statue was a joint effort by the United States and France to celebrate the friendship of the two nations during the American Revolution. Funds were to be raised in both countries, the pedestal to be created in America and the Statue built in France. Fundraising in the United States went very slowly until Joseph Pulitzer, of Pulitzer Prize fame, used his newspaper *The World* in order to galvanise donations.

The French sculptor, Frederic Auguste Bartholdi, turned to Gustave Eiffel who had created the Eiffel Tower to use his expertise to help him with the design problems of a colossal copper-clad female figure with a complex steel frame. Eventually, the Statue was delivered by ship, like a gigantic kit model in 350 pieces, packed in 214 wooden crates. In 1886, it was re-assembled; 31 tons of copper and 125 tons of steel, and erected on the 27,000 ton pedestal. It was exactly ten years too late to be the intended Centennial present from the French people, although nobody seemed to mind.

For 70 years Bedloe's Island enjoyed its fame with its magnificent Statue of Liberty welcoming all to the United States but, in 1956, its name was changed to 'Liberty Island'; probably more appropriate, but rather hard on poor Isaack Bedloo.

See: Alma Underpass, Big Apple, Broadway, Carnegie Hall, Cotton Club, Ellis Island, Empire State Building, Gotham, Harlem, Studio 54, World Trade Center

BERCHTESGADEN
Germany

For centuries, the Bavarian town of Berchtesgaden had been known for only its salt mines, its castle and former Augustinian abbey – the summer residence of the Bavarian kings.

It was Adolf Hitler and his Nazis who thrust it briefly into a different kind of prominence. Suddenly, newsreels made the world all too familiar with the Obersalzberg, 1,600 feet above the main town. At Berchtesgaden, in February 1938, Hitler, having first made it his Southern Headquarters, bullied Austrian Chancellor Kurt von Schushnigg to accept Germany's *Anchluss,* or merger, with Austria. In September, hard on the heels of this victory, his SS Guard of Honour beat its drums to welcome Britain's Prime Minister, Neville Chamberlain. It was the first meeting on the disastrous road to the appeasement of the Munich conference, the sacrifice of Czechoslovakia and ultimately World War II.

It is doubtful if these reluctant visitors ever had the time or inclination to admire the stunning views across the mountains, which we have since seen in Eva Braun's naive colour home movies of her happier times with Hitler. Nor would they have even known about the six kilometres of underground bunkers built as headquarters and air raid shelters under the barracks, and the more conventional buildings like Albert Speer's architectural studio and Hitler's home, the *Berghof.*

Nor would they have taken the brass-lined elevator 400 feet up through the heart of the Kehlstein mountain to the Eagle's Nest, Bormann's 50th Birthday present to Hitler, a chalet with even more breathtaking views.

Eva Braun and Adolf Hitler in happier times at Berchtesgaden

It was to this elaborate and well-prepared 'Southern Redoubt' to which Hitler and his government had intended to withdraw to continue the war. But Hitler decided to remain in Berlin, a city he had never liked (and which had never voted for him) and where he had scarcely spent a night. And there, in the agony of the city's last stand (in which 400,000 Russian troops, let alone Germans, died) was played out Hitler's fate, in the claustrophobic drama of the bunker. There, Goebbels killed himself, having sacrificed his wife and poisoned his six children. After denouncing the German people for 'not deserving him', Hitler, too, killed himself with his bride of a few hours.

How Eva Braun might have wished to return to the simple sunlit beauty of the mountains, we will never know.

See: Bayreuth, Great Hedge, Landsberg, Nuremberg, Unter den Linden

BEREZINA RIVER
Russia

Rivers have always played a crucial role in history. It is strange what barriers they still present, and how vital is the role of the bridges that cross them.

For an army in a hurry, whether attacking or retreating, a river is an even more formidable barrier. Furthermore, if you are in the middle of one of the longest and most devastating retreats in history and the temperature is minus 20°C, getting back across a river before your enemies intercept you is the ultimate challenge. Near Minsk, it was a tributary of the Dnieper, called the Berezina, which Napoleon faced in November 1812.

Napoleon's attack on Russia was not the foolhardy mission that some have painted. His *Grande Armée* was 530,000 strong, of twenty nations. With 1,000 guns, 30,000 wagons and 170,000 horses, in splendid French style, it also took 28 million bottles of wine and two million bottles of brandy.

But Napoleon's advance had not consisted of the expected series of decisive victories; the Russians had not been destroyed and he had lost too many men and good officers, no less than 35 Generals. He had captured a deserted Moscow to find no Czar with whom to negotiate, and the city had then burned down. And the famous Russian winter was approaching. At the end of October, Napoleon decided to retreat. By his return to Europe he was to have lost 400,000 men in Russia.

The French withdrawal was very slow due to Napoleon's initial decision to leave nothing behind. This only succeeded in exhausting the horses which had but one week's feed. On November 2nd, the snow came, and the struggling army, now only 105,000 strong and harassed by Cossacks, began to lose its guns, wagons, horses and men. Napoleon hit his lowest ebb. Heading for the bridge at Borisov, the only crossing-point of the Berezina, Napoleon now ordered wagons and baggage to be destroyed. This included all his *pontons*, boats on which pontoon bridges were built, against the frantic objections of his engineer, General Eblé.

However, Eblé quietly kept two field forges and eight wagons of tools and coal, an inspired decision as – on 22nd November – came the disastrous news that the Russians had destroyed the Borisov Bridge, leaving a raging flood 300 yards wide. But the French pushed across the river with cavalry and small rafts at a narrow unmarked ford five miles further north, and on 26th November, the nearby town of Studenka was torn down to provide the wood for two 105 yard long trestle bridges, with Elbé's men forging the iron work on the spot. Working shoulder-deep in freezing water, and battered by floating ice, Elbé's men finished the first bridge, and infantry and the cavalry crossed just in time to secure the other bank. Four hours later the second bridge for the artillery was finished. Both bridges suffered constant breakages, with Eblé repeatedly leading his exhausted men away from the warmth of their fires and into the darkness and icy water and with his energy returned, Napoleon himself distributing wine to them. Few would survive.

The Russians were now awake to the threat and trying to close in, and though a mob of French stragglers kept blocking the bridges, Napoleon's army eventually crossed to continue its horrific retreat out of Russia and, ever resilient, to fight on for another three years.

See: Bastille, Bayonne, Camerone, Dien Bien Phu, Waterloo

> *'There is only one step from the sublime to the ridiculous'.*
> Napoleon after his retreat from Russia

BERMUDA TRIANGLE
Atlantic Ocean

In 1492, Christopher Columbus was sailing across the Atlantic Ocean on the verge of discovering a new continent and being written into the history books forever. As he sailed through the Sargasso Sea and neared the coast of north America, on three occasions his compass behaved erratically. It is held by some that Columbus was the first to experience what is known as 'The Bermuda Triangle'.

Otherwise known as 'The Devil's Triangle', the phenomenon is said to occur in a region of water between Bermuda, Florida, and Puerto Rico. The precise area covered has never been agreed, but it is certainly estimated at hundreds of thousands of square miles. Though sailors had long regarded the triangle as a threatening place – the Sargasso Sea's floating masses of gulfweed appearing particularly ominous – it was not until the 19th century, when a number of ships disappeared without explanation, that it began to gain the notoriety that it enjoys today. This trend continued into the 20th century, with the USS *Cyclops* vanishing in March 1918. Since then, a broad array of both aircraft and vessels has gone down in the area, most disappearing without warning in generally favourable daytime weather.

Real notoriety was bestowed upon the region in December 1945 with the incident of 'Flight 19'. During a routine training flight, the pilots of a squadron of US navy torpedo bombers broadcast a number of distress messages. Then all five planes totally disappeared from sight. A rescue plane sent out to find them was also to vanish. Six planes and twenty-seven men were lost.

Public interest in the area was fostered in the media, with, in 1964, V. Gaddis writing about it in *Argosy* magazine. Charles Berlitz also published a book, which was named after the phenomenon in 1974 and since then has become a media staple, being pivotal in films such as *Close Encounters of the Third Kind* and *The Addams Family*.

But does it deserve quite such renown? Like many legends, at the very least some of the stories surrounding it can be explained, and it turns out that many of the tales are not quite as mysterious as they first seem. For instance, a number of the mystery so-called 'Bermuda Triangle' disappearances have been mis-marked, placing them well outside the area of the phenomenon.

The 'mystery' of Flight 19 has also come under scrutiny over the years to try and find a credible explanation. For example, it was reported (though the claims later on proved to be unsubstantiated rumours) that the patrol leader had a hangover that morning. Also, the Mariner seaplane sent to look for the pilots did not, as many believed, simply disappear in the middle of the Triangle. At 7.50 pm, twenty-three minutes after taking off on its rescue mission, an explosion was seen about fifty miles out to sea by crew on board the

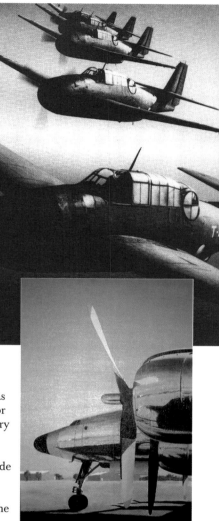

CHARLES FENNO JACOBS / NATIONAL ARCHIVES AND RECORDS ADMINISTRATION

Aircraft similar to those of 'Flight 19' and the Super Constellation

WASHINGTON
Norfolk
UNITED STATES
BERMUDA
BAHAMAS
MIAMI
PUERTO RICO
CUBA
SAN JUAN
HAITI
DOMINICAN REP.

SS Gaines Mill. At the same time, the Mariner disappeared from the radar screen of another ship in the area, the *USS Solomon*. The fact that no wreckage was found from the torpedo bombers could be accounted for by the planes crashing beyond the Continental Shelf, where the ocean floor is some several thousand feet deep, though this does not of course explain why no floating debris was found.

So do the conflicting theories render the Triangle a harmless myth? Perhaps, but then again many enthusiasts claim that the number of incidents and the lack of wreckage must surely point to something out of the ordinary. They also claim that incidents outside the Triangle only prove that its influence is spreading. However weak such claims seem, there are some that are hard to refute. Perhaps the best example of all was the loss of a large four-engined Super Constellation airliner in 1954.

The cargo it carried could not possibly have been more floatable, including pillow-cases, paper cups, and even liferafts, and yet not one piece of debris was ever found. Real or not, now that it has been instilled in the public consciousness, the Bermuda Triangle myth looks like it is here to stay.

BETHLEHEM
Israel

'But thou, Bethlehem Ephratah, though thou be little among the thousands of Judah, yet out of thee shall come forth unto me that is to be ruler of Israel'.

Thus had the mighty prophet Micah predicted, and many people, including King Herod, took his words very seriously.

In fact, the town of Bethlehem (House of Bread), however insignificant it may have seemed, had already had several claims to fame, the most important being as the home of the great King David.

Tax revenue was to make Bethlehem truly famous. Augustus Caesar had decreed that everyone should be taxed, and the orders came down through Cyrenius, the Roman Governor of Syria. Moreover this required a census, which is why Joseph had to leave Nazareth where he lived, to register in Bethlehem, as he was a descendant of David. With Mary so heavily pregnant, it was an inconvenient and dangerous journey, which ended with Jesus being born in a manger in a cave on the outskirts of the village.

It was the 'three wise men' who alerted King Herod that the child had been born, and reminded him of Micah's prophecy. His priests misquoted Micah *'and out of thee shall come a Governor, that shall rule my people Israel'*. Faced by what he saw as a serious political threat, Herod resorted to mass murder, ruthlessly killing all male children under two in the Bethlehem area. But *'The slaughter of innocents'* failed because the Lord had warned Joseph in a dream to escape with his family to Egypt, where they stayed until Herod died.

At least for a while, the families of Bethlehem may have been forgiven for sharing the feelings of the inhabitants of similar martyred places, like Lidice or Oradour, and wishing that Mary had never visited the place and had stayed in Nazareth.

But Bethlehem, like Mecca, is now regarded as a most holy place, and the Church of the Nativity, built above the manger, is one of the most visited spots on earth.

A 15th Century Renaissance nativity scene attributed to Paolo Schiavo

It is therefore tragic that the church was besieged in 2002, when Palestinian fighters were trapped there by Israeli forces, together with clerics and innocent bystanders. Luckily, the impasse was resolved by careful diplomacy and bargaining. But the incident underlines the fact that the story of Bethlehem is by no means over and perhaps never will be.

See: Gethsemane, Mecca

BHOPAL
India

In December 1984, a disgruntled employee of a chemical plant in India decided to get his own back on his supervisor. To spoil some chemicals, he pumped water into a tank containing *Methyl Isocyanate* used for making pesticide, and ran off into the night.

His sabotage created a chemical reaction and a massive leak of lethal gas that spread silently and unseen into the houses and ramshackle shelters that crowded up to the plant's perimeter. Over 3,000 people died and hundreds of thousands were injured. Blame fell upon Union Carbide, whose reputation as one of America's most responsible, innovative and safe companies would be damaged for years.

At first glance, was this an open-and-shut case of a greedy and ruthless multinational exploiting a Third World country? Not quite so. This was an Indian company making pesticide for India's agriculture, in which Union Carbide was an equal shareholder. What's more, no American had, by law, been allowed to work at the plant for years, and therefore, had no say in the safety procedures which, in normal circumstances, were well organised by the experienced Indian staff. Even more importantly, when they set up the plant, Union Carbide engineers had been at pains to point out that, because of the toxic nature of the products, nobody should be allowed to live within half a

UNION CARBIDE

mile of the plant – advice ignored by the Bhopal local authorities, who allowed a shanty town to surround the plant.

The President of Union Carbide was arrested when he came to Bhopal to try to help, and the local police released him. It was an indication of obstructions to come. The millions of dollars immediately offered by the company as compensation were turned down in a highly charged political atmosphere only weeks after the assassination of Prime Minister Mrs Gandhi. It was very convenient to ignore Union Carbide's good record, especially in India, and to try to get at its money.

Investigation into the cause of the accident was obstructed, and it took years 'working backwards' to find the truth. Particularly unedifying were the dozens of American 'ambulance-chasing' lawyers who arrived in Bhopal to try to sign up victims and to get cases held in America, presumably worth billions.

The Indian Supreme Court and Union Carbide settled for $470 million, but when it was paid, the new Indian Government rejected the offer. No money reached the victims until the first trickle in 1993.

A victim waits to discover if she has permanent eye damage after the Bhopal incident.

See: Anthrax Island, Chernobyl, Three Mile Island

'BIG APPLE'
New York, USA

The origin of how New York City became known as 'The Big Apple' has been in dispute for many years.

One of the strongest contenders was the 1937 dance craze, 'The Big Apple' which had become all the rage in Columbia, South Carolina, invented in a synagogue-turned-night club called *Fat Sam's*. This was taken to New York by a group of teenagers, who performed the dance in five or six shows a day to packed crowds of 6,500 fans at the Roxy Theater. After the 'Charleston' and the 'Twist', the 'Big Apple' was the biggest dance craze ever to hit America.

However, New York's Mayor, Ed Koch, always contended that 'Big Apple' was a jazz club name, and entered into a public argument about it with Columbia's Mayor, Patten Williams.

New York City itself has officially disputed both the jazz and dance claim by erecting a plaque at 'Big Apple Corner', at the intersection of West 54th Street and Broadway. This was to honour the horse racing writer, John Fitzgerald, who brought the term from the stables of New Orleans. In his first column in 1924 for the *New York Morning Telegraph,* Fitzgerald wrote, *'The Big Apple, the dream of every lad that ever threw a leg over a thoroughbred. There's only one Big Apple. That's New York'.*

In fact, however much that New York City may not wish to admit it, it is possible that the origin may be even older, but may also involve throwing legs over thoroughbreds.

According to the Society of New York City History, in 1804, a young aristocrat fled the French Revolution and arrived in New York. Evelyn Claudine de Saint-Évremond set up an elegant brothel in fashionable Bond Street. As her friends, admirers and customers insisted on calling her 'Eve', she began describing her beautiful girls as her 'irresistible apples'. Soon, the 'in crowd' was knowingly boasting of 'having had a taste of Eve's apples'.

By 1870, *The Gentleman's Directory of New York City* asserted touchingly that, *'in freshness, sweetness, beauty and firmness to the touch, New York's 'apples' are superior to any in the New World or, indeed, the Old.'* And so New York began to be called the 'Apple Tree', the 'Real Apple' or, worried by its reputation as a centre of vice, by William Jennings Bryan in 1892, the 'Foulest Rotten Apple'.

By 1900, 'Big Apple' or 'The Apple' had passed into general verbal use as a nickname for New York. But in upstate New York, the Apple Marketing Board had started the very first product positioning campaign – with slogans like *'An apple a day, keeps the doctor away'* and *'As American as apple pie.'* Thus, a new and more wholesome image was to prepare the way for the *'I love New York'* tourism campaign for the state, and even the *'Make it in New York'* industrial development project.

No doubt, the 'Big Apple' controversy between jazz, dance, horse-racing and brothel-owning will continue to entertain the world for years.

See:
Actor's Studio,
The Mrs Astor's
Ballroom,
Bedloe's Island,
Broadway,
Ellis Island,
Harlem,
Manhattan

'BIG BEN'
England

For most people, the clock tower of the Houses of Parliament is a symbol of Britain, and they would call it 'Big Ben.' This is an easy mistake, but the tower is actually called St. Stephen's Tower. 'Big Ben' is, in fact, the largest of the bells inside the clock tower – the hour bell – with four smaller bells to sound the quarter.

In 1844, Parliament decided that its new buildings should have a tower and clock. Charles Barry was the architect, and the Astronomer Royal, George Airy, demanded accuracy to within a second a day. It took until 1851 to find a designer who could fulfil this almost impossible specification; Edmond Beckett Denison.

The first, 16 tonne, bell produced to Denison's design, cracked under test. A new bell was cast by the Whitechapel Bell Foundry, featured in the *Guinness Book of Records* as Britain's oldest manufacturing company. Using the molten metal from the first broken bell, it took Master Bellfounder, George Mears, 20 minutes to fill the pre-heated mould and 20 days to let it cool.

Cheering crowds lined the route from Whitechapel as sixteen be-ribboned horses pulled the heavy wagons carrying the bells to Westminster. They first rang out across London on 31st May 1859, and on that day a special sitting to decide the name took place. The *'Chief Lord of the Woods and Forests'*, Sir Benjamin Hall, a large man aptly dubbed by his colleagues 'Big Ben', ended his very long speech. Some wit called out, 'Why not call it Big Ben and have done with it?' The name stuck.

After two months, the new bell cracked too, because Denison had insisted on too heavy a hammer. But George Mears carefully inspected it, and deemed the crack to be shallow. 'Big Ben' went back into service with a smaller hammer, the crack adding a distinctive tone to its dignified and reassuringly accurate marking of each hour for the last one and a half centuries.

It may not be the oldest bell or even the heaviest, but it is easily the most broadcast all over the world.

The statue of Winston Churchill looks at St. Stephen's Tower, containing Big Ben

See: Greenwich, Pisa

BIGGIN HILL
England

There is something very English, sleepy and comfortable about the name 'Biggin Hill'. The village sits on a plateau of the North Downs in Kent, and was for hundreds of years an area of scattered farms. The only one important house, the Manor of Aperfield, was given by William the Conqueror to his half brother, Bishop Odo of Bayeux, to thank him for his support at the Battle of Hastings in 1066.

In the twentieth century, Biggin Hill's location became more significant as an airfield to protect Britain's capital. By 1917, it was part of the inner patrol zone of the London Air Defence Area, when Bristol fighters took off to beat off the Zeppelins and the Gotha bombers.

Between the wars, staff there worked on experiments to perfect Britain's ground defences against air attack, acting as the home of the Army School of Anti-Aircraft Defence and the Searchlight Experimental Establishment.

However, all the time, its vital position was pointing to its destiny as a fighter station, housing a succession of biplanes with very British names like *'Snipe', 'Demon', 'Bulldog',* and *'Gauntlet'*.

In 1938, there were still biplanes at Biggin Hill, and it was probably lucky for them and the British that the Munich crisis did not lead to war that year. By the outbreak of war, the squadrons had re-equipped with Hurricanes, which were much more modern fighters.

THE LONDON BOROUGH OF BROMLEY
Site of
BIGGIN HILL
ROYAL AIR FORCE
STATION
1917 - 1992

TONY COWLAND

Biggin Hill Hurricanes blitzed by the Luftwaffe, one of twelve such attacks on the airfield

Biggin Hill's Battle of Britain Memorial Chapel, with a Spitfire, symbol of the Battle of Britain

With its own radar station, Biggin Hill played a leading role in perfecting collaboration between radar and the fighters, conducting the first exercises with an embryo Sector Operations Room and also creating the new radio language which the RAF adopted: 'Scramble', 'Angels', 'Bogey', 'Bandit', 'Pancake' and 'Tallyho'.

After Germany's invasion of Poland, there were many months of the 'Phoney War', but Biggin Hill's Number 79 squadron was the very first to shoot down an enemy aircraft, in November 1939. It was the first of a thousand. The station's Hurricanes were able to play a vital and unseen role protecting the men struggling off the beaches at Dunkirk, and a few weeks later, as the Battle of Britain started, it had become a Spitfire station with four squadrons. Biggin Hill was blitzed 12 times, and on 30th August

1940, it was reduced to a shambles, with many of its facilities wrecked and 39 killed. In spite of other similar raids, the airfield remained operational throughout the battle, and was reprieved by the Luftwaffe's fatal mistake of turning from its growing success in battering the RAF's over-stretched airfields to bombing the sprawling target of London.

It had been touch and go for four weeks, with exhausted pilots flying mission after mission, landing, refuelling, re-arming and taking off again within minutes. Life expectancy was 87 flying hours; pilots fell asleep as they taxied to a halt.

'Never in the field of human conflict was so much owed by so many to so few', Churchill intoned in the House of Commons. One pilot, not too tired to crack a joke and paid just fourteen shillings a day, quipped, *'He must have been thinking of our officers' mess bills!'*

The Battle was not just *'plucky British boys hammering the Hun'.* It was a technical triumph of the world's finest integrated air defence system. 'Ultra' at Bletchley Park was reading the German *Enigma* codes; radar was detecting the size, direction, speed, and range of the raids; while the 30,000 men and women of the Observer Corps plotted the enemy's movements inland. And all this was co-ordinated calmly and efficiently by the Operations Rooms of Sector, Group and Fighter Command to get the fighters into the right place at the right time.

In Spring 1941, the Germans turned their backs on England and faced towards Russia. Biggin Hill went on the offensive.

By the end of the war, Biggin Hill's pilots had claimed 1,000 enemy aircraft destroyed, and the place with the funny English name would have been no joke in the minds of its enemies.

See: Bletchley Park, Dunkirk, Farnborough, Kitty Hawk, Midway, Pearl Harbor

BIKINI
Pacific Ocean

If we see a pretty girl in a bikini, what crosses our minds? Not often anxiety about nuclear weapons. Still less, perhaps, concern for the people of Bikini.

It was very bad luck for 167 trusting, simple islanders that in 1946 the United States needed their coral atoll to test its atomic bombs. They agreed to give up their island home for a project that would be 'for the good of mankind' but, in reality, would doom them to years of nuclear exile. Only a year after the devastation of Hiroshima and Nagasaki, the US Navy needed to know what would happen to a fleet attacked by atomic bombs. So 'Operation Crossroads' brought 42,000 men, 242 ships and 10,000 instruments to the lovely island.

Ninety vessels were assembled as targets. Everything from tiny submarines and landing craft up to mighty warships like Nazi Germany's *Prinz Eugen*, America's early aircraft carrier. Also included was the well-loved *Saratoga* and the veteran battleship *Nevada,* which had sunk during Japan's surprise attack at Pearl Harbor, but was refloated and repaired. *Nagato,* Japan's only surviving battleship, was a different kind of veteran of Pearl Harbor. She had been Admiral Yamamoto's flagship and it was on her bridge, ironically, in Hiroshima harbour, that he heard Captain Fuchida's cry that they had surprised the enemy, 'Tora! Tora! Tora!' *Nagato* was condemned at Bikini, almost out of spite. In two atomic explosions, *Able* and *Baker,* three weeks apart, many of the moored vessels were sunk – by blast, huge waves or the millions of tonnes of water and sediment that were hurled into the air and then fell to batter the ships.

Just a few days later, the French swimsuit designer, Louis Réard, was to present a revolutionary skimpy two-piece at the Molitor swimming pool in Paris. He considered it so 'explosive' that he named it *'Bikini'*. Revealing the navel for the first time, Réard would not even allow his own wife to wear it. And so shocked was the world that Silvana Pampanini did not win that year's Miss Italy contest because of her *'Bikini'*. And America's swimmer and film star Esther Williams vowed never to we ething that was only for 'disgusting old voyeurs'. But the success of the Bikini was unstoppable, especially after Brigitte Bardot in *And God Created Woman* and Anita Ekberg in *Dr No* and Raquel Welch in the fur bikini which launched her career in *One Million Years BC.* In 1960, Brian Ayland even created the hit *'Itsy, Bitsy, Teeny, Weeny, Yellow Polkadot Bikini'.*

And the Bikinians? Sadly for them, the Americans needed their atoll for another 12 years and another 21 tests, including *Bravo*, the first hydrogen bomb in 1954, 750 times more powerful than the first two naval tests. The hydrogen bomb also deposited cesium that continues to poison the soil, coconuts and the island's other indigenous plants. Long-exiled to Kili, 500 miles to the south-west, the Bikinians are now desperate to return. Said one in 1992, 'I don't want anymore to stay on Kili. If we hear the island is safe, we will swim.' She was probably not planning to use the stylish two-piece that now bore her island's name.

CHRIS CRAYMER

See: Bazaar, Cape Canaveral, Carnaby St, Hiroshima, Jodhpur, Los Alamos

The first test at Bikini. Not a good place for a beach holiday!

BLARNEY
Ireland

Powers of roguish eloquence are claimed if you *'Kiss the Blarney Stone'*.

Blarney Castle, near Cork, is a powerful fortress built in 1446 on the site of previous timber and stone castles. It was built by Dermot McCarthy, King of Munster, and became the stronghold of the McCarthys until Oliver Cromwell, with his cannons, captured it in 1646. The McCarthys won it back when Catholic Charles II returned, and lost it forever after the 'Flight of the Earls' in 1690, when most Irish chiefs were stripped of their power and property after the Battle of the Boyne.

See: Ballingarry, Boyne, Buncombe, Hook & Crook, Laconia, St Germain

The Blarney Stone is believed to be one half of the Stone of Scone, over which the Kings of Scotland were crowned because of its supposed special powers. It was a present from Robert the Bruce in 1314, in return for Cormac McCarthy's help at the Battle of Bannockburn.

The origin of the legend of the Blarney Stone dates back to Elizabeth I. Faced with her demand to occupy his land *'under title from her'*, Cormac Teige McCarthy delayed, but with such charming, amusing and very loquacious reasons, that the Queen complained he was giving her a 'lot of Blarney'.

If you feel you are too laconic, it would be an excellent idea to visit Blarney, climb up on to the battlements, kiss the Stone – and hope it works.

BLETCHLEY PARK
England

In 1938, the Foreign Office stepped in to halt the imminent demolition of a large Victorian country house in the county of Buckinghamshire, destined to become a housing development. The land had once been given to Bishop Geoffrey of Constance by William the Conqueror, a feature it shares with Biggin Hill. But Bletchley Park was to have an even greater significance for Britain than even the famous Battle of Britain airfield.

Below: Bletchley Park Right: The Enigma machine, developed from a toy.

In August 1939, a motley group of people arrived at the mansion under the guise of 'Captain Ridley's shooting party.' They were the first of a band of 10,000 to work at Bletchley Park on what was to be one of the most significant enterprises in British history, for the site was now 'Station X,' the Foreign Office's home for its *'Government Code and Cipher School'* and MI6's most important centre for code-breaking.

The principal task was to open the secrets of Germany's Enigma cipher used throughout its armed forces, a brilliant encoding system which used a machine with frequently moveable rotors. Even though the Poles had been able to create an actual Enigma machine, the odds of breaking the code were 150 million, million, million to one.

But, at Bletchley Park, they succeeded. The fertile brains of an extraordinary group of boffins and intellectuals and the use of Alan Turing's 'Bombes,' electro-mechanical machines first envisaged by the Poles, so reduced the time to decipher the Enigma traffic that Britain's leaders and armed forces could react quickly

BLETCHLEY PARK

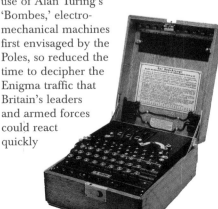

enough to make a difference. To break *Lorenz* – Hitler's own code – 'Colossus,' the first programmable electronic computer was also built.

Bletchley Park was typically British and eccentric. The teams, working in crowded wooden huts, comprised linguists, mathematicians, chess players, crossword champions and technologists – anyone with the lateral thinking to break codes – backed by an army of support staff. The overwhelming majority were women, both service and civilian. They lived in billets in the local countryside, often cycling many miles to work and worked in three shifts covering 24 hours a day.

Churchill used the codename 'Ultra' for the increasingly vital intelligence coming from Bletchley Park. Outstanding examples of Ultra's influence on the successful outcome are to be found in the Battle of Britain, the U-boat war in the Atlantic, Montgomery's victory at Alamein, the D-Day invasion of Normandy and subsequent advance into north west Europe.

Of course, it was crucial to keep the Germans' thinking that Enigma and *Lorenz* were still secure, and great efforts were made to hide the success of 'Ultra' and to trick them into thinking that intelligence had come from other sources.

Information was freely shared with the Americans who had liaison officers at Bletchley Park and who were able to concentrate on their own brilliant effort, 'Magic', to break the Japanese 'Purple' code.

After its vital work had ended, which some estimate shortened the war by two years, and the code-breakers had departed, Bletchley Park, could once again have faced demolition.

But in 1991, 400 code-breakers attended a reunion party and decided to save the site for posterity. Luckily for the nation, they did.

See: Biggin Hill, Dieppe, El Alamein, Mers-el-Kebir, Midway, Mulberry Harbour, Pearl Harbor

BLETCHLEY PARK

'Colossus', the massive computer specially built to beat the German codes

THE BLIND BEGGAR
England

When Ronnie Kray walked coolly up to George Cornell in the Blind Beggar pub in the Autumn of 1965, and shot him three times in the head, it was actually the beginning of the end for the notorious Krays.

The Kray twins were the closest Britain has ever been to organised crime. Ronnie and Reggie, and their brother Charlie, grew up in the East End of London dominated by their doting mother, Vi. Being rather good boxers, the twins' army careers during National Service lasted only a few minutes, when they simply punched the first Sergeant to shout at them. After serving time in military prison, they came back to the East End to begin a life of extreme violence, eventually running nearly 30 drinking and snooker clubs, providing protection rackets and by stealing almost anything they could get. 'The Firm', as it was called, started making inroads into the West End including 'Esmeralda's Barn' in Knightsbridge, fronted by the

aristocratic sixth Earl of Effingham (whose title was rather more respectably earned by a certain Thomas Effingham's role in the defeat of the Armada).

The Krays loved their new social connections, and were publicly photographed with film and sports stars. National notoriety increased when Ronnie's gay friend, Lord Boothby, actually asked questions in the House of Lords about why the Krays were being treated so unfairly.

There was only one other publicly known gang in London, the Richardsons, who certainly did not need to quarrel with the Krays. However, because of the behaviour of one of this rival gang, 'Mad' Frankie Fraser, and a confused and botched

Ronnie & Reggie

shoot-out at 'The Battle of Mr Smith's Club', where a cousin of the Krays was killed, Ronnie decided on revenge and shot Cornell. No witnesses dared identify Ronnie. Thus, the Kray twins became even more confident. But nemesis was at hand. Frances Kray, the childhood sweetheart and now wretched wife of Reggie, cracked after months of misery and killed herself.

Reggie became crazed with grief and drink, and embarked on an orgy of public violence. Goaded by his brother's constant boasting about his 'Blind Beggar' killing, Reggie brutally knifed to death another small-time gangster, Jack 'The Hat' McVitie who cried out, 'Why are you doing this, Reg?' 'Kill him now', snarled Ronnie, and Reggie complied.

Enough was enough. Both brothers ended their days in prison.

Throughout however, their mother Vi never ceased to insist that 'They were such good boys!'

See: Alcatraz, Corleone, Cotton Club, Las Vegas, North Clark Street

BOGSIDE
Northern Ireland

In 30 years, 3,700 people have been killed in Northern Ireland. The equivalent death toll in Britain would be 150,000, and in the United States 600,000 – ten times American losses in Vietnam. 1 in 50 of Northern Ireland's people were injured, equivalent to 1 million in Britain and 5 million in America.

Defiant graffiti in the Bogside in 1984

In many ways, the Bogside is the epitome of the sectarian problems of Northern Ireland. It is effectively a Catholic ghetto outside the walled city of Derry (or Londonderry as the British call it). The city itself used to be an island in the River Foyle, whose western branch ran dry, leaving a marshy bog.

The Bogside district grew up as a residential area of small terraced houses for the Catholics working in the city's factories and docks. It is mostly municipal housing. Northern Ireland until 1985 was unique in the United Kingdom, in that you were not given a local vote if you were not a property freeholder or leaseholder. And there, *local* government was the key because it ruled on who had jobs and houses. So greater Londonderry, 80 per cent Catholic overall, always used to return a

Protestant Council by packing the Catholics into the Bogside, and parcelling the Protestants into the other wards of the city and thus keeping control. That is what the Freedom Marches were all about. The annual triumphalist celebration of the Apprentice Boys Parade did nothing to help, commemorating Protestant resistance to the siege of the City by James II.

So it is not surprising that the District became the focus of confrontation, with the 'Battle of the Bogside' in 1969. As a result, 'Free Derry' was established as a 'no-go area'.

On January 30th 1972, 'Bloody Sunday', a far greater tragedy occurred. A peaceful march through the Bogside deteriorated into a confused riot during which a company of the Parachute Regiment opened fire with live rounds and shot dead thirteen marchers. The effect was to cause outrage throughout Ireland and the rest of the world, severe anxiety in Great Britain, the closing of the Parliament at Stormont, direct rule from London and the worst year of bombings and shootings in the history of the Province. There have been several inquiries, but there can be no doubt that the long and bitter social and political history of The Bogside was bound to mean such a tragedy might occur.

See: Ballingarry, Boyne, Falls Road, General Post Office, Getto

BONNEVILLE
Utah, USA

In Utah, there is a spot that is completely flat and absolutely barren, and it has become synonymous with speed.

The Bonneville Salt Flats and the Great Salt Lake are remnants of an ancient lake. During the last Ice Age, 15,000 years ago, Lake Bonneville was huge – the size of Lake Michigan – and it covered one third of the present state of Utah and parts of neighbouring states. The Flats have been created by wind and water combining to produce a flat surface of salt. Each winter, a shallow layer of standing water floods the surface of the salt flats. During spring and summer the water evaporates, while the winds smooth the surface into a vast, nearly perfect, flat plane of 30,000 acres.

The area is named in honour of Captain B.L.E. Bonneville, whose expedition in the 1830s proved the area was part of an ancient basin. Excavations nearby have discovered that there was human occupation of the area as early as 10,300 years ago, but more recent arrivals have found the place considerably less hospitable.

The first crossing of the desert was made in 1845 by Captain John Freemont's survey party, with scouts Kit Carson and Joe Walker. Next year, young Lansford Hastings retraced the crossing of the salt plain and he convinced several immigrant groups to follow him. Sadly, one of these was the Donner-Reed party who, seeking a short cut to California in 1846, tried the 'Hastings cut-off'. They did not take enough water, lost many of their oxen and were slowed down enough to arrive late in the Sierra Nevada. The result

was tragic death in the terrible snows of the mountains, a fate made worse by the extra horror of cannibalism.

The Salt Flats' potential for speed was first recognised by W.D. Rishel, who persuaded Teddy Tezlaff to attempt a car speed record. Tezlaff drove his *Blitzen Benz* at 141 miles an hour, to set an unofficial record in 1914. By the 1930s, the Flats had drawn international attention as a place to attempt records. Ab Jenkins, who had set records in his *Mormon Meteor*, persuaded Sir Malcolm Campbell to come over from England to use its salt surface, Daytona Beach now considered inadequate for the ever-increasing speeds.

After the war, the raceway at Bonneville became the standard place to break world records and speeds went up from 300 to 600 miles an hour. In the 1960s, jet-powered vehicles entered the fray and Art Arfons (576 mph) and Craig Breedlove (600 mph) became famous. In the 1970s, rocket-cars saw Gary Gabelich (622 mph) stretching the limits ever further.

See: Brescia, Brooklands, Cresta Run, Indianapolis, Kitty Hawk, Le Mans

BONUS CITY
Washington DC, USA

It was the height of the Depression, and many of the 3.5 million American veterans of World War I were desperate and angry. In the summer of 1932 nearly 15,000 of them, many with their families, had come to Washington to

demand early payment of their promised $1,000 war-service bonuses. The 'Bonus Army' or even more cynically 'The Bonus Expeditionary Force' camped in abandoned shacks and tents in 'Bonus City'. All summer they surrounded the

Future General and US President Dwight Eisenhower (right) was worried about MacArthur's actions and very reluctant to be forced to wear full dress uniform during them.

See: Corregidor, Jarrow, Wall Street

Congress, marching slowly in what was called 'The Death March'. But then, because of the need to balance the budget, the Bill which had agreed to pay out early bonuses, or *Adjusted Compensation Certificates*, was defeated in Congress and most of the disappointed 'Army' went home.

Several thousand, however, remained and the atmosphere turned unpleasant, with protests against an unfeeling Government, and near-riots. President Hoover asked for troops to clear the down-town area, and they moved in, led by General Douglas MacArthur, the Army's Chief of Staff, and his then little-known and reluctant aide Major Dwight Eisenhower. Hoover's instructions stipulated that *'women and children should be given every kindness and courtesy'.* What they actually had was Major George Patton's cavalry charging them with sabres, and infantry attacking with teargas.

Then, not for the last time in his career, MacArthur disobeyed the orders of his President and crossed the Potomac at the Eleventh Street Bridge to attack the main camp. Poignantly, two babies died of the gas, and a little boy was bayoneted whilst saving his pet rabbit.

MacArthur then trapped Hoover by calling a press conference, and praising the President for his resolute actions against *'hoodlums, ex-convicts, Communists and a minority of veterans'.* (The reality: 94 per cent had service records, 67 per cent had served overseas and 20 per cent were disabled.)

It was an ugly incident and did little to dispel the impression that Hoover's handling of the Depression was in fact fumbling, complacent and inept. And it helped to ease in Roosevelt and his 'New Deal', although FDR drew the conclusion that MacArthur was 'one of the two most dangerous men in America'.

Years later when, in the Korean War, MacArthur's insubordination finally resulted in his dismissal, President Harry Truman said:

'I didn't fire him because he was a dumb son of a bitch, although he was, but that's not against the law for generals. If it was, half or three-quarters of them would be in jail'.

BOSTON HARBOUR
Massachusetts, USA

By nine o'clock on the night of 16th December 1773, Boston Harbour was littered with tea chests and the surface of the water was covered in tea. Britain was on its way to losing America.

Two men can be blamed for the historic break between Britain and the colonists. Chancellor of the Exchequer Charles Townsend set the scene in 1767 when he thought he had hit on a good way of raising money in the colonies. He decided to tax *'small unimportant things'* like lead, glass, salt, paper and tea.

Three years later, Lord North, a Prime Minister, acidly described by the famous writer and critic, Dr Johnson, as *'filling a chair with a mind as narrow as a neck of a vinegar cruet',* compounded the error. All the Townsend duties were repealed, except for the Tea Tax which would now cost more to collect than the revenue it would raise. Moreover, tea was actually still cheap in America, and taxes were much higher in Britain. In spite of the fears of Members of Parliament that there would be trouble, Lord North kept the tax, *'as a mark of the supremacy of Parliament and as a declaration of their right to govern the colonies'.*

Keeping the tax on tea was also an attempt to help the East India Company which was in financial trouble, in spite of its growing but secret involvement with the Chinese opium trade. The British, in addition to sending tea direct to America, also decided to control smuggling – which annoyed most of the merchants there, especially in Boston, where they were actively engaged in the trade.

So, opposition to the Tea Act grew rapidly and finally exploded in Boston where three British ships laden with East Indian tea were anchored – the *Dartmouth, Eleanor* and the *Beaver.* After a mass meeting earlier in the day, one of

the ships' captains, Francis Rotch, rode off to ask Governor Hutchison for exemption from the tax. When he returned to report that this was refused, a thousand men, many disguised as Indians, burst from the meeting, ran down to the harbour, boarded the ships and hurled the offending 298 tea chests into the water.

John Adams, normally a moderate, was right when he said, *'The people should never rise without doing something to be remembered, something notable and striking. This destruction of the tea is so bold, so firm, intrepid and inflexible, and it must have so* important *consequences, and so lasting, that I can't but consider it an epoch in history'*.

In fact, it was taxation 'without representation' which caused the real indignation. Britain did not make the same mistake in Canada. Six years later, America declared its independence, and six years after that had won it by force of arms.

It would have been much better if Charles Townsend and Lord North had not tried to raise a bit of cash from tea.

Perhaps it is not surprising that Americans, on the whole, prefer coffee.

See: Chinchon, Great Hedge of India, Run, Salem

BOTANY BAY
Australia

In April 1770, Lieutenant James Cook sailed the *Endeavour* into a bay on the eastern coast of Australia. At first he named it Stingray Bay, but his scientific companions Daniel Solander and Joseph Banks were botanists. They were fascinated by the profusion of plants and flowers, and renamed it 'Botany Bay'. On their return to England, Banks, later the driving force behind Kew Gardens, was to recommend it as a naval base and a convict settlement and, in 1788, Captain Arthur Phillip duly arrived with the 'First Fleet'. Unfortunately, Phillip immediately discovered that with its bad soil, no fresh water and poor anchorages, Botany Bay was actually useless for naval and convict purposes and he sailed just nine miles north to discover the narrow entrance of 'The

Heads', landing on 'The Rocks' of Port Jackson, now the magnificent Sydney Harbour.

Thus it was Sydney that became the focus of the extraordinary British phenomenon of 'transportation', whereby those convicted for anything

Nine miles north of Botany Bay, Captain Phillip found his ideal harbour

61

One of the many species of Banksia, named after botanist Joseph Banks, also famous for sending Captain Bligh to collect breadfruit trees from Tahiti which led to the mutiny on the Bounty

CAS LIBER

from High Treason to stealing a chicken were shipped to 'the Colonies'. In fact, the other colonies rejected this practice, South Africa resisting the landing of convict ships by force, so that only Australia was settled in this strange way.

As reported elsewhere, the author's great, great uncle William Smith O'Brien, as a Member of Parliament was unusual, the best-connected felon ever transported who became the natural focus of the anti-transportation movement.

Sydney was the first city to stop transportation, but it is amazing that for nearly a hundred years Botany Bay become the inaccurate but legendary symbol for the unfair and arbitrary sentence of transportation, as the famous Australian song celebrates:

Farewell to old England the beautiful!
Farewell to my old pals as well!
Farewell to the famous Old Bailey
Where I used to cut such a swell.

It's seven long years I been serving,
It's seven I got for to stay,
For beatin' a cop down our alley
An' takin' his truncheon away.

It ain't that they don't give us grub enough
It ain't that they don't give us clothes;
It's all 'cause we light-fingered gentry
Goes about with a chain on our toes.

Now all you young viscounts and duchesses
Take warning by what I do say,
And mind it's all yours what you touches-es
Or you'll land down in Botany Bay.

In reality, not a single convict ever landed at Botany Bay. There's a power station, some suburbs and one of Sydney Airport's runways. Not nearly as romantic.

See: Ballingarry, Chinchon, Kew Gardens

BOURNVILLE
England

George Cadbury, genuine philanthropist

In the 1880's, Britain was reaping the results of its 'Industrial Revolution' in more ways than one.

A unique combination of being a cradle of mechanical invention, having the raw materials and fuel for the Steam Age and being an island with a mercantile history had made Britain the 'Workshop of the World'. A small island had miraculously become the richest country on earth and the ruler of the largest Empire in history. Four out of five ships at sea had been built in Britain and were steaming ahead with world trade.

But there was a darker side. Workers had poured into the industrial cities from the countryside and were now labouring in *'Satanic Mills'*, prison-like factories and mines where women and children worked as hard as men, and all worked incredibly long hours. Sickness, including lung diseases, took their toll (you were lucky if you lasted ten years breathing in steel particles in a needle factory).

Few cities could rival Birmingham for its industrial hardship and pollution, together with its squalid, overcrowded living conditions. It was here that the Cadbury brothers, George and Richard, had their successful chocolate factory.

In 1879, as committed Quakers, they decided that enough was enough and moved the chocolate works to a fourteen acre site, just south-west of Birmingham, on the Bourn Brook in what was then mile after mile of open Worcestershire countryside. But George Cadbury decided to go further. In addition to the site he bought 140 acres on which to build a new and more humanitarian kind of town for both his own and other workers – Bournville Village. In a clever marketing ploy it was given a French-sounding name to reflect the fact that French chocolate was regarded as the best. He planned houses of various sizes with large gardens, and by 1900 there were 313 houses on

300 acres complete with a village green, shops and school.

He deliberately set out to demonstrate that workers – housed properly – could be both productive and happy. In many ways, he was challenging the attitudes of his fellow businessmen, hard-faced and newly rich, who did not really see the point of such kindness, while the landed aristocracy did not really care what went on in the cities.

There have been several famous company towns, steel towns, timber towns and railroad towns in America like Pullman City near Chicago – even another chocolate town, Hershey, Pennsylvania. But they were built for convenience, location and to lock in company loyalties.

Only places like Bournville (and William Lever's Port Sunlight) that were created as philanthropic gestures show that it was possible to rescue workers from really appalling conditions. And with only 40 per cent of the residents having a direct connection to the Cadbury factory, its founder's vision was much wider than simply an interest in his own workers. Thanks to the independent Trust that George Cadbury set up, it can still be seen today.

And, needless to say, we can still enjoy the rich, dark taste of Bournville chocolate.

See: Hershey, Pullman

PICTURES COURTESY OF THE BOURNVILLE VILLAGE TRUST

The spacious houses and gardens of the Bournville estate were a revolution in an age when most workers lived in cramped squalor and poverty

THE RIVER BOYNE
Ireland

Each year, on 12th July, Protestant 'loyalists' in Northern Ireland commemorate an event that took place 300 years ago – the Battle of the Boyne. They march and light bonfires to celebrate the defeat of a Catholic army by William III or 'King Billy', ensuring the Union with Great Britain. Sadly for them, the battle took place not in the British enclave of Northern Ireland, but in the adjacent Irish Republic. The fertile valley of the River Boyne, which drains the county of Meath in the east of Ireland, has in fact been at the heart of the Irish nation for thousands of years.

The infamous battle took place on 1st July 1690, during the War of the English Succession. Deposed in the Glorious Revolution of 1688 by his Protestant son-in-law Prince William of Orange (William III), the Catholic James II tried to regain the English throne by force, with help from Louis XIV of France and mostly Catholic sympathizers in Scotland and Ireland. In March 1690 James had landed at Kinsale; in May he convened an Irish Parliament in Dublin – with both Catholic and Protestant MPs. From April to July his army besieged Derry in the north of Ireland, but William's ships broke through a boom across Lough Foyle and raised the

63

King William leads his army at the Battle of the Boyne.

The mystery of why the Battle of the Boyne is now celebrated on 12th July is explained in the Julian calendar being replaced in 1752 by the Gregorian, losing eleven days.

See: Bael na Blath, Ballingarry, Bogside, Clontarf, Falls Road, General Post Office, Hook and Crook, St Germain-en-Laye

siege. Taking his army south, on 1st July, he met William and an Anglo-Dutch army at a crossing of the River Boyne west of Drogheda.

James was outnumbered and then out-flanked and by mid-afternoon was in retreat. He escaped to France, where he died in 1701 without ever again setting foot in England. Irish resistance never-theless continued until September 1691 under the able command of Patrick Sarsfield, Earl of Lucan, who himself would go into exile with eleven thousand of his soldiers, 'the Wild Geese'. Ironically, in view of today's Protestant hard-line sentiment, James had many Protestants in his army, all loyal to the Stuart cause. And, worried about Louis XIV's support of the French church against papal authority, a delight-ed Pope, of all people, ordered a Te Deum to be sung in St Peter's, Rome, to celebrate William's great victory.

Long before Protestants and Catholics took up the cudgels, the Boyne Valley was an important – and a sacred – place in Irish history. From about 2800 BC Neolithic people were building massive megalithic monuments in Ireland, notably elaborate passage graves – of which the largest and finest are in the Boyne Valley at Newgrange, Dowth and Knowth. These impressive mounds have stone retaining kerbs and a long stone-lined passage that leads to a circular burial chamber, its walls decorated with spirals and zigzags. The chamber held cremated bones, together with pottery, beads and tools for the afterlife. New Grange, dating from 2,500 BC, has

particularly intricate carvings, and the passage is precisely aligned so that the sun only enters at the Winter Solstice. The monuments would be even more impressive but for centuries of erosion by grazing cattle.

Nearby Tara is less impressive, mere grassy earthworks, but with a fabulous view over much of central Ireland. Yet this was once the headquarters of the High Kings of Ireland, a potent and nationalist shrine that evokes an atmosphere of awe and patriotism. It was to Tara that St Patrick himself came to bring the Gospel of Christ to the king and his vassals. During the great Irish rebellion of 1798 (again, Protestants and Catholic fighting together against Great Britain), almost instinctively, large numbers of insurgents gathered here. On 15 August 1843, Irish nationalist statesman Daniel O'Connell, addressed a crowd at Tara estimated to be 750,000 strong.

Thus, among the bones and pottery shards, archaeologists sometimes find clay pipes and whiskey bottles. The 19th century Irish poet Thomas Moore commemorated this affinity with a powerful sense of lost grandeur in his famous poem:

The harp that once through Tara's halls
The soul of music shed,
Now hangs mute on Tara's walls
As if that soul was fled …

And, of course, Tara gave its name to that southern mansion in the novel *Gone with the Wind.*

BRAZIL
South America

Brazil, a vast country named after a tree.

Brazil is the largest country in South America and the fifth largest in the world. Its huge forests influence the world's atmosphere, and it boasts the largest river, the Amazon. With 160 million people, it is also the Continent's economic powerhouse. As one prominent Brazilian pointed out: *'The biggest economy in South America is Brazil, the second São Paulo county, the third São Paulo city and the fourth is Argentina.'*

For a 'corporate identity' specialist, Brazil's name is excellent. It is short, memorable and easily pronounceable in foreign languages.

But it was by chance that the name happened. Early Portuguese settlers wanted to call it *Terra de Vera Cruz* (Land of the True Cross). But there were others, less religious and more practical, who pointed out that the one worthwhile economic benefit achieved in the colony so far was the red dye and wood exported from the local tree, called Pau Brazil (*Caesalpinia echinata*). Why not call the huge country after the useful little tree? And indeed they did.

It is a curious fact that the Brazilwood tree (as opposed to the Brazilnut tree) provides the only wood suitable for violin bows, with the correct density, straight grain, no knots and the preferred colour. Sadly, the tree is under threat from encroaching agriculture and urban development. Other endangered 'music trees' are the Maracauba (used for marimba keys), Ligrum Vitae (used for recorders) and African Blackwood (clarinets, flutes, oboes and bagpipes). So important are these trees to the musical world that there is even a special tree conservation programme called SoundWood created by Fauna & Flora International, whose founding Patron was Yehudi Menuhin, with supporters like classical cellist Robert Cohen and jazz clarinettist Acker Bilk.

LEON MARTIN

A beneficiary of the Brazilwood tree, Miriam Kramer playing at London's Claridge's Hotel

BRESCIA
Italy

'Colui che è in testa a Roma, non vincerà a Brescia' (He who leads at Rome, never wins at Brescia).

This tradition referred to the town of Brescia, once famous for its violins, which was the start and finish point of that most dramatic and dangerous of motor races, the 'Mille Miglia'. Its creation in 1927 was an act of revenge by Aymo Maggi and the Auto Club di Brescia, who had seen the Italian Grand Prix, which they had pioneered in 1921, 'stolen' from them the next year by the Automobile Club of Milan and raced at Monza. With the help and permission of the Fascist Party, a dramatic new race would bring prestige back to Brescia. The Mille Miglia was driven around a thousand miles of Italian roads, closed to traffic but not to people. In the dark of the evening, starting with low–powered sports cars virtually driven by amateurs, every minute a car would roll down the ramp at Brescia, with the fastest cars leaving at dawn.

Over the years the race, mostly dominated by Italians, would have some strange moments. Gianni Marzotto in 1950 won in a smart double-breasted suit, and another winner's car was filled with cigarette ash and empty brandy bottles. The German Rudolf Caracciola sneaked up cleverly behind three over-confident Alfa Romeos with his lights off and became the first foreign winner.

By the 1950s superfast works teams from Maserati, Ferrari and Mercedes were screaming down the narrow roads, blasting past the slower cars. It

The Mercedes SLR of Stirling Moss and Dennis Jenkinson rolls down the ramp at Brescia at the start of their 1955 winning race.

COURTESY OF DAIMLER CHRYSLER

Stirling Moss - his face blackened by a thousand miles of brake dust

was dangerous enough driving along such roads and through typical Italian towns and villages. For the drivers, it was doubly terrifying because the uncontrolled spectators crowded on to the road, only leaping back when the cars came through. So it often seemed that they were driving at 170mph straight at a solid wall of people.

In addition, it was almost impossible to memorise the thousand–mile course which varied every year. The most successful method of knowing what on earth lay beyond the crowd was devised by Dennis Jenkinson, who acted as navigator for Stirling Moss in his Mercedes in 1955. He created an 18 foot scroll, resembling a lavatory roll, on which every corner, bridge or bump on the route had been noted, and for a thousand miles he shouted instructions in Moss's ear, *'Second gear, hump-back-bridge, saucy one left, dodgy one right…'* They broke tradition by leading at Rome and also winning at Brescia.

But, eventually, the inevitable happened to such a dangerous race. Next year, running fourth, Spain's glamorous playboy, Marquis 'Fon' de Portago, pulled in to refuel his vehicle, after having hit a bank, and his Ferrari mechanics told him a wheel was damaged and needed changing. He waved them away and howled back into the race, only to skid to a halt after fifty yards for a kiss with his beautiful girlfriend, the Hollywood actress Linda Christian.

His romantic and Latin sense of priorities had tragic results. Ten miles down the road his tyre burst and his car ploughed into the crowd, killing him, his navigator and 12 spectators.

Under pressure from the Vatican, the high speed Mille Miglia was never run again, and Brescia lost its yearly ritual and its annual few hours of fame.

See: Bonneville, Brooklands, Indianapolis, Le Mans, Maranello

Forty-four years on, Stirling Moss in the Mercedes SLR at Goodwood on his 70th birthday. The number on his car denotes that in 1955 he left Brescia at 7.22 in the morning.

MCvA

THE BRIDGEWATER CANAL
England

Francis Egerton, the third Duke of Bridgewater, has been called the *'Father of Britain's canals'*.

In 1756, as a young man, he had made the traditional 'Grand Tour of Europe' and had been most impressed in France by the 150 mile Languedoc Canal. When, at 22, he had to address the problem of moving coal from his mines more cheaply than by wagon on turnpike roads, he hit on the idea of a cross-country waterway, including an aqueduct over the River Irwell, to go right into Manchester. Having promised Parliament that no public money would be used, the ambitious scheme very nearly ruined him. He mortgaged his

estates, sold his London house and borrowed from friends and family. The canal's construction went on to be surrounded by scorn and ridicule.

But not only did the 'Duke's Canal' include the 40 miles of level waterway to Manchester, it was even dug back into the mines, where another 46 miles of canal, at four levels, reached right up to the actual coal faces. Boats which were very long (47 feet) and very narrow (4.5 feet), with prominent ribs, and which were nicknamed *'Starvationers'*, carried 12 tons each. Six of these were pulled out of the mine and along the canal by one horse or two mules. The Barton Aqueduct, a magnificent structure

The Languedoc canal system which inspired the Duke of Bridgewater

with barges crossing the three arches high above the River Irwell, soon became rather less of a source of ridicule and more of wonder and admiration.

When his canal was opened fully in 1763, the price of coal in Manchester halved at once, and the Duke was able to pay off his debts as his brave venture became a financial success. It was not only coal that was transported, but many other goods, including cotton for Manchester's mills. Passengers were also carried on fast 'packet boats', pulled by three horses at a smooth and steady six miles an hour, with a uniformed 'jockey' sounding his horn to warn slower traffic to drop their tow ropes lest his sharpened bow cut them.

The Bridgewater Canal became part of a complex system of waterways that still exists today, mostly used for pleasure. In 1855, it carried a peak of 2 million tons. Even with the competition from other

canals – and then the railways and the roads – it was not until 1974 that the last freight traffic ceased – over two centuries of commercial success.

The Duke's foresight and courage had paid off handsomely.

The Bridgewater Canal crosses the River Irwell.

See: Chisholm Trail, Cumberland Road, Grand Tour, Great Hedge of India, Promontory, Route 66, Stockton & Darlington, Tacoma, Tay Bridge

BRNO
Czech Republic

No doubt for the Czechs, the city of Brno would be remembered for its famous people – the philosopher and politician Tomas Masaryk, who became Czechoslovakia's first President, Johann Mendel, founder of modern genetics, or Viktor Kaplan, the inventor of the high speed water turbine.

But for a huge number of British and allied servicemen in World War II, the city would be known for the Bren-gun, one of the finest light machine-guns in the world.

As a joint venture between the arms factories of Brno and Enfield, the Bren entered service with the British army in 1937. It was a light, simple, reliable, gas-operated weapon that was as accurate as the army's .303 bolt-action rifle. While firing at half the rate of 1,200 rounds a minute of the German MG34 or MG42, the Bren was a firm favourite with all the forces which fought with it. It played a vital role in many battles and its operators gained many decorations.

The Irish Guards had one such hero, Lance Corporal Kenneally. In North Africa in 1943, they had suffered terrible casualties. At the murderous but successful Battle of the Bou, four

companies were reduced to one, and many of the officers and NCOs were killed or wounded. Kenneally, not just once but again two days later, single-handedly charged with his Bren and broke up whole German companies forming up to attack. During the second charge, he was wounded but continued to hop around the battlefield, supported by a Guardsman, and firing his Bren-gun, which he refused to give up *'as he was the only one who understood it'*. He was awarded the Victoria Cross.

Master of the Bren-gun, Kenneally receives his Victoria Cross from Field Marshal Alexander in Tunis.

IRISH GUARDS

BROADWAY
New York, USA

As a name for a street, the word Broadway is nothing special. It merely denotes a wider thoroughfare than usual – probably for easy access or for driving livestock on market days. There are hundreds, perhaps thousands of Broadways around the world – no less than thirty-three in London alone. But, of course, it is the street that wends its way fifteen miles through Manhattan that the world now calls Broadway. It pre–dated any building in New York, so it does not follow the rigid grid system of the city's streets. It was already a path in 1625 when the Dutchman Peter Minuit bought the island from the Canarsee Indians for twenty four dollars' worth of trinkets, calling it New Amsterdam. By the time Peter Stuyvesant surrendered Manhattan to the British in 1660 it had become the principal cart track between the Bay of what was now called New York and the Bronx.

So it slides and kinks its way up the island of Manhattan, past the Woolworth Building, past City Hall, flanking SoHo and Chinatown, through midtown and on through Harlem – until the Harlem River joins the Hudson and the Bronx is waiting.

However, that still is not the street that we really call Broadway. This is 'the Great White Way', the brilliantly lit and legendary section between 41st Street and 53rd Streets, with its heart at Times Square. Because this is where the theatres are, 38 of them. It is here you find the best theatrical productions, now mostly musicals, which we call plays 'on Broadway'.

'Off-Broadway' plays are performed in 50 smaller theatres in Manhattan. You can even go to 'Off-off-Broadway plays' in 200 small theatres, lofts, clubs or church halls. All the performers aim to get on Broadway and to stay there – unless they get to Hollywood, of course.

A legendary figure on Broadway was the critic for the *New York Times*, Frank Rich. So caustic and devastating were some of his reviews that he was known as the 'Butcher of Broadway'. He could make or break a production.

Not only have innumerable Broadway actors and actresses made their way to Hollywood, but many of the most famous films started out on Broadway. These are just a few:

Thoroughly Modern Millie, Camelot, Oliver!, Sound of Music, Mary Poppins, My Fair Lady, Fiddler on the Roof, West Side Story, King and I, Tea and Sympathy, Annie, Oklahoma, A Chorus Line and *Carousel.*

Not many cart tracks achieve such fame.

There must have been more songs sung about Broadway than any other street. They include:

Lullaby of Broadway
Broadway Baby Dolls
Broadway Caballero
Broadway Jamboree
Broadway Melody
Broadway Baby
Broadway Rhythm
Broadway Serenade
Broadway Gone Hawaii
Broadway Gone Hillbilly
Broadway's Still Broadway
Broadway – The Heart of the World
Say Hello to Broadway
Give My Regards to Broadway
Babes on Broadway
Blue Bells of Broadway
Broadway Prologue to Kokomo, Indiana
Broadway
Can Broadway Do Without Me?
Farm Off Old Broadway
Forty-Five Minutes from Broadway
Goodbye Broadway Hello France
Heart of Broadway
Hello Broadway
Howdy Broadway
I'll Build a Broadway for You
It's Tough to be a Hostess on Broadway
Little Miss Broadway
Look Out Broadway
The Man Who Owns Broadway
Mr Broadway
Song of Broadway
Take Me to Broadway
There's a Broken Heart for Every Light on Broadway
Two Tickets to Broadway
Walking Down Broadway

MICHAEL BURCZYK

BROOKLANDS
England

'The right crowd and no crowding'

Thus proclaimed the posters for events at Brooklands, the first purpose-built motor racing circuit ever built. You could not imagine a more British, upper-class and elitist slogan if you tried. It was the exact opposite of the second circuit built two years later at Indianapolis in 1909.

The idea of Brooklands started at a dinner party in 1906 in Surrey, south west of London. A wealthy landowner, Hugh Fortescue Locke King, was bemoaning the fact no British competitors had taken part in the Targa Florio of 1905 and, indeed, that he had to go to the Continent to see a motor race at all, leaving Britain with its 20mph speed limit. Somehow, by the end of dinner, he found he had volunteered to build a track on his estate at Brooklands.

Allocating 300 acres of swampy meadows and farmland, he probably thought it would be like building a golf course, budgeting £22,000 for the work.

But when Colonel Holden, Royal Engineers, had taken charge, something much more ambitious emerged, with a 100ft wide track and two long high bankings, super-elevated to 29 feet. 2,000 workmen worked 3 shifts, 6 days a week, with 20 steam shovels and seven miles of railway lines. Thirty acres of woodland were levelled, 350,000 cubic yards of earth moved and 200,000 tons of concrete poured.

The effort of this colossal undertaking wrecked the health of Locke King and nearly bankrupted him, but his wife Ethel took over and her family chipped in. The final cost was £150,000 – millions today.

When racing started, on 6th July 1907, horse-racing was the only example to copy. It was called a 'Motor Ascot'. Cars were kept in 'the Paddock', they were 'weighed in' at the elegant clubhouse, given handicaps, and drivers wore coloured smocks like jockeys.

Even before the circuit was finished, Selwyn Francis Edge had booked it for his attempt to race for 24 hours which he completed at the speed of 66mph, a record that stood for 17 years. Soon it was *the* place to beat speed records. Lambert was the first to travel over a hundred miles in one hour.

K. Lee Guinness was the last to create a World Landspeed Record actually at Brooklands, 135.75mph. But from that moment on, it was Brooklands' expertise that took Sir Malcolm Campbell and his Blue Birds to records at Pendine Sands and then Bonneville.

Brooklands is unique in that it was almost equally the home of British aviation, with numerous aircraft sheds and flying clubs which trained many of the pilots in the First World War, when it became the largest aircraft production centre in Britain. Later Barnes Wallis worked on his 'Dam Buster' bombs and his aircraft designs, including the Wellington bomber which was built there.

But Brooklands will always be known for its uniquely British sporting atmosphere. Races of all classes, speed

Cars battled wheel to wheel on the bankings

John Cobb's 24 litre Napier Railton at 143 m.p.h. on the bumpy surface

BROOKLANDS FIRST MEETING

Lavish Prize Money and a Ghastly Failure

Edge's Famous 24 Hours' Record—An Amphibious
Aeroplane Which Swam But Did Not Fly

At Brooklands' formal opening, Mrs Locke King led a procession of 60 famous motorists, including the Hon. Charles Rolls in his racing Rolls-Royce, the Duke of Westminster and Lord Lonsdale

*The Members'
Banking, crumbling
but intact, with the
old entrance bridge*

See: Ascot, Bonneville,
Brescia, Cowes, Cresta
Run, Farnborough, Henley,
Indianapolis, Kitty Hawk,
Le Mans, Wimbledon

trials, record attempts – all by amateurs. With its tennis courts, putting greens, restaurants and 'society' in elegant clothes, it was more like Ascot or Henley than a modern motor racing scene. Some of the names give us the feel; Sir Malcolm Campbell, The Duke of Richmond and Gordon, The Hon. Brian Lewis, Sir Henry Birkin, Lord Montague of Beaulieu, Lord Brabazon of Tara, Sir Henry Segrave, Earl Howe, Count Zborowski. Among the ladies was Barbara Cartland, the prolific romantic novelist, later to be famous as the step-grandmother of Diana, Princess of Wales. While something of a backwater for Grand Prix racing, these amateurs were driving very serious cars. You cannot look at 1935 movie footage of the fastest of all, John Cobb in his 24 litre Napier Railton, high on the bumpy Byfleet Banking lapping at 143mph, without feeling admiration for his bravery.

You might admire even more the fastest woman, Gwenda Hawkes, whose 'Ladies Lap Record' was 135.95mph, in a beautiful little American Miller 91 with a 1.5 litre engine.

World War II ended all motor racing. Aircraft hangars and factories for Hurricane fighters and Wellington bombers were built up and, after the war, the Ministry of Aircraft Production refused to hand Brooklands back for three years. Sadly, the shareholders voted to sell to Vickers-Armstrong, which over the next forty years produced a successful range of civil and military aircraft from Viscount to Concorde.

But Brooklands is still there, and open to the public. The Members' Banking may have grass and weeds growing through it, but the Brooklands Museum Trust has magnificently restored the Clubhouse, the Malcolm Campbell and other sheds, and many historic cars and memorabilia. And now Daimler-Chrysler has plans for a sixty-acre family park and a testing centre. So thanks to the Germans, cars may once again be seen on that very British banking.

BUCK'S CLUB
England

There is only one of London's 'gentlemen's clubs' which has achieved worldwide fame. To be sure, there are many people in Britain who have at least heard of White's or Boodle's or the Turf Club. But only Buck's can claim more – and all because of a pop group named after a drink.

Buck's is the youngest of such clubs, created just after the First World War. Captain Herbert Buckmaster, Royal Horse Guards, sat in a shell-blasted dugout at Guillemont on the Western Front and resolved, if he survived, to create a small, intimate club. In 1919, 'Buck' and his friends bought the lease of a house on the corner of Old Burlington Street and Clifford Street in Mayfair. At the beginning, it had a distinct military base. Three brothers were founder members; two had won

who created for them a memorable and refreshing drink. 'Buck's Fizz', made from champagne, orange juice, and just a touch of grenadine.

Even with 'Buck's Fizz' a staple drink at Ascot and Henley, the club's name would be confined to upper-crust Britain until a pop group was put together specifically to try to win the Eurovision Song Contest of 1981. Mike Nolan, Bobby Gee, Cheryl Baker and Jay Aston of 'Buck's Fizz' duly won with *Making Your Mind Up*, watched by millions of viewers in twenty-five countries. 'Buck's Fizz' went on to be one of the most popular groups of the 1980s with twenty hit singles, including *The Land*

'Buck's Fizz' won the Eurovision Song Contest in 1981.

of *Make Believe* and *My Camera Never Lies*.

Probably not many of the fans knew about Captain Buckmaster and his little club in Mayfair. Not many 'Buck's Fizz' drinkers do either. And please do not think that grenadine is the only magic ingredient added to champagne and orange juice. At Buck's Club they say there is something extra, but they won't give away the secret.

See: Ascot, Cowes, General Post Office, Henley, Wimbledon

Victoria Crosses for gallantry, and the third a DSO and Bar and a DSC, who was known as the coward of the family!

One of the 'characters' of Buck's was John Loder. In 1915, he was the young officer who accepted Padraic Pearse's surrender after the Dublin Easter Rising. Pearse was so impressed by John's kindness that he handed him his cap badge and other mementoes *'in case he was executed'* – which he was. John became a heart-throb cinema actor in the thirties and was married many times, one bride being Hollywood's Hedi Lamarr. Years later, when some Buck's members consulted him about Grace Kelly, he paused and asked, 'Was she one of the ones I married?' 'Buck' himself was partial to actresses, marrying Gladys Cooper and Nellie Taylor.

But it was not 'Buck' and his elegant friends who were to make 'Buck's' so famous. It was McGarry, the barman

BULL & FINCH
Massachusetts, USA

Comedies often have bars or pubs as one of their key locations, from the 'Nag's Head' in the popular TV series *Only Fools and Horses* to the coffee bar 'Central Perk' in the US series *Friends*. But rarely has one been as focal and illustrious as the one after which the television sit-com *Cheers* was named.

With the famous subtitle and theme tune *'Where everybody knows your name'* summing up the ethos of the show, *Cheers* was a stepping stone in the

evolution of comedy. It was part of the movement from family based sit-coms and shows based around a single person to leisure/work place comedy with a wider cast of central characters. The series contained some of the most instantly memorable characters ever. The Boston bar was run by Sam Malone (Ted Danson, who had to be sent to bartending school for two weeks before shooting started), a former alcoholic and serial womaniser, and Diane Chambers

(Shelly Long), a witty English graduate, the two of whom fostered an on-off romance while driving each other crazy.

Other characters included Frasier the psychiatrist, Carla the sassy waitress, and also Norm, so beloved in the bar that everyone shouted his name whenever he entered. Norm, in particular, is famous for his bar-room pearls of wisdom, with a good many internet sites devoted to quoting him.

SAM: *'How's life in the fast lane, Normie?'*
NORM: *'Beats me. I can't find the on-ramp'.*

During its run, starting in 1982, the cast was to become increasingly famous for back-stage water fights and practical jokes, and the show, (the first episode of which was the lowest-rated programme that week), soon went from strength to strength. Kirstie Alley, Bebe Neuwirth and Woody Harrelson joined the cast after the character Coach died, and following a complicated storyline of a love-triangle between Diane, Sam and Frasier, Diane jilted Frasier at the altar and left town.

The exterior shots of the bar were filmed at Boston's 'Bull and Finch'. Now a tourist attraction feeding off the show's successes, and serving dishes such as the 'Cheersburger', it attracts 90,000 visitors a year. Some visitors, however, are disappointed that the interior bears no resemblance to the show's bar whatsoever. In fact, the 'Bull and Finch's' owner, Tom Kershaw, plans to open a new *Cheers* theme bar, which will be an exact replica. So detailed will be the imitation that it is to include Sam's Red Sox jacket and Cliff's mail carrier uniform. Other *Cheers* theme bars already exist, including one in London's Regent Street.

The show itself was not devoid of negative publicity, with Kelsey Grammer (Frasier) being arrested for taking cocaine, and Woody Harrelson (Woody) being an outspoken pro-cannabis activist. But nothing could curtail the show's popularity, and the last episode attracted sixty-four per cent of the viewing public. *Cheers* still lives on to an extent in its successful spin-off, *Frasier*.

Divorced from his wife Lillith (also a character on *Cheers)* Frasier leaves Boston and returns to his home town of Seattle, starring in his own radio phone-in show and living with his father. So successful is this child of *Cheers* that Kelsey Grammer now receives a massive £1.6 million per episode, making him the highest paid television actor ever. In occasional episodes he is even visited by members of the old cast, including Ted Danson and Shelly Long. But though *Cheers* lives on through its spin-off and theme bars, the programme finished its run in 1993 with Sam's famous last line: 'Sorry, we're closed'.

See: Albert Square, Coronation Street, Peyton Place, Ramsay Street

BUNCOMBE
North Carolina, USA

There are famous places which have quite unexpectedly given their names to a language. For instance, 'That was his Waterloo', 'Crossing the Rubicon', 'She's kissed the Blarney Stone', 'The party was absolute Bedlam', 'He's gone doollaly'.

But it's not often that an unknown place stays unknown, whilst at the same time giving us a phrase forever. In 1820, Congressman Felix Walker was making a speech and was being heckled by other legislators. 'I am not talking for your ears. I am talking only for Buncombe', he cried out, referring to his local town in North Carolina.

Thus 'bunkum' or 'bunk', meaning nonsense or humbug, entered the English language, followed a hundred years later by the slang to 'de-bunk' something.

See: Bedlam, Blarney, Deolali, Rubicon, Waterloo

CAMERONE
Mexico

Each year, on 30th April, the men of the French Foreign Legion are paraded, and the most decorated officer relates the story of Camerone. Then a wooden forearm and hand are solemnly carried out to the parade and the Legionnaires march past in salute.

In April 1863, France found herself locked into an ill-fated attempt to impose on Mexico, ruled by Benito Juarez, the Austrian Archduke Maximilian. She soon had 40,000 troops there, including 4,000 of the Foreign Legion. But even the Legion had been ravaged by dysentery, typhus and yellow fever. When a vital convoy of bullion to pay Mexico City's garrison had to be escorted along the road lifeline from the coast at Vera Cruz, the weakened Third Company of the 1st Battalion (only sixty-three men) was assigned to protect it. All the Company's officers were sick, so the Battalion's Adjutant Captain Danjou volunteered (complete with his wooden arm), as did the Pay Officer, Lieutenant Vilain and Second Lieutenant Maudet.

Early in the morning of April 30th, just after passing the deserted and nondescript little hamlet of Camerone, they were suddenly attacked by Colonel Milan's Juarist Mexican cavalry, soon to be followed up by 1,200 infantry.

The Legionnaires conducted a steady fighting retreat, the mile back to Camerone through the dense scrub that luckily protected them a little. But they had already lost eighteen men and, almost worse, the two pack mules with their spare rations and ammunition. Danjou's men desperately fortified the farmhouse. All morning, they beat off assault after brave Mexican assault. They also refused Milan's repeated demands for surrender, swearing to Danjou to fight to the end. But with 2,000 Mexican rifles firing at them, casualties mounted steadily. At 11 am, Danjou was shot dead but Vilain stoutly continued the defence, his men reeling from hunger and, especially, thirst, in the intense heat. Vilain was killed at 2pm and Maudet took command, even resisting an attempt to burn them out.

MINISTERE DE LA DEFENSE, LEGION ETRANGERE

But by the evening only Maudet and five legionnaires were still standing, and with only one bullet left per man. So Maudet drew his sword and ordered them to fix bayonets, and they charged the mass of amazed Mexicans. Maudet and two men were quickly shot down. But the last three were pinned down and spared. Colonel Milan made sure his men cared for them and the other wounded. (Thirty-two survived to fight in other campaigns). The Colonel's chivalry and admiration were all the more impressive when you consider he had lost 300 men killed and 300 more wounded. And by wasting time fighting the Legion, almost as a matter of honour, he had also lost the bullion convoy, which had plenty of time to escape back towards Vera Cruz.

The names of Danjou, Vilain and Maudet are engraved in gold in the Invalides in Paris. And at Camerone itself, a monument was erected in 1892.

Mexican troops salute it to this day.

Captain Danjou's famous wooden hand, which is paraded every year by the Foreign Legion

See: The Alamo, Bayonne, Dien Bien Phu, Mers-el-Kebir, Suez

CAMP DAVID
Maryland, USA

It was President Franklin Roosevelt who chose this country retreat for himself and future United States Presidents. Soon after Pearl Harbor propelled America into war, he directed the National Park Service to find a place which was secure, close to Washington and high enough to avoid the oppressive summer heat. In April 1942, Roosevelt, in a five car cavalcade, set out to visit three candidate sites and quickly decided on the Recreation Demonstration Area

President Jimmy Carter succeeds in creating the 'Camp David Accords' bringing peace between Egypt's Anwar Sadat (left) and Israel's Menachem Begin (right).

1,800 feet up in the Catoctin Mountains, one of the parks created by the Works Projects Administration from worn-out agricultural land. On the $25,000 cost estimate that he had been given, he wrote:

'Fix up one cottage for Miss Hackmeister and any stenogs.
Fix up one cottage for Mr Hassett and other male staff.
Fix up one cottage for Filipinos and Valet - 6 bunks.
Secret Service to sleep in tents'.

While the construction was under way, Jimmy Doolittle's B-25 bombers hit Tokyo – the first symbolic strike against the all-conquering Japanese. Asked from where the planes had taken off, Roosevelt smiled; 'Shangri-La'. And so he named his mountain retreat, which he noted in his 'log' as *'launched July 5th, 1942'*. In fact, everything was rather nautical, with naval crew members of his yacht *USS Potomac* staffing the compound for its 'cruises'.

The cool cabins and sheltered lodges of the camp have seen some of the most vital meetings and most important visitors in history, starting with Roosevelt entertaining and plotting victory with his friend Winston Churchill.

Harry Truman's wife Bess thought it 'dull', but Truman loved to walk the mountains with his Secret Service agents in tow.

It was Dwight Eisenhower who changed the name to 'Camp David', in honour of his grandson David. He chaired the first cabinet meeting to be held there, and was host to Britain's Prime Minister Harold MacMillan and Soviet Premier Nikita Khrushchev. All the Presidents who followed Kennedy – Johnson, Nixon, Ford and Reagan, George Bush and Clinton, used Camp David often and to good effect.

But it was Jimmy Carter who was to give the country retreat its special fame. In 1978, he invited Egyptian President Anwar Sadat and Israel's Menachem Begin to a summit at Camp David. The calming effects of the place seemed to work. It was a triumph for Jimmy Carter, who shuttled back and forth between Sadat's 'Dogwood Lodge' and Begin's 'Birch Lodge' to keep the talks going. Begin praised Carter, saying he had *'worked harder than our forefathers did in Egypt building the pyramids'*.

The 'Camp David Accords', later ratified in Washington, ended hostility between Egypt and Israel. In spite of the fact that Sadat was assassinated three years later for the courage to make such a rapprochement, the long peace process started at Camp David may one day bear fruit.

See: Chequers, Downing Street

CAPE CANAVERAL
Florida, USA

For the Spanish, the Cape had little to recommend it – no treasure and a really fierce tribe of Indians, the Ais. In 1513, the explorer Ponce de Leon retreated from them very hastily and his successor, Francisco Gordillo, had good reason to remember the place, wounded

by an Ais arrow made from cane. It was this bamboo-like plant which gave the Cape its Spanish name, *Canaveral* – 'Canebrake'.

For centuries the Cape's only usefulness was as a vital visual landmark for sailors navigating round Florida by

sites, partly because its position near the Equator could use the high rotational speed of the earth to 'slingshot' the rockets, with less thrust required. It was soon under the control of the National Aeronautical and Space Administration.

Scarcely had the Cape achieved its worldwide fame for all the main rocket launches, when its name was changed. Just six days after John F. Kennedy's assassination, his successor President Lyndon Johnson ordered Cape Canaveral's name be changed to Cape Kennedy, and its complex to the John F. Kennedy Space Center, NASA.

This controversial decision was bitterly debated for ten years and, in 1973, the Florida legislature stepped in and Governor Reubin Askew signed a Florida Statute requiring the Cape to revert to its 400-year old name.

So now there is a compromise, with Cape Canaveral and the Kennedy Space Center both being the places from which we watch rockets and space shuttles lift to the skies and make history.

See: Peenemünde, Roswell

Left: Captured V-2s were tested at White Sands before protests by the Mexicans.

Below: A shuttle launch lifts off.

dead reckoning. It was not wise to make a mistake and join the many shipwrecks along the coast. After all, both the Ais and their more docile neighbours, the Timucuans, were cannibals.

Even with the development of the Flagler railroad and the huge expansion of Florida, Cape Canaveral remained unknown and isolated, accessible only by boat, still with only about 100 inhabitants during World War II.

But the Cape was about to achieve fame. Three thousand miles away in Germany, Hitler's rocket pioneer, Werner von Braun was testing his supersonic V-2 ballistic rockets at the Baltic range at Peenemünde, before dropping a thousand of them on London. He surrendered his team of experts to the Americans, but Peenemünde itself and its secrets were captured by the Russians. It soon became obvious that a rocket and space race was on, and an American testing range was required.

At first White Sands, New Mexico, was favoured, until a stray modified V-2 wandered south over El Paso and crashed in Juarez, Mexico, whose President Miguel Aleman quite understandably refused to allow more rocket testing in the area.

However, America's firmest ally, Britain, agreed to testing over the Bahamas, and offered islands for radar tracking stations. Cape Canaveral was chosen from several other candidate

NASA / NATIONAL ARCHIVES AND RECORDS ADMINISTRATION

CARNABY STREET
England

The 'Swinging Sixties' when Carnaby Street thrilled, or shocked, the world

Why does the name of this tiny street in London's Soho ring bells all over the world? Probably because it epitomised the famously decadent fashion of 60s and 70s 'Swinging London'.

In the 16th century, before the Great Fire of London caused London to 'move west', Carnaby Street was surrounded by fields, used for hunting. The huntsman's cry, 'Soho!' became the name for the area and Carnaby Street owes its origins to a mansion called 'Karnaby House', built in 1683 and to the flourishing Karnaby Market which closed in 1820.

A century later, the first 'boutique' opened in Carnaby Street in 1925, but the street's fashion fame really started in 1955 when Vince Green began to sell the first casual clothes for men. Indeed, his 'Vince' catalogue of that year features a husky male model called Tom Connery, who we would soon know as Sean. Vince Green's Scottish assistant, John Stephen, broke away to open several shops in Carnaby Street, soon to be followed by Warren Gold with his 'Lord John' boutique. This led to a rivalry called the 'battle of the Johns' which was real enough but was helped by public relations 'spin'. Cashing in on the 'Lord John' name was 'Lady Jane', one of the first shops for girls to open on Carnaby Street which was joined by ever more exotic shops, including one with old military-style clothes called 'I was Lord Kitchener's valet.'

In the early days, a young public relations man Tony Edwards, who ended up promoting many of the boutiques, could not quite believe that Carnaby Street would really succeed. He took cash for his fees from 'Lord John' instead of shares. *In an era when streets had butchers, fishmongers, hardware stores, haberdashers and 'men's outfitters' I could not imagine a street full of shops all selling the same kind of thing.'*

One of the most creative of the owners was Sidney Brent of 'Take 6', who had the imaginative idea of serving coffee to his 'Essex boy' customers in his Romford store, asking them what new styles they wanted. This early version of 'focus groups' ensured success and he produced seven new stock turns a year, unheard of in the business.

Soon Carnaby Street was all the rage, an essential part of the 'Swinging London' that the world was talking about, where young people were certainly not interested in wearing the clothes their fathers and mothers used to wear, rather the reverse. Competition for new styles raged. Several shops decided to copy the fashion of Beau Brummell, and young composer Andrew Lloyd-Webber and his partner Tim Rice would make Regency clothes their trade-mark.

The Teddyboys, Mods and Rockers, Hippies, Skinheads, Punks, Gothics and The Old School – all flocked to Carnaby Street, often shocking tourists in between amusing them, and giving newspapers sensational photographic footage. Three national newspapers ran huge features in the same week. Carnaby Street's fame was further enhanced when groups like 'The Kinks' or 'Rolling Stones' were spotted there in their outrageous gear.

Unsurprisingly, the name of the street – and its notoriety – soon spread overseas, so much so that a Frenchman even bought a street in Paris, calling it Carnaby Street, and sold the shortest mini skirts in Europe.

It was not going to last, of course. Many of the pioneers went on to open huge stores in Oxford Street and began to lose their creativity. Many of the others simply went bust, their inexperience and amateur approach being no match for market conditions which 'returned to reality'.

Ever-resourceful Tony Edwards bought

the paving stores from Carnaby Street that Westminster Council were going to throw away and then sold them all over America.

Carnaby Street's chic venues soon gave way to souvenir shops, and the excitement was gone.

But happily, not forever. Recently, popular brands have rediscovered this Soho Street, with labels like O'Neill – a surf and skateboard shop and Ted

Baker, Diesel and Miss Sixty attracting a new wave of young shoppers.

For those of us who remember the street in its heyday, there is still the fashion shop called 'Yesterday's Bread', tucked into a corner behind Foubert's Place.

'If you can remember the sixties, you weren't there', so they say. But if you knew Carnaby Street, it would be hard to forget it.

See: Abbey Road, Bazaar, Bikini, Rotten Row, Savile Row, Sibylla's

CARNEGIE HALL
New York, USA

'How do you get to Carnegie Hall? Practice, practice, practice'.

It was a good thing for the world of music that Louise Whitfield Carnegie's great passion was singing alto with New York's Oratorio Society. In 1884, she persuaded her husband, Andrew, to join the Board of the Society and, together with its young conductor Walter Damrosch, they convinced Andrew to help them create a 'music hall' for orchestral, choral and recital concerts.

Luckily, too, Andrew Carnegie was probably the richest man in the world, based on the toil of his steelworkers in Pittsburgh. *Put all your eggs in one basket and then watch that basket',* he had once said to Mark Twain. He was a strange mixture of ruthless efficiency in business and having a real social conscience. '*The man who dies thus rich, dies disgraced'.*

During his lifetime he gave away $400 million, his entire fortune, to Pittsburgh, to his birthplace Scotland, to England and to America. Having once been barred from free membership of Allegheny City Library, he was determined to bring education to the people, however poor. '*It is the mind that makes the body rich. There is no class so pitiably wretched as that which possesses money and nothing else'.*

The Carnegie Library in Pittsburgh with its carved doorway, *Free to the People,* is but the best known of hundreds of libraries that he created throughout the world. But it is the famed Carnegie Hall which will forever link his name with music. Enrolling another Oratorio Society Board member, William Tuthill, as architect, the 'music hall' was erected in seven years on Seventh Avenue and

57th Street, and on 5th May 1891 the five-day opening festival began, with the raised baton of Peter Ilyich Tchaikovsky. Not only did the cream of New York Society approve, more significant and long lasting was the *New York Herald's* comment, *The acoustics were perfect. There was no echo, no undue reverberation.*

This was one of the best reasons why, since that fabled opening, Carnegie Hall has been graced with every kind of performer. Classical music has seen Sousa, Segovia, Copeland, Casals, Marian Anderson, Ephrem Zimbalist, Pavarotti, Toscanini, Joan Sutherland, Yehudi Menuhin and Daniel Barenboim. Dance witnessed the pioneering Isadora Duncan. Laughs have been raised by Victor Borge, Jack Benny and Groucho Marks. Jazz greats include W.C. Handy, 'the Father of the Blues', Duke Ellington, Errol Garner, Miles Davis and Benny Goodman, whose clarinet resides in the Hall's museum. Popular music is represented by American folk singers like Pete Seeger and Bob Dylan, foreign phenomena like the Beatles, who played their first US concert there and home-grown legends like Judy Garland and Frank Sinatra.

Andrew Carnegie was right as he and his wife laid the cornerstone in 1890, when he stated:

'It was built to stand for ages, and during those ages this hall will intertwine itself with the history of our country'.

Above: Cartoonists extolled Carnegie's generosity in donating libraries and other cultural gifts.

Below: Miles Davis

GRIMSDALE

See: Abbey Road, Bayreuth, Big Apple, Broadway, Cotton Club, Harlem, Manhattan, Motown, Nashville, Storyville, Tin Pan Alley

CASABLANCA
Morocco

Tourism to Morocco has steadily increased in recent years, so quite a few people are familiar with Casablanca, both the old French colonial city and the modern Moroccan one. But many more will have the name Casablanca in their minds for two reasons. First it was the site of the crucial Casablanca Conference between Winston Churchill and Franklin D. Roosevelt in June 1943. This meeting, which Stalin could not attend for military reasons, settled key decisions for the future of the Second World War. Eight months earlier Casablanca had been liberated by General George Patton as part of 'Gymnast', the Anglo-American invasion of North Africa. As Churchill said, 'Now is not the end. It is not even the beginning of the end. But it is, perhaps, the end of the beginning'.

The Casablanca Conference confirmed the British and American view that Hitler had to be defeated before the Japanese and that, reluctantly, the invasion of Europe would have to wait until 1944.

But for most people, 'Casablanca' does

See: Yalta

not mean high strategy, it means a marvellous film, released the same year as the Conference. Set in the city still under Vichy and German occupation, Humphrey Bogart (Rick) abandons his cynicism, and selflessly helps his old love Ingrid Bergman (Ilse) and her underground leader husband to escape from the Nazis. 'Ilse, I'm no good at being noble, but it doesn't take too much to see that the problems of three little people don't amount to a hill of beans in this crazy world. Someday you'll understand that. Not now. Here's looking at you, kid'.

Casablanca is one of the world's most memorable movies, a combination of romance, intrigue, suspense, humour and great lines, 'Major Strasser has been shot. Round up the usual suspects'.

Just one thing. Contrary to public opinion, when Bogart asks Sam, the pianist, to play *'As time goes by'*, he does not say 'Play it again, Sam'. He actually says, 'You played it for her, you can play it for me. If she can stand it, I can. Play it.'

THE CAVERN
England

'The beat groups used to play at the Cavern for nothing in our intervals. John Lennon was very aggressive, then as later, plainly seeing us jazzmen as old farts. 'You're standing in our way', which I suppose we were. But we were soon kicked out of it!'

George Melly with the author when filming 'Smoky Dives'

George Melly, the boisterous, veteran jazz entertainer was describing, in the BBC programme *'Smoky Dives'*, how his jazz music was supplanted by something new which would sweep the world and without which we would never have heard of an underground cellar in Liverpool.

Liverpool's first wealth had come from 'Cheshire Salt'; it had become one of the great ports of the British Empire and the prime entry point for the Irish, indeed the city's famous wit comes straight from Dublin. In this thriving city in the 1950s, youth was emerging

and music was booming, especially jazz. Jazz Club owner Alan Sytner had visited 'Le Caveau de la Huchette' off the Boulevard St. Michel in Paris and he resolved to recreate its sound and cavernous ambience in Liverpool. A former air-raid shelter and wine-cellar in the basement of 10 Mathew Street was to become The Cavern Club. On 16th January 1957, 'The Merseysippi Jazz Band' opened the club with 2,000 teenagers queuing outside, but only 600 of them were allowed in. The club

MEMBERSHIP CARD
1963 SEASON
Ending 31st December, 1963

consisted of three dimly-lit tunnels, and, walls painted black with simple white lightbulbs. It had no liquor licence, but high temperatures, little ventilation and inadequate toilets.

Soon, with 20,000 members, it was one of Britain's premier jazz clubs. The Cavern's bridge to worldwide fame was created by 'Skiffle', folk music with a wash-board, tea-chest bass, acoustic guitar and drums (if you were lucky). In August, 'The Quarrymen' skiffle group played there, led by seventeen year old John Lennon, who sometimes tried to slip in songs from the new American phenomenon called Elvis Presley. He was passed a curt note from Alan Sytner, *'Cut out the bloody rock!'*

But Rock 'n' Roll was not to be denied. Sytner moved to London and the new owner, Ray McFall, was forced to bow to the inevitable as 'beat' music swept Liverpool and Britain.

Beat music was played more and more at The Cavern. Lennon had recruited fifteen year old Paul McCartney, and then fourteen year old George Harrison and later Pete Best. Another Cavern band, 'Rocky Storm and the Hurricanes', featured a drummer who was soon to join them, Ringo Starr. 'The Quarrymen' became 'The Beatles', went to Hamburg, where they vastly improved their act and, at lunchtime on Thursday 8th February 1961, re-launched themselves at The Cavern, for a total fee of £5. They were an instant smash success, soon booked several times a week, with McFall trying pre-purchase tickets to reduce the huge queues. 'The Beatles' were joined by local record shop owner, Brian Epstein, as their manager, and by a host of new bands at The Cavern – 'The Swinging Blue Jeans', 'The Big Three', 'The Searchers' and 'Gerry and the Pacemakers'. Priscilla White joined the club as a cloakroom attendant, but was soon being asked on stage, launching her own entertainment career under her new name Cilla Black (an Epstein suggestion). 'The Beatles' played their last gig at The Cavern on 3rd August 1963 for £300, but the venue continued to boom. In 1964 'The Yardbirds' and Eric Clapton first played blues there. November alone saw the 'Rolling Stones', then John Lee Hooker, Howlin' Wolf and Memphis Slim. The following year the club hosted Gene Vincent,

Sandie Shaw, Joe Brown, Petula Clark, Manfred Mann, 'The Kinks', 'The Who' and Elton John. Key staff included Bob Wooler, the compere and disc jockey, Paddy Delaney, the head bouncer, Tony Buck, the strongest bouncer (he was an Olympic wrestler) and David Bramwell, later one of the world's botanists.

Then, in the midst of all this success, the sanitation system (or the lack of it) revolted! The toilet cistern leaked down into the underground railway. The club's poor finances were too weak to rectify the problem, and on a cold night in February 1966, after one last sad all-night session, the bailiffs moved in.

A new club was soon opened by British Prime Minister Harold Wilson. It was older, sold drinks, smelled of pot but still featured the likes of 'Wishbone Ash', 'Thin Lizzy', 'Supertramp' and Judas Priest. However, the underground railway came back to haunt the venue. Needing an exhaust duct, The Cavern was placed under compulsory purchase order and bulldozed in 1973.

Throughout the 1970s the club bounced back under various guises and various names in a new venue across Mathew Street. Bands such as 'The Clash' led the way in the New Wave and Punk era, and later 'Frankie goes to Hollywood', 'Echo and the Bunnymen' and Elvis Costello typified the local Liverpool bands who continued the city's rich musical heritage. Unfortunately, financial problems once again hit the club, and it was closed permanently.

But though gone, The Cavern was not forgotten. It was John Lennon's death in 1980 which inspired the Council, local business people and Royal Life Assurance to create a shopping centre in Mathew Street with a Beatles theme. Here, using 15,000 bricks from the original venue, they built a replica of The Cavern Club. The whole area is now called 'The Cavern Quarter'. It's not quite the same, but at least Liverpool has honoured itself as one of the cradles of modern music, alongside Chicago, New York, Memphis, Nashville and New Orleans.

Paul McCartney and The Beatles at The Cavern Club

'We're more popular than Christianity now. I don't know which will go first - rock 'n' roll, or Christianity'.

John Lennon, 1966

'Most people get into bands for three very simple rock 'n' roll reasons: to get laid, to get fame, and to get rich'.

Bob Geldof, *Melody Maker*, 1977

79

See: Cognac, Nuits-St-George, Pilzen

CHAMPAGNE
France

In *My Fair Lady* they sing *'The night they invented champagne'*. But to create the magical wine that the world drinks in celebration took rather longer, of course, than one night.

For centuries, the carbon dioxide gas produced from the grapes of the Champagne region's chalky soil had actually been a bit of a nuisance, but eventually was to create its fame.

Since Roman times, the region had been producing excellent red and white wines, so good that the Emperor Domitian, in 92 AD, had decreed the vineyards should be uprooted to eliminate competition with Italy's wine producers. Consequently, for two centuries, the wine was produced secretly, until Emperor Probus ordered the vineyards to be replanted.

By the seventeenth century, the wines of Champagne rivalled those of Burgundy and, because of their monastic connections, were used for the sacrament, for coronations, the royal table and to celebrate treaties.

It was the British and an accident that produced the sparkling wine. Some casks of 'Vin Gris', still white wine, were shipped to the French exile and wine importer Saint-Evremond in England. The wine underwent a second fermentation in the warm weather during the voyage. Bottled with the new invention of the cork stopper, the wine then retained its lively sparkle.

It was two clerics, Frère Jean Oudart and – even more famous – Dom Pierre Pérignon of the Abbey at Hautvilliers at Epernay, who experimented to bring method to the production of the new and increasingly popular clear, sparkling wine, imposing exacting blending standards. Others introduced sugar and then grape juice to create the second fermentation in the bottle, also learning to refine the quantities to avoid both the wastage and danger of huge numbers of exploding bottles.

Soon Champagne was one of France's finest exports, thanks to the efforts of Claude Moët, Philippe Clicquot and Florenz-Louis Heidsieck.

In the 19th century, it was the turn of Perrier-Jouet, Mumm, Bollinger and the famous widows, 'Veuve' Cliquot, Pommery and Perrier.

Champagne has fiercely defended its 'brand image' against all imitators. In 1911, there were riots against fraudulent blending with cheap southern wines – the 'revolt of the vignerons'. And, since then, many successful law cases have been brought.

Cold and deep in miles of caves under Rheims and Epernay, some quarried by the Romans, lie millions of bottles, resting on their sides, slowly maturing for at least three years with their own sediment. They are, over five weeks, brought to the vertical position with the *remuage*, 40 skilled turns of the bottle, to bring the sediment down on to the cork, eventually to be frozen and ejected as a plug of ice. Soon the magic wine is on its way to the markets – and celebrations around the world.

There are 312 wine-producing villages in Champagne – but there are three with names really worth remembering: Bouzy, Rilly and Dizy!

CHANGI
Singapore

An excellent example of a military myth which needs more examination would be '*The guns at Singapore were pointing the wrong way*'.

Singapura, or 'Lion City', was founded by a Sumatran prince, who claimed that he had met a lion – a good omen. It became a minor trading post, first under the Sumatran Srivijaya Empire and later, in the thirteenth century, of the Javanese Majapahit Empire.

But it was as part of the British Empire, that Singapore – founded by Sir Stamford Raffles – was transformed into a flourishing colony with a military and naval base.

In the late 1920s and 1930s, the importance of Changi, the north eastern tip of the island, became ever more obvious as the Japanese threat emerged, and during these years the British worked to create an artillery base which would dominate the eastern Johore Straits and the approach to the newly developing Naval Base. Fifteen inch and six inch guns were sited, capable of destroying almost any ship.

In 1941, 'Changi Fortress' – as the Japanese called it – and the rest of Singapore – complacently awaited events with a somewhat relaxed working day of 7.30 to 11.30.

But key assumptions for the defence of the great port of Singapore had unfortunately been removed. First, by the Japanese occupation of French Indo-China after the fall of France, and then by their brilliant use of air power.

On 2nd December 1941, HMS *Prince of Wales* and *Repulse*, sent there on Churchill's orders, steamed past the guns of Changi to the Naval Base, and seven days later they steamed out again to oppose Japanese landings in the north – never to be seen again. Sharing the fate of the American battleships at Pearl Harbor, they were rapidly sunk by aircraft – flying from Indo-China. It was a disaster that Churchill described as his low point in the war. Soon, in February, the Japanese were just across the Johore Straits, and although the guns of Changi could point in most directions, their flat trajectory and armour-piercing shells, designed for ships, were useless against infantry and artillery. They were ordered to be blown up, and the troops ordered to help defend Singapore City.

Even though outnumbered three to one, desperately short of ammunition and supplies, it was the Japanese, under General Yamashita, who succeeded in bluffing General Percival into surrender – the worst military humiliation in Britain's history.

And so it was that the troops from Changi were soon back, part of a long column of 50,000 prisoners trudging to Changi, which was to become a gigantic prison camp – its real claim to fame.

Civilians, 3,000 men and 400 women, many of whom had been dancing just days before at Raffles Hotel, were housed in Changi Gaol – originally designed for 600 prisoners. The military prisoners

made the best they could of the rest of the complex, maintaining discipline, organising their own food and medicine, and digging forty-foot pits for latrines to combat the dysentery that killed many in the early days.

IMPERIAL WAR MUSEUM

One of the massive 15 inch guns of Changi, but only designed to counter ships

But the Japanese made quite sure that the British, Australian, Indian and Dutch prisoners knew their place, refusing to recognise them as prisoners-of-war, publicly executing the first four attempting to escape in order to force them all to sign a paper agreeing not to try. The medical officers even had armbands inscribed *'One who has been captured in battle and is to be beheaded or castrated at the Emperor's will'*.

Later in the war, many prisoners were forced into labour gangs to build an airbase at Changi, which was horrible work in gruelling heat, especially in their undernourished state. Far worse had been the fate of the working parties on Blakang Mati (Death Island) – or those shipped to Siam (now Thailand) under the promise of better conditions, 'even good enough for the sick to convalesce'. There, they were to work and die on the notorious Siam-Burma railway, hacked through the cholera-ridden jungle along the Kwai River. Altogether 50,000 men died, one for every railway sleeper, in a stupidly brutal effort which ensured that the railway was built so slowly by its sick, emaciated and dying prisoners that it was four months too late to supply the Japanese armies at Kohima and Imphal attempting to break into India. One third of Changi prisoners never returned, and not many of the Japanese either – a poor consolation.

By August 1945, hidden radios and leaflets dropped from the air told the Changi prisoners that the war was over, and it was the turn of the Japanese to be locked up.

It became a Royal Air Force base after the war, and is now Singapore's magnificent civil airport, but for thousands of veterans, the name of Changi would forever blight their lives.

Emaciated Changi prisoners read about the atomic bomb that secured their liberation.

IMPERIAL WAR MUSEUM

See: Andersonville, Andrassy, Corregidor, Dachau, Devil's Island, Gulag, Hiroshima, Kohima, Midway, Pearl Harbor, Raffles, Kwai River, Tsushima

CHAPPAQUIDDICK

Massachusetts, USA

Joe Kennedy ruthlessly groomed his sons for greatness, and fate – just as ruthlessly, dealt with his machinations. Joe Junior was killed in a bomber, and Jack and Bobby were cut down by assassins. That only left Teddy, and Teddy then created his own fate. Of all the brothers, with all their faults – which continue to emerge – Teddy was probably the least gifted and the most flawed, prone to cheating, lying, drinking and making easy decisions.

On 19th July 1969, two people out fishing reported a car upside-down under Dyke Bridge, Chappaquiddick Island. At 8.20 am the local Police chief, James Arena, was informed. He found the car and, at 8.45 am, John Farrer of the Fire Department dived down with scuba gear and, to his horror, found the body of a young woman, Mary Jo Kopechne, which floated to the surface. Word quickly spread, not least to Edward Kennedy and his friends Paul Markham and Joseph Gargan, who pretended they had just heard about the accident. At about 10.00 am, Kennedy went to the police station, where he and his team blocked the two telephone lines calling for help. Eventually, the Police Chief turned up and took down the following statement:

Diver John Farrer searches the partly submerged car

Ever since that moment, most of America has thought that Kennedy's statement was a lie, and punished him for it politically ever since.

At the very least, by leaving it nine hours before reporting the accident, he may have caused Mary Jo to die, because she had not drowned but was found in what had been an air pocket, with virtually no water in her lungs. The poor woman had clung on for 2 or 3 hours in the freezing dark while the oxygen turned to deadly carbon dioxide. If Kennedy had reported the accident within minutes, or even an hour, she might have lived. An autopsy was blocked by Mary Jo's parents, her blood-stained clothes were destroyed and the

car was bought by a Kennedy lawyer and taken away and crushed. All the local investigations were dominated by the Senator's influence. He escaped the mandatory manslaughter charge that in Massachusetts is normally incurred by walking away from a fatal accident without reporting it. This was all bad enough to sully his reputation forever.

But in 1989, Kenneth Kappel came out with an even more startling theory in his book, *Chappaquiddick Revealed. What Really Happened.* His scenario: Kennedy left a party for political helpers and crashed his car on the bridge, which damaged the roof, hood and doors and gave Mary Jo a blow on the back of the head, covering her with blood and knocking her unconscious. At midnight Kennedy came back to the party, then returned to the scene with Gargan and

Markham. They thought Mary Jo was dead, and that the Senator's political hopes would be doomed by his drunk driving. So they pushed the Senator's Oldsmobile off the bridge and into the water and spent the rest of the night alerting friends, preparing alibis and, of course, enabling Kennedy to sober up. If this is true – and the three of them actually killed Mary Jo by mistake – it is, of course, even more of a damning disgrace than anything postulated before. Neither Kennedy nor his two friends have challenged Kappel's book. Presumably, they do not dare.

Whatever the truth, the rumours and mystery do little to enhance the once proud Kennedy name.

See: Ambassador Hotel, Dallas, Texas School Book Depository

CHARLESTON
South Carolina USA

It can be rather unfair, or even undignified, when a town is known for a dance craze. Charleston perhaps deserves more. It is a beautiful city with examples of exquisite Georgian architecture. As its name implies, it was first settled as a mandate from England's Charles II given to eight of his noble grandees, including Lord Anthony Ashley Cooper, after whom are named the Ashley and Cooper rivers that merge at Charleston's harbour.

As Charleston became rich from its cotton and slaves, the city created a completely American architectural style, the 'Single House', one room wide and three deep. To combat the humid heat, such houses usually had a 'piazza', a word that came directly from England and Inigo Jones with his covered design for Covent Garden in 1650.

Charleston survived fire, earthquakes and even the American Civil War. Indeed, it was the forts of Charleston firing on Fort Sumter that marked the start of the whole tragedy. Luckily, years later, when Union General Sherman rampaged through the South, he was in too much of a hurry to raze the city, unlike nearby Colombia and Richmond.

Much of the old architecture also remains because Charleston became

very poor, and did not succumb to that bad habit of tearing down lovely old buildings, only to replace them with something much worse.

Such sleepy anonymity was removed by an extraordinary dance, which started in the city in about 1900 and then spread northwards. First performed in Harlem in 1913, it was part of New York's *Ziegfeld Follies* in 1923. In the same year, *Running Wild* written by jazz pianist James P. Johnson, hit Broadway. The Twenties will always be regarded as the 'Charleston era', with this strange knock-kneed, pigeon-toed, stooping dance and flapping arms giving us the term 'flappers.' Some towns banned it, only adding to the craze. Britain embraced it when the Prince of Wales did. Joan Crawford and Ginger Rogers kicked off their careers by winning Charleston contests.

By 1926, perhaps to the Southern city's relief, the craze was really over. Although, no doubt, Charleston's citizens may have been less pleased with its replacement – the 'Black Bottom.'

See: Big Apple, Fort Sumter

83

MARK FIENNES

THIS HOVSE OF PEACE
WAS GIVEN TO ENGLAND
FOR HER DELIVERANCE
AND AS A PLACE OF
FOR HER PRIME MINISTERS

AND ANCIENT MEMORIES
AS A THANK-OFFERING
IN THE GREAT WAR 1914-18
REST AND RECREATION
FOR EVER.

'This house of peace and ancient memories was given to England as a thank-offering for her deliverance in the Great War 1914-18 and as a place of rest and recreation for her Prime Ministers for ever'.

These commemorative words on a stained glass window mark one of the most generous and selfless acts in British history. Chequers, as the country retreat of British Prime Ministers, is now one of the most famous houses in the world. Yet, curiously, few people know what it looks like, or even where exactly it is. Even fewer would know the names of Arthur and Ruth Lee, who, by their generosity, thrust this otherwise unknown house on to the world's stage.

The house is certainly old. It gets its name from Elias de Scaccario, referring to the scaccarium or chequer-board on which the nation's accounting was calculated. Elias's name was sometimes written as 'Checkers' or 'del Eschekere', because he served as Usher of the Exchequer for 26 years until 1192. The centuries that followed were filled with dramatic moments, not least the 1565

imprisonment there of Lady Mary Grey, whose whole family was under suspicion from Mary I and Elizabeth after the failed attempt at the throne by her sister Lady Jane Grey.

In 1909, Arthur Lee and his wife Ruth took over Chequers and began lovingly to restore it. Lee had a distinguished military career, of which the height must be his presence in Cuba in America's war against Spain, his honorary membership of the 'Rough Riders' and his lasting friendship with their commander Theodore Roosevelt, later Vice President and President. In 1899, as Military Attaché in Washington, he married Ruth Moore, daughter of a wealthy New York banker, and next year became Conservative Member of Parliament for Fareham. Lee fought in the Great War as a Colonel before taking up the post of Director General of Food Production under David Lloyd George. In 1917, it was to Lloyd George that the Lees – who had no children – made their extraordinary proposal. It was to donate their house and its 1,200 acres, plus a running allowance, to the nation

as a country retreat for future Prime Ministers.

In October 1917, the first of many international meetings took place at Chequers to plan the conduct of the War, and its success persuaded the Lees to hand over the house without delay.

In 1921 Lord and Lady Lee left Chequers with some sadness, and Lloyd George was the first Prime Minister to use the house. It has seen every Prime Minister since, and many distinguished visitors, including several American Presidents. During World War II, Chequers became a crucial nerve centre with many of Churchill's greatest broadcasts made there. Years later, Margaret Thatcher conducted the Falklands War from its comparatively peaceful atmosphere, which *'helped to get*

us all together'.

Over the years, the generous impulse by the Lees seems to have worked. As Stanley Baldwin pointed out, *'There are three classes which need sanctuary more than any other: birds, wildflowers and Prime Ministers'.*

See: Camp David, Downing Street

CHERNOBYL
Ukraine

When the news of a nuclear catastrophe at Chernobyl on 26th April 1986 gradually filtered out, there were many for whom it was no surprise. Soviet Russia was slowly changing under the new Premier Mikhail Gorbachev, but old habits die hard. Years under Stalin's iron rule had left a legacy of a strange mixture of industrial success and failure.

The same country that had put the first man in space and had produced gigantic industrial complexes was also bizarrely inefficient – incapable of producing effective washing machines, let alone calculators – and dogged by shortages of materials and supply bottlenecks. Its huge industrialisation programmes had been achieved at terrible human cost, with millions dead or placed in slave camps. Output figures were regarded as all-important, but were often phoney, with real production way behind the official figures. Even Stakhanov's famous feat of hewing 102 tonnes of coal, instead of his allocated seven tonnes a shift, was a cheat. (*Stakhanovites* were given extra perks). Crash programmes, '*shturmorshchina,*' created erratic and inefficient production flows. Quality was constantly sacrificed for output control. When Khrushchev boasted to the West *'We will bury you',* he

was deluding himself.

Electricity was vital for growth, but Soviet power stations could not keep up with demand. Only nuclear energy could bridge the gap. The power stations of Chernobyl were a product of this situation. The RBMK reactors were relatively simple, but there were potential flaws. Only after the Chernobyl explosion was it revealed that disaster had nearly occurred six years before at an RBMK reactor at Kursk, which is why the Americans, after extensive tests, had decided not to go down that nuclear route.

On the night of 25th April, a planned test to create a new safety procedure was postponed because the Kiev grid controller insisted he needed a few more hours of power. When the experienced but now tired operators initiated the test, a series of mistakes began. The emergency AZ-5 button was pressed to shut down the reactor, but all too late. The power shot up from 200 thermal megawatts to 360,000 megawatts, one hundred times more than the reactor could cope with. All hell literally broke loose. The 1,000

Helicopter crews bravely dropping material to seal the reactor

ton steel plate was blown off the reactor and a second explosion blasted uranium fuel, burning graphite and huge clouds of radioactive steam into the air. Incredible bravery by ill-equipped local firemen contained some of the fires. Many knew they were doomed by radiation, as were the helicopter crews who for days flew low over the burning reactor to seal it by dropping 5,000 tons of sand, lead, clay and dolomite and boron carbide. Local hospitals were swamped with radiation victims.

Painfully slowly the 35,000 people from the area of Chernobyl and Pripyat were evacuated, with children sometimes taking weeks to find their parents. Panic occurred in Kiev, the Ukraine's capital, with 250,000 children leaving the city. Meanwhile the radioactive 'plumes' drifted across East and West Europe, causing widespread agricultural and

The spread of radioactive material across the Northern hemisphere

See: Aberfan, Bhopal, Three Mile Island

social damage, not least prompting thousands of women to opt for abortions.

In spite of Gorbachev's desire for 'glasnost', or a new openness, the disaster was shrouded in true old-fashioned Soviet secrecy, with the authorities giving out little real news, and even that too late. The dismal performance of the Chinese government in 2003 over the SARS crisis is typical of hide-bound Communist regimes.

In the cash-strapped countries of the former Soviet Union, accidents continue to occur. In 1999, at Zaporizhia, also in the Ukraine, a scheduled turbine restart was delayed due to lack of money. The Ukraine relies on nuclear energy for forty per cent of its power, but many customers were not paying their bills. Explosions and leakages in Siberia have also caused contamination.

So, alarmingly, the race to industrialise at any cost means it is unlikely that Chernobyl will be the last nuclear town to achieve similar fame, or rather notoriety, by chance.

CHIHUAHUA
Mexico

Most of us would probably struggle to find the state and city of Chihuahua without a map. But we would be able to pronounce it – 'Chiwawa' – because it is the name of the world's smallest dog.

The Toltecs of central Mexico were conquered in the 12th century by the Aztecs, who were enchanted by the Toltecs' tiny dogs and made them into sacred icons in religious ceremonies and as guides for the spirits of the dead.

Another city made familiar by a dog was Lhasa, capital of Tibet. The *Lhasa*

The chihuahua, Mexico's tiny dog

Apso ('barking sentinel dog') was bred exclusively by holy men and nobles. A temple watchdog, it was considered sacred, and a dead master's soul was thought to enter the body of his *Lhasa Apso*. The breed spread through the world because the Dalai Lama used to present them to important visitors from China, often in exchange for tiny *Shih Tzus* (lion dogs).

Canada's province of Newfoundland consists of its island and the mainland of Labrador and is thus famous for two dogs. Introduced by either the Vikings or French fishermen, the *Newfoundland* seemed born for water and it was used as a ship dog and for sea rescue work. *'Nana'* in *Peter Pan* was based on J.M. Barrie's own beloved *Newfoundland*. The *Labrador* also worked in icy water, and was trained by local fisherman to bring in fishing nets to the shore. In 1835, Newfoundland fishermen arrived in Poole, Dorset to sell fish and were persuaded to sell some of their dogs, which have now, of course, turned out to

ANTHONY FITT-SAVAGE

be brilliant gundogs.

A film made Dalmatians really famous, *101 Dalmatians*. The elegant white dog with black spots had long been a fashion accessory in Europe, and particularly in Britain, trotting beside the carriages of the aristocracy. It reached Europe from the East via Dalmatia (Yugoslavia) in what is now Croatia. Unlike leopards, *Dalmatians* do change their spots, being born pure white, developing smudges as puppies, which gradually develop into dramatic black and white.

The *Afghan Hound*, or Kabul dog, is a very ancient breed, found in Afghan drawings 4,000 years old. Very fast, capable of 43 mph, it is tough and agile. Nicknamed 'Greyhound in pyjamas', it was used in the rocky terrain to hunt antelope, gazelles, wolves and snow leopards. The first *Afghan Hounds* arrived in Britain in 1885, four years after British troops had evacuated Afghanistan after decades of warfare, and more than a century before Bin Laden would make us all more familiar with the word Afghan. It was the rather unlikely figure of one of the Marx Brothers, Zeppo, who first brought the *Afghan Hound* to the United States.

An even faster and older breed, the *Saluki*, takes its name from the ancient Arabic city of Saluk, which has long disappeared under the sands of Yemen. Salukis appear on Persian pottery of 4,200 BC, and have been found mummified in Egyptian tombs. King Solomon was but one of the Middle Eastern figures to use *Salukis* for hunting, and the Arabs have bred them as carefully as their horses.

Germany has several places made famous by dogs. It was the red roofs of the Roman fortress town of Arac Flaviae which gave us Rottwil (red villa) and the *Rottweiler*. Originally bred for fighting lions in Roman amphitheatres, it had become an army dog guarding the legions' cattle. During the Middle Ages it was used for hunting wild boar and merchants also avoided robbery by hanging their moneybags round their fierce-looking *Rottweilers'* necks.

Queen Victoria loved her 'Pom', as had Mozart and Napoleon's Josephine. Bred in the Baltic area, the *Pomeranian* was originally a larger dog used to hunt polar bears. But it is now much smaller, with puppies so tiny you can hold three in one hand. Bismarck once remarked that the troublesome Balkans were 'not worth the healthy bones of a single Pomeranian Grenadier'. He probably felt the same way about the dog.

Dwight Eisenhower brought 'Heidi', his *Weimaraner*, to the White House when he became President of the United States. Developed by the nobility in the Grand Duchy of Weimar, it hunted large game, boar, elk and deer and later become a pointer for birds.

The world's most versatile working dog is the *German Shepherd*, once known as the *Alsatian Wolf Hound Dog,* now used as a police dog, guide dog, sheepdog and sadly, a war dog. 25,000 died in two World Wars.

The breed was made famous by the movies, 'Rin-Tin-Tin' in the 1920s and later as Roy Rogers' 'Bullet.' Another famous member of the breed was 'Blondi', Hitler's favourite companion who paid for her faithfulness in the Berlin bunker, used as a 'guinea pig' to test the poison for the suicide of Hitler and Eva Braun.

The British had never liked the German name and always preferred calling the breed the *Alsatian* after Alsace-Lorraine, the disputed border region and one of the places taken from Germany, much to her resentment, in 1919 by the Treaty of Versailles and therefore, ironically, one of the reasons for Hitler's war.

Left: 'A favourite with young and old, who always is as good as gold' reads the postcard of a faithful Newfoundland in 1887. Below: Labradors, Salukis and the Alsatian or German Shepherd

SHELAGH WALTON

CHINCHÓN
Spain

This poster shows how the bullring is erected in the main square with the houses used as stands.

Below: man's most dangerous enemy, the mosquito.
Below Right: Cinchona succirubra, the life-saving tree from the Andes
PHOTOS: BOB GIBBONS, NATURAL IMAGE

In Spain, Chinchón is best known as a pleasant mountain village easily reached from Madrid, famous for its bull ring where Frascuelo founded modern bull fighting and the yearly charity bullfight in the Plaza Mayor, for films made by Orson Welles, and for the sinister series of drawings *Los Desastres de la Guerra* by Goya, who lived in Chinchón and witnessed in 1808 the atrocities and reprisals by Napoleon's French army of occupation. But, worldwide the name of Chinchón is famous for something else, much more beneficial and significant for mankind.

In 1638, in Lima, the Countess of Chinchón, wife of the Spanish Viceroy of Peru, was desperately ill with malaria. As a last resort, the doctor suggested using a local remedy, the extract from the Andean bark, *quinaquina*, and the Countess was saved.

The Spanish Jesuit missionaries in Peru had learned the healing power of *quinaquina* several years earlier and had introduced it to Spain in 1632. But the miraculous recovery of someone of the Countess's prominence meant that Linnaeus and other botanists were to call the tree *cinchona*. Even mis-spelled, it made the Spanish village famous forever. The 'Countess's powder' was brought back to Spain in 1640 by her doctor, but its sale was overshadowed by the larger distribution throughout Europe by the Jesuits. Known as the 'Jesuits powder', it became something of a Catholic monopoly. Indeed, some Protestants stubbornly refused to take it. Oliver Cromwell called it the 'power of the devil' and died, after suffering from chronic malaria all his life, a victim of his own prejudice.

Malaria had been a worldwide scourge since the dawn of history. The invaders of Rome had been almost destroyed – Visigoths, Vandals, Huns and Ostrogoths. A Roman expedition to Scotland had lost half its 80,000 men. Expeditions and colonisation missions from many nations had failed, and armies had been often virtually destroyed by malarial fever. However, it was the British who were to make a real business of quinine, with good reason. With their huge Empire mainly in hot climates, they knew only too well the crippling effects of malaria:
Beware, beware the Bight of Benin
One comes out where fifty went in.

An enthusiastic amateur botanist, Clements Markham, persuaded the Indian office and Kew Gardens to fund an expedition to find *quinquina* plants and reproduce them in India. The £10,000 voted proved to be a bargain for the British Empire. Between 1859 and 1862, Markham brought *Cinchona* trees to India and large scale production began, aiming to protect British and Indians alike at a fraction of the cost of the original Countess's or Jesuits' bark.

Since then, quinine has become the world's main protection against malaria, breaking the cycle by killing the reservoir of parasites in humans before they could be re-transmitted by the mosquito. The British habit of drinking 'gin and tonic' becomes understandable if you use the American version 'gin and quinine water'. In fact, *Cinchona* was the world's first homœopathic remedy.

And Chinchón? Napoleon's armies destroyed its castle and the Countess's family has died out. But the little town's fame by chance will live on in the tree that has saved literally millions of lives.

See: Botany Bay, Brazil, Camerone, Deolali, Devil's Island, Ebola, Havana, Hook & Crook, Lassa, Panama, Timbuktu, Venice

THE CHISHOLM TRAIL
United States

'From two hundred to four hundred yards wide, beaten into the bare earth, it reached over hill and valley for over six hundred miles, a chocolate band amid the green prairies, uniting the North and the South. As the marching hooves wore it down and the wind blew and the waters washed the earth away, it became lower than the surrounding territory, and was flanked by little banks of sand, drifted there by the wind. Bleaching skulls and skeletons of weary brutes who had perished on the journey gleamed along its borders, and here and there was a low mound showing where some cowboy had literally 'died with his boots on'.'

This was the vivid description by Charles Moreau Harger, in 1892, of the greatest cattle trail the world has ever seen.

Jesse Chisholm was half Scottish, half Cherokee. He ran trading posts in what is now Oklahoma, having a working knowledge of fourteen Indian languages. Using well-known Indian trails also used by the Army, he drove 3,000 cattle to trade with the Sac and Fox agency. The trail he began to use for trading was known as 'Chisholm's Trail', but it was soon to become famous for cattle driving on a monumental scale. It was the product of a real need.

At the end of America's Civil War, the plains of Texas were swarming with millions of cattle with no market, scarcely worth a dollar a head. But in the hungry cities to the north, such cattle were worth many times more.

Enter a great American entrepreneur, Joseph Geiting McCoy. Realising that the railroads were the new factor, McCoy arrived at Abilene, Kansas, where the Kansas Pacific Railway had just arrived. In 1867, he described Abilene as *'a small dead place, consisting of about a dozen log huts, low, small, rude affairs, four fifths of which were covered with dirt for roofing.'* All was about to change.

McCoy bought 480 acres to build his corrals, shipping yards and Drovers' Cottage hotel. The first herd was shipped out in a train of twenty stock

'Stampeded by lightning.' Frederic Remington portrays one of the dangers of the trail.

cars, the first of thousands. That winter, McCoy sent leaflets and salesmen to ranchers all over Texas urging them to drive their cattle up the Chisholm Trail to Abilene, while advertising in the North for buyers to come to Abilene to buy their stock. McCoy also marked out the trail with mounds of earth so the ranchers would not get lost and go anywhere other than Abilene! The section from Wichita north to Abilene was called 'McCoy's extension.'

It paid off brilliantly. In 1867, 35,000 cattle were shipped. A year later it was 75,000, and by 1869 it had doubled again to 150,000. By 1872, three million cattle had gone up the vital link from Texas to Abilene.

The long drives were testing ordeals. River crossings, lightning and stampedes were more dangerous than Indians, who could usually be bought off with a few long-horns. After three months in the saddle, the cowboys could hardly wait for the pleasures at the end of the trail, not least a bath.

Abilene was the first of the legendary 'cowtowns', with false-fronted buildings, dusty streets, cattle pens and railroad tracks. By day it was filled with the noise of cattle and locomotives, by night with gunfire and the racket of hundreds of drunken cowboys who had been paid off and were being fleeced of their money in saloons, gambling halls and brothels. Any attempts at respectability usually failed, as when Mayor McCoy ordered

See: The Alamo, Dallas, OK Corral, Promontory, Rock Island

Marshal 'Wild Bill' Hickock to move the brothels to what became cruelly known as 'McCoy's Extension!'

There were other trails and other cowtowns like Abilene – Wichita, Ellsworth, Caldwell, Newton, and, above all, Dodge City, with its famous 'lawmen' Bat Masterson and Wyatt Earp. All, for a while, became wide-open towns before lapsing into respectability or anonymity as the railroads bypassed them, and their brief but spectacular cattle trade disappeared.

By 1925, a journalist wrote of Dodge City, *'Gone are the buffalo, the longhorn steers, the badmen, from this once rip-roaring town, the centre of a vast region of which it was once said that all they raised was cattle and hell!'*

There were 35,000 cowboys at the height of the great cattle drives. Their uncomfortable lifestyle meant that they suffered more from rheumatism, slipped discs and hernias than gunshot wounds!

Their own language included horse wrangler (herder), bronco buster (horse breaker), cayuse (horse), rag proper (dress well), hit the flat (go out on the prairie), slicker (waterproof coat), family disturbance (whiskey), overland trout (bacon). They also inherited words from the Spanish vaqueros (cowboys) like chaps (leather overalls), rodeo (round-up), lariat (rope) and sombrero (wide brimmed hat)

CLIVEDEN
England

Bernard Shaw was ecstatic: *'It was like no other country house in the world....you meet everybody worth meeting, rich or poor at Cliveden'*. He was describing the golden age of a great house looking down across beautiful formal gardens from a wooded cliff above the River Thames.

Cliveden has been owned by some

truly illustrious and interesting figures. In 1666, it was bought by George Villiers, 2nd Duke of Buckingham – rake, wit and minister to Charles II. Later, the Earl of Orkney leased it to Frederick, Prince of Wales, the latter being very keen to be far away from his father, George II. They did not like each other. Frederick's son, George III, was

thought to be the best of the Hanoverians because of the beneficial effects of his childhood at Cliveden and its gardens. The 2nd Countess of Orkney and her husband, William O'Brien, 4th Earl of Inchiquin, moved in. Tragically, in 1795, the house burned to the ground.

It was rebuilt by a great *bon viveur*, Sir John Warrender, known as 'Sir Georgious' or 'Sir Gorge Provender', who then sold it to the Duke of Sutherland. But once again, in 1849, fire destroyed the house and it was rebuilt in the magnificent style that we see today. In 1893, Cliveden passed from the richest man in Britain, the 1st Duke of Westminster, to the richest man alive, William Waldorf Astor, prompting Queen Victoria to write acidly and rather unfairly, *'it is grievous to think of it falling into these hands!'*

But it was in 1904, when William Waldorf Astor gave Cliveden to his son Waldorf as a wedding present for his new bride Nancy, that it jumped from being just another huge, elegant English country house to a place of worldwide fame.

Nancy was one of the five fabulous Langhorne sisters of Philadelphia. One sister, Irene, had married Charles Dana Gibson, who created the 'Gibson Girl',

largely in her image. The divorced, vivacious, beautiful Nancy arrived in England in 1904 and made her mark riding to hounds, *'hunting her horses till their tails dropped off.'* She made early friends with Lady Cunard who had said, 'I suppose you've come over here to take one of our husbands from us.' Nancy replied, 'If you know how much difficulty I had getting rid of my first one, you wouldn't say that.'

She was careful of her reputation, never drinking nor playing cards. Within two years, choosing from a range of eligible bachelors, she had married kindly and quiet William Astor and had begun to turn Cliveden into the social centre of England.

As soon as 120 workmen had completed her changes to the interior, Cliveden was on its way. Politicians like Asquith and his wife Margot, Arthur Balfour, Winston Churchill and Lord Curzon were all invited regularly, with literary and artistic stars like Rudyard Kipling, Hilaire Belloc, T.E. Lawrence, G.K. Chesterton, Henry James, Charlie Chaplin and Bernard Shaw. Soon the King and Queen crowned her social success, describing Cliveden

as *'the prettiest place in England'*.

When his father died, Waldorf inherited his title of Viscount Astor, and had to give up his seat in Parliament. Nancy took over – the first woman MP – and ironically not one of the British suffragettes, but an American 'socialite.' In all the twenty six years she represented Plymouth, she only pretended she had been accepted. *'If I'd only known how much men would hate it, I would never have dared to do it'.*

Among her strongest critics was Winston Churchill. 'If I was your wife, Winston, I'd put poison in your coffee'. 'And if I was your husband', retorted Winston, 'I'd drink it'. Declared Nancy Lancaster, Nancy's niece, 'Two spoiled children'.

But there was a more serious reason why Churchill had become less friendly. The 'Cliveden Set' had become a very public centre of appeasement to Hitler,

A chance meeting between John Profumo and Christine Keeler at Cliveden's swimming pool would create disasters for many

including as it did the editors of *The Times* and *The Observer*, both of which the Astors owned. As war approached, the popular press and the country turned on the famous house, perhaps unfairly, as a nest of traitors. In fact, Nancy Astor was on the Nazi's 'Black List' because of her contemptuous treatment of Ribbentrop when he was German Ambassador.

Cliveden's next problem came in the sixties. Nancy's son Bill was entertaining John Profumo, Conservative Secretary of State for War, and they strolled down to the swimming pool by the cottage rented to the osteopath Steven Ward. They surprised a naked Christine Keeler swimming, and chased her around the pool. It was the beginning of Profumo's brief affair with her that would wreck his career, land Christine in jail, disgrace Bill Astor, kill Steven Ward, and help bring down the Government. According to Christine Keeler, it implicated the Russians, Anthony Blunt and MI5's head, Roger Hollis, in a Soviet spying conspiracy.

It is to be hoped that this great house, now a magnificent hotel, will become famous, rather than infamous again.

See: Chequers, Stowe

CLONTARF
Ireland

King Brian Boru

Clontarf is now a suburb of Dublin, the increasingly prosperous and busy capital of Ireland. But on Good Friday, April 23rd 1014, it was wooded brushland leading down to a sea full of Viking ships. It witnessed the most fateful battle in Ireland's history and the tragic death of her greatest High King, Brian Boru.

Brian seems born to be a hero. He was the younger brother of Mahon, King of Munster, who had tried to live peaceably with the Vikings. As with the English, who paid off the fierce Norsemen with *'Danegeld',* the Irish had offered no coherent resistance to the invaders, and Dublin was now second only to Yorvic (York) as a Viking settlement.

Unlike his brother, Brian hated and distrusted the Vikings, having seen his

mother killed in one of their raids. He conducted continuous and successful guerrilla warfare and inspired Mahon to join him in expelling the Viking King of Limerick, Ivar. But ten years later Ivar took his revenge, returning in 975 to encourage his allies, treacherously, to capture and assassinate Mahon. He paid with his life in personal combat with Brian, who then gradually built up alliances, notably with Malachy, King of Meath, while taking over from him the position of *'Ard Ri',* or High King.

He earned his name Brian Boru (Brian of the Tributes) by collecting taxes from other rulers, and restoring the ravaged monasteries and libraries. Brian's military prowess seems to have been matched by sexual enthusiasm – he had 30 concubines and four wives, of which one, the beautiful and treacherous

Gormblaith, was to prove his nemesis. When he rejected her after four years, she summoned the traditional enemy, the Vikings, for assistance.

Brian, now an old man, marched across Ireland gathering his armies, slightly weakened by his son Donough's contingent away fighting in the south. Not all the Irish would join Brian - he had many jealous enemies. Some would stand aside, some would fight for the Vikings, some would fight for him. At dawn, while Gormblaith, her son and, in agony, Brian's daughter, watched from the walls of Dublin, the two armies began their massive battle. Brian carefully noted the state of the tide and directed the battle, while for once, not participating.

Vicious hand-to-hand fighting raged all day. Brian's son Murrough and most of the leaders on both sides fell. The Vikings finally broke, and tried to make it through the surf to their ships. Few succeeded, because the incoming tide meant that they were now half a mile

out to sea.

Irish victory turned to tragedy. One Viking, King Brodir of Man, with a small group, found Brian Boru praying in his tent and felled him. But the dying King, aged seventy three, struck back and killed Brodir, and their bodies were found together.

While the Vikings were beaten on the battlefield and were eventually integrated into Irish society, the removal of the unifying influence of Brian Boru fatally weakened Ireland, and prepared the way for invasion and domination by the Normans and the English for centuries.

The Death of Brian Boru by Thomas Ryan RHA

See: Ballingarry, Blarney, The Bogside, Boyne, Falls Road, GPO, Hook & Crook, St. Germain-en-Laye

COGNAC
France

'Claret is the liquor for boys; port for men but he who aspires to be a hero must drink brandy'.

For Dr Johnson, the brandy he referred to had to come from Cognac, in France's Charente region. Merchants as far back as the fifteenth century had grown into the habit of distilling wine to reduce the number of casks and shipping space, adding water back at the destination – hence *brandewijn* in Dutch or *branntwein* in German, literally 'burned wine'. In France, distilled alcohol is termed *'eau de vie'*, a more charming and evocative term.

But in the seventeenth century, an unknown distiller in Cognac treated the wine to a second distillation. There is a tale that this was inspired by him waking from a dream where he had faced the Devil and a big furnace. 'I shall burn your body twice in order to extract your soul'. It worked, and 'Cognac' was born.

Cognac, or French brandy, became

very popular in England, and the very mainstay of the smuggling trade. Even Scots loved it, in spite of their own whisky product. There was a religious reason for this rapid spread to other countries. Cognac was a Protestant region, and quite suddenly Louis XIVth, the 'Sun King', revoked the 'Edict of Nantes' that had protected Protestants. Many were to flee to England, Ireland and Holland and there they began to import their relatives' product. The export links were forged.

The raw material, the wine from Cognac, is actually harsh and acid. It is a curious fact that good wine makes poor brandy.

It is not the only curious fact about Cognac.

First, it could easily have been the second town in the region after which the brandy was named. Somehow, Jarnac missed out. Second, Napoleon was abstemious, so all those top-price

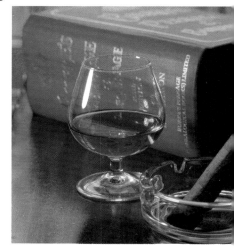

labels such as Napoleon Cognac or Napoleon Brandy, are based on a myth. Finally, there is no link between the regions of Champagne and Cognac. Gradings like 'Grande Champagne' merely refer back to the Roman use of *campania* – a space or field.

The popularity of the spirit, especially in Britain – then the richest country in the world – was vital to the prosperity of Cognac, as it was for Oporto with port, or Jerez with sherry. The English words 'Very Special Old Pale' (VSOP) reflects

the value of this market.

The dreaded *phylloxera* insect nearly destroyed the region, but in 1888 a French scientist went to Dennison, Texas, where the cure was found, grafting European vines with American resistant ones. Now the two towns are linked, and Cognac's region has become France's largest producer of white wine.

But we will all continue to know Cognac for its 'water of life'.

See: Angora, Buck's Club, Champagne, Fray Bentos, Gorgonzola, Hershey, Jodhpur, Pilzen

CORLEONE
Sicily

Ask foreigners to think of Italian words and names, and not far down the list of Ferrari, spaghetti, chianti and pizza would probably come Corleone.

Very few of them would be thinking of the 'City of a Hundred Churches' or its two thousand years of history, with the historic buildings, statues, paintings and fortress walls which dominated Sicily's invasion routes. Far more likely it would be the family name of *The Godfather*, America's movie trilogy of the Mafia.

In the film, Marlon Brando plays 'Don Vito Corleone', whose son 'Michael' takes over his empire, played by Al Pacino. It opens with an apparently charming Corleone family wedding, interrupted by Vito's godson, the singer 'Johnny Fontaine', complaining that he has been cut out of a film part. The family makes the Hollywood movie mogul 'an offer he can't refuse', leading to the horrifying scene of him waking with the severed head of his prize racehorse in his bed beside him.

While many think that 'Johnny Fontaine' was intended to portray Frank Sinatra, Vito and Michael Corleone are an amalgam of some very real and dangerous people.

Vito Genovese and 'Lucky' Luciano would be prime candidates – two of the most feared Mafia bosses. They ended the destructive 'Castellammarse War' between two of the old-style bosses, 'The moustache Petes'; Salvatore Maranzano and Joe 'The Boss' Masseria. Their plan was quite simple. They first killed their own *capo*, Masseria, and then assassinated

Maranzano, opening the way to their own national crime syndicate, with its enforcement arm, 'Murder Inc.'

Both men were tried and exiled to Italy, Genovese becoming friends with Mussolini's son-in-law Ciano and supplying him with drugs, then helping the invading U.S. forces in return for some favours. However, Luciano was never allowed back into the United States.

In 1957, it was Genovese who called the famous conference in Apalachin, New York, where 63 syndicate leaders from fifteen states were to meet; but when interrupted by a couple of local police, they fled through the dark *'like frightened children'*. Among the elderly men panting through the woods were Genovese, San Giancana, Joe Profaci and Joe 'Bananas' Bonanno. Ensuing publicity showed that nationwide organised crime very much existed, however much J. Edgar Hoover of the FBI insisted that it did not, for his own disgraceful reasons.

But Mario Puzo, the author of *The Godfather*, did not pluck the name of 'Corleone' out of thin air. *Mafia* in Arabic meant 'place of refuge', but the Mafia in Sicily had long since changed from patriotic freedom fighters against foreign oppressors in the 13th century to a criminal organisation controlling all aspects of Sicilian life. Corleone, a few miles from the capital Palermo, had a fearsome reputation, with *vendettas* that had destroyed whole generations.

The 'Godfather of Corleone' was

Luciano 'The Faceless One' Liggio, who had become the trusted sidekick of Dr Michele Navarra, Corleone's Mafia boss in 1948. Navarra had killed 57 rival Mafiosi and promoted Liggio after he murdered a prominent trade unionist for him. Liggio became the 'Armed Arm of the Mafia', but decided to branch out on his own. Navarra then tried to kill him, but ended up being ambushed by fifteen men, with no less than 210 bullets in his body.

Liggio was to end up in jail, but not before starting a lucrative kidnapping business which is still flourishing in Italy to this day.

The Godfather series cleverly portrayed the Mafia as at least human, and in many ways attractive, and led the way for the popular T.V. series *The Sopranos,* whose leader is so mixed up that he regularly visits a psychiatrist.

The Godfather series has grossed hundreds of millions to date; good business. The Mafia grosses $200 billion each year; an even better business.

See: Alcatraz, Bay of Pigs, Dallas, Las Vegas, North Clark Street, Texas School Book Depository

Marlon Brando as Don Vito Corleone

CORONATION STREET
England

The longest-running and most popular television soap opera in the UK is Coronation Street. The first episode was transmitted live on the 8th December 1960 from Granada Studios. It is not just renowned in Britain, but round the world. It is also shown in Canada, Australia, New Zealand and parts of Europe.

Coronation Street is set in a fictional town called Weatherfield in Manchester and portrays everyday working class people in everyday situations which are very realistically depicted. This theme of television programme grew out of the 'kitchen sink' drama style which was popularised in the late 50s. The show was created by writer Tony Warren, who drew inspiration from his grandmother living in Salford, and thereafter generated the terraced Coronation Street shown in the title sequence.

The show was originally supposed to run for 13 episodes and was, curiously, to be called Florizel Street. It seems rather ironic now, after 40 years of ratings success. Only one character, Ken Barlow, has been in the show since the first episode. However, the seventies and eighties introduced most of the popular characters who are still in it today, including Curly Watts, Jack and Vera Duckworth and Mike Baldwin. There have also been appearances by many actors and actresses before they were famous, such as Martin Shaw, Ben Kingsley, Joanna Lumley and Prunella

GRANADA VISUALS

Scales. Coronation Street has also cultivated many novice writers such as Jimmy McGovern and Jack Rosenthal, while the award-winning feature film director, Michael Apted, has also been part of the production team.

Perhaps the reason Coronation Street is so successful is because the viewers can relate to its strong sense of regional and local identity, as well as a bond between families and friends in a community. The action takes place in domestic settings of homes, the corner shop and the local pub (The Rover's Return) which, together with its gritty humour, enhances the feeling of every day life. Storylines concentrate on characters rather than being issue-led,

Classic characters from left to right: Hilda Ogden, Bet Lynch, Jack Duckworth and Betty Turpin

95

and from the start the series has always cleverly reflected shifts in social attitudes in Britain.

There have also been some unforgettable television moments. Forty years to the day of the Street's first broadcast, it was shown live for an hour – a feat other soaps wouldn't dare attempt. It had to be perfectly directed and acted, and was watched by an estimated 20 million viewers.

There is no doubt that Coronation Street is the epitome of true Britain, and the fact it is watched regularly by the Queen justifies its position as a leading landmark in British television. No doubt it will be successful for many years to come.

See: Albert Square, Ambridge, Dallas, Peyton Place, Ramsay Street, Truth or Consequences

CORREGIDOR
Philippines

'He may have the bottle, but I have the cork!'

IMPERIAL WAR MUSEUM

Below: MacArthur, flanked by The President of The Philippines (left) wades ashore on his heralded return.

Thus spoke former West Point Superintendent and Army Chief of Staff General Douglas MacArthur, one of the most controversial military figures in history. He was being rather over optimistic. Now commanding all Filipino and American forces, he thought that his strategic position on this 'cork', the Island of Corregidor, would stop General Hommas's encircling Japanese from using Manila Harbour.

The campaign in the Philippines had started only too well for the Japanese. On 7th December 1941, their planes had destroyed most of the US Airforce in the Philippines on the ground – due to MacArthur's indecision. Their pilots were amazed to see the American planes neatly parked below them, since there had been nine hours of warning since the similar attack on Pearl Harbor. Ground forces landed in the Philippines just before Christmas and had closed in on Manila, beating back a mixed force of American and half-trained Filipinos. By 2nd January, Manila had fallen and 15,000 American and 65,000 Filipinos fought to block the peninsular of Bataan. Already ammunition – and quinine – vital against malaria, were short. The 'battling Bastards of Bataan', weakened by sickness and hunger, were forced to give ground, their morale not improved by knowing that MacArthur, despite being brave, had only visited them once in 77 days – and was in the safety of the bunkers of Corregidor, soon to be called 'Dugout Doug'. On 10th March, a reluctant MacArthur was ordered by President Roosevelt to leave the 'Rock of Corregidor', and he escaped 500 miles by torpedo boat – eventually to assume command of the forces gathering in Australia.

In Bataan, 76,000 men laid down their arms on 9th April, expecting to be treated honourably.

Designed and reinforced like a concrete battleship, Corregidor, 'the cork', lasted longer. But Pearl Harbor and the sinking of the British *Repulse* and *Prince of Wales* had shown that battleships were doomed by air power. After a month of pounding from artillery and planes, the Rock's commander, General Wainwright radioed, 'I have fought for you to the best of my ability from Lingayen Gulf to Bataan to Corregidor. Goodbye General'. And the very last message was tapped out, 'Everyone is bawling like a baby. They are piling dead and wounded in our tunnel. The jig is up'.

Indeed it was. As prisoners, they were given no food or water for a week, then

driven like cattle through Manila. The prisoners from Bataan fared even worse; clubbed, shot, stabbed and beheaded on a nightmare 'Death March', which may have killed 10,000 men.

'I shall return', MacArthur pledged to the people of the Philippines. And he did. But it took fifty six amphibious landings and three years of bitter fighting back across the Pacific.

When he did triumph, he received the Japanese surrender in Tokyo Bay with a recently freed and emaciated General Wainwright at his side. Ironically, the ceremony was on the deck of the *Missouri* – a battleship, now yesterday's symbol of power.

See: Bikini, Bonus City, Changi, Hiroshima, Kohima, Kwai River, Midway, Panmunjom, Pearl Harbor, West Point

THE COTTON CLUB
New York, USA

In 1923, on the corner of Harlem's Lenox Avenue and 142nd Street, a nightclub opened which was to become a symbol of New York, a fount of musical and theatrical talent and *the* place for celebrities to go. The proud owner was a serious gangster.

Harlem had been built as a property speculation with fine new buildings and broad tree-lined avenues, intended for middle-class whites arriving on the elevated railways extended north of the Park. But in 1905 there was a property slump, and black tenants were attracted from other overcrowded parts of New York and saved the speculators, to form the largest black community in the US. Harlem was also prosperous, and soon became a musical centre, especially for jazz and blues. Its night-spots took off, and whites began to come up to Harlem, 'slumming it'.

Owen 'Owney' Madden reviewed this situation from his cell in Sing Sing, where he was awaiting his parole while serving time for shooting Patsy Doyle of the Hudson Dusters gang. Slim, dapper and apparently charming, he was born in England and had been a vicious hood all his life, suspected of killing five men and terrifying other gangsters. He knew what opportunities Prohibition would bring, and he had noticed the growing success of all black shows like *Shuffle Along, The Creole Show, A Trip to Coontown(!) and Darktown Follies*. So he decided to create, as an outlet for his beer, a unique nightclub with the finest in black talent, but entirely for white audiences.

Entertainment would be a dazzling fast-paced review with the finest jazz music, superb male dancers and beautiful 'high-yeller' octaroon chorus girls, all over five feet six and none over twenty-one years old. ('*Tall, tan and terrific*', the publicity boasted). The staff were elegant and polite. The place quickly became a smash hit.

In 1927, the resident bandleader Andy Preer died, and the Cotton Club looked desperately for a new band in time for the opening of its new show in December. 'King' Oliver turned the offer down, and someone suggested Duke Ellington. He still had a week booked in Philadelphia, but the theatre owner was made an offer he couldn't refuse: 'Be big or you'll be dead'. Ellington, with his musical genius and innovation, made the club nationally famous. WHW, a local radio station, began to broadcast nightly from the Cotton Club, and soon the Columbia Broadcasting System was transmitting the 'Cotton Club Sound' to listeners across the nation. Everyone in the country knew about the club, and every visitor to New York just had to visit it.

In 1930 Cab Calloway took over, an entertainer made famous for his 'hi-de-ho', words inserted when he once forgot the lyrics!

Even during the Depression, the club was the late night spot for the 'Mink Set', from Mayor Jimmy Walker to the Broadway stars, who headed uptown when their own shows had finished.

Songs beamed from the club became national hits, *I've got the world on a string*, Cab Calloway's *Minnie the Moocher*, and Ethel Waters' and Lena Horne's *Stormy Weather*.

Keep on Truckin' tried to encourage listeners to ignore the Depression, but by 1934 the latter had begun to affect Harlem badly; eighty per cent of its residents were on relief. Incidents of violence increased, as did anti-white resentment. In March 1935, Harlem exploded in a full-scale riot, with the result that the Cotton Club decided to move to Broadway. There, for another five years, it was a glamorous success, before closing in 1940.

But it was the club in Harlem that had been unique and special for everyone: for staff, entertainers and audiences and not least, for a while, the people of Harlem themselves.

See: Abbey Road, Carnegie Hall, Covent Garden, Ibiza, Motown, Nashville, Sibylla's, Storyville, Studio 54, Woodstock

Duke Ellington

COVENT GARDEN
England

Covent Garden in London means different things to different people. We now know that it was once the site of a thriving settlement, Lundenwic, where the Saxons decided to live outside the old Roman city – but which they abandoned as too vulnerable to Viking attacks in the 9th Century.

For hundreds of years, it reverted to agricultural pasture and gardens, owned by the Convent of St Peter of Westminster, hence the name Covent Garden. In 1630, the 4th Earl of Bedford, with the encouragement of King Charles I, decided to commission the architect Inigo Jones to create the first public square in London. The piazza was inspired by Palladian architecture and similar squares in Italy and was a revolution in British architecture and town planning.

Unfortunately, being a public square meant it was frequented by rather an unsalubrious throng, and this began to put off the rich aristocrats for whom Covent Garden was intended. They went to the safety of Bloomsbury and the elegance of Mayfair, leaving the Garden to brothels, Turkish baths, and gambling dens. But a new fame for Covent Garden was in the making. The Earl's son granted the first licence to sell fruit and vegetables – a trade which had started in a small way in 1649, but which had begun to boom when The Great Fire destroyed so many other markets. For three hundred years Covent Garden Market thrived,

Fruit and vegetable traders in the 19th century have now given way to arts and crafts stalls.

The grand elegance of the Royal Opera House

with the covered building in the centre of the square erected in 1830. Every night wagons arrived from the country loaded down with fruit, vegetables and flowers. In Floral Street there was even a 'Carriage Hall', where carts with broken wheels or axles could be hoisted into the upper storeys for the equivalent of 'pit stop' repairs. Such carriage works were the foundation of Britain's car industry.

But there was another reason why people talk about Covent Garden. The financial success in 1728 of *The Beggar's Opera* commissioned by actor/manager John Rich from John Gay provided the money for a new theatre ('it made Gay rich and Rich gay'). In 1732 The Theatre Royal opened to Congreve's *The Way of the World* to begin a long tradition of acting and music, reinforced by Letters Patent granted by Charles II giving Covent Garden and Drury Lane a virtual monopoly to present drama. In spite of two fires, the Theatre Royal became Britain's centre for opera and ballet, in 1892 changing its name to the Royal Opera House.

In 1974, congestion finally forced the Market to move. The planners intended to bulldoze the entire area and erect new buildings of steel, glass and concrete. Luckily, however, a vigorous campaign by residents just managed to stop this vandalism.

Now, with its businesses, shops, bars and restaurants, the restored Covent Garden, has become a huge tourist attraction, with open air theatre and music, the most visited place in Britain.

Fame, by many chances.

See: Abbey Road, Bayreuth, Carnegie Hall, Charleston, Glastonbury, Ibiza, Motown, Nashville, Storyville, Woodstock

COWES
England

As with so much in social Britain, Cowes was influenced and even created by royalty. In 1539 Henry VIII built two castles at 'The Cowe', long a popular sheltered anchorage for shipping. This protected against the French raids that had prevented waterside development and Cowes itself was established in the early 17th Century, supplying Portsmouth royal dockyard and the growing trade between Europe and America. Its strategic position on the Solent ensured it became a shipbuilding centre and customs port. Collector of Customs from 1777 was William Arnold, father of Thomas Arnold of Rugby School fame and grandfather to poet Matthew Arnold.

Royalty re-appeared when Charles I stayed at a 'common alehouse' in Cowes en route to his imprisonment at Carisbrooke Castle and later execution. It was his son Charles II who returned from Holland with a gift, a 52-foot *jaghte*, which he later pitted against his brother the Duke of York in the first yacht race in Britain on the Thames.

By the late eighteenth century, Cowes was being discovered as a smart summer resort, with a number of aristocrats arriving with their yachts. Yacht racing began and in 1815 The Yacht Club was formed, partly to counter the influence of 'Beau' Brummell and his 'Dandies' over the London clubs White's and Brooke's. With the accession to the throne in 1820 of its most distinguished member, the Prince Regent as George IV, it became The Royal Yacht Club and in 1833, under William IV, became the Royal Yacht Squadron, soon called 'the most exclusive club in the world'. The fashionable future and fame of Cowes was assured by chance when Queen Victoria, after childhood holidays there in 1831 and 1833 (during which she went yachting), fell in love with the Isle of Wight. She returned in 1845 after buying the Osborne Estate, and soon Osborne House was one of the social centres of Britain. As well as Royalty, Cowes saw such varied luminaries as Darwin, Tennyson, Keats, Dickens, Marx, Elgar, Garibaldi and Marconi.

In August 1851, fifteen yachts set off round the island and the memorable race was won by the only non-British yacht, *America*, entered by the New York Yacht Club. 'And who is second?' later asked Queen Victoria. 'There is no second Ma'am,' came the reply. And so the America's Cup was born.

Cowes Regatta Week was created by another royal figure, Edward, Prince of Wales. The popular, fun-loving 'Bertie' was the centre of a sparkling social set which transformed Cowes when he arrived, sometimes complete with one or other of his mistresses, Alice Keppel and Lillie Langtry, on the yacht *Britannia*. Queen Victoria watched his 'goings-on' with disapproval from the terraces of Osborne House.

Britannia was soon challenged by Edward's nephew, Kaiser Wilhelm of Germany who built a succession of *Meteors* which finally in 1897 beat *Britannia*. Such races were watched by the Tsar of Russia in *Standardt* and Alfonso XIII of Spain on his *Hispania*. Sadly, history and the world would have been very different, if only Wilhelm had confined his rivalry to yachting.

While some of the glamour went from Cowes when Edward VII died in 1910, his son George V, an avid sailor, raced *Britannia* after the First World War, now like many aristocrats up against the 'new rich'. Today, as Admiral of the Royal Yacht Squadron, Prince Philip continues the royal tradition by competing in events, as have the Princess Royal and Prince Edward.

The America's Cup celebrated its 150th Jubilee at Cowes in 2001, Prince Philip appropriately joined by King Juan Carlos of Spain, Prince Henrik of Denmark and the Aga Khan. The Cup was continuously won by Americans, until their dominance of 132 years was broken by *Australia II* in 1983 and, most recently, by Switzerland.

Cowes Week is an essential part of the social and sporting season and Cowes is lucky that royalty liked the place so much.

The spirit of Twelve Metre racing in the 1960s – Michael Boyle's Vanity V

MCvA

See: Ascot, Aintree, Brooklands, Cresta, Henley, Lord's, Rugby, Savile Row, Wimbledon

99

CREMONA
Italy

By 1550, the town of Cremona in Northern Italy was already well known for its violins, but it was a varnish that really made it famous.

The violin saw its origins in Islam, where the Arabs had developed stringed instruments like the *rebab*, which had then evolved in Spain during the Moorish invasion – with rebecks, viellas, violas, lyres and fidulas – hence, probably, the name for the fiddle.

By the XVII century the violin, reflecting the Baroque age, had become the most important instrument in any orchestra. Three Italian cities, Venice, Brescia

and Cremona, became the world centres for the craft of violin making.

Andrea Amati founded the tradition in Cremona, and it was his grandson Nicola, the only violin craftsman to survive the plague of 1630, who passed

on his skills to his students Antonio Stradivarius and Andrea Guarneri.

In addition to their superlative skills in creating the shape and quality of their violins, the Cremonese had also developed a thin, non-greasy, slow-drying varnish on top of a mineral-rich grounding. And it was this varnish that the master violin makers, including Antonio Stradivarius, used on their violins. The result was a mellow sound that has never been rivalled.

In 1704, when he was 60, Stradivarius decided to write down the composition of the golden-red Cremonese varnish on the inside cover of his bible. Unfortunately, the bible was later lost and, with it, the secret. That is one reason why the 600

surviving violins, 60 cellos and 17 violas inscribed 'Antonio Stradivarius Cremonensis' now change hands for as much as two million dollars. Indeed, a few years ago, a Guarneri violin called The Ladenburg, once played by Paginini, was purchased by violinist Robert McDuffie for $3.5 million. The price was hardly music to his ears – he had to create a limited partnership in order to afford it.

See: Brazil

A superb 'Messiah' Stradivarius violin, made in 1716, is one of the 'Long Strads', complete with its varnish from Cremona.

CRESTA RUN
Switzerland

'The beginnings of the Cresta had the added twist that the conversion from pastime to sport was made by a collection of invalids. No wonder the Continentals are convinced the British are mad! I can only say that I am all for this sort of madness'.

This was the apt description by Prince Philip, Duke of Edinburgh, in a foreword to the book, *The Cresta Run.*

The small Swiss villages of Davos and St Moritz were unknown until a Dr Alexander Spengler, practising in Davos, followed up the 1840s research of Dr Luzius Ruedi and confirmed that Davos was free of tuberculosis, and that infected Davosers, when returning to their village, soon recovered from the disease. His pamphlet of 1869 even advocated the new and bizarre thought that invalids should not only spend the summer there, but the winter as well.

In St Moritz, Dr Peter Berry, a Crimea veteran, agreed with him. His sister, Maria, married Johannes Badrutt, and the couple bought a local hotel and turned it into the 'Kulm' (Summit). Soon after, during a pleasant autumn evening, Johannes made a bet with four Englishmen that the climate in winter was so marvellous that, to convince them, he would even offer them free accommodation. That December, they arrived in blazing sunshine, greeted by Johannes Badrutt in his shirt. So delighted were his guests with their winter stay that the word spread, and hundreds of visitors began arriving every year.

One gentle activity for the invalids which was allowed by the doctors was tobogganing down the snowy slopes. They used 'toboggans' (an American Indian word) which were, at first, simple adaptations of the local 'schlitten', normally used as a handcart. Soon, the enthusiastic English had lengthened the schlitten, and competitions began between the Davos hotels, with the first 'International Race' in 1884. St Moritz was not to be outdone, and Johannes Badrutt hired the geometrician, Peter Bonorand, to lay out a special curved and banked course between St Moritz and the village of Cresta. Because the runners of the toboggans were cutting into the snow, someone suggested deliberately icing the course. Speeds shot up, as they did again when the first competitor decided not to sit on the sled, but to lie down and go headfirst. Next, L.P. Child arrived from New York and built a new, long and low toboggan that he called *'America'* – the pattern for the future.

Soon the Cresta Run was one of the fastest and most exciting sports man (and, for a while, a woman) could undertake, and its competitors were achieving the swiftest speeds in history.

The first iced Cresta Run, 1884

Its fame helped to build St Moritz and Davos into leading centres of the new craze of 'winter sports'.

Every year, when the snow falls, it is lovingly rebuilt with its 85 mph straights and its terrifying curves like 'Thoma' and 'Shuttlecock'. The Cresta Run has always been an amateur sport, and was originally considered to be rather upper class. Although it is now very international, it remains an essentially British creation.

The very concept of enthusiastic British invalids creating a fast and dangerous sport to pass the time is fully in keeping with heroes like the legendary Douglas Bader who, after losing both legs, went into the Battle of Britain as one of the RAF's finest fighter pilots.

No wonder, as Prince Philip said, people think the British are a bit mad.

COURTESY OF THE ST. MORITZ TOBOGGANING CLUB

Urs Natar entering 'Shuttlecock'

See: Augusta, Bonneville, Brescia, Farnborough, Indianapolis, Le Mans, Wimbledon

CRO-MAGNON
France

In 1868, fascinating skeletons were found in the Cro-Magnon caves near the village of Les Eyzies, in the Dordogne, south western France. What was so remarkable was their great antiquity, 25,000 years old, yet great

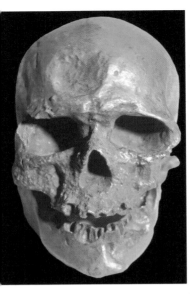

similarity to modern humans. These people were strong, 5 ft 6 inches tall, with skulls featuring high foreheads and jutting chins and no brow ridges, unlike Neanderthal Man, who had populated Europe for 400,000 years.

It became immediately obvious that Cro-Magnon people were much more sophisticated than the Neanderthals. Evidence showed that they had a varied diet, including fish, mammoths, birds, shellfish, fruit and berries, which meant they had the flexible abilities to catch, pick and hunt, aided by the innovation of the barbed spear and fish hook.

Living in the cold of the Ice Age, their facility with tools helped them to build shelters, farm the land, breed animals and cook elaborate food. They were also the first creators of art. Beautiful cave paintings have been found in France and Spain, together with bone carvings, clay models, jewellery and even musical instruments.

Cro-Magnon people emerged from Africa and travelled to Europe, Asia and Australia. Their linguistic competence and cultural sophistication were almost certainly the reason why records of poor old Neanderthal Man disappear about 30,000 BC.

Very much a case of survival of the fittest.

See: Neanderthal, Piltdown

CUMBERLAND ROAD
United States

It is extraordinary to think that roads in America in 1800 were more primitive than those in Europe created over two thousand years earlier by the Romans.

Most American roads were then tracks or trails, impassable for wheeled transport in wet or wintry weather. Indeed, most settlements had clung to rivers or coastlines, and water transport was the preferred method. However, the objective of opening up the hinterland of the Continent was hampered because there were no rivers heading in the right direction.

So, in 1806, Thomas Jefferson and Congress authorised the building of a road to connect the waters of the Atlantic with those of the Ohio River. Although technically beginning in Baltimore, federal funding for the project started in Cumberland, Maryland. This is because Turnpike roads already existed between Baltimore and Cumberland, and so the road ran from there to Wheeling, Virginia (now West Virginia). A path 66 feet wide was carved through forests and mountains, topped with a 20 foot roadway of crushed stone. Rivers and creeks were crossed by stone bridges and milestones (replaced in the 1830s with cast-iron posts) marked the distances.

See: Broadway, Chisholm Trail, Route 66

When the road reached Wheeling, more money was raised by President James Monroe in federal funds because the road was considered to be of benefit to the whole nation. Eventually, 29 years and $7million dollars later, it ended 600 miles from Cumberland at Vandalia, Illinois.

From its inception, the Cumberland Road was a booming success. Soon it was filled with every kind of traffic – stage coaches, wagons, horsemen and endless herds of cattle and sheep. It was punctuated every few miles with taverns renowned for their excellent food and drink. The road was even too crowded for highwaymen to operate!

And it did indeed benefit the nation, opening up Ohio to settlers, reaching Illinois, and eventually acting as the springboard to the west. Now better known as 'The National Road', it played a vital role in building the country, although its importance was soon eclipsed by the transport method that was literally to shape the whole future of America – the railroads.

With the coming of the motor car America built its first generation of automotive highways, and US Route 40 followed the approximate path of the old Cumberland Road. The automobile gave the road a new lease of life, until it was later eclipsed by the straighter and faster highways.

Nevertheless, for its critical first thirty years the Cumberland Road earned its fame and place in history.

DACHAU
Germany

Concentration camps are the most enduring and shocking symbols of the Nazi era. Some are only too famous, a roll call of sinister names: Belsen, Treblinka, Sobibor, Buchenwald, Mauthausen, Ravensbruck – and the greatest killing machine of all time, Auschwitz. Many were smaller and unknown – thousands of them – but one, Dachau, achieved fame by chance because it was the first and the prototype model for all the other horror camps.

On 27th February 1933, the fire in the Reichstag was all the excuse the Nazis needed to turn brutally on their political enemies. Only three weeks later, Heinrich Himmler gave orders for the first concentration camp to be created at Dachau, near Munich. Thousands of Communists, Social Democrats, trade unionists, Conservatives and liberals arrived at the disused munitions factory. Initially, they were guarded by Bavarian State Police, but the SS quickly gained control. That very day, 11th April, the first four murders took place. Amazingly, the local Munich judiciary started to take legal action against the first Kommandant, Hilmar Wäckerle, whom, equally amazingly, Himmler was forced to move.

But his replacement was to be an even more evil and much more important figure, Theodor Eicke. It was this largely unknown man who converted arbitrary terror into a terror system, creating regulations for which many infractions were to be automatic and brutal death. Every day was designed to be filled with methodical and sadistic cruelty.

In June, Hitler decided to get rid of his old comrade and now inconvenient rival, Ernst Röhm, head of the three million Brownshirts of the *Sturmabteilung* or SA. It was the slaughter known as the '*Night of the Long Knives*.' When given a pistol to shoot himself, Röhm sneered, 'If I am to be killed, let Adolf do it himself'. It was Eicke who entered the room and did the job. In gratitude, Hitler and Himmler made Eicke the Chief of Staff for all concentration camps, and he promptly brought to bear all the techniques that he had created at Dachau.

There, things went from bad to worse. In 1936, Kommandant Deubel was dismissed for being too humane, and Hans Lauritz replaced him – with desperate results for the inmates who now included homosexuals, gypsies, clergymen and, of course, Jews. By 1942, Hitler was confident enough to proclaim in a Hanover newspaper: '*Der Jude wird ausgerotted*' – '*the Jew will be exterminated*'.

As Germany annexed or defeated more and more countries, so the first Austrians, Czechs, Poles and Russians arrived. In addition to deaths by shooting, hanging, starvation and cruelty, SS doctors were carrying out cruel medical experiments. By the end, 206,000 prisoners from 27 countries had passed through Dachau.

In spite of losses by typhoid and the removal by the SS of crowds of prisoners on 'death marches', there were still 35,000 prisoners at the main camp of Dachau when it was liberated by appalled American soldiers on 29th April 1945. Three thousand prisoners died of illness within days.

It is not hard to explain the bestial attitude – it had come from the top. From the beginning, Adolf Hitler gloried in it: '*Cruelty is impressive. Cruelty and brutal strength. The simple man in the street can only be impressed by brutal force and ruthlessness. Also women, women and children. The people need*

ALL PHOTOS: CHRISTOPHER AILSBY HISTORICAL ARCHIVE

Eicke, on the Eastern Front in 1943 where he died in action, a more honourable death than he deserved.

Below: the uniform of an SS concentration camp guard, with the K for Konzentrationslager on the collar.

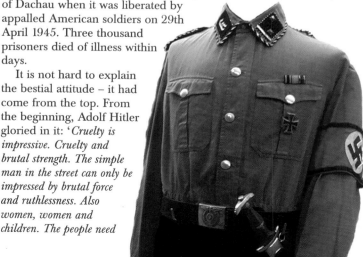

salutary terror. Terror is the most successful political tool. I will not give it up, just because those middle-class fools take offence at it. It's my duty to apply every method in order to make the German people tough and to prepare it for war'.

The result of this attitude was a colossal brutality machine, with over a hundred major concentration camps, among nearly 10,000 other locations, and employing half a million men and women. It killed over six million innocent people and scarred the lives of millions more. Let us hope that a system which started near a village in Bavaria will never be repeated.

See: Anne Frank, Berchtesgaden, Changi, Devil's Island, Getto, Kwai, Landsberg, Lidice, Nuremberg, Oradour, Reichstag, Wannsee

Horrified American journalists view bodies at Dachau after its liberation

DAKOTA
United States

The word Dakota would mean different things to different people. Named after an Indian word, two states, North and South Dakota, are at the very centre of North America – with a stone monument in Rugby, North Dakota marking the exact spot. They have strong agricultural and manufacturing economies. South Dakota, particularly, will be forever linked with the 1874 Gold Rush into the Black Hills and the resulting Great Plains Indian Wars, with names like Little Big Horn, Sitting Bull, Crazy Horse, George Custer and, later, Wild Bill Hickock and Calamity Jane etched into the memory.

But for those outside America, there are two other strong connections. For the millions involved in World War II, the familiar swept-back wings of the wartime version of America's first civilian airliner, the

Douglas DC3, will always be their 'Dakota', flying men and supplies into impossible places and dropping parachute troops at D-Day, Arnhem and the Rhine. Built in huge numbers, many of these rugged twin-engined planes are still flying commercially 60 years on.

For Beatles fans, it will always be the Dakota Building in New York, an apartment block in whose doorway John Lennon was shot down in front of his wife, Yoko Ono, by Mark Chapman, a deranged fan.

Right: John Lennon signs an autograph for Mark Chapman, the man who would later assassinate him.

104

DALLAS
Texas, USA

In 1841, when John Neely Bryan settled on the East Bank of the Trinity River, he would not have known he was founding what is now the seventh largest city in the United States.

Why Dallas has grown is a bit of a mystery. Most of the US cities bigger than Dallas are ports – New York, Los Angeles, San Diego. Houston is both a port and the hub of the oil industry, while Chicago was the railroad and trading centre of America.

By contrast, the growth of Dallas was not due to its Trinity River – which was quite narrow – and was not, contrary to public perception, an oil town. It was a cattle town, and, before the railroad arrived in 1872, was on the route of the great cattle drives to join the Chisholm Trail. It was also a cotton town, and by 1918, had the world's largest indoor cotton market.

Dallas's commercial dynamism is typified by Neiman Marcus, a store made famous above all for its extraordinary and lavish 'His & Hers' gifts as a centre-piece of its famous Christmas Book. These included Beechcraft aeroplanes, hot-air balloons, Chinese junks, submarines and full-size windmills.

However, the driving force of the city has unfortunately been coupled with a reputation for violence. After a shooting in 1875, 'Doc' Holliday was forced to leave town, later to join Wyatt Earp at the bloody gunfight at Tombstone's OK Corral. The Barrow and Parker families lived in Dallas, and 'Bonnie and Clyde's' fifth killing took place there.

1963 was not a good year for Dallas, with the two most public shootings in the history of the world. It is probably unfair to blame Dallas for the assassination of President John Kennedy. The tragedy could have happened anywhere – well, anywhere in the United States, and certainly Texas.

What was even more shaming for civic pride took place two days later. As the suspected assassin, Lee Harvey Oswald, was being led out of the Dallas police headquarters, Jack Ruby, a local nightclub owner, was able to walk up

CAMERA PRESS

Lee Harvey Oswald is shot by Jack Ruby in front of the world's media.

and shoot him in front of the police and the world's media. The fact that there are still many unanswered questions has not helped the city's worldwide notoriety.

Thus, when CBS launched a TV series called *Dallas*, the move was not necessarily welcomed by the somewhat bruised citizens of the real city. The weekly show featured the Ewings, a Dallas oil family who constantly fought each other, while incongruously always meeting for breakfast at Southfork, the family home. Gradually, the players, among them Barbara Bel Geddes, Jim Davis, Patrick Duffy, Linda Gray and Victoria Principal, were overshadowed by the charming but scheming character of 'J.R', played by Larry Hagman - who freely admits he acted constantly under a light influence of champagne. As a cliff-hanger, 'J.R' was shot by an unknown attacker at the end of a series in 1980, boosting Dallas to number one in the ratings.

Great world events taking place at the time – the Iran Hostage Crisis, the crack in the Iron Curtain created by Lech Walesa's Polish shipyard strike and the Reagan/Carter election. But the whole world only wanted to know

Larry Hagman was the scheming and womanising J.R. Ewing.

'Who shot J.R?' Hagman, now a huge star, even refused to tell Britain's Queen Mother the answer. The Dallas episode that eventually revealed the secret was watched by 83 million people in America and 380 million worldwide, then the biggest audience in history.

Nine years later, the Berlin Wall came down. Larry Hagman is convinced that the popularity of Dallas in eastern Europe played a role in the toppling of Communism, with its heady mix of beautiful clothes, big cars and houses and the wealth, abundance and success of America – in marked contrast to the lives of the unwilling citizens of the Soviet Bloc.

If he is right, then the mixed fame of this Texas city may have compensated for all its other problems.

See: Alamo, Ambassador Hotel, Bay of Pigs, Chisholm Trail, OK Corral, Texas School Book Depository, Tombstone, Waco

DAWSON'S FIELD
Jordan

Black September is what the Palestinians called that month in 1970.

It started on the 12th September, when hijackers from the Popular Front for the Liberation of Palestine seized three airliners, a TWA Boeing 707, a Pan Am Jumbo and a Swissair DC8. The Jumbo was blown up at Cairo after releasing the passengers and crew, but the other two planes arrived at a lonely and deserted former Royal Air Force airstrip in the Jordanian desert called Dawson's Field.

However, the planned hijack of an El Al Boeing 707 was thwarted by its alert Israeli guards, who killed one PLO hijacker and overpowered the other - an attractive Palestinian girl called Leila Khaled, who was held at Heathrow. This in turn prompted the hijacking of a British BOAC VC-10, which joined the others in the searing heat of Dawson's Field. There they waited while frantic negotiations took place. The VC10 co-pilot, Trevor Cooper, suspected of trying to signal, was even forced to dig his own potential grave.

Eventually, 255 passengers were released before the planes were blown up, with the remaining 56 only being released on 30th September after Leila Khaled and six terrorists in Germany and Switzerland were released. This gave rise to widespread concern about such apparently supine Western capitulation to terrorism.

Curiously, it was an Arab who was more robust with the Palestinian movement. King Hussein of Jordan was seriously worried by the aggressive PLO behaviour in his country, which was supported by Syria. Exasperated by the hijackings on his soil, he instructed his army to evict the Palestinians from their strongholds. After only ten days, he and Yasser Arafat, both symbolically wearing pistols, signed a truce which effectively destroyed the position of the Palestinians in Jordan. For them, it was indeed 'Black September'.

See: Bethlehem, World Trade Center

DELPHI
Greece

'I will deliver to them all counsel that cannot fail, answering them in my rich temple'.
(Apollo in the Homeric Hymns)

Delphi, at the foot of Mount Parnassus, about a hundred miles north west of Athens, was claimed to be the centre of the world, as proved by the King of the Gods himself, Zeus. He released two eagles in different directions and, when they crossed paths at Delphi, it was designated as the *omphalos* (literally – 'navel') of the earth. Quite why is anyone's guess.

It was originally the site of a temple to mother earth, Gaia. As time progressed, however, it became increasingly associated with Apollo, the god of the lyre, youth, poetry, archery, the sun, and most pertinently, prophesy.

Apollo was heavily involved in the location's mythology. When a vast serpent, Python, had taken up residence nearby, Apollo slew it, using his bow and arrow that had previously only been involved in hunting. *The archer god … destroyed with countless arrows the swollen Python that covered many acres with its plague-ridden belly.* (Ovid)

He founded the Pythian games there, taking their name from the giant snake. He also founded the Delphic oracle. The priestess was called the Pythia, also from the beast. These priestesses were originally young and beautiful virgins but, to assure continuing virginity, older women began to be selected! They would sit on a tripod and breathe in hallucinogenic fumes from a fissure in the rock to enable them to utter their prophesies. Other accounts say that they chewed laurel leaves, the sacred plant of Apollo. Foaming at the mouth, their words would be so garbled that special priests were needed to decipher the predictions.

In 1998 two American scientists, Jelle Zeilingade Boer and John Hale, finally discovered the scientific secret. While methane and ethane gases came out of the fault, the key gas is ethylene, which can produce exactly the symptoms which made the oracle famous.

The prophesies of the oracle were highly respected, if often ambiguous. Private individuals and even heads of state consulted the Delphi oracle. Most famous is the story of Croesus, emperor of Lydia. When he asked the Pythia whether or not he should invade Persia, he received the response that if he did, 'he would destroy a mighty empire.' Delighted, Croesus attacked, but was heavily defeated. When he returned, ruined, to the Oracle, he inquired angrily why he had been deceived. The Pythia replied that he had not. Had Croesus' empire not been mighty, and had it not now been destroyed?

The oracle became increasingly costly to maintain, and eventually Emperor Theodosius announced its official closure in the fourth century BC. However the oracle was still used until the fourth century AD, when a newly Christian Rome shut it down permanently.

The cult of the Delphic oracle, however, has proved virtually indestructible. The expression *'know thyself'*, originally carved into the walls of the temple, is now commonly known. There is even a business forecasting method called 'the Delphi Technique'. Furthermore, visitors to Greece can enjoy the 'New Oracle Of Apollo' experience, with introductory talk, guided tour, and actual consultation of 'James', a modern day Pythia. It is even possible to consult an internet-based oracle, although its predictions are hopefully unreliable; when asked 'Will anyone buy this book?', the response was, *Re-think your career choice before it's too late.*

See: Olympos

DEOLALI
India

ASHEESH SANGAMNHERI

People in Britain still say, *'He's gone doolally'*, meaning that someone has gone a bit nutty or peculiar. In Australia they say, *'Don't do your lolly'*. Both phrases have their origin in a real place. It is not, as you might imagine, some obscure village in the west of Ireland, but a military camp in India.

At the end of the nineteenth century the British Army set up a sanatorium at Deolali, a hundred miles north east of Bombay. Deolali also acted as a transit camp for 'time-expired' soldiers due to go home, and waiting to be shipped back to England from Bombay's port.

But ships only left Bombay between November and March, so some troops were stuck in Deolali for months on end.

With no real soldiering to do, even the best became frantic with boredom and frustration, many turning to drink and some either committing crimes or contracting venereal diseases; in other words, they *'went doolally'*.

Soldiers also used to say *'He's got the Doolally tap'*, because 'tap' was the local word for fever.

'Tap' disappeared and now only a few very old soldiers might remember how a boring camp gave its name to a casual phrase we often use today.

See: Amritsar, Dum Dum, Great Hedge of India, Jodhpur, Taj Mahal, Varanasi

DESIRE
Louisiana, USA

Marlon Brando as the cynical and brutal Stanley Kowalski

Transportation has given us many famous names.

Trains like the *20th Century Limited*, the *Orient Express* and the *Brighton Belle*. Then there were the famous ships, *Great Eastern*, the *Titanic, Queen Mary, La France* and *USS United States*. Or flying machines, from the airship *Hindenburg* to supersonic *Concorde*.

But a streetcar or humble tram?

There is just one – 'The Streetcar named Desire', made famous worldwide by Tennessee Williams' play and movie. The streetcar was real, originated by the New Orleans Railway and Light Company in 1920. For twenty eight years, it served streets we know from jazz tunes – Bourbon, Dauphine, Canal Streets and, of course, Desire Street.

Desire Street, itself, runs down to the Mississippi River and was named after Désirée, one of the two daughters of landowner Robert Montreuil. The Montreuil district contained Andrew Jackson's second line of defence in the Battle of New Orleans against the British in 1815.

The last Desire streetcars were replaced by buses in 1948, but not before they were propelled to fame by Tennessee Williams' play, which opened on Broadway in 1947 directed by Elia Kazan and starring Marlon Brando – the 'method' actor.

Four years later, *A Streetcar Named Desire* hit the world's cinema screens.

Blanche (Vivien Leigh), a fading

108

Southern belle, arrives at her sister Stella's New Orleans tenement, travelling on the Streetcar named Desire. There, she clashes with Stanley Kowalski (Marlon Brando) – crude, cynical and brutal, the very antithesis of everything (or nearly everything) in her past.

The play and film were landmarks, destroying a genuinely neurotic Vivien Leigh and propelling Brando into greatness.

And the streetcar immortalised forever? It is probably coming back.

In 1997, the New Orleans Regional Transit Authority voted $ 1.9 million to study the project, which may be built at a cost of $93 million. It will be called the Desire Corridor Streetcar.

Ask most people why a street is named Desire, and they will surely give you a very different answer.

See: Cotton Club, Harlem, Storyville

DEVIL'S ISLAND
French Guiana

Outside France, few people had heard of Devil's Island until Alfred Dreyfus was sent there. The modern world did not focus on it until the film *Papillon* that starred Steve McQueen and Dustin Hoffman as prisoners, and Patrick McGoohan as the sadistic commandant.

Isle de Diable was one of the three small Islands of Salvation (Isles de Salut) to which the tragic remnants of the first French settlers of 1763 had retreated.

As a colony, French Guiana was proving virtually worthless, so Napoleon III decided to make it into a penal colony. At first the appalling conditions were judged only fit for Africans, Arabs and Annamese, but by 1884 the first white prisoners arrived. Between then and 1946, 56,000 prisoners were sent from France of whom only one quarter made it back alive.

The penal settlement consisted of the administration block and main prison, St Laurent, near Cayenne on the mainland, and prisons on each of the islands of Isle de Diable, Isle Royale and Isle St Joseph, where the solitary cells were. The whole complex became loosely known as Devil's Island.

It was the timber camps on the mainland which were the worst. Naked prisoners with only shoes and straw hats worked in waist-high water attacked by malarial mosquitoes. If they failed to meet their quota of one cubic metre of wood they were punished, starved and faced the same task the next day.

At Koiron, the deadliest camp, 4,000 prisoners died in three years. No wonder they attempted the virtually impossible – to escape. Some tried to swim the Moroni River to Dutch Guiana, often to be returned or to die the horrifying death of being stripped to the bone by piranhas. Some tried to make it by sea in tiny canoes. If you reached British Guiana you could stay – but just for ten days. Some tried to make it overland through hundreds of miles of Brazilian jungle.

In 1936, one prisoner, René Belbenoit, clutching a 20 lb manuscript, took years to reach freedom. Escaping by sea, he reached Panama and waited one year with friendly Indians. Then he went on through the threatening wilds of Guatemala and Honduras, eventually reaching Mexico and then the United States, where his book *Dry Guillotine* became an instant best-seller in 1938, an epic description of Devil's Island.

How could France, with its traditions of culture and civilisation, carry out such barbarity for so long? To condemn your citizens, often imprisoned for minor offences, to the type of horrors we associate with Hitler's concentration camps and Stalin's Gulags was monstrous. But it did happen.

Dustin Hoffman as an anguished prisoner in the film 'Papillon.' We never know if he really escapes.

See: Alcatraz, Gulag, Reading Gaol, Robben Island, Spandau

DIEN BIEN PHU
Vietnam

The French army thought it had created a trap at Dien Bien Phu. It was only partly right.

After the defeat of the Japanese in 1945, the French returned to their colonies in Indo-China to find things had changed. Having seen Asiatics beat Europeans, the peoples of the East were no longer prepared to be colonial subjects. Laos and Cambodia reluctantly accepted independence within the French Union. In Vietnam, formal elections were held and the Viet Minh party won, electing Ho Chi Minh as President. Negotiations on independence broke down in 1946, the Viet Minh moving north to Hanoi, while the people of South Vietnam seemed resigned to being ruled by the French.

A Viet Minh photograph of the last seconds of the siege

From 1946 to 1953, the French fought the Viet Minh to a stalemate. But when the Korean War ended, the Chinese were able to provide Viet Minh with quantities of heavy equipment, including field and anti-aircraft guns. That is when General Navarre decided to launch his trap, 'Operation Castor.' He parachuted French troops into a small valley with a tiny and unknown village – Dien Bien Phu.

The village was completely isolated, and everything had to be flown in to its airstrip. The engineers warned that they needed 35,000 tons of stores. The plan was over-ambitious, because it would have required 2,000 flights. In the event, they received only 4,000 tons, of which 3,000 were barbed wire.

A poster in France reflects the agony of defeat and the loss of empire.

Eventually, 15,000 French Foreign Legionnaires and parachutists, and twelve tanks – built up from kits – waited for an unknown enemy. Colonel Piroth, the garrison's artillery chief, boasted that any gun that the enemy might bring up 'would be destroyed after just three shots'.

As the 'fortress', a series of defensive forts called after girls' names, settled down, many planes flew in, loaded not with vital supplies, but distinguished visitors, including American Vice President Richard Nixon.

What the French did not realise in their complacency was that General Vo Nguyen Giap had surrounded the place with five well-trained divisions, all of them secretly supplied by thousands of peasants using mules and bicycles which could carry 200 lb on their handlebars. Even more shocking would have been the realisation that the French faced twice as many enemy guns, all brought up in pieces, reassembled and then dug into caves on the surrounding hills. Completely hidden, with only their muzzles projecting, their crews could see everything that moved in the valley below and could plot their targets.

The French were not springing a trap, they were firmly in it.

When the siege opened, within minutes the guns on 'Beatrice' were knocked out and the outpost's commander killed. In six hours, it had fallen, losing seventy five per cent of its men. The airport was closed by Viet Minh artillery and the French started rationing precious ammunition. 'Gabrielle' fell next, after bitter fighting. Back at headquarters, Navarre heard with stupefaction that within 48 hours two key outposts had fallen. The over-confident artilleryman, Colonel Piroth, overcome by shame, went to his bunker and killed himself with a grenade.

In the days to come, 'Anne Marie' fell, and 'Dominique', 'Eliane' and 'Huguette' were lost and retaken – but all at the cost of men and ammunition, which the Viet Minh could afford but the French could not. Eventually, after 56 days of brutal hand-to-hand fighting, 7,000

French surrendered, with 2,000 killed and 6,000 wounded or missing. Forced by public opinion 'on the streets of Paris' the French quit Indo-China within weeks; the beginning of the end of their imperial history.

Fifteen years later, Giap tried the same game with the American fire base at Khe Sanh, but this time both logistics and fire-power were on the side of the defenders, with 200,000 shells and 100,000 tons of bombs dropped on to the besiegers. There was not the anticipated second Dien Bien Phu, and Khe Sanh was hailed as a victory. But, once again, public opinion was so shocked by the ability of the Vietnamese to stage the attack on Khe Sanh and by the Tet Offensive, that the Americans eventually left Vietnam in exactly the same way the French had done before them.

See: Arnhem, Camerone, Khe Sanh

DIEPPE
France

A great many people have always thought that there was something very strange about the disastrous raid on Dieppe, a small French port on the Channel coast. In August 1942, fully two years before the Normandy Invasion, it involved almost exclusively Canadian troops, lasted no more than a few hours and left 2,700 killed, wounded or captured. As 4,000 landed, this meant a casualty rate higher than the dreaded Battle of the Somme.

Nor did Churchill's explanation in the House of Commons ring true. 'Dieppe was a reconnaissance in force – to which I gave my sanction'. Indeed, most would have been more likely to agree with the German defenders' comment, 'This affair mocked all rules of military strategy and logic'. Canadian opinion was, rather understandably, more bitter.

The mystery may have been unravelled in a recent and masterful book, *Military Intelligence Blunders*. The author, Colonel John Hughes-Williams, postulates that the raid was a piece of wilful self-aggrandisement and even disobedience by that great British hero, Lord Louis Mountbatten. Mountbatten, aged just 41, had been promoted three grades at Churchill's behest to become 'Chief of Combined Operations'. Churchill needed a hero after the string of British military reverses, and the handsome, dashing, destroyer Captain, a cousin of the King, excellent with the Americans and a friend of film stars – seemed to fit the bill.

The ambitious Mountbatten needed a dramatic success for Combined Operations, which is why *'Rutter'*, the raid on Dieppe, was conceived with three military goals: to see if a port could be held for a short period, to obtain intelligence and to gauge German reaction. Unofficial aims, however, were to bolster Churchill's weak position, second, to draw up the Luftwaffe and hit it hard, and third, to give the over-trained and bored Canadians something meaningful to do.

In May 1942, the Chiefs of Staff approved *'Operation Rutter'*, although the Army and the Navy remained uneasy. On 7th July, because of bad weather, the raid was cancelled and the seasick troops returned to southern England. All were convinced that Dieppe was off, forever. There was, from top to bottom, a sigh of relief.

Mountbatten then did something very strange. With a small staff, he furtively reinstated the Dieppe operation under the new code-name *'Jubilee'*, and kept its planning secret from the Chiefs of Staff. As he said on television in 1972, 'I made the unusual and, I suggest, rather bold decision that we would remount the operation against Dieppe'. It was unusual to say the least. At two meetings, the Chiefs had turned the idea down. But the plans proceeded in secret, and this meant that the normal up-to-date intelligence

Young, handsome and glamorous, but many did not trust Mountbatten

The aftermath. Germans examine one of the wrecked Churchill tanks.

See: Arnhem,
Biggin Hill, Dunkirk,
Oradour

information could not be asked for; nor was the raid cleared with the Inter Service Security Board, who would have known that details of the Dieppe raid had been fed to German double agents.

So, on 19th August, the raid went in and was a murderous fiasco. The allied ships blundered into a German coastal convoy and the resulting 'firework display' fully alerted the defenders of Dieppe. The Canadians were shot to pieces by the hidden guns and machine-guns on their flanks. 27 Churchill tanks scrabbled on

the huge pebbles of the beach, only 15 reached the esplanade, only to get stuck in front of the prepared tank traps – all of which fresh intelligence would have revealed. The French-Canadian reserve entered a 'blizzard of firing.' Out of 600, only 125 returned to England. Even the Royal Air Force failed in its objectives, losing 105 fighters to the Luftwaffe's 44.

Field Marshal Sir Alan Brooke was in Moscow with Churchill, and General Nye, his deputy and the Vice Chief of the Imperial General Staff, the most senior officer in Britain, knew nothing of the attack until the signals started streaming in on that very morning.

Mountbatten got away with it, and went on to a distinguished career as a 'great British hero'. But many would never trust him again. Anyone else would have been court-martialled and sacked for Dieppe. If he had been on the German or Soviet sides, something even more terminal might have occurred. But he did not deserve to die at the hands of the IRA.

DOGPATCH, USA
United States

By 1939, the many and strange activities of Dogpatch USA were probably better known to most Americans than any other place on earth, because Dogpatch was the home of Li'l Abner, the most popular comic strip of all time, syndicated in hundreds of newspapers and eventually read by 60 million people.

Li'l Abner was the brilliant creation of Alfred Gerald Caplin, better known as Al Capp, and featured the handsome, hulking hillbilly, Li'l Abner Yokum, always running from girls – especially the lovely Daisy Mae. This is quite poignant because Al Capp himself lost a leg in an accident, aged nine, which he had felt to be a major disadvantage in his teenage years when trying to run after girls. Indeed, Capp created an American institution, 'Sadie Hawkins Day', named after the ugly Sadie, daughter of the Mayor of Dogpatch, who gave the unmarried men ten minutes start in a chase to net a husband. When they were caught, Marryin' Sam performed a shotgun wedding. Sadie Hawkins 'girl-asks-boy' dances became a craze across

American colleges. Parents even objected to the Dogpatch costumes – especially the Daisy Mae sexy look, with its off-the-shoulder blouse and short ragged skirts, not to be seen again until worn by Jane Russell in Howard Hughes' banned film, *The Outlaw*, or Mary Quant's miniskirts in the 'Swinging Sixties.'

The influence of Li'l Abner went way beyond the comic strip and the Depression era which had launched it. In 1948, Al Capp featured the Shmoos, strange, amiable, bottle-shaped creatures that laid eggs, gave milk, ate nothing and were wonderful to eat – even dying of sheer happiness if you looked at them hungrily. The Shmoo became the largest merchandising success of its era.

Li'l Abner was made into a long-running Broadway musical and two movies, created by Johnny Mercer and Gene de Paul, and several of the numbers became hits. When Daisy Mae finally caught Li'l Abner, the marriage was shock headline news across America. The strip was retired in 1977, two years before Al Capp's death.

For nearly 30 years, there really was a

Dogpatch - in northern Arkansas. It was a town with a Li'l Abner theme park nearby. The park has now closed, and the town has gone back to its original name of Marble Falls. Probably sensible. There's a time and a place for everything.

See: Bazaar, Broadway, Hollywood, Springfield, Truth or Consequences

10 DOWNING STREET
England

A traitor, a brewery, gin parlours, brothels, bombs, builders and the hilariously named Mr Chicken. Surprisingly, these are all chapters in the eventful life of the current home and central office of Britain's Prime Minister. By what chance did 10 Downing Street become Britain's premier political address?

Starting in 1662, Downing Street itself was developed by one Sir George Downing, once Oliver Cromwell's Intelligence Chief. When Downing realised that the restoration of the monarchy was imminent, he did not hesitate to switch sides at once and offer his services to Charles II, thus totally betraying his allies. To increase his personal fortune, he also developed the houses on what is now Downing Street. Building on the site of the Abingdon Abbey brew-house, the road consisted of poor quality, terraced housing with insufficient foundation to support the structures fully on the local boggy ground. The brickwork was so irregular that straight mortar lines had to be drawn up, to give the impression that the bricks were evenly arranged. The house that is now number 10 was at the time number 5, and only in 1779 was it given its modern numeration.

However, this house was only half of the present-day Prime Minister's residence. At the back of Downing Street was a larger, more impressive residence, looking on to Horse Guards Parade. In the early 1730s, King George II evicted an unfortunate Mr Chicken (the last private resident of the building) and presented both buildings (the one in Downing Street and the other facing Horse Guards) to his Principal Minister – Sir Robert Walpole. Walpole ordered the two houses to be knocked together on both floors, leaving the building more reminiscent of its modern form. Walpole had asked the residence to be presented to him in his official capacity – not as Prime Minister, (a term not in popular circulation at the time), but as 'First Lord of the Treasury'. To this day, this is officially the very position through which the Prime Minister resides in 10 Downing Street, and 'First Lord of the Treasury' is inscribed on the letter box.

The house increasingly became the centre of Britain's Government, further confirmed when, in 1828, Number 11 Downing Street became the residence of the Chancellor of the Exchequer. However, the area was very different in those days. It was so filled with brothels and seedy little gin bars that there were very serious plans to knock down the entire street. Instead, the area became progressively 'gentrified', more fitting to its role, especially when the buildings opposite Number 10 were demolished and replaced with the impressive new Foreign Office building at the end of the 1860's. By 1902 the tradition of the Prime Minister actually living in the house became established, with the election of Arthur Balfour.

Centre: Sir Robert Walpole, the first resident as First Lord of The Treasury

During the Second World War, a nearby bomb landing on Treasury Green badly damaged the Downing Street kitchen and killed three servants. Five days later a mine was defused in St James' Park which, had it exploded, could have flattened buildings up to 400 metres away. These threats forced Winston Churchill to move his residence and offices into the relative safety of the underground Cabinet War Rooms in 1940. Most of the building's furnishings were also moved, leaving large parts of 10 Downing Street unfurnished until the war ended.

This was not even the last time that the house would be evacuated. After an IRA bomb attack in 1992, the Prime Minister John Major and members of his staff moved into Admiralty Arch whilst the damage was repaired. Downing Street has now much more security; indeed, the door of Number 10 can only be opened from the inside, and the street itself is blocked off at either end by guarded gates.

In contrast to America's White House or other residences of world leaders, there is something typically British about a great country's affairs being run from behind that familiar black front door of a cosy terraced house, once built by a property speculator.

See: Camp David, Carnaby Street, Chequers, Harley Street, Savile Row

---

DUFFEL
Belgium

The Flanders town of Duffel might never have come to international attention, were it not for the heavy, durable, double-napped woollen material created there in 1667.

For the British, the duffel coat with its hood and its jute rope fastenings and wooden toggles, was to become a symbol of the Royal Navy, which first introduced it in the 1890s. Film buffs will remember stiff-lipped officers such as Jack Hawkins in *The Cruel Sea*, braving out the elements in his stalwart duffel coat.

However, they might be surprised to find that Italians call the duffel coat *'Il Montgomery'* and the French *'Le Monty'*. This was because Field Marshal Montgomery took up the Army version of the rugged, warm garment to ward off the cold of his desert campaigns.

After the war, the duffel would become standard wear for rebellious youth in the fifties and sixties, while the duffel bag is, to this day, absolutely routine camping gear for Americans.

The duffel coat has recently seen a revival as a fashion item, now in bright colours, softer wool and at very high prices.

One of its more charming and eccentric claims to fame is as the essential apparel for that children's favourite 'Paddington Bear'.

See: Angora, Balaclava, Bikini, Gorgonzola, Jodhpur, Nîmes, Pilsen

---

DUM DUM
India

Dum Dum, an industrial suburb of Calcutta, has given its name to a very unpleasant form of bullet.

In the most serious and bloody war of its century – the American Civil War – the rifles were very large calibre, .58 inch, and fired a heavy bullet at low muzzle velocity. But the energy they generated was enough to cause soldiers to suffer horrific and terminal wounds, resulting in twenty battles with the same losses as Waterloo.

As bullets became smaller and travelled faster, military experts noted with some dismay that they were able to pass right through a body – sometimes without inflicting enough damage to stop a man. At Dum Dum, headquarters of the Bengal Artillery, the ammunition factory hit on the idea of a soft bullet that expanded or broke up when it hit someone – capable of causing massive damage.

It was soon realised that such bullets were a fearsome departure, and they were banned by the Hague Convention of 1899 as a '*weapon that created unnecessary suffering*'. Theoretically, they are no longer officially made.

Sometimes, however, soldiers or criminals have improvised their own expanding bullets by cutting a cross-nick in the head of the bullet, causing it to break up when it encounters resistance.

So, the dreaded word '*dumdum*' may linger on.

DUNBLANE
Scotland

On the morning of Wednesday the 13th March 1996, Thomas Hamilton walked into Dunblane Primary School and, in less than 5 minutes, ensured that few would ever forget the name of the Perthshire town, and that Dunblane would have to face the horror of burying 16 of its youngest residents and one of its teachers.

Nestled between the rugged peaks of the Perthshire Highlands and the fertile plain of Stirling, Dunblane had been known primarily for its spectacular 13th century cathedral. It could never have been predicted that such a historical gem of a community should be remembered as the site of one of Britain's worst mass killings.

Dunblane Primary School had 640 pupils, one of the largest in Scotland. At 9.30 am, Thomas Hamilton parked his white van opposite the school and walked in via a side entrance. He was carrying four high-powered handguns and wearing ear protectors. Teachers Mrs Harrild and Mrs Mayor were in the gym hall preparing to start their lesson with Class 1/13, when they heard two shots fired behind a hall full of children, one in the girl's toilet, and one on the stage.

Hamilton burst through the door and fired 29 times. Mrs Harrild was shot four times, but managed to reach an adjoining room with four of the children. Mrs Mayor died instantly. Ambulance driver John McEwan later said that she must have been trying to shield the class, as she was found directly in front of a group of little children who were 'beyond all hope'.

The appalling slaughter continued as Hamilton fired another 24 shots, 16 from '*point blank range*'. Outside, Mrs Gordon, in charge of hut 7, ordered her class to lie down, seconds before Hamilton fired 9 shots into her classroom.

Returning to the gym, he cocked his .357 Smith and Wesson revolver, put the barrel in his mouth, and then pulled the trigger. It was the last of 105 shots.

Fifteen children and their schoolteacher lay dead, and another little girl was dying. Twelve children, and two other teachers, were injured. Fifteen of the dead children were only five years old.

The sense of public outrage and grief was so powerful that even the tabloid media respected the wishes of the town to be left to mourn in peace. Cameras did not attend the funerals, and the people of Dunblane steeled themselves for the aftermath, in private.

The enquiry focused on how someone who could commit such a crime came to be armed with such a veritable arsenal, and why Hamilton had not been spotted as a threat earlier by those who continued to allow him a firearms licence.

Thomas Hamilton was born in Glasgow in 1952. His childhood was far from happy, and he grew up believing that his biological mother was his sister. When his adoptive parents died in 1987 he moved to Kent Road, Dunblane. However, he had already been under police scrutiny for some time, facing suspicion of being a paedophile.

In 1974, he was

Mrs Mayor was killed with many of her class.

A gun control poster in America in 1970. Sadly, the rest of the world now suffers from gun related tragedies.

dismissed as a Boy Scout Master, to his undying resentment, following allegations that he had allowed two young boys to share his camper van.

Later, while running summer camps he was investigated after he had insisted the boys wear small swimming costumes, which he had provided, and that he had photographed them. At this point, he had already run fourteen boys' clubs in Scotland.

When Hamilton was turned down by the Dunblane School, he felt that his career had been deliberately sabotaged by *'a Masonic order'* of Police, and that 'society' in general, was to blame for the misrepresentation of his case.

When he finally snapped, the extra ingredient was his morbid interest in guns. In 1977, he received his first licence for a .22 firearm, 'for target shooting at Callander shooting club'. The licence was amended over the years, so in 1979 he could buy a .357 revolver and, in 1986, a 9mm pistol. Despite his less than savoury history, no one in authority ever questioned the prudence of allowing him so many guns.

It was not as if Hamilton's character had gone unnoticed by the local sport shooting community. Alex Fawcett, of Stirling Rifle and Pistol club, once said to her cousin, 'That's a right weirdo. He talks about guns as though they were babies'. The sight of him 'stroking' his gun had upset her.

After the massacre, the widely-praised public enquiry was led by Lord Douglas Cullen, one of Scotland's most respected judges. He suggested that firearms certificates should only be given to members of recognised gun clubs, and that much more thorough background checks were needed, both in the world of firearms certification, and in childcare.

The Government went further. In the Firearms (Amendment) Bill, 1997, all handguns were banned from private ownership, with the exception of .22 calibre handguns that can never leave registered clubs. Despite a wave of criticism from sportsmen, the Lords would hear no talk of 'watering down' the Bill and handguns became illegal. All of them.

One need only glance at the statistics from across the Atlantic to see that the catastrophe that communities filled with guns can bring. Dunblane's tragedy and the Government Bill gave a message that Britain would never tolerate a gun-toting society.

The nightmare suffered by Dunblane will continue to send a shiver down the spine of all those that can bear to think about it. For those intent on using illegal handguns, however, the nature of the shiver they feel, as the cell door slams behind them, suggests Dunblane left a more powerful legacy than grief and horror alone.

General, later Field Marshal, Alexander commanded the rear guard at Dunkirk.

DUNKIRK
France

Major General Sir Harold Alexander, commanding Britain's First Division, pedalled on to the beach at Dunkirk on a push bike, his car stuck back in a burning traffic jam. The sight that awaited him was not a pretty one. France's third largest port was a shambles and ablaze, with German dive-bombers swooping on the ships that were trying to get in and out. On the beach, thousands of troops waited patiently to be rescued, some up to their necks in water. Alexander promptly ordered his engineers to drive trucks down to form piers, from which the troops could be reached by rowing boats.

What he saw was the British and French trying to escape from a trap set for them weeks before. On 10th May 1940, when Germany attacked in the west, the Allies advanced unopposed into Belgium. But suddenly, further south, the panzers burst from the 'impenetrable' Ardennes forests, battled across the Meuse at Sedan under a howling swarm of Stuka dive bombers and broke out to slice across northern France. Confused and shaken French Generals tried to contact their crumbling armies by talking via village switchboard ladies, from the only place that a respectable chateau had a telephone – the lavatory. Meanwhile, the radios of the clattering tanks and half-tracks of 'Hurrying' Heinz Guderian were reporting that they were fulfilling all the *Blitzkrieg* (Lightning War) predictions of his book *Achtung! Panzer*. They reached the Channel at the mouth of the Somme on 20th May. Achieving in ten days what they had failed to do in four years in the First World War, the Germans had now cut off one million British, Belgian and French troops from the rest of France.

British defenders at Boulogne fought a hard delaying action. Sergeant Dave Smylie of the Irish Guards, (Alexander's old Regiment), wounded, and in a German hospital, was asked by his regiment by an immaculate Oberstleutnant who then, in perfect English, concluded, 'I might have known it that it was the bloody 'Micks' who held us up so long!'

With Calais now under siege, it was obvious to Field Marshal Lord Gort, the British army commander, that there was one chance – evacuation from Dunkirk, the only remaining port. Gort remarked 'You know, the day I joined up I never thought I'd lead the British Army to its biggest defeat in history'. But his brave initiative was to be crucial.

In an office carved from the Cliffs of Dover, Admiral Ramsay pondered the problems as he launched *'Operation Dynamo'*. He only had available 40 destroyers and 129 coasters, ferries and barges. He thought they might be able to bring out 45,000 men, at most.

On 23rd May something strange happened with the Germans. Inexplicably, the tanks paused. It was probably a combination of a German sudden loss of nerve caused by a British counter-attack at Arras, waiting for the infantry to catch up, anxiety about the boggy countryside and a desire to husband the tanks for their thrust south into the rest of France. Or even that Hitler, to the understandable horror of his Generals, planned to leave Britain with her Empire and did not want to

humiliate her too much. Whatever the truth, the panzers stayed put for a vital three days, whilst a vainglorious Goering boasted, 'This is a special job for the Luftwaffe!'

On Monday, 27th May, the whole of the Belgian army surrendered. Frantically, the open northern sector was plugged with French and British troops. Calais fell next day and its defenders became prisoners.

But, back in England, a strange armada had gathered. Yachts, fire floats, lifeboats, tugs and minesweepers, river pleasure boats, trawlers, car ferries and small motor boats, hundreds of them all set off for France and into the inferno of Dunkirk. Naval officers were moved to tears by the sight. Every day and night thousands of starving and exhausted soldiers, still waiting in long lines, were plucked off the beaches by brave volunteer civilians in little boats, while destroyers and larger vessels took off whole units from the wreckage of the quay sides. In spite of the RAF's constant interception, Goering's bombers did their worst. Out of 693 ships, 200 were sunk and many damaged, but on the sandy beaches the bombs did little damage. By amazing good luck, the sea stayed flat as a mill pond. With the normal Channel rollers, things might have been very different.

By the time General Alexander, now in command of the rearguard, toured the beaches looking for stragglers, an amazing 338,226 men, 120,000 of them French, had been rescued, to form the basis of new armies. Churchill said, 'We must be very careful not to assign to this deliverance the attributes of a victory. Wars

Lines of men wade out to the rescue boats.

Boastful Goering was sure that his airforce could destroy the Dunkirk troops.

Unseen by the troops, the RAF did a good job in breaking up the Luftwaffe attacks.
Painting by Ron Freeman

See: Biggin Hill, Dieppe, Sedan

oceans, we shall fight with growing confidence and growing strength in the air; we shall defend our Island, whatever the cost may be. We shall fight on the beaches, we shall fight on the landing-grounds, we shall fight in the fields and in the streets, we shall fight in the hills; we shall never surrender; and even if, which I do not for a moment believe, this Island or a large part of it were subjugated and starving, then our Empire beyond the seas, armed and guarded by the British Fleet, would carry on the struggle, until, in God's good time, the New World, with all its power and might, steps forth to the rescue and the liberation of the Old'.*

are not won by evacuations.' Churchill also dictated to his secretary, almost in tears, a memorable broadcast he was to make to the Americans:

'Even though large tracts of Europe and many old and famous States have fallen or may fall into the grip of the Gestapo and all the odious apparatus of Nazi rule, we shall not flag or fail. We shall go on to the end. We shall fight in France, we shall fight in the seas and

As he turned south for the Battle of France, Hitler sought to reassure his generals that the thwarting of his mechanized legions by a fleet of civilian sailors, the 'Cockleshell Heroes', made no difference, predicting, 'We will not hear much more of the British in this war'. With Dunkirk forever associated with snatching victory from defeat, he could not have been more wrong.

DUNSINANE
Scotland

Humble buildings that inspired writers, as with Alphonse Daudet and his 'Lettres de mon moulin'

Scholars of Saxon forts may know of the one at Dunsinane, between Dundee and Perth. But the rest of us are more likely to remember how the three witches reassured Macbeth that *'none born of woman'* had the power to harm him, nor that he would be vanquished *'till Birnam Wood shall come to Dunsinane'*. But he had not allowed for Macduff, who had been *'from his mother's womb untimely ripp'd'* and whose soldiers cut branches from Birnam Wood for camouflage. Shakespeare loved using places in his work, although he never set eyes on Scotland, let alone Verona or Venice.

With mostly middle-class writers, many names in English literature involve great houses; *Howard's End* (E.M. Forster), *Wildfell Hall* (Anne Bronte) *Brideshead Revisited* (Evelyn Waugh), *Mansfield Park* (Jane Austen), *Grantchester* (Rupert Brooke), *Baskerville Hall* (Conan Doyle) or even Mervyn Peake's crumbling castle *Gormenghast*.

Many have a religious connection which might now seem rather dated, like *Barchester Towers* (Anthony Trollope) *Northanger Abbey* (Jane Austen) *Tintern Abbey* (William Wordsworth) or the *Vicar of Wakefield* (Goldsmith). One feature, the gable, seems to have inspired novelists like L.M. Montgomery with *Anne of Green Gables* and Nathaniel Hawthorne with *The House of Seven Gables*.

Then, there are more prosaic buildings like the *Mill on the Floss*, (George Eliot), Daudet's *Moulin* or even Edward Thomas's charming description of a railway halt, at *Adelstrop*, while Emily Bronte's *Wuthering Heights* is a real, windswept Yorkshire farmhouse called Top Withens.

Some writers focused on the locations they knew well, like Thomas Hardy with England's 'Wessex', or John Steinbeck with California (*Cannery Row, Tortilla Flat, Monterrey*). Others described their places of confinement like Oscar Wilde's *Reading*

Gaol or Brendan Behan with *Borstal Boy.* Both are real, Borstal is a village in Kent, site of the first youth correctional centre. Rugby in *Tom Brown's School Days* (Thomas Hughes) is real enough, while Hogwarts in *Harry Potter* is a figment of J.K. Rowling's imagination. Urban settings abound; *Washington Square* (Henry James), *A Tree grows in Brooklyn* (Betty Smith), *A Streetcar named Desire* (Tennessee Williams), *As I was walking down Sackville Street* (Oliver St. John Gogarty), *The Road to Wigan Pier* (George Orwell), *The Barretts of Wimpole Street* (by Rudolf Besier) and *Brighton Rock* (Graham Greene). A brutal contrast is *Bleak House,* the rotting London tenements of Charles Dickens.

In *War of the Worlds,* H.G. Wells has the martians targeting his town, *'I completely wreck and sack Woking, killing my neighbours in painful and eccentric ways – then proceed via Kingston and Richmond to London, selecting South Kensington for feats of peculiar atrocity.'* John Betjeman is even less kind to what he regards as a horrible new town, *'Come friendly bombs and fall on Slough. It isn't fit for humans now'.*

It is not surprising that others prefer the country, like Washington Irving with *The Legend of Sleepy Hollow* or Henry Thoreau describing his own experiences in *Walden or Life in the woods.*

Nowadays, foreign place names are far more accessible than in Shakespeare's time. *Eyeless in Gaza* (which Aldous Huxley borrowed from Milton's *Samson Agonistes*), *Jamaica Inn* (Daphne Du Maurier), *Our Man in Havana* (Graham Greene) and *Death in Venice* (Thomas Mann) are no longer redolent of the exotic. *Homage to Catalonia* was based on George Orwell's fighting in the Spanish Civil War. *Three Fat Ladies of Antibes* no doubt reflects the locals near Somerset Maughan's house at Cap Ferrat. And then, of course, there are the splendid mythical and allegorical places. The imagination of Jonathan Swift gave us *Gulliver's Travels,* coping with the little people of Lilliput or the mammoth giants of Brobdingnag. *Treasure Island* came from Robert Louis Stephenson, C.S. Lewis was encouraged and influenced by his friend J.R.R. Tolkein when he created *Narnia* and Richard Adams gave us *Watership Down.* And speaking of rabbit holes, thank goodness that Lewis Carroll changed the title of *Alice's Adventures Underground.* Wonderland is what we wanted.

Alice's tea party in Wonderland

Our prize for the finest imaginary place by chance goes to Xanadu in *Kubla Khan,* a poem which Samuel Coleridge wrote, waking from an opium dream. Interrupted by a well-meaning 'person from Porlock', sadly he could not remember another word.

EASTER ISLAND
Pacific Ocean

When the Dutch explorer, Jacob Roggeveen, discovered a strange island, it was Easter Sunday 1722, so he called it 'Easter Island'.

For an inhabited island, it is about as isolated as you can get – 2,500 miles from Chile and Tahiti and 4,300 miles south of Hawaii. The nearest inhabited island, Pitcairn, is over a hundred miles away, where Fletcher Christian and his friends settled after their mutiny on *The Bounty* against Captain Bligh in 1790.

The natives are probably from Polynesian stock, calling the island *Rapa Nui* as it was a bigger version of the Tahitian island, *Rapa.*

But it is the other occupants of Easter Island who have made it famous. These are the *Moai* – huge, brooding, stone, monolithic figures, staring out to sea or watching over the villages. Nobody really knows their purpose, but it is likely that they honour Polynesian gods or ancestors. Most were carved and erected in the 14th and 15th centuries, but some even date back to the 10th century. There are hundreds of them all over the island, with nearly 400 still in their quarry in the volcanic crater of Rano Roraku, where one day the labourers appear to have abruptly stopped work. One explanation is that there were two classes of people – the 'Long Ears' and the 'Short Ears'.

The Long Ears enslaved the Short Ears, whom they forced to carve the giant figures until they rebelled, killing the Long Ears and, of course, ceasing statue carving.

When Thor Heyerdahl, of Kon-Tiki and Aku-Aku fame, found the Moai in 1950, his first question must have been, 'how did these huge statues get to where they were found?' The smallest one weighs several tons and some of the largest are 90 tons.

The Rapa Nui people think it was a magical force called 'Mana', whereby ancient kings simply ordered the figures into place. Others are certain that extra-terrestrial beings achieved it. More likely was a system of sledges, log rollers or skid roads, with the figures levered upright, as may be the case at Stonehenge. They mostly sit on ceremonial platforms called 'Ahu'. Ahu Akiri has seven statues that face towards the point where the sun sets during the equinox. Such astronomical precision makes these giant figures even more mysterious, and has ensured that Easter Island, however remote, has achieved worldwide fame.

See: Skid Row, Stonehenge

EBOLA
Congo

Ebola is a river in the Democratic Republic of Congo (formerly Zaire). It has given its name to one of the most horrific diseases to have been discovered in recent medical history. If the *'heart of darkness'* represented by the perception of the Congo in Stanley and also in Livingstone's era persists today, the concept certainly remains in the shadowy realm of tropical diseases. Few can rival the Ebola virus.

The dreaded Ebola virus, or the 'Ebola Haemorraghic Fever', is defined in the Royal Society of Medicine Dictionary as: *'a highly infectious disease first described among laboratory workers in Marburg, Germany, and occurring later in the Sudan and Zaire. The condition features fever, aching muscles, sore throat, diarrhoea, a widespread rash, bleeding into the bowel, damage to the brain and kidneys, shock, chest pains, and blindness. If untreated, the mortality is likely to be over ninety per cent and even in those patients given good supportive treatment about a quarter will die. All of this will take one to three weeks'.*

To the layman who has ever watched a hospital drama or veterinary 'docusoap', the clue to the nature of this virus lies in the word 'haemorraghic'. Put bluntly – the victim will bleed profusely from virtually every orifice until dead. Combine this horror with unrivalled potential for contagion, and it seems little wonder that Ebola should be ranked alongside Bubonic Plague for instilling fear in the human psyche.

Initially recognised in 1976, it is believed to be native to the rainforests of Africa and Asia, and contracted from contact with wild animals – namely, our closest cousins in the primate world, although there has been some debate suggesting that squirrels, bats, and other small mammals may be also the culprits. By the end of 2000, there were slightly over 1,000 deaths attributed to Ebola.

In 1989 and 1990 a new strain (*Ebola Reston*) was discovered in monkeys in Virginia and Pennsylvania that had been imported from the Philippines. A laboratory worker became infected, but recovered with no adverse affects.

It is a particularly sinister disease in many ways. It has a long infectious incubation and, apart from its sheer speed and extreme aggression, early diagnosis is almost impossible because the signs (rash, itchy eyes, hiccups, sore throat, vomiting), are not specific to the virus. There is no standard treatment except for balancing the patient's fluids, oxygen intake, and blood pressure, and treating any subsequent infections. It is a lonely recovery or a lonely death, because proximity to the dying is so dangerous.

Unfortunately, one of the prime reasons that the outbreaks tend to spread so extensively is the poverty that extends across much of central Africa. In poor hospitals, rodents have easy access to infected excrement, bandages, and even corpses. Also, the danger of uninformed medical workers contaminating both themselves and others is enormous. You almost need spacesuits. Any contact with the body, bodily fluids, or organs of a patient or cadaver can mean infection. Many of the medical facilities where Ebola is present cannot ensure effective quarantine of suspected cases.

The World Health Organisation (WHO) spearheads both research into the virus and education for hospital workers and local people about infection.

There is still an element of mystery to the virus, and a faint glimmer of hope for those that may fall foul of it. Some patients seem to make a miraculous, and full recovery. It is in the physical reaction of this small group that medical science (and the rest of us) places its hopes.

Until a breakthrough is achieved however, Ebola is likely to remain one of the most terrifying diseases in nature's arsenal. It was even recently listed alongside Anthrax, and Sarin gas, as a likely biological threat from terrorism. Thankfully, though, the logistics of attempting to use such a virulent entity as a weapon make a terrorist threat from Ebola the stuff of twisted fantasies. Perhaps, also, the miraculous recoveries documented, and the ongoing efforts of agencies such as the WHO, are what allow us to sleep soundly, as ghastly viruses like Ebola slither about in the darkest depths of our nightmares.

See: Chinchon, Lassa, Panama

The highly contagious nature of Ebola almost demands space suits.

EDEN
Middle East and England

Not all readers will accept what Charles Darwin discovered – and the whole panoply of modern, accepted evolutionary theory – but will instead believe implicitly in the story that the whole world was created by God in six days – as described in Chapter One of the biblical Book of Genesis.

So, taking the story literally, in order to have vegetation quite as lush as that described in the Bible, the Garden of Eden probably lay near large Middle Eastern rivers like the Tigris and Euphrates. We now know that this region was a central part of the cradle of world agriculture in the Middle East, the so-called 'fertile crescent' of crop plant domestication extending from Palestine to Persia. The persuasive snake of the story was perhaps a tree-climbing salamander. After all, only after its transgression was it condemned to crawl on the ground.

The Tree of Knowledge, with its forbidden fruit, was most likely to have been a pomegranate or quince rather than the apple that western society, and all its artists, has envisaged. The hot lowland climate of the Middle East does not suit the apple. Nor is it likely that Adam and Eve would have been white. The pomegranate on the other hand is very heavily imbued with all manner of mystery and association with kingship, the Underworld and fertility ritual. Indeed, its seeds remain a major ingredient of a special cake eaten at Greek Orthodox funerals.

For centuries, people imagined that the biblical Eden might yet exist. Huge double coconuts, reputedly *'fruits of the Tree of Knowledge'*, sometimes washed up on the shores of the Indian Ocean. From there they reached inquisitive people, from Arab potentates to western museum curators. Not just wondrous in size – at up to 50 cm long, and the largest of all fruits – they uncannily resemble the human female pelvic region. We now know

Lucas Cranach the Elder in 1530 portrays the traditional Western view of the Garden of Eden complete with those unlikely apples.

them to be the fruits of Coco-de-mer *(Lodoicea maldivica)*, a palm endemic to the Seychelles.

But there is now another Eden, one that is very real. Entrepreneur and former rock music producer, Tim Smit, turned from his success at the 'Lost Gardens of Heligan' and celebrated the Millennium by establishing a huge new botanic garden in a disused china-clay pit near St Austell, Cornwall. Naturally he named it Eden after

The incredibly successful Eden Project with its gigantic biodomes

the most famous garden ever – and one said to have held all the world's plants. To realise his vision, Smit then assembled a team of experts from the worlds of botany, horticulture and communication,

all dedicated to demonstrating the plant kingdom and the relationship of people and plants to the public, explaining the essential importance of plants in all our lives. At the heart of the Eden Project is a group of gigantic greenhouses landscaped into a clay pit sixty metres deep. Eden divides plants into three groups; an outside temperate garden and two giant geodesic domes, one dedicated to warm temperate zones, the other to the humid tropics. Another dome, dedicated to the world's arid zones, is under construction. The 'biodomes', 50 metres tall, are constructed of hexagonal panels of lightweight transparent polymer.

The project – a brave shot in the dark – has been a runaway success. It has captured the public's imagination and justified over £80 million of investment. Within its first eighteen months the Eden Project had welcomed over two million visitors, and contributed £162 million to the economy of a depressed region. Suddenly botany, a neglected and often forgotten science, is fashionable again: but then it had been waiting for years for somebody with drive and a sense of adventure to apply to botany the dynamic marketing techniques of rock music. The magnificent result is a much needed boost for conservation, biodiversity and sustainable development.

See: Botany Bay, Brazil, Chinchon, Galapagos, Kew, Run, Sissinghurst

EKATERINBURG
Russia

For most people, the Russian city of Ekaterinburg, the centre of the Urals, is not known as the birthplace of Russia's industry, nor the place where Gary Powers' U2 spy plane was shot down in 1960 (deepening the Cold War), nor for it being named in 1721 in honour of Catherine, wife of its founder Czar Peter the Great, nor even as the birthplace of Boris Yeltsin, Russia's President from 1990 to December 1999.

In 1977, it was Yeltsin – then First Secretary of the region who ordered the destruction of the house for which the city is really known. Engineer Ipatyev's house was demolished *'to straighten the*

road', but in reality, because it was attracting too many pilgrims as the place where Czar Nicholas II and his family were murdered in 1918.

Nicholas was a somewhat tragic figure. Since the age of sixteen he had been passionately in love with Alix, Princess of Hesse-Darmstadt, Queen Victoria's grand-daughter, to whom he wrote daily for the rest of his life. When his father died and they were married, he said, 'I am not prepared to be Czar. I never wanted to become one'. As Czarina Alexandra, known as *'the German woman'*, Alix was soon unpopular. Queen Victoria offered gentle advice;

'Every day I think about what I need to do to retain and strengthen the love of my subjects'. The Czarina retorted: 'Here, we do not to need to earn the love of the people. The Russian people revere their Czars as divine beings from whom all charity and fortune derive'.

When their heir, little Alexei, became ill with haemophilia, Alexandra and Nicholas turned in desperation to the help of the dangerous but magnetic 'monk' Rasputin (*'dissolute'* in Russian). During the First World War, with Nicholas away at the front, Alexandra's rule under Rasputin's thrall helped lead to the Russian Revolution. Nicholas was persuaded to abdicate in 1917. Surprisingly for a revolution, the Czar was not killed by the weak interim government of Kerensky. When the Bolsheviks gained power in 1918, they inherited the royal prisoners. Their leaders, Lenin and Trotsky, debated their fate, with Trotsky favouring a trial which would probably have been a mistake. Nicholas, as a rather gentle, religious and reluctant ruler, would have been an object of pity rather than revenge.

There was some intrigue by the Germans, who had smuggled Lenin to Russia, to try to get Nicholas to endorse the Brest-Litovsk Peace Treaty, and even to counter the increasingly dangerous Bolsheviks by reinstating him as Czar. Yankel Sverdlov sent Yakovlev, an emissary, to bring the Czar back from Siberia to Moscow, but their train was stopped at Ekaterinburg by the Ural Regional Soviet. Such local soviets were often a law unto themselves, following Lenin's motto '*Vlast na mestakh*' ('every place its own master'). The royal family was to stay in the Ipatyev house for 78 days.

Soon, counter-revolutionary armies, the White Guards, were approaching the city. In July 1918, hard-line foreign revolutionaries replaced Yakovlev, and the Russian guards - who had begun to admire and respect the dignified Czar and his family, especially his beautiful teenage daughters.

On the night of 16th July, the family and servants were woken and taken into the cellar and quietly lined up as if for a photograph. Eleven strangers suddenly burst in, and the room exploded with gunfire. Some of the bullets apparently ricocheted off the princesses Anastasia,

The Czar and his family were trapped for 78 days at Ekaterinburg.

Tatania and Maria who had sewn hidden diamonds into their clothes. The heir to the throne, Alexei, was lying moaning, but the assassin's leader Yourovsky, soon saw him off. The bodies were thrown down a mine shaft and then explosives were used to try to cover up the crime. Nearby, at Alapayevsk, Grand Duchess Elizabeth and others suffered an identical fate.

The White Guards briefly recaptured Ekaterinburg and investigated the crime, and we know many of the details from Robert Wilton, the dignified and respected correspondent of *The Times*, who escaped with the inquiry's file.

Trotsky justified the killing. 'The execution of the Czar's family was needed not only to frighten, horrify and dishearten the enemy, but also to shake up our own ranks to show there was no turning back, that ahead lay either 'complete victory or ruin'.

For a while, the city was called '*Sverdlovsk*' after the man who had probably ordered the murders, and who, with poetic justice, was himself assassinated by Russian workers.

In 1998, nine bodies of the Royal Family were exhumed, identified by DNA and re-interred in St Petersburg, in a ceremony attended by President Boris Yeltsin. In 2000, the Archbishops' Council of the Russian Orthodox Church canonized Nicholas, Alexandra and the children as '*passion bearers*', a form of sainthood, recognizing their Christian humility and patience in captivity.

There is now a simple cross and grave plate where the '*murder house*' once stood, in a city whose name, by chance, will always be linked to tragedy.

See: Finland Station, Gulag, Katyn Wood, Ladoga, Stalingrad

EL ALAMEIN
Egypt

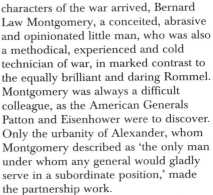

Historians concede that there were three turning points of the Second World War: a city on the Volga called Stalingrad, a Pacific Island called Midway and a railway halt called El Alamein.

By August 1942, Britain had suffered nothing but defeats and losses with Norway, France, Belgium, Holland, Hong Kong, Malaya, Singapore, Burma, Greece and Crete. Her allies, the Russians and Americans, had fared little better. In north Africa, after successes against the Italians, the arrival of the German Afrika Korps and the dynamic Erwin Rommel meant more reverses, and, with the fall of Tobruk, it looked as if Britain could lose Egypt, the Suez Canal and the oilfields of the Middle East. Indeed, military papers were burned in Cairo on the cynically dubbed *'Ash Wednesday'*.

Rommel led from the front, racing across the desert in his command vehicle or flying in his light plane. Often photographed in his captured British goggles, he became a glamorous myth – *'The Desert Fox'*. Even Winston Churchill complimented him in the House of Commons,'We have a very daring and skilful opponent against us, and, may I say across the havoc of war, a great general'.

On 4th August, Winston Churchill himself arrived in Cairo to examine *'the inexplicable inertia of Middle East Command'*. He decided to replace, as the Commander in Chief General Auchinleck, with Sir Harold Alexander, the experienced , steady , aristocratic and charming General, who had commanded in the First War his battalion of the Irish Guards aged 24; had conducted the rearguard at Dunkirk and pulled the British safely out of Burma. His choice for 8th Army commander was General William *'Strafer'* Gott, but within hours, fate intervened. Gott's transport was shot down by fighters under the command of Unteroffizier Hugo Schneider.

So, by strange chance, one of the real

Rommel, 'Desert Fox'

characters of the war arrived, Bernard Law Montgomery, a conceited, abrasive and opinionated little man, who was also a methodical, experienced and cold technician of war, in marked contrast to the equally brilliant and daring Rommel. Montgomery was always a difficult colleague, as the American Generals Patton and Eisenhower were to discover. Only the urbanity of Alexander, whom Montgomery described as 'the only man under whom any general would gladly serve in a subordinate position,' made the partnership work.

Montgomery sat his officers on the sand, and impressed them with a brutal message that there would be no more retreating and no 'bellyaching'. 'I have ordered all plans dealing with further withdrawal be burnt. We will stand and fight here. If we can't stay here alive, then let us stay here dead. Rommel is definitely a nuisance. Therefore we will hit him a crack and finish with him'. He also struck a chord with the fighting soldiers, adopting an Australian bush hat studded with badges of the units he visited, and later, the beret borrowed from his driver. Soon they and the media called him *'Monty'*.

Rommel quickly attacked his new pugnacious opponent on 30th August at Alam el Halfa Ridge, but not quickly enough. Alexander and Monty had used the three weeks to change attitudes and tactics. Now, the British held fast, their dug-in tanks and artillery inflicting heavy losses on the Germans and Italians. Montgomery at once started a seven week intensive training of his army and prepared *'Operation Lightfoot'*, drafting the details himself. 'This is the master plan. Only the master can write it', he said.

Stuck between the sea and the Qattara Depression, an impassable desert , the Battle of El Alamein had to be a frontal assault through 500,000 lethal mines planted in evil sophisticated networks called the 'Devil's Gardens.'

Montgomery envisaged a 'break in' phase with the infantry clearing the mines, an armoured 'dog-fight' phase and then the 'break out'. Refusing to be hurried by the ever-impatient Churchill, Montgomery steadily built up his forces and his supplies. Clever deception helped, with a phoney waterpipe line, tanks disguised as trucks, real tanks replaced by dummies and complete dummy artillery parks with dummy gunners even sitting on dummy latrines. Because Rommel's intelligence predicted the attack would come at the end of November, he felt he could go home on leave to Germany to recover from multiple illnesses. But on the night of 23rd October, a thousand guns in a huge British artillery barrage precisely targeted the Axis lines and the painfully slow advance through the minefields began. For the Germans, bad luck also intervened. Rommel's replacement, General Stumme, fell from his vehicle in an ambush, suffered a heart attack and died. At the critical moment, the Afrika Korps was headless.

Rommel and his wife Lucie were enjoying the fresh mountain air of the Austrian Alps when the news of the offensive came in. At first, Hitler did not wish to shorten the convalescence of his newest and favourite Field Marshal, but within hours Rommel was on his way. *'I have taken command of the Army again. Rommel'* – the signal went to all units on the 25th. But Rommel's presence was no longer a magic wand, and the British continued their methodical advance with both sides losing men and tanks. But Rommel was desperately short of supplies and his too hastily organised counter-attacks failed. He then misjudged where *'Operation Supercharge'*, Montgomery's final phase, would strike.

He had been outwitted and out-fought and with just thirty-five tanks left to him Rommel realised that his position was crumbling. At first, his attempts to extricate himself were blocked by an initial and typical Hitler order: 'as to your troops you can show them no other road but victory or death'. But rain intervened, bogging down the British tanks, and Rommel was able to slip through the net and start a 1,700 mile retreat. In nine days, Montgomery reached Tobruk. He had been made a full General and received a knighthood. Churchill exulted, 'We have a new experience. We have victory, a remarkable and definite victory'.

In fact, the war in the desert was not

over, nor Rommel finished. He would turn savagely on the Americans at the Kasserine Pass. It would take until 12th May 1943 when the Axis was firmly squeezed from both sides for the final surrender to take place. But it was a real turning point. As Churchill recorded, 'Before Alamein we never had a victory. After Alamein we never had a defeat'. At El Alamein, Monty was exactly the right man at the right time.

And, but for that fighter attack of which Hugo Schneider was probably very proud, the world might never have heard of Monty or that little railway halt at El Alamein.

Montgomery at El Alamein

See: Arnhem, Dunkirk, Sedan

The players in the drama of El Alamein had mixed fortunes. Rommel became disillusioned with Hitler and was put in charge of defending France's Atlantic Wall. After the D-Day invasion, he was wounded in an air attack, implicated in the bomb-plot on Hitler and forced to commit suicide, with the Nazis giving him a cynical state funeral.

Alexander continued his partnership with his cocky subordinate. They were visited by King George VI in their desert headquarters. After declaiming how exactly he was going to use *'his'* troops, Monty was called away. Alex apologised to his monarch that neither had been able to get a word in, commenting ruefully, 'I'm afraid he may be after my job.' 'Thank God for that,' replied his Majesty, 'I thought he was after mine!'

'Alex' commanded the long slog up through Italy and became Earl Alexander of Tunis, a much loved and respected figure. One day at the end of the war, outside White's Club in St. James's, a staff car slid to a halt and out stepped the immaculate figure of *'Alex'*, victor of the Italian campaign and acknowledged war hero. Up and down St. James's, officers saluted and men took off their hats. He strode up the steps of White's and disappeared. An American bystander buttonholed the doorman and enquired who the prominent man had been. Puzzled, the doorman replied, 'Oh. That's Lord Caledon's younger brother'. British society and London's clubs certainly have their own sense of hierarchy.

'Monty', after making an enemy of George Patton in Sicily, went on to northern Europe where their rivalry continued, and where his disaster at Arnhem somewhat damaged his reputation. In much later retirement, this unworldly man, Viscount Montgomery of Alamein, insisted to the author's father-in-law that 'all his money was locked in a box in Lloyds Bank in Alton' and, while reading the lesson at Wellington College, added his normal confident views. 'God said to the Israelites, and I have to say I agree with him…'

As Italy's third largest island after Sicily and Sardinia, Elba's early fame was based on minerals - first the granite used to construct much of Rome, and after that iron ore. Over the centuries, it was fought over many times, control of the island passing from the Etruscans to the Romans and, later, to the powerful Italian family of the Medicis. It was so often attacked by pirates that some of its most important towns are sited far from the coast, one fortress even boasting an underground aqueduct to provide water from four miles away in order to resist sieges.

A later claim to fame was the rather unlikely subject of canaries - the result of a Spanish shipwreck in 1550 which released birds of both sexes, breaking a curious monopoly created by the Spanish to corner the canary market by only ever selling male birds!

In 1814 the English frigate *Undaunted* delivered a visitor who was to propel the island on to the world stage, no less than Napoleon Bonaparte. He had been forced to abdicate because Paris had fallen to the armies of England, Prussia, Austria and Russia, and the French themselves were exhausted by years of war. At the Treaty of Fontainebleau, Napoleon was exiled to Elba with a small staff and a financial allowance. Ironically, this imprisonment was so lenient that he was even made the Governor of the entire island.

Typically, instead of sulking, he threw himself into improving the poverty of Elba, starting by making it agriculturally self-sufficient. He paved the streets and installed lighting and even discovered a

Napoleon, once the ruler of an Empire of 120 départements, found himself restricted to a sub-prefecture of one department.

See: Berezina, Trafalgar, Waterloo

sparkling water source. But his spirits were brought down by the death of his friend and former Empress, Josephine, before she could visit him, and also the brief secret visit of his former lover Marie Walewska and their son Alexandre. But his mother and sister Pauline joined him which helped his morale, until the real blow fell when his wife and Empress, Marie Louise did not visit him and, pushed by her Austrian Royal Family, broke off all contact.

Meanwhile the French Government failed to pay his annuity as laid down by the Treaty and he was now in the red. By the winter he was deeply unhappy, but was visited secretly in February 1815 by a messenger in disguise – who told Napoleon that public opinion was clamouring for his return. It did not take long for him to reach a decision. When his principal guard, Neil Campbell, was away he prepared the brig *Inconstant* and six smaller ships and told his mother his plans. 'Paris! Per San Cristino! You are doing the right thing. Better to die sword in hand than in an unworthy retirement.'

Napoleon landed in Antibes, Louis XVIII fled, Paris was retaken and Napoleon, with his peace overtures rejected, elected to strike quickly at his enemies, marching into Belgium, where he would literally 'meet his Waterloo.'

The '100 days' which elapsed between Napoleon slipping away from Elba and his final defeat and exile to St Helena were certainly nerve racking for Europe and the world and ensured that the little island would never be forgotten.

Napoleon's little empire for ten months

ELLIS ISLAND
New York, USA

Nearly half of all the 250 million Americans owe their presence in the United States to a small island in the middle of New York harbour, Ellis Island.

'Give me your tired, your poor, your huddled masses yearning to breathe free, the wretched refuse of your teeming shore. Send these, the homeless, tempest-tossed, to me: I lift my lamp beside the golden door'. These were the words of the poet Emma Lazarus, engraved on the base of the Statue of Liberty, that welcomed the millions of immigrants who sought a new and much better life in the United States.

Ellis Island was originally called 'Oyster Island' by the early Dutch colonists and then given the more sinister name of 'Gibbet Island' because of the practice of hanging criminals there during the 1700s. A New York merchant, Samuel Ellis, acquired the island and, in 1808, the state of New York bought Ellis Island from his family for $10,000.

More and more people in poor and strife-torn Europe began to think of America as a golden land of opportunity. Perhaps learning from the chaotic and unexpected horrors of the Irish 'Famine Ships' arriving in the 1840s, the authorities became relatively well organised. But by 1890, Castle Garden, the original immigration station on the tip of Manhattan at the Battery, was no longer adequate to process the mass of immigrants pouring into New York, and so the House Committee of Immigration took over Ellis Island.

The Immigration Station opened on 1st January 1892, with dormitories, a hospital, kitchens, a baggage station, an electrical plant, and a bath house – and the accommodation needed for large numbers of immigration and naturalisation officers, interpreters, guards, clerks, cooks, doctors and nurses. To create enough room for this massive organisation, the original island was expanded with earth and rock from the digging of New York's subway system and the massive underground Grand Central Station.

Six years earlier, on nearby Bedloe Island, the magnificent Statue of Liberty had been erected, donated by the people of France. The symbolism of the two islands became interwoven, with the Statue of Liberty visually welcoming the immigrants, and Ellis Island processing them with comparative efficiency and lack of corruption.

When the immigrants arrived off New York, both first and second class passengers were inspected on board ship and went on into Manhattan. It was only the 'steerage' passengers, paying the lowest fares, who had to go to Ellis Island to be processed. On board ship, they had to answer a series of 29 carefully crafted questions.

With the ships anchored at the entrance to the Lower Bay of New York Harbour, passengers were examined for contagious diseases like smallpox, yellow fever, scarlet fever and measles. The ships went on to Manhattan, and the steerage passengers, in trepidation, were then transferred to Ellis Island on special ferries. Unknown to them, they were being monitored as they climbed to the second floor of the station for any signs of lameness, shortness of breath, heart condition or mental problems. Once they had passed the further medical

127

The beautifully restored buildings on Ellis Island are now a major tourist attraction.

being detained or deported. It took between two to five hours before the happy and successful immigrants were on their way to their new life.

This processing did not cease until the end of 1954, with over twenty million immigrants having passed through Ellis Island, the peak year of nearly a million being in 1907. In 1982, President Reagan asked Lee Iacocca, Chairman of Chrysler, to raise $230 million to restore the Statue of Liberty and Ellis Island. This was a task close to Iacocca's heart because his own Italian father and mother had entered America through Ellis Island in 1902.

Both Liberty and Ellis Island are now popular tourist attractions and fitting monuments to the remarkable way, unique in history, in which a great new nation was forged from the refugees of the Old World.

examinations, including the dreaded 'eyelid lift' to check for trachoma, they were questioned against the 29 items of information that they had already completed the manifest. Remarkably, 98 per cent passed the test, the remainder

See: Ballingarry, Bauhaus, Bedloe's Island, Big Apple, Cumberland Road, Getto, Harlem, Manhattan, Tammany Hall, Triangle Shirtwaist Company

ELM STREET
United States

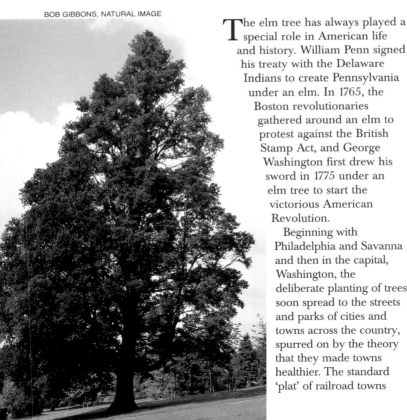

The elm tree has always played a special role in American life and history. William Penn signed his treaty with the Delaware Indians to create Pennsylvania under an elm. In 1765, the Boston revolutionaries gathered around an elm to protest against the British Stamp Act, and George Washington first drew his sword in 1775 under an elm tree to start the victorious American Revolution.

Beginning with Philadelphia and Savanna and then in the capital, Washington, the deliberate planting of trees soon spread to the streets and parks of cities and towns across the country, spurred on by the theory that they made towns healthier. The standard 'plat' of railroad towns

shows Walnut, Hickory, Oak, Chestnut, Poplar and Ash Streets. But, above all, there was an Elm Street.

The American Elm (*Ulmus americania*) proved the most popular urban tree – fast-growing, providing excellent shade, thriving in poor soil, resistant to urban smog, equally at home in icy winters and hot summers. So familiar was Elm Street that when the evil Freddie Kruger appeared in 1984 to star in seven *Nightmare on Elm Street* horror movies, we all knew that he was stalking everyone's small town America.

Sadly, a real nightmare did come to Elm Street. In the 1940s, America's elms mysteriously started to turn yellow, then brown, and finally die. Elm logs on railroad cars imported from France in order to make furniture in Ohio had unfortunately imported something else, a tiny beetle bearing a deadly fungus, *Ceratocystis ulmi,* which we now call Dutch Elm Disease. Forty years later nearly 77 million trees were dead, half of all American elms. Formerly beautiful shady avenues had disappeared and parks were bare, a tragic situation also mirrored across Europe.

Botanical researchers have been working for twenty five years to create elm hybrids like 'Valley Forge' and 'New Harmony', which may be resistant to the disease. Gradually the elm may return and 'Elm Street' in thousands of communities may one day mean something again.

See: Brazil

EL NIÑO
Pacific Ocean

Every few years something happens to the world's weather which turns familiar patterns upside down and as a result can wreak major havoc. Storms and floods occur in California and Central America, ice storms in Canada, snowstorms in Mexico, forest fires in Australia and Indonesia, flash floods in Peru, Ecuador and East Africa, and even the failure of the vital monsoon in India.

First meteorologists and now the general public have learned to call these years the 'years of El Niño'. The name was first coined by Peruvian fishermen, noticing unusually warm water around Christmas time. 'El Niño' (The Child) personifies the baby Jesus.

The strange phenomenon is caused by a periodic change in the east to west trade winds which normally pile up warm water in the Western Pacific, so allowing cold water from the deep to rise off South America. When the winds change, the warm water moves east, blocking the cold water from rising. This does not sound too serious, however calculations show that the heat change is massive. It would take 400,000 hydrogen bombs to have the same heating effect, or 1,500,000 power plants working for eight months.

El Niño years occur regularly but randomly, and can increase or decrease

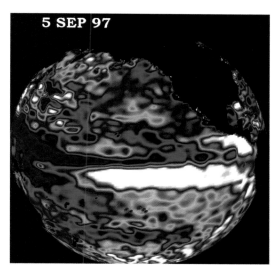

Satellite thermal imaging clearly shows the band of warm water off Peru during El Niño.

the effects of other climate changes, like the fluctuation of anchovy and sardine stocks. Research into corals and sediment indicate that it has been going on for two million years. Historians have even focused on the way battles have been won and lost during El Niño years, and how the Moche civilisation of Peru was destroyed.

Studying and predicting El Niño has become an important branch of science. Hardly surprising. El Niño's effects can be very expensive and life threatening. The more we know, the better.

EMPIRE STATE BUILDING
New York, USA

When John Jacob Rascob, creator of General Motors, first asked his friends to invest in 'the biggest skyscraper in the world', the going was easy. Confidence was high and there was plenty of money about. But when the site was cleared, demolishing the original Waldorf Astoria Hotel at 350 Fifth Avenue, he could not know that it was just one month before the 1929 Wall Street crash.

Despite the crash and the Depression that followed, Rascob bravely pressed on. Amazingly, the Empire State Building took only one year and forty five days to build, thanks to remarkable

planning co-ordination, delivery of materials and the warmest winter on record in New York City.

Rascob was obsessed by another building under construction a few blocks away, his rival Walter Chrysler's Art Deco, 77 floor Chrysler Building.

He therefore insisted on increasing the Empire State's height to 86 storeys, topped by a dirigible mooring mast to make sure his building really was the tallest.

President Hoover opened the magnificent tower on May 1st 1931, but even with rock bottom rental prices there were not enough tenants, so it was soon unfortunately known as 'The Empty State Building'. In the Depression, it remained a major statement of confidence in the future, and its income was boosted by the thousands of visitors who came to marvel at its size, amenities and, above all, its magnificent views of the city. Only in 1941 was it fully occupied.

This very American landmark is also famous for reasons other than its 1,454 ft height. In 1945, an Army Air Corps B-25 twin-engined bomber crashed into the 79th floor at 200 mph in thick fog. Sadly, 14 people were killed and dozens injured. A million dollars' worth of re-construction was needed, but no structural damage occurred and the building survived.

The Empire State Building's fame has also been constantly reinforced by its starring role in films, from Cary Grant waiting for Deborah Kerr in *An Affair to Remember* to Tom Hanks meeting Meg Ryan for the first time in *Sleepless in Seattle,* and a model of the building was used in the 1933 film, *King Kong,* when the giant ape clings to the top of the skyscraper while beating off fighter planes. In fact many New York movies, whether or not they are actually filmed in the city, include the Empire State Building in their establishing shot. Lovers can imitate famous films, because the Empire State Building holds Valentine's Day weddings. What's more, there is so much static electricity at the top during cold winter weather that couples who kiss may find their lips crackling with electric sparks!

Since the terrorist destruction of the World Trade Center, the Empire State Building is once more the tallest building in New York. It represents an incredible achievement of construction, character, elegance and hope.

See: Great Hedge of India, Great Wall of China, World Trade Center

ENTEBBE
Uganda

To the sentry, the sight of the black Mercedes driving out of the inky darkness escorted by two Landrovers, was interpreted as President Idi Amin coming back to visit the hostages. It was an understandable, but fatal mistake.

Entebbe in June 1976 was an obscure small town, its international airport building a reminder that only a few years before it had been the capital of Uganda. Now, it was to be the scene of one of the most daring rescues in history.

The drama started in Athens where a young woman and three young men, recently arrived from Bahrain, boarded Air France 139, stopping off at Athens on the flight from Israel to Paris. Eight minutes after take off, the four took over the aircraft with its 246 passengers at gunpoint, and forced it to land at Benghazi in Libya. Here, it took on fuel and then, surprisingly, flew south. With 77 Israelis and many Jewish tourists on board, it was a nightmare scenario for the Israeli Government.

The plane landed at Entebbe, and it rapidly became plain that Idi Amin was an accomplice in the hijacking. A murderous and unpredictable dictator, he had expelled all Israelis from Uganda when Israel had understandably refused to lend him some Phantom jets to bomb Kenya and Tanzania in 1972. But, by chance, an Israeli contractor had built Entebbe airport. The terminal's old blueprints were to prove extremely useful.

The hijackers, members of The Popular Front for the Liberation of

Palestine, demanded that 53 terrorists must be released from European jails or they would start executing the hostages. They then released the non-Jewish passengers who were flown to France, where they provided vital detailed information of what was to come. The Israelis had decided to pretend to

negotiate, while actively planning to mount a 2,500 mile rescue attempt. While 'friendly' calls were being made to Idi Amin to lull him into a false sense of security, 200 hand-picked men were assembling. Seven aircraft were to be

used, four C-130 Hercules and a reserve, plus two Boeing 707s as command and hospital aircraft. A white Mercedes was borrowed from a Tel Aviv car dealer and quickly painted black to resemble Idi Amin's car. The plan was presented to an astonished Israeli cabinet, who voted for it even as the planes were on their way.

In spite of storms, the rescuers arrived at night at Entebbe after 7 hours, 40 minutes – just 30 seconds off the planned schedule. The Mercedes duly rolled down the ramp and towards the terminals. The ruse worked. The terrorists, confused, were all shot within seconds, together with any of the Uganda soldiers who resisted. Two hostages were killed, and Lt Col Yoni Netanyahu, the commander, was the only tragic military casualty. When the planes took off to safety, it had taken just 58 minutes to pull off this amazing and successful rescue, one that associated Entebbe forever with extraordinary bravery and daring.

Above: Ugandan dictator, Idi Amin, was an accomplice to the hijacking.

Left: Yoni Netanyahu, hero of Entebbe, and the only Israeli soldier killed

See: Anne Frank's Annexe, Dachau, Dawson's Field, Getto, King David Hotel, Lockerbie, Wannsee, World Trade Center

ETON
England

'The battle of Waterloo was won on the playing fields of Eton' avowed the Duke of Wellington after his famous victory. Few such monumental events have been attributed by an old boy to the sterling qualities that his school produced.

George Orwell was more cynical when he wrote, *'Probably the battle of Waterloo was won on the playing fields of Eton, but the opening battles of all subsequent wars have been lost there!'*

In spite of such carping about the intelligence of Old Etonians, the fact is that Eton College is easily the most famous school in the world. In Britain, some people may recognise its rivals, Harrow (Winston Churchill's school), Rugby (probably for the football game it invented), perhaps Winchester – and not many more. In America, people might know the name Eton but probably think of Marlborough as a cigarette! Some of the world's universities are well-known

internationally: Oxford, Cambridge, Yale, Harvard, Princeton, plus military colleges like West Point, St Cyr and Sandhurst – but how many of us could name a single American, French, German, Spanish or Italian school, any more than the bulk of their own citizens could?

The roll call of Old Etonians has perpetuated its fame; more Prime Ministers have come from Eton than all

'A Gallant Gentleman' by JG Dollman depicts Oates' famous self-sacrifice.

The dress code for top public schools could cause embarrassment to even the most self-confident. These pupils are, in fact, Harrovians outside the Eton-Harrow cricket match in the 1930s.

other schools put together, among them Pitt, Walpole, Canning, Gladstone, Salisbury, Balfour, Eden, Macmillan and Douglas-Home. 'Might have been' Prime Ministers would include Lord Randolph Churchill, Curzon, Hugh Dalton, Charles James Fox, Lord Halifax, Quintin Hogg, Jo Grimond, Jeremy Thorpe and Jonathan Aitken.

Nobody could accuse Etonians of lack of courage. No less than 37 have won the Victoria Cross, Britain's highest award for gallantry, from Lord Roberts (and his son) to Colonel 'H' Jones in the Falklands. In fact, no greater example of selfless courage can be imagined than Old Etonian Captain Lawrence Oates saying to Scott in the Antarctic, '*I am just going outside and may be some time,*' sacrificing himself by stumbling out of their tent into the blizzard to his death.

Examples of sheer daring abound, from racing driver and aviator The Honourable Charles Rolls (of Rolls-Royce fame) and explorer Sir Ranulph Twisleton-Wykeham

Fiennes, to World Landspeed Record holders John Cobb and Sir Henry Segrave, who then died trying to beat the world record on water. And, of course, many royal pupils have come and gone, from the King of Nepal (and his old Etonian son who killed him), to Prince William and Prince Harry. Old Etonians number actors, television presenters and jazz men, but there is no greater tribute to the 'brand' of Eton than the way it features in fiction – with, for example, James Bond, Lord Greystoke of *Tarzan*, Captain Hook in *Peter Pan*, Lord Peter Wimsey and Bertie Wooster.

Yet this fame of elitism happened by chance, because 'The King's College of Our Lady of Eton' was never meant for the rich and privileged, but was set up by Henry VI in 1440 with a provost, ten priests, four clerks, six choristers, twenty five poor grammar scholars and twenty five poor men (bedesmen) from Eton, called 'Oppidans' from the Latin *'Oppidum'* for town. Much has changed, but the school is still divided between 'collegers' (scholars) and 'Oppidans', who compete in a strange form of football called 'The Wall Game', which has not seen a goal scored since Harold Macmillan played before World War I. A series of scrums takes place against the 118 yard long wall, and 'sneaking' (offside), 'furking' (passing back), and 'knuckling (hand twisting) are forbidden.

No other school has copied the arcane and baffling 'Wall Game', nor Eton's unique 'Field Game', a mixture of football and rugby. But they have taken up 'Eton Fives' (a hand ball game rather like the French 'Jeu de Paume'), which started with Etonians hitting a ball against the buttresses of College Chapel in the School Yard.

In the past, Eton had enough other strange customs to fill a book, many now obsolete. Wearing top hats, black tails and stiff collars; carrying unrolled 'gamps' (umbrellas), with rolled umbrellas only allowed by members of 'Pop', a self-elected group of Prefects with their colourful waistcoats; walking only on one side of Eton High Street; raising a finger to the 'beaks' (masters) as if doffing an imaginary top hat; always carrying books under one arm with the other hand in the pocket; always putting free hands in pockets; being a 'Dry Bob' or a 'Wet Bob' depending on chosen sports; the boys

being beaten by the Library (house prefects) with canes from Trumper's, the barber; and shouting 'BoyeeUP', the 'fag-call' or cry that would summon the 'fags' – the younger boys who acted as semi-servants to older ones – the last to arrive being given whatever tedious task was required. (Beatings are no longer allowed and fagging was ended twenty years ago.)

As a final claim to fame, Eton is the only school with its own rousing and instantly recognisable song, *'The Eton Boating Song'*. This reflects the school's skill in rowing, and its long history of providing many of the crew members of the world-famous Oxford and Cambridge Boat Race.

> *Jolly boating weather*
> *And a hay harvest breeze*
> *Blade on the feather*
> *Shade off the trees*
> *Swing, swing together*
> *With your back between your knees*
> *Swing, swing together*
> *With your back between your knees.*
> *Skirting past the rushes*
> *Ruffling o'er the weeds*

> *Where the back stream gushes*
> *Where the cygnet feeds*
> *Let us see how the wine flushes*
> *At supper on Boverney meads*
> *Let us see how the wine flushes*
> *At supper on Boverney meads'.*

For a sporting song it is, thus far, charmingly uncompetitive. But Verse 6 gives us a hint at the unique spirit which explains why, even with fees of £17,500 a year, this most famous and largest public school shows no signs of faltering, and will no doubt continue to provide generations of successful men with the unmistakable aura of being 'Old Etonians'.

> *'Harrow may be more clever*
> *Rugby may make more row*
> *But we'll row, row for ever*
> *Steady from stroke to bow*
> *And nothing in life shall sever*
> *The chain that is round us now*
> *And nothing in life shall sever*
> *The chain that is round us now'.*

See: Rugby, Stowe

MOUNT EVEREST
Nepal

Of course, the highest mountain in the world could never have remained obscure for long. But its name was decided in controversy. Called 'Chomolungma' by the local Nepalese and just Peak XV by the British, it was eventually named after Colonel Sir George Everest, who, in 1830, had started his vast 'Great Trigonometrical Survey' of India, which had identified that the peak was the highest in the world. Everest must be regarded as one of history's great surveyors, improving the theodolite and other measuring equipment. His forays included four elephants, 30 horses for the officers, 42 camels and 700 labourers. It is far from certain that Everest ever personally saw the famous peak, but his Surveyor General successor, Andrew Waugh, who had discovered its actual height, determined that he should be honoured, in spite of Everest's own personal objections which he voiced at the Royal Geographical Society in 1857.

Once found, Mount Everest attracted mountaineers. In 1923, George Mallory was asked by an American reporter why he wanted to climb Everest. 'Because it's there', was his immortal reply. Sadly, Mallory *was* mortal, dying the following year 2,000 feet from the summit. His body was not found until 1999, seventy six years later.

After many failed expeditions, it took until 1953 before the summit was reached by New Zealander, Edmund Hillary and the experienced Sherpa, Tenzing Norgay. 'Well, we knocked the bastard off', exclaimed Hillary.

Many have made it since. The first American in 1963, the first woman in 1975, Mallory's grandson in 1995, and in 2001, the youngest (at 16) the oldest (at 64) and the first blind climber.

Everest could not complain that he was forgotten, but he might want us to pronounce him correctly. 'Eve–rest' is what he preferred.

See: Ayers Rock

133

FARNBOROUGH
England

'See you at Farnborough?' This is the question asked by everyone in the aerospace industry around the world, just as anyone in films might say 'See you at Cannes?'

Farnborough is a small town near Aldershot, south-west of London, and just as Aldershot is known as the 'Home of the British Army', so Farnborough is the 'Home of British military aviation'.

It all started in 1862, when Lieutenant George Edward Grover, Royal Engineers, began investigating balloons for military purposes, thus deserving the name as the 'Father of British Military Aviation.' The Royal Engineers dominated those early years under a general rule that any piece of kit more complicated than a spade or a bicycle was their responsibility. (They even had special spades, listed as 'shovels', that no-one else was allowed to use). Similarly, anything you could shoot with, but not pick up, went to the Royal Artillery. This system prevails to this day.

With a grant of £150 from the War Office – the very first Air Estimate – the first military balloon in Britain was designed and built by Captain James Lethbridge Brooke Templer, an imposing and experienced balloon owner in the Militia. The Balloon Factory was created at Farnborough in 1905, and from 1906 an American (later a naturalised Englishman), 'Colonel' Samuel F. Cody, experimented successfully with man-lifting kites, which could be flown in winds too strong for balloons. Cody then fitted engines to his kites, and on 5th October 1908, made the first officially recognised flight in Britain with a heavier-than-air machine in Britain.

The establishment now split; the Balloon Section became successively the Air Battalion, then the Royal Flying Corps and finally, on 1st April, 1918, the Royal Air Force. The Balloon Factory became the Royal Aircraft Factory and in June, 1918, to avoid confusion of initials with the Royal Air Force, the Royal Aircraft Establishment.

In the First World War, the RAE designed a series of rather inferior aircraft for the RFC, until in 1916 it was told to stop and concentrate on research. Ironically, its last design was the highly successful SE5A fighter.

Like all Government establishments, Farnborough suffered in the interwar years from retrenchment, the Depression and bureaucratic neglect. But it did become a research and investigative body that, by the 1930s, had an international reputation and served the RAF and various Ministries brilliantly in the Second World War.

After the Second World War, one of Farnborough's most important tasks became that of accident investigation, first publicly known with its work on the mysterious crashes that ruined the chances of Britain's world-beating jet airliner, 'Comet'. Subsequent cases, large or small, civil or military, were undertaken by Farnborough's Air Accident Investigation Branch of the Ministry of Transport, now renowned world-wide for its expertise. Its most famous case has been than of 'the Lockerbie Bombing' of the Pan American Boeing 747. In 1988 the aircraft blew up eight miles up, and wreckage, some of it minute, was scattered over a huge area. AAIB collected enough to reconstruct almost the whole front end of the 747, and presented a complete and unexpected explanation of the origin of the explosion, a bomb in the baggage compartment.

It was at Farnborough that the world was first presented with Concorde.

While Farnborough has had a long and distinguished history, to the public and the aerospace world it is 'The Air Show'. Once an annual, purely British event, now international, and embracing every form of aviation, it shares this top spot on alternate years with Paris.

As with most major air shows, there have been accidents at Farnborough. In 1968, an 'Atlantique' cartwheeled unbelievably slowly into the RAE area, following an engine problem; the same year the Basingstoke Canal burst its banks after torrential rain, putting one end of the runway under two feet of water. The gap was plugged with an old 'Dove' fuselage filched from the Fire Section, and runway clearance involved the removal of a lot of fish. But only once, in 1952, have spectators been killed at a Farnborough Air Show.

In 1984, one accident turned into sheer comedy. De Havilland Canada had passed a note to John Blake, the commentator, that 'when the Buffalo arrives, it stops the show!' It did.

Blake told the audience 'I want you to watch this landing, it's going to be spectacular'. It was. The plane pancaked, disintegrated, the wings and the engines fell off and the embarrassed crew walked away. Removing the remains, the hookman for the mobile crane shouted to his mate, 'Do you want a wing or a leg?'

See: Biggin Hill, Cape Canaveral, Kitty Hawk, Lakehurst, Lockerbie, Sea of Tranquillity, Peenemünde

FATIMA
Portugal

At the height of the horrors of the First World War, Fatima was a tiny village north of Lisbon. Yet, like Lourdes in France, it was to be transformed by religious apparitions. In early summer 1916, Lucia dos Santos (10) and her cousins Francisco (8) and Jacinto Marto (7) were tending sheep when a vision of a dazzling young man appeared, telling them that he was the Angel of Peace. He appeared again in late summer and in the autumn. The children kept quiet.

But on 13th May 1917, in a pasture called Cova da Iria, there were two flashes and they looked up to see a lady clothed in white, bathing them in bright light. 'Do not be afraid, I will not harm you', she said. Lucia asked her where she came from and the lady pointed to the sky, saying: 'I come from Heaven, I ask you to come here for six months on the 13th day of the month, at this same hour. Later I shall say who I am and what I desire. And I shall return here yet a seventh time'. The Lady finished with a request, 'Say the Rosary every day, to bring peace to the world and the end of the War.' Then she rose into the air and disappeared.

The children tried to think of sacrifices as the lady had asked, resolving to go without lunch and to pray the Full Rosary. One month later, they were followed to the pasture by about fifty sceptical locals who had heard of the apparitions. Once again, there was a flash of light and the vision of Mary appeared, ominously saying that Jacinta and Francisco 'would go to Heaven soon', but that 'Lucia would stay on earth longer' and asking them to return on July 13th. The witnesses reported the apparition, ensuring that on the due date the awaiting crowd now numbered thousands. The vision said, 'I want you to come here on the 13th of next month, to continue to pray the Rosary every day in honour of Our Lady of the Rosary, in order to obtain peace for the world and the end of the War, because only she can help you'. Lucia later revealed that Mary then showed her a horrifying picture of Hell. Mary's exhortations, the *'Secret of Fatima'*, were only announced in 1942.

By August everyone in Portugal knew about Fatima, as the secular press had mocked the apparitions. On the 13th the children were kidnapped by the local Mayor and interrogated about the 'Secret'. Despite his threats and promises of money, they refused to divulge it. In the afternoon they were moved to prison and threatened with death, but said they would die rather than reveal the 'Secret.' The Mayor's action only postponed the August visitation by six days.

On September 13th huge crowds arrived in Fatima. The children had made many sacrifices, praying for hours without food or water. The figure of Mary promised a miracle when she next returned.

This provoked a satirical article in the anti-religious newspaper *O Seculo*, with the result that tens of thousands of pilgrims congregated on October 13th. The vision said, 'I want to tell you that a chapel is to be built here in my honour. The War is going to end, and the soldiers will soon return home'. Then a miracle appeared to occur. *O Seculo* now changed its reporting: *'One could see the immense multitude turn towards the sun. It looked like a plaque of dull silver and it was possible to look at it without the least discomfort. It might have been just an eclipse which was taking place. But a great shout went up and one could hear the spectators shouting: 'A miracle! A miracle!' The sun 'danced' according to the typical expression of the people'.*

See: Lourdes

The movement of the sun was seen by people for miles, ruling out mass hysteria at Fatima. As the War was finishing, Jacinta and Francisco died of the influenza epidemic which swept Europe. Lucia moved from Fatima and became a Carmelite nun, seeing two more apparitions in 1925 and 1929.

Lucia's memoirs contain predictions by Mary, including the end of World War I, the start of World War II, and the rise of atheism in Russia. Six Popes have proclaimed their belief in Fatima, and John Paul II has gone further, crediting 'Our Lady of Fatima' for predicting his 1981 attempted assassination and saving his life. Fatima was truly an unknown place made famous by unknown forces.

FINLAND STATION
Russia

Ever since the first locomotive steamed along pulling its very first passengers, railway stations have played a special role in our lives. They can be magnificent edifices like New York's Grand Central or Washington's Union Station, Paris Gard du Nord or Milan's Stazione Centrale. And they can be beautiful enough to convert into art galleries like the Musée D'Orsay in Paris. Sadly, they can be famous for accidents. They can feature in song – as in Glenn Miller's *Chattanooga Choo Choo* – and star in innumerable farewells, with Noel Coward's *Brief Encounter* probably being the most poignant. For more than a century, all over the world, the station has often been the most important building in town.

But there is one station that is not only famous in its own country, but should be in the rest of the world – St Petersburg's Finland Station.

One evening in 1917, a passenger arrived who was to change the world; Vladimir Illyich Lenin. As Winston Churchill later wrote, *'The Germans turned upon Russia the most grisly of all weapons. They transported Lenin in a sealed truck like a plague bacillus from Switzerland to Russia'.* The German General Staff had indeed organised the journey from Switzerland to make sure Russia was removed from the war, since Germany desperately needed to confine its war efforts to the Western Front. They little knew what destructive forces they were unleashing.

Russia's disastrous handling of the war had led to starvation and revolution. Czar Nicholas II abdicated on 16th March and handed over power to a Provisional Government led by Alexander Kerensky. It was a month later that Lenin's train arrived at Finland Station. He was anxious about his reception, but faithful Bolsheviks had created a huge demonstration of support for him and Lenin made several fiery speeches, one from the top of an armoured car. 'Dear comrades, soldiers, sailors and workers. I am happy to greet, in you, the victorious Russian Revolution!'

But all did not go smoothly. The Bolsheviks' attempted coup in July failed,

forcing Lenin to hide and then leave again for Finland. However in October he was back, riding in disguise on the footplate of locomotive No. 293. This time there was absolutely no mistake, and the October Revolution swept the Bolsheviks into power. The Czar's old Winter Palace was duly stormed and Kerensky's ministers resigned at gunpoint. A bitter, long Civil War began to resist the Bolsheviks. The Czar and his family were butchered at Ekaterinburg to avoid them becoming a powerful focus of resistance, and Lenin began his own reign of terror against the aristocracy and bourgeoisie. As his colleague Zinoniev exclaimed, 'The capitalists killed individuals. We kill whole classes!' Stalin watched and waited.

By December, the Bolsheviks had enough power for the Germans to obtain their peace. Unfortunately, the Russians, and the world, now also had the curse of Communism which Lenin would try to export and which would cast its blight for another seventy years. Lenin himself revealed his hand, 'It is true that liberty is precious – so precious it must be rationed.'

St Petersburg was renamed Leningrad to honour the part it played in the Revolution. It would also endure the most horrific siege in history during World War II.

Locomotive 293 is now preserved at Finland Station. However it could be argued that both this locomotive and the sealed train have a great deal to answer for.

See: Ekaterinburg, Gulag, Ladoga

LAURENCE McDONNELL

Locomotive 293, still preserved at Finland Station

FLATFORD MILL
England

In 1810 it would have been difficult to get to Flatford. The village lies a few miles west of Manningtree on the Suffolk-Essex border. Roads were poor, and the railway had not even been invented, let alone reached rural Suffolk. Yet this tiny place was to influence art all over Europe.

Flatford Mill was owned by a prosperous corn merchant and miller, Golding Constable, who transported his flour to London by barge, Flatford being conveniently situated in Dedham Vale on the lower reaches of the winding River Stour. When his son John went to work there, the locals called him the 'handsome miller'. But his real love was art, inflamed by the local, simple, rustic beauty of his surroundings, and we remember John Constable (1776–1837), as perhaps England's greatest landscape artist. As he himself observed: 'The sound of water escaping from mill-dams, etc., willows, old rotten planks, slimy posts, and brickwork, I love such things…These scenes made me a painter, and I am grateful'.

Later in London, at the Royal Academy, Constable studied relentlessly and carefully, above all looking to the landscapes of Claude Lorraine and Gainsborough. Determined not to *'learn the truth second-hand'*, the locality of Flatford enabled him to bring to life humble but beautiful surroundings and *'to make something out of nothing'*. Above all, again and again, he returned to the haunting inspiration of his childhood, the river and its water-mills and locks, peopled by figures going about their everyday life, especially boys fishing – himself when young.

John Constable's superb 'The Haywain', with the horses resting at the ford created by Flatford's millrace

Flatford Mill today

From 1810 Constable made a series of oil studies of these scenes. His painting *Flatford Mill (Scene on a Navigable River)* of 1816-17 marks the end of the period when Constable painted directly from nature. He then moved to London where he composed in the studio, but always with his heart on his native River Stour.

After many paintings of Flatford, Constable went on to complete his two most famous works, *The Cottage in the Cornfield* and *The Haywain,* wonderful idylls of English rustic life. This last, dating from 1824, is extremely English and yet also had an enormous impact on the development of 19th century art in France, where it was exhibited to great acclaim. For Constable was not yet popular in England, 'struggling with fame and famine', and making so little money

See: Arles, Barbizon, Giverny, Moulin Rouge

that for years he was not able to afford to marry his beloved Maria Bicknell. However, he certainly influenced French painters – especially Géricault, Delacroix, Stendhal and Thiers – and was admired by the Barbizon school and the Impressionists who followed.

Constable had a lofty objective: *'To increase the interest for, and promote the study of, the rural scenery of England with all its endearing associations, its amenities and even its most simple localities, abounding as it does in grandeur and every description of pastoral beauty'.* He was to succeed. Flatford lies at the heart of a stretch of countryside that is forever 'Constable Country'. Most aptly, the Field Studies Council today both owns and runs a beautifully preserved Flatford Mill as a Field Study Centre to teach people from many walks of life about all aspects of the English countryside, its traditions and wildlife.

The world can thank the little village of Flatford for helping John Constable to achieve his aim, and for the lucky chance he was born there amid such beauty.

FLEET STREET
England

Among great cities, London is unique in the way that it has world-famous streets renowned for just one activity. If you are 'off to Harley Street', we know you are a doctor or you have a medical problem. If it's 'Savile Row', it will be for a fine suit of clothes. When you hear 'Whitehall thinks…' it is, of course, code for the Government. For five hundred years 'Fleet Street' meant the press – and still does – even if the last newspapers were scattered to the four winds fifteen years ago, and the street's journalists, printing presses, taverns and coffee houses are already a distant memory.

Fleet Street was named after the small River Fleet which ran into the Thames, but became an open sewer and was then covered over by what is now Farringdon Street. Fleet Street's future as the centre of the newspaper industry was guaranteed by its strategic location running between the Law Courts and the seat of financial power, the City of London. William Caxton may have pioneered printing, but he was over in Westminster serving Church and State.

It was his assistant, Wynkyn de Worde, who set up near St Bride's Church, who was to found the newspaper industry.

The potential power and dangers of the printing press were very quickly recognised by the authorities. For two hundred years the King's Printer at Blackfriars was 'to instruct the nation in its duty and to scotch wild rumours'. But as a trading nation, Britain needed commercial news which was provided by business news sheets smuggled in from Amsterdam and Cologne. Soon translations appeared as in *The Courant* or *Weekly News*, first sold on the steps of St Paul's Cathedral in 1621.

Soon, many news sheets were available but were abruptly suppressed in 1632, to be replaced by a curious Royal Monopoly. The struggles between King and Parliament led to the first press war. *Mercurius Aulicus* or *Court Journal* was matched by *Mercurius Britannicus,* the *People's Paper,* sold by 'Mercury women'. The Restoration under Charles II and James II saw continued repression of the media with the Surveyor of the Press,

'Well, we had a good talk'.
Dr Samuel Johnson

'Yes, Sir. You tossed and gored several persons!'
James Boswell

the fanatical Roger L'Estrange, clamping down because news 'makes the multitude too familiar with the actions and counsels of their superiors and gives them not only an itch but a kind of colourful right to be meddling with the Government'. One printer, John Twyn, was arrested by L'Estrange and duly executed, and his head displayed as an example against sedition.

After the Great Fire of 1666, Fleet Street's influence increased. Its taverns and coffee houses were now filled with famous characters: Daniel Defoe, Editor of *The Review* and, of course, author of *Robinson Crusoe,* Benjamin Franklin, American journalist, scientist and statesman and the mentor of the revolutionary philosopher Tom Paine, whose enemy, William Cobbett, wrote *Rural Rides*; Dr Samuel Johnson, writer,

Dr Samuel Johnson

By that time, advertising had become significant and shorthand had transformed reporting, even of Parliament.

By 1800, *The Times* was a powerful organ, obtaining its information about the Battle of Trafalgar in 1805 days before the Government, who then had to beg *The Times* for news of the Battle of Dresden in 1813. Soon the paper would be called *'The Thunderer'* and would, through William Howard Russell, expose the incompetences of the Crimean War.

Huge press empires would arise; Northcliffe, Astor, Beaverbrook and Kemsley were the 'press lords' of a Fleet Street described as *'a street of hasty judgement, of distorted truth, of elastic morality, of easy conviction'.* Sadly, the street was also a hotbed of industrial unrest, with ridiculous over-manning of the printing process, frequent strikes, refusal to accept new technology, lost production and angry advertisers.

It was to be Fleet Street's downfall. In 1986, Rupert Murdoch moved out with *The Times, Sunday Times, News of the World* and *The Sun,* to his new technology 'factory' at Wapping, from where for months his trucks had to brave a siege of picketing printers. Fuelled with finance from the sale of their Fleet Street properties and, fortuitously, their shares in Reuters, all the others were then to follow, including *The Daily Telegraph,* to the Isle of Dogs. In November 1989, the very last newspaper, a copy of the *Daily Express,* came off a Fleet Street press.

The Wig and Pen, El Vino and Ye Olde Cheshire Cheese are all still very much there, but empty now of journalists. But we still persist in calling the British media 'Fleet Street'.

See: Harley Street, Mainz, Savile Row

critic and creator of the first English dictionary; and his friend and biographer James Boswell. Voltaire, escaping the Bastille by coming to England, wrote in his *Letters on the English* of the Fleet Street tavern, the Saracen's Head: *'Here, the Jew, the Mohametan and the Christian deal with each other as if they were of the same religion. They reserve the word 'infidel' for those who go bankrupt'.*

FORD'S THEATRE
Washington D.C., USA

Ford's Theatre

A play in three acts

The Cast

The President: Abraham Lincoln
The Assassin: John Wilkes Booth
The Wife: Mary Todd Lincoln
Conspirators: Dr. Mudd
John Surratt
Mary Surratt
Lewis Thorton Powell
David Herold
George Atzerodt
The Witness: William T. Kent
Extras: A theatre full of people

Background:

By the time the action begins at the end of the Civil War, Booth, a former actor, is in league with his fellow Confederate conspirators, and has already made an attempt to abduct the President and trade him with thousands of Southern prisoners. Having failed, he resolves to assassinate Lincoln while he watches the popular play *'Our American Cousin'* in Ford's Theatre.

Act 1:

Time: 10:15, April 14th 1865

Setting:
Ford's Theatre, Washington D.C.

(Developed by theatre entrepreneur John T. Ford, in the place of the First Baptist Church, as a music hall. Originally called 'Ford's Athenaeum', it was destroyed in a fire, only to be replaced by Ford's 'New Theatre' in August 1863. (It is in this second theatre that this production is set.)

Synopsis:
While the audience laughs at the comedy, John Wilkes Booth bursts into the presidential box, and shoots Abraham Lincoln with a single-shot Derringer

pistol. Before his wife or guests are able to react, and before the audience is even able to work out what is going on, Booth leaps dramatically from the box onto the stage shouting 'Sic semper tyrannis' ('Thus always to tyrants'). On the way down, he is to catch his spur on a banner, fracturing a bone in his leg. The scene ends with William T. Kent, a man who will later testify against Booth, discovering the gun.

Act 2

Time: *7:22 AM, April 15th, 1865*

Setting:
The Peterson boarding house, across the road from Ford's theatre, where the doctor has taken the mortally wounded President.

Synopsis:
Abraham Lincoln is taking his final breaths. The doctor is unable to help him (indeed, that is why he brought him here, rather than to a hospital), and his weeping wife watches the last glints of life leave his eyes. The President is dead; Booth's single bullet had gouged a mortal wound. *'That dreadful house!'*, sobs Mrs Lincoln.

Act 3

Time:
A few days later, April 26th, 1865

Setting:
A tobacco shed in Port Royal, Virginia777

Synopsis:
John Wilkes Booth and co-conspirator David Herold are trapped in the shed, surrounded by pursuing Union troops. David Herold sees the futility of the situation and surrenders. In the final scene, we see Booth go down fighting, refusing to leave even though the building was burning, and is finally shot dead.

Epilogue:
Many of the other conspirators, Atzerodt, Herold, Powell, Surratt were sentenced to

death, and the rest were condemned to life imprisonment. As for Ford's Theatre, troops were called to stop angry mobs from setting fire to it. The theatre was soon closed, and after subsequent attempts to re-open were met with threatening letters, it was closed for good.

In 1932 it was re-opened as a the Lincoln Museum, and contains artefacts such as the Derringer pistol and the clothes the President wore on that fateful night.

Curtain

See: Andersonville, Appomattox, Arlington, Ballingarry, Charleston, Gallipoli, Gettysburg, Hampton Roads, Harpers Ferry, Little Big Horn, Somme, Waterloo, West Point

FORT KNOX
Kentucky, USA

All in all, the phrase 'as safe as Fort Knox' has proved a reality. In spite of films like James Bond's *Goldfinger*, none of the gold stored there has ever been stolen.

Named after General Henry Knox, a former Secretary of War, there are actually two military camps called Fort Knox. One is in Maine, but it is the one in Kentucky which the world knows, though not for its training centre for armoured forces nor its Patton Museum. It was the decision to move America's gold reserves to a really safe place which has made Fort Knox famous.
The US Mint built the United States

Bullion Depository in 1936. The two storey building is built of 16,000 cubic feet of granite, 4,200 cubic yards of concrete, 670 tons of structured steel and 750 tons of hardened reinforcing steel. Its huge vault door weighs more than 20 tons, and it requires several people to dial in separate parts of the combination in order to open it. Modern and secret security systems abound, and the guards even have a practise pistol range in the basement.

The gold is stored in bars the size of a small brick each weighing 27.5 pounds, and with a statutory value of $16,888. For several years there have been

after the attack on Pearl Harbor and was 649 million ounces.

The security of Fort Knox has meant that other things, perhaps more precious than gold, have also been stored there: America's Declaration of Independence; the US Constitution; Lincoln's Gettysburg Address and Britain's Magna Carta; together with the Crown Jewels of several European nations.

One of the reasons for the success of Fort Knox is undoubtedly its secrecy. Absolutely no visitors are allowed. Only two Presidents have entered its doors, Roosevelt and Truman, and it requires a Presidential Order to obtain permission to visit. In an age of perhaps too much 'openness' and 'transparency' and with some very clever criminals and terrorists around, it sounds a very sensible policy.

147,300,000 ounces stored, worth – at book value – $42.22 an ounce; $6 billion. However, the real value at the current price of gold (of $300 per ounce) is $44 billion. The largest store was just

FORT SUMTER
South Carolina, USA

It was a chance decision by Major Robert Anderson that ensured that we know the name of Fort Sumter.

After a festive Christmas dinner with his unsuspecting friends on the night of 26th December 1860, Anderson moved his little body of United States soldiers quietly by boat from indefensible Fort Moultrie to the empty but powerful Fort Sumter, dominating the mouth of Charleston harbour. What he did not realise was that he had inadvertently broken an informal agreement between the State of South Carolina which, only six days before, had broken away in secession from the Union and President Buchanan of the United States. Indeed, Commissioners from the State were in Washington at that very time to try and reach an amicable solution to the question of the forts.

As soon as Fort Sumter was occupied, feelings ran very high in Charleston, and two officers from the State, Colonel Pettigrew and Major Capers, visited Anderson to remonstrate

Major Robert Anderson

that he had 'altered the status of the harbour' and demanding he return to Fort Moultrie. Anderson, whilst revealing his sympathies 'were actually with the South,' chose duty and declined.

Fast becoming a hero in the North, Major Anderson then began to strengthen Fort Sumter as best he could, with his nine officers, 63 artillery men, 8 musicians, 6 headquarters and hospital staff and 40 labourers. But when the paddle steamer *Star of the West* tried to bring him supplies and troops, she was fired upon by heavy guns now sited at Morris Island and Fort Moultrie and turned back. Anderson did not return fire, but protested in writing to South Carolina's Governor Pickens. A two month truce lasted while the United States waited for its new President, Abraham Lincoln. Fort Sumter was prepared, while the State raised 10 regiments of troops and installed guns in the surrounding forts and islands.

After the secession of more and more States, Confederate General Pierre Beauregard arrived in March 1861 to try to resolve the issue. He wrote to Anderson in the politest of terms: *'...I am ordered by the government of the*

Confederate States to demand the evacuation of Fort Sumter. All proper facilities will be afforded for the removal of yourself and command, together with company arms and property, and all private property, to any post in the United States which you may select. The flag which you have upheld so long and with so much fortitude, under the most trying circumstances, may be saluted by you on taking it down'.

Anderson responded with the same measured courtesy. This was not really surprising – at West Point, Beauregard had been his star artillery pupil and then his assistant.

'...General: I have the honour to acknowledge the receipt of your communication demanding the evacuation of this fort, and to say, in reply thereto, that it is a demand with which I regret that my sense of honour, and of my obligations to my government, prevent my compliance. Thanking you for the fair, manly and courteous terms proposed, and for the high compliment paid me'.

A month after Abraham Lincoln's inauguration, as President, the attitude of the United States stiffened and a small relieving fleet arrived off Charleston. This precipitated open hostilities on 12th April. At 4.30 in the morning darkness, a large mortar shell, trailing its fiery fuse like a prophetic meteor, roared across the harbour and burst above the fort. It was the shot that began the American Civil War. For thirty four hours, guns and mortars pounded Fort Sumter, with Charleston's citizens cheering the guns and even the bravery of the defenders. Swamped by shot and shell, and knowing he had little food, Anderson was forced to surrender. Throughout, both sides exhibited gentlemanly behaviour and, when Major Anderson and his men were evacuated, thousands of Confederate troops lined the shore,

silent and bareheaded. Even more ironic, the first and only fatalities of the whole engagement were two US artillery men killed by a cannon discharging prematurely when Anderson fired a salute as his colour was hauled down.

Sadly, his men were the first of over 600,000 American fellow countrymen killed in a brutal and tragic war that pitted friends, colleagues and even family members against each other.

Sam Houston, Governor of Texas, had desperately tried to warn his follow Southerners, *'Let me tell you what is coming. Your fathers and husbands, your sons and brothers will be herded at the point of the bayonet. You may, after the sacrifice of countless millions of treasure and hundreds of thousands of lives, as a bare possibility, win Southern independence. But I doubt it'.* It is ironic that Confederate officers were encouraged to read Victor Hugo's *Les Miserables*.

Fort Sumter provided a human footnote. There were two convicted Irish patriots (and friends) who had escaped from British exile in Australia. Thomas Meagher became a Union General leading the brilliant Irish Brigade, nearly wiped out in several horrific battles. His friend John Mitchel, however, supported the South and edited its patriotic newspapers. One of his sons died at Pickett's Charge at Gettysburg, the other had fired one of the first shots at Fort Sumter and, three years later, now in command of its Confederate garrison, was killed after an eleven-month siege by virtually the last shell to be fired.

As for Robert Anderson, on 14th April 1865, on the fourth anniversary of his surrender of Fort Sumter, he returned and hauled up its flagpole the now ragged banner that his pupil General Beauregard had generously let him keep. *'I thank God that I have lived to see this day'.*

Fort Sumter, today restored and preserved

See: Alamo, Andersonville, Appomattox Court House, Arlington, Ballingarry, Charleston, Gettysburg, Hampton Roads, Harpers Ferry

143

FOURTEENTH STREET BRIDGE
Washington D.C., USA

On January 13th 1982, the author was involved in a takeover of GELICO, a Washington insurance company by the British insurance giant Legal & General. Two of the American executives, Joe Albert and Tony Shell were heartily annoyed to have had to postpone their Air Florida flight for their nice sales trip to sunny Fort Lauderdale because they had to talk to us 'visiting Brits'. But they were lucky. We saved their lives.

By four in the afternoon the blizzard was so bad that we stopped work and struggled through foot-thick snow to our hotel. Minutes later the live television pictures of the fate of Air Florida flight 90 transfixed us.

The ice and snow at Washington's National Airport

The snowstorm had also sent many hundreds of others home early and the roads and bridges of Washington were gridlocked. National Airport was blanketed by snow and the take-off of Flight 90 bound for Fort Lauderdale had been repeatedly delayed. At 1.40pm, the airport was closed to plough the runway, but Flight 90 continued to board its passengers. At 3pm, Captain Larry Wheaton requested de-icing and the spraying continued until 3.10pm, with a light 'dusting of snow' left on the wings. At 3.23pm, the Boeing 737 tried to leave the gate but the tug failed to pull it out. The Captain then used reverse thrust (this contrary to guidelines), but only succeeded in forcing

storm debris into the engines, where it stayed. Another tug pulled the plane back at 3.38 and it joined the queue to take off, attempting to de-ice itself with the exhaust heat of the DC-9 ahead of it. It was probably another big mistake, because ice formed on the leading wing edges, blocking the engine's probes. The worst mistake was that the engine de-icers were never switched on.

At 3.58pm, flight 90 began to roll, but it was obvious something was wrong. with First Officer Roger Pettit four times raising his concern. He was right; the engines were only providing seventy per cent of the power indicated and required. After forty five (instead of thirty) agonising seconds and 5,400 feet of runway (instead of the normal 3,400), the plane staggered into the air, but the stall warning *'stick shaker'* started at once. The whole plane began to shake, and the passengers now knew that there was trouble.

'Come on, forward, forward! Just hardly climb', begged Wheaton, but instead the plane began to fall, and tail downwards.

'Stalling, we're falling'.

'Larry, we're going down, Larry'.

'I know it'.

Out of the darkness and the snow, the plane hit the stalled traffic on Fourteenth Street Bridge, killing four motorists (one of whom was the lawyer who had completed our insurance deal). The aircraft then sank through the thick ice on the Potomac River until only its tail was left above the water, and we watched the television

drama of the frantic attempts to rescue a handful of survivors emerging from the rear door.

A brave onlooker, Lenny Skutnic, plunged into the icy water to save one drowning passenger, while a hovering Parks Police helicopter passed down a lifeline to others clinging to the tail and wreckage. One really selfless passenger repeatedly passed on the helicopter cable to others, but when it came to his turn he had gone. To mark his bravery, the bridge has now been named after him, the Arland D. Williams Jr Memorial Bridge.

Many of us have sat stalled on bridges full of commuters, cursing the weather and the traffic. But we don't really expect a huge great shape to thunder out of the swirling snow and make the bridge famous forever.

A helicopter trying to rescue survivors from the icy Potomac River

FRAY BENTOS
Uruguay

For generations of British homes, especially during the rationed years after World War II, the words 'Fray Bentos' meant tins of corned beef. If they had thought much about the brand's origin, they would probably have imagined it was from Argentina, and perhaps from a Mr Fray and a Mr Bentos.

They would not have been too far off the mark. The town of Fray Bentos is in Uruguay, Argentina's neighbour, and named after a Friar Bentos, a religious hermit. Its first meat-packaging plant was built in 1861, and the port now handles a large proportion of the products of Uruguay's huge livestock industry.

Brand names emerge in all sorts of ways. Place names like Fray Bentos abound – Gouda cheese, Waterford and Steuben glass, Chantilly lace, Evian water and most malt whiskies. Often, the founder's name is perpetuated, as in Wedgwood china, cigarettes from Philip Morris, Alfred Dunhill, Benson and Hedges, Pullman cars, Winchester rifles, Rolls-Royce, Chrysler and Guinness. They can be disguised – Trebor is Robert backwards – or Tesco, which came from T.E. Stockwell and Jack

Cohen, its founder in 1929.

Sometimes, it's the ingredient – like coca in Coca Cola. Often, it is because they just sound classy. One wonders how many Marlboro smokers think of the town in Wiltshire, let alone the victor of the Battle of Blenheim.

At least Fray Bentos sounds quite acceptable to foreign markets. Sadly, companies are still not paying attention to the translation of their brand names abroad. 'Nova' for a car sounds, in Spanish, like 'No Va' – 'it does not go'. Japanese soft drink 'Poccari Sweat' does not sound too appetising in English and while 'Pschitt' may sound fine in France ....

See: Bath, Bournville, Champagne, Cognac, Gorgonzola, Hamburg, Hershey, Nuits-St-George, Pilsen, Run, Spa, Vichy

GALÁPAGOS ISLANDS
Pacific Ocean

It was an extraordinary series of factors which was to make Charles Darwin and the Galápagos Islands famous. The Captain of the *Beagle*, the ten gun brig destined to make a great voyage of discovery, was Robert Fitzroy, a mere twenty-three years old when he took over from a Captain who had suffered a mental breakdown and shot himself. Fitzroy was also the nephew of Viscount Castlereagh, famous for his subtle restructuring of Europe at the Congress of Vienna, but even more for his duel when he wounded his bitter rival George Canning. Castlereagh, too, had suffered from depression – and despite the best efforts of his friends George IV and the Duke of Wellington to hide all weapons, had stabbed himself to death in 1822.

Fitzroy had already appointed an official naturalist for the voyage, Robert McCormack, the ship's surgeon. What he did not have was a mealtime companion of his own class; rather, the prospect of being condemned by Navy tradition to dine alone for five long years,

Some of the species that intrigued Darwin are still there today.

DAVID BLACKSHAW

and the worry that perhaps inherited melancholy would get to him as it had to his beloved uncle. Thus, he was to ask John Henslow, a Cambridge botanist, who cleverly suggested his aristocratic 21 year old student, Charles Darwin, in his place. The journey was filled with new discoveries,

one of the most important of which was seeing land rise out of the sea during an earthquake. This confirmed for Darwin Charles Lyell's view of the world as a constantly changing environment. Although nowhere near his theory of evolution yet, this was an important step. Then, in 1836, the *Beagle* reached the isolated Galápagos Archipelago. The creatures discovered there astonished Darwin, for they were both unique and diverse. Many of the animals and plants looked similar to those he had seen in South America, but they were not exactly the same. In fact, he would later find out that many species which lived in the islands – the giant tortoises, marine iguanas, cacti and finches – were all unique to the Galápagos. Darwin believed that this endemic diversity had the potential to *'undermine the stability of species'.*

However, the full impact of what had been discovered out on the archipelago was not yet obvious. *The Beagle* returned to England in 1837, and Darwin then began to analyse his findings. Ornithologist John Gould informed him that the finches that he had discovered there were not only unique, but also specifically tailored to their environment. Darwin was very close to formulating his theories on exactly how such species adapted, but the final piece of the puzzle was sparked by a fellow scientist, Malthus. With the current plight of the English poor, locked in workhouses, Malthus' theories that human populations always outstrip the food supply were extremely topical. This finally led Darwin to one of his most important theories, that of *'natural selection',* the idea that the number of creatures being born in any environment will usually be too high for them all to be supported by the local food supply; therefore many must always starve. As he would later write, *'Many more individuals of each species are born than can possibly survive'.*

Any variation, like greater strength or

a differently shaped beak, that helps a creature to compete with its peers increases its chance of surviving, and crucially, of breeding. Thus, its genetic material can be passed on, and after a huge number of generations that animal's advantageous adaptation may have become universal among its fellows. Darwin had hit upon the theory of evolution, although at this time he was calling it *'descent with modification'*; rather less appealing. The isolation of the Galápagos Islands seemed to support his theory. The animals and plants there had become thoroughly individual – almost all of them different to mainland equivalents – and they had all evolved to survive life on the Archipelago.

Darwin's radical hypothesis was not to have a smooth course. For one thing, he knew just how radical the idea was, and how likely it was to be refuted by scholars. There was also the fact that his evolutionary model included humans, suggesting their descent from primates, providing a threat to the powerful forces of the church and the Bible's version of Creation. Evolution disagreed with the very cornerstone belief preached by Christianity that the world and every living thing was created by God in six days. *Man in his arrogance thinks himself a great work, worthy of the interposition of a deity. It is more humble and I think truer to consider him created from animals'*.

Thus, he hid the full force of his discoveries and ideas from the world. Married to Emma Wedgwood, daughter of Josiah Wedgwood, the troubled Darwin disappeared into the Kent countryside, beset by worries about the trauma that his theories could bring him. In fact, the extent of his nerves began to make him ill and depressed, but all the while he was quietly studying. He became interested by pigeon breeding,

seeing how this process of artificial selection worked in a similar, accelerated fashion to the natural selection that he had come to understand. As he became more confident, he began his magnum opus, *Natural Selection*.

However, he had almost delayed too long. Alfred Russell Wallace, a specimen collector, had been on an expedition to the Malay Archipelago, and was now formulating a very similar evolutionary theory. If Wallace had ended up as the more famous and influential of the two scientists, then Galápagos may have never acquired any sort of renown. However, Darwin abandoned his larger work, and began a much shorter one to be able to keep pace with Wallace. In the end, both their papers were read out together to the astonished Linnean Biological Society on 1st July 1858. Darwin, increasingly a recluse, stayed away from the actual reading, but his impact was felt. Darwin quickly published *On the Origin of Species* the next year, which explained his ideas in more detail. The theory of evolution had arrived.

As for poor Robert Fitzroy, his fears were only too well-founded. After a brilliant career as the 'father of meteorology' (the weather area of Finisterre has recently become 'Fitzroy' in his honour) he did succumb to depression and killed himself in 1867.

One writer, the prominent botanist, Stephen Jay Gould, has speculated that if Canning had killed Castlereagh in their duel, Castlereagh would never had committed suicide, and Fitzroy would not have worried about his own mental stability and would not therefore have taken Darwin on his voyage. And so the world might never have heard of Charles Darwin, his revolutionary theories or the Galápagos Islands.

Seven years after his return to England, Darwin wrote to his friend Joseph Hooker, later Director of Kew; 14th January 1844: *'I am almost convinced, (quite contrary to the opinion I started with) that species are not (it is like confessing a murder) immutable. I think I have found out (here's presumption!) the simple way by which species become exquisitely adapted to various ends'.*
Thus Hooker heard about natural selection 14 years before the rest of the world.

Charles Darwin in old age

See: Botany Bay, Brazil, Chihuahua, Chinchón, Easter Island, Eden, Kew, Loch Ness, Run

GALLIPOLI
Turkey

Books, films, TV documentaries and the poetry of World War I usually emphasize the Western Front in France and Flanders. People often forget that Britain and her allies were also at war with Turkey. However, most will have heard of Gallipoli, recalling a 1915 battle

against the Turks that has come to symbolize tragic military failure and human loss.

The Gallipoli peninsula, a long, narrow hilly promontory, extends south-west into the Aegean Sea from European Turkey. It is separated from Asiatic

Turkey by the narrow channel known as the Dardanelles, an historic seaway of great strategic importance as the approach to Istanbul, formerly Constantinople, and the Bosphorus, the only entrance to the Black Sea. In 1915, Britain's First Lord of the Admiralty, Winston Churchill, initiated a bold plan to land troops, seize the peninsula, take a fleet up the channel and knock Turkey out of the war, hopefully to be followed by the collapse of Germany and her central European allies. It was a huge gamble and, sadly, it failed. Instead of ensuring a rapid end to the European war, the campaign ended in stalemate, heavy casualties and the eventual evacuation of the landing force.

Mustapha Kemal, later named 'Ataturk', the innovative ruler of Turkey. His statues can still be seen in every Turkish town, and his image in all public buildings and nearly every home.

Alas for Churchill's grand design, Gallipoli was held by a strong Turkish army, with German officers and, above all, a supremely able and courageous commander, Mustapha Kemal. The Turks – experienced, resilient fighters of high morale, held the high ground and, anticipating the landings, had defended the beaches with mines, barbed wire, entrenched riflemen and artillery, including batteries of heavy guns on the Asiatic shore of the Dardanelles. An unsuccessful attempt in March to sail a naval force up the strait had warned the Turks that an invasion might be imminent.

On 25th April, Empire and French forces landed in strength at Cape Hellas and further north, on Anzac Cove, after the Division of the Australian and New Zealand Army Corps (ANZAC) which fought there. The Allies established beachheads in the face of stiff resistance and heavy casualties, making a slow and bloody advance inland over the next few weeks. Gallipoli was always going to be, at the very least, a close run thing. In those days there were no landing craft: soldiers reached the beach from transport ships via small lighters. Deeply entrenched Turkish positions on high ground overlooked and dominated the beaches. Dense spiny scrub covered a harsh landscape where water was scarce, and the fighting took place during the fierce heat of the Mediterranean spring and summer. Stalemate was inevitable. Indeed it is hard to avoid the argument

that both sides used soldiers as cannon fodder without thought for losses.

On 6th August, the Allies carried out new assaults from Cape Hellas and Anzac Cove. The fanatical resistance of the Turks in the face of both offensives led to fearsome, week-long, hand-to-hand combat – stones, sticks, and fists when ammunition ran out – in which few prisoners were taken. Poet John Masefield, who witnessed the fighting, compared the action to the appalling carnage of the British storming of Badajoz in Spain during the Napoleonic Wars of a century earlier. As weary ANZAC soldiers struggled towards their final objectives, three strongly held hilltops, they could see and hear furious fighting at Suvla Bay, three miles away. Over 30,000 men were landing against yet more stiff Turkish opposition in an attempt to break the military deadlock.

By mid-August it was clear that the Allies would not take the Dardanelles. Both sides settled into trenches and dugouts for a slow war of attrition while dysentery and other illness caused as many casualties as shot and shell. In November, the decision was taken to evacuate. In the Balkans, the central powers had crushed Serbia and the fading Gallipoli campaign was no longer going to shorten the war. A storm on 26th-28th November was the last straw. Trenches flooded and blizzards and bitter cold followed the rain. Frostbite added to the misery of the soldiers. In early December, ships took off the troops from Anzac Cove and Suvla Bay, somehow slipping away without drawing Turkish fire. The last exhausted men left Cape Hellas on 9th January 1916.

Australia and New Zealand still commemorate 25th April as 'Anzac Day'. Although the ANZAC casualties were not as great as those of the British and Irish, they were strongly felt in these two young countries with small populations; the Gallipoli experience weakened affection for the 'Old Country' and helped build strong national consciences for the two nations. Australians and New Zealanders continued to serve the British Empire with great courage and loyalty, especially during World War II, but the link has gradually been lost and the sense of loss and grievance after Gallipoli led indirectly to today's strong republican movement in these two countries.

Gallipoli witnessed much valour and sacrifice on both sides. Australians have never forgotten 'the man with the donkey', John Simpson, an Englishman enrolled in the Australian Army's 3rd Field Ambulance Corps. For the first three weeks of the campaign, day and night, he sought out wounded men and, placing them on the patient shoulders of Duffy (aka Abdul), a stray donkey he had found, he carried them to relative safety at the field hospitals. On 19th May a Turkish bullet found its mark and he died with a shot through the heart.

The most prominent hero of Gallipoli, Mustapha Kemal, was himself the stuff of legend. At one point, as he rallied exhausted men whose ammunition was spent, a bullet hit his chest – but a silver cigarette-case absorbed most of the impact. Just as well, for he went on to command the army that in 1922 drove the invading Greeks out of Turkey. A man of enormous energy and vision, he

is best remembered as Kemal Ataturk, founder of the modern secular state of Turkey. Moving the nation's capital to Ankara, he reformed a backward country, giving women the vote, and dragging the remains of the Ottoman Empire into the twentieth century.

An Australian soldier carries a wounded comrade at the battle of Gallipoli.

See: Angora, Ararat, Maeander, Navarino, Somme, Topkapi, Versailles

GENERAL POST OFFICE
Dublin, Ireland

Most people would associate post offices with mundane things like stamps, parcels and pensions – not drama and conflict. But for 24 hours, one post office filled the headlines and changed a country forever.

Ireland's General Post Office dominates O'Connell Street, the broad principal thoroughfare of the capital, a 19th century classical building built on a grand scale with a portico of massive classical columns. Now the bullet holes have been filled in, it is hard to believe that in April 1916 this grandiose building and Sackville Street (as O'Connell Street was then called) witnessed furious fighting between Irish nationalist insurgents and the British Army. Less a heroic rebellion, more an episode of comi-tragic confusion, the Easter Rising nevertheless proved to be the pivotal moment that created the modern nation of Ireland.

The Rising took place under cover of 'manoeuvres' by the Citizen Army and the Irish Volunteers. For years the British authorities had stood aside as these armed and uniformed men had drilled, just as the 'loyalist' Ulster Volunteers drilled in the north. The Government was apprehensive, but felt matters were under control, especially as Parliament had passed a Home Rule Act in 1914 – to be invoked once the presumably short war with Germany had ended. The nationalist cause lacked broad popular support, and indeed hundreds of thousands of Irishmen were fighting loyally for the British Empire in a World War *'for the freedom of small nations'.* Yet the previous week the Royal Navy had apprehended the *Aud*, a merchant ship packed with German arms headed towards the coast of south-west Ireland. Soon after, prominent nationalist leader Sir Roger Casement was arrested as he landed from a German submarine on Banna Strand, Co. Kerry, ironically to stop the Rising. The military felt the crisis had passed, as the worried leader of the Volunteers, Eoin MacNeill, placed a notice in *The Sunday Independent* to cancel the Easter manoeuvres. The stage was set for failure.

However, plans were too far advanced to halt, and few saw or heeded the warning. Thus, the Rising proceeded as planned, a force of some 1,200 men and women from the Volunteers and Citizens Army seizing prominent strong points from which to pin down military barracks and hold off reinforcements. These included the Four Courts (the law courts on the quays of the River Liffey), Jacobs' biscuit factory and Boland's Flour Mills, the latter to guard canal crossings against troops arriving from the port of Kingstown to the south. The

schoolmaster, read out a proclamation to a somewhat bemused crowd. *'Irishmen and Irishwomen'*, he announced, *'In the name of God and of the dead generations from which she receives her old tradition of nationhood, Ireland through us summons her children to her flag and strikes for freedom...'* Lancers and their mounts, trotting down Sackville Street, were among the first casualties, apparently unaware of the danger.

Once the British had recovered their composure and poured in 30,000 reinforcements an armed cordon slowly tightened around the city centre. The army brought in artillery, with fire directed from the roof of (loyal) Trinity College, and an armed fishery protection vessel on the Liffey also bombarded the G.P.O. and other strong points. By Thursday thousands of soldiers were able to concentrate on the Post Office with machine-guns and artillery. On Friday, the insurgents tunnelled out from the burning building and set up positions in nearby houses. By the early afternoon of the Saturday, they had surrendered. 62 rebels were dead, along with 256 civilians and 116 soldiers and 2,600 were injured. Whole streets had been destroyed.

'The GPO 1916', reproduced by kind permission of Thomas Ryan RHA

General Post Office was to be the headquarters of the Rising.

Up until the last moment, the British did not suspect a thing. It was Easter Monday, the Fairyhouse Races were on and only about 400 soldiers were on duty. At the G.P.O., armed men suddenly expelled the staff and customers and took over the building, barricading the windows and preparing to resist attack.

Padraig Pearse, impressively styled 'Commandant-General and President of the Provisional Government of the Irish Republic', and formerly a patriotic

Initially, the feeling among many Dubliners was that these men were at best misguided, at worst ruffians and blackguards. However, over the next few days, with monumental stupidity, General Maxwell began summarily to court martial and then, day by day, to shoot by firing squad the sixteen leaders of the Rising. James Connolly – hit, ironically, by a marksman from the 3rd Royal Irish Regiment – was too badly wounded to stand up and was shot strapped to a chair. Joseph Plunkett was executed just ten minutes after being married to his fiancée. *'It was like watching a stream of blood coming from beneath a closed door'*. The British Cabinet began to protest, but it was too late. A wave of revulsion gradually translated into fervent nationalism and in the memorable words of Ireland's greatest poet, romantic nationalist W.B. Yeats, *'All changed, changed utterly. A terrible beauty is born'*. Fighting began in earnest early in 1919, when Dan Breen fired the first shots in an explosives raid in Tipperary.

After four years of fighting, killing and repression, in 1922 one of the survivors of the Rising, Michael Collins, helped to negotiate the Irish Free State. Another survivor, Eamon de Valera, fought a tragic Civil War to repudiate the compromise partition of Ireland, the results of which live with us to this day.

The General Post Office is still the principal post office of Dublin. It remains an icon of Irish nationalism, the Rising commemorated inside by a fine

statue of Cúchulainn, legendary Irish hero of Iron Age times – and on Saturday mornings Republicans sell newspapers and political tracts by the great columns of the portico. For Pearse's proclamation at the G.P.O. was indeed the fuse that lit the powder keg of the Irish War of Independence. A few hundred metres away, where there is now a fountain and statue representing the River Liffey ('Floosie in the Jacuzzi' to ever-irreverent Dubliners), once stood another 19th century classical structure – Nelson's Pillar, a Hibernian version of the more famous London monument. In 1966, a bomb demolished the pillar – prefacing a new and grimmer chapter in Ireland's long road to full independence.

See: Bael na Blath, Ballingarry, The Bogside, River Boyne, Buck's Club

GETHSEMANE
Israel

'One is closer to God in a garden than anywhere else on earth'.

The very word 'garden' conjures up an image of tranquillity. It can be a source of admiration as in *The Hanging Gardens of Babylon,* one of the 'Eight Wonders of the Ancient World'.

A garden, as at the Royal Horticultural Society at Kew, can be a source of worldwide knowledge and conservation. It can be an inspiration, as with Monet's garden at Giverny, with its water lily ponds. It can be mythical with Adam and Eve being led astray in the Garden of Eden by a serpent. But Gethsemane, where Jesus spent his last moments of freedom, is real enough, a place of drama and betrayal.

'Gethsemani' is a slightly Hellenized version of two Hebrew words *gath* (press) and *shemanim* (oils). Olives and olive oil were vital elements in the economy of the whole region, and the 'Oils Press' was close to the Kidron gully and the Mount of Olives. In the garden there are still eight ancient olive trees with massive trunks, which are mentioned in writings of six centuries

ago. But though they may be old, they are unlikely to be the same trees that Jesus knew. Jesus knew the garden well, and probably its owner, so he used to cross the Kidron by bridges and to frequent the cave as a place of shelter from the cold and for discussion with his followers.

On the fateful night of his arrest, Jesus led his eleven disciples down from the Last Supper on Mount Zion. At

The garden of Gethsemane today, with Jerusalem's city walls in the background

Gethsemane, he left eight of the men and withdrew with Peter, James and John who watched over his lonely hour of 'sadness' and 'agony'.

Rejoining the rest of his disciples, and knowing what was to happen, Jesus said, 'Rise up, let us go on our way; already he that is to betray me is close at hand.'

Sure enough, Judas Iscariot, whose name would forever stand for treachery, was waiting. He stepped forward and greeted Jesus with a kiss, his sign to the Roman soldiers which man they should arrest.

Treachery ensured that this garden, above all others, would be famous forever.

See: Ararat, Bethlehem, Eden, Fatima, Giverney, Glastonbury, Kew, Lourdes, Masada, Sodom

GETTO
Italy

Venice, the home of the first 'Getto'

The world tends to use the word 'Ghetto' somewhat loosely, referring to any district where people of one race are confined. However, it referred at the outset only to the first Jews who were allowed to settle in Venice, when their money was needed to fight a local war.

In 1516, the *Serenissima*, Venice's ruling Council, decided to restrict its Jewish community to a small area, the site of *getti*, metal foundries. Because many of the Jews were of German origin, they hardened the 'G' when they spoke, so the Italian spelling was altered to 'Ghetto'. There, the inhabitants were restricted to money lending, pawn shops, textiles and medicine. They wore distinctive yellow marks on their clothing – a rule sinisterly repeated four centuries later – and had to return to the ghetto at night. Similar ghettos appeared in Rome, Genoa and other Italian cities.

Such discrimination and segregation were swept away by Napoleon in 1797 and, in 1860, Italian unification was to complete the liberalisation.

After 1939, 'Ghetto' took on a horrible new meaning in Nazi-occupied Europe, most notoriously in Poland with its three million Jews. The Krakow Ghetto was etched into our minds by the film *Schindler's List*. The Warsaw ghetto was worse. Hundreds of thousands of Jews from both the city and the countryside were walled into the ghetto and began to starve to death. 7,000 a day left in innocent hope from the railway station for the Treblinka extermination camp, a handful escaping to come back and warn the Jewish elders of their real fate.

Finally, in April 1943, discovering that the Nazis were to *'liquidate the ghetto'*, the last 60,000 rose and, with pitiful arms, fought from buildings, cellars and sewers. Few survived, but they had the grim satisfaction of killing a few hundred of their overconfident and brutal oppressors.

The end of the Jewish uprising in the Warsaw ghetto. The little boy was one of the only survivors.

The 42,500 Jews in Italy also suffered, although proportionately least during the Holocaust with eighty five per cent surviving. This was at an early stage, due to Mussolini's ambivalence. It is a little-known fact that he had a Jewish mistress, Margherita Sarfatti, until 1935. It may also be that there was none of the rabid anti-Semitism found elsewhere, with Italians protecting their Jewish neighbours, because they had begun to hate the Germans – and also because of an amiable inclination to disobey laws and orders. Moreover, many Italian Jews were educated, resourceful and brave. In the original ghetto of Venice, Dr Guiseppe Jona, the heroic leader of the Jewish community, burned his list of Jews and killed himself rather than help with the deportations.

The nuns and priests of the church, as a whole, came to the aid of the Jews. But a huge question mark still hangs over Pope Pius XII, who made no move to stop the Roman deportations occurring right under his nose, condemning him to be known forever as *'Hitler's Pope'*.

See: Anne Frank's Annexe, Dachau, Gleiwitz, Katyn Wood, Lidice, Masada, Oradour

GETTYSBURG
Pennsylvania, USA

ALL PERSONS FOUND USING FIREARMS IN THESE GROUNDS WILL BE PROSECUTED WITH THE UTMOST RIGOR OF THE LAW.

Thus read the sign on the ornate gate of the old cemetery of Gettysburg, a little town in Pennsylvania. Very soon about 150,000 men were going to break the law.

In July 1863, three years into the American Civil War, General Robert E. Lee, the most able commander of the War – at the head of the Confederacy's formidable Army of Northern Virginia – was determined to take the war north and invade Maryland and Pennsylvania. He hoped to alter the balance of the war, strengthen the 'peace party' in the Union, and at last achieve international recognition for the Confederacy.

Incredibly and by chance, it was footwear that made Gettysburg the site of the most famous and also defining battle of the war. The footsore (indeed, the barefoot) Southerners, searching for a rumoured store of boots in the little town, clashed on the outskirts with cavalry from the Union's Army of the Potomac. The rival armies converged on Gettysburg as if to a magnet, 65,000 Confederates and 85,000 from the Union.

The battle lasted three days, with desperate bravery and losses on both sides, and luck played its usual part. The vital hill of 'Little Round Top' had been abandoned by the foolish advance of Union General Daniel Sickles, a former Tammany politician notorious for shooting his wife's lover. The hill was only reoccupied ten minutes before Confederate infantry would have taken it, and thus dominated the battle. A furious Union defence among the rocks and trees just held on.

On the third day, Lee's blood was up and he decided to attack Cemetery Ridge – the centre of the Union lines – with 15,000 fresh and experienced Virginians under General George Pickett.

However, only seven months before, his Corps Commander, General Longstreet, had commanded the defence of the *'stone wall'* at Fredericksburg. He and Pickett had watched wave after wave of Unionist troops being slaughtered. Pickett himself, after watching General Thomas Meagher's Irish Brigade reduced from 2,200 to 218 men, wrote to his wife, *'Your soldier's heart almost stood still as he watched those sons of Erin. My darling, we forgot they were fighting us, and cheer after cheer at their fearlessness went up all along our lines'.*

Both men knew only too well what riflemen and artillery could do to attackers, however brave, out in the open. Longstreet tried to dissuade Lee, 'There never was a body of 15,000 men who could make that attack successfully'. Lee curtly ordered him to proceed anyway, and when Pickett then asked Longstreet to

The gate to Gettysburg's cemetery

confirm the attack, Longstreet could but nod, unable to speak.

Pickett called out, 'Men, don't forget you are from Old Virginia' and 15,000 men under waving flags marched off, silently and steadily across a mile of gentle open cornfield – 'a beautiful sight.' Cannon and rifle fire continuously tore into them. Just before they reached the Union lines, eleven cannon and 1,700 rifles fired at them all at once. Entire regiments disappeared and *'a moan went up.'* General Lewis Armistead and a few Southerners reached *'the Angle'* only to be shot down, as it happens, by the Irish 69th Pennsylvania Regiment. Dying, he asked that his old friend, Federal General Hancock, should 'look after his effects'.

The shattered Division, having lost half of its number, streamed back to the woods from where they had started, to be met by a distraught Lee. 'It's all my fault, it's all my fault'.

In *'Pickett's Charge'*, 6,500 Virginians were killed, wounded or captured. Indeed, there was hardly an officer not wounded or dead. All fifteen regimental commanders were hit. The next day, the Fourth of July, while Lee's battered army was retreating south, faced by the miseries of a dismal rainstorm, the besieged City of Vicksburg on the Mississippi surrendered to General Grant, splitting the Confederacy in two. Gettysburg and Vicksburg ended a string of Confederate successes and greatly boosted Northern morale. The terrible war would continue for two more years, but the ultimate outcome was already determined.

At 51,000 men, the losses suffered at Gettysburg were even worse than those at Waterloo, but then, several battles in the Civil War exceeded that horror.

Longstreet was one of the few military men who appeared to have grasped that increased firepower had changed battles forever. Generations of such men still seemed not to notice the mounting evidence; at Plevna in 1877, where 15,000 Turks inflicted devastating losses on 150,000 Russians; then the Boer War, where to move a muscle within 600 yards of Boer marksmen was to court death; and, above all, at Port Arthur in 1900, where 60,000 Japanese troops died in the final successful assault alone. The

stage was set for the horrific and totally pointless attrition of millions of men in the First World War. Someone after Gettysburg should have been sketching the design for a tank.

Gettysburg's lasting fame was assured, not just by the great battle, but by Abraham Lincoln's Gettysburg Address four months later – on a field still covered by the wreckage of the battle. Lincoln concluded ...

'These dead shall not have died in vain, that this nation, under God, shall have a new birth of freedom, and that Government of the people, by the people, for the people, shall not perish from the Earth'.

See: Andersonville, Appamattox, Arlington, Ballingarry, Charleston, Ford's Theatre, Fort Sumter, Gallipoli, Hampton Roads, Harpers Ferry, Little Big Horn, Somme, Waterloo, West Point

GIVERNY
France

When most of us look out of the window of a train, we often see little more than the boring backs of houses, apartment blocks or track-side rubbish and graffiti. By chance, in 1883, Claude Monet looked out and saw just the house he wanted to live in. He would make it famous forever.

The village of Giverny is very old, dating back to Roman rule in Gaul. The house that Monet had seen, and at first, rented, was a farmhouse complete with a kitchen garden and an orchard. He became more and more attached to it, buying it in 1890. He began to transform the gardens, with the Clos Normand with 200,000 flowers and a specially dug water-lily pond, filled by diverting a branch of the River Epte.

Monet was one of the great French Impressionists, who had shocked the art establishment with their novel and vibrant use of colour and light. Monet, in particular, loved experimenting with the way that light changed the same scene painted at different times of the day, as with his studies of Rouen Cathedral and Westminster Bridge. He was equally adept at urban scenes and his beloved French countryside.

But never has a painter and his own house and garden been so linked. The pond, with its waterlilies (*nymphéas*), weeping willows, and its little Japanese bridge with its trailing wisteria, are now familiar to the whole world through a series of wonderful paintings, each recording different light and weather conditions, sometimes caught from the bank or from a rowing boat filled with canvasses ready to be painted.

Monet even built an especially long studio for some of the Nymphéas series - huge, panoramic views dozens of feet across.

It is curious to realise that some of these beautiful and peaceful canvasses were painted against a background of trains steaming past with troops and ammunition for the 1914-18 front, close enough for him to hear the *'thudding of the guns.'*

Monet's house is carefully preserved,

complete with the Japanese prints that Monet collected, a charming kitchen and that magnificent garden and lily-pond. Hundreds of thousands of art-lovers come to pay their respects each year.

They must all be very glad that Claude Monet, by chance, glanced up to look out of the window and was not engrossed in a book.

See: Bridge at Arles, Barbizon, Flatford, Moulin Rouge, Sistine Chapel, Vinci

Below: The Japanese bridge and waterlily pond at Giverny are immediately recognisable to art-lovers from across the world.

ARLETTE CAUDERLIER

For over 43 centuries, indeed until the construction of the Eiffel Tower, the tallest building in the world was Pharaoh Khufu's Great Pyramid, the oldest and the only surviving *'wonder of the world'*. Giza, on the west bank of the Nile, had been designated as the royal *'necropolis'* (burial-place) for the Egyptian capital of Memphis. Today, it is part of the modern capital – Cairo.

It seems that this remarkable pyramid

The Sphinx and one of the pyramids at Giza

only took about thirty years to build, with Egyptologists estimating that this included ten years to build a ramp between the Nile and the building site. The site was selected due to its relative proximity to the Nile, needed for the transportation of huge rocks from distant quarries. Its size is almost unfathomable, weighing between six and seven million tons. The vast construction could in fact comfortably house St. Peter's in Rome, the Cathedrals of Florence, Milan, and St. Paul's in London, and still have room for Westminster Abbey. Roughly two million blocks of stone were used, the heaviest of which weighs more than 40 tonnes. The 5th century historian, Herodotus, wrongly estimated that it would have required 100,000 slaves to build the colossal edifice. Further excavation nearby reveals that it was 20,000 men and women enthusiastically working in teams, and housed and fed in a complete workers' city. As impressive

The Rosetta Stone

The most important long-term result of Napoleon's enforced stay in Egypt was his 1799 discovery of a slab of basalt with a decree conferring divine honours on Ptolemy V in 196 BC. Written in hieroglyphic, in demotic and in Greek, it unlocked the secrets of hieroglyphics and the history of Egypt.

as the sheer scale of the building is the precision involved. The four corners of the base point to the four points of the compass, and the difference in height between the shortest and the tallest side is only eight inches, an error of just 0.09 per cent. The stones in the interior are so well fitted that a playing card cannot be put between them.

Khufu's son, Khafre, built the second pyramid complex, including the Sphinx, and the third and smallest was added in turn by his son, Menkaure.

Each structure has its own surrounding temples, along with numerous *masabas* – cemeteries for royal relatives and servants. There were also boats buried beside them, to aid the pharaohs on their journey to the afterlife.

Originally, the pyramids were covered in bright white polished limestone, which must have made them a dazzling sight, but this covering has been torn away to make some of Cairo's buildings. The three pyramids together contain so much stone that it has been estimated that it could be used to build a wall 10 feet high and 1 foot thick all the way around France.

Written on parts of the interiors of the Pyramids are 'hieroglyphics', that are a form of written communication in a pre-literate society. They are, however, extremely difficult to decode. This is because they are a compound of three communication methods. The simplest method is as *'pictograms'*, which simply look like what they portray. They are also *'ideograms'*, depicting something that represents the appropriate idea. Thus, a sun could be 'warm', or a skull could be 'dead'. And to complicate things further, they are also sound signs; the picture portrays the phonetic spelling of what the writer means. So, working from English, if you wanted to say 'I', you might draw a picture of an eye, but of course this could also mean *'eye'* or something like *'see'*. Hence, the difficulty of interpretation, unlocked by the Rosetta Stone.

One of the most interesting aspects of the pyramids at Giza, or indeed ancient

Egyptian culture as a whole is that of *'mummification'*. The embalming process took seventy days, and included removal of all the internal organs, including the brain, which was pulled out through the nose in an astonishingly intricate process.

This practice has helped to contribute to Giza's fame, with mummies displayed for posterity in museums worldwide, fostering awareness and interest in ancient Egypt. Further publicity has been created by numerous films which portray monstrous mummies coming back to life to terrifying the living, like *The Mummy* and *The Mummy Returns*.

The idea of a *'mummy's curse'* gained acceptance on 5th April, 1923, with the death of Lord Carnarvon, who had been part of the team to open Tutankhamun's burial chamber just seven weeks before. It was rumoured that the lights of Cairo went out at the moment of his death, and that his dog, Susie, back in England, had howled and died. Two weeks before Carnarvon's demise, the novelist Marie Corelli had predicted dire consequences for those who entered the tomb. Arthur Conan Doyle, Sherlock Holmes' creator announced that the death was due to a *'Pharaoh's curse'*. One newspaper printed that a curse had been found at the entrance to the tomb, *'They who enter this sacred tomb shall swift be visited by wings of death'*.

However, such an inscription was in fact never found, and many others who opened the tomb lived to a ripe old age. Nevertheless, the idea of a curse of the mummy is yet another factor which contributes to the timeless mystique that has made the pyramids of Giza such a very famous landmark.

See: Actium, Ararat, Aswan, Ayers Rock, Babel, Easter Island, Great Wall of China, Kimberley, Stonehenge, Suez

GLASTONBURY
England

For many people the growing fame of Glastonbury, a fairly small town in Somerset, would be confined to its ever more successful pop music festival. But Glastonbury has been famous for years – mostly for its legends. You do not have to believe in all, or even some of them. The important point is that these legends exist.

The town sits in a cluster of hills and was once called Yns-writrin, the *'Island of glass'* in Celtic, because it was then surrounded by water. Its other name was *Avalon* from Avalloc or Avallach, who ruled the underworld.

Christian Glastonbury was thought to have first been founded by Joseph of Arimathea, the rich merchant who took the body of Christ and placed it in the tomb. Joseph, trading in tin, is said to have visited Somerset, perhaps even accompanied by the young Jesus. He planted his staff, which grew into the famous *'Glastonbury Thorn'*, which flowers twice a year, before Christmas and again in May. The ancient hermit community that built a wattle church then remained and, in 433, Ireland's St Patrick became their Abbot and lived with them until he died.

Then, there is the legend of King Arthur and the Round Table and his search for the Holy Grail – the legendary chalice brought from the Last Supper by Joseph, and which held the blood of Christ on the Cross. According

David Bowie

to the myth, Arthur is buried at Glastonbury, with his Queen Guinevere. Their bodies were said to have been reburied in 1278 in the church of the ancient Benedictine Abbey.

There is nothing legendary about the fate of this abbey. Indeed, it was the second largest in the country after Westminster Abbey, and when Henry VIII dissolved the monasteries for his own gain, it was the last to go in Somerset. Once its silver and gold had been confiscated, its Abbot, Richard Whiting, was dragged by horses to the top of Tor Hill, then hanged, beheaded and cut into quarters as a brutally successful reminder that resistance was futile.

The site of Glastonbury is still visited by thousands of people each year, making their pilgrimage to *'the holiest place in England'*.

It is also visited by thousands of pop fans. The Glastonbury Festival was started in 1970 with 1,500 keen fans attending. It cost £1 for the weekend, including free milk from Worthy Farm.

Over the years the performers, among many others, have included Marc Bolan, David Bowie, Joan Baez, Sky, Van Morrison, UB40, Joe Cocker, The Boomtown Rats, Simply Red, Sinead O'Connor, Tom Jones, Björk, The Manic Street Preachers, Oasis, and Sting.

It now has 115,000 visitors, and tickets cost £105 which does not include free milk! Some people would feel that this Glastonbury Festival is just as worthy a legend as all the others that have made the place famous.

Some would not.

See: Assisi, Bethlehem, Gethsemane, Lourdes, Stonehenge, Woodstock

GLEIWITZ
Germany

In August 1939, Hitler was poised for his next triumph. He had taken over the Rhineland, merged with Austria and first split up and then went on to destroy Czechoslovakia, absorbing its munitions factories into his war effort. Now it was

Poland's turn. As with all his political and military ventures, all was clouded with deceit. In January, Hitler had announced in the Reichstag:
'During the troubled months of the past year, the friendship between Germany

and Poland has been one of the most reassuring factors in the political life of Europe.

Only weeks later in May, he was brutally specific to his Generals at a military conference:

'There is therefore no question of sparing Poland, and we are left with the decision to attack Poland at the first suitable opportunity.

We cannot expect a repetition of the Czech affair. There will be war. Our task is to isolate Poland. The success of the isolation will be decisive'.

And only days before his attack he seemed mainly worried that he might be robbed of his war:

'Now, Poland is in the position in which I wanted her ... I am only afraid that at the last moment some Schweinehund will make a proposal for mediation.'

Germany's perceived quarrel with Poland was the *'Polish Corridor'* to the sea at Danzig, ceded to Poland at the Treaty of Versailles, which blocked Germany from East Prussia. The secret and real objective was expansion eastwards, making the Poles into slaves and exterminating her huge Jewish population. To pull this off, Hitler at first pretended to ally himself, temporarily, with the Soviet Union – in the cynical – and, to the British and French, the shattering Non-Aggressive Pact signed seven days before his planned attack. But Germany still needed a pretext. This was cooked up by Himmler and his scheming sidekick Heydrich, together with the Gestapo.

Heydrich called in Alfred Naujocks of the Sicherheitsdienst (SD). He was ordered to fake an attack on the German

radio station at Gleiwitz in Silesia, near the Polish border. They used twelve Polish concentration camp prisoners ('Canned Goods') dressed in Polish uniforms, with weapons and identity cards. The disguised Polish prisoners were given lethal injections and then shot at the radio station to simulate battle wounds. A member of Naujock's team then broadcast, 'This is the Polish rebel force. Radio station Gleiwitz is in our hands. The hour of freedom has struck'.

The foreign press were taken to the station to view the dead bodies, even as Hitler's Panzers and Stukas were pouring into Poland. How many believed this bizarre, crude and murderous pantomime, who knows? It didn't really matter. Hitler now had his war.

CHRISTOPHER AILSBY HISTORICAL ARCHIVE

Alfred Naujocks, Heydrich's accomplice in the murderous charade at Gleiwitz

See: Anne Frank's Annexe, Dachau, Havana, Katyn Wood, Lidice, Oradour, Tonkin Gulf, Rorke's Drift

GLENCOE
Scotland

There have been many cases of unalloyed treachery in history - the Japanese attack on Pearl Harbor, Caesar's assassination by his best friends, Stalin's elimination of all his Politburo comrades, Hitler's murder of Ernst Roehm and the SA. But for sheer brutal cynicism, the prize must go to the massacre of the MacDonalds at Glencoe.

Many felt it was the *way* it was done that was wrong – not the murder itself –

because the MacDonalds of Glencoe were not short of enemies. As supporters of the exiled Catholic James II, they were not going to find favour with the Protestant King William of Orange. As Highlanders, they would be feared and distrusted by Lowland Ministers, and especially the hated Sir John Dalrymple, the Master of Stair and Secretary of State for Scotland, who had offered the Crown of Scotland to William. Nor could they count on the support of their fellow Highlanders. Years of robbery, raiding, cattle rustling and mayhem had seen to that. Above all, they had ensured, in innumerable battles and skirmishes, the hatred of their neighbours, the doughty Campbells.

As a Dutchman, King William's only interest in Scotland was peace and the provision of troops to help him with his real interest, that of fighting the French to maintain a united Netherlands. As he fought in Flanders, the Highlanders were little more than a potential nuisance.

In August 1691, William – under Stair's urging – issued a proclamation offering amnesty to the Highland clans as long as they swore an oath of allegiance before 1st January 1692. A simple enough request? No, because two Jacobite officers had to go to St Germain-en-Laye near Paris to ask James II to release the clans from their binding oath to him. Typically, he hesitated for weeks and then months. In October the storms came to the glens, in November the snow. None of the clans had come in. In London, the Master of Stair made his preparations for a merciless and brutal lesson. His weapon would be the Earl of Argyll's Regiment of Foot – this virtually a Campbell formation.

With only nineteen days to go before the *'deadline'*, James II released his clans. It took the courier, Major Duncan Menzies, nine days to reach Edinburgh from Paris, exhausted, with the vital dispatch.

On 30th December, Alisdair MacDonald suddenly appeared in front of Colonel Sir John Hill, Governor of Inverlochy, to swear the oath – who could not oblige him. Somewhat sympathetic to the clans, he was forced to send him to the Sheriff who was Sir Colin Campbell of Ardkinglas, but with a note asking him to be received *'as a lost sheep'*. MacDonald rode off into the snow and was arrested for a day. On the 6th January, Sir Colin Campbell, faced by a proud but weeping MacDonald of Glencoe, accepted his oath.

But in Edinburgh, Colin Campbell of Dressalch (who had once lost 12 fine cows to the men of Glencoe) and others, including Stair's father, saw to it that the MacDonald's name was crossed out. The die was cast. The King signed the orders that Stair had drafted, and which were not altered even when Stair heard that the MacDonalds had submitted.

Thus, on 1st February, Captain Robert Campbell, the fifth Laird of Glenlyon, found his company halted by twenty Highlanders. At their head, John MacDonald demanded, 'Do you come as friends or enemies?' 'Friends', Glenlyon replied, then explained the need for quarters. 'You and your men are welcome in Glencoe', McDonald said.

So for twelve days the soldiers enjoyed the hospitality of the Highlanders' families. They ate and drank and played games with them. On 12th February, the final order came, loaded with threats –

The brutal order to kill the MacDonalds

For his Majesty's Service, to Captain Robert Campbell of Glenlyon

Sir,

You are hereby ordered to fall upon the rebels, the MacDonalds of Glencoe, and to put all to the sword under seventy. You are to have a special care that the old fox and his sons do upon no account escape your hands. You are to secure all the avenues that no man escape. This you are to put in execution at five of the clock precisely; and by that time, or very shortly after it, I'll strive to be at you with a stronger party. If I do not come to you at five, you are not to tarry for me, but to fall on. This is by the King's special command, for the good and safety of the country, that these miscreants be cut off root and branch. See that this be put in execution without feud or favour, else you may expect to be dealt with as one not true to King nor Government, nor a man fit to carry Commission in the King's service. Expecting you will not fail in the fulfilling hereof, as you love yourself, I subscribe these with my hand at Ballachulish, Feb 12, 1692.

Robert Duncanson

just in case Glenlyon was to shrink from his unpleasant duty. That night, several of the soldiers were able to hint to their hosts that something bad was to happen – and they should slip away to safety.

At exactly five in the morning, the killing began. Glenlyon's eight hosts, bound and gagged until that moment, were shot and bayoneted. The Chief, Alisdair MacDonald, was shot as he pulled on his trews to say goodbye to his guests. Men were dragged from their beds and killed. Women, some half naked, escaped with their children up the glen through the freezing blizzard.

The final count was thirty-eight, with 300 escaping up into the hills. (In their efficiency and timing, the Campbells would have had much to learn from the SS and the NKVD.)

The soldiers looted the houses and drove off 900 cows, 200 horses and many sheep and goats.

Word of the massacre reached Edinburgh, London and Paris. It was the treacherous abuse of traditional Highland hospitality that caused consternation. As the Commander in Chief said, 'It's not that anybody thinks the thieving tribe did not deserve to be destroyed. But that it should be done by such as were quartered with them makes a great noise.'

The clans, including the MacDonalds, submitted. Nobody was punished for the crime and years later, after the Battle of Culloden and the 'Highland Clearances', the proud and independent Highland life was gone forever.

Indeed the MacDonalds are still not too friendly with the Campbells.

See: Anthrax Island, Gretna Green, Loch Ness, Lockerbie, St Germain-en-Laye, Tay Bridge

GOOSE GREEN
Falkland Islands

Goose Green is a very small hamlet on East Falkland, its one hundred inhabitants outnumbered by geese and by 75,000 sheep. It will always be associated with a military success. But due to political pressure, lack of resources, over-confidence and bad luck, it could easily have been a disaster for the British.

Argentinian claims to the Falkland Islands, or *'Las Malvinas'* are based on the rather flimsy basis that she inherited the title from Spain under the Papal Grants of 1493, whereby Spain claimed South America except Portuguese Brazil. At the time, Spain seemed not to be very interested in 700 tiny uninhabited, windswept South Atlantic islands, 300 miles from Argentina. The first landing did not occur until 1690, when English captain, John Strong, named the islands after the First Lord of the Admiralty, Viscount Falkland. The Spanish *'Las Malvinas'* derives from visiting French sailors from St Malo, 'Les Maloines'.

In 1765, Captain John Byron took formal possession, with the first British settlement established in 1766. For the next 70 years there was confusion – as France, Britain, Spain and Argentina all set up small settlements. Spain withdrew in 1811. Argentina asserts that the rights passed to her by default, although no hand-over by Spain ever occurred. In 1833, Britain resumed permanent occupation. Argentina refuted Britain's claim for the next 149 years, after which regaining 'Las Malvinas' became an obsession.

By the 1980s the British Government was seeking to get rid of this strange outpost, with its 1,800 sheep farmers, as 'impossible to defend'. It proposed that the Falklands should be handed over to Argentina with a long-term leaseback to Britain. Perhaps new generations of the islanders, rather less attached to British heritage, would eventually not mind becoming Argentine citizens. But the proposal coincided with an oppressive right wing military regime in Buenos Aires. Thousands of men, women and children, were kidnapped, tortured and murdered. Many were never seen again; *'los desaparecidos'* (the disappeared). For the islanders, the idea of being handed over to such a country, albeit on a leaseback basis, was considered completely unacceptable.

The Argentine 'Junta' was furious and

felt deceived by British diplomats. It also needed a distraction from the ugly events at home. Argentina was expanding her armed forces – just as Britain was cutting defence spending. At the top of Defence Secretary John Nott's list of casualties was HMS *Endurance*, the South Atlantic ice patrol and electronic surveillance ship. Nott viewed the Falkland Islands as *'peripheral and a non-issue'*.

When the Junta learned of the plans to scrap *Endurance*, it soon sensed Britain's waning interest and seized its chance. The invasion began by stealth with Argentine forces landing on nearby South Georgia as *'scrap merchants'* to dismantle the old whaling station. On one of her final missions, *Endurance* was sent to investigate.

As tension increased, Britain deployed three nuclear submarines to the South Atlantic. The news pushed Argentina into mounting her invasion. On 2nd April thousands of troops attacked Port Stanley, overpowering the tiny Royal Marines garrison and forcing surrender on the Governor, Rex Hunt. Within 72 hours, much to the Junta's amazement, Prime Minister Margaret Thatcher's vengeful Task Force had sailed from Britain.

On 25th May, after six weeks, the British Carrier Battle Group launched its invasion, including the container ship *Atlantic Conveyor*, with her precious cargo of helicopters. The plan was to go into the sheltered waters of San Carlos that night and unload the helicopters.

Admiral Sir John Woodward, the Task Force Commander, brought his plans forward by two hours. It was the very moment when the Argentines launched an Exocet missile attack. The resulting loss of the *Atlantic Conveyor*, and also its helicopters, also lost the means to move troops forward quickly to capture Port Stanley. But Margaret Thatcher was putting real pressure on the army commanders to get the soldiers moving quickly. The only option was to walk.

Before the forces began their punishing battle march to Port Stanley, their commander Brigadier Thompson had really wanted them to dig in at San Carlos and set up a bridgehead. But London disagreed. Nott felt it was vital to move out of the bridgehead to bolster international opinion. The army was irritated by this political pressure, feeling that there was no point in advancing until the logistics were in place. They might run out of ammunition or food and so be defeated unnecessarily. Thompson says: 'We needed to be balanced and ready to go, and, until we were, I was not keen on rushing off to Stanley'.

But the war cabinet in Whitehall wanted victory fast and ordered Thompson to advance. The Royal Marines duly 'yomped' off north, heading towards Port Stanley, 86 miles away. Meanwhile, 400 paratroopers of their 2nd Battalion were ordered to attack the Argentine garrison at Goose Green, where the British would be out-numbered and outgunned by 3 to 1.

London itself was then to remove the element of surprise. Keen to show off British military prowess and boost public morale, Whitehall briefed the British media on the precise route – a full day before the attack – the BBC's World Service being heard by the Argentines.

The Goose Green attack began on the night of 27th May with a short naval bombardment. The plan was for a rapid advance, but with 400 British Paras now facing 1,500 Argentines and a serious malfunction in the naval gunfire support, progress was slow. Due to a lack of resources, the soldiers had only enough ammunition for a raid and very limited mortar fire. 'We were down to relying on courage, bayonets, machine-guns and close gutter fighting'.

Two Para's Commander, Lt. Col 'H' Jones was an impatient, energetic leader who believed passionately in leading his men from the front. As they advanced they were held up, incurring casualties from eleven well-prepared trenches on a ridge. To maintain momentum, Colonel Jones took forward his reconnaissance party and continued to fight through, despite heavy fire. To gain a good viewpoint, he was now at the very front of his battalion. Feeling that desperate measures were needed, he seized the initiative by taking a sub-machine gun and with a small number of men charged up the slope. 'H' was shot in the back from a trench he had already passed. He was awarded a posthumous Victoria Cross.

Second in Command, Major Chris Keeble, received the signal *'Sunray is down.'* He assumed command of a battle which had already fallen badly behind plan, in broad daylight, across bare terrain. One in five of his troops had been injured or killed, but having witnessed the heroism of Colonel Jones, the will of the hungry and conscripted Argentinians evaporated. They gave up next morning, and the local inhabitants were released unharmed.

The Paras had paid a high price for victory at Goose Green. But the battle taught the British some valuable lessons. All fighting now took place under cover of darkness, with better equipped troops and greater artillery support. The capture of Port Stanley and the Argentinian

surrender came little more than two weeks later on 14th June.

Today, Goose Green – still surrounded by sheep – retains its lonely evidence of the conflict, including the Argentinian cemetery, the simple stone memorial to Lt. Col Jones and the memorial to the Parachute Regiment.

THE AIRBORNE FORCES MUSEUM / THE PARACHUTE REGIMENT

See: Arnhem, The Bogside, South Georgia

Lt Col 'H' Jones

GORGONZOLA
Italy

Food has often played a part in propelling places to fame. For example, the tiny village of Gorgonzola, not far from Milan, was saved from obscurity by its moist blue cheese. Close by, the larger town of Parma would still be unknown to most of us but for its ham. Cakes have given acclaim to Eccles and Pontefract in England, Dundee in Scotland, and Battenberg in Germany, where the characteristic yellow and pink cake was created in honour of Prince Louis of Battenberg – whose German name was quickly changed to Mountbatten when his son was Britain's First Sea Lord during the First World War.

Arbroath in Scotland should perhaps be known for its Abbey, scene of the Scottish Baron's Declaration of Independence in 1310. But most of us associate it with *'Arbroath Smokies'*, a delicious hot smoked haddock dish.

On the way to Dover, you pass Sandwich, famous for the 4th Earl, who needed something simple to eat whilst continuously gambling. You could also bypass nearby Whitstable easily enough, but you cannot ignore its oysters, famous for 2,000 years – nor the pies of Melton Mowbray and the tasty tarts of Bakewell.

Worcester, also famous for its china, has produced a sauce recognised all over the world, although foreigners really struggle with the pronunciation of the name, with all its confusing syllables – 'Worcestershire sauce'.

A few of us may be familiar with the

lovely Burgundy town of Dijon, but for gastronomes it means 'French mustard', although they might have more difficulty pinpointing Meaux, regarded by some mustard lovers as even better.

The little town of Vichy, notorious as the seat of power of the collaborationist French government after France's defeat in 1940, has long since washed away its shame in millions of gallons of Vichy mineral water or even the delicious iced soup of leeks, potatoes and onions which we call 'Vichysoisse'.

France is, of course, a wonderful source of food names. General Charles de Gaulle once said, 'How can you govern a country with 246 varieties of cheese?

In Ireland, from Waterford crystal, you can drink whiskey from Bushmills, the oldest distillery in the world. By contrast

163

See: Bath, Bournville, Champagne, Cognac, Fray Bentos, Hamburg, Hershey, Nuits-St-George, Pilsen, Run, Spa, Vichy

Ballygowan is one of the younger spring water successes. A formerly agricultural country is bound to produce names like Cashel blue cheese and Clonakilty black pudding and County Kerry's fame was enhanced by Tony O'Reilly's branding Ireland's dairy products 'Kerrygold'.

With its shorter history, America is perhaps less rich in such places made famous by food. Potatoes have arguably made Idaho a touch more famous. Kentucky, we really hope, has more than just fried chicken. But there is 'Philly Steak', served in Philadelphia, thin beef cuts called a steak so that you could charge more than a Hamburger. 'Long Island iced tea,' was favoured by the young smart set for summer in the Hamptons.

The small white 'Boston Baked Beans' were local, as was the 'Delmonico Steak', named after the famed New York restaurant; 'New England Clam Chowder used potato rather than the usual tomato base of 'Manhattan Chowder'; 'Tex-Mex' spicy foods started in the border towns with Mexico; 'Key Lime Pies' were a custard pie with limes unique to the Florida Keys.

For the origins of 'Mississippi Mud', the chocolate dessert, try looking up the incredibly non-PC lyrics of Bing Crosby's jazz hit of the same name, singing in the Thirties with the Paul Whiteman Band and Bix Beiderbecke.

It is easy to be fooled by some apparent place names. If you thought 'Tabasco' came from Tabasco State in Mexico, you would be wrong. Tabasco sauce was actually created in Avery Island, Louisiana, west of New Orleans. Its inventor, Edmund McIlhenny, was going to call it 'Petite Anse Sauce' after a family island. But, under family pressure, he sensibly then opted for his second choice, the Central American Indian word 'Tabasco' – '*land where the soil is hot and humid*'.

Hamburgers were not first made in Germany, but in New York State. Stilton cheese actually comes from Leicester, but happened to be made famous by the Bell Inn on the Great North Road at Stilton, in the UK county of Cambridgeshire.

And as for 'Bombay Duck' – this is not a bird that flies above the ancient Indian city. It is a dried fish with a strange taste which has now been barred as a health hazard in Europe.

GOTHAM
England

Gotham Church

See: Manhattan, Runnymede

164

Anyone brought up on *Batman* comics, cartoons, and films would regard Gotham City as the archetypal sinister, crime-ridden metropolis – probably New York City. Indeed, by 1800, New York City had achieved its own level of madness as far as its detractors were concerned, and the name of Gotham was given to the city by Washington Irving in his book *Salmagundi* in 1807.

However, the origins of applying the name Gotham to a town of madness go back much further, to six centuries earlier.

Gotham is a village near Nottingham in England. When King John sought to visit the place in 1210 on a Royal Progress – with a view to creating a hunting lodge – the villagers, knowing his rapacious ways, realised they would be financially burdened by this 'honour.'

Thus, when the King's advance party arrived to inspect the village, everyone acted as if they were mad, and the King's plans were changed to avoid 'infection', making Gotham the epitome of madness.

But those they had duped were, perhaps, even more stupid:
'We ween there are more fools pass through Gotham than remain in it'.

The village even became known in English nursery rhymes:
> *Three wise men of Gotham*
> *Went to sea in a bowl*
> *If the bowl had been stronger*
> *My story'd be longer!'*

So the story of madness (feigned) and tax evasion (real) brings us from a little village in England to Batman's fictitious Gotham, a very real New York City, to which both madness and tax evasion may be no strangers.

GRACELAND
Tennessee, USA

To the musical world of the 1920s, Memphis, Tennessee would be best known for W. C. Handy's Memphis Blues, the famous first work for which he was never paid. But these days it is more readily recognised as the home of the very first white man to incorporate blues and black rhythms into popular music. His address – 3764 Elvis Presley Boulevard,

'Graceland', is the second most familiar address in America, the first being the home of the President, 'The White House'. The mansion's status should come as no surprise; after all, Elvis was, and still is, the 'King' of Rock and Roll.

Born in 1935, Elvis Aaron Presley grew up in a poor area of Tupelo in Mississippi. Working as a truck driver in 1953, he was discovered by Sam Phillips of Sun Records, who chanced to hear a private record that Elvis was making for his mother. His superb voice, unique singing style, gyrating hips and sensuous looks propelled Elvis to fame, and, by 1956 he was the most popular performer in America – and soon the world. In 1957, at the tender age of 22, he purchased the fourteen-acre Graceland estate for $100,000. The mansion became the family home for Elvis, his parents, his grandmother and eventually his young wife Priscilla and daughter Lisa Marie. Mary Jenkins Langston, his beloved cook, did not live there but was responsible for making the peanut butter and banana sandwiches that later affected Elvis' slim physique. He was known to say, 'One of

the best joys in life, May-wee, is eating your food'.

Today, the King no longer reigns over just rock and roll; in Memphis he presides over tourism too. Five years after his sad Memphis over $150 million each year.

Graceland is more than the home of a music legend, or even another site on the National Register of Historic Buildings. It is a symbol of the potential success of the 'American Dream'.

Complete with an extraordinary array of memorabilia including his 1955 Pink Cadillac, a shopping centre across the street, and the Heartbreak Hotel, named after one of Elvis' greatest hits, the estate also includes his private jets, the Hound Dog II and the Lisa Marie. A 'Trophy Building' of gold discs is testament to his remarkable musical success while his death is marked by his grave in the 'Meditation Garden'.

Superstar, sex symbol, soldier and screen hero, the small-town boy who shot to stardom remains a unique and enduring legend. Graceland deserves its fame.

See: Las Vegas, Nashville

GRAND HOTEL, BRIGHTON
England

Hotels tend to become famous for their style, quality, service and patronage. Only a few become known for violence, like the King David in Jerusalem or the Europa in Belfast, once the most bombed hotel in the world. In 1984, their ranks were suddenly joined by a conference hotel in Britain's seaside resort of Brighton.

On the 14th September, a man calling himself Roy Walsh checked into the Grand Hotel in Brighton for 3 nights, and left on the 17th just as quietly and unassumingly as he had arrived. But he was not what he seemed. Patrick Magee, under a false name, had carefully planted a large bomb in his bathroom wall, knowing that three and a half weeks later, Britain's Prime Minister – Margaret Thatcher – would be staying in the hotel for the Conservative Party Conference. The bomb was well hidden, and remained undiscovered until it exploded. Magee obviously knew what he was doing; in fact it has been rumoured that he had learned his trade in a Libyan terrorist training camp.

On the night of the 12th September, Mrs Thatcher had just finished working on her speech for the final day of the conference and was preparing for bed when, at 2.54 am, the bomb went off. The devastation was enormous. A massive and terrible explosion thundered through the building, followed closely by the sounds of shattering glass and crashing brickwork. Miraculously, the Prime Minister herself survived because the bomb had been planted too far from her room, but many others were not nearly as fortunate. As she was quickly hurried out of the building, it became evident that much of the front of the hotel had collapsed, and the hotel foyer was clogged with fallen masonry. Five people had been killed, including MP Sir Anthony Berry, and

Right: Margaret Thatcher, determined as ever

Below: The wrecked Grand Hotel

the wife of John Wakeham, the Chief Whip. What is more, Margaret Tebbitt, the wife of the Secretary for Trade and Industry, Norman Tebbit, was paralysed, while he himself had to be pulled from the rubble. Over thirty people were injured, and dazed Cabinet Ministers wandered the seafront in their pyjamas.

Mrs Thatcher was rushed to the local police station, where the decision was made that the conference had to go

ahead. As the Prime Minister would declare in her speech, after the standing ovation she received for her fierce determination, 'This Government will not weaken. This nation will meet that challenge. Democracy will prevail!'

For the Irish Republican Army, it was a daring and extraordinary attack, which very nearly succeeded. As the IRA pointed out, *'Mrs Thatcher will now realise that Britain cannot occupy our country, torture our prisoners and shoot our people on their own streets and get away with it. Today we were unlucky, but remember we only have to be lucky once - you will have to be lucky always. Give Ireland peace and there will be no war'.*

Patrick Magee was tracked down by the careful analysis of the records of everyone who had recently used the hotel and accounting for all of them, except the shadowy Roy Walsh. Arrested in a Glasgow ' safe house', he received eight life sentences, and the judge recommended an absolute minimum of 35 years in prison.

In the event, on the 22nd June 1999, Patrick Magee strolled out of the Maze prison a free man. He had not even come close to completing the eight life sentences that he was due to receive, and this early release, part of the ' Good Friday Agreement', caused a very considerable degree of public and political controversy. Tony Blair said that the prisoner releases were 'very hard to stomach.' Michael Howard, the Former Home Secretary, labelled Magee's release a 'disgrace'. Margaret Thatcher's views on the subject are likely to be even more extreme.

By contrast, the hotel manager has said that Magee, or should it be Walsh, was welcome to stay at the Grand again if he so wished. Forgive and forget? It is hard to fathom why.

How would the United States regard the nearly successful destruction by a terror group of a U.S. President and his team? After the horrors of September 11th, which brought foreign terrorism suddenly very close to home, it is extremely difficult to believe that they would be so pragmatic and forgiving.

See: Ballingarry, Bogside, GPO, Saint Germain, World Trade Center

THE GRAND TOUR
Europe

'If a young man is wild and must run after women and bad company, it is better done abroad'.

Dr Johnson was referring to but one aspect of the education of the first 'tourists'. But he also added, *'A man who has not been in Italy is always conscious of an inferiority from his not having seen what is expected a man should see'.*

'The Grand Tour' was an important ritual in the education of an emerging English gentleman in the second half of the 18th century. Its primary purpose was to expose these young men to the glories of the Renaissance and classical art in Italy.

To get there they had to pass through France, with whom Britain was often at war – and then choose to go by boat from Marseilles (with its danger of pirates) or by mule across the Alps.

Once in Italy the young gentlemen were to study the wonders of art and architecture and also to purchase artefacts or works of art. So much did they spend that many of Britain's finest houses and galleries are full of the results of these aristocratic shopping sprees.

As Dr Johnson hinted, much of their new education was of a sexual nature, and their special sheep-gut condoms made such a favourable impression that King Louis XV ordered a special supply. Some of the 'Grand Tourists' put their discoveries to more practical use. Francis Egerton, the future Duke of Bridgewater, was so impressed by the 150-mile route of the Languedoc Canal in France that he resolved to use such a transport method to move coal onward to Manchester and was later dubbed 'the father of Britain's canals'.

The Grand Tour sometimes took up to five years, which certain parents thought was just fine.

Some never came back, like the poet Percy Bysshe Shelley who died in Italy.

Not all 'tourists' enjoyed the trip which had sometimes been forced upon them. Indeed, one young man responded to a friend who had asked about his experience of the Grand Tour, 'Abroad is bloody and all foreigners are blackguards'.

See: Assisi, Bridgewater, Cremona, Pisa, Venice

CLARE SUTTON

Florence and other cultural Renaissance Italian cities were essential stops on the Grand Tour.

167

GRANTCHESTER
England

Visitors to Cambridge often take in the nearby village of Grantchester; a classic excursion – a two-mile trip up the river Cam by punt – followed by traditional English tea at The Orchard's Tearooms. It is a pleasant enough spot, especially in the summer, with cottages, an old church and pub, the river flowing past green meadows, riverbank wildflowers and quietly munching cows. But that doesn't account for its legendary status. Grantchester's reputation rests, above all, on the fame of one man, the young poet Rupert Brooke, who died in 1915. He was an enigmatic and romantic figure, a last flowering of Edwardian England. Gifted with both magnificent looks and keen intelligence, Brooke still haunts the village that he celebrated in verse. His lyrical and beautifully constructed work was to

First World War poet Rupert Brooke

include some of the most optimistic and patriotic poems of the Great War, for he never witnessed the carnage of the Somme and other battles that would destroy his generation.

Born in 1887, Brooke began writing poetry at Rugby School, where his father was a master. At King's College, Cambridge he read classics, but chiefly immersed himself in literature and the theatre. He also dabbled in socialism, joining the Fabian Society. A brilliant scholar, greatly loved and admired by his peers, and an intimate of the Bloomsbury Group and many of the prominent intellectuals of the time, he was appointed to a fellowship at King's in 1913 for a dissertation on 17th century playwright John Webster. By then he had published his first collection of poetry, *Poems 1911*. It was a considerable success that had 37 editions in 20 years.

He never took up his prestigious academic post; instead he travelled widely and in September 1914, applied for a commission in the Royal Naval Division. As a sub-lieutenant, he saw action at Antwerp, and his spring of 1915 was spent with the expedition to close the Dardanelles by the seizure of the Turkish peninsula of Gallipoli. Fate intervened most cruelly. He died on 23rd April, appropriately St George's Day – not in some glorious battle, as he would have envisaged, but by acute blood-poisoning, apparently from an infected mosquito bite. His death created a legend – as did the funeral that followed. He was buried in an olive grove on a high hill on the Greek island of Skyros. A landing party party climbed the hill in solemn procession, led by a sailor carrying a large white cross with Brooke's name upon it in black. A bugler sounded the last post, and the men covered the grave with marble slabs. He had written his own epitaph the previous year, *The Soldier,* a sonnet included in *1914 and Other Poems:* *'If I should die, think only this of me; That there's some corner of a foreign field That is forever England'* .

The procession marched back to the boat by lamplight. Among four of Brooke's close friends present on Skyros was Arthur Asquith, a son of the Liberal Prime Minister, H.H. Asquith, and one Bernard Freyberg, who would receive the VC, leading the Empire forces in the Battle of Crete in May 1941, and become Governor-General of his native New Zealand. *The Times* published news of Brooke's death a few days later, along with a notice of appreciation signed by 'W.S.C.', none other than Winston Churchill, First Lord of the Admiralty and architect of the Gallipoli campaign. As a friend of Brooke who moved in the same Liberal and Establishment circles, Churchill had arranged that Brooke and several of his friends serve together. In his will, Brooke generously left the royalties from his work to four fellow writers, including war poet Wilfred Gibson and Walter de la Mare, allowing them to live comfortably.

Grantchester was his home from 1909. He first rented rooms at The Orchard, ostensibly as an escape from the hurly-burly of Cambridge life. Later, he moved to the Old Vicarage, immortalized in his poetry. Here, he and his broad circle of friends, who included not just artists and writers like Virginia Wolfe but the philosophers Bertrand Russell and Wittgenstein and the economist Maynard Keynes, read, talked, swam and fell in love. Swimming, especially at night, was a passion for Brooke as it had been his for fellow-poet Lord Byron, commemorated by Byron's Pool nearby on the River Cam. Grantchester continued to dominate his home thoughts from abroad - we all know that feeling. In a Berlin café he wrote one of his most famous poems:

'And, flower-lulled in sleepy grass,
Hear the cool lapse of hours pass,
Until the centuries blend and blur
In Grantchester, in Grantchester ...'

and finished with one of the most heart-felt appeals in the English language:

'Stands the church clock at ten to three?
And is there honey still for tea?'

Half a century later, Grantchester found artistic fame once more. In 1969, the experimental rock band Pink Floyd recorded the song *Grantchester Meadows,* a gentle evocation of the river and the summer meadows for acoustic guitar and voice. Temporarily eschewing sound

amplification and electronic wizardry, the band's bass guitarist Roger Waters, who grew up in Cambridge, wrote and sang a minor classic in the English tradition of pastoral idyll, again putting Grantchester on the map, this time for hippies and hairies.

But life does gravitate from the sublime to the ridiculous. In recent years another larger-than-life personality, alas one far removed from the dreamy cultured world of Rupert Brooke, has dominated the world's perception of the village. Brooke's beloved old vicarage is now the home of best-selling novelist, disgraced former Government minister and one-time darling of the Conservative Party, Jeffrey Archer.

See: Cliveden, Gallipoli, Rugby, Sissinghurst, Somme

THE GREAT HEDGE
India

Salt, sodium chloride, is now so easily available and cheap that we never think about it. We even call it 'common salt.' But it was not always so.

We all need salt – it plays a vital role in our physical health. Our bodies store six ounces of it. If we sweat, we lose it. In hot climates and with physical effort, 2 to 3 ounces can be lost in just a day. If not replaced, the results are serious or even catastrophic. Blood pressure falls, the brain is starved of blood. Lassitude, apathy, muscular weakness and then unconsciousness follow. Before the saline drip was invented, it was impossible to feed unconscious people, so they simply died.

Nowhere was salt more critical than in India, hot and with a mainly vegetarian populace unable to replace salt by eating

meat. So it comes as a shock to find that from the earliest days of the East India Company, the British decided to tax salt and, indeed, to make it the largest source of revenue for the company. It is even more startling to find that British schoolboy hero, Robert Clive, *'victor of Plassey',* enriched himself so quickly and also so outrageously from salt revenues as even to arouse suspicion and envy back in England.

Through the Salt Tax, the British for years allowed the poor of India to be deprived of

Robert Clive was the hero of Plassey, but he greedily used the Salt Tax to enrich himself enormously.

and more effective - made of Babool, Indian Plum, Carounda and Prickly Pear, locked in with Thorny Creeper. As part of the 2,500 mile Custom Line, the hedge was a colossal 1,500 miles long, making it the second largest man-made structure on earth, only surpassed by China's Great Wall. It took 14,000 men to patrol the Line, with a customs gate nearly every mile.

In 1869, at the peak of its perfection, the Line and its Hedge were abandoned, but only because the tax-free Indian States had now been annexed and the tax differences removed, with the Salt Taxes now universal – and which then remained to plague India for decades.

The Great Hedge explains why Britain's salt policy was so hated in India, even sometimes closing Indian salt works to protect imported Liverpool salt. It is exactly why Gandhi later chose salt as a symbol for *'passive resistance'*, leading to his popular and symbolic march on the salt works at Dandi in 1930.

Seventeen years later, centuries of British rule ended.

But salt had been rubbed in the wound.

salt even in times of famine and distress. The price for a family could even rise to half of its income.

When faced by the situation that the Indian rulers, who were beyond their control, refused to tax the salt for their people, the British then did something at once technically brilliant and also morally appalling. As Sir John Strachey (Lytton's uncle) was to write: *'There grew up gradually a monstrous system of which it would be almost impossible to find a parallel in any tolerably civilised country'.*

He was referring to the Custom Line and, more particularly, to the 'Great Hedge of India', for whose rediscovery we should be grateful to Roy Moxham's detective work and his excellent book.

The Hedge was started in 1854, beginning as a dry hedge annually involving 150,000 tons of thorny material. The live hedge was much cheaper

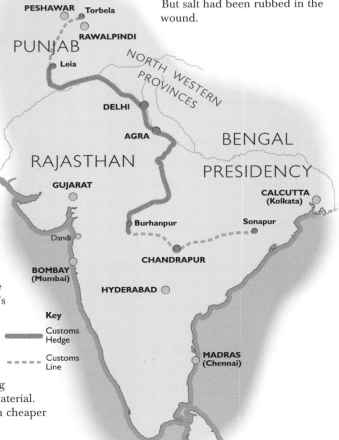

170

SALT OF THE EARTH

The extraordinary importance of salt (for which we recommend Mark Kurlansky's book *Salt, a world history)* is underlined if we list some of the places in our book, famous for other things, but whose original existence was related to salt.

For instance, the only comparable structure to the Great Hedge, the **Great Wall of China**, was financed by the salt revenues that provided half the budget for China's Government. The mummies in **Giza's** pyramids were preserved in salt. **Timbuktu's** trading prominence was based on it. Rome and most of its Empire's cities were built near saltworks; the first Roman road was the Via Salaria and its troops were paid 'salaries.' The naval battle at **Actium** was marked by Cleopatra's purple salt-dyed sails. Rome's Jewish provinces were buoyed by the salt at **Masada** and **Sodom**. When Attila the Hun burst into the Empire at **Mainz**, the one place that survived was **Venice**, which created its salt trading monopoly, building a magnificent city, together with its **Getto**.

Salt helped the cod fishing industry off **Maelstrom**, made the salted **Parma** ham and **Gorgonzola** cheese delicious, and was the first economic boost for **Ibiza, Berchtesgaden** and **Landsberg**. Cheshire salt was carried by the **Bridgewater Canal** and built Liverpool's wealth – without which we might not have had **The Cavern** and the Beatles and **Abbey Road**. Salt provided the healing powers at **Spa, Vichy, Bath** and Hot Springs, New Mexico, renamed **Truth or Consequences.**

In the Americas, it made and then broke the Aztecs, and a salt-works was created by the settlers at **Jamestown**. Captain Cook's voyages without the bane of scurvy were possible because of sauerkraut (salted cabbage), so he could discover **Pearl Harbor** with its later salt beds.

Napoleon's retreat to the **Berezina** was made worse by lack of salt for disinfectants.

Salt taxes usually proved a bad idea, the equivalent of poll taxes, and worse for the poor. The foolish 'gabelle' tax infuriated the French population, with 3,000 people imprisoned or executed every year for salt smuggling. It helped lead to the French Revolution and the fall of the **Bastille**. It was as much Britain's salt taxes that led to the **Boston** tea party and the American War of Independence – which nearly failed for lack of salt.

Slavery was only possible with sufficient salt, much of it coming through New Orleans with its **Storyville** district. In the Civil War, the North blockaded the Confederacy principally to block salt from Liverpool, which rose from 5 cents to 25 dollars for 200 lbs. The battle at **Hampton Roads** off **Charleston** was to break the blockade. Confederate President Jefferson Davis excluded only salt workers form the draft, especially those from the huge deposits at Avery Island where **Tabasco** was created. Salt became so valuable that General Pickett was given a precious little packet of salt as a wedding present before his famous doomed charge at **Gettysburg**.

It was the salt drilling techniques that found oil at **Titusville**; which later powered the record-breaking cars on the salt flats at **Bonneville** and the aircraft at **Muroc**. The worst **Gulags** were the salt mines. And so it goes on ...

THE GREAT WALL
China

If you stood on the moon, apparently you would be able to see just one man-made feature, the Great Wall of China. This incredible structure stretches 4,500 miles, from the mountains of Korea to the flat Gobi Desert.

It would never have been started in 221 B.C. but for the unique and ruthless will of one man, the first Emperor, Qin Shi Huang. His first 3,000 mile fortification was designed to keep

The Great Wall stretches for 4,500 miles.

See: Great Hedge of India, Kwai River, Tiananmen Square

marauding nomads out of China. Emperor Qin ruled his country with an iron grip, burning Confucian literature lest it give people any ideas of not conforming to rigid rules, a capital offence. Intellectuals were sent for years of forced labour on the Great Wall. Qin's 3,000 miles were built in 10 years, nearly a mile a day at a cost of a million people – 300 dead for every mile. But Qin was used to grandiose building works; not only vast and useful irrigation works but also his useless and grandiose Great Tomb, on which 700,000 of his citizens slaved for 34 years, a huge but

miniature empire including the famous 7,000 terracotta soldiers.

In spite of high quality iron swords (not to be rivalled for 13 centuries in the West) and superb crossbows for his army, Qin's dynasty was swept away in 209 BC, by internal revolt only a year after Qin's death. The Great Wall remained and was vastly improved and extended in the Ming Dynasty in 1368, a rule which we now associate with the blue-white porcelain which bears its name – and the early seafaring exploits which brought silk, spices, porcelain and a new drink, called tea, to the Middle East and Europe.

The Great Wall, previously built of compacted earth, was improved by being faced with mass-produced bricks, using the same high-temperature kiln technology that produced Ming porcelain. The wall was not only a barrier but also effectively a military road, with watchtowers every few hundred yards, garrison towns and a signal system of fires burning a mixture of straw and dung. One black column of smoke indicated a small raid, and four columns a serious attack by as many as 10,000 men.

Especially when it snakes up and down across steep mountains and defiles, the Wall is truly impressive and even beautiful, and for centuries it did its job. When China was conquered, as by the Mongols and the Mandarins, it was not the design or the strength of the Wall that failed, but a void of political power and poverty within China.

The concept of a military wall, which was first started 200 years before Christ, with a length the same as Miami to the North Pole, or Paris to Delhi, fully manned and operational for 2,000 years continues to amaze us. Indeed it makes modern transience look feeble.

GREENHAM COMMON
England

Outside Newbury in Berkshire lies a piece of land which shaped political and military history. For nineteen years, between 1981 and 2000, the Women's Peace Camp at Greenham Common was a powerful symbol for the issue of nuclear disarmament.

Before 1938, the land was owned by the Lord of the Manor as part of his Greenham Lodge Estate. A year later it was bought for use as common land by Newbury, with the inhabitants of Newbury granted full access and commoners' rights to the 856 acres. Despite intermittent military use over the next forty years, during both WW2 and the Cold War, the commoners' rights were never revoked.

In October 1977, Chancellor Schmidt of West Germany and British Prime Minister Jim Callaghan asked the United States to deploy more modern deterrent forces to NATO countries. After failing to persuade the Soviets to withdraw their SS-20 missiles, NATO responded with plans for 464 Ground Launched Cruise Missiles (GLCMs) to be in place in five NATO countries by 1986. On June 17th 1980 the British Government announced two British Cruise bases, RAF Molesworth in Cambridgeshire and Greenham Common, which would be the first base in Europe to receive sixteen missiles in December 1983. Taken at face value, it may seem that this was the catalyst which stirred the women's peace campaign into action. In fact, the situation was far more complex and yet also spontaneous.

Influenced by a combination of feminism and anti-militarism, horror over Hiroshima and Nagasaki spurred groups like the Women's Co-operative Guild to raise public alarm to atomic and hydrogen bomb testing. Meanwhile, the conflicts of feminism in the 1950s and 1960s forced women to choose between domesticity or career. This climate, coupled with the intense secrecy which surrounded Britain's development of atomic bombs and alignment with the US over nuclear policy, left many women feeling excluded from issues of worldwide political importance. Feminist writer Elizabeth Wilson summarised that women *'were everywhere – and yet they were nowhere'.*

From 1958, the Campaign for Nuclear Disarmament established itself as a protest organisation – but it was largely controlled by men, and was without the maternalist focus of the Women's Co-operative Guild. As the Women's Liberation Movement developed and women gained greater access to higher education and jobs, contraception, abortion and childcare, it became clear that now that they had found the confidence to speak out, they intended to be heard.

Meanwhile, throughout Europe there was concern over nuclear power. Denmark, West Germany and Holland all saw protests against atomic power sites and towards the end of the 1970s this concern became more specifically focused among the women's movement.

It was from this perspective that Ann Pettitt came. It was her idea for the womens' march from Cardiff to Greenham that snowballed into what we now associate with Greenham Common. Living in Wales with her partner and two young children, her concerns about pollution, radiation leaks and the arms race led her to found a local group called Carmarthen Anti-Nuclear Campaign (CANC). Inspired by a similar event between Copenhagen and Paris, Pettitt hit upon the idea of holding a women-led protest march.

Fellow enthusiast, student, Lynne Whittemore recalled: *'We got the map out and said, 'Where should it go?' … And we decided it should go to Greenham Common, rather than Aldermaston because of Cruise'.* The idea was to publicise the existence of the base and, of course, they also needed a route practical for walkers of varying ages and degrees of fitness. CANC contacted a number of peace,

The cruise missile and its mobile launcher

One of many unorthodox methods of protest as the Greenham Common women block the gate of the airbase with string

environmental and womens' groups and on 27th August 1981 the 120-mile walk began. Thirty six women, four men and three children set off from Cardiff. As they walked through rural Avon and Wiltshire they handed out leaflets. But by the time they were halfway to their destination the women realised that their action was not causing the national media interest they had anticipated. Something more was needed.

After much discussion it was decided that on arrival at Greenham four women would chain themselves to the fence of the airbase. CND speakers and local protest groups greeted them and a rally was held, demanding a televised debate on the subject of Cruise being sited in Britain. The base Commander of Greenham said that, since they were technically on common land, they could stay as long as they liked. Helen John recalled: *'So it was at that moment, it was about six o'clock on the Saturday night, that we decided we would just stay there. It hadn't been planned. That's just literally what happened'.*

After this spontaneous start, the camp took on a life of its own. Despite their serious quest, the women wanted their experience to remain fun, boosting morale by laughing at themselves through humorous songs. Decisions were taken on a collective basis of unanimous consent, and in this way it was decided the camp should become women-only.

Word spread and thousands more women came. Some stayed for months or years at a time; some camped for a few days; others simply visited for the day. They lived in shelters called 'Benders', constructed from branches with plastic to keep them dry.

As the time approached for the arrival of Cruise, the tolerance of the authorities towards the women waned. The direct

action tactics employed by the women included demonstrations, blockades, and incursions into the base by cutting the fence with bolt-cutters. Newbury Magistrates began to charge the women initially with criminal damage, and then with trespass. As relations soured still further, Newbury District Council made numerous attempts to evict them. The right-wing media vilified them as a motley collection of *'squalid misfits, unfit mothers and lesbians'.* The campers claimed that they were exposed to electromagnetic radiation from the microwave security system installed at the base. This caused symptoms such as severe headaches, temporary paralysis, drowsiness, abnormal menstrual bleeding and faulty speech co-ordination. It has never been established whether this 'zapping' of the women was deliberate.

After the end of the Cold War and the fall of the Berlin Wall in 1989, the last missile returned to the United States in March 1991. The Peace Camp remained, however, as a continuing protest against nuclear weapons. The last women did not leave until September 2000.

There are those who still question the choice of Greenham Common from plenty of other bases with atomic weapons. Defence experts have pointed out that Cruise was a real headache for the Russians, who had spent enormous amounts of money on anti-ballistic systems to destroy rockets, and on air defence systems to shoot down conventional bombers. The Cruise Missile, as we now all know, has the extraordinary ability to fly extremely low, hugging the ground guided by the technology that only the Americans can handle, and delivering its payload to within yards of its intended target. As such, the Cruise Missile was for the Russians an extremely unwelcome addition to the arms race and, indeed, probably played a role in making them run out of money while trying to match the Americans.

Most of the women at Greenham Common could probably not have told you the technical significance of the weapon about which they were protesting so vigorously. If so, it does not take a tremendous leap of imagination to guess who might have helped to finance their efforts.

GREENWICH
England

'Can you tell me the time?' A straightforward enough question. But things would be very different if it were not for a simple meridian line running through the Greenwich Royal Observatory.

This corner of London, beside the River Thames, has a history dating back to the 9th century, and one with strong connections to the English Royal family. It was the birthplace of Henry VIII, Mary Tudor and Elizabeth I, and is home to some the finest baroque buildings in the country, including Queen's House designed by Inigo Jones for Queen Anne of Denmark, wife of James I. However, Greenwich is world-famous for 'Greenwich Mean Time' (GMT), the modern equivalent of what is known as Co-ordinated Universal Time, and from which the time zones of the world are calculated.

Until fairly recently, time-keeping was a much more haphazard affair than it is today, because the concept of accurate, standardised time was not used or even needed. Only sailors required a precise idea of the time in order to plot their longitudinal position at sea. Other people rarely travelled out of their own village or town, and so had no need to know the time in other regions.

It was not until 1833, when Britain had both the world's largest navy and merchant marine fleet, that the world's first permanent visual time signal was installed at the Greenwich Royal Observatory. It is known as the 'Timeball' and consists of a 5 foot diameter red ball mounted on a mast on top of one of the Observatory turrets. At five minutes to one each day, the ball is hoisted halfway up the mast. At two minutes to one, it reaches the top of the mast and, at exactly one o'clock, it drops. The original wood and canvas ball was sadly destroyed in 1855 when it was blown into the Observatory courtyard. A replacement, however, is still there – and drops every day (except when there are very high winds). Its position meant that the ball was clearly visible from the River Thames, so that seafarers about to set sail down the Thames Estuary could rely on it to set their chronometers. The reason that one o'clock was originally chosen – and not midday – was that at twelve o'clock, the sailors on the ships in the Thames were busily making observations with their sextants as to the height of the sun - and therefore their position.

Aside from this maritime ritual however, time-keeping prior to the late nineteenth century was still done on a local basis, with each town setting its clocks to synchronise with the transit of the sun. But, because the sun rises and sets at different times, even within the same country, there was considerable variation. In Bristol, for example, the sun rises sixteen minutes later than it does in London, so the local time would be sixteen minutes behind the capital. A clockmaker - or the town clock - would show the 'official' time, and the citizens would set their own pocket watches and clocks to the time of the town.

The idea of introducing a standardised time across Britain had been suggested

The 'Timeball' which used to set the time for every ship leaving London

by several people since the 1820s. Dr. William Hyde Wollaston is credited with the first proposal, when he recommended that all post-office clocks in the United Kingdom should be synchronised *'by means of the time brought from London by the mail-coach chronometer'*.

In addition, he predicted: *'eventually, all the clocks and watches of private persons would fall into the same course of regulation, so that only one expression of time would prevail over the country'*. It was to be several more years, however, before the idea was treated with real seriousness, and over sixty years before standardised time for the whole world was adopted with Greenwich at its heart.

The catalyst for change was the railways. As towns and cities across Britain became connected, running the trains on time – and to the same time – became a priority, quite an irony in view of the notoriously poor time-keeping of today's trains. In 1840, despite the Government's rejections of the introduction of a standard time, the Great Western Railway ordered that London time would apply throughout its network. The other railway companies and the Post Office soon followed suit, and before long, the public clocks in major cities such as Manchester and Liverpool showed London time. In 1847, the railway co-ordinating body officially adopted Greenwich time as the standard. The new system was put to the test four years later when six million people travelled from across the country to visit Crystal Palace for the Great

Greenwich began the movement to standardise time across the world.

See: Rock Island, Promontory

Exhibition of 1851. Most of them travelled by train.

Meanwhile, on a rather larger scale, similar discussions had been taking place in North America. The size of the country meant that it was not practical to use the same time across the whole of the United States. In 1878, Canadian Sir Sanford Fleming proposed a system of worldwide time zones – twenty four in total, each spaced 15 degrees of longitude apart. With the earth turning 360 degrees in 24 hours, this meant that each time zone would be one hour ahead or behind the next.

United States railroads, which also needed precise schedules for signalling and controls, began using Fleming's system on November 18th 1883, and the following year a conference was held in Washington DC to select the location which was to become the Prime Meridian.

Greenwich was chosen, becoming the place that would be measured at zero degrees longitude. The precise position of the Prime Meridian was defined by the cross hairs in the eyepiece of the large Transit Circle telescope built by Sir George Biddell Airy, the seventh Astronomer Royal. The telescope is situated in the Observatory's Meridian Building, and this position continues to be the original reference – even though slight movement of the earth's crust means that the Prime Meridian now moves very slightly from side to side of the official line. It is the place where east meets west, the starting point for the 24 time zone system – and the place around which the whole of the world's maps are orientated.

GRETNA GREEN
Scotland

If you were to ask any American to name a popular destination for eloping couples to marry, they would invariably reply 'Las Vegas', or 'Niagara Falls'. However, ask an Englishman, or a Scot, and they would tell you that Gretna Green had been providing this service for twenty years before America was even born.

In 1754, England passed a law, Lord Hardwicke's Marriage Act – declaring that anyone under the age of twenty-one could only marry with parental consent. Scotland's view on marriage has always been more lenient. If you are over the age of sixteen, all you require is two witnesses, and two 'I do's'.

One of the more bizarre aspects to a

wedding in Gretna Green is that most marriages are performed over a blacksmith's anvil. To many, this is the enduring image of the tradition. The idea stems from melding two metals together over the anvil and, as very important people in the community, blacksmiths could 'forge' together a marriage in much the same way.

Over 4,000 couples marry at Gretna Green each year, representing about thirteen per cent of all weddings in Scotland. One of the oldest surviving marriage certificates from Gretna is dated 11th June 1772.

Situated just over the border (less than twenty miles from Carlisle), directly on the main route from England to Scotland, it is little wonder that there are countless stories of young lovers rushing to Gretna, with an angry father close behind.

One dramatic example is the tale of the Earl of Westmoreland and his lover Sarah Anne Child. In May, 1752, racing northwards, with Sarah's father Robert Child in hot pursuit, they managed to get within a few miles of the border before being intercepted by the furious Mr Child, who leapt from his carriage and shot the horse leading the young lovers' carriage. Undeterred, the couple cut the dead horse free, continued with only three horses, and were married by Joseph Paisley, one of Gretna's best known Anvil Priests.

Sixty years later, Sarah's grand-daughter was to repeat the family tradition when she eloped with Captain Charles Parke Ibbetson. The girl's disappearance was even featured in *The Times* newspaper, under the headline, *'The Mysterious disappearance of Lady Adela Villers.'* Lady Adela's brother, Captain Frederick Villiers arrived in Gretna 24 hours too late. All he could do was acquire a copy of the marriage certificate, and inform their incensed parents. It seems that the parents were finally persuaded of the sincerity of the vows, as the couple repeated the marriage at a London church, with all the usual ceremony, but none of the secretive romance that Gretna offered the first time.

Gretna Green has been the backdrop to thousands of such stories of love, and even today, young couples elope regularly to marry at one of the 'anvils'. Although, thanks to fast cars and modern motorways, only a few hour's headstart will be more than enough to evade even the most disapproving of parents.

GUERNICA
Spain

When judged against the sinister roll call of later bombing raids – Rotterdam, Coventry, Hamburg, Dresden, Tokyo and Hiroshima – Guernica's tragedy *could* seem modest. 1,654 people were killed and 900 wounded by 34 tons of bombs, the load of just four Lancasters six years later. But Guernica was to achieve worldwide fame as the first civilian town to be deliberately targeted, and unfortunately by no means the last.

Guernica is the spiritual heart and centre of Basque cultural tradition, with its famous oak – a 600 year old stump where the Kings of Spain took the oath to respect the rights of Viscaya. In April 1937, this little market town found itself, sadly, all too near the front line in Spain's civil war, with General Franco's Nationalists advancing into the shrinking areas controlled by the Republic.

At 4.30 in the afternoon on a crowded Monday market day on 27th April, the church bell rang. Moments later, the first bombs from a single plane rained down on the main square. Junkers and Heinkel bombers of the 'volunteer' Condor Legion, led by Wolfram von Richtofen, cousin of the Red Baron, then came in steadily and low, having nothing to fear from ground defence. It is claimed that they were trying out the techniques of *'total war'* advocated by Ludendorff and the Italian General Douhet, whereby the deliberate targeting of civilians and their ensuing panic would assist war aims. Ignoring any military targets, for three hours the German bombers unloaded high explosive and incendiary bombs on the blazing centre of Guernica. The hospitals of Josefinas and Santa Clara

Apart from commissioning the painting for the 1937 International Exposition in Paris, the Republic spent a fortune on Guernica as a propaganda

'Guernica', Picasso's famous painting that has made sure the town is still famous

were soon burning ruins, with most of the churches and houses reduced to rubble. Bodies of people and sheep were mixed up in the bloody shambles of the market place. People were machine-gunned in the fields and farmhouses. A panicked procession of ox-drawn farm carts streamed towards Bilbao.

But it was a painting which has kept the name of the town famous – Pablo Picasso's masterpiece, *Guernica*. With its screaming horse and pathetic mother with her dead child, the deliberately monochrome work conveys the horror of the raid on such a defenceless target.

See: Biggin Hill, Hiroshima, Peenemunde

coup. The Nationalists responded by first claiming that the raid never occurred, then insisting that the damage was deliberately increased by the dynamiting of buildings by Basque miners.

Whatever the truth, the name of Guernica will forever be an icon for the ruthless targeting of civilians from the air. It is appropriate that the town has now linked itself with Dresden, the German city in which 100,000 people died in the closing weeks of the Second World War.

GULAG
Soviet Union

'The nation which forgets its history will have to live through it once again'.
- Alexander Solshenitsyn

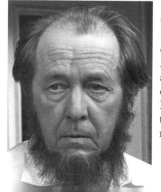

Until 1973 most of the world had never heard the word 'Gulag'. But that year the first volume of a book – *The Gulag Archipelago* – was smuggled out of Russia and published in Paris. Alexander Solzhenitsyn had recorded an account of the vast system of prison camps that he himself had experienced. He was attacked in the Soviet press and then arrested for treason and exiled, to receive the Nobel Prize in December 1974. He was extremely lucky in his

exile, because his book had touched a very raw nerve.

The Gulags were the result of state oppression, starting as soon as the Bolsheviks obtained power in 1917. Those perceived enemies who were not immediately shot went to labour camps, (the first was probably Solovetsky), and, like the first concentration camp at Dachau in Germany, became a prototype for a whole brutal system. In a country which was desperate to expand

and industrialize, Lenin and his Soviet colleagues soon realised that prisoners could be forced to work at virtually no cost to the state. With no wages, and only meagre food and shelter, they could be worked until they died.

The prisoners built canals, railway lines, roads, power stations and slaved in mines for salt, coal, copper and gold. Soon a vast system of camps built up, called the Gulag, shortened from *Glavnoye Upravleniye Ispranitelno-Trudovykh Lagerei* (Chief Directorate of Labour Camps). Literally millions of people disappeared into the maw of the Gulags, often deep in isolated and inhospitable Siberia and the frozen north. At first, they housed common criminals but these were soon joined by the intelligentsia and the Kulaks (wealthy peasants) who resisted collectivisation of their farms. In 1918, Lenin ordered the hanging of one hundred Kulaks just to set an example.

But it was during the Great Terror of Stalin that the Gulags were at their worst, with 25 million inmates incarcerated through no fault of their own. Probably one of the most tragic cases was that of captured Russian soldiers, a few of whom had survived the lethal German prison camps and had

gone back into action when liberated. After the war they headed back to Moscow by train, looking forward to seeing their families for the first time in four years, only to find that the trains failed to stop at Moscow and instead continued to the east and straight to fresh imprisonment in the Gulags. Their crime? According to the Soviet authorities they were tainted by Western influence. Nicolai Getman was one of them, whose unique and shocking visual record of paintings is now carefully preserved by The Jamestown Foundation in Washington.

With Perestroika, the collapse of the Soviet Union and political change, the Gulags are no more. But because of the enormous impact of Solzhenitsyn's *Gulag Archipelago*, the word Gulag is now applied to any system used to crush dissidents and silence citizens.

'Moving Out' shows prisoners sitting in the snow during a halt on the fifteen day journey to the camps. One of fifty Gulag paintings by Nicolai Getman.

See: Andersonville, Andrassy, Bastille, Changi, Dachau, Devil's Island, Getto

HAIGHT/ASHBURY
California, USA

'If you go to San Francisco, Be sure to wear some flowers in your hair'.

Time and again the City of San Francisco has had to replace the sign on the corner of Haight and Ashbury streets in San Francisco. For many, there cannot be a sign more worth stealing. Why? For a brief moment in the 1960s, the intersection was home to a new phenomenon, a counter-culture of youth which would have a major effect on America and the rest of the world.

Up to 1965, the 'Hashbury' was known as a quiet neighbourhood of old Victorian houses filled with blue collar workers, students, black families and orientals all taking advantage of the cheap rents. Some were 'beats' from North Beach, followers of Jack Kerouac

after his book *On the Road* came out in 1957. Following the Russians' success with the first satellite in space, *Sputnik*, journalist Herb Caen had coined a name that stuck, 'Beatnik'. There was also *'Hippie'*, which was the rude word used by black 'hipsters' to describe their white hangers-on.

It was in the month of January 1967 that Haight/Ashbury took off as a focus for the youth movement, propelled by one event in nearby Golden Gate Park. It was the 'Human Be-in', described by organiser Allen Cohen, editor of the underground *San Francisco Oracle*, as *'The Gathering of the Tribes in a union of love and activism.'* Twenty thousand young people listened to 'Jefferson Airplane', 'Quicksilver Messenger Service' and 'The Grateful Dead', while

Allen Ginsberg read poetry, and advocate of the drug culture, Timothy Leary, memorably advised, 'Turn on, tune in, and drop out.'

Coinciding with the height of US involvement in the Vietnam war – to which 540,000 troops had been committed – was the beginning of the 'Summer of Love.' Hundreds of thousands of young people chanting 'make love, not war' flocked to Haight/Ashbury, which had become home to legendary icons of the era. 'The Grateful Dead' lived at 710 Ashbury, Janis Joplin at 635, Country Joe and the Fish at 638, and Jimi Hendrix had an apartment at 1524 Haight.

Sadly, Joplin and Hendrix would soon be dead, the hippies would depart – and the area would decline into poverty, crime and anonymity – today being restored to gentrification. But the influence lived on and spread all over the world. Just as bowler-hatted and square Britain had been bowled over by the Beatles and Rolling Stones, so would buttoned-down America be influenced forever by what happened around one street intersection. The kids, to use their own phrase, had 'left no turn unstoned'.

See: Bazaar, Carnaby Street, Glastonbury, Sibylla's, Studio 54, Woodstock

HAMBURG
New York, USA

There are two world-famous places called Hamburg. First there is the huge city in Germany, built up over hundreds of years to become its largest port. Then, there is the small town of Hamburg in Erie County, New York State, which has given its name to the most famous fast food sandwich in the world.

In 1812, the town of Willink was subdivided into three towns, Eden, Concord and Hamburg. Historians reject

the idea that Hamburg was named in honour of the German city, because no Germans arrived for another eighteen years. They believe it was simply picked from a map of Europe by the State Land Office. Local prosperity increased with the building of the Erie Canal, and roads began to improve the communications for an agricultural community, best known for 'Hamburg Cheese' which was even sold abroad. It was but a hint of what was to come. In 1865, the Erie County Agricultural Society met to decide where to stage their famous annual Fair. After much debate, by just one vote (18-17), they took up Luther Titus's offer of his land at Hamburg, together with its harness racing track. The Fair has remained there ever since.

Twenty years later, Frank and Charles Menches arrived to sell their hot pork sausage sandwiches at the Fair, bringing the new gasoline stove they had created whilst working in railroad yards. Unlike wood and coal cookers, this was clean, and that year they were favoured by a new Fair ruling banning the dirtier cookers, which had been particularly resented by lady visitors with their white dresses. But a crisis threatened. Warm and humid weather had halted local pork butchering, so Andrew Klein, the butcher, offered them ten pounds of beef instead. An anxious Frank Menches decided he would only risk five pounds. When the patties of beef were cooked, Frank thought they seemed to lack something. 'Salt don't seem to develop the flavour'. 'Why not try sugar?' said his brother, half as a joke. A little brown sugar was sprinkled on, and the effect was instant. Customers began to line up, and Frank wondered about a name for their new product.

One customer asked in German, 'Gutte schmeck! Was ist?' ('Good taste!

See: Bournville, Champagne, Cognac, Fray Bentos, Gorgonzola, Hershey, Pilsen

What is it?'). 'Hamburger' was Frank's reply. Within an hour he had tacked up a huge sign with HAMBURGERS written in charcoal. A star was born.

The Menches brothers and their hamburgers hit it really big when they obtained a concession at the 1893 Chicago World's Fair, thanks to their friend, future US President, William McKinley. The popularity of the tasty hamburger was phenomenal, and soon swept the nation. During the First World War, Washington tried to change its German-sounding name to 'Salisbury Steak' (along with 'liberty cabbage' for sauerkraut and 'child's garden' for kindergarten). In vain. The hamburger can be found all over the world, with McDonalds and Burger King perhaps the greatest exponents of this very American export.

The Erie County Fair is now the biggest in America, and in 1992 the great-grandchildren of Frank and Charles Menches served customers their ancestors' invention at Burgerfest '92.

Others may claim the hamburger, including Germany's Hamburg and St Louis, but the citizens of Hamburg, New York, feel they know the truth.

Ohio food vendors Charles Menches, left, and his brother Frank, are said to have invented hamburgers when they ran out of sausage pork at the Erie County Fair in 1885.

Heirs of hamburger inventors revive family trade at festival

By ELIZABETH O'MARA
News Staff Reporter

Descendants of the men credited with inventing the hamburger at the Erie County Fair more than 100 years ago will be in the Village of Hamburg this weekend to serve

BURGERFEST '92 HIGHLIGHTS

The appeal of Burgerfest '92 should extend beyond

Taste of Hamburg," from noon to 8:30 p.m.

HAMPTON ROADS
South Carolina, USA

In London, Henry Adams wrote, *'About a week ago, the British discovered that their whole wooden navy is useless'*. Indeed, it was.

It all began in April 1861 when young Confederate naval Lt. Spottywood had managed to put out a fuse, which was meant to blow up Gosport Naval Yard in Chesapeake Bay, abandoned prematurely by Union forces. Apart from 150 tons of powder and 2,000 precious guns, the yard contained the *Merrimac* – a half-burned steam frigate. Said Confederate Secretary of the Navy, Stephen Mallory, 'I regard the possession of an iron-armoured ship as a matter of the first necessity. Such a vessel could traverse the entire coast of the United States, prevent all blockades and encounter, with a fair prospect of success, their entire navy'. So the

Merrimac was rebuilt, now sheathed with two feet of sloping timber and four inches of steel plate, with a one-ton prow under the water for ramming. News of the iron-clad monster, re-named the *Virginia*, terrified Washington – and the Union turned to the inventor John Ericsson, scarcely on speaking terms with the US Navy after an accident which had killed 2 Cabinet members. But between rows and arguments, he agreed to deliver an armoured vessel in 90 days. It was to be only just in time.

On Saturday, March 8th 1862 in Hampton Roads, it was washday on the Union ships – with laundry drying in the rigging – when the strange, sinister, shape of the *Virginia* steamed slowly but inexorably towards them, *'like a huge, half-submerged crocodile'*, as the pilot of the *USS Cumberland* was to remember.

The Virginia, left, and the 'Monitor' bouncing shells off each other

See: Kiel Canal, Trafalgar, Tsushima

With her shots bouncing off the *Virginia* 'like India rubber balls', the *Cumberland* was rammed, ravaged by gunfire and sunk in shallow water. The *Congress* was then quickly set on fire, and the *Minnesota* damaged and grounded. Luckily, night fell. The *Virginia* intended to finish her work on the Union fleet in the morning.

But the Confederate Navy's rule of the waves lasted just one day, because in the middle of the night, by the light of the

burning *Congress*, a strange vessel moored next to the *Minnesota*. It was Ericsson's *Monitor* which had limped slowly all the way from New York.

So it was that when dawn broke, the confident crew of the *Virginia* saw what looked like 'an immense shingle floating on the water, with a gigantic cheese box rising from its centre; no sails, no wheels, no smokestack, no guns. What could it be?' In fact, the *Monitor* had two big guns in a turret which revolved, and with those she began to fire at the *Virginia*. For four and half hours they battled it out, colliding five times and firing continuously with no effect. It was a stand-off.

Neither ship lasted more than a few more months. The *Monitor* was sunk in a gale and the *Virginia* blown up when Gosport was recaptured by the Union.

But in two memorable days, the events at Hampton Roads changed the naval world for ever.

HARLEM
New York, USA

Harlem, the area of New York City that we know today, was the direct result of a property boom and bust.

It was Peter Stuyvesant, the Dutch Governor of New Amsterdam, who called the northern part of the island of Manhattan 'Nieuw Haarlem', after the city of Haarlem in Holland. There were prosperous farms on the flatter eastern side and large estates on the western side owned by rich city families like the Delanceys, Bleekers, Rikers, Beekmans and Hamiltons. Broadway, a wagon track, wended its way through them.

In the 1830s, both the farms and the estates declined, and much of Harlem became the home of poor immigrants living in shanty towns. New York's increased prosperity after the Civil War led to massive property speculation, especially when both the Lenox Avenue subway and the elevated railway were built north of Central Park. Harlem was designed to be a prosperous white middle-class area, particularly for the Germans and British.

But disaster struck in the form of a collapse in the real estate market in 1904

and 1905, leaving the speculators and builders with a real crisis on their hands.

By chance, an enterprising black entrepreneur, Philip Payton, and his recently formed Afro-American Realty Company were on hand to benefit both sides. He was able to acquire the leases and then offer middle-class black families accommodation at low cost in a 'better' neighbourhood previously denied to them. Four years later, the construction of Penn Station brought the demolition of a large part of overcrowded 'Hell's Kitchen', and thousands of the black residents were evicted. They, too, went north to Harlem. Within ten years Harlem had become an almost entirely black community, attracting thousands more each year.

The area became the natural centre for political improvements. The National Association for the Advancement of Coloured People (NAACP) was founded in 1910, and Marcus Garvey's Universal Negro Improvement Association in 1916.

In art, literature and theatre, Harlem created a cultural renaissance and with clubs like Small's Paradise and the Savoy Ballroom, Harlem continues to be associated with music, especially jazz. Names like Fats Waller, Willie 'The Lion' Smith and Eubie Blake, together with big bands like Fletcher Henderson and Chuck Webb, are all part of the legend. The success of black shows like *Shuffle Along, Liza, Running Wild* and *Chocolate Dandies* created white enthusiasm for jazz and dancing. Among the five hundred jazz places, there were eleven nightspots that *Variety* called, *'class white-trade nightclubs'*, with *'high yeller girls in chorus lines, comedians and dancers'*. The most famous of all was the Cotton Club, with its strange combination of black musicians and staff and whites-only audiences, and with Duke Ellington's music beamed by CBS radio to the nation.

The Depression hit Harlem hard, with eighty per cent on benefit, and in 1935,

frustration over jobs and discrimination led to a full-scale riot which helped to drive out business – including the Cotton Club. The 'Mink Set' led by Mayor Jimmy Walker and the Broadway stars were no longer willing to go up to 'slum it'.

Today, Harlem has poor schooling, high unemployment, drugs and crime. Its sudden growth by chance, and its subsequent fame by chance, may have led to a ghetto which may take a long time and a great deal of effort to change.

GRIMSDALE

See: Big Apple, Bedloe's Island, Broadway, Cotton Club, Ellis Island, Empire State Building, Getto, Gotham, Menlo Park, Studio 54, Tammany Hall, Tuxedo Club, Wall Street, World Trade Center

HARLEY STREET
England

In London there are some streets whose names have become synonymous with particular trades. 'Downing Street' and 'Whitehall' mean Government, 'Savile Row' denotes fine gentlemen's tailoring, 'Fleet Street' was once the press and 'Harley Street' is medicine.

In 1668, Samuel Pepys, the diarist, recorded visiting the village of St Mary-le-Bourne: *'a pretty place called Marrowbone'*. He probably walked up Marylebone Lane, a narrow footpath crossing the fields from the northern edge of London, which was Soho Square. Soon afterwards, Edward Harley married the daughter of the Duke of Newcastle, Henrietta Cavendish, and her estate was steadily built upon. Harley became Chancellor of the Exchequer and, in 1711, was made Earl of Oxford. The old Tyburn Road became Oxford Street, and other streets were named for family connections – Wimpole Street, Cavendish Square, Portland Place, Mortimer Street and Welbeck Street.

The great Regency period saw the realisation of the plans of the Regent's favourite architect – John Nash – for his particularly fine Regent Street, and the completion of the elegant streets north of

Wigmore Street, one destined to become the byword for medical skill – Harley Street.

It was in the mid-1850s that the first doctors and surgeons arrived in Harley and Wimpole Streets. At first they lived there, using the ground floors for their consulting rooms. Other private clinics moved into the area, adding to its fame, with the oldest medical society in the world – the Medical Society of London – created in Chandos Street to bring together the physicians, surgeons and apothecaries who were then at loggerheads. Joseph Lister also fought his long campaign with such men for sterilisation in the surgery and operating theatre.

Florence Nightingale, too, struggled against the convention that English women could not use their education to go beyond either lightweight frivolity or domestic routine. After many years, in 1853, her father relented and she applied her knowledge of nursing abroad in her new post as 'Superintendent of the Hospital for Invalid Gentlewomen' in Harley Street. It was just in time for her revolutionary

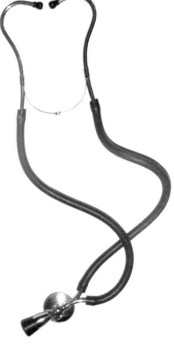

183

role in the hospitals of the Crimean War, where the grateful wounded called her 'The Lady with the Lamp'.

By the 1930s, such was Harley Street's reputation that the area became known as 'Pill Island'. After World War II, the custom grew of each house being shared by several medical men and women – who number in total 1,500 today.

Indeed, modern Harley Street is almost entirely medical, and the leases, issued by the Howard de Walden Estate, encourage only medical practices and clinics. However, the few people who do live there must surely feel in very safe hands.

See: Carnaby St, Fleet St, Getto, Lloyd's, Savile Row, Storyville, Tin Pan Alley, Wall St

HARPERS FERRY
West Virginia, USA

Harpers Ferry lies in Jefferson County, West Virginia, at the confluence of the Shenandoah and Potomac rivers. For most of its history, this small community was relatively unknown, although it was here that John Hall invented and perfected interchangeable parts for rifles. But it was the autumn of 1859 that really put Harpers Ferry on the map when it became forever associated with the name of a courageous, uncompromising civil rights activist – John Brown – immortalised in song (to the tune of 'The Battle Hymn of the Republic'):

John Brown

John Brown's body lies a-mouldering in the grave,
But his soul goes marching on…'

Brown was a wool trader born in the year 1800 at Torrington, Connecticut. He had a lifelong, all consuming hatred of slavery, which he passed on to his children; and together they were more than prepared to take up arms in defence of the freedom of black Americans. In 1854, Brown and some of his sons moved to the newly-formed state of Kansas to campaign against slavery. One of his sons died in a fight with pro-slavery opponents, and at Osawatomie in 1856, Brown and his followers, fought and won a pitched battle against pro-slavery raiders from nearby Missouri. Kansas was to vote against slavery.

On 16th October 1859, with a party of 16 white and 5 black men, he attacked the Federal Arsenal at Harpers Ferry, seizing weapons and ammunition and holding 17 hostages in the fire engine house until the arrival of US Marines. Alas for him, the 90 US Marines, under the command of Robert E. Lee, surrounded the insurgents. Ten of Brown's men were killed, including two of his sons, and he and a number of others were captured. Brown was quickly brought to trial for *'treason, conspiring with slaves and other rebels, and murder of the first degree'.* He was hanged on 2nd December.

Brown's death placed the issue of slavery firmly on the political agenda, and within two years Union and Confederate States were at war. Ironically, Robert E. Lee, his opponent at Harpers Ferry, would opt to lead the armies of the slave-owning Confederacy, and prove to be its ablest commander. Many of the Virginia Militia – living in a state torn between the two factions – would fight on both sides.

See: Andersonville, Appomattox, Arlington, Charleston, Fort Sumter, Gettysburg, Hampton Roads, Little Big Horn, West Point

HASTINGS
England

When Halley's comet was first seen on 24th April 1066, the Anglo - Saxons saw it as a bad omen. Sadly, they were correct.

King Edward the Confessor died on 5th January 1066. The throne passed, as was often the case, not to any relation of his – but to Harold, son of Earl Godwin and leading noble of England. It seems Edward had nominated him as his successor, and almost more importantly, he had been chosen by a council of England's nobles, who believed that he was the strongest and also the most just candidate.

But as far as William, the ruler of the Normans, observing events from across the channel, was concerned, he had no right to keep it. Harold had stayed at the court of William in 1065, and paid homage to him. Whether this was at all voluntary is unknown, but it certainly led William to believe that Harold would hand him the English crown.

The Bayeux tapestry, a 70-metre long artefact created soon after the Norman Conquest, records the whole story. The tale it tells is not merely a historical one; it is a human tragedy. Telling the tale of of Harold, a basically good man who allowed ambition to overtake his promises. Harold refused to hand the throne over to William, who was so angered that he immediately began construction of an invasion fleet. Harold, ever confident, raised his own army, and prepared to resist the attack.

Neither plan ran smoothly. Adverse winds and storms in the channel prevented William from leaving Normandy, while Harold was distracted by a separate invasion in the north. Harold Hardrada, the Norwegian king, had been provoked into an attack by Tostig, Harold's renegade brother. Having been exiled, he also wanted England's throne. Harold was forced to abandon his position in the south and march his men at breakneck speed to Yorkshire, where the Norwegian army had already defeated Edwin and Morcar, the local earls. Harold crushed the invasion at the Battle of Stamford Bridge, one of the bloodiest battles of the time, and killed off a whole generation of Norwegian nobles, from which the country did not recover for centuries. Harold's losses were also critical, and he was beset by a further problem. The weather had cleared, and William's fleet had crossed the channel and was ravaging southern England.

The Norman army had all the advantages. A large proportion of William's knights fought on horseback,

The Bayeux Tapestry. Curious arrows and an even more curious riding position.

whereas the Anglo Saxon cavalry was token.

Also, after refusing to acknowledge a tribunal from the pope, Harold had so alienated himself that William had been given full papal support. Not only was there a psychological advantage in carrying the pope's battle standards, but soldiers flocked to William's army from all over Europe, eager to save their souls by fighting under them. When 50,000 Norman knights and many other lesser soldiers landed in southern England, with Harold's exhausted and depleted army still in York, it seemed there was no hope of repelling the invasion.

However, as Harold travelled as fast as possible to London, his casualties were partially replaced by men joining him on the way. Furthermore, when he arrived, men from all over the south of England struck out for the capital to add to his army, moved by the valour of their king. If he had waited for these men to arrive, he may have amassed a force large enough to stand against William. But either through over-confidence or through a genuine concern for the lands that the Normans were ravaging, he did not wait – staying in London for only six days. As soon as a small force had gathered, he left to engage the invaders. Even now, Harold's captains advised him to retreat, leaving the Normans to run out of supplies and also weakening them with famine and disease. The re-assembled English fleet had moved into the channel, and cut off

A sign that could be misconstrued

The battlefield today, with Battle Abbey, built by William the Conqueror as 'penance' for the slaughter

eventually they drew the exhausted English line from its hilltop position with a feigned retreat, and gained the upper hand on the flatter ground. As the Norman attack reached Harold's personal retinue, the king himself was killed by an arrow through the eye. In this section of the tapestry, captioned with the Latin words, '*Harold rex interfectus est*' – we see Harold at the point he was slain.

Harold is probably not only the figure with the arrow in his eye, but also the one being cut down by the horseman. It seems that after he was incapacitated by the arrow, the English were over-run, unable to prevent him from being slaughtered by the Norman troops. After night fell on the lengthy battle, the Anglo-Saxons realised that their king was dead and abandoned Hastings. The country was William's.

any chance of William getting any fresh supplies from Normandy.

Unfortunately, Harold was determined to fight, and drew up his small force on a little hill in a region called Hastings. The Norman cavalry tried through repeated uphill charges to dislodge the English line, but the line was not broken. The Anglo - Saxons repelled the attacks with huge axes, said to be so heavy that they could cleave through both horse and rider in one stroke. At one point the Norman army was poised for flight, believing their king to be dead. But when William lifted his helmet to show his men that he was still alive, his army's spirit returned, and

When William the Conqueror took the throne of England, it was more than the exchange of one king for another. All the higher places in both state and church were given to Norman nobles, and soon the Anglo-Saxon language was spoken by none of the country's nobles, and used only in rural areas. Thus, today, there are more English words of Norman descent than Anglo-Saxon. The battle of Hastings had signalled not only a change of ruler, but also a change of the very nature of English nationality.

HAVANA
Cuba

On February 16th 1898, the cruiser USS *Maine* had been at anchor in Havana for three weeks, ostensibly 'showing the colours' as a sign of friendship with Spain, which was attempting to put down a Cuban rebellion. At 9.40 pm, a huge explosion ripped out the bottom of the ship, killing 252 officers and men. This was enough to start a war.

In America, there had been agitation for months to intervene in Cuba, even after Spain had recalled its brutal Governor General, 'The Butcher' Weyler, and made moves to give Cuba home rule. William Randolph Hearst, the powerful publisher of the *New York Journal* had been rabidly advocating action. However, his man in Cuba, the

famous Western artist Frederic Remington, complained by telegram EVERYTHING QUIET, NO TROUBLE HERE. THERE WILL BE NO WAR. I WISH TO RETURN. REMINGTON.
He received the response,
PLEASE REMAIN. YOU FURNISH THE PICTURES AND I WILL FURNISH THE WAR. HEARST.

On 2nd April, the United States eventually declared war – which Spain certainly did not want. President McKinley, a gentle man, was pushed into the war less by firebrand politicians than the public opinion fostered by newspaper barons like Hearst, Pulitzer and Gordon Bennett – the eccentric sportsman who sent Stanley to find Dr

Livingstone. 'We'll whip the Dagos until they howl' was a typical cry of thousands of volunteers who flooded the recruiting stations; (the US army normally only had 30,000 men).

In the far-away Philippines, Admiral Dewey annihilated the Spanish fleet riding at anchor in Manila Bay. In Cuba, led by the bellicose future President Theodore Roosevelt and his 'Rough Riders' to cries of 'Remember the Maine', US forces overcame the now outnumbered Spanish at San Juan Hill. 'Fighting Joe' Wheeler, a former Confederate commander, appeared to be somewhat confused when he encouraged his troops by shouting, 'The damn Yankees can't stop us'.

HOW DO YOU LIKE THE JOURNAL'S WAR?, gloated the headlines. The Americans were in a hurry. They knew the wet season was coming and, with it, the threat of yellow fever and malaria which had stopped the British in the 18th century. In July, the surrounded city of Santiago, with no prospect of relief from Spain, was to surrender. Exclaimed Roosevelt: 'A grand time to be alive. A bully time'.

'Bully' may be the right word. The United States had effectively 'got itself an empire.' Its expansionist faction forced Spain to give up not only Cuba, Puerto Rica and Guam – but insisted on the whole of the Philippines – President McKinley needed a map to locate them. The Filipinos were less than happy to trade one colonial power for another,

rather sanctimonious one, and rebelled. Soon 56,000 US troops were fighting in the Philippines for two years before the rebellion was crushed.

There have been many investigations as to what really happened to the *Maine*. Several ships of the period had been destroyed by the spontaneous explosion of coal dust in bunkers. Many believe that this may have occurred at Havana, leading to a more serious explosion in the *Maine's* magazine. It is a great deal more plausible than a complex underwater sabotage operation by the Spanish, who had no earthly reason to antagonise the United States.

But for whatever reason the *Maine* did blow up at Havana, for the newly expansionist United States it had been – as Secretary of State John Hay had called it – 'A splendid little war'.

The devastating but mysterious explosion that sank The Maine

See: Gleiwitz, Rorke's Drift, Sarajevo, Tonkin Gulf

HENLEY
England

A nyone who has ever taken a train to Henley during the Regatta will undoubtedly realise that something unusual is going on. The carriages are packed every year, with the women in an array of hats and high-heels, and half the men in some of the smartest clothes imaginable and the other half in some of the strangest, with multi-coloured blazers and caps that might normally qualify as fancy dress.

The original Henley Regatta was held in 1839, as much a fair as it was a rowing spectacle. The location is ideal, since the Henley Reach is the longest

stretch of the non-tidal Thames that is straight. Over the years, the amateur rowing has become increasingly focal, and the Regatta has gradually extended from one to a full five days, with preceding qualifying sessions. The number of races is now huge, with almost a hundred being conducted on the main days of the proceedings.

Prince Albert became the Regatta's Royal Patron in 1851, and every reigning monarch since has automatically followed

Veteran official in pink Leander cap

suit, which is why it is called the 'Royal' Regatta.

The dress code for the smartest area, the Stewards' Enclosure, is very specific. Women

The young generation from one of the great rowing schools, Pangbourne College. Tim Eckersley (left of the boat) was later selected for the British team.

are conducted on an unorthodox, one-on-one 'knock-out' system, as opposed to multi-lane races. And, as the event, (costing nearly £2 million a year), is funded primarily by the fees paid by members of the Stewards' Enclosure, it requires no sponsorship or subsidy.

Henley's church looks down on Matthew Pinsent and James Cracknell, Olympic Gold Medallists.

See: Brooklands, Lord's, Wimbledon

must wear skirts below the knee, and men are instructed to wear jacket and tie.

An interesting aspect of the Regatta is its detachment. The distance of the race: 1 mile 550, yards is slightly longer than the standard international distance of 2,000 metres. Furthermore the races

And every year, after the Regatta, the huge stretch of enclosures and tents on the banks of the river are packed away, leaving almost no indication that Henley is anything other than a quiet little town.

HERSHEY
Pennsylvania, USA

For the children of liberated Europe and Asia, the Hershey Bars that American G.I.s handed out were symbols of a rich, bountiful and generous America. The bars were even sometimes used as currency.

Indeed, Milton Hershey must surely be counted among the more generous and philanthropic of the American capitalists.

Descended from Swiss and German stock, he was to get no further than fourth grade at school, but then became an apprentice to a candy maker. After several years in the business in Colorado, New York, Chicago, New Orleans and Philadelphia, he settled finally in Pennsylvania and created the very successful Lancaster Caramel Company.

However, at the Chicago International Exposition in 1893, he became fascinated by German chocolate makers and also their equipment – which he then installed to coat caramels with chocolate. Soon he went further, declaring, 'Caramels are only a fad, chocolate is a permanent thing'. Eventually, in 1900 he sold the caramel company for the then huge sum of a million dollars.

With the money, he created not only the world's largest chocolate factory but also a whole town in the heart of Pennsylvania's dairy country – Hershey. It became the ultimate in successful company towns, with tree-lined streets, homes, shops, a transport system, school, bank, medical facilities, zoo and a park. The main street is Chocolate Avenue and the large hotel was the Cocoa Inn.

The town and its attractions are now visited by nearly three million tourists each year.

Milton and his wife Catherine were childless and created a home for orphan boys, one of whom, Bill Dearden, became President of the company. When he died in 1945, Milton Hershey left everything to the schooling system and to a trust for philanthropic purposes which controls the Hershey Foods Corporation and benefits from its income.

So when you tuck into a 'Hershey Bar' or 'Kisses', you really can feel that your chocolate habit is doing some good!

See: Bournville, Pullman

HEYSEL
Belgium

Fate conspired that an old rundown football stadium near Brussels would be famous for a major tragedy.

On 29th May 1985, the European Cup Final between Liverpool and Juventus of Turin was to be played at Heysel, where the neutral Belgian hosts were far from equipped to deal with the problems to come.

First of all, this was an era of unprecedented football hooliganism, when thousands of rival supporters – often drunk – regarded matches as an excellent and fitting substitute for nationalistic, clan, or even, in the case of Glasgow's Celtic and Rangers, ethnic and religious warfare. Britain's clubs were notorious, especially Millwall, Chelsea, Newcastle, Cardiff, Swansea, Sheffield and Manchester United. The 'Inner City Firm' of West Ham was probably the worst, pinning their ICF calling cards on the bodies of their victims left unconscious on the street. In fact, Liverpool supporters were not particularly bad, except when playing Manchester United when, once, they threw golf balls studded with nails at each other. But probably unknown to the Belgian organisers, there was also bad blood between Liverpool and the Italians. Their previous year's successful European Final against Roma had been marred by serious attacks on the English supporters by armed scooter gangs and even the Roman police.

As the whistle blew for the start of the last match ever scheduled for the neglected, crumbling and condemned stadium, the Belgian preparations were revealed as wholly inadequate. Tickets for the Belgian 'neutral area' between the rivals had been sold by touts to British and Italian supporters, now strengthened by hooligans from other British clubs looking for 'payback time', and Fascists from Italy.

Within minutes open warfare started, and suddenly a mass of Liverpool supporters charged into the Juventus fans. A weak wall collapsed and hundreds were crushed and trampled. Fighting broke out all over the stadium, and even the pitch, until police reinforcements and the Belgian army restored order. Reluctantly, the players continued the match to avert even more bloodshed. Thirty nine spectators had died. The Queen and Prime Minister, Margaret Thatcher, apologised to Belgium and to Italy, and Britain was banned from European competition for five years, Liverpool two years more. Soccer had to change. It was no longer tenable to lock up tens of thousands of rival fans in concrete areas to 'let off steam'. It would need more lessons.

A Juventus supporter attacks a Liverpool fan with an iron bar. The violence at Heysel left 39 people dead.

Two weeks before Heysel, a grandstand at Bradford had caught fire and had exploded in flames, killing 56 men, women and children. The reasons included poor maintenance – with rubbish piled under the stand; no available fire extinguishers because fans had a tendency to use them as weapons; and locked turnstiles to keep out gate crashers - a tragic echo of the fire at the Triangle Shirtwaist Company, and unfortunately, other disasters since. Inadequate policing and poor crowd control would mean that 96 Liverpool supporters would be crushed to death at Hillsborough in April 1989.

Football hooliganism has not gone away. It has changed, with 'firms' often from smaller clubs, using the occasion of matches to fight each other. Led by 'Top Boys' and 'Main Lads', they dress up for the occasion in designer labels such as Lacoste, Burberry and Stone Island, reconnoitre the town in advance, and use mobile phones not only to co-ordinate amongst themselves but to ring up the opposition to arrange the venue for the

See: Balaclava, Brescia, Hillsborough, Le Mans

fighting. Millions are spent on the police just trying to hold the line.

It is a curious thought that if normal, respectable citizens decided one day to smash cars, break shop windows and assault other citizens with deadly weapons on the street, they would go to jail for years. But if you are a football hooligan or an anarchist, you get packed off home with a minor slap on the wrist. Except, perhaps, in Turkey.

HILLSBOROUGH
England

Mention 'football' and 'England' in the same breath, and sadly the first thought might be that of hooliganism. It is a bad reputation perpetrated by a minority, who feel a sense of tribalistic machismo on entering the turnstiles. But on 15th April 1989, when Liverpool met Nottingham Forest for the Cup Semi-Final at Hillsborough Football Ground, it was not crowd violence that led to the

Young fans are crushed as the fence becomes a deathtrap.

deaths of 96 supporters, but something far more unbelievable – over-crowding and lack of police control.

Ever since that sunny afternoon, even those who have no interest in football will know of that football stadium in Sheffield, ironically chosen because of its

geographical 'neutrality' for the supporters of the opposing teams. On that day, those watching the disaster on the early evening news could have been forgiven for initially thinking they were witnessing, as the *Sun* newspaper's Kelvin McKenzie tagged them, *'drunken hooligans,'* attempting to climb over the barriers and storm the pitch. In reality, it was Liverpool fans, including women and children, desperately trying to avoid being crushed and suffocated by the ever increasing pressure of fans entering behind them.

Just before kick-off at 2.45pm, the Police Superintendent on duty at gate C received permission to open the two Lepping Lane turnstiles leading to the terrace. Within about five minutes, 2,000 impatient Liverpool fans had descended on a tightly-fenced pen in the Lower West Stand. The police tried to ease congestion by opening a larger gate, and a domino effect ensued, as thousands pushed into an already full pen, literally crushing those at the front to death. The only desperate means of survival was to climb over the perimeter fence on to the pitch. Those who attempted it were at first pushed back in by police. Shockingly, as people suffocated and began to die, the game began and play continued for six minutes before the referee noticed people in distress. It was only then that an apparent crowd control problem officially became a major disaster.

David Lacey of *The Guardian* newspaper wrote, *'Hillsborough was no Heysel because there was no riot, it was not*

Bradford because there was no fire, it was not an Ibrox because there was no crush of fans going in opposite directions. The biggest question of all is how was it possible?'

The South Yorkshire Police, under the guidance of lawyers, changed their initial statements weeks later for the Taylor Inquiry. Included in the amendments of the officers on duty that day were deletions, direct falsifications and distorted recollections. The changes made removed any criticisms of the actions of the police force. Those former criticisms would have amounted to police mismanagement and ultimate culpability for the tragedy. Undoubtedly, the police were exemplary in their assistance of the victims once they were aware of the disaster but, in the end, hiding responsibility became paramount.

In a further inquest in 1990, the conclusion was that the eleven changed statements proved it was simply a case of accidental death, and no-one was held accountable.

Nine years later, with Tony Blair's Labour Government in power, a new report into the disaster headed by Lord Stuart Smith was commissioned, and the conclusion was the same, even though PC David Frost told the Inquiry that he and other un-named officers had refused to sign the 'amended statements'. Frost described the amendments as 'an attempt by senior management to sanitize and protect themselves'.

Eleven years after the event, two former policemen were tried for manslaughter in a private prosecution brought by the Hillsborough Family Support group at Leeds Crown Court. They also walked free. Finally, the judge ruled that there would be no retrial.

Many victims did receive compensation for the trauma they experienced. In one instance, the police were forced to pay £1 million to a man who suffered permanent brain damage. However, it is also true that some police received compensation in six figure sums.

Hillsborough will be forever etched into the collective consciousness as the most unnecessary tragedy in British football history.

See: Brescia, Heysel, Le Mans

HIROSHIMA
Japan

Unknown to them, the citizens of the city of Kyoto had every reason to bless their enemy, Henry L. Stimson, the United States Secretary of War, and the citizens of Hiroshima would have every reason to curse him.

Brigadier General Leslie Groves, the Director of the 'Manhattan Project', which had created the atomic bomb, favoured Kyoto as the first target in Japan. But Stimson, after twenty five years in public service, was fiercely adamant that Kyoto's historical and religious significance to the Japanese would be important for American relations when the war ended. He even involved President Truman in approving the decision. Thus, Kyoto was saved and Hiroshima doomed.

It was Albert Einstein in 1939 who had warned President Roosevelt that Germany was working on the atomic bomb. At first dismissive, the President was finally convinced by the famous story of Napoleon rejecting American inventor Robert Fulton's offer of steamboats to beat the British. 'What Sir, you would have my ships combat the wind and waves by lighting a bonfire under their decks? Pray you, excuse me, I have no time for such nonsense!' On 6th December 1941, Roosevelt received a joint British-American report on the definite possibility of producing an atomic bomb, and authorised substantial funds. The very next day, Captain Mitsuo Fuchida signalled back to Admiral Yamamoto, moored in Hiroshima Harbour, 'Tora, Tora, Tora!' This was the message that complete surprise had been achieved by the air attack on Pearl Harbor.

Infuriated, the Americans swung into action. At Los Alamos, New Mexico, Robert Oppenheimer assembled the formidable team of Niels Bohr, Edward Teller and Enrico Fermi, who had produced the first 'chain reaction' in a

Paul Tibbets on his way to destiny

See: Bikini, Changi, Corregidor, Kohima, Kwai, Los Alamos, Midway, Pearl Harbor, Tsushima

disused squash court at the University of Chicago. Millions of dollars would be secretly spent on the 'Manhattan Project' and on the training of special aircrews in a desperate race to beat the Germans and Japanese – and in July 1945 the race was won. That month, the first atomic bomb exploded with awesome power in New Mexico. A shaken Robert Oppenheimer remembered the Hindu scripture: *I am death to the destroyer of worlds.*

The Japanese had been given a formal warning, more than they had given before Pearl Harbor. The 'Potsdam Proclamation' of 26th July had 13 carefully worded points that advised Japan to surrender. It was ignored.

On the morning of 6th August, three silver B-29 bombers arrived high over Hiroshima. The lead plane was named *Enola Gay* after the mother of its commander, Colonel Paul Tibbets. Even then, had the weather been bad, the plane could have been directed to Kokura or Nagasaki, and other names would have been forever associated with this first tragic moment. But the weather was clear, and at 8.15am the bomb dropped from the *Enola Gay* and fell for forty seconds, while the plane banked and raced away. It exploded 1,890 feet above the centre of the city, killing 80,000 people and destroying all in its path. After the blinding flash, the crew

of *Enola Gay* stared transfixed at 'a vision from hell' as the blast wave nearly knocked them from the sky, and the now-familiar fiery red mushroom cloud rose to 60,000 feet.

The next day, the very man who had literally led Japan into war, Captain Fuchida, who by a stroke of chance had been called away from a conference in Hiroshima, flew back to the city. Receiving no radio response from the control tower, he landed safely. Then, in his immaculate white uniform, he walked into the devastation, past a procession of blackened people who seemed 'to have come out of hell.' Stunned, he must have reflected that surprise attacks could be two-edged weapons.

Nagasaki was spared for only three days.

On 9th August, it suffered the same fate as Hiroshima, and it was the Emperor himself who, on 15th August, 'bore the unbearable' and told his people to accept the Allied terms in one of the greatest understatements of all time, 'The war situation has developed not necessarily to Japan's advantage'.

There is a small plaque at 'ground zero' in modern, thriving Hiroshima. 200,000 *hibakusha,* bomb victims, have since died. A shrinking number of survivors are now outnumbered by young people, some of whom do not even know when that fatal day by chance occured.

HOLLYWOOD
California, USA

It was Mrs Daieda Wilcox who decided to call her husband's new piece of land 'Hollywoodland'. In 1886, he had bought part of an old agricultural settlement called Rancho La Brea – and began to lay out a property development for wealthy Midwesterners to 'Winter in California'. Wilson duly paved Prospect Avenue (now Hollywood Boulevard) and it was soon lined with large houses, while his wife built churches, schools and a library. Only a shortage of water forced Hollywood to become part of the City of Los Angeles in the year 1910.

Just one year later something happened to propel this prosperous,

unknown little community on to the world stage – quite literally. An old yellow citrus barn on the corner of what is now Vine Street and Selma Street was turned into a film studio by New Yorkers Jesse Lasky and his director Cecil B. De Mille to shoot the interior shots of *The Squaw Man,* the world's first full-length (six reel) film. One investor was Lasky's brother-in-law, Sam Goldfish, who was born Schmuel Gelbfisz in Warsaw and was now a glove salesman in New York. A visit to a nickelodeon had inspired his interest in film-making, but otherwise, like his partners, he had no movie experience at all. Before they left, Lasky organised for De Mille, who had been on the verge of quitting the theatre, to spend one afternoon at the Edison Studio in Brooklyn to see how movies were made.

They set off to film in Flagstaff, Arizona, but De Mille looked around, felt it was not right for *The Squaw Man*, and they climbed straight back on the train, and thus ended up in Hollywood, almost by chance.

Apart from the weather, which meant they could film all through the year, Hollywood had another priceless advantage. It was three thousand miles away from 'The Trust', the Motion Picture Patents Company, which had a stranglehold on production on the East Coast. After a saboteur broke into his laboratory, De Mille decided to shoot two negatives and transported them himself on horseback, packing a revolver which he twice used to fire at mysterious gunmen, probably 'Trust' men.

The Squaw Man made it to become a legend, and Hollywood became the centre of movie-making and the stuff of dreams; 'Tinseltown'.

Within three years, Sam Goldfish had broken away to form a film company with the theatrical Selwyn family, and so liked the merged name of the new company ('Goldwyn') that he adopted it for himself. Sam Goldwyn later founded MGM, went independent and became one of the truly great characters of Hollywood, with a strange way of expressing himself – although most 'Goldwynisms' were bogus. However, there were enough genuine gems to create a legend, for example: 'Don't call him Arthur. Every Tom, Dick and Harry is called Arthur'. 'Pictures are for entertainment, messages should be delivered by Western Union'.

Lasky and Goldwyn were typical of an extraordinarily creative phenomenon. Hollywood would become, almost overnight, dominated by Jewish enterprise and talent. Producers and directors would include David Selznick, Walter Wanger, 'Pop' Lubin, Carl Laemmle, Harry Cohn, Irving Thalberg, Louis Mayer, the Warner brothers, Jo Mankiewicz, William Wyler and Lee Strasberg.

Early stars who were also Jewish included the original silent vamp Theda Bara, Douglas Fairbanks, Eddie Cantor, Jack Benny, Al Jolson (who ushered in 'the talkies'), the Marx Brothers, Sophie Tucker, and Edward G. Robinson. Later, the tradition was to continue with Kirk Douglas, Rod Steiger, Walter Matthau, Lauren Bacall, Barbra Streisand, Dustin Hoffman, Tony Curtis, Bette Midler, Woody Allen, Paul Newman and Goldie Hawn.

The film industry became huge and, of course, many of the studios were built outside the original area of Hollywood. Warner Brothers and Disney are in Burbank, Columbia Pictures in nearby Culver City, and Universal Pictures, home to Steven Spielberg's *Jaws*, *E.T.* and *Jurassic Park* , is in Universal City – once a large chicken farm.

Nor is the whole area confined to the

CLARE SUTTON

The pavement outside Mann's Chinese Theatre with the hand prints of Charlton Heston, Sophia Loren, Jane Russell and Marilyn Monroe

movie business; it also became the centre of radio and later television. RKO Radio is in Culver City, although *Gone with the Wind* was shot on their site. CBS used Charlie Chaplin's studio, where all his greatest classic films were made. NBC radio expanded into television and Johnny Carson's *The Tonight Show*, now hosted by Jay Leno, is still broadcast from Hollywood. Every year the world gathers to watch the Academy Awards, the 'Oscars' (possibly named because Margaret Herrick, an Academy librarian and eventual executive director, thought the figure looked like her uncle Oscar). The ceremony takes place in Hollywood. Where else? But it might have been New York or, maybe, even in Flagstaff, Arizona.

See: Actor's Studio, Broadway, Casablanca, Las Vegas, Motown

HOMEBREW COMPUTER CLUB
California, USA

From 1974, a lot of young men met every Wednesday night in a hall rented from Stamford University in California's Silicon Valley. They called it 'The Homebrew Computer Club'. It had an extraordinary effect on the growth of personal computers that, in twenty years, became the world's third largest industry.

Kids had always wanted their own computers. But until Gordon Moore and Robert Noyce of Intel created the micro-processor, the world was doomed to have computers with thousands of vacuum tubes - and as big as houses. In 1949, *Popular Mechanics* forecast that computers might one day weigh less than five tons, although the big computer makers scoffed. One main frame-manufacturer, Kenneth Olsen, stopped any development of personal computers at Digital because he didn't see '*any reason why anyone would want to have a computer at home!*'

The silicon chip, created in 1971, launched the personal computer revolution in the rather unlikely shape of the Ed Roberts' simple computer, the Altair 8800, which did not do very much, but drove the 'nerds' into endless experiments at the Homebrew Club. Two kids who had bought an Altair, Bill Gates and Paul Allen, struggled with BASIC, their software and, nervously feeding it into the Altair on a paper roll, made it work. Without that success there might never have been the gigantic Microsoft and its products we use today.

Everybody shared their triumphs on those Wednesday nights – a rather endearing habit, and one reason why Silicon Valley took off so fast.

Two other regulars at the Homebrew were Steve Wozniak and Steve Jobs. Their first Apple computer was put together for Wozniak to impress his friends at the Club. In 1976, a fellow member ordered 50 units, built by hand. A bearded, 19 year old Steve Jobs then went off to Arthur Rock who had funded Intel, and obtained enough capital to move out of his garage and order 1,000 machines. As Steve Wozniak put it, the Apple II took computing from '*guys with big beards who thought a good use for the computer was controlling a model train set*' out into the business world. VisiCalc, the first 'spreadsheet', became a business crystal ball, transforming the computer's uses and the prospects for the industry. It also transformed the finances of many of the Homebrew members. Steve Jobs was worth a million dollars at 23, and $100 million two years later.

Bill Gates soon became the richest man in the world, worth $35 billion, with Paul Allen close behind.

The personal computer is arguably the most important invention of the last century, transforming the way we work and live. And we all owe a great deal to that funny club where, every Wednesday, enthusiastic nerds shared their hopes, dreams and technical breakthroughs.

Two results of the Homebrew Club, right: Apple and below: Microsoft

Microsoft®

See: Kitty Hawk, Mainz, Menlo Park, Nimes, Nokia, Stockton & Darlington, Titusville, Vinci

HOOK & CROOK
Ireland

The phrase 'By Hook or by Crook' is an old one, thought to refer to the wood a tenant could once collect from the Manor using a shepherd's crook, and cut with a bill-hook. It is mentioned in Edmund Spenser's poem *Faerie Queene; 'In hope her to attaine by hooke or crooke'.* The poet wrote this in Ireland in 1586, in Kilcolman Castle near Cork – given to him as a reward for helping to 'crush Irish rebellion'.

It is therefore ironic that the phrase became a real part of the English language because of the crushing of another Irish rebellion.

Near Waterford lies Rinn Dubhain which, in Celtic, meant the Point of Dubhain, but Dubhan means fish hook -

so the headland became known as Hook Head. In 1649, England's Oliver Cromwell, fresh from his brutal 'triumphs' of Wexford and Drogheda, vowed to take the City of Waterford 'by Hook or by Crooke' – Crooke being a small village on the estuary opposite Hook Head. In fact, Cromwell failed, blocked by the staunch defence of Duncannon Fort, which delayed him long enough for winter rains to incapacitate his army's heavy guns.

Waterford did succumb eight months later because of plague and starvation, but, in Cromwell's absence, General Ireton behaved honourably to the citizens and defenders of both Waterford and heroic Duncannon.

Whatever satisfaction the Irish might take in the personal thwarting of Cromwell's 'by hook or by crook' plans, it is a sobering thought that between 1641 and 1652 Ireland suffered 600,000 deaths out of a population of just two million – proportionately a far greater toll than during the Great Famine of two centuries later.

No wonder Cromwell is still the most hated name in Ireland.

See: Chinchon, Old Kinderhook

Cromwell, reviled in Ireland to this day

IBIZA
Spain

For an island whose image seems to epitomise all that is modern, Ibiza is surprisingly steeped in history. As a useful trading post of the Mediterranean, it has changed hands on numerous occasions, held at some point in history by Phoenicians, Carthaginians, Romans, Byzantines, Arabs, and finally the Spanish. It was the Arabs who brought with them the island's modern name, calling it *Yebisah*.

Centuries of constant attack, especially by the Saracens, led to the extensive defences built on the coasts. Coastal churches were often fortified, and even had cannon on their roofs. Italian architect Calvi build the 1,931 metre long walls of Ibiza town, (which can still be seen) in the sixteenth century.

There was even a system of beacons all along the coast of the island, each in sight of its nearest neighbour. If a pirate attack were in progress, the nearest beacon would be lit, causing all the others to be lit in sequence, and placing the whole island on alert.

The roots of the island's cosmopolitan character originated during the Second World War. Many Central European artists, having fled their homes, saw Ibiza as a place to escape, and settled there to avoid the horrors of the conflict. After the War, Europe began to notice that Ibiza was, as yet, relatively untouched by civilisation, and its tourist industry began to swell. An important cultural influence came from the late sixties and early seventies, when large groups of hippies moved to the island, helping to create a hugely liberal atmosphere. Indeed, their influence can still be felt at the still-existing hippie craft market based at Es-Cana.

But it was music that would grant the island the stratospheric fame it enjoys today. Until the later eighties, Ibiza was a relatively quiet resort. The primary DJ on the island was Spanish Alfredo, who played a mix of pop, 'new wave' and '80s 'house'. In 1987, as a birthday celebration, four friends from England took a trip to the Balearic island. The birthday boy himself was none other than the now legendary DJ Paul Oakenfold. The strange mix of music that Alfredo played was like nothing that people had ever heard before, and it gave the young Paul an urge to recreate this sound back home.

Upon his return he persuaded the owner of 'Project', the club where he worked, to allow him to replicate the mix of styles that he had heard on his holiday. The night was a success, and 'Acid House' had finally arrived. The venture led to the creation of one of the country's first genuine Acid House nights, 'Spectrum' at 'Heaven' in Charing Cross.

The importing of Balearic sounds did not just affect the club scene in England, but also back in Ibiza. Many of dance

Consciousness and Robert Miles' *Children* originated on the island, and would dominate the dance market when exported. The resort fed off the success of the music, and vice-versa. Ibiza also pioneered the genre of 'Chillout music', born with the release of the first *Café del Mar* album in 1994.

Today Ibiza is splashed across holiday brochures, album covers, and television documentaries alike. Other resorts such as Ayia Napa in Cyprus have followed the clubbing trend but as long as Ibiza continues to create so much of the dance music that is popular around the world, then people will continue to make pilgrimages to visit its source.

music's classic tunes were written for, and first played on, the island. As the music itself became increasingly popular, so Ibiza's popularity as a holiday destination rocketed. Nightclubs began to sprout all over the island, the largest of them evolving into the now legendary superclubs.

Undoubtedly the world's original clubber's paradise, Ibiza has been the birthplace of influential dance music. Tunes such as Josh Wink's *Higher State of*

See: Elba, Cavern Club, Harlem, Milo, St. Louis, Sibylla's, Storyville, Studio 54, Tin Pan Alley, Tulsa

INDIANAPOLIS
Indiana, USA

'Gentlemen start your engines'.

Founders of 'The Brickyard'. Carl Fisher is first from right.

Those are the words that begin one of the greatest sporting spectacles in the world, the Indianapolis 500-mile race. Ever since cars had been invented, men had wanted to race them. The first race was as early as Thanksgiving 1895; Paris to Rouen. The same year, the *Chicago Times Herald* sponsored the first

American race, Chicago to Evanston and back - at a brisk 6.5 mph!

Paris became the starting point of European races, and 3 million people cheered the 1902 Paris-Vienna event. But Paris-Madrid in 1903 was a disaster, with many killed, precipitating 20 mph speed limits on Europe's roads and casting doubts on motor-racing's future. Closed circuits were the obvious answer.

Newspaper proprietor James Gordon Bennett and William K. Vanderbilt pioneered motor-racing in the United States, whilst in Britain, motor-racing began at Brooklands, built in 1907 by rich landowner, Hugh Fortescue Locke King. But in spite of its two enormous bankings, Brooklands was basically the home of the wealthy amateur. *'The right crowd and no crowding'* was not simply the unspoken attitude, this slogan was actually printed on the

programmes and advertising.

Meanwhile in Indianapolis, then home of America's motor industry, other ideas were emerging. Carl Fisher of Prest-O-Lite, carbide headlight makers, together with three motor industry friends, bought 320 acres outside the city and build a 2.5 mile rectangular track, paved with tar and crushed stone. This surface created a disaster during the first 1909 race, with five deaths. Fisher at once resurfaced the track with over three million bricks, the reason it is called *The Brickyard*. Racing fervour created plenty of competition, from county fair dirt tracks to the 'The Boards', steeply banked wooden tracks used in professional competition, similar in design to bicycle velodromes.

But Carl Fisher made two inspired decisions. He decided on just one race a year, over 500 miles, and then created the richest purse in the world. The result: the most important single motor race in the world. An Indy winner could earn more in a day than Babe Ruth in a whole baseball season.

At first European cars dominated the Indy 500, although American expertise gradually took over with names like Miller, Duesenberg and Offenhauser. But technical progress was slow. In 1960 all the big, long, front-engined 'roadsters' were powered by identical 4-cylinder Offenhauser engines, as they had been since 1949!

Suddenly in 1961 a funny little mid-engined car arrived from England, the Cooper-Climax which Jack Brabham took to ninth place. Such cars had already swept the field in Grand Prix racing, but were a real shock at Indianapolis.

By 1965, the mid-engine revolution was complete, with Britain's Jim Clark winning, and in the year 1966 Graham Hill became the first 'rookie' to win for almost forty years. Most of the Grand Prix innovations were implemented as quickly as they appeared: improved tyres, wings, ground effect. Only the gas turbine was squeezed out by the regulations. And some innovations travelled in the opposite direction across the Atlantic. Turbo-charging, for example, began at the Indy in the late 1960s but did not appear in Grand Prix cars until 1978.

A race that had sometimes only speeded up by 1 mph between years suddenly jumped 30 mph between 1970 and 1973. Soon something else amazing emerged. Five out of six of the engines used were from overseas, and all three of the car types were made in England. It is as if all the European Grand Prix cars and all their engines were made in Indiana. Southern England had created a dominant expertise in motor racing which it has never lost – an industry worth £3 billion a year.

But the Indy 500 marches on. Run every Memorial Day, it is as American as the Tour de France is French.

Racer Lewis Strang looks at a model of the track in 1909

See: Brescia, Brooklands, Le Mans

Jack Brabham's Cooper. The tiny shape of things to come.

Roger Ward leads Jim Rathman in nearly identical Watson roadsters (1959 and 1960).

JAMESTOWN
Virginia, USA

The very course of American history was altered at Jamestown by the kindness and love of one girl – and the unexpected success of a crop.

The fort, set up in May 1607 by 100 men and four boys and named after England's King James I, was not the first

NATIONAL PARK SERVICE, COLONIAL NATIONAL HISTORICAL PARK, JAMESTOWN COLLECTION

The tiny settlement on the James River. Painting by Sidney King

European settlement. Since Columbus had sailed in 1492, the Spanish had settled in the south and the French in the north, although there was no permanent British settlement. But the destruction of the Spanish Armada in 1588 suddenly altered the naval balance of power in the Atlantic. Now the British could try their hand at creating an empire in America.

However, the first attempt was a disaster. Sir Walter Raleigh, who had named the territory he discovered 'Virginia', after Queen Elizabeth, 'the Virgin Queen', had created a colony on Roanoke Island in 1584, but in 1591 it was found deserted – and called the 'Lost Colony.'

At first, Jamestown looked set for success. John Smith, one of the seven councillors, said, 'Heaven and earth never agreed better to frame a place for man's habitations.' But soon came blistering heat, disease, poor water, freezing winters and attacks from the Powhatan Indians.

When John Smith was captured by the Algonquian Chief Powhatan and was apparently about to be clubbed to death, his little daughter, Pocahontas, rushed forward and lay her head on Smith's, reputedly saving his life. The resulting friendship with the Indians saved the colony for a while, but its troubles were certainly not over. First, a relief fleet with the proposed leaders of the colony was wrecked and stranded in Bermuda (Shakespeare based *The Tempest* on the disaster); Smith was shipped back to England after an explosives accident, and without his leadership the winter of 1609 was so bad that it was called the 'Starving Time', during which the settlers even turned to cannibalism. A tragic majority of them died.

On 24th May 1610, two little ships from Bermuda picked up the 60 gaunt

Left: Bodies being taken for burial during 'The Starving Time.'
Painting by Sidney King

survivors and, in despair, headed for England down the James River – but luckily met a boat that told them that relief was at hand.

The colony struggled on, but what Jamestown needed was a profitable cash crop.

Farmer John Rolfe began to grow tobacco, using seeds smuggled from the Caribbean (there was a death penalty for selling seeds to non-Spaniards). Pocahontas, 'the playful one', had been rewarded for her continuous kindness to the settlers by being captured and held to ransom. Now a young woman, she fell in love with John Rolfe, converted to Christianity and changed her name to Rebecca. They were married with Powhatan's approval, if not with that of King James.

In 1614, the first shipment of tobacco arrived in London and was soon all the rage. And so was the exotic Pocahontas when she arrived with Rolfe in 1616, once again meeting her friend John Smith, whom she thought was dead – and even being presented to Queen Anne as a Princess, because James had crowned Powhatan 'King of Virginia'.

The fairy story romance ended seven months later in tragedy, with Pocahontas succumbing, possibly to smallpox, at Gravesend on her journey back to Jamestown.

Through Pocahontas' generosity and kindness she had enabled the colony to survive, while Rolfe's tobacco was to transform Virginia, creating a 'tobacco coast' of wealth. But the crop was setting the scene for future problems. Unlike the northern states, with their manufacturing and merchant classes, the southern states would develop large plantations for tobacco and later cotton, importing a servile work force – first white indentured servants and then thousands of African slaves. Thus when Rolfe planted his first tobacco seeds, he unwittingly planted the seeds of a tragic Civil War 250 years later.

See: Bedloe's Island, Botany Bay, Cape Canaveral, Cumberland Road, Ellis Island

JARROW
England

In the late 1920s, the Great Depression had hit Britain as hard as any other country. By 1930, only months after the Wall Street Crash that had withdrawn American credit and brought the world to its financial knees, there were 2 million British unemployed. One man paraded through the streets with a sign saying, *'I know 3 trades, I speak 3 languages, fought for 3 years, have 3 children and no work for 3 months, but I only want one job.'* Government spending cuts had done worse than nothing. In 1931, national bankruptcy threatened and sterling was devalued. Even the Royal Navy mutinied. Unemployment hit 3.1 million. Food riots broke out. In spite of the euphoria around King George's Silver Jubilee in 1935, the gradual return to prosperity was patchy and slow.

Until the 1930s, Jarrow in Durham would have chiefly been known to ecclesiastics as the birthplace of the Venerable Bede. But its wider fame was to be made as an industrial town that had been nearly destroyed. Catastrophic declines in shipbuilding and heavy iron and steel work, and also the dreadful

199

collapse of the largest local employer meant that unemployment had reached 68 per cent. On 6th October 1936, 200 men set off from the despairing town to march to London, carrying a petition with 1,572 signatures. The march was blessed with a church service by the Bishop of Jarrow, and a fierce supporter was the young Labour party MP, Ellen Wilkinson. Led by a brass band, it set off for London.

The 'Jarrow Crusade' and other hunger marches caught the public's imagination. They did a great deal to alert the more prosperous southern half of Britain to the desperate problems still affecting much of the country. But it was only re-armament and the Second World War that brought employment back to suffering towns like Jarrow.

See: Bonus City, Wall Street

JODHPUR
India

The links between India and Great Britain go back a long way, first with private enterprise with the East India Company, then as the 'Jewel in the Crown' of the British Empire. It is therefore hardly surprising that places in India have become worldfamous not just for themselves, but also for the products they have exported. Jodhpur, in Rajasthan, the home of polo has given us the name for riding breeches.

'Let other people play at other things. The King of games is still the game of Kings'.

That is how an ancient plaque on a polo ground in India described the attitude of the east to the oldest organised game in the world. For 2,500 years polo was played by Kings, Emperors, Shahs, Sultans, Khans and Caliphs. Polo is first recorded in art and literature in Persia, and the polo stick appeared on the royal coat of arms in China and in Islamic heraldry. Shah Abbas the Great built a whole city at Isfahan around a vast central square that enclosed his polo field, overlooked by his seven storey palace, with stone goal posts eight yards apart – still the official width of a goal.

But no place in Asia is more famous for polo than Jodhpur, which seemed to provide as many Indian State players as Silhet now provides Indian chefs! From 1922 until World War II, the Jodhpur team not only dominated Indian polo, it went on, under the Captaincy of the

GRIMSDALE

Maharaja of Jaipur, to beat the world.

Every time someone puts on their 'jodhpurs' to go to a 'gymkhana' (there's another one) we are reminded of perhaps one of the most 'pukka' (first-rate) Indian names used worldwide, but there are many other examples of our language links.

'Dum-dum' bullets, 'chitty' (a note) 'Bangalore torpedoes' (demolition charges) 'mufti' (civilian clothes),'khaki' (dust-coloured uniforms) and 'puttees' (anklets) are all words passed on from the Indian military. Dungri, a district of Bombay, made rough calico, and its dungri trousers are now known to us as 'dungarees.' Kashmir has given the world the rather softer 'cashmere' sweater. Single-storey houses, as built in Bengal, have given us the 'bungalow', while 'calico' is named after the cotton made in Calicut on the south west coast of India. In fact, the English language is littered with textile and clothing terms from India: 'chintz', 'gingham', 'pyjama', 'bandana', 'goni' (as in gunny sack) and 'kamar-band' (cummerbund).

Curry comes from'kari' the Tamil word for sauce and it is reported that Chicken Tikka Marsala is now Britain's favourite dish. It is certainly true that Indian words are among the favourite ingredients of our modern vernacular.

Prince Charles has carried on a British tradition of playing the Indian game.

MCvA

See: Amritsar, Bhopal, Deolali, Dum Dum, Nîmes, Taj Mahal, Varanasi

JONESTOWN
Guyana

On 18th November 1978, in the jungles of Guyana, 914 men, women and children died suddenly, apparently from suicide. A strange megalomaniac man calling himself the Reverend Jim Jones had ordered them to drink a potion containing cyanide. Jones himself was found dead from a gunshot.

There are those who find it difficult to believe that so many people, however drilled and brainwashed, would all kill themselves and, especially, would kill 300 children. Stories still continue to emerge which make such a simple explanation even less believable.

In 1999, Jeff Schnepper revealed a very different tale in *USA Today*. Jim Jones had created his first 'People's Temple' in 1956 in Indianapolis, a predominantly black cult church, where he earned the reputation for healing people. He was apparently respectable enough to be made the 'Director of the City's Human Rights Commission.' In 1985, the Temple moved to Ukiah, California, partly 'to be safer from atomic warfare'. There, according to Terri Buford, Jones' mistress, a very unreligious pattern emerged. In 1975, Jones used his 20,000 Temple members to influence California politics, using vote-rigging to help George Moscone became Mayor of San Francisco, his opponent backing down from his fraud allegations when he was threatened with violence. Sexual traps by the girls of Terri Buford's 'diversion unit' ensured the silence of other politicians. Temple members were soon in leading positions

The grim sight of bodies found at Jonestown

See: Waco

It is hard to know quite what Jones's eventual plan was; whether just to leave the Temple one day in his helicopter or whether to murder all his members. Whatever it was, it went wrong when Democrat Congressman Leo Ryan decided to investigate what was going on in Guyana. When he tried to leave with four Temple members after just one day, Ryan was shot dead at Port Kaituma airport along with several others, while Richard Dwyer of the US Embassy and Tim Reiterman (with the *San Francisco Examiner*) were wounded.

Within hours the 'suicides' had been enacted. After two days, the death toll jumped by 400. Were desperate Temple members simply killed in the jungle, as Guyanese coroner Leslie Mootoo plainly thought when he testified that 700 of them appeared to have been forcibly killed? Why was Jones's gun found 60 feet from his body? And why were Mayor Moscone and politician Harvey Milk gunned down nine days after the Jonestown massacre? Who silenced their killer, Dan White, who was found dead seven weeks after he left prison? Why is Terri Buford still in hiding, with the money still missing? There are lots of people who seem not to wish to talk.

All in all, if you have to belong to a religious cult, it would be better not to choose Jim Jones's 'Peoples Temple Full Gospel Church'.

in local government, while Jones even managed to be elected as head of San Francisco's Housing Authority. Why was this useful? Because the Temple then took over millions of dollars worth of property, tax exempt because of its religious status. With these profits and many stolen from Temple members, a nest-egg of $26 million was amassed.

The Temple moved to 'Jonestown' in Guyana in 1977, comprising 600 adults and 300 children, together with Jones's own armed guard, equipped with semi-automatic weapons, shotguns and crossbows. According to the account of Terri Buford, she flew regularly to Paris and Zurich, with suitcases full of money, depositing millions in her own name.

KATYN WOOD
Russia

In the year 1943, an elderly Polish man reported to the occupying Germans that there was a huge burial site in the woods at Katyn, near Smolensk. In front of a team of international doctors, a horrifying discovery was made. The bodies of thousands of Polish officers and civilians were found, layer upon layer, quite well preserved and easily identified. Most had been shot in the back of the head. There were 4,250 of them. The Nazis had been methodically carrying out such atrocities for months in Russia but, this time, it wasn't they who were the murderers.

At the same time, in 1943, the Russians were reeling back from the

German onslaught, and urged on by Churchill, they had begun to gather a Polish army from the 1.5 million prisoners they had shipped off in 1939 to Gulag camps – after the defeat of Poland and its division between Russia and Germany. Almost at once, General Anders and his Polish staff realised there were soldiers but no officers. Where had they disappeared to? The ghastly truth has slowly emerged.

When Russia took over their half of Poland, they put all the surrendered Polish officers, plus leading politicians, administrators and policemen into three camps, Kozielsk, Starobielsk and Ostashkov. There, under appalling conditions, were kept nearly 15,000 men, the best hope for the Polish nation if it could be rescued from the German yoke. After the spring of 1940, all contact with their families ceased. From early March, in groups of 60 to 240, they were taken away 'to rejoin their families'. In fact they were taken by Russia's NKVD into the woods, shot and dumped in huge pits.

One can imagine the terror felt by these trained officers arriving in small groups at the burial pits and knowing exactly what was to happen to them.

All the Kozielsk prisoners, including six Generals, were found at Katyn. Where were the others, the 'lost 10,000'? The answer was that they too had been executed in cold blood – on the direct orders of Stalin – who had no interest in the survival of such leaders in his planned post-war Poland.

We now know, after more than fifty years, what happened to the 'lost 10,000'. The prisoners of Starobyelsk, about 4,000, were shot and buried near Kharkov and those of Ostaschkovo, almost 6,400, near Bologoye.

In 1991 and 1992, under Gorbachov's 'glasnost', the Soviet Union finally admitted the crime. And in 1974, through London's German Embassy, the NKVD report below was revealed.

Germany's Heinrich Himmler, the greatest liquidator in history, would have been most impressed with the cold destruction of the leadership of a whole nation. He would even have approved of the crispness of the report.

See: Andrassy, Dachau, Getto, Gulag

Stalin wanted to destroy Poland's leadership.

Secret
10 June 1940

Union of the Socialist Soviet Republics.
People's Commissariat for
Internal Affairs.

Headquarters of the NKVD.
region of Minsk.

To: The Headquarters of
the NKVD, Moscow.

Official Report

By Order of the Headquarters of the NKVD of February 12, 1940 the liquidation of the three Polish prisoner-of-war camps was carried out in the regions of the towns of Kozielsk, Ostaschkovo and Starobyelsk. The operation of liquidating the above three named camps was completed on 6 June of that year. Comrade Burjanoff, who had been seconded from the Central Office, was appointed to be in charge.

Under the above-mentioned Order, the camp at Kozielsk was liquidated first of all by the security forces of the Minsk headquarters of the NKVD in the area of the city of Smolensk during the period between 1 March and 3 May of that year. As security forces, territorial troops, in part from the 190th Rifle Regiment, were employed.

The Second action under the above Order was carried out in the area of the town of Bologoye by the security forces of the Smolensk headquarters of the NKVD, and was also covered by troops of the 129th Rifle Regiment (Velike Luki); it was completed by 5 June of that year. The Kharkov headquarters of the NKVD was entrusted with carrying out the third liquidation of the camp of Starobyelsk. It was carried out in the area of the Dergachi settlement with the assistance of security forces of the 68th Ukrainian Rifle Regiment of the territorial troops on 2 June. In this case, the responsibility and leadership in this action was entrust to the NKVD Colonel B. Kutschov.

A copy of this report is being sent simultaneously to the NKVD Generals Raichmann and Saburin for their attention.

The Organizational Head of the Office of
The NKVD area of Minsk.

TARTAKOW

KENT STATE
Ohio, USA

Opposition to the Vietnam war was a hallmark of 1960s youth culture, especially on university campuses. It was mostly peaceful, a picturesque medley of long hair, badges, beads, denim, buckskin and bright Paisley shirts, in a haze of cannabis smoke and with an exciting, throbbing rock soundtrack. But it could turn sour, especially when hotheads incited riot or, when more frequently, the authorities felt threatened – and over-reacted against people they totally failed to understand. On Monday 4th May 1970, they did so with a vengeance.

Kent State University in north eastern Ohio suddenly emerged from obscurity to hit headlines worldwide. President Nixon had unfortunately set the scene, describing student protesters as 'campus bums'. Vice President Spiro Agnew went further, telling police: 'Just imagine they are wearing brown shirts and act accordingly'.

jungle network of roads, tracks, footpaths and storage dumps, down which the insurgent Viet Cong hauled supplies from Communist-ruled North Vietnam and into the South. The invaders enjoyed short-term military success, but the episode was a political disaster that sparked massive protest across the United States, notably on the campuses.

At Kent State, there was serious unrest, with broken glass and showers of missiles in the town and on the campus beginning on 1st May. Then on May 2nd, protesters at an anti-war rally torched a university building holding the Reserve Officer Training Corps (ROTC). Martial Law was not declared, but the Mayor of Kent summoned help from the Governor of Ohio, James A. Rhodes. A contingent of reservists from the Ohio National Guard attempted to clear the area for two days, armed with tear gas, helicopters, powerful M-1 rifles and bayonets. Just after midday on the 4th, a group of them panicked and fired 61 random bullets into a crowd of students. They killed four and wounded nine, all unarmed, several merely passers-by. Shortly after, folk-rock band Crosby, Stills, Nash and Young would angrily sing in *Ohio*, their anthemic song, *'What if you knew her, and found her dead on the ground?'* – for two of the dead were girls. Another was even a ROTC cadet. The pictures flashed round the world.

Whatever the President and the authorities may have thought of the students, the young saw things differently, and protests exploded across the nation. Over 400 campuses shut, and two million students cut lectures. In Jackson State College, Mississippi, police fired on a crowd of black students, killing two and wounding eleven. Divisions racked the nation. In New York, construction workers laid into students protesting at the events at Kent State; 70 were injured. The 'Children of God' religious hippie group circulated pamphlets lambasting an America of hard-hats in league with President Nixon (who had been presented with a worker's hard hat as a symbol of freedom and patriotism).

John Filo, a photography student, captured this shot as a girl screams over a fellow student.

On May Day 1970, an army of 75,000 US and South Vietnamese troops had invaded Cambodia. Their mission: to disrupt the Ho Chi Minh trail, a vast

So powerful was the imagery of the 'Kent State Massacre' that by two months later US forces had evacuated Cambodia, on the orders of Congress.

A County Grand Jury blamed the University authorities for failing to clear the protesters, and indicted 25 Kent State students and staff for affray, but absolved the National Guard of any blame.

However, a Presidential Commission described the National Guardmen's firing as 'unnecessary, unwarranted and inexcusable'.

See: Amritsar, Khe Sanh, My Lai, Tiananmen Square, Tonkin Gulf

KEW
England

The Royal Botanic Gardens, Kew, has not always been a botanic garden – but it has always been royal.

For both George II and Queen Caroline, it was, as usual, infuriating that their son Frederick (widely known as 'Poor Fred') should do something like set himself up on the Kew Estate – right next door to their Richmond Estate by the River Thames. 'My dear first-born is the greatest ass, and the greatest liar, and the greatest canaille, and the greatest beast in the whole world, and I most heartily wish he was out of it', was Caroline's motherly opinion.

Frederick needed to settle down. One of his many mistresses was Madame d'Elitz, who had been the paramour of his father and grandfather. 'There's nothing new under the sun' retorted George Selwyn, the noted wit. 'Or under the grandson!'

The Prince of Wales eventually settled on Augusta of Saxe-Gotha, and it was she who started the first small gardens at Kew, with the support of Lord Bute and the architect Sir William Chambers, whose Orangery, Ruined Arch and Pagoda still stand – where the temporary gardener was a young William Cobbett, later to be famous as a radical politician, the founder of Hansard and author of *Rural Rides.*

However charming Kew was as a Royal Garden under George II and Queen Caroline, it was to Sir Joseph Banks that the credit must be given for its international fame. Banks had been with Captain James Cook on the voyage of the *Endeavour,* and was the botanist who gave the name to 'Botany Bay' in Australia. He had, with the King's approval, started the policy of sending collectors all over the world to bring plants back to Kew, where temporarily

The Palm House

the King was confined, as depicted in the film *'The Madness of King George'.*

Kew's policy of collecting plants, and either bringing them to Kew or sending them to other parts of the British Empire, was to lead to Cook's tragic death in Hawaii in 1779 and, even more dramatically, the 1789 Mutiny on *The Bounty,* when Cook's former sailing Master, Captain Bligh, was transporting breadfruit trees from Tahiti to the West Indies as a food for the slaves of the sugar plantations. The small boat in which Bligh and 18 men were cast adrift travelled 4000 miles, and his 'strongest helper' was the Kew botanist David Nelson.

After some years of decline, the Government took over Kew, and first under William Hooker and then his son Joseph, friend and supporter of Charles Darwin, Kew continued to expand with its magnificent Palm House and its continuing policy of worldwide collection of plants.

At least two of these plants changed the world. It was a Kew gardener, Robert Cross, who joined the expedition to Ecuador to bring the chinchona plant *(Cinchona)* to Kew, and then to Ceylon

The Pagoda

and India to create quinine in order to combat malaria – which was killing a million people a year. Rubber, too, owes its success to Kew. Seeds of *Hervea brasiliensis* were brought back from Brazil and sent to the Far East to create one of the world's greatest industries.

Kew's huge scientific pre-eminence and influence in distributing plants throughout the world has been called 'the NASA of botany'. Kew Gardens remains one of the world's great botanical centres – and 'Kew' is a byword for botany.

See: Botany Bay, Brazil, Chinchón, Galapagos

KHE SANH
Vietnam

By 1967 the Americans and the South Vietnamese were beginning to win the Vietnam War. Secret Vietcong (VC) and North Vietnamese Army (NVA) reports reveal disillusionment, terrible casualties, little food and ammunition, fear of the devastating US bombing and low morale.

The US forces had their own problems. Under the baleful influence of Secretary of State for Defence, Robert McNamara, who arrogantly ran the war as he used to run Ford, US troops only stayed a year, waiting for their DEROS (Date Expected Return Overseas). Thus green troops and officers were fighting men who had fought in the country all their lives. Certainly, except for the Marines and other élite units, they had little of the comradeship and pride provided by the British regimental system. They were also fighting on two fronts – against the enemy and against the media and public opinion back home. Nevertheless, their personal bravery, mobility and firepower had worn down their enemy, who then decided in the winter of 1967 to 'go for broke' and to conduct a spectacular all out offensive throughout South Vietnam.

In great secrecy, they planned to attack villages and towns during the ceasefire of the Tet Festival, the most sacred day in Vietnam, on 31st January

Khe Sanh under attack

1968. An American obsession played into their hands – the catastrophic French defeat in 1954 at Dien Bien Phu. This obsession was fed by the first diversion at Dak To near Cambodia, to which the Americans quickly moved a division. Then it was Khe Sanh which became the focus, a fire support base close to the North Vietnamese border. 'Unattended Ground Sensors' had detected 15,000 NVA troops massing.

Soon, General Westmoreland was convinced that Khe Sanh was the critical point, pointing out, 'Attempts would be made elsewhere in South Vietnam to divert and disperse US strength from the real attack at Khe Sanh.' As attacks began on 21st January President Johnson even had a model of Khe Sanh built in his basement to follow the progress of what was to be a 77-day siege.

But Khe Sanh was, in reality, a brilliant diversion. In the towns and villages, the first wave of 67,000 VC and NVA attackers quietly moved into position for the real attack. There had been plenty of warnings. Truck movements on the Ho Chi Minh trail had gone up from 500 to 6,500 a month. Captured documents had revealed *'a great offensive to win the war'*. Vietcong leaders had been captured with tapes to be played over radios announcing 'the uprising.' Luckily, General Weyand had persuaded Westmoreland to bring back some US troops to the cities, and many South Vietnamese forces had tried to cancel the traditional leave over Tet.

But, with the South Vietnamese revellers waiting 'to celebrate a dying

ASSOCIATED PRESS

not winning the war, but losing it'. It did not matter that the battle became a US victory and a horrific defeat for the NVA and the Vietcong, who lost a crippling 33,000, with 60,000 wounded and 6,000 captured, nor that they did not hold one of their objectives (while deliberately butchering about 5,000 civilians in the holy city of Hue). Sadly, as one American put it, 'It all came unglued at Tet'.

One of the most horrifying pictures from the Vietnam War, as the Police Chief of Hue executes a Vietcong prisoner.

war', the happy firecrackers set off on the night of 31st January covered more sinister noises. Saigon's radio station was attacked but, intelligently, cut its own power off. The Palace was successfully defended, as was the Joint General Staff building. The US Embassy's grounds were penetrated by a small group, but the building itself was defended.

After six hours, General Westmoreland arrived at the Embassy and surveyed the damage – that one US officer described as 'a piddling platoon action'.

However, the trouble was that the US media were close by and also saw the Embassy, and gave the impression that Westmoreland, McNamara and President Johnson were lying. *'They were*

In the meantime, the Americans had bravely held Khe Sanh, thanks not least to 24,000 fighter-bomber missions and 2,700 B-52 missions, dropping 100,000 tons of bombs. 5,000 NVA attackers were killed or wounded. Again, the Americans had won. But it didn't matter. Opinion at home now swung against the war. McNamara resigned. A thoroughly disillusioned Johnson announced he would not be re-elected.

Khe Sanh was abandoned two months after the siege was lifted. Five years later the last American troops left Vietnam, and in 1975, the North Vietnamese took Saigon and South Vietnam.

Khe Sanh was indeed a hollow victory.

See: Kent State, My Lai, Tonkin Gulf

KIEL CANAL
Germany

WWW.KIEL-CANAL.ORG

The Kiel Canal is one of the most important artificial waterways ever built. It is now the world's busiest canal and, like many man-made constructions, it originally had a military purpose.

Completed in 1895, it was sixty miles long and joined the North Sea to the Baltic Sea, shortening the distance by about 200 miles. More importantly, it gave the German Fleet two ways to emerge into the North Sea, making the planning of its potential enemy, Britain's Royal Navy, very much harder.

As warships grew larger, the canal, now called the Kaiser Wilhelm Kanal, had to be widened and deepened. The work started in 1907, and was finished in 1914. Warships from many navies attended the Kaiser's splendid opening ceremony, including three from the Royal Navy.

At the height of the festivities, the Kaiser received a cable from Austria on his Imperial yacht. His cousin, the Archduke Ferdinand had been

assassinated at Sarajevo. Nobody yet knew for certain that this signalled the start of the Great War. But, out of respect, the ceremonies stopped and the foreign ships saluted their Imperial host and sailed away.

A few months later, the Kaiser's High Seas Fleet did indeed steam down the Kiel Canal and do battle with the British Grand Fleet at Jutland.

'You will find as the children grow up that, as a rule, children are a bitter disappointment. Their greatest object being to do precisely what their parents do not wish and have anxiously tried to prevent'.
Queen Victoria, to her daughter Victora, Crown Princess of Prussia, 5th January 1876. Her grandson, Wilhelm, the wilful future Kaiser, was only 17, and had yet to get up to real mischief.

KIMBERLEY'S 'BIG HOLE'
South Africa

In 1867, young Erasmus Jacobs found a glittering stone on his father's farm and gave it to his sisters to play with. It would change South Africa forever. When he saw it, the Colonial Secretary of the Cape prophesied: 'This diamond is the rock upon which the future success of South Africa will be built'.

Much of the story of Africa is one of greed: greed for slaves, for land, and for minerals. The rush for diamonds would rival anything that California had seen. By 1870, 10,000 diggers were frantically hacking at the soil. When diamonds were found on a farm owned by the De Beers brothers and at Colesberg Kopje, the British quickly annexed the territory of Griqualand West, first by an alliance with the Griqua tribe and then by a survey which 'moved' the boundaries away from a furious Orange Free State.

Colesberg Kopje was the top of a 'pipe' of diamond-bearing rock, whose hill was soon dug away. Within months the miners had excavated their little plots deep into the earth. The roadways between the plots collapsed, and soon a huge hole in the ground appeared with a vast network of ropes and pulleys taking buckets of ore up to the rim of the mine. The little town, and its big hole swarming with miners, was called

Right: Cecil Rhodes

Below: The 'Big Hole' at Kimberley , with the modern city in the background

Kimberley after Britain's Colonial Secretary, the Earl of Kimberley.

Soon control of the mine passed to just two men, Barney Barnato, a cockney from the East End of London, and Cecil Rhodes, whose De Beers company eventually bought out Barnato for £5,338,650 – at that time the largest cheque ever issued.

The 'Big Hole' eventually went down 1,000 feet and produced over 14 million carats of diamonds from 22 million tons of rock. It is the largest hand-dug hole in the world. At one time, it was producing 95 per cent of the world's diamonds. Cecil Rhodes used his wealth to play a major role in South Africa's gold rush, became Prime Minister of the Cape Colony and, hoping for more mineral finds, annexed Rhodesia, which is now the troubled nation of Zimbabwe.

The story of the greed for diamonds in Africa is unfortunately not over. In Sierra Leone, the bloodthirsty Revolutionary United Front, which inspires terror by amputation, has killed 50,000 people and created the term in the diamond industry of 'blood' or 'conflict' diamonds, which the industry is trying not to buy. Thousands of Africans have also died in Angola and the Democratic Republic of Congo in the

lust for diamonds, and Robert Mugabe's rule in Zimbabwe has been propped up by his military involvement in Congo.

A continent of mostly peaceful farmers was transformed by diamonds, with war, theft of land and apartheid the direct results. It might have been better if Erasmus Jacobs had never picked up that stone.

See: Nome, Rorke's Drift, Robben Island, Run, Silk Road, Sophiatown, Sutters Mill

THE KING DAVID HOTEL
Israel

'I am speaking on behalf of the Hebrew underground. We have placed an explosive device in the King David Hotel. Evacuate it at once. You have been warned'.

On 22nd July 1947, a female voice gave this warning to a British official in the hotel, and a similar message was sent to the French Consulate next door to open the windows to avoid flying glass.

Part of the luxurious 200-bedroom hotel in Jerusalem had been taken over by the British, exercising their somewhat thankless Mandate over Palestine. The hotel housed the military command, the Mandate's Secretariat and a military communication centre.

It was thirty years since the 'Balfour Declaration' had promised a Jewish homeland in Palestine. Having suffered the horrors of the Holocaust, Jewish activists were now united in their efforts to remove the British.

Menachem Begin (later Prime Minister of Israel) received the orders to blow up the hotel, and assembled his group. Six 'porters', disguised as Arabs, delivered milk churns each containing 50 kilograms of explosive to the side entrance, where the food for the 'La Regence' restaurant was delivered. Guards were overpowered, timers were set and the staff told to leave after ten minutes. Thirty minutes later, a huge explosion destroyed all seven storeys of one wing of the hotel. It killed 28 British, 41 Arabs, 17 Jews and 5 others.

It is still a mystery why the British did not take the warning seriously, turning the bombing into a real tragedy instead of a symbolic gesture. It may have been the usual military sin of underestimating an enemy, coupled with contempt. One officer apparently sneered, 'We don't take orders from Jews'. But hearing others joking about the threat in the bar,

Troops look for survivors in the wrecked building.

another officer sensibly left and survived.

While the British briefly tried to claim they had never received the warning, their case was not helped by the plainly anti-Semitic views of the British Army commander, General Sir Evelyn Barker, who issued an order which included, *'The aim of these orders are to punish the Jews in a way the race dislikes as much as any, namely by striking at their pockets.'*

The order was rescinded, but not before the damage was done – not least in Britain.

A year later the British were gone, leaving the Jews to fight against their Arab neighbours. And the King David Hotel may have hastened their departure – rather more than the Brighton hotel bombing did for Northern Ireland.

See: Anne Frank's Annexe, Armageddon, Aswan, Dachau, Getto, Grand Hotel, Masada

KITTY HAWK
North Carolina, USA

Actually, it was a telegraph that made Kitty Hawk famous.

While Orville and Wilbur Wright had made the remote North Carolina village their headquarters, it was not at Kitty Hawk that the first powered flight took place on 17th December 1903. It was at Kill Devil Hill, just four miles away. Nevertheless, Orville's mis-spelled telegraph message to his father was made from Kitty Hawk, the newspapers picked up the dateline and the world has remembered the name ever since.

Probably named from the Algonquian Indian word 'Chickahauk', Kitty Hawk is on the spit of land called the Outer Banks on North Carolina's Atlantic shoreline. Orville and Wilbur Wright

running a bicycle shop, they became inspired by the career – and the death in 1896 – in a glider accident, of the German pioneer Otto Lilienthal. They were particularly struck by the lack of controls in early flying machines, and after carefully watching eagles and pigeons, created a wing-warping system which they first tried out on kites at Dayton, Ohio, and then in a wind tunnel of their own design. Having solved the control problems, they designed and built a lightweight 12-horsepower petrol engine, driving two propellers.

On 14th December, Wilbur first flew 'The Flyer', but stalled it. Three days later Orville and Wilbur made four successful flights at Kill Devil Hill, the last of 852 feet and history was made. The plane was damaged and never flew again, and now resides in the Smithsonian Air and Space Museum.

The Wright Brothers carefully improved their design, Wilbur launching it publicly during August 1908 at Le Mans, France, and Orville a few days later at Fort Meyer, Virginia. The era of powered flight, with

See: Biggin Hill, Dakota, Farnborough, Lakehurst, Muroc, St Louis

arrived in 1900, deliberately choosing it for its wind, its sand for soft landings and its privacy; because the Wright brothers were working on something momentous – powered and controlled flight. After success with printing and

all that it implied for the civilian and military future, had begun.

But it will always be Kitty Hawk that the world will associate with the birth of flying – erroneously, but never mind.

KOHIMA'S TENNIS COURT
Burma

In Central Assam, the green mountains and spectacular peaks reach to 10,000 feet. The area contains the wettest place on earth, with no less than 800 inches a year. During the rains of the monsoon the jungle paths become torrents, while leeches, ticks, sandflies and mosquitoes are a constant torment.

The charming bungalow and tennis court of Deputy Commissioner Charles

Pawsey was situated 5,000 feet up in the Naga Hills, on a hairpin bend on the winding road between Dimapur and the local capital, Imphal. For the local mountain people, the Nagas, in their traditional mountain-top fortified villages, Pawsey was like a father figure. In March 1944, it was towards his remote home that 100,000 Japanese troops were laboriously but steadily advancing through Assam's thick jungle.

Having swept the British from Malaya and the rest of Burma, the Japanese saw no reason why they could not continue their successful advance towards India, which they hoped would rise against the British. They even called it 'The March on Delhi'. A confident, battle-hardened Japanese Army fell on the garrison of Kohima, manned at first by a scratched together group of British, Indian and faithful Assamese troops. For nearly six weeks the battle raged. Shelling and mortaring ripped the leaves from the thick green trees, so eventually the place looked like the barren waste of the Somme. Men on both sides were unshaven and filthy. The water ration was a pitiful pint a day. Bodies lay and rotted where they fell. Flies covered everything. The wounded suffered horribly. Fanatical battles were often conducted by sections and platoons, so difficult was the terrain.

Incredibly, as the battle raged, its central point became Pawsey's tennis court, with enemies occupying each end. First it was the Japanese, attacking with showers of grenades and fanatical banzai charges. Then, gradually, the British became stronger, but in no way could they shift the Japanese from their end of the tennis court. The narrow road up to Pawsey's bungalow was only just big enough for his tiny car, let alone a tank. However, after weeks of trying, Sergeant Waterhouse's Lee tank was winched up and suddenly appeared on 'our' baseline and blasted the bunkers from his end of the tennis court. It was the beginning of the end of the battle.

Unknown to the British, the Japanese were quarrelling about their own horrendous problems. It was not just their terrible battle casualties; their supply chain had completely broken down and they had virtually no food,

An Indian soldier looks at the Kohima battlefield, the lush vegetation completely blasted away.

ammunition nor medicine arriving, partly due to the appalling terrain. Another problem was their much-needed Thailand-Burma railway, with its notorious Bridge over the River Kwai. It was built four months too late, due to Japanese stupidity and cruelty in callously mistreating their slave workforce of British, Dutch, Australian and Asian prisoners, who through illness and starvation, worked slowly and died quickly.

Kohima was now to witness something unheard of; a confused and desperate Japanese retreat, with the troops ravaged by starvation, dysentery and virulent malaria. The wounded killed themselves rather than suffer more. A fraction of the bedraggled, sick army, tottering like old men with canes, made it back to its starting point.

It was the last offensive by the Japanese, whose veterans to this day go silent when anyone mentions the name Kohima.

On Kohima Hill there is a monument inscribed:
WHEN YOU GO HOME,
TELL THEM OF US AND SAY,
FOR YOUR TOMORROWS,
THESE GAVE THEIR TODAY.

See: Bikini, Changi, Corregidor, Hiroshima, Kwai River, Midway, Pearl Harbor

KRAKATOA
Sunda Strait

Volcanic eruptions like Vesuvius, Etna and Mount St Helens in Washington State, act as timely reminders of the colossal destructive power of nature. Whole civilisations

have been destroyed by volcanoes – as with Santorini in the Mediterranean, one of the supposed sources of the story of Atlantis.

It was fortunate that the island of

Krakatoa was comparatively isolated, in the Sunda Strait between Java and Sumatra, in what we now know is on the junction of the Indo-Australian and Eurasian tectonic plates. In 416 AD, an ancient eruption had created three islands; Rakata, Sertung and Panjangall, which steadily grew in size.

In May 1883, eruptions began, but they were just a foretaste of what was to come. On 27th August, the walls of the volcano collapsed and sea-water rushed in, meeting the red hot lava in the magma chamber. The result was the ultimate example of a 'steam eruption'.

Krakatoa exploded with the force of 100 megatons, 500 times more powerful than the atomic bomb at Hiroshima. It was heard in Alice Springs in the centre of Australia, and even in Madagascar, 2,200 miles away. The ash was blown 50 miles into the air and, blocking the sun, cooled the world's weather for a year – as well as creating beautiful sunsets.

Many were killed by falling ash and pumice, but much more tragic were the four waves or 'tsunamis' which raced silently towards Java and Sumatra, rose to 130 feet and hit their coastal villages, killing 36,000 people. The Dutch gunship *Berouw* was picked up and

See: Atlantis, Bikini, Chernobyl, El Nino, Maelstrom, Mount St. Helens, Pompeii

smashed down two miles inland.

The danger of tsunamis is the most lasting lesson of the fame by chance of Krakatoa. Caused by eruptions or underwater earthquakes, they can arrive without warning, travelling at 400 miles an hour from a peaceful sunlit sea, or out of the quiet night.

The world's scientists are beginning to focus on Gran Canaria, where a whole section of the island is in danger of suddenly sliding into the sea. In 1964, the strongest earthquake ever to hit the United States created a tidal wave 50 feet high, which travelled 8,000 miles. If Gran Canaria goes, a wave ten times bigger could destroy America's eastern seaboard before it could be evacuated, destroying everything from Boston to New Orleans, including New York, and Europe would not be untouched. The Bay of Naples may be equally threatened by a potential landslide off the slopes of the volcano Vesuvius.

As for Krakatoa – a new island, 'the child of Krakatoa', appeared in 1927. It is already 200 metres high and 2 kms in diameter. It is just a tourist attraction now, but history tells us it will one day be known as more than that.

KWAI RIVER
Thailand and Burma

They even took a grand piano. In April 1943, 7,000 British and Australian prisoners were told by their Japanese guards at Changi camp on Singapore that they were 'to go up country to a nice place in the mountains' where their 2,000 wounded could recover. They were cruelly deceived.

After a long train journey, they abandoned their piano and even their medical supplies as they faced an appalling 200 mile march over 17 nights. They arrived at a filthy camp site to start work the next day. They had come to work as slave labourers on the notorious Thailand-Burma railway along the River Kwai. 69 per cent of the Australians and 29 per cent of the British were to die – of cholera, beri-beri, malaria, but mostly of malnutrition and starvation which made the prisoners fatally susceptible to typhus, dysentery, scabies and tropical ulcers.

The railway was vital to the Japanese, both to supply Burma and also its armies who were trying to break into India at Kohima and Imphal. 12,000 allied prisoners were to die, together with innumerable 'romusha', conscripted Asians. Someone calculated that there was a dead body for every railway sleeper – 55,000.

The Japanese were desperate. 'Speedo, speedo', they kept repeating to the sick, hollow-eyed skeletons staggering in the jungle dressed in loincloths. 'It will be built even if it is over the dead bodies of each and every one of you.' The brutality of the Japanese should come as no surprise – they treated each other as badly, and also their Korean allies. They had already committed major acts of bestiality – 200,000 civilians slaughtered in 'The Rape of Nanking' in 1938 and 6,000 Chinese in Singapore. Gang rape was regarded as soldierly bonding, like bayonet practice on live prisoners. Only 4 per cent of allied prisoners died in German camps, but in Japanese ones it was 29 per cent, and for the Australians an appalling 36 per cent. Half the Australians who perished in the war against Japan died as helpless prisoners.

What is extraordinary about the 'Death Railway' is the short-sightedness of the cruelty. Given enough food and medicine, the prisoners would have built it so much faster. With their work- force sick and dying, the schedule fell months behind. Simple, practical mistakes added to Japanese inefficiency. Wrong surveys meant cuttings and embankments had to be changed. One leaking radiator on a compressor, instead of being repaired, required three elephants to bring water to keep filling it up. The Alec Guinness film *The Bridge on the River Kwai* only hints at the real horror of the badly built railway.

When the lines from Thailand and Burma finally met, the Japanese wanted to make a propaganda film of the 'last spike' ceremony. The film crew was appalled by the appearance of the naked, emaciated men and quickly gave them costumes – equally quickly snatched back when the filming was over.

The railway never even achieved its purpose. At Kohima, after 64 days of battle, General Sato desperately signalled to his superiors, 'Since leaving the Chindwin, we have not received one

bullet from you, nor a grain of rice', and he ordered withdrawal, which became a horrific and unheard – of retreat that was to be the greatest disaster in Japanese military history.

The line is no longer used, and the jungle has reclaimed most of the 'Death Railway', a project which will never be forgotten or forgiven, above all perhaps, in Australia.

See: Andersonville, Andrassy, Changi, Dachau, Gulag, Hiroshima, Kohima's Tennis Court

Top: Alec Guinness in 'The Bridge on the River Kwai.' He looks much fitter and plumper than any real prisoner.
Bottom: The cemetery of the Dutch prisoners who died building the line.

LACONIA
Greece

In 338 BC, Philip II of Macedon threatened, 'If I enter Laconia, I will raze Sparta to the ground.' He received the terse reply, 'If'.

Laconia's capital, Sparta was the most military and disciplined of the Greek city states, whose well-drilled Spartan phalanx had led to many victories. It was also the most austere and sparing with words, in contrast to her more flowery Hellenic neighbours.

Famous 'Laconic' replies have to include the response from General McAuliffe, during the 1944 'Battle of the Bulge', to the German demand for the

Americans to surrender at Bastogne, 'Nuts!' More of a classicist was General Sir Charles Napier, who captured Hyderabad and the province of Sind in 1843. His laconic report in Latin to the Governor General of India was 'Peccavi', (I have sinned).

Another might be Lord Sainsbury, furious that the American Poultry Association had cancelled a conference in London because of fears of personal safety, just after Britain had obligingly let the US use British airfields for their planes to bomb Colonel Gaddafi. He confined his cable to 'CHICKEN!'

Calvin Coolidge, the US President famous mainly for his taciturn nature, said, 'I have noticed that nothing I have never said ever did me any harm'. Once he was told by a gushing girl at a party 'I've bet my friends I can get more than two words out of you, Mr President'.

'You lose'.

When the famous wit Dorothy Parker was told that Coolidge had died, she responded, 'How can they tell?'

There are times when it is worse to say nothing than to say little. The citizens of Amyclæa were so frightened of the prospect of being attacked by Sparta that they issued a decree forbidding anyone to even mention the subject. So, when they saw the Spartan army approaching, nobody would report it. The 'Amyclæan Silence' doomed the city.

Even though they have 158 verses in their National Anthem, the Greeks have continued their tradition of Laconic replies. They even celebrate a national holiday and festival called Óhi Day each 28th October. This marks the crisp reply of Prime Minister Metaxas to Mussolini's 1940 ultimatum – 'Óhi!' (No!).

LADOGA'S ICE ROAD
Russia

One of the first German bombs to hit Leningrad in 1941 killed 'Betty', the elephant in the zoo. The citizens could well have done with Betty a few months later, because by then they were eating cats, dogs and rats.

Formerly St Petersburg, the beautiful and imperial city of Leningrad had been caught by surprise by the rapid success of the onslaught of Hitler's 'Operation Barbarossa'. Since 22nd June 1941, the German panzers had fought their way a distance of 500 miles, and by the end of August were only a few miles from the city. Leningrad's party boss, Andrei Zhdanov, once tipped as Stalin's successor, was at first primarily worried about air attack and evacuated 300,000 children, tragically sending no less than a third of them straight into the path of the Germans. Leningrad's factories had immediately converted to turning out munitions. They never stopped, regardless of the horrors to come.

In spite of desperate resistance by the Russian armies, the Germans kept coming, confident enough to issue tourist guide books to their troops, to print parking permits and, of course, to plan a victory parade.

Food rationing had started on 18th July, in common with the rest of the Soviet Union – quite generous in retrospect. Plans were made to evacuate 700,000 women and children from Leningrad. They never made it. Disaster struck on 8th September. The Germans from the south and their allies, the Finns from the north, cut off the city from the rest of the Soviet Union. Nearly three million civilians and 500,000 troops were trapped, and doomed to begin an ordeal arguably unparalleled in history.

The same bombing raids that killed Betty burned down the huge wooden Badayev warehouses. Two and half thousand tonnes of precious sugar melted into the cellars. Vital tons of meat, grain, lard, butter all went up in flames. Food reserves dropped to 15-25 days supply. Rations were cut. No food could be obtained without ration cards, which were soon to be the difference between life and death. Half a million civilians, women and children slaved to build fortifications. The brutal battles continued, but the Germans then had to divert troops to the Battle of Moscow and decided to starve Leningrad. On 22nd September, Hitler secretly ordered, 'Leningrad should be razed from the face of the earth. It is not to be allowed to surrender'.

Hunger was really biting by October. The daily issue of flour fell from 2,100 tons in September to 510 tons in December. For many subsisting on two slices of bread a day, this was a death warrant, especially for the old and the children. Some food was able to come from the 'mainland' across Lake Ladoga by boat, but by 15th November ice began to form. It was, in fact, to be Leningrad's salvation.

Gradually, the ice thickened. On 17th November, a team of engineers, roped together, tested the ice. Days later, with

Leningrad down to two days food supply, the first sleds drawn by weak and emaciated horses crept across the frozen, windswept lake. The military Automobile Highway 101, the 'Road of Life', was open. On 22nd November the first trucks delivered 33 tonnes of flour, to the starving city. Soon the road had first-aid stations, repair depots, traffic control, anti-aircraft guns. 800 tonnes a day were getting across, but death still now stalking Leningrad. 12,000 died in November, 53,000 in December, either from starvation or the diseases caused by it. Desperate to keep up public morale, Zhdanov boldly increased the ration a tiny amount, counting on the ice road to prove him right.

Leningrad was now dark and ice-cold, the coldest in memory. On children's sleds, the dead were dragged slowly to the morgues. Piles of bodies were everywhere; in the hospital, the parks, the theatres, the cathedral. Apartments were full of frozen corpses. People were murdered for their ration cards or for food. Without fuel, the power stations wheezed to a halt, and water pumps and sewerage stopped. The radio fell silent. Rats disappeared, either dead – or sensibly leaving for a morsel of food in the German lines. Sparrows dropped dead in flight. Cannibalism began, privately, or in the mysterious meat patties sold by unpleasant people in the Haymarket.

But while the number of people to be fed was dropping, the ice road was still improving, achieving 2,900 tons a day. By the time the ice turned to slush in April, the road had saved the city. It really was 'The Road of Life'.

But, in that winter alone, over a million people died of starvation and cold. Incredibly, as the corpses were removed in the spring and the power returned with a few trams clattering into life, it was not the final chapter in Leningrad's misery. It took until January 1943 for the German ring to be broken, and another whole year of constant deadly shelling and siege before the Germans staggered back in retreat.

'The Nine Hundred Days' of the longest and most horrible siege in history had ended. It was the courage and ingenuity of those who kept the ice road running that made it possible.

The first food came across the lake on sleds pulled by emaciated horses.

See: Berezina, Ekaterinburg, Finland Station, Gleiwitz, Lidice, Stalingrad, Unter den Linden

LAKEHURST
New Jersey, USA

By 1937, at Lakehurst, New Jersey, the majestic sight of airships was almost routine. The mooring mast at the Naval Station had been the destination for the German transatlantic airship service for nine years. The *Graf Zeppelin* had now completed 144 flights across the Atlantic in perfect safety and great comfort – a real competitor to the ocean liners. It had also flown round the world and had started a passenger and mail service to South America.

Its successor, the *Hindenburg,* was twice as big: 804 feet long, ten storeys high and with four massive diesel engines capable of driving it 11,000 miles at no less than 84 miles per hour.

Its fifty passengers travelled from Europe in 48 hours, cosseted in first-class luxury, with bunks, hot and cold water, and air conditioning, and were treated to velvet upholstery, Japanese silk, walnut fittings and even a (very light) grand piano. It was the Concorde of its era and, at $400 a ticket, appealed to the same kind of affluent passenger. Throughout 1936, *Hindenburg*, which also flew to South America, arrived at Lakehurst every few weeks, having sailed over Boston and New York. Here was the wonder of the age, and also a potent symbol of Nazi Germany's technological skills.

But there was a flaw. Dr Hugo Eckener, the Zeppelin company's designer, had intended to fill the gas cells with non-flammable helium. However, most of the world's helium came from a small part of Texas – and it

mooring lines. Suddenly, an explosion ripped through the gas cell near the rear section and flames started spreading forward in a flash. Passengers and crew began leaping for their lives as the blazing wreckage sank to the ground.

was rare and expensive. The American Government, worried about the Zeppelin company's links with the Nazis, had indeed made sure it was too expensive – demanding $600,000 ($7,500,000) today. Thus Eckener, who had actually quarrelled with the Nazis, was forced to use seven million cubic feet of cheaper, but volatile, hydrogen – turning the *Hindenburg* into a potential bomb.

Every precaution against fire or sparks was taken, including hemp-soled shoes, anti-static uniforms, and passenger searches for incendiary materials before boarding.

On 6th May 1937, *Hindenburg* approached Lakehurst several hours late because of thunderstorms over New York. At seven in the evening, watched by newsmen, the magnificent airship approached the mast and dropped her

Herb Morrison, a Chicago reporter, there to record the docking for coast to coast radio, created history with one of the most anguished and memorable broadcasts of all time:

'It's burning, bursting into flames and falling on the mooring mast and all the folks.

This is terrible. This is one of the worst catastrophes in the world.

Oh, the flames, 400 or 500 feet into the sky. It's a terrific crash.

Oh, the humanity and all the passengers. I can't talk, ladies and gentlemen....'

From the first spark it had taken just 34 seconds for the stately *Hindenburg* to become a smoking ruin on the ground. Amazingly, 62 of the 97 on board survived. But the horrifying sights and sounds of that evening at Lakehurst made sure that airship passenger travel did not.

See: Biggin Hill, Cape Canaveral, Farnborough, Kitty Hawk, Lockerbie, Muroc, St. Louis

LANDSBERG
Germany

Landsberg in Bavaria has had many visitors, some more welcome than others. In 1158, when Henry the Lion built a castle and a bridge over the River Lech, he was welcoming a special type of visitor, the Austrian salt merchants from Salzburg who needed to cross the river. Here was the opportunity to levy several taxes – not just the bridge toll, but for weighing the salt, checking it and even storing it for three days. This was the unusual beginning of the wealth of the town.

Less welcome visitors were the soldiers of Swedish General Torstenson, who besieged the town in 1638. Before its fall, some of Landsberg's women were sufficiently worried about their fate to throw themselves pitifully from the castle battlements, now charmingly described by locals as the 'Virgin jumping place'.

But in 1923, a much more significant visitor was to put Landsberg on the world stage for ever – Adolf Hitler.

Four years after the Treaty of Versailles, Germany was desperate. It had defaulted on timber reparations to France, which had occupied the industrial Ruhr. The resulting general strike drove the Reichsmark in weeks down from 7,000 to the dollar to billions, then trillions. Savings were utterly destroyed and public confidence shattered.

Hitler and his quite small National Socialist German Workers' Party saw their opportunity. And Bavaria seemed just the right place, with its leadership publicly ready to declare independence. At a meeting at the *Buegerbraukeller*, Hitler interrupted the Commissioner Gustav von Kahr by firing a revolver into the ceiling. He then tricked Kahr and his two triumvirate colleagues, at pistol point, that the war hero General Eric von Ludendorff was 'forming a Bavarian or even a national Government'. A bemused and annoyed Ludendorff arrived just in time to complete the false impression. Hitler left, and Ludendorff swore the three officials, 'as ex-officers', to remain there. They promptly disappeared, and overnight proclaimed on posters that they had been under duress. The 'Beer Hall Putsch' had begun to fall apart.

Next day, facing failure, Hitler then agreed with a suggestion by Ludendorff that they try to rescue the revolution by marching to the centre of the city. 'No one would dare to fire at us', predicted Ludendorff. He was only partly right. The 3,000 Nazi storm troopers bluffed their way through one road block, but at the second, a shot was fired. A blizzard of firing left 16 Nazis and three policemen dead; Goering was hit (a wound requiring drugs that would cause his later addiction) and Hitler retreated ignominiously, to be arrested two days later. Only Ludendorff had marched on, dignified and unscathed.

At first glance, the fiasco appeared to have finished the Nazis and Hitler. Not a bit of it. For 24 dramatic days, Hitler dominated the court in Munich with his rhetoric, and soon became famous far beyond Bavaria and even Germany. He ended his defiant defence, 'It is not you, gentlemen, who pass judgement on us. That judgement is spoken by the eternal court of history'.

But he was sentenced to five years in Landsberg Prison, where he spent several months in comparative luxury, dictating 782 pages of his book *Mein Kampf* ('My Struggle') to his faithful Rudolf Hess. It was a book that exactly predicted the fate envisaged for Germany and her enemies. Its great length, turgid style and Hitler's apparent unimportance meant that few moderate Germans, or world leaders, bothered to read it at the time. If they had, history would have been very different.

Hitler was to be released after thirteen months, and set about rebuilding his Nazi party. The terrible poverty of the Depression in 1933 gave him his second

> '*The broad mass of the nation will more easily fall victim to a big lie than a small one*'.
>
> Hitler, Mein Kampf, 1925

> '*That man for a Chancellor? I'll make him a postmaster and he can lick the stamps with my head on them*'.
>
> President Paul von Hindenburg

217

chance – and Germany marched towards World War II, the Holocaust and, eventually, total defeat and ruin.

For a while, Landsberg briefly returned to provincial obscurity. Then, the victorious Allies decided to send most of the Nuremberg prisoners and the more evil of convicted war criminals to the same prison in which Hitler had stayed in such comfort. Their fate was very different. 284 were executed there.

Landsberg has probably now had its fill of unwanted guests.

See: Alcatraz, Andersonville, Andrassy, Bastille, Dachau, Devil's Island, Gulag, Landsberg, Robben Island, Reading Gaol, Sing Sing, Spandau, Wannsee

LAPLAND
Finland

The northern province of Finland, Lapland, is a sparsely inhabited land of mountains and tundra, but for millions of children it has one very important inhabitant – Father Christmas.

Some parts of the legend of Santa Claus are extremely old. As with so many mythical figures, he is a mixture of a number of characters from several countries. However, the overall origin appears to be Bishop Nicholas of Smyrna, in Turkey. Living in the 4th century AD, Nicholas was a very rich man, and also a generous one, particularly towards children. The multitude of tales concerning his munificence include giving money to three young penniless girls in his village so that they could eventually marry – using the gift as a dowry – and throwing presents through the windows of poor children. So renowned were his deeds that he was honoured by the church after his death, being made the Patron Saint of children and seafarers.

Every December 6th his name was venerated. This, together with his status as a figure for kindness and warmth, is the most probable reason that he became absorbed into the Christmas

legend, gradually being referred to as 'Father Christmas'. His image tended to differ slightly between countries. In France, for instance, he had a tough sidekick, ' Pere Fouettard' – 'Father Spanker' who would accompany him on Christmas Eve and punish bad children, while Father Christmas would reward the good ones.

As a Christmas institution, however, Father Christmas did face some opposition. In England, in 1642, the Puritans decided that he detracted from the religious side of the celebration. For this, they simply banned Christmas that year, and there were countrywide riots as the shops were forced to stay open. Conversely, in Communist Russia, he was regarded as too religious. The poor chap's name was promptly changed to 'Grandfather Frost', and his red garb, thought to be too like that of a bishop, was altered to blue.

The name Santa Claus itself was a result of the European settlement of the New World. Dutch settlers brought their version of Saint Nicholas, 'Sinter Klaas' across the Atlantic with them, and the name 'St. A Claus' occurred in the American press as early as 1773.

His image evolved over time. Writer Clarke Moore, author of the poem *The Night Before Christmas,* portrayed him as an elf. Later, in the 1860s, the illustrator Thomas Nast of *Harper's Weekly* portrayed Santa as the rotund, bearded figure now familiar to us, showing him with Union Troops to help President Lincoln. As his physical image changed, other details were added to the legend, such as the helper elves, the lists of good and bad children, and the names of the reindeer. *Rudolph the red-nosed reindeer,* incidentally, was invented long after the others, being created in 1939 by Robert L. May, a writer for the Montgomery Ward Company. Ten years later, Gene Pitney recorded Johnny Mark's hit tune.

The idea that Santa's workshop existed in Lapland, however, is a relatively new addition. Nast had depicted him as living at the North Pole, but even small children questioned this for the rather practical reason that it would leave the reindeer nowhere to graze. Thus, in 1925, his 'home' was moved to Lapland in Finland, which is conveniently filled with grazing reindeer.

Indeed, in 1927, on his *Children's Hour* radio show in Finland, 'Uncle' Markus Rautio announced his exact location: the mountain Korvatunturi. In Finnish, this means 'Ear Fell'. The mountain itself resembles three giant ears, through which Santa is said to listen to all the world's children to see how well they are behaving. At Rovaniemi, there is now a Santa Claus village – a theme park and Santa Park, a cave which doubles as an atomic shelter. As a result of mixed up legends, the Finns, rather unfortunately even call Santa 'Jouluppuki', which translates as 'Christmas stud goat'

Today, Santa's image is attached to every form of advertisement and blatant commercialisation. However, although the original Bishop Nicholas was as detached from such an ethos as possible, it is worth noting that the Lapland legend, seen as such an integral part of the Santa Claus story, was only created six years before he appeared in his first Coca-Cola advertisement!

See: Nokia

LASSA
Nigeria

In 1969 in the town of Lassa, a disease was identified that had been infecting and killing people for several years in the west African countries like Nigeria, Liberia, Sierra and Guinea.

Lassa fever, in its early stages, can be easily confused with familiar health problems like severe malaria, septicaemia and yellow fever, and with even more dangerous viral fevers like Ebola. Its gradual symptoms include fever, headache, sore throat, coughing, vomiting, diarrhoea and general pain. 15 per cent of patients admitted to hospital die and, more alarmingly, 80 per cent of pregnant women lose their babies.

Contamination is caused by direct or indirect contact with the faeces of the wild rat, *Mastomys natalenisis,* the initial culprit – but once people catch it, they too can pass it on in all sorts of ways, and for many weeks.

The World Health Organisation (WHO) recommends many ways to limit Lassa Fever's effects, including exterminating the rats, strict isolation, high quality disinfecting procedures, and monitoring places the patient has been and any other contacts made. But words like 'strict procedures', 'auto-claving' and 'bio-safety

See: 'Anthrax' Island, Ebola

containment' may not be too well known in the jungle, so it is not surprising that about 5,000 people die from the disease each year. As the S.A.R.S virus has recently demonstrated, with a relatively long incubation period and modern air travel, one of these days Lassa may become even more famous.

LAS VEGAS
Nevada, USA

For 'Bugsy' Siegel, the little town in the barren heat of the Nevada desert had two attractions. It was two hours from Los Angeles, and you could legally gamble there.

As the underworld's West Coast leader, Siegel had recently made quite a name for himself – perhaps too much of a name.

Handsome and charismatic, he had teamed up with an old pal, the 'gangster actor' George Raft, himself a former bootlegger. He had 'made friends' with the local social leader, Countess Dorothy di Frasso, who had introduced him to the cream of Hollywood society; Clarke Gable, Jean Harlow, Norma Shearer, Gary Cooper. Siegel had made his own friends too, mostly beautiful actresses, in spite of a wife and two daughters.

His attractiveness and boyish charm hid a dark history. His career in crime began as a boy in New York, as part of a protection racket – setting fire to pushcarts if the owners did not pay. Then he befriended a skinny kid called Meyer Lansky, and they created the 'Bug and Meyer Mob', running gambling and stealing cars. Ben Siegel was already called 'Bugsy' for his unpredictable violence, and he always hated the name. But it suited him well. Lansky hired him out as a contract killer, and his reputation was further enhanced in April 1931 when he played a notable role in the Coney Island shooting of Joe 'The Boss' Masseria – in the distinguished company of Vito Genovese, Joe Adonis, Albert Anastasia

and Lucky Luciano. He then created 'Murder Inc.', a team of Jewish assassins which enforced the crime syndicate's demands – while his charm was used to win over politicians and celebrities.

By 1937, Siegel had become a bit too 'hot' for New York, and he was moved to Los Angeles, successfully taking over for Lansky the Dragna brothers' wire service, linking betting shops and gambling dens, netting $8 million a year for the Mob.

It was then that a beautiful, green-eyed redhead came into his life. Virginia Hill, a syndicate courier and a blackmailer, became his partner – both sexually and commercially – with Virginia helping Siegel to start the heroin and opium traffic up from Mexico.

In 1945, Bugsy Siegel also conceived his grand dream,

'The Flamingo', a lavish casino and hotel on dusty Highway 91, in the desert outside the tiny railroad town of Las Vegas, whose population had been boosted by Boulder Dam workers. He obtained rather reluctant backing from Lansky and Luciano, but with Siegel inexperienced, distracted and overworked, the costs soared. Materials were expensive, plans were changed and trees were sold to him many times over. After one bout of frustrated fury, he reassured the contractor, 'Don't worry Del, we only kill each other'. He was close to the truth. At a conference in Havana, a furious Lucky Luciano found that not only had the expenses rocketed from one to six million dollars, but also that Virginia Hill had been flying to Switzerland to deposit huge sums. Luciano, Genovese, Adonis and Frank Costello were all for contracting Charlie Fischetti to 'hit' Siegel at once. But his old boyhood friend and mentor, Meyer Lansky, convinced that Siegel was more an incompetent dreamer than a thief, begged them to hold off and await results until after 'The Flamingo's' opening, the day after Christmas 1946.

Unfortunately, the opening was dogged by bad luck. Two planes full of Hollywood stars and celebrities were grounded by Los Angeles fog. It poured with rain at Las Vegas, and for weeks gamblers' interest was tepid. Losses mounted. With suspicions not allayed that some of the money was sitting in Swiss banks, Luciano called Siegel and demanded that $5 million be returned. An overconfident Siegel told him to 'go to hell', and added that he would pay 'in his own good time'.

Enough was enough. On 30th June 1947, as he sat in Virginia Hill's mansion while she was away, Benny Siegel was hit through the window by three bullets from a rifle.

'The Flamingo' was taken over by Siegel's underworld colleagues and, curiously, the notoriety of his death contributed to its success.

Within a decade, a whole lavish city

CANDY MAGUIRE

had risen out of the desert. It has several million visitors a year and has now earned $100 billion, despite a population of just half a million.

By the 1970s, organised crime had left Las Vegas. 'The Flamingo' has grown under Hilton to 3,642 rooms, the fourth largest hotel in the world. During its 50th Anniversary celebrations a spokesman said 'The Bugsy image was not something that was particularly endearing to the Flamingo or Hilton. This was not George Washington or Abraham Lincoln. We're talking about a robber, rapist and murderer. These are not endearing qualities'.

But still, there is something endearing about Benny Siegel pursuing his dream, and without it Las Vegas might still be a little village in the desert, and none of us would ever have heard of it.

The Flamingo is now one of the world's largest hotels.

See: Alcatraz, Cotton Club, North Clark Street

LEAVENWORTH
Washington, USA

If you say 'Leavenworth' to most people, they usually remember Fort Leavenworth, with its prison in Kansas. But Leavenworth, Washington State, is a small town in the Cascade Mountains named after Captain Charles Leavenworth, who laid out the town to profit from its position on the Great Northern Railway's trans-continental line to Seattle.

Prosperity for the railroad was further

boosted in 1904 by the Lamb-Davis Lumber Company building a large sawmill, fed by 29 lumber camps.

But the good times did not last long. In 1922, the Great Northern decided to move its 'Division Point' from Leavenworth to Wenatchee, thirty miles down the track. The status of being a 'Division Point' had been one reason for the economic success of the town and losing it meant the loss of numerous jobs

A shopkeeper with a sense of humour

connected with the repair workshops, stores and the divisional headquarters of the railroad.

Five years later, the sawmill closed with further job losses, and four decades of gradual decline began. By 1950, Front Street had 24 empty stores, crammed with broken glass and rubble.

In 1962, The University of Washington advised Leavenworth's Chamber of Commerce to organise local citizens to work together to save the town. After a year's study into various themes, the 'Gay Nineties', 'The Wild West', 'Railroad' or 'Scandinavian', an extraordinary decision was made.

'We have to go Bavarian'.

Little by little, Leavenworth was persuaded that the downtown area should look exactly like somewhere in the Alps – and so it does today. It is effectively a theme town. You get out of your car, and you begin to hear the yodelling and Germanic music from the bandstand in Front Street Park. People are all dressed in dirndls or leather shorts – like a bizarre but realistic parody of Switzerland, Austria or Southern Germany. Shops and bars overflow with Bavarian-type wares.

All the buildings are in Bavarian style, helped in authenticity by German-born architect Heintz Ulbricht. Even the Safeway supermarket sign is in Gothic lettering, as is the Chevron gas station. The only person with a sense of humour about all this seems to be the owner of a sausage shop who has a sign which reads, 'The Best of the Würst'.

But this image make-over has transformed Leavenworth from an obscure, fading railroad and lumber town into an international attraction, with over a million visitors from all over the world and a booming economy. Maybe some other towns should try it.

LE MANS
France

Until 1923, the cathedral town of Le Mans might have been known as the birthplace of England's Henry II, and not much else. But ever since 1923, once a year the roads around town become the famous home of one of the most demanding and evocative motor races in the world – the Le Mans 24 hours. At 4pm on a June Saturday afternoon, the world's fastest sports racing cars roar into life, to begin a gruelling drive which will last until 4 pm on Sunday, over 3,000 miles later.

The idea came from Georges Durand, Secretary of the Automobile Club de l'Ouest, who wanted to organise a race long enough to demonstrate the reliability of ordinary touring cars. He took his ideas to Charles Faroux, editor of *La Vie Automobile*, during the Paris motor show in 1922. Faroux enlisted the help of Emile Coquille, the French agent for the Rudge-Whitworth detachable wire wheel, who put up a trophy, the Rudge-Whitworth Cup, and a donation of 100,000 francs.

Cars were to be standard touring cars – complete with wings, hoods, mirrors and lamps. All tools used had to be carried on the cars. Because headlights were thought to be inadequate, for the first race in 1923, military searchlights lit up the major corners of the circuit.

A seven car pile-up during the 1927 race. One of the three crashed Bentleys went on to win at 61 m.p.h.

The cars became faster and ever more specialist.

In the '30s, Britain's gentlemen drivers – 'the Bentley boys' – dominated, then after World War II, factory teams like Jaguar, Ferrari, Ford and Porsche used Le Mans for its glamour and publicity.

However, even using alternating drivers, the strain of racing through the night,

DONOUGH O'BRIEN

often in heavy rain, in the company of drivers of varying ability and cars of varying speeds, takes its toll.

On June 11th 1955, Le Mans raced from famous to infamous. Veteran driver Pierre Levegh had so impressed the Mercedes team with his single-handed near victory two years earlier that they gave him a place on their team. Travelling at 150 mph, Levegh could not avoid hitting another car swerving in the congested pit area. His silver projectile somersaulted into the crowd like a lethal scythe, killing 80 spectators and injuring more than a hundred. Horrified by the carnage, Mercedes pulled out of the race and, indeed, out of racing.

Le Mans, despite the tragedy, is still a major feature in the annual motor racing calendar. And after 73 years it is great to see Bentley winning again.

Sunset at Le Mans. A Jaguar and Mercedes like these would be involved in the fateful crash.

Top left: the traditional Le Mans starts with the drivers running across the track to leap into their cars.

Left: Ford came to Le Mans in 1968 and dominated for years.

See: Brescia, Brooklands, Indianapolis

LESBOS
Greece

The basis for the terms 'Lesbian' and 'Sapphic' rests purely on an interpretation of poetry, and a debated one at that.

In ancient times, calling someone a 'lesbian' would merely point out that they came from the Island of Lesbos, now called Lesvos, the third largest of the Greek islands. It became famous in antiquity, primarily as a cultural centre. In the 7th century B.C., it gave rise to two of the most illustrious lyric poets ever, the contemporaries Alcaeus and

Sappho. 'Lyric' poetry, accompanied by the lyre, was deeply personal, concerned primarily with the private feelings of the poet, and can still be evocative today.

The legendary explanation of the poetic gift associated with the island was that the legendary bard Orpheus, someone so powerful that mountains and trees would strain to hear his song of mourning for his lost love Euridice, was torn to shreds by spurned Thracian women. Subsequently, his head washed up on the shores of Lesbos and was buried there.

The work of Alcaeus lives on only in tiny fragments, much about fighting, lamenting and the loss of his shield upon the battlefield. To lose your shield indicated flight and cowardice, as the shield would be too heavy to carry at a run. The stigma is clear from a stern demand, uttered by a Spartan mother to her son leaving for war, 'Return with your shield or on it!'

Alcaeus also wrote of love, and of drinking, which he clearly regarded to be the cure for just about anything.

Sappho, however, is far more famous than her male contemporary. For one thing, she is one of the only known female poets of the ancient world, on which her poetry made a powerful impact. The people of Syracuse erected a statue of her, coins of Lesbos were minted in her image, and Plato, struck by the beauty of her writing, described her as the tenth muse. In fact, her work moved Solon, a ruler of Athens, to such an extent that he said of one of her poems: 'I want to learn it and die'.

Slightly more of her poetry survives than that of Alcaeus, but still only one poem exists in its complete form, along with numerous fragments, whereas at one time there had been nine volumes. Some of the material that we have today was found on papyrus used for wrapping Egyptian mummies.

Sappho's preferred topics were love, her friends and family, and especially the women in her life. Her poetic gift became so well-known that young girls were sent to her for an education. This group may also have acted as a religious cult, and it is thought that they worshipped Aphrodite, the Greek goddess of love. Sappho addressed extremely affectionate poetry to this circle of women, for instance composing their 'epithalamia' – marriage hymns – when they took husbands.

It was the Greek poet Anacreon, living a generation later, who first wrote that the island's name carried an implication of homosexuality, now popularly believed. But did Sappho's poetry ever actually contain allusions to homo-eroticism? And is she what the modern writer would call a lesbian? Certainly, she writes in one poem about envying the husband of one of her circle. She writes of her passion, describing this woman:

'Her tongue will not move, a subtle fire burns under her skin, her eyes see no longer, her ears ring, she breaks into a sweat, she trembles, she is as pale as death which seems so near'.

It certainly sounds as if she could be in love with this student. Nevertheless, it is far from concrete evidence. Furthermore, the story of Sappho's death, if it is to be believed, is that she killed herself out of love for a man. When the boatman Phaon spurned her, she leapt heartbroken into the sea from the cliffs of Cape Leucas. Thus we have no way of knowing whether the allegations about her sexuality are true, but they have stuck. If false, this interpretation of Sappho has entwined her name, and the name of her island home, with female homosexuality – preserving them in an inaccurate link forever.

See: Ibiza, Milo

LIDICE
Czech Republic

Of all the Nazi leaders, the icy, blond and slit-eyed Reinhard Heydrich was arguably the most evil and the most dangerous. Secretly feared by even Hitler and his own SS boss Himmler, he was physically brave and had gathered a unique triple power base; as second in command of the SS, Head of the Sicherheitsdienst (SD) and Controller of the Reichsicherhaupstamt (RSHA), the overall security umbrella of the Reich. It was Heydrich who was to unleash 'Kristallnacht', the first public attack on the Jews, and Heydrich who engineered the phoney assault on Gleiwitz radio station – the excuse to attack Poland – which started World War II. In addition, it was Heydrich who was to chair the notorious lakeside Wannsee Conference which planned the 'Final Solution' of no

The light railway carts away the rubble of Lidice's homes.

In response, the British backed a Free Czech attempt on Heydrich's life. He was ambushed over-confidently driving his open car to work in Prague, and a grenade drove debris deep into his body. His wounds turned septic and killed him after days of agony.

The Nazis took a terrible revenge for the death of a favourite son. One morning they surrounded an innocent Czech village called Lidice. All 173 men and boys were shot, 114 women sent to concentration camps, and nearly all the 82 children sent to the gas chambers. Dogs were shot in their kennels, houses dynamited, and the rubble shipped away on a special light railway. Finally, the place was ploughed flat. All this the Nazis gloatingly photographed and filmed, ensuring that Lidice became forever a symbol of one nation's brutality to another.

less than eleven million Jews, and who directly commanded the Gestapo's 'Jewish expert' Adolf Eichmann, who succeeded in killing 6 million. When Heydrich was sent to Prague as Czechoslovakia's brutal master, he cleverly started to use 'the carrot and the stick' method – combining rewards and harshness which quickly gained him the title 'The hangman of Prague'. Vital Czech production actually started to rise.

MONUMENT PHOTOGRAPHS: SOCIETY FOR THE CHILDREN'S CASUALTIES OF WAR

Part of the superb, evocative sculpture by Marie Uchytilova of the 'Children of Lidice' about to be transported to death camps

See: Anne Frank's Annexe, Dachau, Gleiwitz, Oradour, Wannsee

LITTLE BIG HORN
North Dakota, USA

With his long fair hair, and his exuberant if arrogant personality, George Custer was both glamorous and popular. History records that he was also

one of the most dangerous men with whom to go into battle. Armed with reckless courage, his heroic exploits in the American Civil War certainly earned

Top: General George Custer
Right: Crazy Horse

See: West Point, Wounded Knee

him wide publicity and the rank of General at the age of just 26, but often at the expense of needless losses. Nor, later, did he learn from the man whose death brought him out of disgraced semi-retirement. The foolish young Captain William Fetterman had boasted; 'Give me 80 good troopers and I will ride right though the Sioux nation'. On the Bozeman Trail, the brilliant young Sioux leader, Crazy Horse finished him and his 81 troopers off in about twenty minutes.

So it is hardly surprising that when Custer himself met Crazy Horse by a sleepy stream called the Little Bighorn, disaster was about to strike. After many exhausting days riding, Custer looked down and could only see part of what was a very sizeable camp of Sioux and Cheyennes. He therefore sensed an easy, surprise victory – mostly against women and children – like his dubious exploit at the Massacre of the Washita. Against orders to wait for reinforcements from the infantry, Custer impetuously split his forces and plunged 225 tired cavalrymen down towards the camp, to realise – at once and with horror – that 4,000 united, prepared, fresh and well-armed braves were thundering up towards and around him. Losing the race for protection from the nearest hill, Custer was killed, as was every single man in his command, all of them overwhelmed by heat, exhaustion and superior firepower. A recent brush fire revealed 9,000 artefacts of the battle, which showed that the Indians were using 40 types of rifle and had more than enough Winchesters, while some of the unfortunate cavalrymen had not even had time to fire their weapons. While a new monument is being erected to honour both sides, The Little Bighorn still remains a symbol of the excellent old military maxim, 'Never underestimate your enemy'.

LLOYD'S COFFEE HOUSE
United Kingdom

By 1650, the coffee houses of London had become a vital part of Britain's trade, and a primary source of reliable maritime information. Indeed, the famous diarist, Samuel Pepys, thought the news he received about shipping in his coffee house was much more valuable to him than that gleaned from his job in the Admiralty.

Edward Lloyd's first coffee house in Tower Street near the river Thames became so popular with tradesmen and mariners that in 1691 he had to move to bigger quarters on Lombard Street. He realised the immense value of the information that was changing hands on his premises, and five years later launched *Lloyd's List*, full of shipping news that was provided by correspondents around the world.

Insuring ships and their cargoes became vital, and brokers would visit 'risk takers' in the coffee houses, who would sign the deal by writing their names under the contract. Nowhere was more popular with these marine 'underwriters' than Lloyd's, confirming its dominant position in mercantile shipping.

In 1771, seventy-nine underwriters subscribed £100 each, to form the Society of Lloyd's. Later, the members became known as 'names', committing their wealth to cover their customers'

potential losses. Recently, many 'names' have suffered badly after several disasters worldwide – linked with shipping, hurricanes and, especially, asbestos. The collapse of the twin towers of New York's World Trade Center in September 2001 may prove to be the single largest insurance problem the world has ever seen.

But Lloyd's still remains the centre of world insurance. Not bad for a coffee house.

See: Bedlam, Fleet Street, World Trade Center

LOCH NESS
United Kingdom

'Many a man has been hanged on less evidence than there is for the Loch Ness Monster'.
G.K. Chesterton

In the first century AD, the Romans arrived in Scotland, a region inhabited by the fierce Pictish people. When they discovered Loch Ness, they discovered a series of standing stones, each one featuring a different animal carving. However, although most of the carvings portrayed ordinary and recognisable creatures, one of them presented a total mystery. With a beak, flippers and a spout, it was described by some scholars as a swimming elephant. The concept of the 'Loch Ness Monster' has been with us ever since. Scottish folklore contained aquatic beasts called 'water-kelpies,' which were the mythological prototype for 'Nessie'. Whereas the modern creature is often viewed fondly, these were far from benevolent. They were said to use their sinister magic to entice children to ride on their backs. As soon as the unsuspecting youngsters acceded, they were dragged under the waves to be savagely drowned. The monster's press could only get better.

The first famous sighting of a potential Loch Ness Monster was one by Saint Columba in 565 AD. While making the journey to visit a Pictish king, the Saint, who was reputed to have introduced Christianity to Scotland, passed by the Loch. There he apparently saw a swimmer about to be devoured by a terrifying monster, and only by ordering it to retreat in the name of God could he save the fortunate man.

However, despite these scattered tales, the legend of the Monster fully established itself in 1933. Mr and Mrs Spicer were driving beside the Loch when a 'prehistoric creature' crashed past the car and plunged into the murky waters. From that point the fame of the story increased rapidly, as did the frequency of the sightings. Circus owner Bertram Mills offered a reward of £20,000 for the Monster's capture.

Nessie was even spotted during the war. C. B. Farrel of the Royal Observer Corps, posted to watch for German air activity, caught sight of the creature, partially out of the water. As in many accounts, he described a long neck, a small head and fins. Other sightings report a blowhole above the mouth, a tail, and occasionally, several hoops of the beast's body protruding from the surface of the Loch.

Since then many photos have been

The 1934 Hugh Gray photograph, later admitted to be a hoax

published, claiming to be of the Monster. The most notorious one, taken by Hugh Gray in 1934 has since been admitted to be a hoax. There have also been claims of sonar images, and even videos. Various theories abound, including the famous hypothesis that the Monster is an evolutionary survivor from the age of the dinosaurs. In 1933, the *Daily Mail* sent a film crew and big-game hunter Marmaduke Wetherell to find the creature. The expedition appeared to be a tremendous success when Wetherell discovered several large footprints, and sent plaster casts to the Natural History Museum to be analysed. Unfortunately, when the results came back, it became apparent that the tracks were those of a hippopotamus. Some wit had used a stuffed hippo's foot to make the prints. By this stage, hundreds of people had flooded to Loch Ness to be a part of the discovery. It was all rather embarrassing.

Seventy years on, still no concrete evidence has been found of a monster dwelling within the Loch. Submarines, nets, sonar and underwater cameras have all failed to provide sufficient evidence. In fact, the bookmakers William Hill face a payout of over £1 million if the creature is ever actually discovered. Despite widespread scepticism, some of the 'witnesses' seem disturbingly respectable, including priests, teachers, policemen and a Nobel Prize winner. Many quote the sheer scale of the Loch, 24 miles long and almost 1,000 ft deep, as the reason for Nessie's elusiveness. Perhaps it would be better if the riddle were never solved. After all, if we did ever find 'Nessie', what on earth would we actually do with her?

LOCKERBIE
Scotland

Nestling in the lowlands of Scotland, the little town of Lockerbie was mostly known only to those travelling between Glasgow and Carlisle. But its quiet anonymity was cruelly shattered

See: Dunblane, World Trade Center

on the evening of 21ˢᵗ December 1988. High in the air above, Pan America's flight 103 was just levelling off at 31,000 feet after its climb from Heathrow on the way to New York. At 7 o'clock a bomb exploded in the baggage hold and the giant Boeing 747 blew up and disintegrated. In a hail of fire and debris from the sky, pieces of aircraft, luggage and 259 bodies rained down to earth, scattering over an area of 500 square miles. Lockerbie bore the brunt with sections of fuselage, wings and engines cascading in flames – demolishing rows of houses and killing 11 of its inhabitants.

Years later, a Libyan was convicted of planting the bomb, revenge presumably against the United States and its position in the Middle East (although evidence in the author's possession may be used, belatedly, in an appeal). But, whatever the blame, seldom can a close community have suffered so abruptly, so terribly, and so innocently for some distant quarrel in which it played no part.

THE LOO
Ireland

The name we use for one of our most important rooms can cause social agonies. 'Lavatory', 'toilet', 'the bog', 'crapper' (see panel), 'the potty', 'closet', 'John', 'restroom' and even 'khazi' are joined by rather twee and self-conscious euphemisms like I'm going to 'powder my nose', 'spend a penny', or use the 'little boy's room'. So the simple word 'loo' has come to the rescue. It started as British upper-class slang, and has seeped into general usage because of its very versatility.

Patrick, the present Earl of Lichfield, some of whose photographs appear in this book, and James the present Duke of Abercorn, reveal the origin. In 1867, the 1st Duke of Abercorn was Viceroy of Ireland and hosted a large house party at Viceregal Lodge in Dublin. His guests included the Lord Lieutenant of County Roscommon, Edward King Tennison, and his wife Lady Louisa, daughter of the then Earl of Lichfield.

Lady Louisa was not, apparently, a very lovable person, especially to children. In revenge for her attitude, the two naughty youngest Abercorn sons, Lord Frederick and Lord Ernest, removed her name card from her bedroom door and placed it on the door of the only 'water-closet' in the guest wing.

Once her outrage and their laughter had dissipated, the family continued to talk about 'going to Lady Lou' and the phrase gradually spread from such ducal circles – so that now the rest of us are happy to announce that *'we are going to the loo.'*

Thomas Crapper

For many years the author lived in the King's Road, Chelsea, opposite the showroom of Thomas Crapper. The charming book, *Flushed with Pride* by Wallace Reyburn, reveals how the word 'crap' evolved. Although in Britain it may come from the old Dutch 'krappe', old English 'crappe', as used by Americans, it really did come from the sanitary products of Crapper, the eminent Victorian. Thomas Crapper invented water closets as we know them today, providing them for the Royal Family, the aristocracy and later, humbler folk. During the First World War, American soldiers were very impressed with the superior lavatories they used in their British barracks and military hospitals, all marked 'T. Crapper, Chelsea'. They took home the phrase 'Going to the crapper', and by 1930, the *Dictionary of American Slang* reported that it was in common usage, as were the derogatory words 'crappy' for inferior and 'crap' for nonsense.

LORD'S
England

Most famous sporting venues have kept the names of the sometimes quite ordinary towns, boroughs or villages where they happen to be located like Wimbledon, Indianapolis, Old Trafford, Flushing Meadows, Cresta, Daytona and Landsdowne Road. Some are named for their shape – the Orange Bowl, the Oval and the Nurburgring. But few have been named after the person who founded them, like Lord's Cricket Ground.

Bearing in mind cricket's aristocratic beginnings, you could be forgiven for thinking that Lord's had been named in honour of some cricket-loving peer. You would be partly right.

The game of cricket was indeed a game for aristocrats, and in London they were to play at White Conduit Fields in Islington, often betting huge sums on the results. Deciding they wanted more privacy, they asked one of their humbler players, Thomas Lord, to find them a quieter and more exclusive spot.

It was Lord Winchilsea who helped Thomas Lord to lease Dorset Fields in Marylebone. Thus was founded, in 1787, the Marylebone Cricket Club, the MCC, which then laid down the laws of cricket that we know today, and specified that the wickets should be 'pitched' 22 yards apart.

In 1805, Thomas Lord moved the MCC to a ground which was then out in the country near a duck pond at St John's Wood, which is where you will find Lord's today. To keep down the grass on the pitch, sheep were let in to graze, but after a while a mower was purchased, and after a few more decades, in 1864, a groundsman was finally appointed. As fans of the sport will know, cricket is a game where things happen slowly.

Showing that Lord's can break with tradition, it now has this space age press box - the Nat West Media Centre.

Lord's became the home of the Eton-Harrow cricket match, an essential part each Summer – along with Ascot, Henley and also Wimbledon – of Britain's social and sporting 'season'.

The county club of Middlesex was to adopt Lord's, while internationally, the MCC was on the road to becoming the arbiter of cricket throughout the world, with the first 'Test Match' played by an English side in Australia in 1877, against former convicts who had taken up the game.

What differentiates this game of cricket created by Thomas Lord and the MCC from other games is its leisurely elegance. As Lord Mancroft wrote, *'Cricket – a game which the English, not being a spiritual people, have invented to give themselves some conception of eternity'.*

So it is perhaps no coincidence that the legendary bearded figure who stares down on The Long Room at Lord's is called W.G. Grace.

See: Ascot, Brooklands, Cowes, Cresta Run, Henley, Wembley, Wimbledon

LORRAINE MOTEL
Tennessee, USA

Of all the 25,000 motels in America only one of them is truly famous. Built in 1925, the Lorraine Motel in Memphis, Tennessee had once been 'whites-only', but from 1945, it was a minority-owned establishment. Situated in the south end of Downtown Memphis, not far from Beale Street (made famous by W. C. Handy's *Beale Street Blues*), the Lorraine was rather unremarkable except as the haunt of such musical guests as Cab Calloway, Nat King Cole, Count Basie and Aretha Franklin.

However, on the evening of 4th April 1968, this otherwise obscure motel was catapulted to worldwide notoriety. As the Reverend Martin Luther King leaned over its second floor balcony to talk to his colleagues, Jesse Jackson and Ralph Abernathy, a single rifle shot rang out, mortally wounding him in the neck.

Many Americans, and especially black communities who rioted in 124 cities, were appalled that the respected, non-violent Civil Rights leader and Nobel Peace Prize winner had been murdered. 'America is shocked and saddened by this brutal slaying', announced President Johnson.

But this was not true of all America. One FBI agent in Atlanta leapt to his feet and shouted exultantly, 'We finally got the son of a bitch!' Indeed, the assassination at the Lorraine Motel must be seen against the horrific personal vendetta pursued for seven years by the Federal Bureau of Investigation, and by the FBI's veteran Director, J. Edgar Hoover. Once an American hero, Hoover has since been revealed as one of the most peculiar and malevolent public servants ever to have power.

Hoover (whom it is said may have had a mixed race ancestral past) was a racist, like some virulent anti-Semitic Nazis who were secretly part Jewish. He was obsessed with King, and was to use the same techniques against him that he had used years before on the black leader Marcus Garvey and the singer Paul Robeson – even branding King as a Communist and using stool pigeons and electronic bugging. The tapes revealed no evidence about Communism but, unfortunately for King, a lot about his sexual philandering. Tapes and transcripts were sent to Attorney General Robert Kennedy and President Johnson, but nothing stopped their strong commitment to

CLARE SUTTON

The Lorraine Motel, now the National Civil Rights Museum. The wreath marks the place where Martin Luther King was shot.

Civil Rights. Hoover also failed to stop the Pope meeting King, and sent a tape and a threatening note to his wife, Coretta King, trying to block his Nobel Prize for Peace in 1964, (something Hoover had tried to win for years). Thus, jealousy also fuelled his hatred.

A number of highly suspicious things happened before King's assassination. Pressure from leaked news stories led to King switching hotels from the Holiday Inn to the black-owned Lorraine, and a mysterious 'advance security' man had King's room changed from the front to the back, facing a boarding-house from where the shot came.

King's apparent assassin was James Earl Ray, a minor criminal on the run whose convictions included stealing a typewriter and money orders, and holding up a cab driver and a supermarket. When he escaped from Missouri State Prison in 1967, the reward was a paltry $50. Ray fled the boarding-house, saw a police car and abandoned personal items, his expensive Remington rifle and binoculars and his white Ford Mustang. Two FBI men later spotted him, reported it, and were amazed to be told 'to take no action'. Such behaviour meant that Ray was not caught in America but at London's Heathrow Airport on his way to Rhodesia with a Canadian passport, having also made a mysterious trip to Lisbon.

Ray pleaded guilty and was sentenced to 99 years, but the next day retracted his plea and changed his lawyer. His father said, 'He couldn't have planned it alone. He's not smart enough'.

In 1978, the House Select Committee on Assassinations was told by Russell Byers from St Louis that he had been offered $50,000 to arrange King's death by John Kauffmann and John Sutherland (the latter dressed bizarrely as a Confederate Colonel). Both men were now conveniently dead. The FBI had known about this since 1973, but had not passed on the information.

Ray himself claimed in 1988 on television that he had only confessed under FBI threats against his father and brother, and that he had been framed to cover up 'an FBI plot to kill King'. He died in jail ten years later, still protesting his innocence. Perhaps we will never know the unsavoury truth.

For the Lorraine Motel, the result of the assassination was a severe decline in business. In 1982, when it was a foreclosed property, a group of Memphis businessmen formed the Martin Luther King Memorial Foundation in a bid to save it. In December of that year, through fundraising, donations, and a bank loan, they bought it for $144,000 – and in 1991 it became the National Civil Rights Museum. The balcony, now refurbished, bears a single wreath in honour of a great man.

> ***Movie Footnote:***
> The film world was affected by the King assassination. Not only were the annual Academy Awards postponed for two days, but two pictures dealing with race won Oscars that year. *'In the Heat of the Night'*, with Sidney Poitier as Virgil Tibbs, was voted Best Picture, with Rod Steiger as the 'redneck' Sheriff winning Best Actor. *'Guess Who's Coming to Dinner'*, also with Sidney Poitier, gained an Oscar for Best Screenplay – and Katherine Hepburn won the Best Actress award.

See: Ambassador Hotel, Montgomery, Texas School Book Depository

231

LOS ALAMOS
New Mexico, USA

There can be few laboratories in history that can claim to rival the fame of Los Alamos, in New Mexico. Julius Robert Oppenheimer selected the site, while he was a Professor of Physics at the University of California – at the Berkeley and California Institute of Technology, in 1943.

Set against the backdrop of the Second World War, Oppenheimer had been charged with the task of leading a project, (and simultaneously, a race with Nazi physicists), to create an atomic explosion. The success of 'The Manhattan project' has resulted in the name of Los Alamos being interwoven into the very fabric of modern life. With history's first atomic explosion, came irrevocable changes in the culture and politics of the entire planet.

As such, it is impossible to consider the fame, or infamy, of the laboratory without first examining the role played by Oppenheimer in its creation.

Oppenheimer was born in New York on 22nd April, 1904. He graduated from Harvard in 1925, and then travelled to Cambridge University, England, where he carried out research for the University's Cavendish Library. In 1927, he was to receive his doctorate from Gottingen University, in Germany, and to return to the United States, where he took the position at the University of California at Berkeley that would lead him to New Mexico, and ultimately into the history books.

Robert Oppenheimer and General Leslie Groves survey the remains of the tower at 'Ground Zero.'

When given the task, Oppenheimer was already something of a hero among physicists and other intellectuals across America, and despite his lack of administrative experience, he was the perfect candidate to lead the experiment.

Throughout the two years that it took Oppenheimer's team to succeed, it wrangled with the ethical principles, and considered the ideological implications for the future, but never once wavered from the goal, reminding itself that the Nazis were known to have discovered nuclear fission, and that the deadline was therefore 'as soon as possible'. Oppenheimer himself was known to have placed great credence in the theory of 'complementarity', championed by his long-time friend and colleague Niels Bohr, whom he had met at University in Germany.

Bohr's theory was that two findings in physics, though different and unrelated, can be equally true when applied morally. And, to Oppenheimer, the death and destruction that his project would theoretically cause, would also be 'counterbalanced' by the security and stability that it would then be able to provide.

Some have alleged that it was with this theory in mind that Oppenheimer and his colleagues chose to name the first test of an atomic device 'Trinity' – after lines from the writer, John Donne, that deal with death and resurrection.

On the morning of 16th July 1945, the military leader of the Manhattan Project, General Leslie Groves, had taken the pessimistic precaution of preparing a statement in advance, explaining the deaths of all the scientists, and advising the Governor of New Mexico that he should be at the ready to declare Martial Law. In the desert, a brilliant flash ushered in the nuclear age. The bomb had a five-foot outer sphere, and contained 13.6 pounds of plutonium. And, as the stories go, it was held together with tissues, and sticky tape.

The awestruck scientists watched their project turn the desert sand to glass, and were dumbfounded at the might of their creation. When the detonation occurred, the oldest member of the team was 27. One of the group, Kenneth Bainbridge, described the spectacle as 'a foul and awesome display', and Oppenheimer is reported to have said, 'Now we're all sons of bitches'.

Shortly afterwards, Nagasaki and Hiroshima were subjected to the unrivalled ferocity of this newborn, with the effect of ending the war with Japan.

Time magazine called those who had worked on the project in Los Alamos *'the world's guilty men'* and, with the success in 1946 of the first Soviet Atomic device, Oppenheimer commented that 'our 20,000th bomb will not offset their 2,000th' – a grim prediction of the arms race that was to characterise the coming Cold War. Perhaps, also, this can be construed as an admission on the part of Oppenheimer that, (as said by the writer, E.L. Doctorow), *'No emperor or fiend from the past – not Caesar, not Alexander, not Attila the Hun – ever claimed the sovereign right to determine the life and future of the entire universe. Yet, that power is now claimed by every graduate engineer who steps into a nuclear weapons laboratory'.*

In more recent times, the laboratory has continued to maintain its academic excellence, and specialises in research into, and control of, nuclear arms as well as an array of other highly specialised fields. It has also proved invaluable to the local community, having purchased an estimated $357 million in goods and services from the surrounding counties of New Mexico in 2001.

Having survived a large brush fire in May 2000, the Los Alamos laboratory is still, arguably, the most famous – or infamous – laboratory in history.

See: Bikini, Hiroshima

LOURDES
France

In the 1850s, Lourdes was a small, unknown town in the French foothills of the Pyrenees – whose agricultural economy was suffering from drought and from the new competition for its water mills from steam power. What is more, cholera had killed and maimed quite a number of its 4,000 inhabitants.

Today, Lourdes is not actually very much bigger, with 17,000 people. But each year it receives five million visitors, has an international airport, and its hotel industry is second only to Paris. All because of one young girl.

Bernadette Soubirous was a typical child of the town, born at the Boly Mill, which her father, the miller, then sadly lost. She nearly died of cholera, suffering from asthma for the rest of her life. The poverty-stricken family was reduced to living in a room in the 'Cachot', a disused prison. Bernadette could not read or write or even speak French – just the local language of Provençal.

On 11th February 1858, just after her fourteenth birthday, Bernadette was collecting firewood with her sister Toinette and their friend Jeanne. She lagged behind from crossing an icy stream because of her asthma, and suddenly heard a rushing wind. Looking up towards a grotto known as 'the pigs' shelter', the startled girl saw a young lady dressed in white, who smiled at her and then vanished. The same happened three days later. On Thursday 18th February, the vision appeared again and, this time, spoke. In response to Bernadette's request for her to write down her name, the figure responded 'That is not necessary', and then invited Bernadette to come for the next fifteen days to the grotto, adding, 'I do not promise to make you happy in this world, but in the other.'

On her eighth appearance on Wednesday 24th, the figure said, 'Penance, penance, penance. Pray to God for sinners. Go, kiss the ground for sinners.' The next day, Bernadette was instructed 'Go, drink of the water and wash yourself there', thus uncovering, from the mud, a spring of fresh water. On Tuesday 2nd March, at the thirteenth Apparition, she was told, 'Go, tell the priests to bring people here in procession and have a chapel built here'. On Thursday 25th, the lady in white announced *'Que soy era immaculada conceptiou'.* ('I am the immaculate conception').

The Bishop of Tarbes set up an immediate inquiry which at length reported in 1862, *'We remain convinced*

Bernadette Soubirous, now known to millions of pilgrims as St. Bernadette

that the Apparitions are supernatural and divine, and that, by consequence, what Bernadette saw was the Most Blessed Virgin. Our convictions are based on the testimony of Bernadette but, above all, on the things that happened here, things which can be nothing other than divine intervention.'

The Bishop was referring to the apparently miraculous cures that had simultaneously started. Some pilgrims judged incurable were permanently restored, especially when they drank the waters from the grotto. The water itself was analysed and revealed nothing chemically out of the ordinary. A Medical Bureau was set up to authenticate 'the cures', first started by Doctor Pierre Dozous, who recorded a hundred during 1858. Abbé Bertin then went on to record 4,445 more between 1858 and 1914.

Today there is an International Committee made up of thirty surgeons, professors and heads of medical bodies, who meet up in Lourdes once a year to go through the cases, some going back

many years. If there is no valid scientific or medical reason for the cure, it is then passed to the Bishop to be judged a miracle and 'sign from God'. Since 1954, nineteen cases have been so judged.

After the eighteenth Apparition, the long inquiry and her increasing fame, Bernadette retreated into the Convent of Saint Gildard in Nevers where, after years of prayer and sickness, she died in 1879.

There she can still be seen, because when her body was exhumed, it was, amazingly, quite perfectly preserved. There is just a thin layer of wax applied to her face and hands, and she is called 'the Sleeping Saint of Nevers' – because she was made a Saint in 1933.

Whatever the truth, there are five million people every year who believe enough in her story to feel compelled to make the pilgrimage to the little town of Lourdes, whether to obtain a cure or because of the strength of their faith.

See: Assisi, Bethlehem, Fatima

LYNMOUTH
England

Lynmouth is one of many picturesque villages on the cliff-girt coast of North Devon and Somerset in western England. With wooded cliffs 500 feet high, rushing waters, rocky dells, and ferny glades, a quaint main street and miniature harbour with a toy tower on the mole, it was long a favourite spot for those on holiday or honeymoon. Originally the fishing harbour for Lynton, a larger village atop the cliff to the west, from the early 19th century Lynmouth attracted Romantic poets like Shelley and Southey.

Lynmouth has other engineering claims to fame – England's first funicular railway, linking Linton and Lynmouth, and the largest hydro-electric power generator then in use in England, which was overwhelmed by the rising waters and damaged beyond repair in the disaster of the 'Lynmouth flood'. This horrifying natural event shocked Britain and the world just weeks after the widespread rejoicing at the accession of the young Queen Elizabeth II.

The summer of 1952 was extremely wet. On Exmoor, rain fell steadily – water which the moorland peat soaked up like a gigantic sponge. On 15th August 1952, rain fell both steadily and heavily in Lynmouth for much of the day – even at midday local people were switching on lights in their homes. At 8.30 that evening, an almost tropical cloudburst caused 5 inches of rain to fall on the district in a single hour. In all, 9 inches of rain – an estimated 90 million tons of water – fell on just 40 square miles of Exmoor, massively swelling the streams feeding the East Lyn and West Lyn rivers that converge at Lynmouth to flow into the sea.

During that fateful night, the waters of the Lyn rivers – which fall over 1,200 feet in 10 miles – rose rapidly to sweep trees, soil and massive boulders down upon a defenceless Lynmouth. Pounding, swirling waters undercut banks and stone walls, rocks and boulders smashed roads, buildings and cars, and great water surges raced seawards as bridges that had temporarily dammed the torrent collapsed under intolerable pressure. A small force of local police and firemen, together with RAF and other military personnel, worked desperately through the night, much hampered by hilly terrain and just two (very steep) access roads.

Morning revealed a scene of hideous devastation: ruined buildings, great piles of debris and a beach strewn with wood, smashed cars and other wreckage. It also brought helicopters and urgent reinforcements, and the area was effectively placed under military government, not to re-open to the public until a month later. The final death toll in Lynmouth and surrounding villages was thirty four, including several tourists, with ninety three buildings and twenty eight bridges destroyed. There were many heroes that night, notably P.C. Harper, then 24 years old, recipient of a George Medal for a twenty four-hour duty shift in which he saved several lives. Henry Williamson, who lived nearby, vividly described the events of the Lynmouth flood in his 1969 novel *The Gale of the World*.

Once the news broke, money and gifts poured into Lynmouth and district, from not only Britain, but the Commonwealth and the rest of the world. Jamaica generously sent five tons each of bananas, sugar and coffee, not to mention arranging a visit from Mr Bustamante, the island's large and jovial Chief Minister. As he handed out bananas – doubly welcome, as England was only just just emerging from post-war austerity and rationing – to local children at a public meeting in the adjacent village of Lynton, he loudly exhorted his young friends to eat them, 'Banana good for Bustamante, banana good for children. Make you big and strong like Bustamante!'

However much this tiny touch of humour may have lightened the sombre mood in Lynmouth, the population may have reflected on the fact that their ancestors a millennium ago may have seen the shape of things to come: the linguistic root of Lyn is 'Lynna'. It is Anglo-Saxon for torrent.

Water rages past the wreckage of Lynmouth's houses

MAEANDER
Turkey

One often talks of a river that 'meanders' or wanders lazily along its winding course. The verb derives from the River Maeander or Maiandros in the eastern Mediterranean, famous in ancient times for its many sinuous bends and curves. This river was almost sacred in the Greek world, its convoluted wanderings even said to have inspired Daedalus to build the legendary 'Labyrynth' – an intricate maze of palace rooms – for King Minos of Crete. Later, having quarrelled with Minos, Daedalus, with his son Icarus, attempted to flee Crete using wings of feathers and wax that he had constructed. Alas, however, Icarus flew too near the sun and plunged fatally to earth.

The river, now western Turkey's River Menderes, divided the ancient kingdoms of Lydia to the north and Caria to the south, as it flowed from Central Anatolia to the Aegean Sea. The mouth lies to the east of Patmos, the Greek island where St John the Divine wrote the Book of Revelations. A major river valley with rich agriculture, the Maeander basin supported several ancient cities, linking as it does, the Aegean with the interior. In the second millennium BC, it was an important zone of contact between the Mycenean world of Greece and the Aegean and the Hittite kingdom of central and southern Anatolia. The most important of the Maeander's cities was Miletus, built on a fortified promontory at the mouth of the river – but today high and dry, four miles from the sea. The ruins lie south of the modern mouth, the river's course having shifted as silt accumulated in the estuary. From the Bronze Age onwards, Greeks colonised the district around the mouth of

Turkish statuette, reflecting the Maeander River and its link to the labyrinth of Daedalus

the Maeander, where Miletus became the mother-city of the Greek lands of Ionia along the western seaboard of Anatolia.

The Maeander Valley saw fierce fighting during the 1919-22 war between Greece and Turkey, as the Greeks attempted to secure north-western Anatolia within a Greater Greece. After

their advance up the valley in June 1920, the river became an axis of the fighting between Greeks on the north bank and Turks to the south. In 1922, the once-confident Greeks fled in total disarray from the triumphant troops of Kemal Atatürk, hero of Gallipoli.

See: Angora, Gallipoli, Manzikert, Marathon, Topkapi, Transylvania

MAELSTROM
Norway

Norway's Lofoten Islands project out into the sea like a string of rocky pearls. Often battered by gales and storms, they are also luckily touched by the warmth of the Gulf Stream, thus enjoying a special benefit – the finest cod fishing harvest in the world. The cod are spawned in Vestfjord, between the islands and mainland, and each year the shoal returns by instinct in its thousands from the Barents Sea five hundred miles away.

But it is not the island's fishing industry, with its exports of 'stockfish' and cod liver oil, which is the truly notable thing about the Lofotens.

The strong currents and the shallow seas have created the Moskstrammien, or 'Maelstrom', between the islands of Mosken and Vaerøy, and twice a day, midway between high and low tide, whirlpools begin to appear – soon with speeds reaching up to six knots.

The Maelstrom is highly dramatic to

watch, and locals have always been happy to climb the mountainside just to gaze in awe. 'It was our television when we were children'.

However, what made the Maelstrom really famous were the splendidly exaggerated descriptions of its power by writers who perhaps should have known better.

In 1539, Olaus Magnus published his 'Carta Marina' with a dramatic illustration of the Maelstrom, and in 1555, his *History of the Nordic People* described, *'the ocean vortex that runs up and down the sea every day, devouring great ships and spewing them up again.'* In 1591, a local bailiff said, 'When the Maelstrom is at its peak, you can see the sky and sun through the waves and breakers, because they are as high as mountains'.

The world's popular imagination was fuelled by Jules Verne and Edgar Allan Poe with such gems as:

'The world's most dangerous stretch of sea'.

'A current that howls, that rumbles like a buffalo herd on the prairie, that drags ships under, smashing them to smithereens against the sea bed'.

'Great whales bellow as they submit to the Maelstrom's vortices, while the houses shudder at their foundations'.

In reality, the locals have learned to shrug off such hyperbole and live with the predictable dangers, and, above all, to cash in on the Maelstrom's genuine advantage, the fabulous crop of fish.

Although one does wonder how the nearest village came by its name of 'Hell'.

The Maelstrom in the Carta Marina of Olaus Magnus

See: Atlantis, El Nino, Krakatoa

MAFEKING
South Africa

The siege of Mafeking is a very extraordinary story, not least because the outcome was so unlikely. When the Boer War began on 11th October, 1899, the local commander, Colonel Robert Baden-Powell, had just over 1,000 soldiers at his command, and the only two guns in his possession were obsolete old 7-pounders. As the Boer force sent to capture the town numbered in excess of 6,000 men, and possessed a gigantic 94-pounder siege gun known to the British as 'Old Creechy', the situation did not look very promising.

Mafeking (the British mis-spelling of the seTswana word *Mafikeng*, 'the place of stones') was an important railway siding, and a key supply depot for the British forces, and thus was a likely target for an early Boer attack. However, even when war loomed, Baden-Powell was forbidden to fortify the town openly. He was forced to employ a variety of deceptions. For example, instead of sandbags, he stockpiled innocuous empty grain sacks, and although fortification of the town's highest point, Canon Kopje, was not allowed, he managed to do so anyway by pretending to construct a rifle range. These sort of ingenious tactics of illusion epitomise the methods that Baden-Powell would employ throughout the siege to even the odds.

The most pressing concern was to stop the Boers from storming at night, which would certainly have proved to be unstoppable. To prevent this, a visiting seller of acetylene lamps was employed to construct a searchlight. Using biscuit tins as reflectors, the lamp was rushed around the town and shone out upon all areas of the Boer lines, giving the impression that the defenders possessed an entire array of searchlights, which would make a night assault difficult. Then there were the 'landmines'. His men buried metal containers all round the town as ostentatiously as possible. By the time that a 'test' was conducted, an explosion of a stick of dynamite nearby, the Boers had been convinced that the landmine threat removed the possibility of a mass attack. And even though the British soon ran out of barbed wire to protect their lines, Baden-Powell realised that, at long distance, if they mimed laying it out, and then crawled under the areas where the wire was supposed to be, it would prove an effective deterrent. And so the Boers resorted to continuous shelling of the town. Often they would seem to have struck a fatal blow, as their artillery fire destroyed one of the defending forts. But this was yet another bluff; the forts were dummies, manned by dummies, whose movements were induced by pulleys and string. Again, the thin defences of the town were bolstered by bluff and trickery.

However, even though not over-run, life in the town was becoming extremely difficult. The donkeys, which were at first used to carry messages, soon found themselves in various kitchen pots, as the food supply began to dwindle. To replace the donkey messaging service, young boys, mostly on bicycles, were employed as couriers. The responsibilities of these khaki-clad youths began to grow. Soon, as well as message carriers, they were also used as hospital assistants and lookouts. These boys were the prototype of the modern Boy Scouts. Mafeking was their baptism of fire.

As the siege dragged relentlessly on, and the shelling of Mafeking continued unabated, Baden-Powell continued to do everything in his power to keep the townsfolk's spirits up, with sport matches on Sunday (when an unofficial weekly truce had developed) and competitions to see who could build the most convincing dummies to man the forts. Whistling

Baden-Powell, hero of Mafeking and founder of the Boy Scouts

See: Robben Island, Rorke's Drift, Sharpeville, Sophiatown

tunes, even in the most pressing situations, above all, Baden-Powell tried to inspire by example. He was famous for being awake almost all the time, snatching only a few hours of sleep a day. Furthermore, as the food crisis worsened, he and his staff had smaller rations than the rest, so as to show how little food was needed for survival. Spurred on by their commander, the locals never cracked, no matter how long the siege dragged on.

Baden-Powell's confidence in his men was evident when, in his reply to a Boer message suggesting an inter-army cricket game, he replied, 'Mafeking, in the game it is playing at the moment, is 180 (the number of days the siege had lasted) not out against the bowling of Cronje, Snyman and Eloff. Don't you think you had better change the bowling?'

Outgunned to the end, the British managed to bolster their firepower a little bit. One new gun was hastily constructed from the steam pipe of an engine mounted on the wheels of a threshing machine. The other addition was an ancient cannon, found being used as a doorpost. It fired a ten-pound shot that was often described as 'bouncing along like a cricket ball.' The makeshift artillery force was rushed around the town, and fired from as many angles as possible to give the impression of a large defensive battery.

On 12th May 1900, the Boers, increasingly frustrated with their inability to over-run such a feebly defended post, finally made a direct attack on the town itself. At first it seemed that all of Baden-Powell's guile and heroics had been in vain, as the attackers pushed into the very heart of the town. But they had over-stretched themselves, and soon found themselves surrounded. The British captured Eloff and 108 Boers. It was to be the besiegers' last attack.

Far off gunfire could be heard from the town on the 16th, and on the next day the British army arrived, and Mafeking had finally been relieved. The town, during the 217 days of the siege, had been hammered by 20,000 shells, and suffered 813 casualties. The bravery and inventiveness of the inhabitants, and especially that of Baden-Powell, became famous back in Britain. Crowds rejoiced in the streets at the happy ending of such an amazing tale, and thronged outside the house of Baden-Powell's mother to cheer and applaud. In fact, the word 'mafficking' was coined to describe such joyous scenes. Queen Victoria herself had been keeping a close eye on the town throughout, and sent Baden-Powell the following telegram, I AND MY WHOLE EMPIRE GREATLY REJOICE AT THE RELIEF OF MAFEKING AFTER THE SPLENDID DEFENCE MADE BY YOU THROUGH ALL THESE MONTHS. I HEARTILY CONGRATULATE YOU AND ALL UNDER YOU. Fame, respect and legendary status; all were bestowed upon the townsfolk of the little town of Mafeking. And they had certainly earned it.

MAIN STREET
United States

All across the United States there are towns, large and small, which boast a 'Main Street'. The name probably came from settlers from Scotland and Ireland, the English favouring the rather grander-sounding 'High Street'. There were Main Streets before the railroads, but it was the railroads that quickly created hundreds of little towns across the Continent, often regularly spaced at the intervals needed by steam locomotives to stop for water – 'water plug towns'. Often, Main Street was actually built by the railroad, parallel to the tracks, together with the depot, maybe a hotel, and even a bandstand.

In the great grain-producing parts of the United States and Canada, there are the so-called 'T-towns', where Main Street runs down at right angles from the tracks and the depot in the shape of a 'T'. If you fly across the prairie, you can see them with their grain elevators and little grids of streets, spaced only nine miles apart, close enough for the farmers to deliver their grain to the elevator in horse-drawn wagons.

Main Street would contain the General Store, the bank, the local lawyer, and the saloon, barber's shop and drug store. It was the street that farmers came to on Saturday to buy provisions, pick up their mail, and listen to gossip in the saloon. It was the street where the kids hung out at weekends, (as we saw in the film *American Graffiti*), and the street where the Fourth of July was celebrated. Of course, less salubrious people and activities were located 'the other side of the tracks'.

Main Street became associated with an attitude to life, perhaps a little on the conservative side, rather provincial. 'Main Street would never accept those fashions'. But so very typical is Main Street of the 'American Way of Life' that one has been built at Disneyland, albeit somewhat sanitized – with no bars, for instance.

By the end of the 1970s, the growth of Interstate highways, out-of-town shopping malls and the 'flight to the suburbs' meant

LIBRARY OF CONGRESS

that the 'downtown' area of thousands of towns and thousands of Main Streets were in decay, with empty stores and boarded-up buildings. Luckily, residents began to realise that they were allowing their town centres to disappear, and with them, their sense of community. So, there is now even a National Main Street Center created by the National Trust for Historic Presentation. Forty three States and 1,800 communities are actively working on a 'Main Street Program'.

Just in time. It is vital that 'Main Street, USA', such an essential part of American life, is preserved.

See: Broadway, Cumberland Road, Elm Street, Route 66

MAINZ
Germany

Our world has been changed forever by a handful of inventions; the wheel, gunpowder, steampower and, more recently, the aeroplane, computer, microchip and internet. Mainz was to be made famous by the momentous invention of printing with movable type. And its fame was by chance.

The city on the Rhine had a darker past, twice the gateway for invasions. It was one of the fortress towns meant to protect the Roman Empire from marauding Germanic tribes and it was here in 406 that the Vandals crossed the ice, sacked the town and broke into the Empire. They pillaged their way right through Gaul, (now France), and ended up in Spain and North Africa from whence they would sack Rome itself. 406 was also the year Attila the Hun was born, a yet more terrible threat. The Huns had ridden out of the east, pushing

all other tribes before them, and the Romans even tried to bribe them to keep the peace.

When the ambitious Attila became their King in 433, aged just 27, Marcian, the new Emperor of the Eastern Roman Empire, refused to pay the usual tribute. In his fury, Attila fell on the easier option, the weaker Western Empire.

Once again, it was poor Mainz that felt his brutal wrath, sacked along with Strasbourg, Cologne, Worms, Trier and Rheims. Fortunately, after his sudden death, the Huns then dissolved as a force.

So Mainz was twice the doorway through which the primitive eastern hordes smashed into sophisticated western Europe, plunging it into the Dark Ages. But exactly a thousand years later, Mainz took its place on the world stage, as the birthplace of one of the

239

Gutenberg printing his Bible

See: Fleet Street, Manzikert, Venice

most important inventions in history – movable type and the printing press.

It took some time for the Genfleisch family to feel safe in adopting the name of their house, Judenberg or 'Jewish Hill', because, in spite of the fact that Mainz was the centre of European Jewry, the bubonic plague of 1348 had been hysterically blamed on the Jews. But by 1400, when Johannes was born, he was able to take on the name Gutenberg. He became a coin maker and thus familiar with the skills of striking an impression on to metal. In 1434, Mainz was bankrupt and Gutenberg moved to Strasbourg where he began to work in secret on his 'big idea'. The market was provided by the needs of the Church, in the form of his old acquaintance Nicholas of Cusa, now a Cardinal. There was a desperate need for unity and uniformity and the slow production and inaccuracy of scribes could not provide this. Compared with others who had tried printing like the Chinese, Gutenberg realised he had everything to hand, a simple alphabetic language, paper and vellum, screw presses, inks, pieces of metal with type, frames to hold them and a customer. What he did not have was money and

this was provided by Johannes Fust, later to be his nemesis.

Gutenberg planned to produce his 'bestseller' – his Bible – in Strasbourg, but, by chance, an army of unemployed French mercenaries, the 'Armagnacs', threatened the city. Thus in 1448 he returned to Mainz. With encouragement from the Church and yet more money from Fust he began to produce his Bible, 30 copies on vellum 180 on paper. In 1455, with the Bibles printed and pre-sold, in a spectacular piece of business treachery, Fust sued for his money and took over Gutenberg's printing works, becoming, with his son-in-law Peter Schöffer, the provider of the Church's printing for years.

However, Gutenberg's influence was immense. Printing spread across Europe like wildfire, and it was an essential force behind the Renaissance, liberating science, technology and commerce. When Martin Luther's '95 Theses' were nailed to his church door, the effect was as nothing compared to the *printed* copies which triggered the Reformation, and which split the Church that printing was meant to unite.

In England, Caxton at Westminster and the growth of Fleet Street would unify English and make it the world's most significant language.

As for Mainz, it was a lucky chance that drove her most famous son back from Strasbourg.

MANHATTAN
New York, USA

New York City, and particularly Manhattan, can claim to be the greatest and most famous piece of urban real-estate on earth. And yet there are several ways in which its fame might never have been achieved.

The dark rocks in Central Park tell us that the area dates back to the very formation of the earth's crust during the Archaeozic Age between 5,000 and 1,500 million years ago. Animal life, including dinosaurs and mammals, were to flourish until the area was covered by the creeping ice of the great Laurentide Glacier, which only retreated 17,000 years ago. Native American tribes then took over, and it was they that the first

explorers were to encounter.

Distant Manhattan was always going to be dominated by events in the Old World. The Protestant Dutch – like the French Huguenots – were escaping from the oppression of the Catholic Spanish and French after the St Bartholomew's Day Massacre of 1572, and the 1685 repeal of the liberal Edict of Nantes. The English victory over the Spanish Armada in 1588 had made it suddenly possible to challenge Spain everywhere including the New World. The Jews were expelled from Spain and Portugal, and had moved to Holland and then to Brazil. When the Portuguese recaptured Pernambuco in 1654, the first 27 poor penniless Jews arrived in New Amsterdam.

Above all, the riches of the east meant that European powers were sending explorers to America to find a short sea route in that direction, the fabled but non-existent 'North West Passage'. Verrazano was trying to reach Cathay and died in Central America. Jacques Cartier reached as far as present day Montreal. Henry Hudson, in 1609, tried going west up the river that now bears is name. Next year he died in Hudson's Bay, cast adrift by his mutinous crew. But his report to the Dutch of the area's abundance of valuable furs led to their own arrival.

In one of the greatest bargains in history, in 1626 the Dutch purchased Manahatta (the 'small island' or the 'hilly island') from the Menates tribe for 24 dollars worth of trinkets, naming the island New Amsterdam.

The remaining Indian tribe, the Lenapes, introduced them to maple, sugar, tobacco, maize and corn. Oysters generated the shiny shells they used for currency, as in De Peral Straet, present day Pearl Street. At what is now the Battery, the Dutch built a fort which could dominate both the Hudson and East Rivers, pushing the tiny settlement up an old, wide Indian trail which they called De Heerewegh or Broadway.

They created good trading relationships with the 'Five Nations' of Indians, spoilt by the arrival of Director-General Kieft who very nearly ruined the colony by quarrelling with the Algonquins. The Dutch were lucky they had just erected a protective palisade across the island, supplied by a road called Wall Street.

The new Director-General, Petrus Stuyvesant, vigorous but arbitrary, rebuilt the colony's fortunes, but even he could not resist the increasing power of the English, who were locked in wars with the Dutch, mostly over the spices of the distant East Indies. In 1664, four British naval ships arrived in the name of King Charles II, and New Amsterdam was renamed after his brother the Duke of York. Despite the brief recapture of

'Manhattan Purchase, 1626' after the painting by Alfred Fredericks. Peter Minuit buys Manhattan for $ 24 in beads and trinkets.

New York in 1673 by a large Dutch fleet, once again events thousands of miles away intervened. At the Treaty of Westminster the Dutch – unbelievably – agreed to give up Manhattan forever, in exchange for the tiny nutmeg island of Run in the Spice Islands.

Under the British, New York was to prosper, in spite of Governors like William Hyde – who tended to wear his wife's clothes in public! In the American Revolution, New York was never taken back from the British in spite of the Battle of Harlem Heights, but was finally entered by George Washington in 1883, and 'Evacuation Day' became a national holiday for years.

Manhattan was set to boom, the main entry point for immigration into the United States. Ellis Island was to see tens of thousands of immigrants of every race including waves of Irish (especially after the 1848 famine) and Jews after the pogroms and persecution. African-Americans came north. The way was open for one of the most polyglot, dynamic and prosperous places on earth.

But what if? What if the Dutch had elected to give up Run and to keep Manhattan?

Leaving aside the possibility that America would surely have been a very different place with less English influence, Peter Stuyvesant might well have gone back to his original wish to exclude Jews. The Dutch would surely have banned Catholics (who after their experience with Spain and France, they hated) so there would be no Irish, Spanish or French.

In spite of its wonderful location as a port, Manhattan might have stayed a little Dutch backwater, and Boston or Philadelphia would have become the premier city of the East Coast. What if?

See: Alma Underpass, Bedloe's Island, Big Apple, Broadway, Carnegie Hall, Cotton Club, Ellis Island, Empire State Building, Gotham, Harlem, Run, World Trade Center

MANZIKERT
Turkey

On the morning of Friday 26th August 1071, Alp Arslan, Sultan of the Seljuk Turks, robed himself in white. In the Moslem world, however, this colour was not the livery of celebration: white proclaimed the martyr. Although very afraid, he was resigned to whatever Allah determined. He solemnly bequeathed his kingship to his son Malik Shah. Everything was in readiness for what he, and many, believed would be his last ride. Before him stood the legions of the Byzantine Empire – still, despite many vicissitudes, the mightiest power in the Middle East.

Across the plain of Manzikert, then and now an insignificant village in eastern Turkey, the Byzantine Emperor, Romanus Diogenes, sweated through a very different fear. After months of preparation, a motley army of 70,000 men should have assembled, and yet, for reasons no historian has ever quite unravelled, Romanus was missing a contingent of 30,000. The rump which remained was hardly inspiring, being composed largely of disgruntled mercenaries and ill-equipped provincials from Asia Minor, feeling little loyalty and less love for this Emperor from far-off Constantinople. Romanus had found the once great Byzantine army in a pitiable state. Years of contempt and negligence from the civil aristocracy in the capital had stripped the force in the east of money, morale and self-esteem. But the Emperor, unlike his predecessors, was determined to end this trend, to mark an end to cowardice and compromise and, above all, to arrest the continued attacks from the new menace of the east, the Turk. This victory would have to be decisive; he had too many enemies in the capital. The day before, a detachment of his men had been ignominiously routed by the retreating Turks.

This most influential of battles is hardly documented – as if the hideous confusion that marked the actual battle was echoed in the chronicles. Some maintain that the Byzantine force was at first victorious, capturing the Turkish camp, and others that the army was betrayed by treachery. The story must be hewed from what facts we have.

The Emperor advanced towards the vast crescent of the Turkish army, all mounted. The Emperor formed his legions into the customary blocks dictated by the military manuals, which were written for those who had only to engage in pitched battles. Yet, before them, the Turkish host retreated. The Emperor pressed on – confused, then frustrated, then perhaps fearful. Ahead, the light from a myriad of spears winked at him. The only tokens of the enemy's intentions were the bands of archers who harried the Byzantine flanks. At last, baffled by this unnerving indifference to the rules of combat, the Emperor ordered the standards to be reversed. The army was to retire, hopefully in good order.

The result was catastrophic. The mercenaries, lacking training and cohesion, thought this was the signal for retreat, downed their weapons and fled. The Emperor's treacherous subordinate, Andronicus Ducas, led off his entire division. The Emperor, with little more than his bodyguard beside him, looked upon his beloved empire's doom as the Turks finally struck.

When the slaughter was over, the Emperor, fighting heroically, was wounded, disarmed and then brought before the victorious Sultan who, after a few perfunctory humiliations, raised his foe to his feet and treated him with all courtesy.

'And what would you have done, had providence given you the victory?' asked the Sultan. Romanus, whose many qualities did not include tact, nor it

seems, an instinct for self-preservation, replied, 'I would have had you flogged with chains'. 'It may be so', replied the Sultan cheerfully, 'yet I have heard that your Christ taught you to show mercy. I will do the same'.

The Sultan was as good as his word, but the damage was done. While the Turkish army did not advance, hordes of

turcomans now poured into undefended Asia Minor. The luckless Emperor was caught and blinded by his enemies.

Thus, a battle which no-one had sought, and which would otherwise have been merely a minor embarrassment, led to the fall of Constantinople, the destruction of Byzantine power in the east, and to the establishment of the greatest Moslem State since the time of the Caliphs – the Ottoman Empire.

The Turkish victory at Manzikert would lead to one of the greatest Empires in history.

See: Angora, Gallipoli, Maeander, Marathon, Topkapi, Transylvania, Venice

MARANELLO
Italy

If you were cruising along in a little Fiat on the road from Maranello towards Abetone and not watching your mirror, the blur of red and the howl of twelve cylinders from a projectile passing at three times your speed would undoubtedly come as a shock.

When Duke Francisco III of Modena employed Pietro Giardini and 3,000 men to build his magnificent road to Tuscany in 1776, he could scarcely have envisaged the speed of the vehicles that Enzo Ferrari would one day create in the little town of Maranello – which was named, it is said, after the beautiful rich Mara and her impoverished lover Nello who drowned themselves rather than be kept apart.

Enzo Ferrari was born in industrial

Modena. The son of a metal-working railway engineer, he became passion-ate about racing cars, first racing in a hill climb in 1919. Soon he was helping Alfa Romeo to domination, and the legend of the 'Cavallino Rampante' – the Prancing Horse – was born. According to Enzo, in 1923 Contessa Paolina Baracca asked Ferrari to paint his car 'for luck', with the emblem which had adorned the plane of her dead son, Francesco Baracca – Italy's top fighter ace. The truth is more ironic. First, Enzo did not put it on his car for nine years and, second, it was actually Baracca's unit that displayed the symbol. There is also the theory that it was taken from a vanquished German pilot from Stuttgart (once Stutengarten, or Garden

Enzo Ferrari testing an early Alfa Romeo in 1924

See: Brescia, Indianapolis, Le Mans.

of studs) – a city whose double horse symbol was changed to a prancing horse in 1642. Stuttgart is the home of Ferrari's deadly rival, Porsche.

In 1929, the Scuderia Ferrari was formed in Modena, racing with cars lent to them by Alfa Romeo and giving the brilliant young Tazio Nuvolari his first chance. But in 1933, Alfa Romeo pulled out of racing and locked up its best cars, refusing to sell them to Ferrari until they relented, when Nuvolari left in disgust. But soon the Italian cars would be outclassed by the 'silver arrows' from Mercedes and Auto Union. Desperate, in 1938 Alfa Romeo re-established Alfa Corse and employed Enzo Ferrari as team manager. It did no good. The German teams, backed by unlimited money and the Nazi party, were unbeatable, and after nearly twenty years Ferrari was dismissed by Alfa Romeo in 1939, a gigantic blow to his ego. He returned to his native Modena, while Italy lurched into war.

It was industrial decentralisation caused by Allied bombing which forced Ferrari to move his machine tool factory to a plot of land he happened to own ten miles away at Maranello. Ferrari himself began a double life. At his home in Modena was his virtually estranged wife Laura and his sickly son Dino. Near Maranello was his mistress Lina Lardi and their son Piero – a clandestine liaison which would continue for the rest of his life.

Maranello began to produce world-beating cars – Formula One, sports racing and road cars. Enzo Ferrari, curiously, was hardly ever an innovator, with the caution of the 'peasant' that he was. Over the years, he managed to resist nearly every technical innovation until it was almost too late – disc brakes, magnesium wheels, fuel injection, coil springs, monocoque chassis, mid-engined layouts, even good aerodynamics. His only real interest was in horsepower, 'I build engines and attach wheels to them'. He was a manipulator of people and a megalomaniac, having difficult relationships with his designers and, above all, his drivers – whom he some-times seemed to regard as expendable. They included some of the greatest: Fangio, Ascari, Farina, Ickx, Lauda, Surtees, Gurney and Phil Hill. Over three years Collins, Musso, De Portago, Castellotti and Hawthorn died.

He also treated valued customers with disdain. While early clients like the Aga Khan, King Leopold, the Shah of Iran and King Feisal would presumably have been given some deference had they turned up at Maranello, others would not be so lucky. Future team drivers Olivier Gendebien and Eugenio Castellotti, rich young men who had each bought six of his cars, were made to wait in the scruffy reception shack near the gate, freezing in winter and boiling in summer. After the same casual treatment, millionaire industrialist Tony Vandervell, who had supplied Ferrari with 'thinwall bearings', vowed to beat 'those bloody red cars', and, with his green Vanwalls succeeded. Another customer, the tractor tycoon Ferruccio Lamborghini, was sufficiently angry to go off and create his own rival luxury sports car company. Luigi Chinetti, who for years was Enzo's loyal American distributor and responsible for half his sales, was once thrown out into the road by a shouting Enzo because of a small financial problem.

Nowadays, with Michael Schumacher coupled to Ferrari, we think of the marque being unbeatable. But, in Enzo's declining years, things did not go well. Long distance sportscar-racing was suddenly dominated by Ford, while his Grand Prix cars were being beaten by the genius of what he contemptuously called the British *'garagistas'*, Cooper, Lotus and McLaren.

In 1988, Pope John Paul II visited the Maranello factory to pay tribute to a great Italian, but Enzo was now too ill – and could not be there to greet him and to accept the honour. Two months later he was dead.

But this strange, driven man, flawed in so many ways, had created at Maranello something unique. No other marque has competed in every Grand Prix for 50 years, and also made road cars of such speed and luxury. Maranello deserves its fame.

The author (right) with his Dino, a jewel of a Ferrari, named after Enzo's son

MARATHON
Greece

Every year, in most big cities, thousands of runners take part in 'Marathons'. As they pound their agonising way to the winning post twenty six miles away, how many of them think of a small Greek town or a big battle?

Marathon is an undistinguished community in Attica, 24 miles from Athens. In summer, its inviting sandy beach – backed by cool pine woods – is a playground for Athenians, and a nearby marsh inland is an important landfall for migrating birds. The name Marathon is from the ancient and demotic Greek for fennel, a tall herb that grows there abundantly on the dry waysides.

In 490 BC, Marathon witnessed one of the most significant battles of world history, a decisive east-west clash between Greeks and Persians. The fleet of Darius I, King of Persia, landed a large army at Marathon as a punitive expedition against Athens – which had supported revolt in the Persian provinces of Asia Minor. It was a second attempt. A fleet two years earlier had been wrecked in a storm before any troops could be landed.

A small Athenian army, including a contingent from their ally Plateia, under the command of Miltiades (mercifully acting alone, rather than, as was the Athenian custom, in committee with nine other generals), opposed the Persians on the coastal plain. The Greeks ran bravely at their superior enemy. At first, the Persians drove back an over-extended Greek centre, but as the Greek wings closed in, the Persian line broke. Routed Persians fled towards their ships only to be mired in a lagoon and its surrounding marsh – then deeper and much more extensive. A third of the army failed to return home. Many drowned, and others were killed by the triumphant Greeks. Free citizens had triumphed over the acolytes of a despot.

Marathon rid Athens and Greece of a deeply-held fear of Persian arms. Although Darius was to plan another expedition, rebellion in Egypt forced its cancellation. He died shortly after, deferring the task to his son, Xerxes, who invaded Greece in 480 BC with a fine fleet, shattered at the Battle of Salamis, and with an immense army, which was defeated a year later at Plateia. No Persian soldier ever set foot in Greece or Europe again. Some 140 years later, Alexander the Great would unite Greece and conquer Persia.

The beach at Marathon today, with stone pine (Pinus pinea)

Before the Battle of Marathon, Athens had sent the athlete and courier, Pheidippides, to seek aid from Sparta, their rival city 120 miles to the south. This splendid fellow apparently ran all the way – and claimed to have conversed en route with Pan, a god who supported the Athenians. The Spartans, for once, were sympathetic, although they were unwilling to break an

Pietri staggers across the line at the end of the 1908 Olympic Marathon in London.

See: Maeander

revived in 1896, the feat of Pheidippides after the battle was commemorated in the well-known long distance event over the same distance as Pheidippides's last run from Marathon to Athens – 24 miles – extended at the London 1908 Olympics to 26 miles, 385 yards, to ensure that the runners would start at Windsor and finish opposite the Royal Box!

At the Paris Olympics of 1900, an enthusiastic (if unfit) Frenchman, steeped in patriotic fervour rather than athletic prowess, emulated his Greek hero by expiring during the marathon.

Ironically, for the 2004 Olympic Games in Athens, the Greek Government has chosen Marathon as the location for rowing and water sports – requiring construction of a huge boating lake. Thus the ancient battle field, site of a pivotal day in European history, may yet be destroyed for the sake of the Games that honour its name!

eccentric religious taboo forbidding them to go to war before a full moon. Having won the battle, the Athenians again called upon the athletic services of the unfortunate Pheidippides. He ran back to Athens, announced a glorious victory, warned of an impending sneaky Persian attack on the city by sea, and it is said, promptly died of exhaustion.

When the Olympic Games were

MASADA
Israel

'Fortified by Heaven and man alike against any enemy who might wage war against it'.

Thus was Masada described by Yossef Ben-Matityah, a Jewish historian who later joined the Romans as Josephus Flavius.

Not far from Jerusalem, overlooking the Dead Sea, is an isolated mountain 1,200 feet above the Judean Desert with steep rocky sides – a natural fortress. And there King Herod, patronised by the Roman Empire, built such a fortress – but with luxurious palaces, with pools and bathhouses supplied by an intricate water system using winter flood water,

in an otherwise arid wasteland.

In 66 AD a Great Revolt against Rome broke out, and the Zealots captured Masada. Gradually, more and more Zealots and their families arrived in this last refuge. Three years after the Destruction by the Temple by the Roman Procurator Flavius Silva, he turned to Masada, arriving with 15,000 men including the Tenth Legion. They surrounded the mountain with eight camps and laid siege, thinking at first that the 967 men, women and children would surrender, faced after all by impossible odds. It was not to be. It needed the whole elaborate Roman system of siege engines and the building of ramps to get the Romans into position, after several months, for the final direct assault. The doomed Jewish garrison then made its terrible decision.

Its leader Elazar Ben-Yair gathered the people together on the evening before the Roman's final assault and made his moving speech.

'Brave and loyal followers! Long ago, we resolved to serve neither the Romans nor anyone other than God himself, who

alone is the true and just Lord of mankind. The time has now come that bids us prove our determination by our deeds. At such a time, we must not disgrace ourselves. Hitherto we have never submitted to slavery, even when it brought no danger with it. We must not choose slavery now, and with it penalties that will mean the end of everything if we fall alive into the hands of the Romans… God has given us this privilege, that we can die nobly and as free men. In our case it is evident that daybreak will end our resistance, but we are free to choose an honourable death with our loved ones.... Let our wives die unabused, our children without knowledge of slavery. After that, let us do each other an ungrudging kindness, preserving our freedom as a glorious winding-sheet. But first, let our possessions and the whole fortress go up in flames. It will be a bitter blow to the Romans, that I know, to find our persons beyond their reach and nothing left for them to loot. One thing only let us spare - our store of food: it will bear witness when we are dead to the fact that we perished, not through want but because, as we resolved at the beginning, we chose death rather than slavery….Come! While our hands are free and can hold a sword, let them do a noble service! Let us die unenslaved by our enemies, and leave this world as free men in company with our wives and children.'

After which, as Josephus Flavius, who was with the Roman besiegers, tells us:

'They then chose ten men from amongst them by lot who would slay all the rest; every one of whom laid himself down by his wife and children on the ground, and threw his arms about them, and they offered their necks to the stroke of those who by lot executed that melancholy office, and when these ten had without fear slain them all, they made the same rule for casting lots for themselves, that he whose lot it was should first kill the other nine, and after all, should kill himself… and he who was last of all, examined the mass of those who lay on the ground, and when he had perceived that they were all slain, he set fire to all corners of the royal palace, and with the great force of his hand ran his sword into his body up to the hilt, and fell dead beside his kinsmen. Thus they all died believing that they had left no living soul behind to bear the Roman yoke…'

Next morning, the Romans finally assaulted Masada. First puzzled, they were shocked and then moved to find nothing but an eerie silence, dead bodies in little family groups and burned buildings. Only a few women lived to tell the tale.

Masada has been a symbol of sacrificial defiance ever since.

See: Bethlehem, Gethsemane, Mecca

MECCA
Saudi Arabia

The western world uses the word 'Mecca' very casually. We talk of 'the Mecca of racegoers' or the 'Mecca of vintage car enthusiasts'. In Britain a leading entertainment company even calls itself Mecca, best known for ballrooms and even bingo.

But, for a quarter of the world's population, the city in Saudi Arabia has a deep significance unmatched in any other religion. Five times each day Muslims turn towards the city of Mecca to pray. Each year, millions arrive there to fulfil the command in the Koran that at least once in their lifetime they should make the *Hajj*, the pilgrimage to the Holy City. It is this devotion to one place that has led us to the half-admiring use of 'the Mecca of…'

It is an extraordinary fact that the original founder of Mecca, Abraham, born in 2000 BC, is regarded as the founder of three great religions – Islam, Judaism and Christianity. By his first wife Sarah, he was the father of Isaac; by Hagar, Sarah's hand-maiden, the father of Ishmael; and by Ketivah, he had six sons who were the ancestors of the Arab tribes. It was Ishmael who helped Abraham to build the first House of God, the cube now called the Ka'bah. And it was from Ishmael that the prophet Muhammad was descended.

Muhammad was born in Mecca in about 510 AD, but his relationship with the city would be stormy. In about 600 he began to receive revelations of the word of Allah, 'the one and only true

Pilgrims circle the Ka'bah at the Mosque at Mecca during the annual Hajj.

Left: Mecca Cola has been created, with some of the profits to go to Palestinian children.

See: Bethlehem, Varanasi

'*Labbaika – Allahumma, Labbaika*' ('Here I am, O God, at thy command, here I am').

As a pilgrimage, the *Hajj* is a remarkable and huge event. Tens of thousands of pilgrims from all over the world, and from dozens of countries, now arrive each day by air at Dahran, Riyadh, Jizan, Najran, Medina and Jedda, where the Hajj Airport terminal is the world's largest roofed structure. It is a huge task for Saudi Arabia which finances and organises the *Hajj*.

At Mecca, the pilgrims, with the men dressed all in white, go straight to the Sacred Mosque, where they will perform seven *shawts* or circuits of the Ka'bah, the first three at jogging pace which Muhammad did to show he was not weakened. With hundreds of thousands present, the massed moving human whirlpool is daunting. As the prophet said to his wife Aisha, 'to perform the *Hajj* is an exacting combat'.

Mecca is only part of the ritual of the *Hajj*. At Arafat, where Muhammad preached his last sermon, it is absolutely essential to be there when the sun rises. 'Missing' means that all other worship rites are nullified, and it is a time of great anxiety for the hurrying pilgrims. At Muzdalifah, forty-nine small stones are

God' which resulted in the Qur'an or Koran, which dictated that the pagan idols be destroyed and the rich should give to the poor. For the priests and rich merchants of Mecca, this was scarcely welcome and Muhammad, facing potential assassination, was forced to move to Yathob (Medina). In 623 he went to war with Mecca, gaining control in 629, and was recognised as chief and prophet. It was the beginning of a dynamic religion which would take Islam, with its culture, military might and organisation deep into Africa, Asia, the Far East and Europe.

gathered to be thrown in Mina the next day at three pillars which represent Satan. Colossal walkways have been specially built. The final part of the *Hajj* is a visit to Medina to view the tomb where Muhammad is buried.

Every year, pilgrims make their way to Mecca in greater numbers. In 2002 it was more than two million – all in a few days. Perhaps it is not surprising that we use the word with admiration.

MEDELLIN
Colombia

There are three cities that outsiders could probably name in South America that are not capitals: huge SãoPaulo and glamorous Rio de Janeiro in Brazil, and Medellin in Colombia –

tragically know for drugs and murder.

Medellin first came to the world's attention in the 1970s, when 'suitcase smuggling' to the United States of, first, marijuana and then cocaine began to make the smugglers very rich. A kilo of cocaine processed in the jungle for $1,500 was worth $50,000 on the streets of America. The so-called 'Medellin Cartel' was a mixed lot. Among its members, Rodriguez Gacha had been an emerald trader, the Ochoa brothers were ranchers, and Carlos Lehder was a marijuana smuggler who suggested using small aircraft to fly directly to the United States. But it was the incredibly violent, former street thief Pablo Escobar who really hit the world's headlines.

It was America's huge appetite for drugs that helped to wreck the beautiful country of Colombia and ruin the lives of its 42 million people. In 1981, *Time* magazine's front cover featured a martini glass full of cocaine, with the headline 'HIGH ON COCAINE'. Inside, it reported the booming trade to America's middle-classes. *'Today, coke is the drug of choice for perhaps millions of solid, conventional and often upwardly mobile citizens'.* Small wonder that despite all efforts at crackdowns, the 'Medellin Cartel' was booming.

By 1986, Medellin was the murder capital of the world. That year, a city of approximately 1,500,000 people saw 3,500 of them killed. Greater New York, with 18,000,000, saw 700 murders, while same-size London only 210.

Attempts to capture the Medellin leaders and to extradite them to the US met a furious and murderous response, particularly from Escobar. Anyone who did not take the advice, *'Plato o Plombo'* ('silver or lead' – take the bribe or the bullet), received the latter. Hundreds of judges, policemen and journalists met a grisly fate. A bus filled with dynamite killed 80 people and injured 700; an airliner was bombed out of the sky with 107 more fatalities. In the year 1985, the Colombia Supreme Court building and all the extradition files were destroyed.

The dominance of Medellin declined with the jailing of the Ochoas and the shooting of Gacha - and at last Escobar himself in 1993. It was the cartel from the rival city of Cali with quieter and more subtle criminals, who helped to bring it down, but sadly it too would soon succumb. However, the cocaine trade has in fact continued to increase with 300 separate smaller organisations involved. The authorities have even found a high-tech smuggling submarine under construction, designed by Russian and American experts.

For a brief period, the brutality of Medellin propelled it on to the world stage, and was so much on the public mind that when a hapless Colombia soccer player scored an own goal in the 1994 World Cup, and was later shot to death in a bar, people just assumed he was being punished for his error.

The role of Colombia and Medellin as the drug centre of the world may indeed never end until America's appetite for drugs is itself reduced.

See: Alcatraz, Blind Beggar, Corleone, North Clark Street

MENLO PARK
New Jersey, USA

'Genius is one percent inspiration and ninety nine percent perspiration'.

Thus spoke Thomas Edison, a man who knew something about genius and invention. And at Menlo Park in West Orange, New Jersey, Edison would not only create many world-changing innovations, but would also change how the whole process of invention was carried out.

Edison patented his first invention at twenty-two, and had spent valuable time as an itinerant telegrapher which later helped him as an inventor of telegraph equipment. After five years of creating inventions, he decided he needed a special environment – and his father helped him to build a laboratory at Menlo Park that was to be the home of some of his most fruitful ideas.

But why Menlo Park? By chance, of course. Edison needed a place just far enough outside New York City to be devoid of distraction, but near enough so that investors and businessmen could flock there to buy inventions. The estate at Menlo Park, on the railroad line to Philadelphia, with a mere six houses, just happened to fit the bill.

The laboratory was certainly not the conventional inventor's workshop, with one inventor and his assistants. Though Edison was definitely the most important mind there, Menlo Park employed many other scientists and workers. At its peak, his eighty employees were working in teams, each one of them containing an experimenter and several specialists backed by the most modern equipment. Indeed, this was a prototype for a modern research station, and it was thoroughly efficient. During his 7 years working there, the man who was to become known as 'The Wizard of Menlo Park' applied for over 400 patents; *'a small invention every ten days and a big thing every six months'*, claimed Edison, who worked long hours, often late into the night. These efforts were aided by his ability to take quick, refreshing 10-minute naps, and his wife's tendency to bring the employees a midnight snack when they were working late. And as he worked, Edison was changing the world around him. The inventions he created at Menlo Park would shape the future.

Some of the more important innovations were the telephone and a principle called the Edison Effect, which foreshadowed the development of radio. But the most famous and significant area Edison explored was the domestic use of electricity. He was not the first to try to make a light bulb, but earlier ones were both too small and too short-lived. The key would be the type of filament. Edison needed a material that would remain incandescent, burning to

Right: Thomas Edison's Menlo Park laboratory
Below: Edison at work

PHOTOS: NATIONAL PARK SERVICE
EDISON NATIONAL HISTORIC SITE

give off light for long periods of time. After experiments with platinum and silicon, he realised that carbon would be the most effective material. In October, 1879, his first carbon-filament bulb burned for 45 hours. Two months later, 3,000 people came to marvel at the laboratory – and the local village street lit by these miraculous new inventions. Within his newly formed company, The Edison Electric Light Company, the modern light bulb had been born.

However, Edison had a problem on his hands. A light bulb is totally useless without an electrical supply, so he needed to both invent and establish an entire electrical system. He set his genius towards this goal until, in 1882, the Pearl Street generating station was activated, and began to supply power to a small area of New York. Edison was making electricity very real indeed. He continued to pioneer projects in this area, including batteries, an electric railway, generators, light sockets, fuses, and an electrical billing meter.

In 1887, after he married his second wife Mina Miller, Thomas Edison constructed a new research facility in West Orange, New Jersey. Though also a large-scale operation, with around 60 workers, Edison always said that Menlo Park had been the place where he had come up with his best ideas. Eventually, the derelict building collapsed, and now exists only as a re-creation which Henry Ford constructed in Greenfield village as a museum to the great inventor.

In his eventful lifetime, Edison would go on to patent a staggering 1,093 inventions. Menlo Park had helped to foster and harness one of the greatest minds in history.

See: Acol Road, Bazaar, Kew, Kitty Hawk, Mulberry Harbour, Nîmes, Nokia, Stockton and Darlington, Titusville, Vinci

MERS-EL-KEBIR
Algeria

'A hateful decision, the most unnatural and painful in which I have ever been involved'.

Winston Churchill sat down in the House of Commons with tears streaming down his cheeks. He had just finished explaining 'a Greek Tragedy' which had occurred at Mers-el-Kebir on July 3rd, 1940.

Britain had her back to the wall. Above London, her pilots were battling the Luftwaffe; many of her ships had been sunk off Norway and then Dunkirk; invasion was expected in days and France had capitulated. A vital part of France's fleet, the fourth largest in the world, was moored in the harbour of Mers-el-Kebir, a port near Oran in French Algeria with a long but strictly local maritime history, now about to be projected on to the world stage.

It was crucial that this fleet should not fall into the hands of the Germans. If it had, Britain might have lost control of the Mediterranean, the Middle East oilfields and perhaps even the war.

'Force H' arrived off Mers-el-Kebir, commanded by a reluctant Vice-Admiral Sir James Somerville, who sent Captain Cedric 'Hooky' Holland in to negotiate with the very pro-British French Admiral Gensoul. The negotiations should have succeeded, because Holland was very pro-French, spoke the language well – having been the Naval Attaché in Paris – and was even involved with a French woman.

In Gensoul's stifling cabin, Holland put four alternatives on the table:

Sail the ships to British harbours and join the fight alongside Britain.

Sail to a British port, from which the crews would be repatriated to France.

Sail to the West Indies, with the ships entrusted to the neutral United States for the duration of the war.

Scuttle the ships.

In a disastrous mistake, the most attractive 'West Indies' option was not signalled to the anti-British Admiral Darlan, who ordered French ships to rally to Gensoul – a signal immediately intercepted by Britain's code-breakers.

At 5.15 pm, Somerville was forced to give a 15-minute ultimatum, 'Accept, or I must sink your ships'. At 5.54 pm, the battleships *Hood, Valiant* and *Resolution* opened fire with huge 15-inch shells. In ten minutes, several of the French ships were sunk in the harbour, with 1,300 Frenchmen dead. The battlecruiser *Strasbourg* and five destroyers escaped to France where, ironically, in 1942, the Vichy government kept its promise and scuttled them.

The incident horrified all but the Germans, who exploited its propaganda value to the full. Somerville wrote to his wife: *'An absolutely bloody business, the biggest blunder in modern times.'*

However, after reflection, the Free French leader, General Charles de Gaulle, in his broadcast to the French people, called the action *'déplorable et détestable',* but added that it was better the ships be sunk rather than join the enemy.

The most important effect was actually

in America. The very ruthlessness of the decision against a former ally and friend convinced Roosevelt and his Government of Britain's absolute determination, and strengthened their desire to help.

In France, on the other hand, it would only be understandable if the tragedy of Mers-el-Kebir continued to feed those with anti-British leanings, and to convince them that it was merely typical of 'Albion Perfide'.

See: Casablanca, Dieppe, Dunkirk, Sedan, Versailles

251

MIDDLE EARTH
Middle Earth

That world between worlds, soaked in a history so ancient that it makes our own seem rootless and childish, Middle Earth never existed. But perhaps it should have; perhaps, somewhere it does.

Even the fiercest critics of the writer J.R.R Tolkien have acknowledged his central achievement. More than any other writer, he truly created an alternative world. Like many other writers of his generation – Orwell, Vonnegut and C.S. Lewis – Tolkien served in the Great War, observing at first hand the savagery of modern, mechanised conflict, before which the old morality seemed to stumble in helpless horror. So he and his fellow veterans turned to fantasy.

He created another kind of conflict, a different kind of world. Drawing deeply upon his profound, indeed unparalleled, knowledge of Norse and Old English culture, he set about the creation of a landscape which was to have affinities with our own and yet be entirely separate, familiar but remote.

In the Tolkien mythology, as demonstrated in *The Silmarillion*, Middle Earth was made by music, by the song of Eru, the One, who sang and made angels, and whose angels, in turn, fashioned the world with their song. There is one discordant note, Melkor, Tolkien's Satan, who wishes to sing his own tune. The world is marred even as it is made.

Hill by hill, mapping each mountain, carefully planting his legends like foundation stones, Tolkien developed his melody until it burst out, loud and plangent, in his masterpiece, *The Lord of the Rings*, where Sauron, servant of Melkor, is finally defeated and the world begins to mend. Elves, dwarves, goblins, all these seemingly trivial characters from folklore, acquire dignity and reality. Tolkien found wings of gossamer but left them with blood and bone.

And yet this extraordinary world would never have caught the public imagination were it not for the creation of one particular race, a race so odd, so eccentric, so English, that it alone merits Tolkien a place in literary history. After weary days marking exam papers, Tolkien found to his delight that one student had left a page bare. He looked down at it, baffled as writers often are by the cold, unblinking blankness of the empty page, before picking up his pen and writing a short sentence. He was never able to explain it:

'In a hole in the ground lived a hobbit'.

See: Utopia, Valhalla

MIDWAY
Pacific Ocean

For Japan it came quickly – the promise of victory slipping away to be replaced by the threat of defeat.

For the Germans, it had taken nearly three years – from easy victory over Poland to disaster at El Alamein and Stalingrad.

It was just six months before the sweet fruits of the Pearl Harbor success turned to the bitter ashes of defeat at Midway. And the key moments lasted five minutes, 300 seconds which changed the world.

Midway is a speck of a coral island roughly halfway between Japan and Pearl Harbor and, by June 1942, it was one of the few places not flying the flag of the Rising Sun. Japan had raged through the East. In the weeks after the raid on Pearl Harbor, her troops had taken Hong Kong, Malaya, Singapore, the Dutch East Indies, the Philippines and had reached New Guinea and half way up Burma – apparently on their invincible way to India. Even Darwin in Australia had been bombed.

But Japanese confidence had been dented by the daring Doolittle Raid on Toyko by US Army B-25 bombers launched from carriers. The Japanese were stung into trying to extend their territory for self protection. In the Coral Sea, the American aircraft carriers that had so luckily been absent at Pearl Harbor inflicted at least a draw, sinking one Japanese carrier and damaging another, with the loss of many experienced pilots. It was the first major naval battle in which the ships never saw each other.

Admiral Yamamoto needed to lure the remaining American carriers into a trap to eliminate them, and he chose tiny Midway as a place the Americans would defend.

Japan's unexpectedly rapid expansion had brought a crucial problem. Her new naval code book could not be distributed fast enough to far-flung ships and bases. So its planned introduction was fatally delayed – twice. By brilliant American cryptoanalysis, the old code had been broken by the allies, so the Americans knew that the Japanese were to feint at the Aleutians, with the main attack at 'AF', which was probably Midway. They tricked the Japanese by broadcasting that Midway's water distillation plant was broken. Sure enough, two days later, intercepts heard that 'AF was short of water'. Thus, Admiral Chester Nimitz could confidently send his three carriers to 'Point Luck', 350 miles north east of Midway to set his ambush for the unsuspecting Japanese. *Hornet* and *Enterprise* were joined by the *Yorktown,* its Coral Sea damage miraculously repaired, not in the expected 90 days, but in one frantic, brilliant weekend.

At 5.30 am on June 4th, a reconnaissance Catalina spotted the Japanese carriers through the clouds, as they launched their planes against Midway. Soon, Admiral Nagumo was thunderstruck by a report of a similar sighting of the American carriers of whose close presence he was unaware. He had to re-arm his second wave of aircraft from bombs to torpedoes to meet the threat, while his first wave of aircraft returning from Midway was desperate to land. Low level torpedo planes from the American carriers and from Midway were also attacking, but were nearly all shot down by the swarming Zero fighters. In one flight, 29 out of 30 American crewmen were killed, the only survivor watching

TIMKEN AEROSPACE / SMITHSONIAN INSTITUTION

'SBD Dauntless over the Akagi' *by R.G. Smith.*

the remainder of the battle floating in the sea.

With all attention focused on the low level activity, and just as Nagumo's planes were ready to take off, crowding the decks with armed and fuelled aircraft, a piercing howl came from the sky. Horrified, Commander Fuchida, who had led the Pearl Harbor raid, looked up: 'Black objects floated eerily from their wings. Bombs! Down they came, straight towards me!' From 15,000 feet, dive-bombers screamed down and ripped open *Akagi, Soryu* and *Kaga,* setting fire to the massed planes, exploding their bombs. It took just five minutes for 3 out of Japan's 8 carriers to be wrecked. Only *Kiryu* survived long enough to launch planes to cripple the *Yorktown,* whose own dive-bombers took their revenge. For 7 hours, *Kiryu's* crew fought the flames, before the doomed Admiral Yamaguchi ordered submarines to sink her, turning to Captain Kaku and saying, 'Come, let us enjoy the beauty of the moon'.

The Japanese had lost half of their heavy carriers and, more importantly, hundreds of expert and irreplaceable air crews. The tide had turned. Japan, unknown to its people (who did not even hear about Midway until after the war) was already on the defensive.

Admiral Yamamoto had said to his Prime Minister before the war, 'If I am to fight, I shall run wild for the first six months or a year, but I have absolutely no confidence for the second and third years'.

It was a tiny piece of coral in the Pacific that proved him right.

Aftermath of Midway
The Japanese people never learned the truth. All news was suppressed and the wounded smuggled back to Japan. An injured Commander Fuchida – six months earlier hero of Pearl Harbor – revealed, 'I was not taken ashore until after dark on a covered stretcher and through a side entrance. My room was in complete isolation and I could not communicate with the outside world. It was like being a prisoner of war among our own people'.

See: Changi, Corregidor, Hiroshima, Kohima, Pearl Harbor, Raffles, Tsushima

MILO
Greece

Deep in a cave, in 1820, a Greek peasant called Yorgos made a startling find – a beautiful semi-nude marble statue of a woman, but with both arms missing.

For a while, he was able to keep this exquisite work of art secretly in his barn on the Island of Melos in the Aegean Sea, knowing he should hand over such an antiquity to the Turkish authorities. However, his secret was discovered and, to his anguish, his sculpture confiscated. His anguish no doubt increased when the statue was loaded on to a Turkish vessel and then transferred, out at sea, to a French warship. He may have felt some feelings of grim satisfaction when the greedy and corrupt Turkish official involved was publicly whipped for parting with a potential masterpiece. However, the deed could not be undone. The statue had been sold to the French Marquis de Rivière, who sent it to France as a gift for Louis XVII. There, it became known as the 'Venus de Milo'.

Dating from the second century B.C., it was one of numerous such pieces depicting the Greek Goddess of Love, Aphrodite, whom the Romans called Venus. The missing arms somehow gave her an extra, enigmatic appearance. At first, the King's advisors commissioned French sculptors to try and replace them, and they experimented with examples that held apples, clothes and lamps, and others which merely pointed in various directions. Luckily, the King became convinced that the statue's beautiful form should not be spoiled by such attempts.

Scholars disagree about the sculptor. It could have been Alexandros of Antioch-on-the-Maeander. Or it may have been Praxiteles, whose other sculptures of Aphrodite were sufficiently erotic to inspire real lust. His completely nude Aphrodite, in a temple on the Island of Knidos, was certainly exciting enough to be visited by people from all over the old world.

Now occupying pride of place in the Louvre in Paris, the 'Venus de Milo' is arguably the most famous statue in the world.

See: Laconia, Lesbos, Marathon

MONTGOMERY
Alabama, USA

It is hard to choose. There are so many places in the southern states that were propelled onto the world stage by the Civil Rights crisis of America: Little Rock, Selma, Birmingham. A fitting choice is Montgomery with the same name as a British general, a name appropriately perhaps, from another place with age-old community tensions, Northern Ireland. It was also the town which saw the first success of the Civil Rights movement and the emergence of its most famous and charismatic leader, Martin Luther King.

Since slavery was abolished after the American Civil War, little had improved for the African-American. In spite of fighting for their country in two world wars, blacks, especially in the south, suffered apartheid-like discrimination. Everywhere was segregated; schools, colleges, hospitals, restaurants, parks, swimming pools, elevators, buses, cinemas, bars and prisons. The result of this was that black citizens received the worst of everything. Five times more was spent on white schools; fifteen times more on white colleges. In 1958, a black college teacher was committed to a mental asylum simply for applying to work at the University of Mississippi. A quarter of blacks were illiterate. Blacks were denied, effectively, the vote.

Ten years after Jesse Owens' 1936 triumph at the Berlin Olympics, there was not a single black player in major league baseball. And there was real fear and hatred in some white attitudes. One woman from the Ku Klux Klan said after four little girls had been killed in a church bombing, 'They weren't children. Children are little people, little human beings and that means white people. They're just niggers and if there's four less niggers tonight then I say good for whoever planted the bomb'.

Any attempt to demand freedom was grotesquely equated with Communism and treason in an America which would see the hysteria of McCarthyism. The singer and actor Paul Robeson had been vilified and nearly ruined for eight years. If you throw in the racist J. Edgar Hoover as head of the FBI, it paints a horrifying and depressing picture.

And all this had passed by most of the white nation, even in the north where the discrimination by custom was still there to see. The progress by successive Presidents in tackling the issue was very patchy. Truman made a first step when he abolished inequality in the armed forces. Eisenhower said 'The biggest damn fool mistake I ever made', was his appointment of Earl Warren as Chief Justice to the Supreme Court when Warren went on to de-segregate schools in 1954. But Eisenhower did, reluctantly, send in paratroopers to protect the first black students of Little Rock High School in 1957.

John Kennedy made great speeches about freedom but was usually looking for the political advantage. It was during his presidency that a tired Captain Colin Powell, one day to be America's most senior General and later Secretary of State, was told to 'sneak round the back' of a restaurant in Georgia. Only Lyndon Johnson, to his eternal credit, was to take the cause seriously.

In Montgomery on December 1955, Rosa Parks was arrested on a bus for failing to give up her seat to a white man. 'Why do you push us around?' she asked the arresting officer. She knew only too well. Rosa Parks was a seamstress, but she was also the secretary to the local chapter of the National Association for the Advancement of Colored People. By a technical blunder her case became a Federal matter. Much more important was the boycott of the city's buses. That Monday morning, thousands walked to work or used a well-organised car pool. 'My feets is tired, but my soul is rested'

Rosa Parks keeps her place on the buses.

said Mother Pollard to the newly-elected President of the Montgomery Improvement Association, 26-year old Martin Luther King Jr. The first night of the boycott he stamped his mark on the audience who roared its approval when he cried,

'And you know my friends, there comes a time when people get tired of being trampled over by the iron feet of oppression'.

But he quietened his listeners when he said, 'Now let us say we are not here advocating violence. We have overcome that. I want it to be known throughout Montgomery and throughout this nation that we are Christian people. The only weapon we have in our hands this evening is the weapon of protest'.

Out from Montgomery went the words that would begin to change everything, 'We are not wrong in what we are doing. If we are wrong – the Supreme Court of this nation is wrong. If we are wrong – God Almighty is wrong! If we are wrong – Jesus of Nazareth was merely a Utopian dreamer and never came down to earth! If we are wrong – justice is a lie'.

The boycott lasted a whole year and was ready to be beaten, when King was handed an Associated Press wire with the news that the Supreme Court had declared Alabama's bus segregation unconstitutional. There was still a long way to go. But what had started in Montgomery was unstoppable and long overdue.

'Being a star has made it possible for me to get insulted in places where the average negro could never hope to go and get insulted'.

Sammy Davis Jr
1965

See: Ambassador Hotel, Dallas, Harlem, Lorraine Motel, Motown, Texas School Book Depository

MOORGATE
England

As mysterious as it was horrific, the Moorgate train crash was the worst train disaster which has ever occurred on the London Underground. The oldest underground railway in the world, it may be rather hot, crowded and uncomfortable, but at least it is normally fairly safe.

In 1975, work was underway to connect the isolated Northern Line to the main line services, and Platform Ten at Moorgate, named after one of the old gates into the City of London, was not being used as a result. Instead, platform nine – which terminated in a dead-end wall – was more than large enough to accommodate the trains that would stop there, with the driver changing ends and walking back up the platform to take the train out again.

When train number 272, crowded with people working in the financial district of the City, approached the station on February 28th, 1975, instead of slowing down as usual, it appeared to accelerate and came hurtling into the terminus at full speed. Disaster inevitable, the train ploughed through the sand at the end of the platform, kicking up clouds of debris. Finally, slowing only slightly, the train smashed into the far wall. As the tunnel itself was a high one, built to contain larger trains, the second and the third carriages had room to ride up over the first, which was itself almost completely crushed. Dead passengers in the first two were found still holding on to straps, newspapers and briefcases. Death had come as a complete surprise.

In total, 42 passengers lost their lives along with the driver, while 70 more were badly injured, and some died later as a result of their injuies. The rescue operation was painfully slow, despite a surgery set up on the platform to tend to the critically wounded. The firemen could not get their equipment into the confined tunnel, and the breakdown train could only winch the stricken carriages away at one inch every 10 minutes. As *The Daily Telegraph* described it: *'The platform was choked with helmeted firemen, police, ambulance men, doctors, nurses and welfare workers'*. The dead were still being discovered and removed on the 4th of March.

One of the things that has made this tragedy so infamous is that nobody has ever discovered why it occurred. The train's brakes were found to be in perfect working order, and it had undergone a routine examination the previous evening. The driver was in excellent health, had been with the Underground for six years, and was known as a careful driver. He was found to be under the influence of neither drugs or alcohol, and there appears to be no motive for him to have killed himself deliberately. Those on the platform had seen him holding his controls in the normal way. In fact, he held them right until the end, never even raising his hands to his face at the moment of impact.

The London Underground has since introduced a new signalling system, called 'Moorgate Control'. This ensures that a train stops at a dead-end, regardless of the driver's input, and should prevent a similar disaster from ever occurring again.

See: Aberfan, Bhopal, Chernobyl, Fourteenth Street Bridge, Three Mile Island

THE MOTHERS' CLINIC
England

It opened without publicity on March 17th 1921, at 61 Marlborough Road in London's Holloway, a converted house between a grocer and a sweet shop. 'The Mothers' Clinic' at first only attracted about three women a day, but it was soon to have a huge influence not only in Britain but throughout the world.

Created and financed by Marie Stopes and her husband, The Mother's Clinic was designed to give poor mothers access to birth control and to gather scientific data about contraception.

Dr Marie Stopes is arguably one of the greatest and most influential women in history. In an age where women had only just won the right to vote and few went to university, she was already quite unconventional – with her two first class university degrees – together with studies in Germany and a doctorate. She also managed to follow exactly her childhood ambition; to devote the first twenty years of her life to science, the second to social issues and the third to poetry.

It was her first and disastrous marriage to an impotent husband that convinced her that the veil of ignorance must be lifted from the taboo subject of sex. In 1918, she wrote *Married Love* which was, in fact, the first sex manual in Britain. While an instant hit with readers it shocked the church, the medical world and even members of the press. One wrote, *'The idea that women can actually enjoy sex is a disgusting aspersion on British womanhood'*.

Stopes went on to marry Humphrey Roe, a Manchester industrialist, who had seen his female workers suffer unwanted pregnancies. With his encouragement and financial backing and after meeting Margaret Sanger – the American

advocate of birth control – she went on to write *Wise Parenthood*, which was an explicit guide to the subject.

It was three years later that The Mothers' Clinic opened, with its reassuring, all-female staff and free cervical caps for married women. Marie Stopes disapproved of chemical contraception, with the blunt phrase, 'Never put anything in your vagina that you would not put in your mouth!'

Eventually, the Clinic moved to Whitfield Street and mail order contraception was started, which outraged the Catholic Church still further. Affiliated clinics were then started in South Africa, Australia and New Zealand, and eventually Marie Stopes International would open in thirty countries worldwide.

Unconventional as always, in later life, with her husband's contractual consent, Marie Stopes took younger men as lovers and, as she had predicted, began to write excellent poetry.

But her great legacy was her campaigning, her books and that building in Holloway, called 'The Mothers' Clinic for Constructive Birth Control'.

Marie Stopes

See: Greenham Common, Harley Street, Triangle Shirtwaist Company

MOTOWN
Michigan, USA

When the French explorer, Antoine Laumet de la Mothe Cadillac, beached his boats on the banks of the Detroit river in 1701, he could scarcely have imagined what might be there two centuries later.

Detroit duly passed from the French to the British, and then in 1796 became part of the United States. In 1837, the new state of Michigan abolished slavery, a very significant move because Michigan, and especially Detroit, was to become important on the escape route for slaves fleeing from the south – the 'Underground Railroad'.

Always, therefore, a haven for black Americans, Detroit was transformed forever by the automobile industry, and especially by Henry Ford, who deliberately recruited plantation workers as being robust enough to handle his

strenuous and repetitive new assembly line methods.

Detroit's black population rocketed far faster than other northern cities, with the employment first provided by Ford, then General Motors in 1908, and later by Chrysler in 1925. The city had truly become the home of the gigantic American car industry – 'Motortown'. Not surprisingly, with such a population, Detroit became a centre for music; Blues, Gospel, Jazz and Jump Blues.

Berry Gordy was a car assembly line worker, and then a jazz shop owner. In 1959, he decided to borrow $800 from his family to start a record company called 'Motown', in a modest house at 2648 Grand Boulevard, which he less modestly called 'Hitsville USA.' His ambition was to 'cross-over' black music to white audiences. Elvis Presley had, after all, softened up the market by singing Rhythm and Blues like a black man. And the Rolling Stones were set on their road to fame by covering the songs of Muddy Waters, Bo Diddley and other black bluesmen.

Gordy hired experts to train his artistes as professionals, with coaching including deportment, dancing and enunciation. The rest is legend. All through the '60s and into the '70s, star after star with hit after hit was to pour out of Motown – Smokey Robinson, Stevie Wonder, The Contours, The Temptations, The Isley Brothers, The Marvelettes, Gladys Knight and The Pips, The Spinners, Martha Reeves and the Vandellas, Mary Wells, Jimmy Ruffin, The Jackson Five, Marvin Gaye and Tammy Terrell, Brenda Holloway, Kim Weston and, of course, The Supremes.

Diana Ross lived a few doors away from Gordy's friend Smokey Robinson in Detroit's Brewster Projects, and worked as a secretary at Motown before she, Mary Wilson and Florence Ballard

See: Abbey Road, Broadway, Carnegie Hall, The Cavern, Cotton Club, Covent Garden, Glastonbury, Harlem, Nashville, Mull of Kintyre, Penny Lane, Route 66, Storyville, Tin Pan Alley, Tulsa, Woodstock

were allowed to record *Where Did Our Love Go?* – a smash hit that was followed by five consecutive 'number one' records, unmatched even by The Beatles. Multiple appearances on the *Ed Sullivan Show* helped them to become glamorous role models for black women, inspiring, among others, a young Oprah Winfrey to realise she could make it. Motown rivalled the British invasion of The Beatles and The Rolling Stones with 'The Sound of Young America.'

It is sad that the glamorous, positive and hip image created by Motown did not always reflect Motortown. In 1967, one of the biggest riots in American history left 43 dead, 1,189 injured and 7,231 arrested. Among those who eventually fled the city was none other than Berry Gordy, who moved the company to Hollywood, eventually selling it for $61 million.

Detroit has since embarked on an extensive and successful programme to rejuvenate itself. The Motown Museum is still there, at 2648 Grand Boulevard – a memorial to one of the most innovative periods of American music.

MOULIN ROUGE
France

A Lautrec poster featuring the dancer, La Goulue, 'The Glutton'

Mills have played a role in our lives for centuries. They fill our literature – George Eliot's *Mill on the Floss,* Longfellow's poem *The Mills of God grind slowly, Don Quixote* ('tilting at windmills'), Daudet's *Lettres de mon Moulin,* and even our songs, like Nellie Dean's *Old mill by the stream* and Sting's *Windmills of your mind* in the film *The Thomas Crown Affair.* They provide inspiration for paintings like Constable's *Flatford Mill* or Van Gogh's *Moulin de la Galette,* (although the Dutch mills are mostly pumping water). But one mill became world-famous for very different reasons, a red mill called the 'Moulin Rouge'.

As the 19th century drew to a close, Paris was a glorious place to live, 'La belle epoque.' Advances in technology and increasing prosperity had led to a general

feeling of optimism, and the city became the perfect place to enjoy yourself. Leisure facilities of all kinds sprang up, from circuses to operas, cafés to dance halls. In the upbeat ambience, young men flocked to Paris, abandoning the straitlaced social mores of their parents, and revelled in their new identities as 'Children of the Revolution' – painters, sculptors, students and musicians, together forging their own bohemian world that epitomised the spirit of the time, and the four concepts of BEAUTY, TRUTH, FREEDOM, LOVE, a modern code for a modern revolution.

Montmartre ('the hill of martyrs') was an extraordinary amalgam of lowlife and creativity, with impecunious artists and writers living and working next to dancers and prostitutes. On top of the hill, the 'pure-white' cathedral of Notre-Dame du Sacre-Coeur was specifically built in 1881 to try to counter the influence of the brothels, nightclubs and dance halls. This noble concept, however, did not work.

In October 1889, all Paris turned out for the opening of what was to be the most famous(or infamous) dance hall and nightclub of the era, the 'Moulin Rouge', referring to the prominent structure that made the club so visible. It had an immense dance floor, viewing galleries, exotic décor and a garden with a giant wooden elephant, large enough to house an Arabian-themed room, this complete with belly dancers and opium. A microcosm of the contemporary breakdown of social barriers, within the gaudy halls of the Moulin Rouge, aristocrats (including even the Prince of Wales) would rub shoulders with artists, high-class courtesans, prostitutes and dancers. Best-known were the can-can dancers, the most titillating spectacle of the day. The *Guide des Plaisirs à Paris* said of the performers *'...with a physical elasticity as they do the splits, which promises just as much flexibility in their morals'*. In such an environment, almost anything was available for the right price. In a country that was drinking in quantities that had never been seen before, the Moulin Rouge was no exception. The tipple of choice was a potent green spirit called absinthe, known also as 'The Green Fairy' among its cult following. One ingredient was wormwood, a powerful herb widely believed to have hallucinogenic qualities, making it highly popular among young artists looking for inspiration. It was certainly dangerous enough to kill off some of the greatest talents of France.

However, it was not only the Moulin Rouge's wild reputation that would make its fame so enduring, but the patronage of one of its best customers, the brilliant and aristocratic Henri de Toulouse-Lautrec. A tragic childhood accident had given him a bone condition that left him at the meagre height of 4' 11", 'a queer top-heavy little man, swaying on his stunted legs like a ship at sea'. Lautrec would spend much of his life in the Montmartre club, drinking absinthe, and vividly and sardonically painting all that he saw around him, in all its attendant wealth and squalor, decadence and beauty. His work remains a snapshot of a place that represents a time, a generation, a revolution. He helped the Moulin Rouge to keep history's attention not only for what it was, but what it stood for.

Australian film director Baz Lurhman chose to add more weight to the legend, with his film *Moulin Rouge* in 2001, starring Nicole Kidman and Ewan McGregor. It contains several real life characters, including Toulouse-Lautrec and Charles Zidler, the club's owner (although in the film he is curiously renamed Harry), and even has singer Kylie Minogue playing 'The Green Fairy' herself.

Over a century after its opening, you can still visit the famous Moulin Rouge, boasting 'a hundred dancers and a thousand costumes'. It merely involves parting with hundreds of euros or dollars.

See: Arles, Barbizon, Broadway, The Cavern Club, Cotton Club, Nashville, Sibylla's, Storyville, Studio 54

MOUNT ST. HELENS
Washington, USA

Mount Rainier

If you want to imagine what the area around Mount St. Helens used to look like, look at Japan's Mount Fuji. Mount St. Helens was known as 'The Fuji of the west'. Alternatively, drive up through the magnificent green forests and beautiful lakes at the base of the snowy white cones of nearby Mount Hood or Mount Rainier.

Mount St. Helens is named after an eighteenth century British ambassador to Spain, Alleyne Fitzherbert, whose title was Baron St. Helens. The man who chose the name was Commander George Vancouver, who with his fellow officers aboard HMS *Discovery*, surveyed the northern Pacific coast from 1792 to 1794. The mountain was known by the native northwest Indians as *La-We-*

Mount St Helens, still erupting weeks after the initial explosion

Lat-Klah meaning 'smoking mountain,' and legends explain the volcanic activity through stories of a tragic love triangle between spirit gods, resulting in the creation of Mount St. Helens and its two nearby peaks, Wyeast (Mount Hood) and Patu (Mount Adams).

Flying above the Cascade Range, it is easy to imagine the volcanic violence that created these mountains. Crater Lake is huge, a water-filled relic of a colossal eruption. Although at around 50,000 years, Mount St. Helens is a relatively 'young' volcano, its foundation was constructed during three eruptive stages, each separated by periods of dormancy ranging from 6,000 to 16,000 years. However, the visible cone was created during the most recent, fourth stage, which began 3,900 years ago. The volcano experienced seventeen major eruptions during this period. Before 1980, the last major activity occurred in 1857.

Like the other mountains in the surrounding Cascade Range, Mount St. Helens is a 'stratovolcano', in essence a great cone of rubble, made up of lava rock and interlayered with pyroclastic deposits such as dacite magma.

Starting in March 1980, trouble was brewing. Intense seismic activity at Mount St. Helens caused more than 10,000 small earthquakes and hundreds of steam-blasts (phreatic explosions). As molten rock rose up into the volcano, it found a weak spot on the north flank, causing it to swell sideways at a rate of five feet per day for almost two months. This magma created an ominous bulge, a mile wide and up to 450 feet high.

Local people were told to evacuate their homes, although some refused to leave. Luckily, photographer Gary Rosenquists' motor-drive camera was on hand to record the graphic events which suddenly occurred on 18th May.

At 8.32 am an earthquake measuring 5.1 on the Richter scale triggered a massive landslide as the north face and summit collapsed. Millions of tons fell from the volcano and seconds later, a 350 degree Celsius, stone-filled blast shot out of the side at 450 mph. It shattered over 230 square miles of forestland in three minutes.

Melting snow and ice turned to raging floods of concrete-like debris that swept through the river valleys below, choking the channels with tons of sediment, rock and trees. The landslide surged through ethereal Spirit Lake, causing the water to rise 800 feet up the hillsides on the opposite end of the lake. As this gigantic wave sloshed back down into the lake basin, it carried thousands of trees with it. A fifteen mile high plume of ash rose from the mountain to be blown by the wind across 20,000 square miles of the western United States.

With the fallout, darkness fell in daytime Portland and other towns. The once majestic white mountain was reduced in elevation from 9,677 to 8,365 feet, and the surrounding green forest landscape was dramatically transformed into a grey wilderness of mud and ash.

The eruption continued for nine hours, but it was the initial blast that was the most catastrophic, killing 57 people and wiping out the wildlife population of birds, deer, elk, bear, most small mammals, twelve million salmon from nearby fisheries and enough trees to build 300,000 two-bedroomed houses.

Since the 1980 eruption the area has been declared a National Volcanic Monument, and whereas visitors used to flock there because of the beautiful countryside and opportunities for hiking, camping and sailing, now they come to witness the extent of the destruction. The Monument was established to allow nature to recover at its own pace, and trees, plants and wildlife are now returning. As a study site, the volcano provides much significant scientific data for the prediction of future eruptions, but, above all, Mount St. Helens now stands as a symbol of nature, suddenly and by chance deciding to remind us of its potential cataclysmic power.

Trees like these were flattened like matchwood.

See: Atlantis, Krakatoa, Nome, Olympos, Pompeii, Sodom

MULBERRY HARBOUR
France

Churchill said: 'Let me have the best solution worked out. Don't argue the matter. The difficulties will argue for themselves'.

If you stand on the beach of the little town of Arromanches in Normandy and look out to sea, you will see a curious sight – a semi-circle of long grey shapes. They have been there ever since 1944.

The Allies' invasion of Europe was always going to be a tricky operation. The English Channel can be one of the stormiest seaways in the world, and the German defenders were counting on their enemies needing at least one big port wherever they landed. As a result, Field Marshal Rommel put most of his efforts of his 'Atlantic Wall' into massive defences for ports such as Cherbourg, Calais and Caen, figuring that he would have time to bring up his fearsome Panzer divisions to throw the Allies back into the sea. In order to get ashore and then break out into France, the Allies knew they needed 'critical mass' – in this case, over 26 divisions, 2 million men, 500,000 vehicles and millions of tons of supplies.

The answer? Bring the harbours with the invasion force; one for the British beaches and one for the Americans.

The Mulberry Harbour was one of the most ingenious and technically successful British achievements of the entire war. It consisted of a complex system of block-ships (rather charmingly called 'gooseberries'), breakwaters, floating piers and bridges. Most impressive of all were the 'Phoenix' units – huge, hollow, concrete caissons, 200 feet long, 60 feet wide and 60 feet deep, and weighing 7,000 tons each. It took 20,000 British workers to build this massive system, in locations as far away as Glasgow. The two hundred components were towed south of the Solent and, soon after the D-Day beaches were secure, on to France where they were flooded, settling on the seabed to form artificial harbours. Twelve days after the first land-ings, the Mulberry Harbours were in place, and only just in time. When the worst storms for years hit Normandy, the Mulberry off the American beaches was damaged but the one at Arromanches was able to pour men and material into France.

Rommel's calculations had been upset by a piece of brilliant lateral thinking, and a truly impressive technical effort.

One of the huge concrete Phoenix caissons ready to be towed to the Normandy beachheads

See: Arnhem, Dieppe, Oradour, Peenemünde

MULL OF KINTYRE
Scotland

As a name, the 'Mull of Kintyre' has long been familiar as a weather station to insomniacs or mariners who listen to the BBC's shipping forecasts in the middle of the night. Thirty years ago nobody would have dreamed that this remote hilly moorland peninsula in western Scotland would shortly emerge as an icon of popular culture.

Then in the year 1970 the depressed, disillusioned, heavily-bearded former Beatle, Paul McCartney retreated to the farm that he and his supportive wife, Linda, had bought on the Mull of Kintyre. Press, radio and TV had announced the final demise of the Beatles, the legendary group that had brought him such fame and fortune, after its last blaze of glory on the album *Let it be*, a magnificent (if flawed) swan-song. McCartney appeared to be about to quit the music scene he had helped to create. As he later wrote:

I felt washed-up and it was a very traumatic time for me. It was one of the heaviest periods that I have ever had in my life. It completely knocked me for six. In losing the Beatles, I'd lost the framework for my whole working life. I just didn't know what to do, I didn't know if I had any future in music.

The Scottish peninsula proved to be just the tonic he needed. Now a family man, no longer working

within the partnership of genius with John Lennon, he nevertheless went on pouring out songs, many of them of high quality. And always a true rock 'n' roller, he wanted to be back on the road and so created 'Wings', a makeshift band that included wife Linda (enthusiastically learning keyboard as she went along) and Denny Lane, who had been a founder member of 'The Moody Blues' in the early '60s. McCartney was now right back to his roots, rebuilding a musical career from scratch. 'Wings' started by gigging in clubs, colleges and universities, taking a hard road, but gradually building up a mighty international reputation both live and on record.

The band needed material, and McCartney's post-Beatles isolation, and bolt-hole from rigorous touring, inspired its very biggest hit. *Mull of Kintyre*, co-written by McCartney and Lane, and with deceptively simple, almost banal lyrics and melody was released as a single in 1973. What elevated the song to popular acclaim was augmenting 'Wings' with a traditional Scottish pipe-band, touching the emotions of patriotic Scots as well as sentimental Sassenachs. The video (just film-clips in those days) that went with the song when the band featured on TV pop shows, showed the pipe band performing on a beach against a background of loch and romantic castle – a Scottish Tourist Board dream.

See: Abbey Road, Carnegie Hall, Covent Garden, Dakota, Motown, Tin Pan Alley

Paul later revealed that he wrote *Mull of Kintyre* to say thank you to Scotland for helping him through his depression. 'I wasn't trying to write a big hit, I just wanted to write a love song to the area really, just about how I love being there and imagining myself travelling miles away and wanting to get back to it'.

Bucking the musical trends of the time – punk, heavy metal and the ubiquitous disco - *Mull of Kintyre* was to become the fourth best-selling pop single of all time, and the first to top the two million mark in the UK. Paul was to say:

'I remember Alan, one of my guys in my London office, phoning me and saying, "It's selling 30,000 a day." I still wasn't convinced and as a joke I said, "Don't phone me back until it's selling 100,000 a day".

Sure enough, a week later, Alan's on the phone again saying, "It's selling 100,000 a day". It was crazy and to tell the truth, I was very surprised how big it became'.

History has not judged it kindly, and the song can never compare with masterful McCartney classics such as *Yesterday* and *Eleanor Rigby*, but all those punters can't all be wrong. A still youthful-looking Paul McCartney has continued a great musical career, but he has never again enjoyed the sheer mainstream commercial success of *Mull of Kintyre*.

MUROC
California, USA

It was a very long and boring assignment and the three exhausted technicians must have been heartily relieved to reach Muroc. For 8 days they had crossed the continent in an old railroad baggage car from Buffalo, New York, to this isolated place. Their mission: to escort the priceless secret cargo of two of General Electric's first jet engines. To protect the bearings from vibration, General Electric had decided to use a compressor to keep the engines slowly turning over at 200 r.p.m.

Muroc, California, is in the remote Mojave Desert, and its curious name comes from its first settler family, Corum, spelled backwards. In 1942, it

had been selected to test the Bell XP-59, America's first jet, in order to catch up with the British and Germans. The little base had nothing but a hangar and some outbuildings on the edge of a huge dry lakebed, but with its isolation and fine weather it was soon to be America's flight-testing centre.

Five years later, former World War II fighter ace Captain 'Chuck' Yeager arrived at Muroc to fly the Bell X-I in an attempt to break the 'sound barrier', (Mach1), a challenge which had already killed one British test pilot. Thirty one feet long, the rocket plane was dropped from the belly of a B-29 Superfortress bomber high above the desert like a bomb, before lighting up its 600 gallons of volatile liquid oxygen fuel.

Yeager's wife, Glennis, described her own arrival at Muroc. 'Well, a garden spot it definitely was not. We went past the guarded gate and drove for miles and miles. Nothing but scrub and lakebeds and Joshua trees. The desolation took your breath away'.

As speeds were increased, Yeager discovered that at Mach .94 the controls froze due to the shock waves. His boss and mentor Colonel Boyd said, 'Well, it looks as if we've reached the end of the line'. But engineer Jack Ridley sat in the corner and puzzled out that some limited control could be achieved by moving the plane's normally fixed horizontal stabiliser. It seemed to work.

Just two nights before the scheduled attempt to break the barrier, Yeager fell off a horse and broke two ribs. He hid his painful injury from everyone except his wife and Ridley, who cleverly improvised a broom handle to enable him to reach up and lock the door of the orange Bell X-1 – with 'Glamorous Glennis' painted on the nose. On 14th October 1947, the plane went smoothly through the barrier, Mach 1.07, 700 m.p.h. and a boom was heard on the ground. It was to be the first of many.

Yeager worked for sixteen years at Muroc, joined by more and more pilots and ever faster aircraft. They hung out at 'Pancho's Fly Inn' – a motel, restaurant and bar run by a former woman stunt flyer, Pancho Barnes, a lady of fierce loyalties and even fiercer language. It was the only fun and recreation for miles around.

Once the historic barrier breaking was announced, a very reluctant Yeager was forced into speech-making all over the country, with his face on the cover of *Time* magazine. But unlike the civilian test pilots who were paid huge salaries and vast bonuses, Yeager was still earning $250 a month as a Captain – just $2 an hour for flying frightening rocket planes like the X-1.

Soon the sleepy, isolated Muroc ceased to exist, becoming Edwards Air Force Base in honour of Glenn Edwards, one of Muroc's best test pilots who had been killed. Its growing streets and roads were also named after dead heroes. By 1954, ten thousand people worked at the base, and every high performance American aircraft was tested there.

One Muroc pilot, Neil Armstrong, went on to be the nucleus of NASA's space programme – and became the first man to land on the moon.

The desolation of Muroc must have been good familiarisation.

GEN. CHUCK YEAGER INC.

Above (top): Chuck Yeager after breaking the sound barrier.
Below: The Bell X-1

See: Biggin Hill, Cape Canaveral, Farnborough, Kitty Hawk, Lakehurst, Peenemünde, Sea of Tranquillity

MUSTIQUE
West Indies

When Princess Margaret announced her engagement to Anthony Armstrong-Jones in 1960, her old friend the Honourable Colin Tennant, gave her a choice of presents: one 'wrapped in a box' or ten acres on his new Caribbean island, Mustique. By choosing the land, she helped to start a legend to which two of the most overused words in the English language can genuinely be attached – 'unique' and 'exclusive'.

Mustique is a small island in the Lesser Antilles, part of St. Vincent and the Grenadines. Like the other islands, it was first settled by the Arawaks in AD 700, who were displaced five hundred years later by the far fiercer Caribs,

THE MUSTIQUE COMPANY

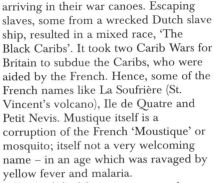

Patrick Lichfield, whose photographs first put Mustique on the map

LICHFIELD

Above: Colin Tennant Right: one of the 1970s assets of Mustique, Bianca Jagger

264

arriving in their war canoes. Escaping slaves, some from a wrecked Dutch slave ship, resulted in a mixed race, 'The Black Caribs'. It took two Carib Wars for Britain to subdue the Caribs, who were aided by the French. Hence, some of the French names like La Soufrière (St. Vincent's volcano), Ile de Quatre and Petit Nevis. Mustique itself is a corruption of the French 'Moustique' or mosquito; itself not a very welcoming name – in an age which was ravaged by yellow fever and malaria.

For a while, Mustique prospered as a sugar island, until the steady decline of Caribbean cane sugar due to sugar beet and other competition.

In 1958, the now run-down and poor island was owned by the Hazell family, who raised cows, sheep and goats. It was a real backwater when Colin Tennant arrived from Trinidad. Tennant was an eccentric member of an eccentric family, made wealthy in 1799 by a new bleach, and later by an empire of chemicals, mines, railways and steel. He bought the island for £45,000, not as ridiculously cheap as it sounds today. His father, Lord Glenconner, had cabled, 'Full agreement if plenty of water'. There was no water, nor a jetty or road or anything much else – but plenty of mosquitoes.

When Princess Margaret turned up on honeymoon on the royal yacht Britannia in 1960, she described a somewhat forlorn picture. 'It looked like Kenya, burnt to a frazzle. We drove down a path, the only road on a tractor, and sat in the brush whacking mosquitoes. We took Colin Tennant and

his wife to the yacht and gave them a bath. They were in tough shape'.

After trying unsuccessfully to re-sell Mustique, Tennant then decided to make something of it. A photographic feature in *Queen* magazine by Patrick Lichfield first put the island on the map, and Tennant began to develop the island. Oliver Messel, the well-known stage designer, helped to create The Cotton House, the island's hotel, and to design the houses, starting with Princess Margaret's 'Les Jolies Eaux'. The first manager, Hugo Money-Coutts, now Lord Latymer, learned to fly in a period of just two weeks to help to improve communications with the outside world.

Soon, the concept of a limited number of building plots being sold to an international clientele emerged. Tennant ran the island by his rules, some charming, sometimes impossible. There were many who could never be allowed to buy in to the island, including the Marcoses, the Shah of Iran and Club Med. But many of the 'right type' did, like Sir Mick and Bianca Jagger, Lord Lichfield, David Bowie, and Viscount Linley. In 1977, Queen Elizabeth dropped in to visit her sister, which finally put the island on the world stage. 'Exclusive but not excluding' was Tennant's philosophy (a nice echo of the motto of Brookland's motor racing circuit, 'The right crowd and no crowding'). Fabulous parties, theatrical

LICHFIELD

LICHFIELD

LICHFIELD

and 'naughty', were soon reported by newspapers, and especially by Nigel Dempster in Britain's *Daily Mail*, who sometimes devoted whole pages in his diary to Mustique's exotic goings-on.

The financial and personal strain of running Mustique as a one-man island took its toll on Tennant, now Lord Glenconner, who eventually sold most of the company and the island to a consortium of home owners.

The beautiful green island is still small, but will always remain uncrowded because only 120 homesites will ever be made available. Visitors and residents will always be in the hundreds not the

thousands. They now have an airstrip, plenty of water, electricity that works, a medical clinic and an equestrian centre.

And they should all be thankful for the willpower and vision of an eccentric aristocrat who bet on Mustique when it was a very different place.

Above: Princess Margaret at 'Les Jolies Eaux'
Above left: Nigel Dempster devoted whole pages to Mustique in the Daily Mail.

MY LAI
Vietnam

For American television viewers, it should have been a time of pride, because CBS was covering the second moon landing in late November 1969. But suddenly the screens were full of images of something dreadful, which had occurred 18 months earlier in far away Vietnam in a little village called My Lai.

They were right to be shaken. History records some spectacular and horrible acts of murderous barbarism by soldiers on unarmed, helpless civilians. Most were in the distant past, with 'barbarians' like Genghis Khan, or Attila the Hun or Tamerlane. More recently, we can blame the worst type of Nazi Germans for Oradour and Lidice, or the Japanese for Nanking. But the massacre at My Lai was carried out by ordinary, young Americans. A few hours of collective madness was to lose America any of its rights to morality, to weaken its resolve

to continue the Vietnam war and to begin years of self-doubt. By 16th March 1968, when C Company of the 11th Light Infantry Brigade of the Americal Division entered My Lai, the Americans were frustrated. They had been fighting an undeclared war in Vietnam for thirteen years. Despite growing protests back home, more than 500,000 young Americans were now in Vietnam, part of eight million who passed through with the sole justification that they were saving Vietnamese civilians 'from Communism'.

They faced a hidden enemy, often lost in the local rural population, who were themselves caught helpless in the middle. Brutal methods crept in. Most of My Lai's neighbouring villages had been razed to the ground. Coming right from the top, the need to produce 'kills' was felt by every soldier. A Marine described

265

Ron Haeberle's photograph captures the moment when a mother tries to protect her daughter. Seconds later this whole group was dead.

Calley at his Court Martial

See: Amritsar, Changi, Dachau, Dien Bien Phu, Glencoe, Kwai, Lidice, Oradour, Srebrenica, Tianamen Square, Wannsee, Wounded Knee

the atmosphere. 'Our mission was not to seize positions or win terrain but simply to kill. Victory was a 'high body count', defeat a 'low kill ratio', war a matter of arithmetic. The pressure on unit commanders to produce corpses was intense, and they in turn communicated it to their troops. It is not really surprising, therefore, that some men acquired a contempt for human life and a predilection for taking it'. As one American infantryman also put it: 'They were gooks, spooks, Charlie. We never looked at them as being other human beings'. So here we have Americans talking just like SS men on the Russian Front of 1942.

'Charlie' Company was an above average unit, with good results in training. It had been just four months in Vietnam under its respected commander, Captain Ernest 'Mad Dog' Medina. When he briefed his men, Medina ordered that everything in 'heavily fortified' My Lai should be destroyed. No prisoners. The company had lost some men recently, and Medina hinted that they 'could get their revenge'.

Leading the assault would be Lt William Calley, in civilian life a failed diner cook, car wash attendant, insurance clerk and railway ticket collector. Also taking part, by chance, were photographer Sergeant Ron Haeberle and reporter Jay Roberts, to record the action for the Brigade's newspaper.

In My Lai on that warm morning, children were playing, women cooking, men going off to the fields. Suddenly the calm was shattered, as 155 mm high explosive and phosphorous artillery shells slammed into the village. Moments later, Charlie Company – having landed in helicopters – came marching through the paddy fields, already shooting. Military photographer Haeberle testified later:

'A woman's form, a head, appeared from some brush. All the other GIs started firing at her, aiming at her, firing at her over and over again. She had slumped over so that her head was a propped-up target. There was no attempt to question her or anything. They just kept shooting. You could see bones flying in the air chip by chip'. From hut to hut Charlie Company moved, grabbing terrified inhabitants by the hair, shouting 'VC? VC?' and then murdering them. In the middle of the village, Calley gathered 45 civilians and, when his men hesitated, started the automatic fire. Private Paul Meadlo then also helped Calley kill another 75 men, women, children and babies in a ravine. 'Just outside the village', said reporter Jay Roberts, '…there was this big pile of bodies. This really tiny little kid – he only had a shirt on, nothing else – he came over to the pile and held the hand of one of the dead. One of the GIs behind me dropped into a kneeling position and killed him with a single shot'.

Worse than 'just' killing occurred. Scalping, mutilation and rape. One of Ron Haeberle's photographs was to go round the world. A thirteen year old girl holding the remnants of her clothing, hid behind her mother. Haeberle's presence stopped the rape, but the whole group of women and children were then machine-gunned to death.

The soldiers took a lunch break before starting to kill again. By nightfall, the body count was 504 civilians.

It took months for the story to emerge, after a soldier had written to politicians. At first the Army tried to believe that there had been a real battle, with civilians caught in cross-fire. But CBS ensured that a proper inquiry took place, with Sgt Haeberle's photographs providing horrific evidence.

However, of the 45 men involved, only five were tried and only Calley was convicted for a 'specimen' 22 murders and sentenced to hard labour for life. Three days later, he was released from prison on the orders of President Nixon and went to work in a jewellery shop in Georgia. He has never once expressed remorse, although some of his men have gone through agony.

My Lai now welcomes tourists from an America which should never forget its own day of infamy.

NASHVILLE
Tennessee, USA

Nashville, Tennessee, with its Appalachian Mountain hinterland and its remote, self-sufficient and conservative communities, has long been a hotbed of traditional music. On the evening of Saturday 28 November 1925, George Dewey Hay launched a new music show on Nashville's WSM radio. The show, which became the longest running music programme on American radio, was based on the National Barn Dance that he had established in 1924 on WLS radio in Chicago. Hay's passion for country music had been fired at a log cabin hoe-down in the Ozark Mountains. He believed in old time, no-nonsense music – 'Keep it down to earth!' – with a wholesome, folksy, hillbilly image.

Two years later, the radio barn dance acquired a famous name, when on 10th December 1927 it followed a broadcast by the NBC Symphony Orchestra. This gave Hay a chance for an enduring play on words. 'For the past hour we have been listening to music taken from Grand Opera – but from now on we will present the Grand Ole Opry'. George D. Hay, the 'Solemn Ol' Judge', presided over his baby until he retired in 1951, attracting the cream of country performers. The house rule was a minimum of 26 appearances per year, giving new acts a helpful contract and much-needed exposure.

In 1938, the Opry at last found a really big star, Roy Acuff, whose records sold massively through the 1940s, a period when Opry began to attract a host of 'big stars with string bands.' The legendary Hank Williams joined in 1949, and the list of artists progressively became a Who's Who of country music: Williams himself, Jim Reeves, Dolly Parton (with a debut at 13), Flatt and Scuggs ('Foggy Mountain Breakdown' from the film *Bonnie and Clyde*), Johnny Cash and the Carter family.

With more and more radio stations syndicating the music, Opry put Nashville firmly on the map as the home of country music. Capitol Records arrived in 1950, and the town soon attracted the recording studios and offices of other major record companies. A select band of session musicians, initially playing mostly banjo, fiddle and the trademark steel guitar, later incorporating more rock-orientated electric guitars and rhythm sections, provided the smooth distinctive 'Nashville Country Sound.' This reached its fullest development in the 1960s, when even mainstream acts such as Bob Dylan (notably his *Nashville Skyline* LP) and the Byrds flirted with country music.

The rise of rock'n'roll both threatened and strengthened the country scene (Elvis Presley himself was a country boy who fused this music with the black man's blues). The Grand Ole Opry was the only barn dance radio programme to survive this cultural upheaval. Indeed, it went from strength to strength. It began in a studio, moving to various theatres, notably thirty years in the Ryman Auditorium. Its home is now a custom-built theatre at Opryland USA, a few miles outside Nashville, where it continues to provide country music to the nation's airwaves, including, sometimes, the live commercials with which the Opry started.

Music may only be Nashville's ninth largest industry but for most of us it means 'country', a commercial stylised but perfectly genuine manifestation of American folk music which remains a perennially popular musical form in North America, Britain and the world.

The original Grand Ole Opry in downtown Nashville

See: Abbey Road, Big Apple, Broadway, Carnegie Hall, Cotton Club, Harlem, Motown, Storyville, Tin Pan Alley

Dolly Parton, country music superstar

NAVARINO
Greece

Navarino Bay is an attractive natural harbour on the coast of the Peloponnese, the southern peninsula of Greece, providing a wide and deep anchorage, protected by the narrow island of Sphakteria. Today, the bay and the town of Pylos (once home of Nestor, Greek hero in the Trojan War) are popular holiday destinations set amidst vineyards and groves of olives and citrus fruits. But it was not always so peaceful. On 20th October 1827, Navarino witnessed, by chance and almost by mistake, a naval defeat for Turkey so catastrophic that it led directly to the modern Greek state breaking away from the Ottoman Empire. The Greeks would be a free people for the first time in more than two millennia.

Nor was this the first significant clash of arms in the bay. Back in ancient Greece, during the long and hard-fought Peloponnesian War between Athens and Sparta, here the Athenians decisively defeated the seemingly invincible Spartans in a combined land and sea operation. An Athenian fleet arrived by accident, storm-bound en route for Sicily, but decided to establish a naval base at the old Mycenean town of Pylos at the northern end of the bay. At first besieged by Spartans, they turned the tables, and following a naval victory, trapped a contingent of 420 Spartan hoplites on Sphakteria. Landing on the island to finish the job, they captured 292 of the Spartans, a considerable bargaining chip – as Sparta was always short of manpower. Sadly, Athens eventually lost the war.

But Navarino's finest hour was rather more recent. During the 1821-30 War of Greek Independence, the Sultan of Turkey arranged for Egypt, a Turkish vassal state, to send a fleet and army under Ibrahim Pasha to the Peloponnese to fight the Greek insurgents and terrorize the population. The Egyptians captured the old Turkish fortress at Navarino in 1825, during fierce fighting with the Greeks in the bay and on Sphakteria. The following year, Ibrahim Pasha captured Mesolonghi, the base in central Greece of Lord Byron, who had died the previous year. The Greeks appeared to be on their last legs, and liberals and Philhellenes throughout Europe were aghast.

In July 1827, a Triple Alliance of Great Britain, France and Russia, nominally neutral but mindful of numerous Egyptian and Turkish atrocities, decided to settle the Greek question once and for all. Instead of complying with an ultimatum to quit Greece, the Sultan reinforced the Egyptian fleet in Navarino Bay. An Alliance fleet under Admiral Sir Edward Codrington was ordered to Navarino as a show of force, but Ibrahim Pasha still ignored the ultimatum. Finally, at midday on 20th October, Codrington took his 27 ships into Navarino Bay, where 91 Egyptian and Turkish ships lay at anchor. Not only did the enemy outnumber the Alliance but also possessed twice its total weight of ordnance, not to mention shore batteries in the castle. However, the British ships, especially, mounted huge state-of-the-art cannon.

Codrington was under strict orders to coerce rather than engage the enemy. But the Egyptians, defiant to the last, rashly fired on the crew of a boat dispatched by HMS *Dartmouth* to request it to move a fireship. All the crew were killed or wounded. After further shooting incidents, Alliance ships opened fire with all the force that they could muster. By the end of the day they had sunk 55 ships, including 12 frigates, and disabled all the others. Codrington, remarkably, lost no ships. Alliance casualties were 174 dead and 475 wounded, whilst Turkish and Egyptian losses were 6,000 dead and 4,000 wounded. After such a one-sided performance, the Sultan's men wisely surrendered.

The Battle of Navarino settled the outcome of the Greek War of Independence. The Russian and French Governments were well pleased – particularly the Tsar of Russia who had unfinished business with Turkey in the Caucasus, and declared war in April 1828. In Britain, a Conservative Government, under the Duke of

Wellington, was more concerned about Russia's strength at the expense of that of Turkey, and MPs called for Codrington to go on trial for over-reaching his orders. Failing this, they made sure he lost his command the following year. However, the Liberals saw things differently, and Lord John Russell praised 'the greatest naval victory in history' – only equalled 80 years later by the Japanese at Tsushima.

The Triple Alliance demanded that Turkish and Egyptian troops leave the Peloponnese and south-central Greece, enabling the Greeks to set up their new nation. Greek independence was enforced in 1828 by a French military mission to the Peloponnese. French soldiers from the garrison at the castle in Pylos built the modern town, its attractive seaside square shaded by plane trees, and a 12-km stretch of road south to Methoni – the first road constructed in modern Greece. It would be more

than a century – and many wars – before Greece attained its present-day boundaries.

As well as a colourful history, Navarino Bay boasts an oddity of Greek natural history – a flourishing colony of chameleons. These fascinating creatures lay their eggs in the hot sands by a lagoon at the northern end of the bay. Chameleons are rare in the European part of the Mediterranean, and biologists generally believe them to be introduced from north Africa. One wonders whence they came to Navarino, but is it just too fanciful to imagine that they might have been brought in by the Myceneans? No doubt Nestor, by repute a wise and thoughtful ruler, would have regarded them as amusing pets for his grand-children, and a curiosity exotic enough for a royal palace!

See: Delphi, Manzikert, Marathon, Milo, Mount Olympos, Topkapi, Troy

NEANDERTHAL
Germany

On the autobahn near Düsseldorf you will see signs for Neanderthal, where the little river Düssel, over the ages, has carved a ravine through the limestone. Originally it was called 'Hundsklipp' or Dog's Cliff, later 'das Gestein', the Rocks, and, in 1679, was renamed after Joachim Neander, a local scholar and hymn writer. The beauty of the little valley attracted painters, but

soon its limestone was extracted for use by the local railway, and then a marble mining company began to destroy its beauty forever, starting in 1854.

However its fame was still to be made. In a cave in the Neanderthal valley, a skeleton was unearthed in 1856 that was to set the scientific world ablaze. The bones were thick and powerful and the skull had a brow ridge, with a brain

capacity larger than that of modern man. Later, there was also evidence that 'Neanderthals' had created fire, used stone tools and conducted burial rites.

For years, it was thought that 'Neanderthal Man' was a direct ancestor of *Homo Sapiens Sapiens*, the modern human. But 'he' is now believed to be one of two separate species, descending from *Homo Erectus*. The Neanderthals survived 350,000 years through numerous hardships and appalling weather, including that of the Ice Age, but then died out 35,000 years ago – probably under competitive pressure from the Cro-Magnons, who were our real human ancestors.

See: Cro Magnon, Piltdown

NÎMES
France

Nîmes, capital of France's Gard département, was already an important town before Christ was born. As Nemausus, it was one of the finest cities in Roman Gaul, and its magnificent arena, seating 24,000, is still used. Its Maison Carrée (Square House) is regarded as one of the most beautiful of surviving Roman temples.

But it could be argued that it is more famous for a product that is worn all over the world. *Serge de Nîmes* was a fabric woven in the town and exported in the 17th century to England, where it was called serge de Nim, soon shortened to denim.

In 1853, Bavarian immigrant Levi Strauss moved from New York City to San Francisco to open a dry goods wholesaling business, selling clothing and other soft goods to small retailers all over the American West. In 1873, he and a Nevada tailor, Jacob Davis, received a U.S. patent to put metal rivets in men's denim work pants, thus inventing the blue jean. By the early 20th Century, Levi's® jeans were the leading working men's trousers of the West, and by the 1930s Hollywood saw to it that they became associated with the individualism of the cowboy. By the '60s, *American Fabrics* was to write *'What was once a fabric only for work clothes has now become an important fabric for play clothes'*. It had, in short, become a fashion item for men and women alike, a symbol of youth and the subject of pop songs like *Venus in Blue Jeans*, and *Blue Jean Baby*.

Nîmes is not the only place that is perhaps less famous worldwide than its fabric product. Few of us have visited Al-Mawsil in Iraq, or Zaitun in China, but we do know what muslin and satin are. However, it is fair to say that after years of turmoil in the Middle East, Damascus, as capital of Syria, remains better known than its richly coloured cloth, damask.

See: Angora

NOKIA
Finland

The name 'Nokia' sounds Japanese, which may have been no bad thing in the early days of the mobile phone revolution. But it is, in fact, Finnish, and the story of how it became the largest company in Europe – let alone Finland – is an inspiring one.

It started in 1865, in a little sawmill by the side of the Nokia River, deep in the forests of southern Finland. The 'Nokia' company was soon producing pulp for paper, timber, matches, cellulose and plywood, and starting a tradition for exporting – initially to Russia, Germany and Britain – which was to stand it in good stead. The company also built a power plant and was soon selling electricity.

The steady growth of Nokia was achieved against continuous political change in Finland, a country which had been under Swedish dominance for centuries, then became a Russian Duchy, and finally achieved independence. Even its independent status was fraught with difficulties. In 1918, reflecting the neighbouring drama of the Russian Revolution, there was a vicious Civil War which claimed the lives of one per cent of the population, but in which the 'White Guards' finally prevailed over the Communist 'Red Guards'.

Somehow, Finland survived its 'Winter War' when invaded in 1939 by its giant neighbour Russia; 'The Continuation War' fighting on Germany's side against Russia; and then the 'Lapland War' to expel the Germans. And so did Nokia.

Then, during the 'Cold War', the company continued its steady progress of becoming a big conglomerate in a small country, pincered politically and economically between Europe and the Soviet bloc. Its rubber company produced studded winter tyres for cars and bicycles, and even rubber over shoes, *Only buy Finnish galoshes in Finland* was the rather patriotic advertising headline.

Cable manufacturing ultimately led to electronics with digital switchboards and television sets, but what was to really transform Nokia was its instinctive grasp of the concept of the mobile telephone. The firm pioneered car phones, then the bulky 'Talkman' which could be

transferred from the car, then 'Cityman' which, though still big and heavy, was genuinely mobile. Yet more significant than this early hardware was the creation of the Nordic Mobile Telephone System and its network equipment.

FINLAND NATIONAL BOARD OF ANTIQUITIES

Suddenly, you could talk on mobiles to folk in other countries. This was the precursor of the European GSM (Global System for Mobile Communications) which we now take for granted. Finland was to score another 'first'. Finnish teenagers took to mobiles years before their counterparts elsewhere, even in America where the mobile was envisaged as a business tool. *'Yuppinalle'* ('yuppy toy') became the pet name *KANNYKKA* (a hand extension) and a social phenomenon was born. 'Texting' became far more important for gossip and dating than for business.

Nokia is not only the world market leader; having ousted Motorola and Ericsson, it is one of the world's most valuable brands and the only non-American one in the top ten.

Not bad for a country with lots of trees and only five million people. A classic case of 'coming out of the woodwork!'

COURTESY OF NOKIA CORPORATE COMMUNICATIONS

See: Finland Station, Ladoga, Lapland

NOME
Alaska, USA

The native Aleut Eskimos called Alaska 'Great Land'. It is indeed America's largest state, with America's highest mountain. It was bought by Secretary of State William Seward in 1867 from the Russians for $7,200,00 (two cents an acre). The Russians were delighted to be rid of it because they thought they had exhausted its only obvious resources; fur seals and other pelts. 'Seward's Folly' came into its own

when Joseph Juneau discovered gold in 1880. For a few years it was boom time. Now it is oil that has made Alaska prosperous again.

The distant Alaskan town of Nome, only a few miles from the Bering Strait and Siberia, has seen its ups and downs too. In 1900, it had its own gold stampede to rival the Klondyke that briefly took its population up to 20,000, with the normal mixture of prospectors, saloon keepers, gamblers and prostitutes. The riproaring town even attracted a well-known figure from Tombstone, Wyatt Earp, who briefly ran a saloon called the 'Dexter' that made him more money than most miners. But within three years the boom was over. By 1920 the town had only 852 people.

In 1925, Nome was threatened with diphtheria, to which the local Inuit Eskimos were particularly vulnerable, and was dramatically rescued by the heroic 'race for life'. Whole villages nearby had been wiped out by measles and flu. The serum was running out, and three children had died. Serum was rushed by steam locomotive from Anchorage to Nenana, and then a relay of dog teams took on the remaining 674 miles by sled. Gumnar Kaasen made the

See: Kimberley, Sutter's Mill

last 53 miles through blinding blizzards, letting his lead dog, 'Balto', do the navigation.

Then there was the fire that destroyed the town completely in 1934.

But perhaps the most extraordinary thing about Nome is how it got its name.

A British naval mapmaker in the 1850s did not know the name of a nearby cape, so he wrote '?Name' beside it on the map. Forgetting to follow up the enquiry, he sent it off to the printer who thought he meant 'C. Nome' or 'Cape Nome' and marked it in accordingly. So the town, which had really wanted to call itself Anvil City, has been Nome ever since.

NORTH CLARK STREET
Illinois, USA

On a freezing 14th February 1929 (St Valentine's day), a black Packard touring car with detective markings pulled over to the kerb outside the nondescript CMC Cartage Company at 2122 North Clark Street, Chicago. Two men in police uniforms and two in plain clothes entered the warehouse. Up the street, George 'Bugs' Moran paused along with his two bodyguards, thinking it was a routine police raid on their headquarters. He decided to wait it out and have a cup of coffee. It saved his life.

'Bugs' Moran's North Side Gang had been the biggest problem for Chicago gang-leader Al Capone for a decade. Capone had killed its leader, Dion O'Bannion, in 1924, and then 'Hymie' Weiss in 1926, but Moran remained.

It is a little-known fact that the Irish had dominated organised crime in America for a century, until the Sicilians and Italians muscled in during the 1920s. But Moran was not as Irish as he sounded. In fact he was Polish, changing his name to fit in with the Irish street gangs. By 1929, at the height of Prohibition, he controlled bootlegging liquor distribution in the lucrative 42nd and 43rd wards of Chicago. Simple rivalry

'Bugs' Moran

272

was only half the picture. Moran and Capone were bitter enemies. Moran called Capone the 'beast' and despised his involvement with prostitution, referring to his rivals as 'dago pimps and spaghetti benders'. Moran had also never forgiven Capone for killing his beloved mentor, O'Bannion.

Shootings between the gangs culminated in the amazing cavalcade of cars, filled with 50 Weiss/Moran hoods driving slowly past Capone's Cicero headquarters, the Hawthorne Inn, riddling it with 5,000 rounds of machine-gun, rifle and shotgun fire. Amazingly, Capone survived the 'Bootleg Battle of the Marne'. Finally, he decided to eliminate Moran for ever, using out-of-town killers under the direction of 'Machine-Gun Jack' McGurn (real name James Vincenzo De Mora).

Thus, on St Valentine's Day, seven men were waiting for their boss Moran at the warehouse in North Clark Street, expecting a supposed whiskey delivery. When the 'uniformed police' entered, Moran's men willingly lined up, facing the wall to be searched. The 'plain clothes detectives' (actually Capone's Albert Anselmi and John Scalise) then entered the room with Thompson sub-machine-guns and literally shot the Moran men to pieces. They calmly walked out, the uniformed men appearing to march the two others out with their hands up. After a while, the howling of the pet dog, 'Highball', alerted people that the noise had not been pneumatic drills – and revealed the dreadful scene inside.

One of Moran's men, Frank Guesenberg, amazingly lived for a few hours but would not betray his killers. Moran, shaken, retreated to a hospital bed where he was finally goaded by a reporter into breaking the underworld's code of silence, 'Only Capone kills like that'. Safe in Florida, Capone smirked, 'They don't call that guy 'Bugs' for nothing'.

The 'St Valentine's Day Massacre' was such a brutal and brazen event that at last the authorities moved against the hoods of Chicago. President Hoover kept asking, 'Have you gotten rid of that fellow Capone yet?' The slow but sure process of jailing Capone for tax evasion began.

'Bugs' Moran caught up with the 'Machine-Gun Jack' McGurn in a bowling alley in 1936, on the eve of the seventh anniversary of the Massacre. Moran placed the customary five-cent piece in his right hand, and in his left a comic Valentine card:

The appalling scene at 2122 North Clark Street

You've lost your job
You've lost your dough
Your jewels and handsome houses.
But things could be worse, you know.
You haven't lost your trousers.

But Moran's own days as a big time gangster were numbered. After years as a petty burglar, he died in 1957 in Leavenworth Penitentiary, convicted of a small-time robbery.

Nobody sent flowers.

See: Alcatraz, Blind Beggar, Corleone, Cotton Club, Las Vegas

NUITS-ST-GEORGES
France

Imagine a field with just one crop. Now imagine that this field is known all over the world.

For some reason, when the British began to drink fine French red wine after World War II, they picked on Nuits-St-Georges as the symbol of Burgundy, which is a little unfair to the other wines regarded as even better.

Ever since the Gallic leader Vercingétorix surrendered to Julius Caesar at Alesia (now Alise Ste. Reine) in AD 52, the Romans began to appreciate the wines of Burgundy (hence

Romanée). By the eleventh century, the monks, who were allowed to drink a little wine, were developing it in the cloisters (Clos de Vougeot) and it was the Cistercians who invented Chablis.

Nuits-St-George was to be given a major boost when the doctor of Louis XIV recommended that he drink, with every meal, *'a few glasses of Nuits and of Romanée'*. The whole Court at Versailles then quickly followed suit. Red wines from Burgundy were soon exported all over the world, with names like Vosne-Romanée, Romanée-Conti, Gevrey-Chambertin, Aloxe-Corton, Pommard, Volnay and Puligny-Montrachet, which Alexander Dumas thought was so magnificent

Signs of good wines

that *'it should be drunk on your knees, with your hat removed'*.

Condemned to death by his brother the King of England, the Duke of Clarence pleaded 'I should like to drowned in a vat of Beaune wine, so my death is effortless and good.'

Burgundy's Meursault, Puligny and Chassange-Montrachet are also regarded as some of the finest white wines in the world.

The number of double-barrelled names should give rise to caution when buying wine. Villages added the names of their grand-crus; thus the village of Gevrey added Chambertin to its name to become Gevrey-Chambertin.

If you are looking for the finest wine of all, you should choose Le Chambertin as one of the tiny quantity of the grand-crus (great growths) like Le Corton,

Le Musigny, and Le Montrachet.

In 1863, a tiny insect *Phylloxera*, arrived from America and reached Meursault in 1878, ravaging the region and threatening its whole being. Luckily, immunised vines also came from America and the Burgundy wine industry was saved.

In 1934, at the chateau of Clos de Vougeot at Nuits-St-Georges, the Chevaliers de Tastevin was formed. This brotherhood, for those who appreciate and can taste fine wines, has a motto: *'Never in vain, always in wine'*, and 10,000 wine-lovers from all over the world aspire to belong, giving a further boost to the reputation of Burgundy. Maybe the place deserves its leading reputation after all.

NUREMBERG
Germany

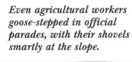

Even agricultural workers goose-stepped in official parades, with their shovels smartly at the slope.

IMPERIAL WAR MUSEUM

Nuremberg or 'Nürnberg' as the Germans call it, has many claims to fame. Before 1927, historians would have linked the city to its 500-year long importance to the Holy Roman Empire; artists would remember Albrecht Dürer; and tourists would appreciate its medieval walls, Gothic churches, gingerbread biscuits and bratwürst sausages and also admire its famous toy makers – among the finest in the world.

But after 1927, the city would forever be associated with the rise and fall of Hitler and the Nazi party. That year Hitler moved the *Parteitage* or 'Party Days' from Munich to Nuremberg, where for the next eleven years they were held every September. In the early years the speeches, parades and music were joined by the 'flag ceremonies', when the original bloodstained party flag from the 1923 Munich Beer Hall Putsch was ceremoniously touched by other flags.

Gradually, the week-long events became more spectacular, with huge stands being designed by Albert Speer and constructed on the Zeppelin Field outside the city, the largest stadium able to contain 400,000 troops and workers.

The 1934 Nuremberg rally was immortalised by the film *Triumph of the Will*, created by Leni Riefenstahl, a brilliant actress turned director who was later to become even more famous for her magnificent film of the 1936 Berlin Olympics. *Triumph of the Will*, captures unforgettably the colossal size and magnificent orchestration of the Nuremberg rallies, and it is easy to imagine how even the most sceptical German would have had difficulty in avoiding being swept along in the euphoria.

While Germany and the world were being dazzled by the ceremonial, the music, the speeches and the torch-light parades, Nuremberg was already associated with something much more sinister. In 1935 and 1938, the Nuremberg Laws moved to isolate the Jews and rob them of their jobs, money and freedom. Soon Hitler's Third Reich would plan to rob them of their lives, with the secret Wannsee conference plotting the murder of the eleven million Jews in Europe.

After Germany's collapse and the Americans' symbolic blowing up of the huge swastika on the grandstand at the Zeppelin Field, it might be thought that the choice of Nuremberg for the 1945 War Crimes Tribunals was in revenge for the city's association with the Nazis. The reason was more mundane. Nuremberg's large Palace of Justice and prison were among the few suitable buildings in Germany undamaged by Allied bombing, which had buried 20,000 civilians under the flattened buildings of Nuremberg alone.

There, the world watched for nine months as the surviving Nazis tried to defend themselves against their monstrous crimes – 218 days, 240 witnesses and 300,000 declarations. As the full horror of the Holocaust emerged, the defendants squirmed, denied knowledge or avoided responsibility, claiming to have been 'just obeying orders'. Goëring would now commit suicide, as Hitler, Goebbels and Himmler had done earlier. Others would hang or be imprisoned. For four years, Nuremberg would witness follow up trials, with justice catching up with hundreds of less famous figures.

The city had truly seen the rise and fall. It is not surprising that its museum,

The Nazi defendants at Nuremberg with a slumped Hermann Goering, perhaps planning his suicide

See: Anne Frank's Annexe, Berchtesgaden, Dachau, Getto, Landsberg, Lidice, Oradour, Reichstag, Wannsee

opened in 2001 by Germany's President with the extraordinarily ponderous title of *DokumentationszentrumReichsparteitagsgalände,* contains a section with the rather shorter and very appropriate *Faszination und Gewalt* – 'Fascination and Violence'.

OK CORRAL
Arizona, USA

Apart from the one in Bethlehem there has probably never been a stable as famous as the OK Corral, located on Fremont Street in Tombstone, Arizona – itself probably the most famous of all American mining towns.

Tombstone was virtually the creation in 1878 of one man, Ed Schieffelin. Hired to guard two men as they carried out assessment work on the old Brunckow mine in the San Pedro Valley, Schieffelin looked over the bleached, grey granite Tombstone Hills and became sure that rich minerals were there. With little money, he struggled until his brother Al, and Dick Gird – a professional assayer – agreed to join him as partners after Gird checked some of the chunks of ore that Ed had found. Further tests revealed silver worth $15,000 a ton – potential fortune.

After many negotiations, deals and partnerships, Tombstone became one of the most spectacular mining centres on earth, with prospectors and miners in a rush like that in California, Nevada and Colorado – followed, naturally, by a rush of lawyers.

The first houses in the town of Tombstone went up in 1879. With only a hundred residents, the local population was really much larger, with suburbs like Hog-em, Goug-em and Stink-em.

But soon, the town had thousands of residents and was booming, with a brewery, two banks, two newspapers – *The Nugget* and *The Epitaph* – a hospital, a school and lots and lots of restaurants, gambling halls and saloons. There were two theatres, Schieffelin Hall and the much racier The Bird Cage, where *Uncle Tom's Cabin* was once being performed

Morgan

Virgil

Wyatt Earp

Doc

when a drunken cowboy shot dead the (real) bloodhound so Eliza could escape!

Tombstone also had one of the world's most aptly-named graveyards, Boot Hill, because so many had died violently – still with their boots on.

Lawlessness was a problem, not helped by smuggling and rustling problems with nearby Mexico, with which even US President Chester Arthur became embroiled. But what was to propel Tombstone into the headlines was the feud between a cowboy faction, the Clantons and McLowerys, backed by Town Sheriff John Behan and the five Earp Brothers. Virgil Earp was City Marshall, and his more famous, dominant brother Wyatt had been a saloonkeeper, cardsharp, policeman, bigamist – and churchwarden. His best friend was the tubercular gambler, Doc Holliday.

What happened at the OK Corral on October 26th 1881 has been glorified by

Hollywood several times, notably with Burt Lancaster as an upright Wyatt Earp and Kirk Douglas as Doc in *Gunfight at the OK Corral.* The truth was rather closer to an ambush of unprepared, defenceless men (see panel). Indeed, citizens draped the coffins with a banner declaring, *'Murdered in the streets of Tombstone'.* The town turned against the Earps.

Six months later, Morgan Earp was shot, and moments after his funeral in Tucson, Wyatt gunned down his killer. Indicted for murder, he left Arizona forever, re-emerging all over the West – and later in the gold rush in Nome, Alaska.

Almost as soon as Tombstone became respectable, its prosperity and its population of 12,000 began to decline. The price of silver dipped, then fires broke out in the mines in 1886, and arguments among the mine owners stopped the pumping and the water rose to cover the lower workings. After $80 million, its days as a silver town were over – a short-lived 'flash in the pan'.

But thanks to romantically distorted books, pulp magazines and several over-imaginative films, Tombstone and its OK Corral will never be forgotten. In a valley of ghost towns, it has at least created a booming tourist industry.

A clean shaven and heroic Burt Lancaster (right) with Kirk Douglas as Doc Holliday in 'Gunfight at The OK Corral'.

See: The Alamo, Chisholm Trail, Nome, Old Kinderhook, Sutter's Mill

'The Earps – Wyatt, Virgil and Morgan – and Doc Holliday had stepped suddenly out on to Fremont Street from the rear entrance of the OK stable lot and immediately commenced firing on the cowboys who were preparing to leave town. Frank McLowery was sitting on his horse and at first fire fell mortally wounded. The other two cowboys lay dead in the street. Tom McLowery had his hands up when a load of buckshot cut him down. It was all over almost as soon as begun. A play enacted by the Earps to wipe out those cowboys under the pretence of enforcing the law – and carried out under the manner of shooting first and reading the warrant to the dead men afterward. But in this case I doubt if there was ever a warrant issued. The Earps called out, 'Hands up' and began firing simultaneously'.

Witness: John P. Gray

OLD KINDERHOOK
New York, USA

There is no American phrase more universally used than 'OK' or 'Okay' and speculation has raged first as to its origins and then why it has stuck. Three United States Presidents are involved in the story. The first was Andrew Jackson, whose poor spelling had been a problem for him in his 1828 campaign. Whig

journalists spread the malicious and probably untrue rumour that Jackson used 'OK' as a short form of O-L-L K-O-R-R-E-C-T. The story grew after the craze in newspapers at the time for faddish abbreviations as in O.K.K.B.W.P (one kind kiss before we part) and deliberate mis-spellings K.N.O.W.U.S.E (no use) or K.K.K. (commit no nuisance).

Forty five years later President Woodrow Wilson believed another Andrew Jackson story, that 'Old Hickory' during his Indian-fighting days had borrowed the word 'OKEY' from the Choktaw Indians. Wilson insisted on writing OKEY on documents to indicate approval, thus perpetuating a Jackson version.

However, it was America's eighth President who was responsible for 'OK' and its rapid growth. Martin Van Buren was a pleasant and even-tempered man, the son of an innkeeper and farmer. He rose to be President Jackson's Secretary of State, and became President himself in 1837. To support him in his 1840 campaign, New York's Tammany Democrats created an OK Club derived from 'Old Kinderhook', based on Van Buren's home town, Kinderhook in New York State. The political OK's were rowdies during the campaign and their behaviour pushed the phrase 'OK' into newspapers across the whole country. Van Buren lost the election and his enemies cruelly dubbed his departure, OK or 'Off to Kinderhook'.

Of the three, it was the most obscure President, Martin Van Buren, and his little home town that finally propelled the initials OK across the world.

NATIONAL PARK SERVICE, MARTIN VAN BUREN NATIONAL HISTORIC SITE.

Martin Van Buren's home at Kinderhook, New York

See: OK Corral, Tammany Hall

OLD TRAFFORD
England

'The most handsomest, the most spacious and the most remarkable arena I have ever seen. As a football ground it is unrivalled in the world, it is an honour to Manchester and the home of a team who can do wonders whenever they are so disposed'.
(Sporting Chronicle:1910)

In their origins, Manchester United were not the worldfamous, showbiz football team that they are today. Originally a small club by the name of Newton Heath, their first ground was North Road – widely known as the worst ground in the league, with a pitch that alternated between rock-solid and water-logged, and with changing rooms half a mile away.

Matters, of course, were to change. First, there was a popular call for the club to be renamed. Originally the name 'Manchester Central' was proposed, but it was decided that this sounded too much like a railway station, so the team's new name became Manchester United. Soon later, thanks to the huge £60,000 investment of J.H. Davies, a new stadium was built, and ready for use by 1910. It was named Old Trafford, the second ground by that name, the first being the Old Trafford Cricket Ground built in 1884, giving Manchester two famous Old Traffords.

The new football stadium was one of the finest in Britain with a capacity of 80,000 and such luxuries as tip-up seats and tea-rooms. However, by the Second World War, little real improvement had been made, and the ground had begun to fall behind. Things took a turn for the worse in 1945, when German bombs, intended for Trafford Park industrial estate, almost destroyed the entire stadium.

In the years following, both the club and their ground have changed beyond recognition. The team went on to include such illustrious names as Duncan Edwards, George Best, Denis Law, Nobby Stiles, Mark Hughes and Eric Cantona. Manchester United have also had two of history's most famous managers, Sir Matt Busby and Sir Alex Ferguson. They have finished top of the Premiership 7 times, and won the FA cup a record 10 times. Probably their finest hour came in 1999, winning the famous treble, and also becoming Premiership League champions, and winners of the FA and Champions League cups. The team is also sadly remembered for the Munich air disaster of 1958, when returning from an

Former star of Old Trafford, David Beckham (right), now transferred to Real Madrid, with Kevin Campbell

away match against the European team Red Star, the plane carrying the team crashed after refuelling in Munich. Almost a whole generation of young star footballers, sometimes named the 'Busby Babes', was wiped out, along with many of the team's staff. It took many years for Manchester United to recover.

The ground itself (dubbed 'The Theatre of Dreams' by Bobby Charlton) has constantly evolved, with the 26,000 seater North Stand now having the largest cantilevered roof in Europe. It has a total capacity of over 68,000, and the long-term plans, which may rebuild the South Stand and fill in the corners of the stadium, could boost it to a massive 90,000. The team has become world famous, with the names of some of its modern generation players – Roy Keane, Ryan Giggs, Ruud Van Nistelrooy, and, of course, David Beckham – becoming household names.

Manchester United is also a symbol of sporting Britain, and their glamour and success are quoted by asylum seekers as prime reasons they want to come to Britain (coupled bizarrely with the strong will of Margaret Thatcher!). They are the most valuable sports team on the London Stock Exchange, reaching a peak market capitalisation of £835 million in 2000.

Football is an ever-changing world, but one thing is certain; Old Trafford's team will continue to be one of the most revered (and most hated) football teams in the world.

See: Augusta, Beckingham Palace, Brescia, Brooklands, Cresta, Henley, Indianapolis, Jodhpur, Le Mans, Lord's, Rugby, Tour de France, Wembley, Wimbledon

OLYMPOS
Greece

Olympos, the reputed seat
Eternal of the gods, which never storms
Disturb, rains drench, or snow invades but calm
The expanse and cloudless shines with purest day
(Homer, Odyssey)

Metaphorically, the concept of Mount Olympos is complicated. Did the ancient Greeks really believe that their gods lived on a mountain? The truth is that they would not have stuck to this concept in a literal fashion, any more than Christians believed that Adam and Eve actually spent most of their lives in a garden.

Belief eventually became associated with one specific mountain range, the Olympos massif, even though many other peaks are named Olympos. Its height makes it a natural choice, with the tallest peak at 2,918 metres disappearing into the clouds, thus forming a bridge into the heavens, a link between the worlds of men and gods. Just as important was the ancient Greek perception that some of the peaks happen to resemble huge chairs – the thrones of the gods.

Olympos is surrounded by a wealth of ancient mythology. Not only was it the seat of divinity, but also the epicentre of cosmic wars. The original god of heaven, Uranos, was overthrown and castrated by his tyrannical son Chronos, in turn banished by Zeus, the ruler of the 'Olympian' gods.

Zeus and his two brothers, Hades and Poseidon, cast lots for possession of the world. Thus Zeus became lord of heaven, Poseidon ruler of the sea, and Hades, who lost out somewhat in this process, was made king of the underworld. Zeus' position was by far the most powerful, and so he became the king of the gods.

Though the gods of Olympos were never again overthrown, they were still occasionally challenged. Most threatening was the invasion of the giants, a barbaric race, in league with monsters known as 'The hundred handers'. Piling mountains together, they made a gigantic ladder all the way up to the summit of Olympos. With the aid of the mortal hero Hercules, the gods managed to repel the invasion, and eventually Zeus toppled the ladder, crushing the giants underneath. So much blood was spilled, that from it, was born a second race of men.

With the arrival of Christianity in Europe, the myths of Olympos were repressed, and began to be forgotten. The large numbers of real pilgrims who came to the mountain began to dwindle. Now, it is visited by a limited number of hikers and tourists, its true significance as a metaphorical link between heaven and earth obscured.

ORADOUR
France

Until one warm summer afternoon in 1944, the Second World War seemed to have passed by the little village of Oradour-sur-Glane. There were no Resistance fighters, the immediate area was peaceful, and the Germans had left the village alone – even though four days earlier the Allies had invaded Normandy two hundred miles to the north.

On Saturday 10th June all that changed. Oradour was crowded with more people than usual. The children from the area were still in school, the farm workers had returned from the fields, fishermen had arrived on the little tram from Limoges to try their luck on the Glane river and some of the professional families were lingering over lunch at the Milord Hotel.

At 2.15, the rumbling arrival of a convoy of trucks and half-tracks full of SS men caused no particular alarm, until the troops, shouting, began to push and jostle the men, women and children into the square called the Champ de Foire. Children were calmly led by their teachers in orderly crocodiles, although one seven year old boy was scared enough to bolt and was pursued by a volley of shots. He pretended to be dead and later made it across the fields to the river.

By 2.45, the terrified and confused villagers stood covered by the German machine guns, ever more fearful now because they could hear sporadic shooting from the outskirts and the fields. Abruptly, the prisoners were divided into groups, the men being herded into garages and barns in groups of fifty, and the women and children, 450 of them, packed into the village church.

The men were asked about arms and 'prohibited merchandise'. At 3.30, a shot rang out. At this signal, howling as in battle, the Germans began to machine-gun the groups of men, finishing off the wounded with single shots – again after questioning them about 'prohibited merchandise'. In the church, the horror was worse. They tossed grenades at the screaming crowd of women, children and babies and then began to machine-gun them. The altar and walls are still pocked obscenely with bullet holes. The church was set on fire, and every single one of Oradour's 254 buildings was blown up.

The next morning, the Germans left – loaded with loot – and the survivors crept back into the village to make the horrifying discovery that all their friends and relatives were dead.

Why did it happen? And why was quiet Oradour chosen for this bestial act?

The perpetrators were from the 2nd SS Panzer Division, *Das Reich*, on the way to Normandy. For them, the savagery itself was of little importance. After all, in Russia they had often committed similar crimes against civilians, and only two days before, at nearby Tulle, 99 Frenchmen had been hanged by them as a reprisal. But the obvious question remains. Why on earth was *Das Reich*, one of Germany's finest armoured divisions, its 15,000 men, 3,000 vehicles and precious Panther tanks desperately needed in Normandy to repel the Allies – wasting time in such a senseless, random act of brutality?

In December 1982, UK businessman, Robin Mackness, best known for his company 'Slumberdown', which introduced the duvet to Britain, was

The ghostly main street, just as it was in 1944, with a tramline that now goes nowhere

Above (top): 450 women and children died in the church.

Above: The local doctor paid with his life when he drove his car into the main square.

Right: General Lammerding, whose lost booty may have caused the massacre.

arrested for trying to smuggle 20 kilos of gold out of France. He was imprisoned for two years for not revealing his client. His client was 'Raoul' – an elderly Frenchman – who was in fact a German Jew who had escaped from Leipzig in 1934. Raoul had asked for help from Mackness – and told an amazing story.

On the night of 9th June 1944, Raoul was with a group of over-eager resistance fighters when a little convoy of a car, a truck and a half-track full of SS men came down a lane. The French attacked, and Raoul was the only survivor – except one German who ran away. The truck contained thirty small wooden boxes, each with a bar of gold. Raoul buried them by the side of the road before setting fire to the wreckage.

What has emerged is that three *Das Reich* officers, General Lammerding, Majors Otto Dickman (who led the massacre) and Helmut Kämpfe, had been carrying out *ratissages*, or raids, ostensibly to find resistance fighters, but actually to loot French gold, of which they now had half a ton. It was planned to be the secret nest egg of Lammerding and his friends for after the war, and when they heard about the ambush, they were desperate to get their booty back.

Nearby Oradour, just four kilometres away, seemed the only likely hiding place – and that is why it was chosen to be attacked. Of course, the tragic inhabitants knew nothing of the 'prohibited merchandise' (the gold) and, after interrogation, paid for their ignorance with their lives.

Today, Oradour has been preserved as a ghost town, exactly as it was in June 1944, a poignant witness to a place chosen by chance, by greed and by mistake.

See: Dachau, Getto, Lidice, Katyn Wood, Masada, Nuremberg

PAMPLONA
Spain

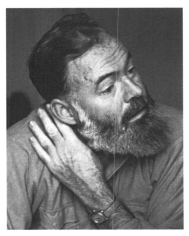

Ernest Hemingway

For centuries the festival of San Fermín has taken place in the Navarre town of Pamplona. But it took one man to bring it to the world's attention.

The Sanfermines were mentioned as early as the thirteenth century, and over the years their religious festival was combined with a commercial fair and then a bullfight series. The attendant revelry could cause tensions - with the clergy in the eighteenth century already complaining of drinking and the 'permissiveness of young men and women'. By the 1800s, fairground attractions included a female cannonball, wax figures and the 'Company of Giants' – and great excitement was added by the frequent sight of bulls escaping from the single-walled bullring, which then ran amok through the streets.

In 1923, Ernest Hemingway first arrived in Pamplona. The now formal 'running of the bulls' impressed him so much that he featured it in his novel *Fiesta*, that we know as *The Sun Also Rises*.

From the 7th until the 14th July, every morning at eight o'clock, a rocket goes up over Pamplona. The six bulls to be fought that afternoon – with two herds of tame bulls – are ready to set off down 325 metres of Pamplona's streets from the Santo Domingo corrals to the bullring. Hundreds of youths dressed in traditional white shirts and red belts, sing three times, 'We ask San Fermín, as our patron, to guide us through the bull run and give us his blessing'. For a very fraught three minutes they run ahead of, and in amongst, the bulls. Thousands of intrepid foreigners join them.

The practice was always dangerous even before such overcrowding. Hemingway witnessed the first fatal goring in 1924 and described it in his book *Death in the Afternoon*. This was the first of fourteen deaths and 200 injuries, some recorded for puzzled and shocked international television audiences.

Hemingway came to Pamplona nine times, a friend of bullfighters like Antonio Ordonez. His *Death in the Afternoon* reflects his passion for the drama of bullfighting, shared with fellow Americans like Orson Welles, Ava Gardner and Arthur Miller.

Pamplona certainly recognises his role in transforming a local, hometown festival into worldwide fame. In the 'Avenida de Ernest Hemingway' there is a monument whose inscription reads:

To Ernest Hemingway, winner of the Nobel Prize for Literature, friend of this town and admirer of its fiestas, which he discovered and made famous. The City of Pamplona. San Fermín 1968.

The running of the bulls

See: Chinchon, Havana

PANAMA
USA

Ferdinand de Lesseps must have felt he was 'on a roll'. First, he had triumphantly completed the Suez Canal, one of mankind's greatest achievements, and now a similar opportunity presented itself in the Americas.

The Isthmus of Panama is in a very important position, the crossroads not only between the Atlantic and Pacific, but also between North and South America. Thus, it was highly valued by the Spanish as a central link and marketplace for their American Empire. Even in the early 1850s the Spanish Government had considered constructing a channel to link the two oceans, to help trade with her colonies in Peru and the Philippines. The massive westward traffic after the Californian gold rush re-awoke the idea, but instead a less effective trans-Isthmian railway was built.

But in the year 1879 the renowned canal builder, Lesseps, began construction. Unfortunately, things were already going wrong. Lesseps had attempted to raise 400 million francs to finance the project, but had only managed to obtain 30 million, an unimpressive eight per cent of the total needed. This would mean that Lesseps, who was now in his seventies, was forced to travel back to France several times to scrape up funds – taking out a number of loans – and even using a lottery to raise capital. But incredibly, these were not the most serious of his problems. Lesseps insisted for a long time that the canal, like Suez, should be at sea-level and contain

no locks, which proved to be impractical. The area itself – hard volcanic rock – proved extremely difficult to cut through, and the bulk of Culebra Mountain was a nigh-on insurmountable obstacle. Worst of all, the workers were ravaged by diseases, the most dangerous of which were caused by the swarming mosquitoes, malaria and yellow fever. A catastrophic toll of almost 30,000 men died. By 1889 Lesseps was transformed from the 'Hero of Suez' to the 'Villain of Panama'. He and his shareholders were ruined, his son was jailed and even the great engineer Eiffel was heavily fined. The project had failed, as had its founder.

The next chapter of the Panama story begins in 1903 with the province's rebellion against its parent country, Colombia. The United States had long expressed an interest in this most well-placed of locations, having noticed that, during the war with Spain, the battleship *Oregon* had taken so long to travel round South America that the war was nearly over. President Theodore Roosevelt, famous for his phrase 'talk quietly and carry a big stick', sent American warships to protect Panama's sovereignty. The new republic had shaken itself free of Colombia, but had become very firmly part of the sphere of influence of the USA. Since Lesseps' failure, thoughts of a trans-American canal had been focused on Nicaragua. Now,

President Theodore Roosevelt proudly astride a crane at Panama

however, William Cromwell and Philippe Bunau-Varilla, the pioneers of the new project, used a range of publicity to ensure that the canal was once again to be located in Panama. The Canal Zone in the Hay-Bunau-Varilla Treaty of 1903 was granted to the USA 'in perpetuity', and the construction was almost ready to begin.

Almost. The errors made by Lesseps could not be repeated. To prevent mosquitoes spreading yellow fever and malaria, methodical efforts had to be made to cover stagnant water with a layer of oil and insecticide. This, as advised by American doctor William Gorgas, would then prevent the mosquitoes from reproducing. It was also made compulsory to put screens on all windows, not just to protect the inhabitants, but to stop them being reservoirs of diseases.

A narrow 'Panamax' sails past the jungles of Panama

See: Botany Bay, Chinchon, Kew, Suez, West Point

The Americans also carried out renovation of the local towns, Panama City and Colon, providing them with decent sewerage and road-paving, decreasing the health risks still further. It was finally time for construction work to begin on the actual canal.

Thirteen years later, with even Culebra Mountain beaten by massive locks, the 51-mile canal was complete – on time and under-budget – a triumph by a team of West Point trained engineers. In August 1914, the concrete ship *Cristobal* was the first vessel to pass from one ocean to another, although the SS *Ancon* was officially the first. The success was somewhat muted by the events in Europe, where the First World War had just begun.

After a long-stirred cocktail of success and failure, effort and ingenuity, the canal has become an incredibly important stretch of water, able to handle almost any ship, except for the largest supertankers. Indeed, there is now a generation of large (but long and thin ships) called 'Panamax', specially designed for the canal. A ship sailing from New York to San Francisco cuts 7,872 miles off its journey by using Panama, which takes only 8-10 hours to traverse. Tolls are charged for using the channel, and even Richard Halliburton, who swam it in 1928, was made to pay a price of 36 cents for the privilege! A total of over 80,000 people had taken part in the canal's construction, and between them, the French and Americans had spent a colossal sum for that time, of $639,000,000. There has been some tension in the relationship between Panama and the United States, ending in the ousting of Manuel Noriega in 1989. Panama's history has certainly not been easy, but it has been remarkable.

PANMUNJOM
Korea

Every day buses leave Seoul, the capital of South Korea, and travel the thirty miles to Panmunjom, loaded with tourists wanting to visit the hut where for nearly two years negotiations dragged on to end the hostilities in Korea.

The fact that it took twice as long to argue as it did to fight is but one of the strange aspects of the tragic and inglorious war which killed two million, including nearly as many Americans as were to perish in Vietnam – in a third of the time. It is theoretically not even over today; only a 'ceasefire' was signed in July 1953.

It started at dawn, on a quiet Sunday, 25th June 1950, when tanks and infantry of Kim Il-Sung's Communist North Korea poured across the border of the 38th Parallel. South Korea's inexperienced forces reeled back, and the intervention of its ally, the United States, was hardly propitious. The American army in Korea and Japan was a half-trained garrison; many of the troops had simply enlisted for the educational opportunities. They found themselves fleeing from the Soviet and Chinese-trained North Koreans just as fast, as far and as ignominiously as their allies. Only American airpower saved a desperate situation and helped to stabilise a defensive line way down south round the port of Pusan. United Nations forces also began to arrive to help, including the British.

America's General Douglas

American gunners at one of the desperate battles in Korea

MacArthur had accepted the surrender of the Japanese in 1945, and was now their ruler; a regal and revered 'shogun'. Despite being 70 years old, he rose to the Korean challenge. Against advice from all sides, he staged a daring and brilliant landing at Inchon, near Seoul, halfway up the country. The North Koreans were soon in full retreat back up the peninsular, trying to escape being cut off by his trap.

But then the Allies went too far, crossing the 38th parallel and advancing northwards with the Yalu River, the Chinese border, in their sights – which they reached on 25th October. Communist China, through various channels, had tried to warn the Americans not to continue. In vain. The Chinese then infiltrated 130,000 troops through the snow and, on 1st November, struck the leading American forces, backing off, however, after a few days. Amazingly, the warnings of a *'real new enemy and a real new war'* were not heeded. On 24th November, the Americans were eating their lavish turkeys 'with all the trimmings', specially flown in for Thanksgiving Day. The very next day the Chinese, with thirty divisions – 300,000 men – attacked from where they had been carefully hidden in the snowy mountainous spine of Korea.

Briefly, there was contemptuous and ridiculous Allied talk of 'not being afraid of Chinese laundrymen', ignoring the fact that most Chinese troops had been fighting all their lives. In the west, the allied armies collapsed, and in panic, 'bug-out fever' took hold. One American Colonel said to his Executive Officer, 'Look around here. This is a sight that hasn't been seen for hundreds of years: the men of the whole United States Army fleeing from the battlefield, abandoning their wounded, running for their lives'.

In the east, the US Marine Corps, with British Royal Marines fighting with them, performed much better, conducting an orderly, if murderous, retreat. Soon they were all back to the 38th parallel, and all this had happened in less than six months. When a shaken MacArthur insisted on a wider war, perhaps with atomic weapons and then, against orders, took his views to the media, President Truman dramatically dismissed him.

In spite of fresh attacks by the Chinese and North Koreans, especially at the Imjin River where the British 'Glorious Glosters' fought so well, the war gradually became a stalemate and at Panmunjom, on the original parallel, some huts were erected. There, for months and months, negotiators tried to make the unofficial ceasefire work, arguing mostly about 50,000 allied prisoners who had gone missing. The trouble was not over. Hostilities kept flaring up, bombing and aerial dogfights continued, Chinese offensives and vicious battles like 'Pork Chop Hill' raged. While talks ground on with agonising slowness, elsewhere the world moved on. Mau Mau terrorism had started in Kenya; Britain's Winston Churchill was back at Number 10; George VI had died and his daughter Elizabeth had become Queen; Gene Kelly had delighted US audiences with *Singing in the Rain;* 'Little Mo' Connolly had won Wimbledon; King Farouk of Egypt was deposed; the 1952 Olympics had taken place in Helsinki; Nixon had made his 'Checkers' TV speech; Ike had won the election; America had exploded the H bomb; Stalin had died; Marilyn Monroe had posed in the nude; and Hillary and Tensing had conquered Everest.

But only in July 1953 was the Panmunjom truce signed. One year of real fighting and two years of talking and still, fifty years later, the two Koreas are glaring at each other across the fortified parallel, while tourists are happily visiting the nondescript set of huts at Panmunjom to look at a green baize table with a microphone cable which still marks the official border.

See: Bonus City, Corregidor

The talks at Panmunjom dragged on for nearly two years before the ceasefire was signed.

PEARL HARBOR
Hawaiian Islands

To the farmers working in the rice fields of Oahu, the planes looked no different from usual as they roared overhead. If they had looked more carefully they might have noticed the red circles on the wings. But then not enough people were being careful on that Sunday morning of 7th December 1941, 'a date that will live in infamy' and which propelled the name 'Pearl Harbor' onto the lips of the whole world.

Pearl Harbor, part of the Hawaiian archipelago, was first discovered by the British explorer Captain James Cook, who called them the Sandwich Islands after the Earl of Sandwich. The islands were to cost Cook his life, for it is said that he was stabbed during a quarrel about his sailors using the precious iron nails that held together their boats to pay for sexual favours from the beautiful Hawaiian girls. There really were pearls at the deep estuary called 'Wai Momi' (River of Pearls), but their beds were soon exhausted and then poisoned by polluted run-off from the hills, first from sandalwood and later sugar production.

It was the vast natural anchorage, the best for 2,000 miles in any direction, which made Pearl Harbor desirable, and then essential, for the United States, especially after its acquisition of the Philippines from Spain. Its harbour was dredged, and it became a huge military and naval base.

So on that fateful December morning in 1941, over a hundred ships lay at anchor, including eight battleships moored alongside Ford Island in the middle of the estuary. Vast fuel storage tanks, repair facilities and dry docks were theoretically protected by aircraft and even newly-acquired radar sets.

For what happened next, there are many to blame. First, of course, the Japanese, whose Army war faction, under General Hideki Tojo, 'The Razor', was determined to thwart the peace efforts of moderate Prime Minister Prince Konoye. The army, trained in the previous century by the Germans, had a narrow, insular attitude, leading to over confidence. The Japanese Arms intended to continue its brutal war against China, America's friend, and moreover to seize the rich resources of the colonies of the defeated French and Dutch, and of the distracted and embattled British.

The Japanese Navy, formerly trained by the British, had always acted as a restraint. Well-travelled and familiar with a wider world, it knew the huge military and industrial potential of America, a country with, for instance, twelve times the steel industry of Japan.

The architect of the Pearl Harbor attack, Admiral Isoroku Yamamoto – educated at Harvard and formerly Assistant Naval Attaché in Washington – knew full well that Japan would lose a protracted war, but finally persuaded himself that one bold strike, 'a fatal blow', might succeed.

On then to US President Franklin D. Roosevelt and Secretary of State Cordell Hull, who cut off Japan's supply of vital scrap metal and aviation fuel, and then ignored their experienced Ambassador in Tokyo, Joseph Grew, when he tried to advise them of how to help Konoye against the war faction. Konoye duly lost power to Tojo.

We can also blame the Japanese Foreign service. When the vital 14-part coded signal breaking off negotiations arrived at the Embassy in Washington, the staff paused in their decoding efforts to go to a party, then assigned

Japanese 'Val' dive-bombers turn towards Ford Island.

TONY COWLAND

security-cleared but slow amateur typists to prepare the document. Their Ambassadors, Normura and Korusu, were not told that the raid was imminent. The result was that they delivered the Declaration of War more than an hour after the raid had actually begun, stimulating fury.

We can also blame US Intelligence Services. The Army and Navy had done a brilliant job in decoding Japanese signals and then, as usual, did not talk to each other. The commanders at Pearl Harbor, traditionally a relaxed, 'cushy billet', must also take their share, although perhaps not as much as was assigned to them. Admiral Husband Kimmel and General Walter Short were warned repeatedly, if incompletely, of a potential attack. Yet ships had no torpedo nets out, ammunition was locked up, planes were parked wingtip to wingtip, radar sets were manned only part-time and, above all, not a single reconnaissance flight was made.

And when one of the new radar sets did pick up 150 planes coming in from the north, we have to blame poor young Lieutenant Kermit Tyler, who, assuming they were 12 American B-17s from San Diego, told its operators to switch off and get some breakfast, adding one of the most memorable lines in warfare, 'Well, don't worry about it!'

Whoever was to blame, 235 miles to the north, after an undetected voyage of nearly 4,000 miles, six aircraft carriers had turned into wind and launched 350 dive-bombers, torpedo bombers and fighters. At 7.49 am, after flying for 90 minutes, Commander Fuchida tapped out his famous 'Tora, Tora, Tora' signal, indicating complete surprise, and proceeded to reduce much of Pearl Harbor to a shambles. 300 of the 400 American planes were destroyed or damaged, lined up on the ground. All eight of the battleships were sunk or damaged , together with several other ships. In just a few minutes 2,400 Americans were dead and 1,178 were wounded. America was propelled into war.

In England, when the BBC News vaguely reported 'some kind of attack' to a stunned group at the Prime Minister's house at Chequers, Winston Churchill did not even know where Pearl Harbor was, and even muttered, 'It must be the Pearl River in China', until Ambassador

Averell Harriman put him right and Roosevelt came on the line to confirm it. In spite of his horror, Churchill saw at once that what he had been trying to achieve for months had now occurred as a result of Japan's rashness. As he later wrote: '*No American will think it wrong of me if I proclaim that to have the United States at our side was to me the greatest joy. I could not foretell the course of events. I do not pretend to have measured accurately the martial might of Japan, but now at this very moment I knew the United States was in the war, up to the neck and in to the death. So we had won after all!'*

The shambles of sunken ships

Ultimately, Pearl Harbor was a Japanese failure, strategically and even tactically. The vital fuel tanks and repair facilities were untouched, and several of the battleships were re-floated. Above all, the three American aircraft carriers, which had been luckily saved by being at sea, would soon defeat the Japanese at Midway only seven months later.

Yamamoto himself recognised that the treacherous attack had backfired, '*I am afraid that all we have done is to wake a sleeping giant and fill him with a terrible resolve*'.

But for Japan's risky and ultimately suicidal move, Pearl Harbor might have remained just a naval base like San Diego. As it was, so ingrained is the sneak attack in the American psyche that when sixty years later Bin Laden's Al Qaeda suicide planes hit the World Trade Center and the Pentagon on 11th September 2001, it was hardly surprising that everyone should at once call it 'a second Pearl Harbor'. The sorry revelations of the intelligence failures slowly emerging since Nine Eleven make the comparison doubly apt.

The Pearl Harbor memorial built over the wreck of the battleship Arizona

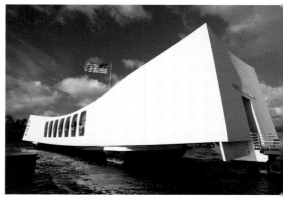

See: Corregidor, Hiroshima, Kohima, Midway, Tsushima, World Trade Center

PEENEMÜNDE
Germany

Soon after the beginning of the Second World War, a mysterious parcel was delivered to the British Embassy in Norway. The 'Oslo Report' found its way to Professor R.V. Jones, Britain's leading scientific intelligence expert. The parcel contained a glass tube, the very advanced electronic trigger for Germany's anti-aircraft proximity fuses, together with a huge amount of other secret information, and the very first mention of rockets and an unknown place called Peenemünde.

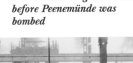

V-2 rockets being assembled before Peenemünde was bombed

R.V. Jones took it very seriously, but for a while the army, navy and airforce Ministries considered it a hoax or 'plant'. Soon everyone, including Winston Churchill would learn to listen more carefully to R.V. Jones. He was to unmask the secrets of *Knickebein* and the other beams that guided German bombers, new radar systems; 'Heavy Water' for making atomic bombs and, above all, the V-1 and V-2, Hitler's *Vergeltungswaffe* (revenge) weapons, which were tested and perfected at Peenemünde. Two German Generals, Von Arnim and Cruewell, were recorded in British captivity: 'Wait till next year and the fun with the rockets will begin'.

The RAF bombing the secret Peenemünde testing station

FRANK WOOTTON

Gradually, the significance grew of Peenemünde – the tip of the Usedom Peninsular on the Peene river. General Dornberger and his brilliant colleague Werner von Braun and their élite scientific team needed a safe, secret testing range. Peenemünde was ideal, facing 200 miles of open water up the Baltic.

Foreign labourers added to the flood of reports about Peenemünde. Jerzy Chmielewski, the head of Poland's underground army, cycled 200 miles with recovered rocket parts in a sack which were to be flown to London. Intercepts of Enigma codes discovered that Peenemünde was even being given priority for petrol coupons, and *Würzburg* monitoring radars were detected being installed down the coast. Peenemünde was indeed a hive of activity, with the cream of German scientists and many hundreds of foreign workers labouring to make the *Heeresversuchsanstalt* or 'Army Proving Site' a success for the supposed 'war-winning' V-1 and V-2.

Reconnaissance Spitfires came back with pictures on which the skilful eyes of Flight Lieutenant Constance Babington-Smith found a V-1; a small, strange, aircraft on what looked like a 'ski-ramp'. Then, R.V. Jones discovered V-2s standing vertically.

The V-1 was to be the first 'cruise missile' - a simple, cheap, pilotless aircraft propelled by a ramjet at 400 mph and launched from a steam catapult. The V-2 was much more sophisticated, the first ballistic missile, bursting through the stratosphere at 3,500 mph. Both weapons, with one ton warheads, were destined for the sprawling target of London.

Now thoroughly alarmed, in August 1943 the RAF struck Peenemünde with 500 bombers, wrecking the facilities, killing 130 German scientists and, sadly, 600 foreign workers – some of whom were providing vital information.

Werner von Braun survived, bravely rescuing the drawings from the flames. The raid delayed the programme by a vital 2 months, as did the Allies' massive bombing of

the sinister 'ski-sites' now mushrooming along the French and Belgian coasts and the railways on which agents reported trainloads of V-1s.

The first products of Peenemünde hit London on 13th June, seven days after D-Day. On 15th June, 200 V-1s were launched. The 'Doodle-bug' droned in like an old motorbike until, when the fuel cut off, there were terrifying seconds of silence before a huge explosion shattered whole city blocks.

British and American fighters had to learn how to knock them down, shooting them or tipping up their wings with their own. Frantically, 800 anti-aircraft guns with 23,000 men and women were moved to the coast. The bombing of the 'ski-sites' intensified, and 'Tallboy' earthquake bombs collapsed the storage caves, burying the waiting bombs. The planned 7,000 flying bombs a day never achieved a tenth of their aim and the defences worked. R.V. Jones also tricked

the Germans into making the V-1s drop short, despite Herbert Morrison's objections that, *'Kensington, Westminster and Belgravia were being spared at the expense of more South London proletarian boroughs!'* But it saved lives.

Then, on 8th September, a strange double bang echoed across London, the first V-2. Supersonic, it arrived without warning. More than a thousand were to follow until the Allied forces pushed the Germans out of range, meaning that Antwerp was hit more than London.

In the final days of the war, Werner von Braun and his top scientists cleverly surrendered to the Americans – and he became the 'father of the US space programme.' The Red army captured Peenemünde and destroyed it. A restricted area still, it is covered in grass and trees with only the odd sign of its former worldwide significance.

The V-2, the world's first ballistic missile

See: Biggin Hill, Bletchley Park, Cape Canaveral, Guernica, Hiroshima

PEYTON PLACE
New Hampshire, USA

Peyton Place, the mythical New England 'small town USA', was the setting for an extraordinary publishing phenomenon. The novel written by Grace Metalious in 1956 was a blockbuster. *Peyton Place* lifted the lid on the shocking goings-on in a small New Hampshire town and has been described as *'probably the most controversial novel ever written'*.

Not only did it become the biggest selling novel to date, but it spawned a motion picture; a sequel; *Return To Peyton Place;* a movie of the sequel; a long running TV series; plus a day-time soap opera and two TV films.

The first film, directed by Mark Robson and released in 1957, starred amongst other notables Lana Turner, Arthur Kennedy, Hope Lange, Diane Varsi, Russ Tamblyn, and Lorne Greene. The film and several of the cast were nominated for 'Oscars'. The 1961 sequel, was directed by Jose Ferrer and featured the likes of Jeff Chandler, Brett Halsey, Carol Lynley, Eleanor Parker, Mary Astor, and young newcomer Tuesday Weld. The TV series was also a great hit, running to 514 episodes from 1964 to

1969, and boosting the career of Dorothy Malone and launching Mia Farrow and Ryan O'Neal to stardom.

Why the success? It was probably not the writing style since Grace Metalious, born Grace De Repentigny, was castigated by the literary world for its poor quality. Some claimed that she was not even the real author, and had more than a little help from her good friend, journalist Laurie Wilkens.

But the fact was that its scandalous nature meant that a literary storm was created. Well brought-up young people – whose reading habits were subject to parental or school control – found themselves wrapping the book in plain paper or reading it covertly under the bedclothes, with a torch. One prissy girls' school in England even paraded one poor pupil at Assembly for the crime of having *Peyton Place* in her possession. And the contents? Just the everyday story of the goings-on in a small New England town, but with characters who indulge in rather more than their fair share of hanky-panky. Pretty tame by today's standards.

Mia Farrow and Dorothy Malone

See: Albert Square, Ambridge, Coronation Street, Ramsay Street, Truth or Consequences

PILSEN
Czech Republic

It was King Wenceslas II, a successor to the 'Good King' in our carols, who pointed the 260 citizens of the tiny town of New Pilsen in western Bohemia towards their destiny. In 1295, he gave them the right to make beer and to sell it from their houses. The citizens used this privilege well, building their first brewery twelve years later, followed by joint breweries and a community malthouse.

Soon, they created guilds to pass on the accumulated knowledge and a great tradition had been born. But Pilsen could have remained just another brewing centre like Dortmund in Germany or Burton-on-Trent in England, with Pilsner quality being not even particularly good. But, in 1839, two hundred Pilsner brewers decided to improve the standards and make a real change from their traditional top-fermentation system to the bottom-fermentation process favoured by Bavaria.

They also decided to build a new brewery – and to recruit a new master brewer, Josef Groll. The combination of his experimental genius and the unique

See: Champagne, Cognac, Nuits-St-Georges

Czech malt, hops, and the very soft Pilsen water produced a new, clear, light beer, Pilsner Urquell (German for 'original source'). This beer emerged in 1842 and was to change the whole pattern of brewing, partly because the recent introduction of mass-produced clear drinking glasses favoured a clear, golden and attractive beer. The new understanding of yeast fermentation, coupled with the 'lagering' process at low temperature which was perfected at Pilsen, has created what we now call Pils, Pilsner or, more simply, ninety per cent of what we now call lager beer. Railway distribution also ensured that the new product's popularity spread very quickly, and soon emigrants took it all over the world. Chicago even has a neighbourhood called Pilsen.

Today, most of the world's great brands – Heineken, Becks, Coors, Stella Artois, Fosters, Carlsberg, Miller, and even Budweiser, (which originally came from nearby Ceské Budejovice), all trace their origins to the little Czech town whose wise King gave them such encouragement.

PILTDOWN
England

In 1856, when the first Neanderthal fossil was discovered, scientists the world over threw themselves into the quest to find remains of our distant ancestors. The case of the 'Piltdown Man' illustrates just how keen scientists were to discover the 'missing link'; an ancient creature that would mark the mid-point of evolution between ape and man.

Between 1912 and 1917, a number of fossils were found in the Piltdown quarries in Sussex. As the findings were collected, it became increasingly apparent that the site contained the remains of an animal with a large, human cranium, but also the long jaw of an ape.

Furthermore, some of the teeth were worn down in the manner of human teeth, not that of an ape. Although many

scientists were sceptical, particularly French and American palaeontologists, the Piltdown Man's mix of features seemed to fulfil all the expected criteria of the long-awaited 'missing link'. The new genus was named *Eoanthropus dawsoni* after Charles Dawson, the amateur archaeologist who had discovered the fossils.

However, as other remains of early man were found around the world – such as 'Peking Man' – the 'Piltdown Man' increasingly failed to fit into the growing picture of humanity's evolution. By 1950 it was being predominantly ignored by the scientific community, and in 1953 it was barely mentioned at all at the prestigious international conference of palaeontologists.

Nevertheless, though interest in the

fossil was dwindling, the possibility of outright forgery had not been conceived. However, a new dating technique, called the *'fluorine absorption test'* had become available in 1949, and in 1953 had revealed that the bones were not old enough for 'Piltdown Man' to be an ancestor of humans. Furthermore, upon microscopic examination, the teeth were found to have a criss-cross scratching pattern. As scientist Le Gros Clark wrote, *The evidence of artificial abrasion immediately sprang to the eye.*

It turned out that the skull bone was from a human, and the jaw from a modern orangutan. The bones had been soaked in a solution which made them appear convincingly old.

This most famous of hoaxes threw up a large lists of suspects, ranging from Charles Dawson himself, W.J. Solass, a professor of geology at Oxford, and even Arthur Conan Doyle, the creator of Sherlock Holmes and author of *The Lost World.* However, the evidence for each case is fairly circumstantial, and today we are no closer to discovering the perpetrator of the hoax.

Whoever created the Piltdown man must have had a comprehensive understanding of palaeontology and biology. Furthermore, he or she must have made the effort to plant the evidence diligently over a number of years. Even more intriguing is the lack of conventional motives, such as the desire to make money by selling the fossil, or even to confirm the theories of a researcher. This makes it even harder to theorise as to the daring culprit.

So why was the deception so successful? One vital reason is that scientists were not actually allowed to examine the evidence. The bones themselves were locked away in the British Museum, and anyone wanting to look at the 'Piltdown Man' had to make do with plaster moulds, which gave nothing away. Also, the technique of fluorine absorption testing was not invented until 1949, so the age of the bones could not be precisely tested.

However, it is crucial to understand that the reasons behind the long life of the hoax were not solely practical and scientific, but also psychological. The scientific community was simply not prepared to believe that someone would be so malicious as to manufacture such a web of lies. Furthermore, scientists wanted to believe that 'the missing link' had been discovered; it fitted every theory of evolution that they had espoused, and especially seemed to confirm that man's large brain had evolved before any of his other features, casting intelligence as the factor which has allowed humanity to evolve so far. Seen by some as proof that science can never be trusted, by others as a blip caused by deficient palaeontological technique, the 'Piltdown Man' lived a long, illustrious life as one of the world's most famous and successful hoaxes.

A curator from the British Museum pronounces that the Piltdown skull in fact comprises the remains of a relatively modern human and an orang-utan.

See: Baker Street, Cro-Magnon, Neanderthal

PISA
Italy

All over the Christian world, there are bell towers; steeples in Britain, campaniles in Italy, and many more – all symbols of faith. Unluckily, or maybe luckily, ground subsidence caused one of them to start leaning over, making it one of the most famous and most recognizable buildings in the world.

Pisa was one of the trading cities of Italy, with its wealth based upon its mercantile strength, and its fate locked in continuous trading and military rivalry with other cities – particularly Florence.

The bell tower of Pisa was designed as a dramatic gesture, part of a group of buildings called the 'Piazza de Miracolo',

comprising the cathedral, baptistry and cemetery. Just how dramatic it was emerged almost immediately after construction began in 1173, when a pronounced lean appeared in the structure. Builders tried to compensate, but the lean then reversed the other way. The tower took a very long time to complete, no less than two hundred years, because of interruptions caused by wars with Florence and Genoa, with the bells only being installed in 1392. Already the lean was 2.5 per cent from the vertical.

The problem arose because the tower is built on an ancient river bed of soft, sandy soil and the foundation is too shallow for

a structure of 14,000 tons. Despite all efforts to correct it, the lean increased, making 'The Leaning Tower of Pisa' a splendid tourist attraction. During 1989, when the lean was 5.5 per cent, a million visitors climbed its 294 steps, but experts then warned that it was now too dangerous. For twelve years it was closed, while methods were worked out to stop the lean and even to straighten it, just enough to preserve the building, but not enough to ruin its tourism appeal.

It was a British engineering team who came up with the complex solution. First, 870 tons of lead weights were placed on the north (higher) side of the tower's base. Then, steel bands were wrapped around the first vulnerable level, and in addition a giant belt was looped round the whole building and anchored to blocks hundreds of feet away.

Finally, forty one tubes were sunk diagonally into the earth, and drills were inserted which very carefully removed tons of soil over many months. Little by little, the tower settled back on to the reducing soil, eventually stopping at a 5 per cent lean.

In June 2001, with a great fanfare, the tower was re-opened to the public on the Feast of Pisa's patron saint, San Ranieri. Now guaranteed for three hundred years, 'The Leaning Tower of Pisa' has kept its unique drawing power to those who lean towards the Christian faith, or simply as a building that should never have survived the course of time.

POMPEII
Italy

'Many raised their hands to the gods, and even more believed that there were no gods any longer, and that this was one last unending night of the world'.

(Pliny the Younger, letter 6.20)

CLARE SUTTON

Thus did Pliny the Younger describe to Tacitus the eruption of Vesuvius in 79 AD. It remains our best report of Europe's most famous volcanic disaster. He and his mother ran through the streets of nearby Misenum, filled with people panicking at the darkness that the volcano had brought. His uncle, Pliny the Elder, was killed by the eruption. As Commander of the fleet at Misenum, he had sailed to Pompeii (against the advice of his ship's Captain), hoping to rescue survivors, and the thick cloud of descending ash choked up the old man's weak lungs. The ash buried the nearby towns of Stabiae, Herculaneum, and most famously Pompeii, under 20 to 100 feet of mud and ash. These towns had prospered primarily because volcanic ash makes land very fertile and Pompeii, especially, had a standard of living unrivalled for centuries. The pressure build-up had already caused an earthquake in 62 AD, but most of the inhabitants of the surrounding area were unaware that Vesuvius even was a volcano. The eventual eruption was so savage that six cubic miles of the mountain were blown off and spread over the entire region at over 100 mph. Pompeii was buried so quickly that thousands were caught before they had any chance to evacuate. Those that were not killed by the toxic gases were crushed by a weight of ash so huge that it smashed in roofs and walls. The forms of those trapped have been preserved in the volcanic pumice, and plaster casts made by archaeologists show them chillingly contorted in their final agonising moments. More than three thousand people were killed. It is unsurprising that, as Pliny tells us, so many lost all faith in the gods.

So deeply was Pompeii buried that it was almost two millennia before it was re-discovered. The abruptness of the disaster made Pompeii fascinating for archaeologists as, preserved by the volcanic rock, it gives us a unique view of Roman life.

Vesuvius has erupted many times since killing 18,000 people in 1794. Worryingly, scientists feel that it could erupt again. It is not an extinct volcano, merely in what volcanologists call 'quiescence' or rest. The estimated casualties of a similar eruption in today's crowded Gulf of Naples would be around three million, almost a thousand times those killed in Pompeii.

See: Atlantis, Krakatoa, Mount St. Helens, Nome

PROMONTORY SUMMIT
Utah, USA

The 'Great Race' was nearly over. From east and west two armies, well-drilled and organised, were steadily approaching each other. But they were not there to fight. They were there to meet and to complete one of the greatest feats in American history. And, by chance, the place was to be a lonely, arid desert of sagebrush in Utah called Promontory.

Two railroads – the Union Pacific, starting from Omaha, Nebraska, and the Central Pacific – starting from Sacramento, California – were about to link the east and west Coasts of America. Both had to overcome enormous difficulties; technical, political and financial. Both were controlled by small groups of powerful men who created lucrative construction companies 'on the side' which were to make them very rich, but would later taint the railroads with scandal. Both had used bribery and political favours described by a wit in Washington as *'scrupulously dishonest'*. Both had rushed the frantic track laying, and even made it longer – in order to cash in on the Federal loans awarded for each mile of track laid, and the land grants which would finally net them 21 million acres, the equivalent of Vermont, Massachusetts and Connecticut. Both would struggle with the understandably suspicious Indian tribes and with the desperate terrain, whether the snows and mountains of the Sierras or the waterless plains. Every mile counted financially and politically. No wonder it was called the 'Great Race'.

On 28th April, 1869, just before the meeting at Promontory, the Central Pacific even staged 'Ten Mile Day' for a $10,000 bet with their Union Pacific rivals. Eight husky Irishmen – backed by their Chinese colleagues – laid a record ten miles of track in twelve hours, spiking 3,520 rails to 25,800 cross ties, and with rail handlers each lifting 250,000 pounds of iron rail.

So frenetic had the race become that first the surveying teams passed each other by 200 miles, and then the grading teams actually overlapped – even laying down parallel road beds. Someone had

to stop this wasteful rivalry, and U.S President Grant stepped in, forcing an all-night meeting in Washington between the companies, which decided that Promontory should be the place where the lines would meet.

At Promontory, on 8th May, the Central Pacific's group was ready for the ceremony, but the Union Pacific's team was apparently delayed by a 'washed out track'. In fact, U.P.'s Dr Thomas Durant had actually been kidnapped by his own furious unpaid track workers in Wyoming, and was not released until the wages were wired through.

On 10th May, construction workers and dignitaries duly assembled, complete with four infantry companies and two bands. Two locomotives, C.P.'s *Jupiter* and U.P.'s *No. 119*, faced each other across the last rail gap. Special gold and silver spikes were ready, together with an iron one linked to the telegraph key to alert the nation. C.P.'s Leland Stanford raised the silver sledge hammer – and missed. So did Thomas Durant. Finally, U.P.'s Grenville Dodge slammed it in, and the telegraph tapped out DONE. While the hundreds of

Hundreds of spectators, four infantry companies, two bands, two locomotives and two dogs gather for the 'joining of the rails' on May 10th 1869.

291

spectators at Promontory celebrated with champagne, whiskey and beer, the rest of the country went wild. In Chicago, a seven mile parade jammed the streets, a hundred guns roared a salute in New York and Wall Street suspended business.

The railroads were to create and form America, and for many decades were the most significant social, political and economic influences on the continent. However, Promontory, like so many railroad towns, never grew big. In 1965,

See: Greenwich, Rock Island, Stockton and Darlington

the Golden Spike National Historic Site was created and four years later the Centennial drew 28,000 visitors, including John Wayne. Fittingly, there is now a museum complete with replicas of the two locomotives.

As San Francisco's Bret Harte's first verse of his poem asks:
What was it the Engines said,
Pilots touching, – head to head
Facing on the single track,
Half a world behind each back?

PUDDING LANE
England

The London of 1666 was, in many ways, an accident waiting to happen. While the skyline was magnificent, with the old St. Paul's Cathedral and 109 parish churches pushing their bell towers and spires above the houses, a closer look would have presented a desperate picture. While there were large halls and mansions – built by aristocratic nobles, merchant adventurers, wealthy tradesmen and the guild and livery companies – much of the city was mean and squalid with tortuous, dark, evil smelling ways. Crowded and densely packed timber-framed dwellings were built on a web of cobbled streets, an open channel ran down the centre of lanes into which householders threw their kitchen water, refuse and garbage. Worse still, the overlapping storeys above these evil-smelling streets meant that there was often only a narrow shaft of daylight piercing through to the fetid scene below. Little wonder that, in these overcrowded and insanitary conditions, the Great Plague had recently killed

56,000 people in the City of London.

The Great Fire of London was thus not entirely unexpected. King Charles II himself had repeatedly written to the Lord Mayor, warning of the dangers, seers had foretold of fire, and preachers had promised, 'Repent or burn'. There was even a plot by Republicans that envisaged setting fire to the city. But in the event, it was nothing more than an accident that caused the famous conflagration.

Pudding Lane, one of the narrowest streets in the city, was a line of tottering houses running down a steep hill towards the Thames. The houses were timber-built, old and dry, and the wood was coated with pitch. One resident, the King's baker called Farynor, had gone to bed thinking that his oven was safely damped down. However, at 2 o'clock in the morning, he awoke with his house full of smoke – and he and his wife and daughter escaped by climbing through a window and across a roof to reach a neighbouring house. His maidservant - not so brave - remained behind, and became the first victim of the fire.

At first, the fire went slowly but after an hour, hay in the yard of the Star Inn opposite blazed up. Gradually, the flames moved down Pudding Lane and Fish Street Hill towards the river quays, engulfing the first church. London's Lord Mayor, Sir Thomas Bloodworth, arrived on the scene after only an hour, and at first was confident that this was just one of the many regular fires that would soon be under control. 'A woman could piss it out' he said. But he had not

allowed for the fact that the flames were carried by a rising wind down to Thames Street. Here was the perfect place to start a real conflagration – in the cellars and warehouses with their stores of tallow, oil, spirits and hemp – and on the open wharves with their hay, timber and coal. Luckily, the fire did not cross Old London Bridge to the other side, and burned itself out after destroying the Gate Tower. However, less good news was that the bridge road was blocked, and no one could cross the river to combat the flames. For a while, the shaken Mayor hesitated to pull down houses to create a fire-break, worrying about 'who would pay to renew them'. As a result, the fire rapidly became unstoppable and, eventually, even St. Paul's Cathedral was consumed, its stones splitting apart in explosions and throwing chunks of up to a hundred pounds in weight a considerable distance. Molten lead poured from the six acres of lead on the roof, and ran down the streets in a red stream. The bankers hurried their gold away from Lombard Street, but the shopping area of Cheapside was gone in an afternoon.

Gradually, the wind fell. By the Wednesday night it was dead calm, and the fire came under control at last. One after the other the burning buildings were successively extinguished.

There is a famous epigram that says 'the Fire of London began in Pudding Lane and ended at Pie Corner'. Unfortunately, the fire burned a long way after Pie Corner had been levelled to the ground.

The Great Fire of London raged for four days and four nights, but on the Thursday the sun rose over a still smoking city and the exhausted people could rest. The whole city was covered in ash and dirt – sometimes inches thick. About 450 acres of housing had been burned, over 13,000 houses were destroyed in 400 streets and 87 parish churches were also destroyed. So many people were ruined or made destitute that four debtors' prisons had to be built. But, incredibly, only six people died.

While a tragic event, the Great Fire destroyed a thoroughly unsuitable and dangerously insanitary warren of houses – unworthy of a great city. Much of the city was soon rebuilt, dominated by a magnificent new St. Paul's Cathedral designed by Sir Christopher Wren.

In 1940, the Luftwaffe came to London, and its bombs did a fair job of emulating the destruction of the Great Fire. Once again, huge gaps appeared between the buildings.

Today, the City of London is almost unrecognisable, with glass and steel monuments to mark its position as one of the world's leading financial services centres. Only the names of streets and tube stations remain to remind us of the city that burned down by chance.

See: Biggin Hill, Fleet Street, Triangle Shirtwaist Company

PULLMAN
Illinois, USA

Nobody could ever accuse George Pullman of not being an innovator.

It was Pullman who brought long awaited and inexpensive comfort to America's railways. In 1864, his *Pioneer* sleeping car appeared with his ingenious system of the upper berths – which were let down for night time travel, and folded away during the day.

Four years later his first dining car, called *Delmonico*, appeared, named after the famed New York gourmet restaurant. Pullman was soon leasing his cars to railroads all over the country, fully staffed and equipped by his Pullman Palace Car Company. His dining cars set culinary standards as superb as the finest big city restaurants, with 12-course meals not unusual. Another Pullman custom, paternalistic but self-serving, was his almost exclusive hiring of black staff – whose smiling helpfulness became a legend for a century.

In 1880, George Pullman decided on another innovation for his workers - the ultimate 'company town.' He purchased 4,000 acres in open prairie near Chicago, put up a new factory and surrounded it with houses, all with indoor plumbing, gas and electricity, and built by company workshops and Pullman employees. The broad, tree-lined streets and parks of Pullman, Illinois were very pleasantly landscaped and there was a gas works, a

hotel, library, theatre, post office, schools, parks and a tree nursery.

For ten years it seemed to work, but there were some drawbacks to this rather claustrophobic life. Designed to keep workers from the evils of Chicago, there was no drinking allowed in Pullman, (except in the Hotel Florence), although some residents smuggled beer in from nearby Kensington. All residents were employees, their pay cheques drawn from the Pullman Bank, their rent – set by the Pullman Company agent – required to be paid at the same time. George Pullman plainly regarded it as another money-making enterprise: 'We are landlord and employers. That is all there is of it'.

In late 1893, there was a nationwide economic depression, and orders for Pullman cars declined. 2,200 of the 5,500 workforce were laid off, and piecework wages for the rest cut by twenty five per cent. But the rents were not reduced, and were deducted as usual. Trapped, the furious Pullman workers went on strike. The American

It was probably a good thing that the residents of Pullman did not get together with those of this French town, whose company makes explosives.

See: Bournville, Duffel, Getto, Hershey, Leavenworth, Nuits-St-Georges, Storyville, Tin Pan Alley

Railway Union supported them, and their members refused to work trains that had Pullman cars – disrupting the whole network, including the mail. Violence broke out in the railyards of nearby downtown Chicago, 12,000 troops were called out, 2 men were killed, and Eugene Debs, the American Railway Union President, was jailed.

Within weeks George Pullman went from being one of the respected men in America to one of the most hated.

The town's pastor, the Rev William Cawardine, pointed out he *'was destined to be regarded as stubborn, ungenerous, autocratic and a prime example of all that was worst about capitalism at that time'.* Pullman, when he died four years later, was buried under tons of steel and concrete lest his grave be desecrated.

Today, George Pullman's town is a landmark district within the City of Chicago, and in an enthusiastic experiment, many residents, new and old, are trying to restore and preserve architect Solon Beaman's original design of the houses and buildings.

RAFFLES
Singapore

There are few places left which bear the name of the founder of a nation, and even fewer which are hotels. But the world famous Raffles Hotel celebrates the achievements of Sir Stamford Raffles, who founded the Singapore we know today.

The island was first maintained by the third century Chinese as *Pu Ino Chung,* ('island at the end of a peninsular'). Four centuries later, the Sumatran Empire called it *Temasek* (sea town). It was a member of the Royal Family, Sang Nila Utama, who, in about 1250, named it 'Singapura', Sanskrit for Lion City, having mistaken a tiger for a lion and considering it a good omen – which it indeed turned out to be.

In 1819, Great Britain was locked in deadly rivalry with the Dutch, especially over the trade in spices. Needing a trading station in the Malacca Strait, Lord Hastings, the Governor General of India, told

Raffles Hotel today

COURTESY OF RAFFLES HOTEL

Sir Stamford Raffles of the East India Company to search for a location. It was Raffles who chose Singapore for its potential deep water harbour and was to negotiate with the Sultan of Johore. Five years later, he bought the Sultan out with a treaty ceding the port to Britain – which he made duty-free, attracting many entrepreneurs from all over the world. They traded in tea and silk from China, timber from Malaya, opium and fabrics from India and, of course, spices.

Among the foreign entrepreneurs were the Sarkies, four enterprising brothers from Armenia who decided to create a hotel, starting with a ten-room bungalow called 'Beach House', soon renamed 'Raffles'.

It soon became the only place to stay, a symbol of colonial Singapore, *'standing for all the fables of the exotic East'* as Somerset Maughan described it. As a frequent visitor, his name is on the door of one of the ten 'Personality Suites', as are those of Charlie Chaplin, Ava Gardner, Noel Coward and Rudyard Kipling.

In 1915, a bartender at Raffles, Ngiam Tong Boon, created a new pink cocktail especially for female guests, named the 'Singapore Sling', another of the hotel's claims to fame.

With Singapore independent, first from Britain in 1957 and then from Malaysia in 1965, it has become an economic miracle. While there are now plenty of excellent hotels, it is still a temptation to stay in the one named after the country's founder, and maybe even try one of those delicious pink cocktails.

See: Bucks Club, Changi, Run Island

RAMSAY STREET
Australia

If ever a place were more likely to be obscure than famous, it must surely be the road that is now a household name – Ramsay Street – and only a long string of circumstances, chances, and decisions have granted it the fame it has today.

It is, of course, the location of Australian soap opera *Neighbours*, and, unlike the settings for many such shows, it is actually a real street, with houses lived in by real people. Pin Oak Court, as the cul-de-sac is actually called, is to be found in a Melbourne suburb called Nunawadding, chosen by a location scout for the show. (The show itself, brainchild of Reg Watson, was originally to be called *One Way Street*). The scout asked the residents if they would object to a few months of inconvenience, as he was sure that this would not be a long-running show. And indeed it almost wasn't. Early ratings were poor, partly because many Sydney residents refused to watch, owing to the established Sydney-Melbourne rivalry. After 170 episodes, Channel Seven had had enough and pulled the plug, so there was every chance that the name of Ramsay Street would be swept away and forgotten. However, Ian Holmes, who worked for Grundy, had more faith in the show, and resurrected it on Channel Ten, using extensive promotion to boost the ailing rating figures, and finally give it a hold in Australia.

But while the show had, at last, made its mark on its native country, it was unknown on the global stage. This was all to change however, in 1986, when the BBC were looking for a new soap opera to fill an empty lunchtime slot. It just so happened that the company's Director, Michael Grade, had recently visited Australia and, impressed by the antics of Ramsay Street, thought that *Neighbours* would be ideal as the second soap (after *Crossroads*) to be shown five days a week. For the UK, it was a far cry from the better-known *Eastenders* and *Coronation Street,* with splendid sunny Australian weather, and more glamorous but still down-to-earth characters. Furthermore, it proved to be much lighter in style, without the gritty British soaps' plot lines of rape and murder. Standard *Neighbours* crises were more along the lines of being caught smoking, or losing the dog – but only for a while. As the show began to catch on, its blossoming popularity among school children led to an epidemic of pupils arriving at school late after their lunch break. By chance, Michael Grade's daughter Alison was one of the followers of this trend, and when this was brought to the attention of her father, the show was given a second slot at 5.35pm, to allow it to be watched after school, and giving it yet more airtime on British screens. The soap had finally arrived in the pervasive form we know today, and managed to establish itself on two opposite sides of the world.

But it would be very wrong to say that the programme's, and therefore the street's fame, comes solely from this televisual success. Born from the smart houses of Ramsay Street were the pioneers of a new trend in the music industry – soap stars becoming pop stars. When young, glamorous, and award-winning actress Kylie Minogue turned up at the doors of record producers Stock, Aitkin and Waterman, she was about to pave the way for a host of other illustrious names. But it was only chance and speedy endeavour that allowed this meeting to

From tom-boy 'Charlene' to international pop princess, Ramsay Street launched Kylie Minogue on to even bigger things.

take place. In fact she had only an hour before she had to fly back to Australia – and her producers managed to compose the song *I Should Be So Lucky*, and actually record it, all within that time. In doing so, they created a song that would top the British charts for five weeks and launch a glittering music career for the Brit Award-winning princess of pop. Following her example, other former Ramsay Street residents became musical stars in their own right, including Jason Donovan, Natalie Imbruglia and, more recently, Holly Valance. *Neighbours* stars have even

See: Albert Square, Coronation Street, Peyton Place, Truth or Consequences

made it in Hollywood, in the form of Guy Pearce, of *Memento* and *LA Confidential* fame. Even *Gladiator's* Russell Crowe had a few guest slots in the show.

Through so many twists and turns, *Neighbours* has managed to etch Ramsay Street on to minds on both sides of the world, known to television watchers and music fans alike. After 17 years, and still with no signs of the show or its stars losing any of their recognition, one unassuming little Melbourne cul-de-sac still feels like just next door.

READING GAOL
England

In the late nineteenth century, the British Empire was basking in the sun which, proverbially, never set upon it. Her dominions covered a fifth of the world's surface. Queen Victoria – the grandmother of Europe – had just been declared Empress of India. Britain made and unmade realms as she pleased and represented a political monolith of a kind not seen since the age of Genghis Khan.

But it is not for nothing that we remember this 'golden age' as a period marked by morbidity and cruelty. The East End of London, the 'stinking pile', was notorious for its criminality and poverty. The British were infamous throughout Europe for their callous delight in putting the feeble-minded or deformed into circuses, for the gloating delight of a coarse and violent populace or even making a paying spectacle out of a lunatic asylum like 'Bedlam'. The Boer War was soon to break out, and the world would be introduced to the Concentration Camp – a British invention. And then there were the prisons.

It was the opinion of disinterested observers that British prisons were the most appalling in Europe. The regime alone is inconceivable today. Pointless, humiliating tasks alternated with pointless, humiliating punishments. The prisoners would be ordered to pick oakum until their hands were bleeding, only to see their efforts burned in the

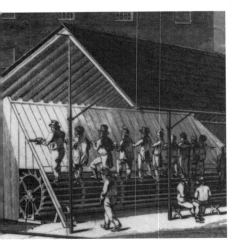

The treadmill, one of the totally pointless activities in Victorian prisons. Six hours a day and more than 6,000 feet - the equivalent of climbing Ben Nevis one and a half times.

yard as they trooped out for the hour-long walk which was their only sight of the sun. They would be forced to turn a crank handle 10,000 times a day, which could be screwed down to make it harder (the origin of the word 'screws' for warders). The treadmill, upon which the prisoners were made to march, is now a proverb for any work that is useless and soul-destroying. The diet of fatty soup and bread made with lime resulted in constant and enervating diarrhoea, a condition made still more distressing by the fact that they were only allowed to empty their 'slops' twice a day. Prison warders, entering the cells at dawn for the daily inspection, would frequently vomit at the stench from the overflowing buckets.

Of all the prisons, Newgate was the most notorious in its time. But Reading Gaol is now the most famous. And its fame was assured by the most unlikely of chroniclers.

In 1895, Oscar Wilde – socialite, wit, and consummate playwright – was found guilty of 'indecent relations' with young men. An unsuccessful lawsuit against the Marquess of Queensberry, father of Wilde's lover, Lord Alfred Douglas, had resulted in him being tried and convicted under the terms of the Labouchère Amendment, a law which made sexual relations between men illegal. The story of this law is intriguing in itself. Henry Labouchère, an urbane and genial MP, became so frustrated with the puritanism of a new law on sexual morality that he offered this sarcastic suggestion: *'If the state* is to interfere so grossly in the private mores of its citizens, then why not extend its scope to include sex between men?' But his learned colleagues failed to see the joke and proceeded to implement his suggestion in deadly earnest, to the ruin of many a reputation – and the delight of blackmailers.

Wilde served two years in prison, first in Wandsworth, then in Reading. 'A fiendish nightmare', he described it to his friend Frank Harris when he visited, but was too terrified to elaborate. 'Promise me you won't say anything', he begged, 'I never complained'. He saw a half-witted man regularly flogged for 'shamming', children in oversized prison garb crying for their mothers, a prison warder dismissed for giving some food to them, and the strange, silent figure who inspired his most famous poem, *The Ballad of Reading Gaol*. The man was a guardsman awaiting execution for killing his wife in a fit of jealous rage. The poem records the man's final days in verse that is often brilliant, sometimes banal, occasionally sublime:

'He did not wear his scarlet coat,
For blood and wine are red,
And blood and wine were on his hands
When they found him with the dead:
The poor dead woman whom he loved
And murdered in her bed'.

For all its flaws, this extraordinary portrayal of prison life has ensconced itself in the world's imagination like no other. No-one who has read it could forget lines like, *'Yet each man kills the thing he loves;'* the description of the noose, *'And feel upon his shuddering cheek*

the kiss of Caiaphas;' or that chilling condemnation of prison piety, *'And twice a day the chaplain called And left a little tract'.*

Towards the end of Wilde's sentence, a new and more humane Governor took over at Reading Gaol. But even he could not mitigate the severity of prison rules. Upon his release, Wilde began sending letters to the Government in an effort to secure better conditions for prisoners, and it is a comfort to reflect that many of his suggestions – particularly regarding children – were later implemented.

But for Wilde, it was too late. *The Ballad*, published all over the world in 1898, was, with one, insignificant exception, his last poem. 'Something is killed in me,' he confided to a friend. The imagination which had enchanted children in the stories, *The Happy Prince* and *The Selfish Giant*, and titillated adult audiences in *The Importance of Being Earnest*, was crushed by the horrors of prison life. And the man himself did not long survive his muse.

The Governor of Reading Gaol had told Robert Ross, Wilde's friend and executor, that men of Wilde's breeding and temperament could expect to survive four years in the outside world, so terrible would their ordeal have proved. In 1900, Oscar Wilde died – only two years after his release, from what he plainly regarded as his ultimate horror.

See: Alcatraz, Bedlam, Devils Island, Robben Island, Savoy, Spandau

REICHSTAG
Germany

Considering its part in the most nationalist era of Germany's history, it is both amazing and amusing that Germany's Parliament building has been redesigned and rebuilt by a British architect, Sir Norman Foster.

The Reichstag was built between 1884 and 1894 by Paul Wallot, and in 1916 the inscription 'Dem Deutschen Volk' (to the German people) was added to the front.

After the First World War in September 1919, the assembly moved in to the Reichstag. However, the area in front of it was often the scene of riot and mayhem.

Twelve years later, Germany's Weimar Republic was still in turmoil, and was the worst economic victim of the Depression, her currency worthless. Adolf Hitler's Nazi party was the largest in the Reichstag, but both the Social

The Reichstag burns. It was all the excuse the Nazis required to seize total power.

See: Anne Frank's Annexe, Berchtesgaden, Dachau, Getto, Landsberg, Lidice, Nuremberg, Oradour, Wannsee

Democrats and the militant Communists were a force to be reckoned with. President Hindenburg, half senile, had allowed Hitler to become Chancellor, who called for new elections on 5th March 1933. On the night of 27th February, the empty Reichstag building stepped into history. It caught fire. A deranged Communist arsonist from Holland – Marcus Van der Lubbe was found and arrested, but it was almost certainly Nazi storm-troopers, using a tunnel from Hermann Goering's residence who did the real job of torching the building.

The Nazis grabbed their opportunity. Hitler said it was a beacon from heaven. 'The German people have been soft for too long. Every Communist official must be shot. All Communist Deputies must be hanged this very night. All friends of the Communists must be locked up. And that goes for the Social Democrats and the Reichshammer as well!'

He was as good as his word. Many were murdered, thousands soon locked up by the truckloads of stormtroopers who roared through the streets and burst into homes. Next day, a befuddled Hindenburg was persuaded to sign an Enabling Act which removed all civil liberties. It stated bluntly that:

'Restrictions on personal liberty, on the right of free expression of opinion, including freedom of the press; on the rights of assembly and association; and violations of the privacy of postal, telegraphic and telephonic communications and warrants for house searches, orders for confiscations as well as restrictions on property, are also permissible beyond the legal limits otherwise prescribed'.

Two days before the election Goering was ranting, 'I don't have to worry about justice; my mission is only to destroy and exterminate, nothing more!' Amazingly, on election day, 5th March, the Nazis did not get the two thirds majority they needed for dictatorship. At forty four per cent, (17 million votes), they still had to contend with four million for the Centre Party, seven million for the Social Democrats and over four million for the Communists.

No matter. In July, all other parties were simply forbidden. The long agony for Germany, and Europe, under the Nazis had begun. The Reichstag building fell into disuse, used only by Hitler for propaganda speeches – as a final humiliation for what he regarded as the hated Weimar Republic.

During the War it became a Luftwaffe headquarters, and was heavily bombed.

On 2nd May 1945 it was from the roof of the shattered Reichstag building that the Soviet troops made sure that they raised their flag as a symbol of the final overthrow of the Nazis.

RILLINGTON PLACE
England

Ten, Rillington Place – a nondescript London house in a Notting Hill cul-de-sac, was the chilling location of several murders. But what makes the place even more sinister, and far more remarkable, is that it may have been the home to not one, but two killers.

Our two main protagonists are John Christie and Timothy Evans, two very strange, and yet two very different men.

Evans, with an IQ of around 70, was almost retarded, with a meagre education. Those who knew him said that his most notable traits were temper tantrums and compulsive lying. He and

his wife – living in 10 Rillington Place – had a tempestuous relationship that often exploded into physical violence.

For Christie, a combination of his abusive father and over-protective mother had turned him into a hypochondriac; over the course of 15 years he had made 173 visits to doctors. He also visited prostitutes and had a perverted attitude to women. Christie had been an odd child, who seems to have genuinely enjoyed playing in graveyards. Once he and his wife moved into the building, they kept themselves very much to themselves, with John having no real friends.

IMPERIAL WAR MUSEUM

It was in 1949, with the disappearance of both Evans' wife Beryl and their first born child, that suspicion fell on both men. Evans' aunt eventually confronted her nephew, and Evans reported to the Merthyr Tydfil police station, where he wrote a statement: '*I have disposed of my wife. I put her down the drain*'.

However, when police investigated the house, they found no body in the drain as Evans had described. Instead, after further searches, they discovered Beryl's corpse inside the wash-house behind Rillington Place, along with the body of the baby.

All concerned found Evans' statements exceedingly confusing. Much of the complication stemmed from Beryl's unborn child (she was pregnant at the time of her death). Evans claimed that Christie had attempted to perform an unlicensed abortion on his wife, and that the drugs he had given her had turned out to be lethal. These claims made no sense, as they did not account for the infant, nor the fact that Beryl appeared to have been strangled.

Evans later changed his account entirely, confessing to the murder of his wife (apparently for running up debts) and his child, before reverting once more to claiming that Christie was the perpetrator. At his trial, the jury was won over by Christie's quiet, thoughtful testimony, especially when weighed against that of Evans' – riddled with contradictions and struggling against his previous confession of murder. The jury swiftly returned with a guilty verdict and Evans was executed on March 9th, 1950.

Life returned to normal in Rillington Place, new tenants moved in, and for a few months it seemed as though the terrible murders had never occurred. But in December, Christie's wife Ethel went missing, and the house began to develop a strong smell of disinfectant. He told neighbours that his wife had 'moved to Sheffield, and was not going to return'. Then, on March 20th, Christie moved out, and a new tenant, Beresford Brown, moved in, not suspecting the horror story he was about to enter. But he soon discovered a hidden cupboard, and the unmistakable shape of a human body.

The police returned to 10 Rillington Place to find that the atrocities they had discovered a year ago were only the beginning. It was the body of Ethel, Christie's wife, that Brown had discovered, and she was not alone. Three other dead women were found within the hidden alcove, and two more buried in the garden. After Christie was arrested (he had been moving around various parts of London until recognised by a policeman), he eventually confessed to strangling these women, some with the help of poisonous carbon monoxide gas, and having sex with most of them at some stage before – or even after – their deaths. His excuses for the murders ranged from 'putting his wife out her misery' (she was apparently having some sort of fit) to 'defending himself from Rita Nelson', whom he claimed was trying to steal money from him. Described by his own lawyer as a maniac and a madman, he pleaded insanity. And just as the jury had been quick to attribute guilt to Evans, so, after a trial only 4 days long, the plea of insanity was rejected and Christie was also sentenced to death. He was hanged on July 15th, 1953.

The crimes of Christie threw up the crucial question that has made Rillington Place so famous: if Christie killed all those women, was he also responsible for the deaths of Beryl Evans and her daughter? If the answer to this question was yes, it would reveal a further tragic aspect to the whole affair; Timothy Evans was sent to the gallows for a murder committed by another man.

So what is the truth? Did Christie kill Beryl and the child and frame Evans for his crimes? If so, why did Evans confess to the murders? (He did once claim that the police beat the confession out of him). Or was 10 Rillington Place really the home of two killers? The story of Rillington Place endures because, whether it is a story about one man's unjust execution, or a tale of two murderers under one roof, the mystery remains as baffling as it is famous.

John Christie

See: Katyn Wood, Lidice

299

RIVER ROUGE OVERPASS
Michigan, USA

'A picture speaks a thousand words'.

It is often the visual impression created by an artist or a photographer that catches the key moment that can make a place famous and change history. So it was in May 1937 on the overpass at Ford's gigantic River Rouge plant.

It was merely the best recorded in a series of violent battles between capital and labour in the United States of the 1930s.

After the Wall Street Crash of 1929 came the Depression, and workers counted themselves so lucky to have a job that they would work for a pittance and under appalling conditions, cowed by company gangs and spies. But in 1933 things began to change, with a new generation of union leaders and the introduction of Section 7a of the National Industrial Recovery Act, which made it patriotic to join a union.

The result of this was a series of confrontations, like that at the Republic Steel works in Chicago. The police, against Mayor Edward Kelly's orders, shouted, 'You got no rights. You Red Bastards. You got no rights'. Moments later, they opened fire on men, women and children, killing 10 and wounding 30, and clubbing down 28 more. It took five years to get redress.

In the car industry, things were just as bad. At General Motors, Alfred Sloan had squeezed and bullied his 250,000 workers so badly that they had rebelled and occupied the Fisher Body plants in Cleveland and then at Flint, Michigan, using the novel and effective method of the 'sit-down strike'. They also closed the vital Number 4 plant producing all Chevrolet engines, and when Michigan's Governor Frank Murphy refused to let the National Guard assault the plants, Sloan eventually recognised the union. As did Chrysler.

Not so Henry Ford. He was no longer the hero whose Model T had brought mass mobility to America. Always a bit strange, ('History is more or less bunk'. he once said), and by now really eccentric and consumed with hatred, he ran his plants with a combination of fear and the thugs of Harry Bennett's 'Service Department'. It was these men who were to confront three United Automobile Workers officials on the River Rouge Overpass trying to hand out leaflets. The thugs attacked Robert Kanter, pulled Richard Frankenstein's coat over his head while they punched him, and struck Walter Reuther on the back of the head. All three were hurled down the 39 steps of the overpass. Luckily, *Detroit News* photographer James Kilpatrick was on hand and, when threatened by the Ford 'goons', equally luckily handed over the wrong film. His pictures marked the beginning of the end for the tyranny at Ford. Henry Ford, under the urging of his gentler son Edsel and of his own wife Clara, (who threatened to leave him if he reneged on the deal), settled with the union. 'Don't ever discredit the power of a woman'.

> **'History is more or less bunk'.**
>
> Henry Ford, before he became really difficult and eccentric

The first in a series of pictures which revealed Ford's brutal methods. The Union officials on the right are just about to be attacked by Harry Bennett's thugs.

FORD MOTOR COMPANY

See: Tolpuddle, Triangle Shirtwaist Company

ROBBEN ISLAND
South Africa

Most people would never have heard of Robben Island but for its most famous inhabitant, prisoner 466/64, Nelson Mandela – future President of South Africa.

Robben Island, 'Seal Island' in Dutch, is six miles across a shark-infested cold sea from Cape Town. It was first discovered by the Portuguese explorer Bartholomeu Dias in 1488, and was later used as a place of banishment by the Dutch, who even brought prisoners from their colonies in the Far East – including, in 1748, Indonesian royalty. In 1844, the British, now masters of the Cape, made the island a leper colony, which it remained for nearly a hundred years. As a convenient place of isolation, Robben Island served for years as the dumping ground for those the colonists wished to forget – cancer patients, epileptics, the insane, lepers and political prisoners. The most prominent of these were the Xhosa chiefs, after the blatant annexation of their land by the British colonists. The Xhosa chief Makama drowned in the most famous escape attempt from Robben Island. Generations of Xhosa chiefs, and then Zulu leaders, found themselves banished to the piece of land, agonisingly close to the city of Cape Town and beautiful Table Mountain. The similarity with the prison on the 'Rock' of Alcatraz in San Francisco Bay is only too obvious.

During World War II, huge guns on the island protected Cape Town from any German or Japanese naval threat, and in 1958, the South African Navy left the island. The stage was set for its years of infamy. In 1959, hard-faced Justice Minister, John Vorster, designated the island as a maximum security prison for 'non-white males', one of the very harsh measures to enforce Prime Minister Hendrick Verwoerd's *apartheid* or 'apartness' policy, whereby civil rights were denied to black, Asian, and coloured citizens. Africans had only thirteen per cent of the land, passes had to be carried by them at all times, and over half of the African population lived below the poverty line. In 1963, Vorster introduced a law permitting detention in solitary confinement without trial for 90 days, but which he could extend 'to this side of eternity'.

Nelson Mandela was one of the victims of the repression, and found himself on Robben Island under appalling conditions – with some of the poor-white Afrikaner warders behaving with atrocious brutality. But gradually his courteous and dignified approach won over everyone. Over the years, his friendly, but not over-familiar bearing became the almost regal one by which the world now knows him.

South Africa became increasingly isolated with the 1960 Massacre at Sharpeville and the Soweto township uprising in 1976. The 1980s saw four States of Emergency, with prisons filled – forty per cent by child inmates, and even death squads emerged. A poll showed that fifty four per cent of whites would support Mandela's release. Apartheid was plainly not working.

ELENA SANCHI

Partly because he was becoming too identified with Robben Island, in 1982 Mandela and some of his fellow political prisoners were moved to Pollsmoor Prison in Cape Town. Two years later, the first tentative and secret talks with the Government and the very worried big business leaders began. In 1989, the courageous F.W. de Klerk became Prime Minister, and a year later Mandela was released after 27 years in prison – 18 of them on Robben Island.

When Nelson Mandela was elected President in 1994, he invited three of his

So near and yet so far. The view of Cape Town from Robben Island

Nelson Mandela (left) with Walter Sisulu. Note the rows of squatting prisoners in the background, breaking stones.

Robben Island warders to his inauguration; an unprecedented act of forgiveness. But then, the whole story is extraordinary: a man incarcerated for nearly three decades emerging to change the whole face of his country – both peacefully and successfully.

The last prisoners left the island in 1996, and the island has become a World Heritage Site. But, it will always be a symbol of suffering and ultimate triumph.

See: Alcatraz, Reading Gaol, Rorke's Drift, Sharpeville, Sophiatown, Spandau

ROCK ISLAND
Illinois, USA

*'The Rock Island Line is a mighty fine road
The Rock Island Line is the road to ride
The Rock Island Line is a mighty good road
If you want to ride it, got to ride it like you find it
Get your ticket at the station for the Rock Island Line'.*

Abraham Lincoln at the time of the Rock Island Bridge Case

For many music fans, Rock Island was epitomised by the Leadbelly song, and later the Lonnie Donegan 'skiffle' hit which reached number eight in 1956 on both the US and British charts. The style of this new music was to influence many musicians, including the Beatles, adding the name of at least one American regional railway to their knowledge. However, Rock Island deserves much more serious recognition.

The growth of the railways was even more important to the United States than to Europe. In Europe, they were superimposed on an established society, and on existing cities and villages.

By contrast, the railroads helped to build America, and were a pivotal force in the creation of half of America's cities and industries. What is more, they superimposed a standard time system on the Continent, created the mail order industry and gave birth to a language. If you feel you've been *'side tracked'*, are getting *'steamed up'* and might *'blow your stack'*, you're talking railroad vocabulary. Even the phrase 'rock 'n' roll' may owe its origins to the swaying motion of articulated steam engines in 1915.

Most people know the story of the railroads forging across the Continent, propelled by land grants and, sometimes, by appalling financial skulduggery, but few know the story of one of the key political changes created by the railroads.

In 1855, the dominant transport system in the US was provided by the two great rivers flowing south; the Mississippi and the Missouri. Steamboats ruled these waters, with the steamboat towns being key economic centres, especially for the southern states.

It became absolutely apparent to the South that if railroads were able to go from east to west, it was going to undermine one of the financial strengths of the south in the favour of the north. St. Louis, Memphis and New Orleans would lose out to New York and Chicago forever. A sympathetic Mississippi Senator and Secretary of War, Jefferson Davis, encouraged his friends – the steamboat men – to try to ban the 'bridging of navigable rivers'.

The Chicago and Rock Island was the first railroad to reach the Mississippi and

The first train to cross The Rock Island Bridge

it was decided that a bridge would be built at Rock Island. Unfortunately, Rock Island was right opposite the fanatically protective steamboat town of Davenport, Iowa. With the bridge about to open, the Davenport steamboat men resorted to dirty tricks. They loaded a ship called the *Effie Afton* with inflammable materials, set fire to it and floated it down towards the bridge. In the event, it did no serious damage, but the Mayor of Davenport was quick to announce that it posed dangers to navigation and that 'his side of the bridge should be taken down.

The Chicago and Rock Island Railroad hired its usual troubleshooting lawyer, Abraham Lincoln, who fought the case all the way to the Supreme Court – and won. Important men in the east noticed him and backed his political career.

Not only did this mean that the railroads did 'go West' and that the northern states became ever more dominant, but it is also an interesting thought that Abraham Lincoln might not have become famous except for this case, or end up as President of the United States, fighting a Civil War against Jefferson Davis as President of the Confederacy – and for the same economic reasons for which he had fought the Rock Island Bridge Case.

Rock Island owes its importance to rather more than just a song.

See: Abbey Road, Cavern, Fort Sumter, Gettysburg, Greenwich, Harpers Ferry, Promontory, Stockton & Darlington

RORKE'S DRIFT
South Africa

The world should have heard of Rorke's Drift just a little earlier than it did. The two thatched buildings and kraal constructed by Irish trader Jim Rorke were on a ford of the Buffalo River, the border between Zululand and Natal. There, in 1878, a Boundary Commission was convened by Sir Henry Bulwer, the Lieutenant Governor of Natal who was desperate to avoid a war which was plainly being engineered by Sir Henry Bartle Frere, the British High Commissioner, with little support from the British Government. For Frere, with his Indian Mutiny memories, the powerful Zulu Kingdom was a major and dangerous obstacle to his plan to create a confederation of white-ruled states. Frere was horrified when, in July after five weeks, the Commission ruled in favour of the Zulus. He locked up the report. Frere then used as a pretext the crossing of the Buffalo River by a group of Zulus, to take back and kill two wives of Zulu Chief Sihayo who had eloped with young warriors.

The Zulus were summoned to Rorke's Drift on 11th December, expecting to hear a favourable verdict, and were dismayed to read an ultimatum insisting that they dismantle their military machine, an impossible demand which also had family implications.

One remarkable man, Shaka, had created the 300,000-strong Zulu nation with its 50,000 warrior army. It was he who transformed inter-tribal warfare from the equivalent of village cricket to ruthless conquest. He had personally perfected the deadly stabbing assegai, the *iXwa*, had trained his men to be so physically fit that they could run down a horseman, and manoeuvre smoothly as regiments with the tactics of the 'head' and the 'enveloping horns', and had imposed mortal discipline that no African (or European) had ever known. Then, there were the 'age-sets' of his regiments, recruited by age and not by location or family. Crucially, men were only allowed to marry when they were well over 30, and then only after 'the washing of the spears', proof of bravery in battle. That is why, fifty years later, the meeting at Rorke's Drift broke up – and why Cetchewayo – crowned Zulu King with the approval of Queen Victoria and a British ally for decades, reluctantly ordered his army to resist.

It was once again at Rorke's Drift, on 12th January 1879, that an illegal invading British Army, under Frere's confident

BRYAN COODE

The regiments which attacked Rorke's Drift were of older men who had not fought at Isandlwana

How Isandlwana must have looked. An anniversary re-enactment.

BRYAN COODE

Behind a Victorian myth.

Rorke's Drift was a heroic action, but consider:
• Colonial Secretary, Sir Michael Hicks Beach to Frere:
'By the exercise of prudence and by meeting the Zulus in a spirit of forebearance and reasonable compromise, it will be possible to avert the very serious evil of a war'.
• Duties of High Commissioner:
'He is not to declare war or to make war against any foreign state'.
• The last parts of Frere's ultimatum were not copied to Hicks Beach, especially: '5'. 'The Zulu army is to disband and every Zulu is free to marry'. An absolute negation of Zulu culture.
• Cetchewayo sent 7 peace messages to Chelmsford, all ignored.
• Col. Glyn, handing over command of 2/24th Regiment said 'Isandlwana was as vulnerable as an English village'.
• Chelmsford was desperate to use Rorke's Drift to counteract his performance over Isandlwana. He tried to blame Col. Durnford (conveniently dead, who had backed the Zulus at the boundary commission). He then tried to blame Glyn.
• Unlike the media and public, the rest of the army did not approve of the 11 VCs awarded for Rorke's Drift and 3 for Isandlwana. Sir Garnet Wolseley even said that it was 'monstrous'.

friend and accomplice Lord Chelmsford, crossed into Zululand. Past British success against the Xhosa, and notably a skirmish with some Zulus at 'Sihayo's Stronghold' convinced Chelmsford that not even the Zulus would face European fire power. The classic military mistake of 'underestimating your enemy' was about to take its toll.

Under the mountain at Isandlwana, the British made camp. Chelmsford, fatally, decided to overrule his officers and did not to bother to dig trenches and laager the wagons, in direct contravention of *Regulations for the Field Forces in South Africa*. The next day he took half his army to seek out the Zulus, whom he was anxious 'would not give battle'. He need not have worried. At noon, firing from the camp alerted him that something was wrong, although telescopes revealed that 'bodies of men were moving about and the tents were standing'. But at 3 pm, in galloped Commandant Lonsdale with the dreadful news. 1,700 men had been overwhelmed by thousands of Zulus, the greatest defeat for British arms in a century.

Rorke's Drift's final and greatest claim to fame happened by chance, because the Zulus never intended to invade Natal, merely to block the invasion of their homeland. But as one Zulu later laconically stated, *'The Undi and Udhloko regiments went to Rorke's Drift to plunder the post and failed and lost very heavily after fighting all afternoon and night'*.

The settlement, now a store and hospital, was commanded by Major Spalding who had just gone to fetch reinforcements. He left Lt John Chard with the immortal words, 'I see you are senior, so you will be in charge. Although nothing will happen and I will be back this evening'. Chard, an engineer, had been maintaining the pontoon bridge and was supported by Lt Gonville Bromhead

with his Midlanders, Irishmen and Welshmen from the 24th (2nd Warwickshire) Regiment of Foot. The hospital was full of wounded and sick. Firing was heard from Isandlwana, ten miles away, and soon survivors rode through, including the Natal Native Horse who refused to stop. Indeed, the garrison's own Natal Native contingent fled with them. Chard wrote of the remaining 139 men, including the wounded, *'we seemed very few now'*. Commissary Officer James Dalton, an experienced former Sergeant, sensibly advised Chard and Bromhead to stay and fight, and to create a defensive position, linking the two buildings with overturned wagons and a high parapet of bags of maize. Just in time, because only 75 minutes after the news of Isandlwana, lookout Private Hitch reported 'thousands of Zulus approaching'.

The first wave of Zulus was stopped by the defender's Martini-Henry rifles. This first attack was followed by another, and then another. The Zulus, with their deadly assegais, were kept at a distance – but the British were sometimes forced to fight on the very perimeter, with rifles and bayonets, barely preventing the Zulus from climbing over the walls. Zulu gunfire from the Oscarburg Hill made the British position worse. And no matter how many Zulus were mown down, nothing seemed to stop their relentless attacks. Colour Sergeant Bourne recounted, *'One cannot but admire their fanatical bravery'*. The hospital caught fire and had to be evacuated, and Private Henry Hook was just able to hold back the Zulus from pouring through the holes they had carved with their bayonets in the mud brick walls, although Private Joseph Williams was dragged back and disembowelled before his comrades' eyes.

The light was now fading, but the fighting did not. Chaplain Smith and the wounded methodically handed out ammunition. Assistant Commissary Walter Dunne constructed a last redoubt of 'mealiebags' in the centre of the compound, giving the British a last bastion. The soldiers never stopped firing their jamming, red hot rifles, their targets illuminated by the hospital fire. At 2 am, a desperate British sally rescued the vital water cart. Soon, the Zulu attacks began to wane. As the sun rose, the British soldiers saw the destruction. Hundreds of corpses were stacked round the buildings.

But nobody could relax yet. A huge force of Zulus could be seen massing on the Kwasingqindi Hill. Exhausted, the British braced themselves for a last defence. But the attack never came. The Zulu army turned and disappeared over the horizon as Chelmsford's column returned. Just over 100 men at Rorke's Drift had done what a British army had failed to do at Isandlwana, resisting the most savage attack of the sons of Shaka. Eleven of them were awarded the Victoria Cross, the most ever awarded for one battle. Seventeen men had lost their lives. The heroism of this most remarkable of battles has been famously recorded in the film

Zulu, starring a young Michael Caine as Bromhead and Stanley Baker as Chard, and has one of the great lines in the cinema. Colour Sergeant Bourne (Nigel Green) orders one very frightened soldier, staring at 4,000 advancing Zulus, 'Do up your tunic lad! Where do you think you are?'

There have been bigger, more significant battles, but the bravery at Rorke's Drift, especially after the disaster at Isandlwana, captured British hearts. As Queen Victoria herself said, *'The Defence of Rorke's Drift is Immortal.'* But it would have been better all round if we knew the place for a successful treaty.

BRYAN COODE

See: Bayonne, Gleiwitz, Robben Island, Sarajevo, Sharpeville, Sophiatown, Tonkin Gulf

ROSWELL
New Mexico, USA

History is filled with legendary creatures. Ancient ships' captains used to claim that they saw gigantic serpents swimming around their keels. According to folk-lore England used to resound with the beating of dragon wings. In all these cases, fact and fiction become indistinguishable. Reason and evidence seem to disprove them all, even to their contemporaries, and yet people believe.

But surely the civilised, cynical 20th century would be immune to such myths. In July 1947, the modern world was given a modern legend.

While tales of extra-terrestrials have been around for centuries, the phrase 'flying saucer' had only been around for two weeks before Roswell. On June 24th, a businessman called Kenneth Arnold saw nine glowing objects flying through the sky 'like a saucer would if you skipped it across water.'

Very quickly the term was taken up by the media. In the following weeks hundreds of UFO sightings were reported across North America. Flying saucers had captured the public's imagination. At the height of this obsession, Mac Brazel, a rancher, claimed that he saw some strange debris scattered across a field near his home town of Roswell, New Mexico. This would have been just one sighting among hundreds, but 24 hours later the Air Force issued an official statement that would make this occasion very different. They said they had found a *'Flying saucer'*

(*Roswell Daily Record*, July 8, 1947). A day later they retracted that statement, and declared that it was the wreckage of *'an ordinary weather balloon'* (*Roswell Daily Record*, July 9th, 1947).

The Air Force's about-turn changed a run of the mill UFO sighting into something much more interesting.

The story became increasingly famous and elaborate. The US Government was said not only to have taken possession of the alien ship and the alien bodies within, but also to have taken them to a legendary secret airbase by the name of Area 51. Videos and pictures have since been released of a supposed alien autopsy, although their validity is incredibly dubious.

The US Air Force has ever since denied that anything remarkable happened at Roswell. They have issued several reports, including their most recent, and final, one: *'The Roswell Report, Case Closed.'* In it they describe the object as a *'radar target',* a balloon made out of aluminium foil. Another report says that any bodies that were discovered were not the corpses of aliens, but dummies used in parachute tests. Their report presents reams of evidence against any UFO activity, and seems, as with all great legends, to prove rationally that nothing ever happened.

Yet people still believe. They continue to doggedly pick holes in the arguments of the establishment. Why, they ask, did the Air Force issue that first statement?

Alien autopsy. Real or phoney?

Why were the parachute dummies, that were supposed to have been found at the site, part of tests that occurred a full decade after Roswell? And would people have really confused dummies with aliens? The incident was bound to create a conspiracy theory.

The Roswell incident has since been featured in every form of media, key to the plot of Hollywood blockbusters *Men in Black* and *Independence Day*. Such films probably only serve to trivialise what some would see as a genuine issue, and the more the media uses Roswell as a fantasy device, the more people forget how seriously it was once seen. The only conclusion must surely be the famous subtitle of the *X-Files*.

'The truth is out there'.

See: Cape Canaveral, Peenemünde

ROTTEN ROW
England

There can be very few thoroughfares whose name so belies the reality as Rotten Row. It sounds like a condemned row of houses in some blighted, dreary and industrial city. Nothing could be further from the truth.

Rotten Row was the creation of royalty. It is in London's Hyde Park, acquired first as a hunting domain by Henry VIII in 1536, and its name was derived from 'Route du Roi' or 'route of the King'. When Charles II returned from exile in 1660, Hyde Park became the place where 'society' should be seen, and the practice of showing off one's fashionable attire and elegant carriages on Rotten Row began. The diarist Samuel Pepys recorded how he tried to get noticed by the King and the important Lady Castlemaine, but his horse spoiled the fashion show by bolting.

When William III moved his court to Kensington Palace, his direct route to Westminster, Rotten Row, was plagued by crime at night. He therefore installed 300 oil lamps, making Rotten Row the first illuminated highway in Britain.

Rotten Row continued to be the focus of fashionable London. Gentlemen sported the finest riding habits tailored in Savile Row, ladies were the epitome of elegance, and their polished carriages, like the Phaeton, were specifically designed for the leisurely, very public parade. This took place in the middle of the day throughout London's 'Summer Season' and was an event from which nobody in 'society' would wittingly absent themselves.

One young lady, Catherine 'Skittles' Walters, the most famous 'kept mistress' in London, used to wear such a skintight Savile Row riding habit that crowds gathered to watch her ride, blocking the roads. Letters in the newspapers even suggested that *'this pretty creature and her pretty ponies'* might be persuaded to

ILLUSTRATED LONDON NEWS

exercise somewhere else.

Rotten Row was the elegant 'tip of the iceberg' of the use of horses in London, which dominated the streets until about 1915. The coming of the railways in 1850 may have replaced horses for long-distance travel, but actually increased their numbers in the capital, as visitors and trade increased. The number of private carriages went from 60,000 in 1814 to half a million in 1901. Together with carts, omnibuses and hackney cabs they filled the streets, and the resulting tons of manure required hundreds of 'crossing sweepers' and 'bootblacks'.

For the upper classes, a complex system of transport handling was needed, including 'mews' stables close to their smart houses, advance briefings for servants as to which carriages would be required for Rotten Row, and invitations to all social events indicating the time for collection – 'Carriages at twelve'.

With the coming of the motor car, Rotten Row lost its social relevance and the carriages disappeared. People still go riding in Hyde Park, and Rotten Row is still there – a broad, sandy, shady, tree-lined track. What memories it must have.

Catherine 'Skittles' Walters

See: Aintree, Ascot, Chequers, Cliveden, Downing Street, Jodhpur, Lords, Savile Row

ROUTE 66
USA

Dramatised in many a road movie, it is one of the most enduring and evocative images of that enormous country, the United States of America.

It is the romantic vision of riding endless highways with the roof down on the convertible, rolling toward distant horizons dominated by mountain ranges that never seem to come any closer, and accompanied only by line after line of lonely telegraph poles. And perhaps there will be a single road sign, probably somewhat battered, but proudly bearing the designation 'Route 66.'

This is the great road that has become an American legend, a route that is often described in almost mystical terms as 'an icon of free-spirited independence 1inking the US across the Rocky Mountains divide to the shores of the Pacific Ocean'.

Certainly it was a visionary enterprise, conceived in 1926 to wind 2,400 miles across the country, the first all-weather highway to bring the east within easier reach of sunnier climes and, snaking across eight states, much beloved of that hardy breed the American trucker for shortening the endless trek by a good 200 miles.

There is solid reason for US Highway 66's iconic status in American history. From Chicago, Illinois to Santa Monica, California, the road linked the isolated, rural west with the densely populated midwest. Performing an invaluable and ongoing role in the countrywide transport of goods, it was applauded by historians and economists alike as one of the great arteries that helped pump the lifeblood into a rapidly developing America.

In the '30s, it became the fabled escape route, the 'road of opportunity', for those who fled the rigours of the Dust Bowl for California, thus becoming celebrated as 'The Mother Road' in John Steinbeck's 1939 novel *The Grapes of Wrath* and the subsequent 1940 movie. Later in the '40s, it became a

The narrow road that crossed a Continent

307

ALL PHOTOS: NATIONAL HISTORIC ROUTE 66 FEDERATION

One of hundreds of motels that lined Route 66

See: Broadway, Chisholm Trail, Cumberland Road, Main Street, St. Joseph, St. Louis

thoroughfare for troops and supplies bound for war.

And, for many years, it was the most popular tourist route in the country for those thousands who simply felt the irresistible urge to 'motor west.'

To all who rode it, Route 66 symbolised the kind of restless and enterprising spirit that has always been an intrinsic part of the American psyche, ever since early pioneers drove herds of cattle huge distances from state to state, or navigated dust-clouded wagon trains across endless and unforgiving prairies.

It was not surprising that, in 1946, Route 66 became immortalised in song with Nat King Cole's rendition of composer Bobby Troop's 'lyrical route map' of the great highway, and the phrase *Get your kicks on Route 66* thus entered the musical language forever.

And, in the it '60s, Route 66 became the subject of its own TV series.

Eventually however, the road was superseded by new generations of Interstate freeways. After years of neglect, much of it fell into disrepair, de-commissioned and often obscured. Today however, after almost a decade of preservation work by the National Historic Route 66 Federation, over eighty-five per cent of the old route is driveable once again.

And, in every state en route, preservation societies publish guides as to what remains, erect signs to help those in search of its continuing mystery and stay determined to perpetuate an enduring legend, a legend of over 2,000 miles of tarmac that, poetically, has also come to be called 'America's Main Street'.

RUBICON
Italy

W e say we are 'Crossing the Rubicon' when we commit ourselves to an irrevocable course of action, and from which there is no turning back.

On 11th January, 49 BC, Julius Caesar led his 13th Legion across the Rubicon, passing the point of no return on the road to an increasingly inevitable civil war. The triumvirate, a governing body of three men, Crassus, Pompey, and Caesar, which had been created in the belief that it could maintain a balance of power, had collapsed.

Crassus was the richest man in Rome, having made his money from silver mines and slaves. He became a huge property owner, partly by ownership of the fire service and his unpleasant habit of negotiating slowly while houses were burning, with the owners selling at a knock-down price. He had also put down the Spartacus slave revolt, and was especially renowned for the even more unpleasant act of lining the Appian Way for a 100 miles with crucified slaves, after which he set up 10,000 banqueting tables in the Forum and fed Rome for days. Perhaps that is why we use the word 'crass'.

Crassus suddenly decided that he wanted real military prestige and, without authority, and at his own expense, invaded Parthia. In 52 BC, at Carrhae, Crassus and his son lost their lives along with 20,000 Romans, many victims of the 'Parthian shot'- arrows fired backwards across the horse's backs, which we now record as 'a parting shot' in a conversation.

By contrast, Julius Caesar had enjoyed a brilliant and continuous military career. In 61BC, with financial help from Crassus, he was given command in Spain and the Triumvirate began its rule based on military power, mob rule and money, which the Senate could do little to curtail.

Caesar's conquest of Gaul may have had the same motives of personal prestige and political power as that of Crassus, except that he succeeded. He defeated the Helveti (modern Swiss) the Sueli (Germans) the Belgi (Belgians) and finally the Veneti (Maritime Gauls) at a naval battle commanded by Decimus Brutus, later to be one of Caesar's assassins ('You too, Brutus'). He also successfully invaded Britain before the much tougher battles against a

> *'I had rather be first in a village than second in Rome'.*
>
> Julius Caesar

rejuvenated Central Gaul under the redoubtable Vercingetorix, culminating in the critical and near-run victory at Alesia.

Pompey was a similarly brilliant General. The Mediterranean had been infested with pirates in the late republic, and he was the first to have made those waters safe for travel. So prestigious were his military successes that he gained the name 'Magnus' ('The Great'). He was known for his ruthless tactics as 'Carnifex' – 'The Slaughterer'.

Thus, when Crassus died, Rome was left with two brilliant, ambitious, and powerful men who both had control of the state in their sights. Caesar's ambitions were obvious, 'I had rather be first in a village than second in Rome'.

Eventually, through fear of his potential domination, the Senate ordered Caesar to disband his army and return to Rome as a private citizen. Faced by political or actual suicide, he violated the *Lex Cornelia Maiestratis*, forbidding a General to lead an army out of his province. 'Alea iacta est' – 'The die is cast', he remarked as he crossed the small stream separating Cisalpine Gaul from Italy, the Rubicon. War was now impossible to avoid. Caesar and Pompey, father and son-in-law, would fight to the death for rule of Rome. The tribunes who were loyal to Caesar fled Rome, meeting with him at Ariminum,

Caesar crosses the Rubicon.

regarded by many as the moment that spawned the Roman Civil War, a conflict that stained Rome's memory and literature for hundreds of years to come. After Caesar defeated Pompey at Pharsalus, he would be murdered by Cassius and Brutus, who were defeated at Philippi by Antony, who in turn was defeated by Octavian at Actium. The cycle of civil war would be a terrible one. The greatest work written about the civil war, Lucan's *De Bello Civili* (see right), laments the crossing of the Rubicon as the moment that released all the evils of the world.

See: Actium

Caesar, ut adversum superato gurgite ripam attigit, Hesperiae vetitis et constitis arvis, 'hic' ait 'hic pacem temerataque iura relinquo te, Fortuna, sequor'.

Caesar, when he crossed the stream and reached the far side, halted in the ancient fields of Italy and said, 'Here, here I cast aside peace and soft laws, and I follow you, Fortune'.

RUGBY
England

Rugby is an industrial town in Britain's Midlands, and it was the nearby school, founded in 1567, which was first to achieve real fame in Thomas Hughes's book *Tom Brown's Schooldays,* which portrayed the brutal life in the British public school of the early 19th century. The theme has now been wonderfully spoofed by George McDonald Fraser who had the brilliant idea of making the fictional school bully 'Flashman' into a cowardly but attractive, womanising rogue, getting into outrageous scrapes all over the world and being consistently and undeservedly honoured.

But something happened in 1823 which was to take the name Rugby to the furthest corners of the earth. During a game of football at the school, a boy

called William Webb Ellis picked up the ball and ran with it. After the initial shock, this unusual practice became the norm, and within years, running with the ball was joined by H-shaped goal posts, the 'try' at goal, the oval ball and the distinctive jerseys and caps, all reflecting the sport we know today.

Rugby football also became somewhat violent, sometimes with 200 people in 'Big Side' games, with forwards 'hacking' at the ball and at the players with their boots, which often inflicted injury.

Thus, in 1863, meetings were held in London to try to sort out the rules of football. Many clubs wanted to follow the 'Cambridge Rules', banning 'running in' and 'hacking'. When both were banned, some clubs withdrew to play 'Rugby Football'. Others remained to form the 'Football Association', which effectively created 'soccer'.

The game of rugby spread quickly through the expanding British Empire. The first 'away' game was played in far away New Zealand, in 1870. Twelve years later, the first Australian team,

See: Augusta, Cresta Run, Dunsinane, Eton, Henley, Heysel, Hillsborough, Jodhpur, Lord's, Old Trafford, Stowe

'New South Wales' toured New Zealand and in 1888, the first British team arrived in New Zealand.

Then, in 1895, another split occurred, when clubs in the north of England created the professional 'Rugby League', as opposed to 'Rugby Union'.

Today, Rugby is one of the most popular games in the world, with France and Italy now major forces, joining the more traditional nations.

How many places have achieved such fame – simply by a schoolboy breaking the rules?

RUN
Spice Islands

'Sugar and spice And all things nice…'

It is hard for us now to grasp the huge economic and political importance of spices. Ever since people learned to cook, they have had an ever-increasing role.

Two thousand years before Christ, the spice trade from the east was already fully developed. In 950BC, the Queen of Sheba visited King Solomon. Why? She was worried his fleet would bypass her kingdom (now Yemen), ruining her wealth as a spice route. The Egyptians and Romans were prolific users of spices, whose use briefly declined in the Dark Ages – but soon, contact with the Arabs revived the trade. The cynical Fourth Crusade was mounted by Venice, in reality, to capture Constantinople as a spice centre. The growth of Venice and Genoa was mainly based on the spice trade, and the cultural explosion of the Renaissance was only possible because of the massive wealth that spices created.

At first, it was Portugal and Spain – dividing up the world, that dominated the trade, but two new players, England and Holland, soon intervened. For year after year, they competed and fought, especially over the 'Spice Islands' of Molucca and Banda, and it was nutmeg

Short-term nutmeg wealth exchanged for the future New York.

that provoked the confrontation – and one of the strangest twists of fortune in history.

To speed up the journey to the 'spiceries', sailors searched for the 'Northeast' or 'Northwest passage'. Britain's Henry Hudson was attempting this, when he arrived in a river the Indians called 'Manna-hata'. Now we call it the Hudson River and its island Manhattan. The ever-present rivals, the Dutch, trading for fur, created New Netherland there.

The tiny nutmeg island of Run was ceded to the British in 1616 by the Bandanese islanders. As the only island not under their control, it was besieged by the furious Dutch. A British hero, Nathaniel Courthope, led the defence for three long years until he was trapped and killed. His followers and many other British traders were horribly tortured by the Dutch at the 'Massacre of Amboyna'. It took years of conflict for Britain to take back Run by the Treaty of Westminster in 1654, and its possession did not last long. Charles II's brother James, Duke of York, captured that other Dutch island, Manhattan, and, at the Treaty of Breda in 1667, the Dutch decided that Run was *much more valuable*, and so the British acquired the whole of New Netherland, re-naming it New York.

Run is still a tiny, sleepy island, its nutmeg monopoly and wealth long lost to Grenada and other places. New York, while no longer British, has proved rather more important on the world stage.

See: Big Apple, Ellis Island, Gotham, Great Hedge, Manhattan

RUNNYMEDE
England

Runnymede is a picturesque borough in Surrey, by the River Thames. It is also the birthplace of the Magna Carta, the oldest documented declaration of human rights and civil liberties in British history.

In 1215, there was a great deal for the King of England to fear, not least his own barons, eager to see an end to (or greater share of) the anarchic violence that had ruled the land for as long as anyone could remember.

King John was cruel, avaricious, cowardly, lecherous and incompetent. He had been born into an era of violence and treachery, and continued his career in the same spirit. He had quarrelled with his father, with all his brothers – including Richard 'the Lionheart' – with the French, with the Pope and with the Church, resulting in 'Excommunication'. Above all, he had treated his barons badly, taxing them, fining them and even violating their wives and killing their children as hostages. He may even be the only English King to murder a rival, the young Arthur. However, the appalling scale of his misrule was to change everything.

After years of twisting and turning, breaking alliances and reneging on agreements, he had only a few knights still loyal to him. The writing on the wall suggested if he did not at least pretend to compromise with the rebels that had gathered against him, civil war was inevitable, as was his defeat.

Realising that he was cornered, the King sent William Marshall, Earl of Pembroke, and other 'trustworthy' messengers to tell the barons that for the sake of peace, and for the honour of the kingdom, they would be granted the laws and liberties that they demanded. All that the barons needed to do was choose a place and date where the two parties could meet to discuss the details.

The King's messengers all returned with the same instructions; the day would be the 15th June, and the place would be a field between Staines and Windsor – Runnymede Meadows.

King John, waiting in Windsor Castle, agreed. Runnymede Meadows offered a large enough space to house both armies, and was in itself symbolic of compromise – lying, as it did, halfway between the Castle in Windsor and the forces of the rebel barons camped in Staines.

On 15th June, by the banks of the River Thames, the King signed the historic agreement that has long been the most powerful symbol of personal freedom in the western world. The rights, instantly bestowed on every man, included the statement that: *No free man shall be imprisoned or outlawed except by the lawful judgement of his peers of the land. To no one will we sell, to no one will we deny or delay right or justice.* The King was now theoretically subject to the same laws as every free man in the country.

However, he immediately (and predictably) backed off the deal, persuading the Pope to excommunicate the barons, and recruited an appalling mercenary army from France which devastated Kent. Louis, the King of France, then also invaded.

But fate intervened, and John died of dysentery on 16th October 1216. His son, Henry III, having united the country at last, reissued the Magna Carta. Its principles were to shape the American Constitution half a millennium later. For that reason, Runnymede has a memorial erected by the American Bar Association, maintained by the Magna Carta Trust and chaired by the Master of the Rolls, a leading figure in the British judicial system.

While the Magna Carta now resides at The British Library, the National Trust maintains the meadows themselves and, combined with various memorials (to the nameless dead of the Second World War, and to John F Kennedy), the fields continue to attract thousands of tourists every year.

King John is forced to sign the Magna Carta.

See: Downing Street, Gotham

ST. ANDREWS
Scotland

If you were drinking with your friends in Scotland in 1458, a conversation about golf would be conducted in hushed, nervous voices. Those brave enough to venture out on to the courses would spend as much time looking over their shoulders as looking for the ball. The reason? James II, had made the sport illegal through an Act of Parliament. If you were a golfer, you were now an outlaw. This harsh Act did have a serious purpose. The King had realised that the sport's blossoming popularity was having a worrying effect. In their free time, the young men of Scotland were neglecting their vital archery training to enjoy themselves on the golf courses. And James' concern was justified. The pastime's prevalence endured, despite two more Bills to ban it, and the effects came home years later in 1513, where the under-trained Scots were defeated by the English at the Battle of Flodden. The power and popular appeal of golf had been proved to be insurmountable. James IV of Scotland had long since decided that, if he could not beat them, he would join them. Royalty was evolving from golf's enemy to its strong devotee, and the 1502 Treasury records show that James IV splashed out 14 shillings on his first set of golf clubs which he took south with him when he became James I of England. Golf was here to stay.

The roots of the sport itself are somewhat difficult to pin down. Did it come from Paganica of ancient Rome

WWW.STANDREWS.ORG.UK

inspiring the Dutch 'kolfen', or the French 'jeu de mail', where a ball was knocked from one point to another (perhaps two doors in a village) in the least number of strokes possible? Or was it an evolution of Scottish fishermen knocking along stones on their walk home? One thing that is certain is that, fortunately, it is not really an acronym of the words *'Gentlemen only, ladies forbidden!'*

St. Andrews, more than any other course, has its name etched into the archives of golfing history. Though records

of the game being played there only appear in 1552, it is widely believed that it had taken root long before, perhaps even earlier than the University's foundation in 1411. The rough surface of the links may well have led to the bunker and the hole. And residents of the town are quick to assert their claim that it is indeed the 'Home of golf'.

The legend began to shine brighter than ever with the foundation of The Royal and Ancient Golf Club at St. Andrews in 1754. Though it was the golf club at Leith that drew up the first set of golfing rules in 1744, St. Andrews, was asked in 1897 by other clubs to draw up a truly uniform code of regulations, which included the stipulation that 18 holes should be a standard course. St. Andrews became the epicentre of golfing rules, and has remained their arbiter ever since, now in collaboration with the American ruling body.

But chance nearly intervened to remove St. Andrews' pre-eminence. In 1797, the town council was in such severe financial difficulties that it was forced to sell its golf links to local merchants, who in 1799, to the horror of all the local golf enthusiasts, converted their beloved courses into rabbit farms. After years of squabbling, and even the odd brawl, the courses were finally resurrected in 1821, when James Cheape of Strathtyrum bought back the land, and returned golf back to the ancient buildings and dramatic spires of St. Andrews.

Today, the town demonstrates its perennial symbiosis with golf in the local British golf museum. The Old Course (now one of the five 18 hole courses at St. Andrews Links) is possibly the most famous golf course on earth, and is renowned as being as glorious as it is historic. St. Andrews is a frequent home to the Open Championship, and by 2005, it will have been held there 27 times.

From a sinister, illegal practice to a worldwide omnipresent pastime, golf, and indeed St. Andrews, have come a long way.

See: Agincourt, Augusta

ST. GERMAIN-EN-LAYE
France

Take the 'A' train out of Paris, and after half an hour, you arrive at a prosperous suburb, St. Germain-en-Laye. With good shops and several excellent restaurants, the town is dominated by a handsome castle which is now an archaeological museum. There is little to explain its former political significance.

In 1691, after their defeat by King William at the Battle of the Boyne and several other disasters, the Irish Catholics surrendered at the Treaty of Limerick. 18,000 Irishmen left for France with their commanders, and became known as the 'Wild Geese', a wonderful and romantic name, but probably just a cover by Irish shipping clerks to disguise the human military exodus. Soon 30,000 Irishmen were in the service of Louis XIV, as the 'Army of King James'.

It was at his castle at St. Germain-en-Laye that Louis generously invited James II and his fellow Scottish and Irish Catholics to stay, and which they took over completely when Louis moved to rather larger premises in Versailles.

The 'Wild Geese' were to repay Louis well, distinguishing themselves in innumerable battles. Charles, Viscount Clare, fought at Blenheim and died at Ramillies, and his son fought so well at Dettingen and Fontenoy that he became the famous Maréchal Clare.

Fontenoy was not the first or last time that the Irish Brigade would save a battle:

> On through the camp the column trod
> King Louis turns his rein;
> 'Not yet, my liege', Saxe interposed,
> 'The Irish troops remain'.
> On Fontenoy, on Fontenoy
> Like eagles in the sun,
> With bloody plumes the Irish stand.
> The field is fought and won!

There was a real human sadness in all this conflict, with Irishmen fighting on opposite sides. The Duke of Berwick, Clare's brother-in-law, also lived in the castle, and was the son of James II and Arabella Churchill – the sister of the Duke of Marlborough – their enemy, and the victor of Blenheim. Marlborough pointed out that at Malplaquet:

> *In the depths of the wood, by one of the strange coincidences of history, the Royal Irish met and defeated the French Royal Irish Regiment, famous in the war as the 'Wild Geese'.*

It would not, of course, be the only time Irishmen would serve on opposite sides. The fate of India was decided by the British victory of Wandewash in 1760, in which Sir Eyre Coote beat the French, commanded by his fellow Irishman Count Thomas Arthur Lally-Tollendal (O'Mullally). Thousands of Irishmen fought fiercely on both sides of the American Civil War – and further south, 'Wild Geese' were individually even more significant. *To him, more than to any other man, Chile owes her independence* was written of Bernado O'Higgins, who liberated Chile, and inspired Peru and Argentina to throw off the yoke of Spain.

He was but one of hundreds of Irishmen who fought with Bolívar – the Liberator of Venezuela – and in other campaigns. And Latin America's navies were nearly all founded by men with names like Brown, Keating, Cowan, O'Grady, Wright, Campbell and O'Brien. But, the most famous Irishman in Latin American history abandoned his Irish name. We now know Ernesto Guevara Lynch as 'Che Guevara'.

It is a pity that at St Germain-en-Laye there is not more to show for Scottish, and even more, Irish loyalty to France. After all, Rudyard Kipling was to record for the Irish Guards in the First World War:

> 'For we carried our packs with Marshal Saxe,
> When Louis was our King.
> But Douglas Haig's our Marshal now
> And we're King George's men.
> And after a hundred and seventy years
> We're fighting for France again'.

The castle donated by Louis XIV

One of the wildest of 'The Wild Geese', Che Guevara, descendant of an immigrant from Galway

See: Bael na Blath, Ballingarry, The Bogside, River Boyne, Clontarf, General Post Office, Versailles

ST. JOSEPH
Missouri, USA

A Pony Express rider on the next stage

See: Chisholm Trail, Cumberland Road, Promontory, Rock Island, St Louis

'Father of the Blues', W.C. Handy

RONALD McDOWELL / ALABAMA MUSIC HALL OF FAME

On the banks of the Missouri Joseph Rolidoux opened a trading post and by 1842 had laid out the town which was not called after him – important as he was – but after his patron Saint.

St Joseph was just in time for the great migration to the west caused by the Californian Gold Rush of 1849.

Every spring the population of the town grew immensely, with settlers determined to set off along the Oregon Trail. Most had made it by railroad to St Louis, and then by steamboat to where the Missouri went north and they could go no further by water. There they paused in 'the jumping off places', the townships of Independence, Westport, Omaha, Council Bluffs and St Joseph. By April, the grass along the trail was high enough for grazing and the wagons set off, often into a huge traffic jam. They were not the huge Conestoga wagons but smaller, more versatile farm wagons, usually loaded to the brim. After a few miles many emigrants realised they were too overloaded and, days later, scavengers from the towns had often collected tons of surplus supplies and abandoned equipment, much to be resold to the next wave of departing settlers.

But something extra was to make St Joseph famous. The population west of the Rockies had jumped by 1860 to half a million, and folk were demanding a letter mail service faster than the two stagecoach routes – and the even slower one by sea in Panama, which took a month. The three owners of the company running the 'Central Overland Route' decided they needed something to convince the Government to give them the main mail contract worth $1million. Their answer was the Pony Express.

At 7.15 on 3rd April, John Fry galloped out of St Joseph heading west, and the next day Billy Hamilton left Sacramento in the rain heading east. In ten days they delivered the mail – 20 pounds of special, thin, lightweight letters. They were the first of 186 riders who were to ride in relays of 75 to 100 miles each, changing horses every ten miles or so, using 400 horses and 165 stations along the 2,000 mile trail.

'Buffalo Bill' Cody, as he was later known, was just fifteen when he was one of the riders who delivered the mail to California with news of the outbreak of the American Civil War – for which he nearly paid with his life, jumped by an Indian war party. Like many young men, he had answered what must be one of the frankest notices in advertising. In spite of the ominous tone of this recruiting, only one rider was ever killed and one mail bag lost.

For 18 months, the Pony Express brought fame to St Joseph. But progress sadly intervened. The telegraph line across the continent was completed in October 1861, and doomed the ponies and their intrepid riders overnight. Buffalo Bill went on to slaughter buffalo for the railroads, and was later to star in his Wild West Show. The prominence of St Joseph and the other Oregon Trail towns did not last long, but was certainly dramatic.

ST. LOUIS
Missouri, USA

As a city, St Louis, Missouri has more claims to fame by chance than most. In 1764, Pierre Liguest and his young scout Auguste Chouteau set up their fur trading post near the confluence of the Missouri and Mississippi Rivers in the name of Louis IX. Thirty nine years later, following the Louisiana Purchase, it was the only American city to fly three flags on one day – French, Spanish and US.

That same year, 1803, saw St Louis as the 'jumping off' point for the Lewis and Clark expedition which forestalled the British, and secured the whole of the West, the 'Oregon Territory' for the United States.

Because it was the most westerly railhead, most of the emigrants flooded through St Louis during the gold rush of the 1850s, but the improvements in rail traffic created by its Eads Bridge in 1874 came much too late to stop Chicago becoming the rail and food centre of America. Nevertheless, by that time, St Louis was its fourth largest city, qualifying for another unique event in 1904, the only time a city has hosted the Olympic Games and a World Fair at the same time, with 20 million visitors following the song *'Meet me in St Louie, Louie'*. A more dubious distinction at the time was the world's first petrol station and the first car accident.

Then two things happened which ensured the name St Louis would become familiar to millions who might not have had the slightest idea even where it was.

William Christopher Handy had just written his first blues, *Memphis Blues.* Visiting St Louis, he met a black woman on the street loudly complaining of her husband's faithlessness, 'Ma man's got a heart like a rock cast in de sea'.

She was the inspiration of *St Louis Blues,* the most famous blues in history and the world. At first, all publishers turned it down, so W.C. Handy decided to publish it himself. After two years it took off, with Ethel Waters, the Original Dixieland Jazz Band, Bessie Smith, Louis Armstrong, Cab Calloway and Benny Goodman and many others all playing it. In 1917, Sophie Tucker made it the very first blues to sell a million records. It appeared in innumerable films and it was even made socially respectable by European Royal Families, with King Edward VIII having it performed with Scottish pipers.

Only *Silent Night* beat it as the most recorded song up till 1954 in America. As *Stille Nacht* is really German, it means that *St Louis Blues* is the most recorded American song.

With *St Louis Blues* playing in everyone's ears, a young fresh-faced 'barnstorming' stunt pilot called Charles Lindbergh was getting bored flying mail

from St.Louis to Chicago, although that was dangerous enough in the so-called 'flying coffins'. St Louis now had the claim to fame of also being the centre of American aviation, with the St Louis Air Meet of 1923 attracting no less than 125,000 enthusiasts.

The daring Lindbergh, the only man whose life had been saved four times by parachutes, determined to fly from New York to Paris non-stop – trying to beat many others who were competing for a $25,000 prize. The local *St Louis Post-Dispatch* would have nothing to do with such a reckless stunt, but a group of St Louis businessmen helped to buy a specially-built single-engined plane built by the unknown company in San Diego. Needing 400 gallons of fuel for the 3,600 mile flight, Lindberg elected to fly alone. On the side of the huge extra fuel tank blocking his forward vision, was painted SPIRIT OF ST LOUIS.

The media took to this brave, shy and good-looking 'Kid Flyer', also calling him the 'Human Meteor' or the 'Flying Fool'.

At 7.54 on the morning of May 30th 1927, the two ton flying fuel tank staggered into the air. After hours desperately trying to stay awake, he spotted fishing boats. 'WHICH WAY IRELAND?' he shouted, circling. No answer. But soon the coast of Dingle Bay appeared out of the mist. At 10.39 at night, after 33 hours 39 minutes, he rolled to a stop at Paris, Le Bourget, thunderstruck by the 150,000 people flooding onto the airfield.

He had become the most popular man in the world, and put St Louis on the map forever.

Lindbergh circles above the Irish fishing boats. Painting by Roger Middlebrook.

The arch that commemorates the role of St Louis as the principal gateway to the west

See: Farnborough, Muroc, St. Joseph, Sissinghurst, Storyville, Tin Pan Alley

ST. TROPEZ
France

'A charming and simple daughter of the sea, a lovely, modest little town, grown from the water like a shellfish, fed on fish and sea air' – Guy de Maupassant.

ST. TROPEZ TOURISM

See: Barbizon, Bikini, Ibiza, Hollywood

St. Tropez has become better and better known in a fascinatingly progressive fashion. There was no one event that propelled it on to the world stage, no battle or invention or landmark, but the steady influx of well-known characters. It is famous people that have made St. Tropez a famous place.

Back in 1892, the painter Paul Signac sailed his yacht to the village to investigate his ancestry. The stay was meant to be short, but the natural beauty and vivid colours of the place inspired him. He remained, and painted some of his most impressive pieces. The scenery that captivated him drew other artists, including Bonnard, Braque, Seurat and Matisse. St. Tropez was to become an artistic haven. Pianist Franz Liszt and romantic writer Guy de Maupassant also fell under its spell, and the process gathered momentum. Between the two World Wars, the French writer Colette set up residence in the village, and praised it in her *La Treille Muscate*. For the first time, this charming seaside retreat was also earning a reputation as a destination of the rich and famous, with Errol Flynn among its regular guests.

It was a place stars and artists alike visited to get away from the world. But after the Second World War, this was set to change. In 1956, the young filmmaker Roger Vadim created a movie here, *Et Dieu Créa la Femme* (And God Created Woman), starring the now legendary Brigitte Bardot. The film itself was very influential, paving the way for the 'Nouvelle Vague' directors. And although Vadim would never be quite as famous a director as his early career had

Brigitte Bardot at St. Tropez in the unspoilt early days

promised, Bardot became a household name. She would personally adopt the village as her favourite haunt, and increasingly it became the place to be for celebrities, from Picasso to Jane Fonda, and now such names as Robert De Niro, Elton John, Barbara Streisand, Jack Nicholson, Joan Collins, Julia Roberts, Eddie Jordan and many, many more. The streets are as filled with beautiful people as the harbour is with luxury yachts, and those not in magnificent cars are above in private helicopters. As the celebrities came, so did the tourists and fans. Many of the village's 30,000 daily visitors are people hoping to soak in the atmosphere of fame, and to see one of their idols, perhaps on the legendary beaches, like the Tahiti. Huge sums of money are flashed around like small change in a town where a plate of spaghetti bolognese in La Voile Rouge Bar will set you back £80. Glamour is as abundant as £250 champagne.

So is this the most perfect place on earth? For the locals, some of whom have lived there all their lives, St. Tropez has changed, and not for the better. Prices have become astronomical, with a beer often costing £15, and ordinary, essential shops like butchers and bakers have been squeezed out by fashionable designer boutiques. Parking has become difficult with long traffic jams. Even the din of helicopters has become an irritation. So while the secluded haven of artists has become a glamour-filled paradise for some, it is both over-crowded and over-priced for others.

For many, the jewel has been tarnished through its fame and popularity. Even Brigitte Bardot, the pioneer of St. Tropez's modern image, seems to have changed her mind about her old haunt, *'I can no longer live in what St. Tropez has become, I am leaving it to the invaders. It has been taken over by yobs. The sunny little port of the 1960s, with its pretty girls, its cover girls, has disappeared. Today, sausages and chips reign'.*

SALEM
Massachussetts, USA

In 1792, in the village of Salem, Massachusetts, two young girls were behaving very strangely. The local community became increasingly concerned at what appeared to be no ordinary illness. Abigail Williams and Elizabeth Parris, daughter and niece of the local priest, were suffering from fits, arching their bodies, thrashing violently and screaming nonsense. As their condition became more inexplicable, the town murmured about supernatural powers; someone was hurting these girls, using powers granted to them by the devil. Who would do such a thing? This question festered in every mind in Salem, and suspicion spread.

The finger was first pointed at Sarah Good and Sarah Osborne, two old women on the fringes of the community, and Tituba, a Caribbean slave. Meanwhile more young girls were beginning to be afflicted like Abigail and Elizabeth. Perhaps others were in league with Satan? Trials duly began with courts established to hunt down the witches in Salem and hang them. The situation became worse than anyone could have imagined. Whereas the first few people suspects had been dubious figures, now some of the most respectable, church-loving, pillars of the community were targeted. Some of the most unlikely people were turning out to be 'witches'. Even Rebecca Nurse, a frail, God-fearing woman of 71, and Dorcas Good, a 4-year old girl, were found guilty and imprisoned. Yet all the while the girls' attacks continued, with eight of them afflicted with fits and appearing to see horrifying visions. Without any provable evidence, the inhabitants of the village continued to be accused, imprisoned and condemned.

Salem had become a dark and terrible place. Hangings were held on what was becoming known as 'Gallows Hill', and for his refusal to confess, Giles Cory was killed in perhaps the most awful way of all, crushed by great rocks. 'More weight', were his defiant last words. Almost 150 languished in prison, and the local fields, unattended, began to reek with decay. Five had died while incarcerated, and twenty had been put to death. The only way to avoid the death sentence was to confess to 'consorting with the devil'. While this would save your life, it would certainly damn your soul. Nobody was safe. No matter what their character or reputation, anyone could be accused of witchcraft. But relief from the witch hunt was coming. The Massachusetts Governor, Sir William Phipps, stepped in, and officially ended the trials on October 29th. The prisoners were released, and the ex-communications were rescinded.

What explanation, other than the supernatural, can be provided for Salem? Arthur Miller's play, *The Crucible,* portrays the girls who claimed to be attacked by witches as spiteful and dangerous children, feigning their fits and accusing all around them. Then, there is the rivalry between Salem Village and Salem Town. Over the previous years, while the village had held on to Puritan values of sharing and community, those in the town had become increasingly prosperous. These economic inequalities were frequently lamented by the new village Reverend, Samuel Parris, unsettling the locals. Many of the accusations came from the villagers, aimed at those near the town. Could the horrors of Salem really be a simple case of local rivalry?

There is a modern, more scientific conclusion. Linda Caporael, a behavioural psychologist at the Rensselaer Polytechnic Institute, New York, has postulated that the attacks were biochemical rather than paranormal. She notes that a cereal fungus called ergot, from which LSD is derived, may have been responsible. Bread made from rye that is tainted with ergot provides all the symptoms of the Salem girls; hallucinations, muscle contractions and skin sensations. Furthermore, the warm damp summer of 1691 provided perfect conditions for the fungus. Indeed, research has tracked such weather conditions to similar outbreaks of witch hunts over the centuries in Europe,

> *'You are God's instrument put in our hands to discover the Devil's agents among us'.*
>
> The Reverend Hale in Arthur Miller's *The Crucible*

the last in 1956 in France. So did ergotism result in the tragic deaths of 25 people by poisoning the minds of a few Salem girls? Even if this is the case, the lack of trust that raged through the community still has no excuse.

See: Assisi, Bethlehem, Fatima, Lourdes

Perhaps the most significant lesson to be learned from Salem is that, no matter how dangerous the powers of the supernatural, suspicion, distrust and panic can be far more destructive.

SANDHURST
England

The motto of the British Army's Royal Military Academy Sandhurst is *'Serve to Lead'* – and it is the underlying philosophy of every course undertaken by the officer cadets who study there. But this was not always the case. In the 18th and 19th centuries, it was assumed that the 'gentleman cadets' naturally possessed all the skills and qualities necessary to lead men into battle. But with the strange practice of officers being able to purchase their commissions, together with the increasing complexity of warfare, this was proving to be rather over-optimistic.

As in other countries, it was the specialist skills that first needed to be formally taught. The Royal Military Academy at Woolwich was founded in 1741, to train fee-paying young men from largely wealthy families for a career in the Royal Artillery and Royal Engineers. It was known by its students as 'The Shop' probably because its first building was a converted workshop. This resulted in the expression 'Talking Shop' passing into common language, meaning to 'discuss subjects not understood by outsiders'. The game of snooker also has its origins in the RMA. It was invented by a former cadet who named his new game after the title given to new arrivals, 'snookers', a corruption of 'les neux' (the new guys).

The Academy Sergeant-Major is the senior Warrant Officer in the British Army. Below is WO1 (ACSM) Ronnie Convery, Scots Guards

But the size, complexity and movement of armies in the Napoleonic age quickly showed that the infantry and cavalry also needed trained officers.

St Cyr (1802), West Point (1802), and the Kreigsakademie (1806) in Prussia were the results, as was the Royal Military College. Founded in 1799 by Guernseyman, Major General John Gaspard Le Marchant, it began life in High Wycombe as a school for staff officers, and two years later expanded by opening a Junior Department for younger officers at Remnatz, a country house at Great Marlow. The new department was successful, but it was clear that a different site was needed.

Sandhurst Park was on the old Exeter coaching road, 450 acres of sandy woodland in Windsor Forest. It had been owned by Prime Minister William Pitt, 'the Younger' and was then sold to the Government. The Park was chosen for the RMC because it was then considered far enough from London to prevent cadets being tempted by the distractions of the capital. The building now known as Old College was built in 1812. A century later, in 1912, New College was completed and a third, Victory College, was added in 1969.

Both the RMA and the RMC closed on the outbreak of World War II and

re-opened in 1947 under the single name and location as the Royal Military Academy Sandhurst (RMAS). It combined the best features of its two predecessors with a chief aim to train the leaders of the future.

The Academy provides a mixture of the academic and the military basics. Drill is taught mainly by the top instructors from The Brigade of Guards, and the Academy Sergeant Major is the Senior Warrant Officer in the British Army. Sandhurst's Department of War Studies is also legendary, and helped to launch the careers of academics like Richard Holmes, famous for television's *War Walks,* and Sir John Keegan, who has observed that, *The atmosphere and surroundings of Sandhurst are not conducive to the realistic treatment of war.* However, the fact is that Sandhurst has

provided Britain with most of her finest military leaders, as well as politicians, including Churchill, and foreign rulers like King Hussein of Jordan and the Sultan of Brunei.

And among all the seriousness, the cadets are allowed some fun. One indulgence is to pull a stunt at the full dress rehearsal for the Sovereign's Parade (The Passing Out Parade). The Adjutant's horse was often spirited away, but more dramatic was the year that elephants from a circus joined the parade and another occasion when the A30 road was diverted through the drill square.

Perhaps this healthy balance is one of the reasons why Sandhurst's reputation as one of the world's leading military institutions has endured for so long.

Academy Sergeant Major J.C. Lord was one of the Sandhurst legends, greeting new cadets with:
'My name is Lord. He is Lord up there, (pointing his pace stick skywards) but I am the Lord down here'.
He further explained:
'I will call you, 'Sir' and you will call me 'Sir'. The only difference is that you will mean it'.
He also confidently admonished monarchs:
'Mr King Hussein, Sir. You are the idlest King I ever did see'.

See: West Point

SAN SERRIFFE
Indian Ocean

The readers of *The Guardian* who rang in to find out more about lovely San Serriffe in 1977 could be forgiven. After all, it had been featured in a special anniversary seven-page supplement full of interesting articles and lively advertisements. Anyone in the worlds of advertising, journalism and print should have smelt a rat when they noticed the country was divided between two islands, Upper Case and Lower Case. Others should have paid more attention to the date – 1st April.

One of the more elegant of April Fool's jokes ever, San Serriffe was cooked up between the London office of the leading advertising agency, J.Walter Thompson, and its client *The Guardian.* What was really clever was to persuade several other clients to actually pay for advertisements. Thus, British Airways announced new direct flights into Bodoni International Airport; Texaco offered a holiday competition; and Kodak asked readers to send in San Serriffe snaps.

Articles of welcome were written, apparently by the Minister of Tourism and the country's President, General Pica (a size of type). The detailed map listed pleasant-sounding towns like Bodoni, Clarendon, Garamondo (all popular typefaces). The northern cape on Lower

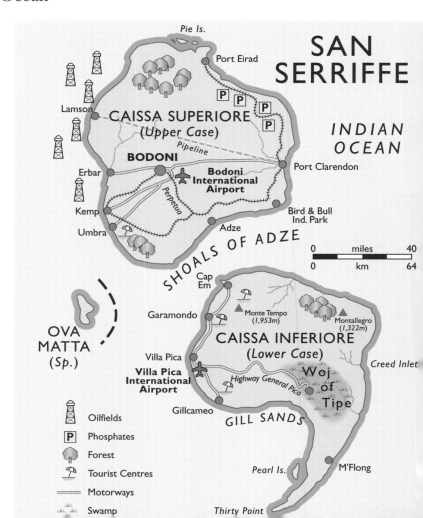

Caisse, Cap Em, overlooked the body of water called Shoals of Adze. Tourists were invited to visit the Woj of Tipe, or stroll along the beach of Gill Sands, (another typeface). Boats could visit Ova Mata ('over matter'– too much copy) or sail round Thirty Point, (the type size of a newspaper headline).

The other British medium which allowed itself the indulgence of playing an April Fool's prank on the public was no less than the world-renowned BBC in 1957, and, equally improbably, in the form of a serious Richard Dimbleby of the *Panorama* programme. He strolled through an orchard of Swiss spaghetti trees, while a family harvested strands of spaghetti hanging from them, whilst bemoaning the competition from the 'vast spaghetti plantations' in Italy.

Hundreds of viewers called in to find out how to grow spaghetti at home. The BBC advised them to 'place a sprig of spaghetti in a tin of tomato sauce and hope for the best'. In fairness, it must be pointed out that in 1957 spaghetti was seen as a rather exotic delicacy, so maybe the stuff did grow on trees. But still ....

SARAJEVO
Bosnia

> *'If there is ever another war in Europe, it will come from some damned silly thing in the Balkans'.*
> Otto von Bismarck

'The Balkans are not worth the healthy bones of a single Pomeranian Grenadier'.

Prince Otto von Bismarck, the great Prussian statesman and founder of Germany, was only too prophetic. The world would regret not worrying about his second prophecy (on the left).

On June 28th 1914, the heir to the throne of the Austro-Hungarian Empire, Archduke Franz Ferdinand, was visiting Sarajevo, the capital of Bosnia. On the way to an official reception, a bomb was thrown into his car – which he threw back into the road, protesting later to the Mayor for 'this unfriendly welcome'. He did not survive this lucky escape for long.

On the return journey, a 19-year old student, Gavril Princip, darted from the crowd and fired straight at the Archduke, hitting him in the neck. His second shot killed the Duchess Sophie, who had flung herself across her dying husband to protect him. Almost immediately suspicion for the outrage centred on the Serbs and their ' Black Hand' secret society.

Europe was in shock and revulsion, Pope Pius X fainted, Emperor Franz Josef broke down crying, 'No sorrow is spared me'. *The Times* commented, *'It shakes the conscience of the world'*. But for most of Europe, life – briefly and comfortably – went on as normal. In Britain, 'society's' thoughts turned to Ascot Week, the Henley Regatta and preparing for the grouse-shooting season. The French were more interested in whether Madame Caillaux would be acquitted for shooting the Editor of *Le Figaro* for attacking her cabinet minister husband in print. The French President went on a state visit to Russia, the Serbian Prime Minister was away, the German Kaiser was on his usual yachting holiday – and General von Moltke, his army chief, was taking a cure at a foreign spa. Suddenly, nearly four weeks after the assassination, the Austrians presented impossible demands to the Serbian Government which had to be answered in 48 hours. Britain offered to mediate, which the Kaiser decided was 'insolent', and the Austrians, encouraged, declared war on the Serbs. Russia, Serbia's ally, mobilised, as did France and Germany.

By 1914, 'mobilisation' meant huge and complex railway mobilisation. Railways were now so important that, in Germany, the best staff officers were given the honour of going to railway school. 'The Schlieffen Plan', the huge movement of German troops through Belgium and France was worked on by Field Marshal Alfred von Schlieffen for 13 years, right down to the last platform, set of points or culvert. As such, mobilisations had become unstoppable, and Europe chuffed clumsily to war. On 1st August, the Kaiser declared war on his cousin Czar Nicholas. Two days later he declared war on France, and just 24 hours later the Schlieffen Plan sent the first troops into Belgium. Britain came back from her August Bank Holiday and

After the assassination, Princip is captured.

declared war on Germany.

The world had lurched into the most horrible war in its history. It would kill tens of millions, and wipe out the flower of Europe's youth. It would engulf whole monarchies, destroy the great Austro-Hungarian and Ottoman Empires, bring Communism to Russia and the world – and lay the seeds of Fascism and the Nazis. Gavril Princip, languishing in gaol for four years, must have wondered what he had unleashed.

For seven decades, Sarajevo returned to obscurity – until the dismemberment of Yugoslavia brought a city which had hosted the Games back on to our television screens, with the Serb forces of Slobodan Milosevic shelling it for weeks. Finally, the West decided enough was enough - and air power and artillery forced the Serbs to lift the siege. They went on to attack Eastern Serbia, and the world would get another Bosnian town made famous by chance – Srebrenica.

It is difficult to stand aside from the tensions and problems in the Balkans, but one does have sympathy with Bismarck's intention to do so.

See: Gallipoli, Somme, Srebrenica

> *'I constantly wonder whether it really pays to bind ourselves too tightly to this phantasm of a state that is cracking in all directions'.*
>
> German Ambassador to Vienna, 1914

SAVILE ROW
England

The name of Savile Row is now so associated with fine tailoring worldwide that even today in Japanese the word for a suit is *Sebiro*.

This originates from 1871 when the first Japanese Embassy staff arrived in their kimonos, and were promptly sent around to Henry Poole & Co to be fitted out with Western attire suitable for the Court (to whom Poole was the main tailor).

Two men and a woman helped to create the street's original fame. The tailor Robert Baker created Piccadilly, named after the ornate Elizabethan shirt collar, the *pickadil.* He also helped to develop the rest of the Earl of Burlington's estate – of which Savile Row was part of his Lordship's kitchen garden – named after the Earl's wife, Lady Dorothy Savile.

But it was the legendary dandy, Beau Brummell, who encouraged tailors to gather in Cork Street, Old Burlington Street, and above all, in Savile Row. Brummell, a close friend of the Prince Regent, became the arbiter of Regency taste, and set the trend for elegant, bespoke tailoring in wool. After the end of the Napoleonic Wars in 1815, trade and fashion boomed, and Savile Row became the place to have your tailor. As younger tailors broke away from the established houses, they too needed to stay close, hence the continuing concentration in one street.

Ever since Beau Brummell's friend became King George IV, royal patronage has been a vital ingredient of Savile Row's success, right up to the present Queen and Prince Charles. Most of Europe's royalty in the last century came to this famous venue. And in this century, the new 'royalty' – film stars – reinforced its image and not just our own stars like Roger Moore and Sean Connery – but also Gary Cooper, Cary Grant, Clark Gable, Bing Crosby and Frank Sinatra. Indeed, Fred Astaire's morning coat in 'Top Hat' was created by Gieves & Hawkes.

When the firm of Kilgour, French and Stanbury created the uniform of Captain Bligh for Charles Laughton in the film *Mutiny on the Bounty*, every detail was completely accurate. This was hardly surprising; the real Captain Bligh had been a former customer.

If you look carefully at the morning suit at Ascot or weddings, or the evening tail coat, you will detect the influence of the 18th century rural gentleman on Savile Row style, the cutaway front to clear the knees while riding, the tails to clear the horse's back, and those two little buttons to pin up the divided tails if the horse were muddy! Savile Row also created, and then gave true style and elegance to that most egalitarian of male attire, the 'lounge' suit.

Another innovation was the dinner jacket, or 'tuxedo', also created in Savile Row. The Prince of Wales ordered a short and informal jacket in 1865 from Poole's, and James Brown Potter – an American financier – had one run up quickly before staying the weekend with the Prince. He later wore it, with royal

The official Court Dress designed by Henry Poole

COURTESY OF HENRY POOLE

approval, at his club – The Tuxedo Club of New York – and the fashion spread.

Something which has not changed over the centuries is how tailors were always hopeless at collecting their money. Accounts were often still unpaid when the word *'dead'* appeared in customer ledgers. Given their royal patronage, *'Assassinated'* was also not an uncommon indication that the account was unlikely to be settled.

'Clothes don't make a man…but they go a long way to making a businessman', said Thomas Watson, the head of IBM, reflecting the most important role for modern fine tailoring.

See: Ascot, Carnaby Street, Cowes, Fleet Street, Harley Street, Tuxedo Club, Wall Street

Some streets lose their special fame; Fleet Street is no longer the centre of Britain's press. Some keep their niche; Harley Street is full of doctors and Wall Street of brokers.

Today, Savile Row has more tailors than ever before. At one end is Issey Miyake, with his revolutionary Japanese style and – at the other – is the more traditional Gieves & Hawkes. Even its bank, once the Bank of England's West End branch, has become a Jil Sander fashion store. And Terence Conran's 'Sartoria' restaurant at number twenty says it all.

THE SAVOY
England

It was a very good thing that Richard D'Oyly Carte changed his mind. Otherwise, the Strand might have had a nondescript apartment block rather than the most famous hotel in the world.

As a concert and lecture agent, D'Oyly Carte had created one of the great musical partnerships with William Gilbert and Arthur Sullivan. So very successful were the Gilbert & Sullivan operettas that all three sank the profits into a new theatre. It was built on the site of the former Palace of Peter, Count of Savoy. Overlooking the Thames, this had been dubbed the *'fayrest Manor in Europe'*, and was later passed to John of Gaunt, Duke of Lancaster, who made an invaluable contribution to English literature by paying Geoffrey Chaucer £10 a year, enabling him to write his 'Canterbury Tales'. Savoy Palace was burned down in Wat Tyler's Peasant revolt of 1381, where 32 trapped and starving men drank themselves to death in its cellar.

Five hundred years later, in 1881, The Savoy Theatre opened to great acclaim, and was another financial success. D'Oyly Carte's next idea was an apartment block, to be called 'Savoy Mansions'. However, halfway through construction, he suddenly changed his mind. Now it would be a hotel, and what is more, a great one, requiring an exceptional manager. He persuaded César Ritz to spend half his time at The Savoy (Ritz was already running two hotels and a restaurant on the Continent).

Among the team that Ritz brought with him was another legend, Auguste Escoffier, a great chef, and also a great innovator. Escoffier promptly decided to abandon meals *à la française*, where all main and side dishes arrived at the same time, because, whilst looking impressive, he felt it blunted the palate, caused gluttony and indigestion, and, of course, made the food cold. Instead, he served food *à la russe* with each main dish served separately. He shopped for food and ingredients from all over Europe, and reorganised kitchen systems, not least by banning a constant problem – alcohol. Known as 'the King of chefs and the chef of Kings,' Escoffier, with Ritz, was to create a revolution.

Opened in 1889, The Savoy Hotel was full of innovations; electric lights and lifts, bathrooms throughout, even its own soft water from its very own well. Throughout, Ritz and D'Oyly Carte were determined that their new creation should combine the best of American technology and European service.

Soon, The Savoy was setting every kind of trend. 'After-theatre parties' meant that women came to dine – natural enough on the relaxed Continent but then unheard of in strait-laced London. Moreover, nobody in English 'society' ever went out on Sunday night, until The Savoy made Sunday dinner the place to be seen. In 1896, the very first woman to smoke a cigarette in public in Britain did so at The Savoy.

The connection with theatreland and the nearby opera was crucial. Indeed, it was for the great Australian diva, Nellie Melba, that Escoffier was to create the delicious 'Peach Melba', although he and Ritz always had to keep Nellie Melba and her hated opera rival Adeline Patti at opposite ends of the restaurant.

Having persuaded D'Oyly Carte to invest in Claridge's and the Grand Hotel in Rome, Ritz was becoming rather overconfident and began neglecting his work. Finally, he overreached himself – and started ruining The Savoy's profits by lavish spending on his own projects. Sadly, both he and Escoffier were duly dismissed in 1898 for *'gross negligence and breaches of duty and management',* although this did not seem to spoil their careers too much, as they went on to create Ritz-Carlton.

Their successor 'Joseph', had been somewhat scarred by his unappreciated spell as the private chef of the American railroad magnate, William Vanderbilt, and was wont to remark, 'Americans don't dine, they eat'. Nevertheless, despite this early bias, Americans were to make The Savoy their own, usually arriving at nearby Waterloo Station from the great Atlantic liners docking at Southampton.

During the twenties and thirties, many a couple learned to dance at home to music from The Savoy. Thanks to the new British Broadcasting Corporation which started at Savoy Hill, the music from the 'Savoy Opheans' was soon beamed to two and half million households.

The location of the hotel was a huge advantage. Without his balcony at The Savoy, Claude Monet might never have given us his superb paintings of the Thames in a foggy and atmospheric London. And, but for the comfort of his suite, Oscar Wilde might not have become so involved with 'Bosie' Douglas and thus might not have been ruined by Bosie's vengeful father, the Marquess of Queensberry.

Close to the Palace of Westminster, the hotel was full of peers and politicians from the start, including every Prime Minister. Winston Churchill and F.E. Smith started the unofficial political 'Other Club', which meets at The Savoy to this day.

However successful the hotel has been for politicians, millionaires, and royalty, it is the original and continuing connection with the performing arts which has helped to distinguish this famous venue from its competitors. Starting with Henry Irving and Escoffier's friend Sarah Bernhardt, there has never been a moment when stars are not staying or dining here.

Hollywood, especially, took to the hotel. Before the war it was Dorothy and Lillian Gish, Fred Astaire, Cary Grant, Douglas Fairbanks and Groucho Marx. Stars of Westerns included Gary Cooper of *High Noon,* Tom Mix and Gene Autrey (who both rode horses into the hotel) and Tex Austin, who defined his version of a perfect rare steak, 'Get a bullock, wound it slightly and drive it in!' Mae West used to arrive with 150 dresses and sixty pairs of shoes.

During the Second World War, Noël Coward moved into the hotel permanently, and was soon joined by other stars eager to help the war effort: Bob Hope, Ingrid Bergman, Al Jolson, Danny Kaye and Gregory Peck. In uniform was Clark Gable, as were, of course, military guests like Eisenhower, Montgomery and de Gaulle.

The list of screen idols who have insisted on The Savoy is endless: Charlie Chaplin, John Wayne, Marilyn Monroe, Frank Sinatra, (whose idea of a room was fifteen of them), Greta Garbo, Marlon Brando, Jack Nicholson, Steve McQueen and Louis Armstrong, who asked for a soundproof room.

It is probably fitting that the launch of the first Harry Potter film was celebrated by 480 guests at The Savoy – and in line with the hotel's tradition – on a Sunday.

LICHFIELD

Marlon Brando consults with Charlie Chaplin at The Savoy.

See: Fleet Street, Pudding Lane, Raffles, Reading Gaol

SCOTLAND YARD
England

The origins of the birthplace of the modern English police service are uncertain. The name of the place called 'Scotland Yard' derives either from a home of Scottish ambassadors, or simply because the original dwelling was once owned by a man called Scott in the middle ages. However, Scotland Yard's role in history is far more significant than its unassuming beginnings would indicate.

Early English law enforcement was designed to police a feudal society, and so was as decentralised as the crime scene itself. Without regular, organised crime, there seemed no need for a powerful police presence in the county, and the constables were untrained, unskilled, and unpaid. The situation changed in 1748 when Henry Fielding established the Bow Street Runners, often regarded as the world's earliest detective service. *'Wanted'* posters were brought into frequent use for the first time, and believing that 'it takes a thief to catch a thief', Fielding employed several ex-convicts to fill the Runners' ranks.

However, this new service was still far from a modern police force. To earn a living, the Runners were forced to charge heavy fees, known as 'blood money', to those whose valuables or safety they succeeded in protecting. For this reason, they were only effective for those few who could afford their expensive services. Furthermore, their numbers never exceeded 12 men, and London was a growing city, which would soon need a suitably expanded law enforcement service.

The history of today's police begins in 1829 with The Metropolis Police Improvement Bill. The crime levels in London had recently escalated to alarming levels, and three Parliamentary committees had been established to look into how to deal with the problem.

Robert Peel, proposer of the bill and founder of the new police force, had some very new ideas. Among them was his belief that harsh punishment itself was not enough to prevent crime, *'The certainty of detection is a far greater deterrent from crime than severity of punishment'*.

The new policemen, who were all retired army officers, were called 'Bobbies' after their founder, or similarly 'Peelers', with the added idea of keeping their eyes 'peeled.' However, they were given less friendly nicknames by those who believed that they would threaten public liberty, such as 'Blue Devils' and 'Raw Lobsters.' (The word 'Coppers' does not actually come from England. It became used to describe New York policemen around 1844, whose badges were made of copper).

The headquarters of the police had now been established at Scotland Yard. The location has since been moved twice, most recently in 1967 to Westminster, after which both new buildings were called New Scotland Yard.

The sweeping powers of the police to arrest, 'All loose, idle, and disorderly persons' caused problems. The lack of prejudice the police showed in arresting anyone they deemed suspicious thoroughly irritated the upper classes, who believed they should be totally above suspicion, though they themselves were usually idle, often loose and even occasionally disorderly. There were definite feelings all round that the new powers of the police were potentially very frightening, especially when such police sayings were in circulation as: 'Necessity is the mother of invention; so when you find it necessary to make a charge against someone you have locked up, invent one'.

However, to the credit of the police force, it received strict instructions not to attempt to force a confession out of suspects, and that a statement should only be received voluntarily.

The police became increasingly successful, and their numbers swelled to 18,000 by 1840. In 1842, Scotland Yard set up a force of detectives, although this constituted only eight men. Even by

1878 there were not more than 40. Sir Arthur Conan Doyle, (also writer of *The Lost World*, would set his tales of Scotland Yard's most famous fictional detective around this period; the stories of Sherlock Holmes. Brilliant, eloquent and fair, Holmes became the idealised epitome of all a detective should be, and his assertion on the nature of police work is perhaps one of the most expressive statements ever made on the subject, *'The law is what we live with; justice is sometimes harder to achieve'*.

See: 221b Baker Street

SEDAN
France

The name of Sedan carries few happy memories in 19th and 20th century French history, because its fame marks how two German armies, and in two separate wars, invaded and defeated the French.

In 1870, Germany was not yet even a proper country, but a confederation of states, with Prince Otto von Bismarck striving to ensure that Prussia would be at the head of a newly formed nation. He had already achieved much of his goal, using wars against both Denmark and Austria. But he had been unable to entice the southern German states into the fold. What Bismarck needed was a common cause, a threat that would unite all the German states, particularly if they needed the protection of the fearsome Prussian army. But where would he find such an opportunity?

As it happens, the opportunity presented itself. When a Hohenzollern candidate for the newly-vacated Spanish throne was put forward, Napoleon III did everything he could to sabotage this bid, lest it tip the European balance of power in favour of Prussia. Though he was successful, it was to be his undoing. The French ambassador Benedetti tried to persuade the King Wilhelm I of Prussia to make an official promise that the Prussian candidate's application would not only be retracted, but never again be issued. He even returned to the Spa town of Ems and confronted Wilhelm in the park, and went as far as to demand an official apology. Bismarck saw this as an opportunity too good to miss. He published a report of the incident, the famous 'Ems Dispatch', and edited it to make Benedetti's demands sound even more aggressive and arrogant. The doctored telegram was regarded by France as a 'provocation'. France was tricked into declaring war.

The German princedoms united in the face of their new foe, and the last phase of German unification was underway. As it rolled onward into France, the German army, still predominantly Prussian, was intimidatingly large; 400,000 men. The French army on the other hand, through poor organisation and slow mobilisation, was half the size. After a number of German victories, the French were crushed at Sedan on 1st September 1870. The following day, Napoleon, with 83,000 troops, surrendered to the Germans.

For the unhappy French, their troubles had just begun. Paris was besieged, and, beset by starvation, with people eating their cats and dogs, it surrendered. Even though the Minister of the new French Government, Léon Gambetta, made a dramatic balloon escape from Paris and tried to establish resistance in Lyon, the Germans were too strong. The newly established Commune of Paris was not powerful enough to overthrow them. The French were humiliated as Wilhelm was crowned the King of Germany in Versailles, and awarded Alsace-Lorraine as the spoils of war.

But, seventy years later, Sedan was once again the hinge of defeat.

In 1940, Germany was once again poised to attack France but there were several people critical of the army's *Fall Gelb* ('Plan Yellow'). One of them, instinctively, was Hitler; the other was General Eric von Manstein, who wrote, *'I found it humiliating, to say the least, that our generation could do nothing better than repeat an old recipe'.* The old recipe was a broad push into neutral Belgium and Holland north of the Maginot Line, designed to create a major battle in Flanders and perhaps to wheel south to

First Sedan aftermath: Napoleon III (left), surrenders to Prince Otto von Bismarck. Painting by Wilhelm Camphausen.

Rotting near the Meuse, the concrete bunkers that failed to stop the Germans crossing in 1940

325

Belgium's newspapers report the latest 'Hitlerian crime', the invasion of their country.

Second Sedan aftermath: Hitler's triumph at the French surrender in 1940

IMPERIAL WAR MUSEUM

See: Biggin Hill, Dieppe, Dunkirk, Oradour, Vichy

Paris – almost exactly the plan which had failed in 1914.

Hitler himself started to talk about the Ardennes Forest and Sedan on 30th October 1939, while Manstein was bombarding the irritated staff with his similar plans. In January 1940 a staff officer, against the rules, flying with details of *Fall Gelb,* crashed in Belgium. The Allies thought it a bluff. But it was Manstein's lunch with Hitler which changed the plan completely, to a thrust through the 'impassable' Ardennes Forest towards Sedan and beyond.

On May 9th, a French pilot reported *'60 miles of traffic coming through the Ardennes.'* Nobody believed him. Then, to the north, Holland was attacked, Rotterdam was bombed, and Belgium's 'impregnable' fort at Eben Emael on the Maas River was overcome by glider troops. The British duly advanced as planned into Belgium to confront the expected main thrust. But all these were diversions. The real thrust was further south, where the Germans had swiftly reached the same river there called the Meuse. On 13th May, the daring Rommel was across the river at Dinant with a few troops. French

counter-attacks were constantly postponed. Reinhardt struggled across at Monthermé. But it was at Sedan that the decisive moment came. The French – facing the great Panzer advocate, Heinz Guderian – even rationed their shells, waiting for the Germans inevitably 'to bring up artillery'. They failed to grasp that the Germans would use their terrifying Stuka dive-bombers as artillery to swamp the defenders, and would soon have infantry across the river.

Then something terrible happened to French cohesion. Unconfirmed reports of *'tanks'* led to withdrawal, which became a rout. A fatal gap appeared. It was the greatest tank victory of all time, because in fact Guderian had not yet managed to get one single tank across the Meuse. But next day he did, and like a dagger, was through the gap with a torrent of swiftly moving armour, speeding into the rear of the French and setting off for the coast. Only at Arras did British tanks delay the panzers for a couple of days. The Germans had split the allies in two.

Just 9 days later, Calais and Boulogne had fallen, and the world watched the amazing drama of the Dunkirk evacuation. It was indeed *Blitzkrieg,* 'lightning war.' Sedan had once again become a black word for the French.

SHARPEVILLE
South Africa

For a black township, Sharpeville was regarded as something of a model community by Vereeniging Town Council. It was named after John Lillie Sharpe, an immigrant Scot who had, ironically, shown considerable concern for the local black population.

It was only twelve years since the Afrikaner National Party had achieved power and had implemented its hated *'apartheid'* policies. Eighty seven per cent of the land was kept by the minority whites, and the black population had been reduced to a subservient race of low-paid menial or manual workers, rigidly confined by the 'pass laws' to their own 'townships', and indeed buses, trains, public seats and toilets.

The Sharpeville township provided workers for the nearby steel industry, and had been quiet, stable and non-political. The African National Congress had received little response in 1950 from Sharpeville for its 'May Day stay away', nor the bus boycott of 1955. Residents were keener on soccer, boxing and jazz. The facilities, schools and clinics were quite good: 'A happy Bantu, is a housed Bantu' was the compliant white attitude.

But conditions deteriorated, especially with the sudden arrival of hundreds of forcibly evicted residents of nearby Topville in 1959. Unemployment and criminality increased, rents escalated and so did police raids.

The Sharpeville Police Station became

the centre for local repression and enforcement of the 'Pass Laws', whereby all blacks had to show their pass to the police at any time. Significantly, it was the only police station isolated in the heart of a black township. During random interrogations about a small arms cache found in December 1959, a petty thief called 'Geebooi' was beaten, tortured and abused, before being released uncharged. He was to re-appear to play a sadly wider role.

In 1960, The Pan Africanist Congress, a militant breakaway from the ANC, decided that a mass demonstration by residents to burn their pass books and offer themselves for arrest should occur at Sharpeville Police Station. This nondescript building was normally manned by 35 African policemen and a handful of white officers, themselves young, poor and badly educated Afrikaners. In spite of warnings from informers, little was done in preparation to counter this demonstration, and both sides drifted towards disaster during the sunny weekend of 18th to 20th March.

By Sunday night, the authorities at last became alarmed by the growing crowds, and began sending reinforcements to Sharpeville. A genuine fear of being besieged by a huge mob took over. One group of police had already opened fire on a crowd near the beer hall in an ominous change from non-violence. More reinforcements arrived, mostly white, armed with .303 rifles and 'Sten' sub-machine guns. A new element was heavy Saracen armoured personnel carriers, which the Sharpeville residents, especially the children, regarded with some interest. The PAC organisers were fast losing control of the huge crowd, now about 25,000, many of them women and children, who were pressed against the low fence round the Station.

The police and the PAC faced a dilemma. The police could not peacefully disperse the crowd, and the crowd was not going to disperse itself.

Nor could, or would, the police arrest anyone for breaking the Pass Laws. Colonel Spengler tried to negotiate, and put his hand on the arm of one red-shirted man and stumbled over something. At that very moment, the thief Geebooi spotted one of his brutal interrogators. He pulled a little pistol, drunkenly mumbling, 'I will shoot that

pig!' A friend restrained him, but two shots rang out into the air. Someone shouted, 'Skiet' ('a shot', or 'Shoot!'), and all hell broke loose.

For 15 seconds the police, without orders, fired straight into the crowd which evaporated. Some of them then reloaded and fired at the fleeing, panicked people, many of whom were shot in the back. It lasted for one disastrous, murderous minute. One thousand rounds had been fired.

Dead and wounded moments after the shooting

There was complete silence, with not even a moan from the wounded that littered the ground. Some white police officers finished off the wounded with a pistol shot. Some black constables, from out of town, deliberately stabbed the wounded with assegais, even women, until stopped by white officers saying, 'We are in enough trouble already'. Some of the dead were killed hundreds of metres away, hit by stray bullets when in their houses and gardens.

Officially there were sixty-nine dead (18 of whom were women and children) and probably 400 wounded. But at least 20 bodies 'disappeared', because they displayed the classic huge exit wounds associated with 'dum-dum' – expanding bullets. The wounded figure is probably much higher too, because any injured who could move, quickly hid or left hospital after they heard that the police had began shackling and arresting any wounded as 'agitators'.

The South African Government showed little shame after the massacre and merely tightened its paranoiaic grip further. Abroad, the reaction was overwhelming, with the US State Department and the

> '*The South African police would leave no stone unturned to see that nothing disturbed the even terror of their lives*'.
>
> Tom Sharpe
> *Indecent Exposure, 1973*

United Nations futilely urging equal rights. Foreign capital began to dry up. Virtually nobody could now publicly defend apartheid. South Africa, expelled from the Commonwealth, was rapidly becoming a pariah state. British Prime Minister Harold MacMillan's very unwelcome speech about *'the wind of change in Africa'*, made in Cape Town just weeks before Sharpeville was to be only too prophetic.

The Sharpeville massacre was not a planned deliberate act of state terror like those at Lidice or Oradour. It was rather the result of the police's fear, panic, lack of planning, inexperience, divided command and racialism, coupled with lack of control by the PAC 'stewards' over a huge crowd.

Whatever the complex reasons, a peaceful protest, in a place of which none of us had ever heard, turned into a slaughter which started the long road to freedom four decades later – and a successful multi-racial state in South Africa.

See: Amritsar, The Bogside, Dum Dum, Kent Ohio, Lidice, My Lai, Oradour, Robben Island, Rorke's Drift, Sophiatown, Srebrenica, Wounded Knee

SIBYLLA'S
England

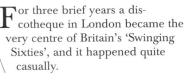

For three brief years a discotheque in London became the very centre of Britain's 'Swinging Sixties', and it happened quite casually.

Up until then there had only been two stylish establishments to replace the fading, upper class dinner-jacketed night spots of London. These were Mark Birley's *Annabel's*, still going strong all these years later and the first genuine lively sixties-style discotheque, the *'Ad Lib'*, in Leicester Square.

One night in 1965 at the *'Ad Lib'*, Beatle George Harrison turned to his friend, Terry Howard and said, 'You know, we are spending too much money in this club. Why don't we start our own?'

So a new club was born, with George Harrison as a shareholder and named after Terry Howard's girlfriend Sibylla Edmonstone, a beautiful Marshall Field heiress. Designed by the leading new interior designer David Mlinaric, it was not only an elegant club but it had the major advantage that the cleverly designed sound system was extremely loud when you were on the dance floor and much quieter three feet away, with the speakers pointed vertically down and very carefully controlled so you could talk where you were sitting down. This sensible concept seems to have been lost for modern clubbers.

The role of Sibylla's as a trend-setter was obvious right from the opening night.

Sibylla's founders, above, Terry Howard, and Left: George Harrison

Guests included all the Beatles and all the Rolling Stones, rising actors and actresses like Michael Caine, Julie Christie, Charlotte Rampling, Sue Lloyd, Edina Ronay, Leslie Caron, Jacqui Bissett and Anita Harris, plus TV personalities like Lance Percival, and pop-music gurus Cathy McGowan and Alan Freeman. The new wave of photographers was represented by David Bailey, Terry Donovan, John d. Green and Patrick Lichfield. Models Celia Hammond, Joanna Lumley and Annagret were wearing clothes designed by fellow guests Mary Quant and Sue Locke.

However, unlike any similar event in today's hyped-up celebrity-mad world, there was no media and no photographs. There was however one slight media glitch. Writer Anthony Haden-Guest, who was planning a feature for *Queen* magazine, (now *Harpers & Queen*) dropped in and asked who was coming to the opening party. Terry Howard casually gave him the draft list that was lying on the table,

Sue Lloyd

JOHN d. GREEN

forgetting that this was a working list that included cryptic notes about the people invited, and what is more, a reserve list of 'less interesting people' to be invited only if any of the first 200 could not turn up. Unfortunately, the whole list was typeset word for word and reproduced in *Queen*, which caused sensational offence to the reserve list.

Unlike many discos, Sibylla's also featured live

music, and among performers were Bill Haley & the Comets, José Feliciano, The Four Tops, and an unknown lead singer with the Small Faces called Rod Stewart.

Many attributed Sibylla's success to the loyalty of the 45 staff – none of whom left – and the lack of crime. This was partly due to Laurie O'Leary, the doorman, who booked groups through a legitimate agency owned by the notorious Kray Brothers. Other protection gangs assumed the Krays had 'got there first'.

All too soon the club was gone, replaced by others – but perhaps without the style and flavour of the decade Sibylla's represented.

See: Abbey Road, Bazaar, Carnaby Street, Cavern, Ibiza, Studio 54

Some of the future stars at the Sibylla's opening party. Left to right: Jacqueline Bisset, Charlotte Rampling, Joanna Lumley, Cilla Black, Michael Caine

SILK ROAD
Asia

The words ' Silk Road' evoke an Indiana Jones-style adventure; excitement, danger, romance and all things exotic. It was indeed that very thing, an ancient 5,000-km trade route for man and beast across Central Asia that once linked the great civilizations of China and the West. In ancient Rome, of the Empire's five great trade goods – amber, incense, ivory, pepper and silk, the wealthy particularly prized silk for its luxury and status. It proved so popular that Emperor Tiberius had to ration it, even banning its use for men's clothes, ostensibly on the grounds of effeminacy.

Legend has it that it all started when Xiling Shi, the wife of the Emperor Huangdi who ruled China in the third millennium BC, was strolling in her garden and idly plucked a white cocoon from a white mulberry tree. Later, as she took her tea, she happened to drop the cocoon into her steaming cup, and,

reaching in to fish it out, unravelled a long white thread. She had stumbled on the silkworm, a caterpillar which is the larva of *Bombyx mori*, a heavy, flightless moth that is the only member of *Lepidoptera* domesticated by man.

Each cocoon can produce nearly a mile of filament, which is joined to several others to produce a 14 denier thread, which weighs a mere half ounce for 30,000 feet. Indeed, 30 mulberry trees produce just one kilogram of silk. The miraculous fibre; light, glossy, long lasting and as strong as steel, soon became one of the world's most precious products – sometimes used, as by the Han emperors of China, as international currency. It remained for centuries a Chinese Imperial monopoly, and its production the most jealously-guarded secret in history.

The Silk Road linked China, which the Romans called Seres, 'the land of

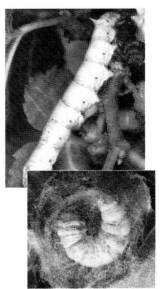

The silk worm and (below) its cocoon

Silk' with the Roman Empire and the Mediterranean Greco-Roman world, via an extensive chain of intermediate independent states. After the decline and fall of Rome in the 5th century, the Silk Road remained the principal route from the east to Constantinople and the Byzantine Empire, and subsequently all the kingdoms of medieval Europe. Roman art and artefacts have been discovered far along the Silk Road, even as far as Korea, demonstrating the cultural importance of this two-way link. Goods – silks, gemstones, ceramics and rugs – reached the shores of the Mediterranean at Antioch, Tyre and other ports. An Indian Ocean sea route, which developed slightly later, took ships from ports in south China eventually to Hormuz and other ports on the Persian Gulf and Red Sea.

The big fly in the ointment for Rome was Persia, a powerful adversary that firmly blocked eastward expansion of Rome and later Constantinople. From the first century BC – at about the time that silk began to arrive in the Mediterranean world from China – Persia was ruled by the Parthians, formidable fighters whose speciality was rapid-fire archery on horseback - often backwards ('The Parthian Shot'). Parthian rulers, and their even more powerful successors of the Sassanid dynasty, closely regulated the silk trade by levy, or periodic veto.

The overland Silk Road was closed in the early Middle Ages, with the expansion of the Arabs into Persia and the Turks into Central Asia, but re-opened with the rise of the mighty Mongol Empire during the 13th century. Under the stern but efficient rule of the Mongol khans, it was said a virgin with a bag of gold could travel in complete safety from China to eastern Europe.

During the next three centuries, a succession of traders, missionaries and adventurers went back and forth along the Silk Road, linking east and west. Perhaps most famous was Marco Polo, the Venetian merchant who in 1271–94 travelled extensively across Central Asia and China, and who wrote up his travels with verve, enthusiasm and a touch of the philosophy that truth should never spoil a good yarn.

By the late Middle Ages, Europe was producing its own silk. Then, in 1492, Christopher Columbus landed in the Americas, and in 1499 Vasco da Gama reached India. Caravans continued to travel the Silk Route, but its glory days were over.

In 1347, the Silk Road brought a horrible unwanted product to Europe. Galleys from the Genoan port of Kaffa in the Crimea, terminus of one branch of the overland Silk Road, sailed into Messina in Sicily. Many of the sailors were dead or dying of bubonic plague, which ravaged Europe for the next two years, de-populating many districts and leading to severe labour shortages. This hastened the collapse of the feudal system of land tenure, as labourers demanded cash wages rather than enforced service to overlords.

But perhaps the most significant long term legacy of to-and-fro along the Silk Road was religious faith. In the medieval period, Christian missions reached China, and the Pope was able to establish a bishopric there. A millenium or so earlier, a Hellenized Afghanistan, ruled after Alexander the Great by Indo-Scythians, had become a centre of Buddhism. From here, Buddhist missionaries travelled via the Tarim Basin to China, where the new religion became established from the 1st century AD – a curious legacy of an ambitious Greek king.

See: Great Wall, Rubicon, Tiananmen Square, Topkapi, Venice

SISSINGHURST
England

Chance played a major role in the story of Sissinghurst in Kent, one of the most famously romantic gardens in the world. If Vita Sackville-West had not fallen for, first the charms of Harold Nicolson, and second, for a derelict twin-towered castle and wasteland in Sissinghurst, this glorious garden would certainly have been lost to us forever.

Their marriage in 1913 led to a great half-century collaboration of visionary planting (Vita) and extraordinary design talent (Harold) and produced a stunning combination of abundance and restraint. Unusually, the garden is divided into 'separate rooms', and features 'one colour areas' the most famous being the 'White Garden', where the lack of any other colour not only produces a rare feeling of tranquillity, but also persuades the eye to look more closely at the structure of the plants.

As Vita said herself in an article in the journal of the Royal Horticultural Society: *'I could never have done it myself. Fortunately I had, through marriage, the ideal collaborator… He had a natural taste for symmetry, and an ingenuity for forcing focal points or long-distance views where everything seemed against him, a capacity I totally lacked'.*

Both saw the garden as another house, creating room after room of intimate spaces (in Harold's words, 'a succession of privacies'), each surrounded by walls or high hedges, and each embracing a formality of shape with an exuberant freedom of planting. And both were prolific writers and diarists, so the history of the garden and its creation have been kept for posterity, from when the land was little more than a wilderness of weeds.

Their treasure-trove of writing was certainly not confined to diaries. A novelist, poet and essayist of distinction, Vita wrote numerous works throughout her life, the most famous of which are the novels *The Edwardians* and *All Passion Spent*. She also contributed for fourteen years to a weekly gardening column in *The Observer* newspaper, describing her horticultural failures as well as her successes, and building up a legion of avid and loyal readers.

Both were as unconventional in their private lives as they were in their garden, indulging in extramarital, homosexual affairs – Vita, famously, with Virginia Woolf and Violet Trefusis. However, the marriage of Vita and Harold remained strong.

But for the lucky chance of these two eccentric and charismatic personalities coming together, working together and having the means to pursue their dream, there would be no Sissinghurst. Indeed, even Harold himself had strong initial doubts about the scale of the project. On 24th April 1930, after first seeing the plot, he wrote to Vita: *'My view is that it is most unwise of us to get Sissinghurst. It costs us £12,000 to buy and will cost another good £15,000 to put in order. This will mean nearly £30,000 before we have done with it. For £30,000 we could buy a beautiful place, replete with park, garage, h. and c., central heating, historical associations, and two lodges r. and l.* However, he also added the telling phrase: *'We like it'.*

How supremely fortunate for the world's gardeners that they did.

See: Giverny, St. Louis

Sissinghurst Castle Garden has been open to the public since 1938, when Vita Sackville-West nicknamed the visitors 'shillingses' after the admission price.

When they moved to Sissinghurst the Sackville-Wests leased their previous home, Long Barn, to the family of aviator Charles Lindbergh, desperate to escape the publicity of his baby's kidnap and the controversial execution of Bruno Hauptman

331

SISTINE CHAPEL
Italy

It is a rare chance when two people meet to create something sublime, especially if the partnership is between an obdurate patron and a reluctant artist, bullied into creating a masterpiece – almost against his will.

In 1508, Michelangelo arrived in Rome, assigned by Pope Julius II to a job that he did not much relish. Whereas he prided himself on his abilities as a sculptor, having completed his huge and spectacular statue *David* in 1504, this new commission required him to paint. And what was worse, to paint the immense and uneven ceiling of the Sistine Chapel, which at the time was designed to look like a starry sky. But despite Michelangelo's objections that 'painting is not my art', and suggestions that Raphael was more suitable, the Pope was as persuasive as he was powerful, and the project soon began.

It is interesting in itself that he had so great a preference for sculpture. A medium that Leonardo da Vinci once described as a 'most mechanical exercise', it took a great deal of physical exertion, and left the sculptor both filthy and exhausted. However, his new project looked to be every bit as demanding. As he decided to be the sole painter of the ceiling, the only real help he had was assistants to bring him materials and paint. And to work on such an inhospitable surface, he would

was a huge and daunting task.

First commissioned by Pope Sixtus IV (1473-1484), the Sistine Chapel already boasted work by some of the most important artists of the day; Sandro Botticelli, Luca Signorelli, Il Ghirlandaio and Pinturicchio. But the ceiling's decoration would prove to be the most famous.

Once he had actually embarked on the project, Michelangelo quickly began to take to it. This was fairly unsurprising since, as an artist, he was known for being enthusiastic and doggedly industrious. During days of constant work he would often lose a worrying amount of weight, and, in the years before he painted the Sistine Chapel ceiling, he had even risked the death penalty by performing autopsies in order to gain a better understanding of human physiology. As he said himself, 'If people only knew how hard I work to gain my mastery, it wouldn't seem so wonderful at all'. For a tough job, the Pope had found a tough man, with whom he constantly quarrelled about the time the project was taking.

After four long years, the epic work was finally completed in 1512, and it appeared that all the time and effort had been thoroughly worthwhile. Thrones of the Seers, consisting of a combination of Christian prophets and classical sibyls, divide the vault into nine sections, which progressively tell the story of Genesis, beginning at the altar end and ending at the entrance. Depicted here are scenes such as the separation of darkness and light, and the famous *Creation of Adam*, whose outreaching hand almost touching the fingers of God is an image familiar to most. Around the larger sections, other early biblical stories like the battle between David and Goliath and Haman are gloriously portrayed.

Pope Julius, although suffering from wounds from military campaigning, just lived long enough to admire the wonderful ceiling which he had so constantly pushed his artist to complete.

But Michelangelo was not finished with the Chapel. He would return in 1534, on another papal commission, to

need to work constantly lying face-up on a scaffold, staring upwards at what he was creating. To paint a surface of this kind, covering almost 10,000 square feet,

paint the wall behind the altar. *The Last Judgement*, as this creation is called, was to be one of his most brilliant works yet. The dead are seen to rise from their graves, and ascend up to the focal figure of Jesus Christ, who is poised with one hand to cast down the wicked souls and raise up the righteous. The amount of nudity in both religious works made them controversial, which only added to the Chapel's fame. Michelangelo has left the Sistine Chapel with a gallery of artistic brilliance. These masterpieces and their creator would ensure the Chapel's emergence as one of the world's most famous buildings.

See: Arles, Barbizon, Flatford, Giverny, Grand Tour, Vinci

SKID ROW
USA

Nowadays we refer to 'Skid Row' as a place full of down and outs, and we judge that a failure is 'on the skids'. In fact, the term comes directly from one of the most successful and dramatic periods of American history, the logging and timber boom in the Pacific North West.

When the first loggers arrived at the shoreline of Washington and Oregon, they were stupefied by the density of the forests and the immense size of the trees, twice the height and five times the width of trees back east. At first, they felled the trees that grew right down by the water, creating little settlements like Seattle and Portland. But in order to bring trees from deeper in the forest, the 'Skid Road' was developed, making its initial appearance on Puget Sound in the early 1850s. The Skid Road was made of foot-thick logs, twelve feet long, laid crosswise like railroad ties or sleepers, and half buried in the ground. It was carefully engineered, leading generally downhill, and gently banked to help the logs ride down it. Along these roads, cut through the forest, came teams of sixteen oxen heaving a chained-together string of a dozen enormous logs, fifty tons in all. The skilled 'bullwhacker' in charge was the most highly paid man in the forest, and was assisted by a boy called the 'skid greaser', whose dangerous task was to run behind the rearmost oxen and just in front of the leading logs, lubricating the skids with fish oil, grease, old butter or water.

The oxen could only haul for about two miles, and the technique was obviously useless for steep terrain, so methods to get the logs to the sawmills were invented. Logs came out of the forests smoking down long dry chutes. Water-filled flumes, much as we see in a modern swimming pool, snaked out of the hills and ravines – bringing logs and lumber down at 50 miles an hour. But the skid road kept its place, with the oxen now replaced by 'donkeys' – not the animal, but the small steam engine created by the naval engineer, John Dolbeer, soon capable of pulling the heaviest log for miles along the skid roads. Later, geared locomotives would arrive to haul whole trains of logs out of the wilderness. Thanks to these innovations, the logging and timber industries became the biggest in the north west, ten times more valuable than the Gold Rush which they served. For it was the Gold Rush of 1849 which had brought hundreds of thousands of people to the west, with huge demand for timber – for mine props, houses, stores, factories and railroad ties.

The skid roads, which had led right down to the waterside sawmills, then became the places of entertainment for the loggers, starting with Mill Street in Seattle. 'Skid Rows', as the brightly lit honky-tonk streets were now called, provided everything the loggers would need – dentists, barbers, tailors, restaurants and tattoo parlours. But what a lumberjack really needed, of course, was to be found in the saloons. The grandest of all was Erickson's in Portland North Side, with the biggest bar in the world, 200 yards long,

Bullwhacker and skidgreaser with their train of logs on a skid road.

Seattle (below) and Portland (left) cities made prosperous by the skid roads

jammed with men, with a concert stage and dozens of gaming tables.

But, after lonely weeks in the forest, whiskey was not enough. Naturally, many of the buildings in the Skid Rows were devoted to the provision of female company. Until the 1860s, most settlements had the ratio of one woman to ten men. Some philanthropic people devised schemes to bring respectable young brides out from the east, but others indulged in the easier tradition of the

See: Leavenworth, Mount St. Helens, Nome, Promontory, St. Joseph, St. Louis, Sutter's Mill, Tacoma Narrows Bridge

setting up of Skid Row bawdy houses, with many of the proprietors quickly becoming some of the richest people in town.

The Skid Roads, in both senses, have long gone, and the cities they helped to create – Seattle, Portland, Tacoma, Everett, Vancouver – are now huge and respectable. Only the derogatory term 'Skid Row' reminds us of that dramatic and hell-raising era.

SODOM
Israel

When the Marquess of Queensberry, furious with his son Bosie's supposed homosexual affair with Oscar Wilde, accused Wilde of being a 'Sodomite', he may have been unfair to the city of Sodom, or at least inaccurate.

Sodom was one of five cities in what was once a fertile valley on the Jordan River. In the Bible its inhabitants are accused of many transgressions. Ezekiel says, *She and her daughters had pride, overabundance of bread and leisure but they did not extend their hand to the poor.* Peter says, *They have eyes full of adultery and are increasingly sinful.* Jude criticises, *Sodom and Gomorrah and the nearby cities fornicating and going after other flesh.* So while we have a general picture of arrogant over-indulgence, only once are same-sex practices in Sodom mentioned. In Genesis 19, we have the men of Sodom demanding that Lot sends the angels out to them so that they might 'know them' (have sex with them), and Lot offering his two virgin daughters instead. This has unpleasant resonance with the men of Gibeah, the Benjamites, surrounding the house where the Levite is staying, and him handing over his concubine, who died of rape. Yet we do not talk of 'Benjamites' as we do of 'Sodomites.'

Nor, incidentally, do we hear criticism of the rather unchivalrous practice of sacrificing one's womenfolk. While no doubt grateful to be spared outrage, the angels could well have reported to the Lord that Lot was morally no better than the rest of the citizens of Sodom, and

'Don't Look Back.' From a painting by Raphael.

See: Armageddon, Great Hedge of India, Lesbos, Masada

therefore had little reason to be spared.

Whatever the truth of the real sexual habits of Sodom, we know of its final fate, *'Then the Lord rained down burning sulfur on Sodom and Gomorrah.'* Lot escaped with his family, but his wife, looking back, was turned into *'a pillar of salt'.*

Scientists have looked closely at the area south of the Dead Sea. Sodom was probably a town built on the prosperity of digging and shipping salt up the (then navigable) Jordan River to Jericho, a salt centre thought to be, at 10,000 years, the oldest city in the world.

Apart from the salt which still drains off present day Mount Sodom, the other local natural deposit is petroleum-based bitumen. While Hebrews called the Dead Sea *Yam Hamelah* (The Salt Sea) and the Jordanians *Lot's Lake*, the Romans called it *Asphaltites Lacus* after the bitumen or asphalt with which they caulked their ships. Some scientists now contend that an earthquake caused bitumen to gush out, ignite and fall as a hot burning mass. They think they have found the remains of two cities reduced completely to ash, with ash skeletons with vaporised gold, and have analysed evidence of sulphur balls which would have burned at 6,000 degrees Fahrenheit. Other scientists contend that the cities are under the surface of the Dead Sea.

Science will one day give us the truth of the cities' cataclysmic fate. Tourists can still visit Mount Sodom and see the columns of salt which eventually break away with erosion, and are called 'Lot's wife'. Meanwhile gays will no doubt continue to be called 'Sodomites' by those that hate them.

SOMME RIVER
France

All over Britain in July 1916 thousands of telegrams began to arrive to inform wives, mothers and sweethearts that they would never see their men again. For the British, 'the Somme' is the symbol of the tragic and terrible losses, incurred for so little result, that typified the mincing machine that was the First World War's Western Front.

'The machine-gun is an over-rated weapon', said Field Marshal Douglas Haig. The Somme was to prove him wrong. From the American Civil War onwards, battle after battle had shown that defenders would inflict appalling losses on attackers however brave – even with rifles. But now the water-cooled, belt-fed machine-gun was equivalent to fifty trained riflemen, and could be fired continuously and effectively by even half trained men. By July 1916, the Germans, French and British all had plenty of them.

The reason for the Somme offensive was to take pressure off the French, who were locked in to the hellish battle at Verdun. Primarily an artillery battle, Verdun was to kill or wound over 300,000 on each side, nearly a third listed as just 'missing', literally blown to nothing.

The choice of the Somme was curious. Compared with an attack at Ypres, with its vital German railhead, success at the Somme offered little of tactical importance or strategic significance except attrition. After considerable argument, it was decided that a seven day artillery barrage would 'soften up' the formidable and well-prepared German defences. 3,000 guns would fire a million and a half shells. This sounds impressive. But, on quite a long frontage, it was half what the French would consider necessary – and faulty fusing, poor weather for observation, and

inexperienced artillery crews made the barrage even weaker. Thus, the German barbed wire was not cut properly, and the German troops sheltering in 30 foot deep bunkers were not killed.

Nearly 200,000 British infantry climbed out of their trenches on 1st, July, expecting to walk steadily into the crippled German defences. Some were kicking a Rugby ball ahead of them. Suddenly, all hell broke loose. One British officer recalled. *'I raised my head as the Highlanders rose to their feet, bayonets gleaming in the morning sun. My eyes swept the valley-long lines of men, officers at their head, in a half crouching attitude … moving forward over a three-mile front. For a moment the scene remained as if on an Aldershot manoeuvre. Two, three, possibly four seconds later an inferno of rifle and machine-gun fire broke from the edge of High Wood, from the tops of its trees and from all along the ridge to the village of Martinpuich. The line staggered. Men fell forward limply and quietly. The hiss and crack of bullets filled the air and skimmed the long grasses. Looking across the valley I could see men of the 1st Queens passing up the slope to Martinpuich. Suddenly they wavered and a few of the foremost attempted to cross some obstacles in the grass. They were awkwardly lifting their legs over a long wire entanglement. Some two hundred men, their commander at their head, had been brought to a standstill. A scythe seemed to cut their feet from under them, and the line crumpled and fell, stricken by machine-gun fire…'*

It was the same everywhere. At Fricourt, one lone German machine-gun wiped out two battalions. Near Thiepval, two whole Northumberland Fusiliers companies were reduced to eleven men. Thirty two battalions lost over 500 of

The monument at Mouquet Farm (Mucky Farm) where the Australians, having lost 17,000 at Pozières a mile away, lost another 6,000 advancing the 300 yards to the farm on the crest.

'See that little stream. We could walk to it in two minutes. It took the British a month – a whole Empire walking very slowly, dying in front and pushing forward behind. And another Empire walking very slowly backwards a few inches a day, leaving the dead like a million bloody rugs'.

F Scott Fitzgerald
Leader in the Night, 1934

The Tyneside Irish moving up. Most of them would be dead or wounded a few minutes later, including most battalion commanders.

The piles of empty shell cases look impressive, but the artillery barrage was inadequate.

Newfoundland's dead are watched over by several poignant statues of caribous.

Eighty years later, the cemeteries are still kept superbly, with flowers on every grave.

See: Agincourt, Bayonne, Gallipoli, Sarajevo

their men. Even in the second line, the 1st Royal Newfoundland Regiment lost 700 men before it had even reached 'no man's land'.

On that horrible day, 19,000 British were killed and 38,000 wounded, and it was only the first day. The Somme was to cut down the flower of Britain's and her Empire's youth, from public school aristocrats to the hopeful volunteers from industrial communities like the 'Leeds Pals' and the 'Accrington Pals'. Families with missing fathers, sons and brothers were blighted. The Prime Minister's son, Lieutenant Herbert Asquith, was killed, as was W.J. Johnson, an Australian Member of Parliament serving as a private soldier, just one of the appalling losses of 23,000 Australians who fell taking Pozières and Mouquet Farm, casualties that were to taint for ever the opinion of *'British staff, British methods and British bungling'.*

The battle was to last until November, dominated as ever by the machine-gun. One British detachment of ten Vickers guns fired *one million bullets* in twelve hours in August.

After four and a half months and seven phases of the Battle of the Somme, the British had lost 419,654 casualties, the French 200,000. Of 73,000 of the British dead, no trace was found. 680,000 Germans were also killed or

wounded. It certainly was attrition.

It was a German officer who wrote: *'The sunken road now appeared as nothing but a series of enormous shell-holes filled with pieces of uniform, weapons and dead bodies. The ground all round, as far as the eye could see, was ploughed with shells... Among the living lay the dead. As we dug ourselves in we found them in layers stacked one on top of the other. One company after another had been shoved into the drumfire and steadily annihilated'.*

The appalling dominance of the machine-gun, 'The Grim Reaper', was all too evident. A few months later, the French began to mutiny rather than face certain death. It was not until the tank arrived, ironically first during the Somme, and was later properly used, that the machine-gun's dreadful power was partially tamed.

But a river valley in northern France, full of huge, sad, military cemeteries, will be etched into the British soul forever as a symbol of brave but tragic futility.

The monument at Thiepval, designed by Sir Edwin Lutyens, commemorates the 73,000 British and South African men whose remains could not be found.

SOPHIATOWN
South Africa

Rather like New York's Harlem on the other side of the world, Sophiatown had been designed to be a white township, but its location next to a sewage works meant that its houses were soon reluctantly sold to black residents in 1903, as were the houses in next-door Martingdale in 1905, and Newclare in 1912. They were the first, and last, places in South Africa where blacks could own

a freehold property and sell it on – albeit to other blacks.

For years Sophiatown, some miles from Johannesburg, prospered and grew until by 1950, it had 50,000 inhabitants. It was overcrowded but it was home. But, the mining city's prosperity meant that it now butted on to white areas and, indeed, was visited by whites who enjoyed its jazz clubs – again an echo of Harlem.

All this was anathema to the Afrikaner National Party, whose Government took power in 1948, and it was determined to implement its policies of racial 'apartness' or *apartheid*, as the world was to know it.

The Government purchased a tract of land at Meadowland several miles away, in order to re-house, forcibly, the inhabitants of Sophiatown. The African National Congress collaborated with other ethnic groups – like the Indians and the Cape Coloureds – to protest. Such co-operation was another worrying threat for the Government. The legendary Father Trevor Huddleston lent his voice to the protesters, who adopted the slogan *'over our dead bodies'*.

On the evening of 8th February 1955, faced by overwhelming forces of the state, Nelson Mandela and other ANC leaders reluctantly advised the young and militant men of Sophiatown not to take the slogan to its logical conclusion and fight the authorities.

The next day, 4,000 police and army surrounded Sophiatown and evicted the sad and miserable people, many of them

home-owners for generations. They were trucked and bussed to Meadowlands. Nowadays we would call it 'ethnic cleansing'.

The scene was set for forty years of racial segregation and conflict, with the Massacre of Sharpeville in 1960, the killing of children in Soweto in 1976, the jailing of Mandela and others for nearly thirty years – and then the very sudden collapse of the iniquitous policy of apartheid in 1992 and a better future at long last.

Peaceful Sophiatown before it was destroyed

See: Harlem, Lorraine Motel, Robben Island, Sharpeville, Storyville

SOUTH GEORGIA
Atlantic Ocean

The Endurance stuck fast and then crushed in the ice.

The island of South Georgia is about as isolated and desolate a place as you could ever find. A World Fact Book points out that it has no indigenous inhabitants, no telephones, no radio station, no arable land, crops, pastures or woodland. It is 1,000 km east of the British Falkland Islands (which administer the island and are coveted by Argentina) and the same distance north of Antarctica. And yet twice in history it has played a dramatic role.

The island was first discovered by chance by a London merchant, Antoine de la Roche, who found shelter there in 1675 after the rigours of rounding Cape Horn. Exactly a hundred years later, Captain James Cook was trying to find the Continent of Antarctica, and thought he had done so at South Georgia. On sailing further, rounding the south-eastern corner and realising it was just an island, he called the point *'Cape Disappointment'*.

But his reports of the vast populations of seals created a seal industry that nearly destroyed the Fur Seal, quickly followed by a similar destructive and ultimately suicidal industry, whaling.

There are two ships called *Endurance* in our story. The first was the ship which the extraordinary explorer Sir Ernest Shackleton planned to use as his base for a trans-Antarctica expedition. However, in December 1914, *Endurance* became stuck in the ice – and remained there for fully eighteen months before the ice began to crush her to pieces.

'It is hard to write what I feel', wrote Shackleton. *'To a sailor a ship is more than a floating home. Now straining and groaning, her timbers cracking and her wounds gaping, she is slowly giving up her sentient life at the very outset of her career'.*

The statue of Ernest Shackleton outside the Royal Geographical Society

The tiny boat that Shackleton used to reach South Georgia and save his men

See: Eton, Goose Green

A born leader, Shackleton at first camped his men on the ice for another five months, then set out in three small, open boats reaching Elephant Island after an appalling voyage through icebergs. He then took one boat, the *James Caird,* and with seven men sailed for another sixteen horrific days across 850 miles of monstrous seas, to arrive in a violent storm on the wrong side of South Georgia. There, he left three men sheltering under the upturned boat and with a minimum of equipment, clothing and food, the remaining four scaled the central mountains and eventually walked into Stromness Whaling Station, their appearance terrifying the first people they met. The three men they had left behind on the other side of the island were quickly rescued, but it took four expeditions through the pack ice to reach the rest of his men on Elephant Island, not one of whom was lost. Fittingly, the intrepid Shackleton is even buried on South Georgia, having returned in 1922 and sadly died there of a heart attack.

Sixty years later, in a cost-cutting exercise, the British Government publicly decided to withdraw another *Endurance*, the Royal Navy's Antarctic patrol ship, from service in the South Atlantic. As a result, the Argentine Junta, needing a foreign adventure to distract her population and detecting weakness in the British resolve to keep the Falkland Islands, decided to invade. They started with South Georgia.

So, on 19th March 1982, an Argentinian scrap metal dealer with the unlikely name of Constantino Davidoff arrived, ostensibly to dismantle the old disused whaling stations he had bought. Unusually, however, he arrived with special military forces. A few days later the Falklands themselves were invaded, and a strange and tragic little war began. It took scarcely a month for British forces to take back South Georgia, albeit with some very dramatic moments in the traditionally appalling weather. As mute evidence, two Wessex helicopters still stick out of the ice of the island's Fortuna Glacier.

South Georgia has now returned to its important ecological role. Each summer, ninety five per cent of the world's southern fur seals crowd on to the island, together with half of the world's elephant seals and half its wandering albatrosses – not to mention millions of penguins and other birds.

South Georgia is extraordinarily demanding. It takes true character to be a wandering albatross chick sitting all alone on a nest at minus thirty degrees Celsius, in a one hundred mile an hour gale, desperately hoping your parents don't wander too far.

SPA
Belgium

See: Bath, Truth or Consequences, Vichy

Since the 16th century, the therapeutic mineral springs and healing baths of the small town of Spa in eastern Belgium have given the name 'spa' to similar watering places all over the world, like Leamington Spa and Bath Spa.

Some spas, like Vichy and Vittel, have made themselves more famous – because of the mineral waters they have so cleverly persuaded us to drink instead of tap water.

And for motor racing fans, Spa-Francorchamps has won its place as one of the great motor racing circuits for both Formula One and long-distance sports cars. However, it used to be considered one of the most dangerous, as it swooped through the thick trees of the Ardennes. Its only slow corner, a hairpin bend, is appropriately called 'La Source' (The Spring). Approached at 160mph, braking down to 35mph, it has been known to eliminate half the grid on the first lap.

Spa is also the circuit where Michael Schumacher became the world's most successful Formula One driver, notching up his 52nd win to beat Ayrton Senna's record.

SPANDAU
Germany

Spandau was not a totally obscure place before the Second World War. It had already been known as a munitions factory for some time. In 1722, King Friedrich Wilhelm built the first gun factory there, and by the beginning of World War One, it was a key manufacturer of German machine-guns. However, it was not until the Second World War had ended that Spandau became a household name, due to the shadowy figure of Rudolf Hess.

Hess was one of Hitler's earliest supporters, and had been arrested with him after the attempt to seize power in 1923. While incarcerated, he helped the future Nazi leader write his famous book *Mein Kampf* by writing the text as it was dictated. From the time that the two men were released, Hess remained Hitler's personal assistant. Although he never achieved a sweeping administrative position, he continued to create Hitler's daily personal schedule and control visitor admission, right up to 1941. In that year, one of the strangest and most mysterious events of the Second World War was to happen.

On May 10th, Hess flew from Germany to Britain, alone in a Messerchmitt 110. He bailed out of his aircraft in Scotland, and parachuted into the Duke of Hamilton's estate. Why had he come? It seemed that he was trying to arrange some sort of peace treaty. Perhaps this was a genuine attempt to end the war, or maybe it was designed to take the pressure off Germany as she prepared to invade Russia. The official statement released in Berlin was that 'Hess had gone mad', and his flight to Scotland was without a sensible reason. Whatever his motivation, Hess' reception was not a warm one. He was quickly locked in the Tower of London, where he had no choice but to wait and see what was to become of him. His official trial would come at Nuremburg. Despite his attempts to distance himself from Germany, Hess would be tried and sentenced along with the most heinous of Nazi war criminals.

And so, in 1945, Hess was condemned to a lifetime of captivity at Spandau prison. The sizeable ex-fortress had the capacity to hold hundreds, but now seven prisoners, bereft of their identity, were the only inhabitants. Hess was 'Prisoner Number Seven'. His claims that the Nuremburg trials had no real validity did not help him, and he was doomed never to leave Spandau. The prison guards were supplied by Britain, America, France, and Russia, and were rotated in regular shifts.

By 1966, six of the original prisoners had died, and Rudolf Hess was alone. As Prisoner Number Seven spent his days trapped in Spandau, a movement petitioning for his release developed. Including Lord Geoffrey Lawrence, previously President of the International Military Tribunal, and even Hess's own son, the group protested not only that Hess was a peace petitioner and therefore should not be punished, but also that he was becoming a very old man, and his imprisonment no longer served any purpose. But Hess was never released. In this case, life meant life.

As mysterious as his original flight were the circumstances of his death. In 1987, it was announced that the 92-year old Hess, in a moment when he was unsupervised, had managed to hang himself with an electric cable on 17th of August. He had spent 41 years in Spandau. Controversy over this statement still rages. Is it possible for such a frail old man to hang himself? Or was he killed? There is even a theory that Prisoner Number Seven and Rudolf Hess were not in fact the same person. Soon after Hess' death, Spandau prison was destroyed, perhaps for fear that it might become a shrine. The group who had clamoured for the old man's release did not forget his lonely days in the prison, however. Thirteen years after his death, on August 17th, 2000, police broke up a procession in Rostock and other German towns in his honour. Leaflets and banners were distributed, with the claims that Hess was a 'martyr' of peace. It seems that the memory of the Spandau incarceration of this most enigmatic of men will not be destroyed as easily as the prison itself.

Rudolf Hess, intimate of Hitler and then a traitor?

See: Alcatraz, Nuremberg, Reading Gaol, Robben Island

SPRINGFIELD
United States

As a name, Springfield has a pleasant feel to it, hopeful and rural, which is why it is a popular choice for a town. There are no less than three American Springfields that have achieved fame.

First, there is the State Capital of Illinois, probably most renowned as the birthplace of President Abraham Lincoln. Then, for those who enjoy military history, there was the 'Armory at Springfield' in Massachusetts, which first stored, repaired and maintained weapons and supplies for the United States during the American Revolution starting in 1777. Ten years later, it achieved major and long-term significance because of its attempted capture by 'Regulators' – dispossessed citizens in rebellion against the Massachusetts Government, leading directly to the creation of the Federal Constitution. The principal arms factory of the United States, and even the subject of a poem by Longfellow, it became famous for the 'Springfield 03' rifle used in the First World War and the 'Garand M-1' of the Second World War. 4.5 million of the latter were produced, described by General George Patton as *the greatest battle implement ever devised.*

But only one Springfield has achieved worldwide fame – the home of *The Simpsons*. Back in 1987, on its TV debut, the now legendary family looked different, sounded different, and only played for 30 seconds at a time. It featured in a series of short spots, spread among the various sketches of the *Tracy Ullman Show*, and it would take 3 years before making it in its own right.

The creator, Matt Groening, was already well known for his comic strip series *Life in Hell,* but it was the Simpsons that would make him a household name, as it would their hometown of Springfield. One of his more original touches is the family's yellow skin, which instantly set the show's look apart as unique, and to prove a subtle signpost for the casual channel surfer. When former Director, David Silverman, was asked about the unusual colour, he claimed that it was necessary because Bart, Lisa, and Maggie had no hairline, so the artists had to find a hue that could be skin and hair. Otherwise, if they were painted in a flesh tone, the characters would appear to have 'a serrated forehead!'

Groening named the entire family after his own (except Bart, an anagram of 'brat'.) It was dysfunctional from the very beginning, and perhaps it is this that has led to its perennial popularity. This is not an idealised set of people by any means; the Simpsons are neurotic, lazy, anarchic, stupid, and anti-social, but nevertheless are seen as one of the most genuine and human depictions of the average American family. The show was quick to receive official recognition, winning the 1990 and 1991 Emmy Awards for 'Outstanding Animated Program'.

Springfield's most famous family has not lived free of controversy. Never afraid to attack political figures, former Vice President Dan Quayle was far from immune. His well-known mistake of correcting a school child's spelling – telling him that 'potato' was wrong, and 'potatoe' was right – was reflected in 1997, when Bart scrawled 'potato, not potatoe' over the blackboard as a punishment. To this day, Matt Groening claims it was Bart's idea.

Barbara Bush once said in an interview for *People* magazine that *The Simpsons* was the 'dumbest thing' she had ever seen. Strong words from high places.

NATIONAL PARK SERVICE,
SPRINGFIELD ARMORY

The church organ at the Springfield Armory made out of muskets

Matt Groening with his Simpson friends. Left to right: Lisa, Maggie, Marge, Bart and Homer.

However, it is hard to keep a good show down. With a running total of over 300 episodes, and contracts signed to produce more, *The Simpsons* is the longest running prime-time series ever shown internationally. Its fame and influence is such that, when the unwise members of a school council in Greenwood South Carolina allowed the children to choose the name of the new school, it was titled Springfield

> **Comedian**: I finally got around to reading the dictionary. Turns out the zebra did it.
>
> **Homer**: It's not easy to juggle a pregnant wife and a troubled child, but somehow I managed to squeeze in 8 hours of TV a day.
>
> **Ralph**: Me, fail English? That's unpossible.
>
> **Mr Burns**: Smithers, for attempting to kill me, I'm giving you a five per cent pay cut.
>
> **Homer**: Maybe for once, someone will call me 'sir', without adding, 'you're making a scene'.

Elementary. Truly, the cult of Springfield is unstoppable.

See: Albert Square, Coronation Street, Peyton Place, Ramsay Street, Truth or Consequences

SREBRENICA
Bosnia, Herzogovina

Wim Kok, Prime Minister of the Netherlands resigned on 16th April 2002 because of Dutch action, or rather, inaction, at Srebrenica in 1995. As a gesture, it was weakened by the fact that his term of office only had days to run. But it did at least reflect the agony and guilt his country was feeling after a damning report by the Netherlands Institute of War Documentation.

Also in Holland, in The Hague, the War Crimes Tribunal had indicted two men for Genocide and Crimes Against Humanity, including the worst mass murder since 1945: Radovan Karadzic, President of the Bosnian Serb administration in Pale and his military Commander, General Ratko Mladic. Both remain in hiding, unlike their ultimate chief Slobodan Milosovic, now behind bars awaiting trial for crimes in Croatia, Bosnia, and later Kosovo.

After the death of strongman Tito, Yugoslavia had fallen apart, with the Serbs bent on dominance. Croatia had been attacked first, then Bosnia, with its capital Sarajevo under siege. The Serbs were also determined to break the Muslim corridor and conquer eastern Bosnia. As her forces approached Srebrenica it was declared a 'safe area', and two hundred Dutch soldiers were meant to guard its safety, protecting the thousands of Muslim refugees there.

The Serbs shelled the area, blocked United Nations aid convoys, and cut food supplies. Massacres went on all over the countryside. At Glodzanje, the Serb commander said to his men 'You must kill everyone. We don't need anyone alive'. On the Bratunac-Milici road, 'They must surrender their weapons, then shell the group and destroy it.' In a forest, another intercepted order said, 'Kill them slowly'. One hundred Muslims including women and children were killed with knives.

But the real horror was in Srebrenica itself. When the town surrendered, General Mladic, who pathologically hated Muslims, threatened the Dutch and forced them to comply with his orders that the women and children be separated from men and boys, some as young as ten. He even obtained fuel for the buses that took the men away. For the next five days, seven thousand men and boys were slaughtered, shot in the back of the head as they knelt. Lights were rigged to enable the executions to continue at night, and bulldozers were used to push the bodies into mass graves and to cover the crime.

General Mladic left) confers with Radovan Karadzic. Both are still on the run.

Hundreds of Muslims were also killed in the building across the street from the Dutch troops. *Concern about their own survival in this hell meant more to the Dutch troops than the fate of the Muslim men*, commented the report.

The recriminations roll on. Criticisms were levelled at the French UN commander General Janvier for striking a deal with the Serbs agreeing not to call in protective air strikes if hostage soldiers, some French, were released – a deal which sealed Srebrenica's fate.

The Dutch Government has been accused of trying to boost its international prestige by sending a small force on an ill-defined mission. The Bosnian women who had lost their menfolk knew what was happening,

'When we saw the peacekeepers running away, then we knew we had to run too'. One said, 'Right before the massacre I saw one Dutch soldier sitting and crying. It seemed he knew what would happen to us. But they failed'.

Stacked in a Bosnian warehouse called

See: Sarajevo

'The House of Death' there are still four thousand skeletons waiting to be identified by DNA sampling, so that their grieving families can lay them to rest. No wonder Wim Kok resigned.

STALINGRAD
Russia

Selective amnesia might be the best way to describe Hitler's approach to his Stalingrad disaster.

When the Germans invaded 'her ally', the Soviet Union, on 22nd June 1941, they were confident of success. Four million men, 3,350 tanks, 600,000 horses and 2,000 aircraft poured across the borders of the Soviet Union. The Russians, including Stalin, appeared paralysed. 1,200 of their planes were destroyed on the ground in hours, great pockets of troops were cut off, or – as one General put it, – 'running with suitcases across broken ground'. Hitler seemed right in his prediction, 'Smash in the door and the whole rotten structure will come crashing down.' Russian officers dared not use initiative. (After all, Stalin had killed 37,000 of their senior comrades in his purges). Whole armies were destroyed, and within three weeks, the Red Army lost two million men, 3,500 tanks and 6,000 aircraft. Then Smolensk and Kiev fell – another million men lost.

But there were worrying signs for the Germans. The same huge distances that had defeated Napoleon began to take their toll. Troop losses by the end of August were 400,000; vehicles were breaking down in the dust. Soviet equipment, like their T-34 tanks, were plainly superior, German estimates of the number of Russian divisions actually *went up* from 200 to 360. Stubborn, brave Soviet resistance by 'Ivan' was visibly stiffening as news of German brutality to civilians, Jews and Russian prisoners filtered out. The NKVD began to shoot Russian deserters and create suicidal 'penal companies'. It was to be a war like no other.

The Russian winter arrived early, and the German troops found themselves stalled in front of Moscow, shivering in their thin clothing, while their tanks and

German troops fighting in the rubble. It was going to get much worse.

'Visiting the town is forbidden. Curiosity endangers your life as well as the life of your comrades'.

guns ceased to function. A quarter of a million horses had died, and with temperatures dropping to minus 40 degrees celsius, 100,000 German soldiers were already out of action with frostbite. Then, completely unexpectedly, fresh Soviet armies from Manchuria counter-attacked and the Germans reeled back – only surviving the horrible winter through their extraordinary resilience and tenacity, and Hitler's willpower to stand fast, including his decision to supply encircled pockets by air.

When spring and summer returned with fresh victories, for Hitler (if not for his men), both the horrors and the lessons of the winter seemed like a bad dream, easily forgotten.

At his 1st Junconference to plan the great summer offensive, an industrial town named after Stalin was hardly mentioned, except to eliminate its armaments factories and to secure the Volga river on his way to the Caucasian oil fields. But as the Germans tramped across the steppe, their horses coughing in the dusty heat, Stalingrad was ordered to prepare, and on 28th July Stalin issued his draconian Order 227 – '*Not one step backwards*'.

Tsaritsyn (Tartar for town on the Yellow River) had been changed to Stalingrad to honour Stalin's (fictitious) role in the revolutionary war. It sprawled 20 miles along the west bank of the Volga, with several large factories. 200,000 civilians started to dig fortifications. The Red Army had a new breed of general, Zhukov in overall command and Chuikov in charge of the 62nd Army.

On 23rd August, three days after the German public ever heard the word 'Stalingrad', 1,200 bombers under General von Richthofen (cousin of the Red Baron) started a huge assault, killing

IMPERIAL WAR MUSEUM

40,000 civilians and turning the whole town into a shambles, which was to prove a killing ground in the coming weeks. In the fighting amidst the rubble and wrecked buildings, German mobility was lost, casualties rocketed, and six battalion commanders were killed in one day. The railway station changed hands 15 times in 5 days, some buildings had Russians and Germans on different floors like a layered cake. 'Rattenkrieg' had become a war of stationary annihilation. Clinging to the west bank, the Russian troops dared not retreat a yard towards the NKVD troops behind them, who killed 13,500 of their own Soviet soldiers for supposed 'cowardice'.

As the appalling fighting raged, Hitler became obsessed with Stalingrad, and waited desperately for news of its fall – even making a speech on 8th November underlining its importance. Meanwhile, the Russians had planned an audacious move: to leave Stalingrad as a bait in a huge trap. They planned to attack the weak and vulnerable flanks of the Salient, a hundred miles back so that the panzers would not have time to react. On 19th November, Lt Gerhard Stock, Javelin Gold Medallist at the 1936 Berlin Olympics and now Liaison Officer with the IV Romanian Army Corps, rang General Paulus's Headquarters to report tanks in the mist in front of him. 3,500 Russian guns and mortars then blasted the Romanian troops, who repulsed the first Russian attacks bravely enough, but with few anti-tank guns, could not stem the tide of T-34s which swept over them. The German response was sluggish, and

the next day another Russian offensive cut through their lines south of Stalingrad. On 25th, the two pincers met and the attackers were now besieged.

Instead of making urgent efforts to relieve his encircled troops, Hitler relied on his willpower, falsely buoyed up by Goering's irresponsible boast that he could supply the 270,000 men in the *Kessel* (cauldron) by air. In spite of the bravery of his Luftwaffe crews, never more than a quarter of the bare minimum ever got through, further reduced when the Russians captured the key airfield, with tanks rampaging among the escaping planes.

Any chance that Stalingrad could be relieved by 'Operation Winterstorm', by Von Manstein's armies to the west, were ruined by yet more Russian offensives. Soon, the Germans were too weak from starvation, lack of fuel and disease to be able to walk – let alone fight their way out. A truly nightmarish Christmas in freezing bunkers for emaciated, lice-covered soldiers was followed by a final assault on the 11th January. By 2nd February 91,000 Germans and 22 generals had surrendered, although initially Goebbel's propaganda pretended that they had all died. Only 5,000 prisoners returned to Germany.

This battle, in which 485,000 of the *victorious* side were killed and 600,000 wounded, was the turning point of the war. Stalin's victory at the town on the Volga was to strengthen his hand with his allies and give him a free hand in the east, and made the Soviet Union into a superpower.

General Paulus surrenders to the Russians. He was in much better shape than most of his troops.

See: Berezina, Ekaterinburg, Finland Station, Gulag, Ladoga

STOCKTON AND DARLINGTON
England

If there was one person who did not deserve to have his name associated with the very first passenger train, it was the Third Earl of Darlington.

In the early nineteenth century, the South Durham owners of coal mines – without easy access to the sea – had a real problem of competition. Coal carried in panniers on horses, or even, as the roads improved, in wagons, was very expensive. But a horse could do 30 times the work when pulling a barge. In Darlington, George Dixon experimented

with a short canal in 1767. (George is much less famous than his younger brother Jeremiah, who created the Mason-Dixon Line in America which separated the slave-owning states from the north, and from which we get the words 'Dixie' and 'Dixieland').

It took decades for the canal idea to gather strength with, amazingly, the grandchildren of Dixon's original partners – Edward Pease and James Backhouse – still pushing the concept in 1818. But in order to include Darlington,

343

The centenary celebrations of the first passenger journey of The Stockton & Darlington

See: Greenwich, Promontory, Rock Island

their engineers now concluded that only a railway would work. The Stockton Canal group had their local landowners on their side, Lord Stewart and Lord Castlereagh, and even they eventually backed a railway.

Not so, Lord Darlington. Obsessed with fox hunting, he envisaged the railway ruining his precious fox coverts, and therefore his sport. He even tried to break the Backhouse Bank in Darlington by getting his tenants to present hundreds of notes one morning, but Jonathan Backhouse had rushed to London and obtained enough gold to cover the notes. Lord Darlington managed to defeat the first Stockton and Darlington Bill in Parliament, but only by 13 votes. A fellow peer advised him, 'Well, if the Quakers, when nobody knows anything about railways, can raise up such a phalanx, I should recommend that country gentlemen be very wary how they oppose them'.

In the event, Lord Eldon, the Lord Chancellor, was bought off with a very generous price for his land, and Lord Darlington's fox coverts were avoided, but only by making the route 'rather crooked'. As Edward Pease, the hero of the railway, who had thrown in his own money, explained, *'Thee must remember that they were the crooked ones with whom the railway had to deal'*.

The Bill passed in 1821, and that week Edward Pease was disturbed at night by two cold callers, one of whom was George Stephenson, an engineer from Killingworth Colliery, where steam engines were used. It was Stephenson who joined Pease as Engineer for the railway and who persuaded him that steam locomotives were the answer for the new line. Stephenson additionally recommended malleable iron rather than cast iron for the rails, starting a bitter quarrel with his old iron works partner William Losh, who was to have built the locomotives. Thus he was forced to start an engine building works with his son Robert, once again with the pioneering financial backing of Edward Pease. Robert Stephenson and Company was to be famous round the world. However, the Stockton & Darlington really had to pester the Stephensons to get their locomotives on time, because they were too successful and therefore overstretched. Wrote an exasperated Pease, *George shouldn't place our property at risk by the application of his time and talent to other objects and while his talent and ingenuity is great, his execution is torpid, defective and languid as to promptings.*

But at last, on 16th September 1825, *No 1 Locomotion* was delivered in pieces on three wagons down the Great North Road. It was quickly assembled and fired up, and on 26th November, hauled the Stephensons and Peases in the world's first passenger coach, *'The Experiment'*.

The next day, the official opening saw the first train in history to carry paying passengers. The world had changed for ever, but it was not much thanks to the Earl of Darlington.

STONEHENGE
England

Time is unbelievably destructive. Monuments of the ancient world, no matter how magnificent when created, become worn down by wind and rain, or destroyed in wars or building projects. Of the original 'Seven Wonders of the World', only the Pyramids now remain, with time having wiped the other six off the face of the planet.

However, standing in the fields of Salisbury Plain, just 2 miles west of the town of Amesbury, are the remains of a monument – the first parts of which were built around 5,000 years ago. The original parts of Stonehenge were a circular bank and ditch, surrounding 56 'Aubrey Stones', which are now invisible from the surface. Several other parts including the 'Slaughter Stone' and the 'Heel Stone' are also believed to date from this period.

The large stones we see today are part of Stonehenge IIIb, constructed between 2000-1550 BC, including the semi-circles of 'bluestones'.

What makes this structure so impressive is the lack of technology available to construct it. Neolithic man had nothing like the equipment of the

Romans when building the Colisseum centuries later, where metals and sophisticated tools were available. Whoever constructed Stonehenge had to carve out the stones by using large, sharp chunks of the same material – obviously a time-consuming and strenuous exercise. To dig the ditches they had to use the antlers of red reindeer and the shoulder blades of oxen. Furthermore, transporting the stones, the heaviest of which weighs almost 50 tons – the weight of six elephants – must have been a daunting task. It is thought that much of the transportation was by sea and river, but some of the journey would have had to be made by land on sleds. Under these circumstances, its construction is nothing short of miraculous.

Who, you wonder, would do such a thing? English antiquarian John Aubrey suggested that it was built by the Druids. This seems all the more feasible as Druids still cultivate the site today, some visiting as many as eight times a year to celebrate the changing seasons. However it seems that Druids, perhaps formed from a Celtic priesthood, came along about two thousand years after the first stage of the monument was built. With a structure so ancient, it is simply not possible to ascertain the original creators.

But what is it actually for? This is a question that has caused endless debate, and one that has never been conclusively answered. Many believe it may be some sort of calendar. On the longest day of the year, the summer solstice, an observer in the centre of the structure can see the rising sun perching just on top of the 'Heel Stone', while on the winter solstice, the setting sun does the same in the opposite direction. Both days mark a change of season.

In the 20th century, a theory developed that it marks the movements of both the sun and the moon. Gerald Hawkins proposed that Stonehenge, which he called an *'astronomical computer'*, could track both heavenly bodies, and predict eclipses. Such an ability would clearly give great power to the controller of the monument, able to terrify the ignorant populace with its respect for the mystical.

Others say that it is only a temple, or some sort of place of worship. A rather more complicated theory is that the original Stonehenge was an astronomical calendar, while the new additions were not.

Whoever built it, and whatever it does, Stonehenge continues to fascinate, surviving as one of the oldest glimpses of a truly ancient age.

See: Giza, Great Wall of China, Pisa, Pompeii, Troy

STORYVILLE
Louisiana, USA

If there were two things that New Orleans Alderman Sidney Story really hated, they were prostitution and jazz music. So how he must have resented the fact that his name would be forever linked to the largest brothel area in the United States, and the birthplace of New Orleans jazz.

For years in America there had been a battle between licence and prudery as far as prostitutes were concerned. Such women had been slipped in by foreign Governments or had flooded in of their own accord to San Francisco and the mining towns like Cripple Creek, Colorado and Butte, Montana, where the 'light-ladies' accounted for ten per cent of the 10,000 population. Many of the legendary names of America's growth had a very close relationship with bordellos. Calamity Jane was the daughter of a prostitute, 'Butch Cassidy' and 'The Sundance Kid' worked out of a brothel in Fort Worth, and Doc Holiday

Future giant of jazz, Louis Armstrong delivered coal to the Storyville brothels.

GRIMSDALE

was a friend of 'Big Nose' Kate and 'Squirrel Tooth' Alice.

But New Orleans had established its leadership in vice decades before. By the middle of the eighteenth century, its name was established in this area, not least because of the women shipped in from France by Louis XIV and Louis XV. Puritan morality elsewhere in America only served to boost the city's attraction. In New Orleans there was a complete class of women, quadroons and octaroons, deliberately raised to fill the brothels. Light-skinned girls set themselves up as mistresses in the Rampart Street area – witness, fifty years later, the jazz classic *South Rampart Street Parade.*

In 1857, the 'madams' of New Orleans were required to buy licences, and soon several blocks on Canal Street were lined with brothels, ranging upwards in style from Clip Joints, Cribs, Bordellos and Whorehouses, to Houses of Assignation, Sporting Houses and Mansions.

Thus, in 1897, Alderman Sidney Story stepped in and said, 'If you can't eliminate prostitution, at least you can isolate it'. The Board of Aldermen defined a 'District' that legalised brothels, outside of which prostitution became illegal.

This ultimate 'red light' district also helped the birth of New Orleans jazz. While full bands played in dance halls, many jazzmen, especially pianists, played in the bordellos in what was immediately and rather cruelly, for the Alderman, dubbed 'Storyville'.

The tunes they played sound like a street map, *Burgundy Street Blues, Dauphin Street Blues, Bourbon Street Parade, Basin Street Blues, Canal Street Blues, St Phillips Street Breakdown, Perdido Street Blues.*

And *Beale Street Blues* does a good job in explaining the morals of Storyville, even if W.C. Handy was actually talking about Memphis.

'If Beale Street could talk

If Beale Street could talk
Married men would have to take their beds and walk
Except one or two, who never drink that booze
And the blind man on the corner singing the blues'.

Mahogany Hall Stomp salutes the finest brothel in the whole country at 235 Basin Street. Mahogany Hall was listed in the *Blue Book*, the 'Guide for Gentlemen', and, like many of the elegant and relaxing Storyville establishments, boasted sumptuous décor, delicious food, the finest wines and spirits, and of course, the most beautiful girls. Ragtime was played by piano players like 'Jelly Roll' Morton (and you should be able to guess what a jelly roll was!). Indeed, jazz itself was used as a word for sex. Musically, jazz was an amalgam of black work songs (the Blues), New Orleans marching music and Creole classically-trained sophistication. The names of those who learned their trade in Storyville echo with us 80 years later: Kid Ory, Bunk Johnson, Sidney Bechet, 'King' Oliver and, of course, a kid who delivered coal to the brothels, Louis Armstrong.

We might never have heard of these giants at all if America had not entered the Great War in 1917, and if the US Navy, fearful of Storyville's potential health or crime effects on its young recruits, had persuaded the city to close the 'District' down.

Thousands of girls were forced to go north to Chicago, no doubt to fill the brothels of 'Big Jim' Colisimo, Johnny Torrio and Al Capone.

Much more lasting in its effect was the economic migration of the jazzmen, who in Chicago and other cities in 1920, first began to put on record the wonderful music we call 'New Orleans Jazz'.

See: Big Apple, Broadway, Carnegie Hall, Cavern, Cotton Club, Desire, Motown, St Louis, Tin Pan Alley, Tulsa

STOWE
England

Stowe's modern claim to fame is that it is arguably the most beautiful school in the world. A huge Palladian palazzo, it is 300 yards long with 400 rooms, set in 450 acres of grounds in England's

county of Buckinghamshire. Any boy or girl with artistic inclination would glory not only in the main house, but in the lovely temples carefully designed into Arcadian valleys and vistas.

Two centuries ago, Stowe House was no less than the centre of political and social Britain. It was started in the year 1677 by Sir Richard Temple, and was steadily expanded by his son Viscount Cobham and his heir Richard Grenville, Earl Temple. Architects included Vanbrugh (soon to create Blenheim Palace), William Kent, Gibbs, Robert Adams, Giovanni Battista, Borra, George-François Blondel and Thomas Pitt. The greatest gardener of the age, 'Capability' Brown, created the lovely valleys and walks, and the lakes reflecting the house and its many temples.

The result was, in the opinion of one expert, *'the largest and most completely realised private neo-classical building in the world'*. Everything was done on a grand scale by the Temple Grenville family who were now Dukes of Buckingham. Thousands of workmen dug out the Grecian Valley, and dumped the earth in what had been a lake. Evidence of minor quarrels are still to be seen. The 'Temple of Friendship' – deliberately built in ruins after a family row - the long earth mound, raised so the Duke did not have to look at a neighbouring landowner, the little temple with a monkey looking in a mirror – dedicated to a disgruntled relative who 'felt left out'.

The great house echoed to the talk of great men: The Earl of Chatham (Pitt the Elder), Sir Robert Walpole, William Pitt 'the Younger', Alexander Pope, Benjamin Disraeli and Sir Robert Peel, the creator of Britain's police. The house and its families produced 4 Prime Ministers in 50 years.

Superb paintings graced the ornate walls of *'some of the finest rooms perhaps in Europe'* and there was a style of hospitality which was praised in 1765, *'I never saw so large a house so well conducted; servants that have no 'embarras', no noise, but all attention and respect'*.

But a century and a half of amazing expenditure was not to last. It was the visit in 1845 of Queen Victoria which sealed the financial fate of Stowe as a private house. The second Duke of Buckingham had inherited a colossal sum, and had succeeded in frittering it all away, not least by trying to buy all the land on each side of the road from Stowe to Chandos Square in London - so that he could refer to the 60 miles as his 'carriage drive'.

The bailiffs were already in residence during the Queen's visit, which was costing £1,000 a day. They refused to move out but they sportingly agreed to wear the Duke's livery and to pretend to be his servants.

As *The Times* wrote acidly: *He has thrown away his high position for the baubles of a pauper and the tinsels of a fool'*. Another newspaper described him as the *greatest debtor in the world*. Hundreds of paintings and artefacts together with 40,000 acres were sold in a month-long 'Sale of the Century' in 1848, helping, incidentally, to launch Christie's as an auction house.

But the Duke's foolishness was eventually to be the school's opportunity. The magnificent home and its hundreds of acres of grounds were purchased in 1921 for the comparatively miniscule sum of £50,000.

Two of the first pupils to arrive were the author's father, Toby O'Brien and the future actor David Niven, who started a little business together to cash in on the vast numbers of rabbits that over-ran the grounds. They stashed dogs, snares, ferrets and even guns out in the woods, and pretty soon their partnership provided the rabbits for both workers

Stowe's south and north Fronts, with royal patron George IV

David Niven, distinguished 'Old Stoic'

LICHFIELD

347

who were refurbishing the school and the butchers of Buckingham. They became mysteriously rich pupils until the headmaster put a stop to it.

As a school, the house has not only survived, it is being steadily and beautifully restored – thanks to the National Trust and a volunteer group of former pupils, the Stowe House Preservation Trust. Stephen Spender's father, Harold Spender, wrote in 1924, *The Grenvilles lost us America, but I verily believe that they thought England sufficiently compensated by gaining Stowe.*

See: Camp David, Cliveden, Chequers, Eton, Rugby

STRATFORD-UPON-AVON
England

William Shakespeare

From all over the world people flock to a town in Warwickshire. Its claim to fame is, of course, as the birthplace of William Shakespeare, arguably the greatest playwright of all time.

Chance played more than a small part in this fame. First, Shakespeare's father, John, was rich and successful. His glove and wool business enabled him to become Bailiff or Mayor of Stratford, so his son could attend King Edward VI school, where he became a familiar with Virgil and Ovid. The second chance was the touring troupes of players which came through Stratford. Having married Anne Hathaway and now with three children, William followed the players and sought his fortune in London, firstly as an actor, then as a playwright and finally as a theatre owner, eclipsing even the established hero, Christopher Marlowe.

As an actor he became a 'sharer' in the 'Lord Chamberlain's Men', performing for Queen Elizabeth I, and later as the 'King's Men' for James I. As a writer, he is best known for his plays – a brilliant and prolific output of comedies, tragedies and histories – although his 154 narrative poems were also works of genius. His plays opened his new theatre, The Globe, on the south bank of the River Thames, now beautifully and authentically re-created on its original site. His writing had a huge and unrivalled influence on the English language (see panel).

Shakespeare was able to repay his father by using his own newly-gained wealth to save him from the bankruptcy of his business and the threat of debtors' prison and to help John to become a 'gentleman', paying for his 'grant at arms'. After 25 years of success, William Shakespeare returned to Stratford in 1612 to settle down at his house, New Place. He was to die just four years later. The world can thank two of his fellow actors, John Hemminge and Henry Condell for retaining and publishing his collected plays in the 'First Folio'. Otherwise much might have been lost because Shakespeare himself was far too casual about the legacy he would leave us.

Over the years there have been doubts that Shakespeare, a country boy with limited education and no foreign travel, could produce so much sophisticated work. Some have postulated, as the true writers, Francis Bacon, the Earl of Oxford, or even his rival Marlowe, (somewhat unlikely since Marlowe was killed in 1593 before many of Shakespeare's best plays were written). For the moment though, the flags above the playhouse of the Royal Shakespeare Company fly proudly over Stratford-Upon-Avon. But if it is ever proved that they fly in error, if the man they celebrate was in fact nothing more than a prosperous local burgher, then Stratford must surely stand as the greatest example of fame by chance in literary history.

Bill Bryson in his excellent book on the English language, *Mother Tongue,* points out that Shakespeare created 2,000 words never used before and numerous phrases we still use today. Here are a few: *Foul play, salad days, tower of strength, budge an inch, cold comfort, one fell swoop, fast and loose, flesh and blood, primrose path.*

See: Agincourt, Broadway, Hollywood

STUDIO 54
New York, USA

Frank Sinatra sang, 'If I can make it there, I'll make it anywhere. It's up to you, New York'. What he really should have sung was, 'It's up to you Steve Rubell', at least in the late '70s, because it was Rubell who decided who was to be a celebrity for 15 minutes. Steve was not an agent or film maker, but a Brooklyn boy who grew up to be the co-founder of 'Studio 54', the Big Apple's pleasure palace disco – that came to epitomise the hedonism of the latter part of the decade.

In April 1977, Rubell transformed the former theatre, casino and CBS radio Playhouse and Television Studio, located in Manhattan, calling it Studio 54 – because it was number 254, West 54th Street. Pandering to the excesses of the time, he created the first 'superclub'. What made it famous was his method for ensuring its popularity, which was simple – keep the 'grey people' out. The red velvet rope leading to the entrance became an élitist selection parade, which Rubell monitored vigorously, dubbed 'Mr Outside'. It did not matter if the approaching hopeful was a millionaire or a film star if he felt a person was not 'happening' enough; he turned them away. To get in, women sold their bodies, and men sold their women. Even Cher was once rejected (this was before her reported surgery). As a result, anyone who wanted to prove they were 'someone,' would line up for endorsement – from Rod Stewart to Andy Warhol.

Even Warhol himself described the experience as, 'dictatorship at the door and democracy on the floor,' because once inside nothing was off limits; including a large 'man in the moon', a puppet dangling from the ceiling that would receive nightly doses of fake cocaine via an oversized spoon, to

raucous applause from the people taking real cocaine below. It has been described as, *'like real-life theatre, with a fascinating cast of characters being selected for each night's grand cabaret performance party'.*

'The path to excess leads to the palace of wisdom', Mike Myers said when portraying Rubell in the Miramax film *54*, in 1998. Although it was morally questionable, the crowds were happy to follow it religiously.

Sadly, the 'innocent' age of unaccountable debauchery had to come to an end, but it did so in a fittingly dramatic style, with Rubell and his partner Ian Schrager imprisoned for tax evasion in early 1980, in spite of being defended by Roy Cohn – formerly the notorious sidekick of Senator McCarthy during the anti-Communist witch-hunts of the 1950s. Then, in 1989, Rubell died of AIDS, (as did Cohn), while Schrager has gone on to become a successful hotelier.

Meanwhile, the club which had been closed since 1989, re-opened nine years later, once again as a theatre – but what you pay to see inside will never be as theatrical as when it housed 'the party the world will never forget'.

Crowding round the entrance, hopefuls wait to be 'selected.'

Liza Minelli with Mikhail Baryshnikov

See: Astor Ballroom, Big Apple, Cotton Club, Gotham, Manhattan, Sibylla's, Tin Pan Alley.

SUEZ
Egypt

'Stagnant ditch' is a cynical phrase that French engineer Ferdinand de Lesseps was greeted with time and again when he appealed to England for financial backing – to dig out of the dusty desert in what is now the Suez Canal.
It seemed at the time as if the project would never get off the ground.

However, the concept was not even a new one. Senosert III, the Egyptian Pharaoh in 1874 BC, had linked the Red Sea and the Mediterranean through the branches of the River Nile. Throughout the centuries, the stretch of water was alternately neglected and then re-dug. But, despite the sporadic efforts of the

Greeks, Romans and Arabs, by the eighteenth century the canal had once again been allowed to fill up with sand.

In 1798, Napoleon Bonaparte proposed the idea of creating a new navigational canal, but left Egypt before he could take it further.

Over 50 years later, despite resolute opposition, Ferdinand de Lesseps managed to strike a deal with the Egyptian government to construct the canal, and the ambitious project finally begun. Unfortunately, it was to be founded on the sweat and blood of those who worked on it – the Egyptian Pasha created a system of forced labour. In the

Between the battles of The Pyramids and of Aboukir, Napoleon surveyed the ancient canal route, nearly drowning in the process when caught by the tide. His engineer, Charles Le Père, made a report which helped the decisions of de Lesseps years later.

ten long years of digging between 1859 and 1869, over 2.4 million Egyptian labourers toiled away, and more than 125,000 perished under the extreme conditions. The epic success of Suez contains tragedy.

By joining several large lakes together, the ninety-mile channel was to be the longest canal without locks in the world. In 1865, the stream was already large enough for a small boat, and on August 15th, 1869, the canal was officially opened. The critics had prophesied that the canal would silt up, or that the banks would fall in, or even that it would be more efficient to unload goods into railways on one side, and back into boats on the other. The English newspapers had long remained sceptical, seeing the stories of the canal's impressive progress as a trick to encourage investment. This cynicism was to be mis-placed. The channel exceeded the budget by 100 per cent, reaching £19 million, but the utility of the canal was easily worth its cost. The gap between east and west had been slashed; the distance of a journey between Jeddah and the Black Sea port of Canstanza (which would previously been conducted around Africa) had been cut by eighty six per cent. For Britain, which in 1880 had 80 per cent of the world's merchant marine and its vast Empire held together by maritime and naval strength, the canal was absolutely vital.

A project that succeeded against all the odds, the Suez Canal now has an annual capacity of more than 25,000 ships. Crucial for world trade, it now transports 26 per cent of all the world's oil exports and forty one per cent of the total volume of goods that reach Arab Gulf ports. Its importance, however, in both trade and strategic terms, was to make it a target for controversy and conflict in the years to come. For one of the objectives of the Afrika Korps and of Rommel was to reach and to cut the canal – luckily thwarted by the Battle of El Alamein. Later, in 1956, when Nasser nationalised the Suez Canal, it was to result in a war, with Britain, France and Israel attacking Egypt. Once the resulting blockages were cleared, Egypt, contrary to many expectations, ran the Canal with perfect efficiency and it has worked well for the country and for the world ever since.

See: Actium, Aswan High Dam, El Alamein, Panama

SUTTER'S MILL
California, USA

In January 1848, Captain John Sutter's sawmill at Coloma was not working properly, so his partner James Marshall diverted extra water down the tail race, which widened the channel to let the mill wheel work. A mass of sand and gravel was thus displaced. Next morning, Marshall strolled down the stream, and something glinted and caught his eye. He hurried to tell John Sutter, confessing, 'Do you know, I positively debated within myself two or three times whether I should take the trouble to bend my back to pick up one of the pieces and had decided on not doing so when, further on, another glittering morsel caught my eye.

James Marshall picks up the first gold.

I condescended to pick it up and to my astonishment found that it was a thin scale of what appears to be pure gold'.

Sutter came to the mill and found gold everywhere. He then begged his crew, mostly Mormons, to keep the discovery quiet for six weeks so that he could complete his flour mill. No chance. Within two weeks, the secret was out – but not at first believed. The fever really started in May when the Mormon leader Samuel Brannan rode down the streets of San Francisco with a bottle of dust shouting ' Gold, Gold from the American River!' The little hamlet of Yerba Buena, only recently changed to San Francisco, was the first to get gold fever. Sutter himself was a typical victim of the mania; 'My labourers began to leave me, in small parties first, but then all left, from the clerk to the cook'. Sutter's mill, tannery and fields emptied of workers overnight. It was a microcosm of the whole of California.

On 14th June, *The California Star* reported *'Every seaport as far south as San Diego, and every interior town has become suddenly drained of human beings. Americans, Californians, Indians and Sandwich Islanders, men, women and children'*. Four days later, *The California Star* ceased publication. All the staff had left for the goldfields.

Outside California, news spread more slowly, partly because it was difficult even to muster a crew to sail a ship to the east. But soon, the rumours and then the confirmation had spread throughout the United States and abroad, and the following year the 'Forty-niners' poured into California from all points of the compass.

The population of San Francisco jumped from 900 in 1848 to 100,000 the next year. 42,000 had come overland, 35,000 by sea – and 3,000 were sailors; indeed most ships that arrived in San Francisco were at once abandoned by their crews. At one stage, 200 were left tied up and deserted. 'The Gold Rush' was probably the single largest example of mass greed the world has ever seen.

However, once the first easy surface pickings had played out, it is doubtful if many of the prospectors and miners became really rich. In fact, the people who did were more likely to be selling picks, shovels, fruit and food, whiskey and women. The biggest beneficiaries of all were the loggers. The wood required

for housing, buildings, mine props and railroads meant that the 'timber rush' was ultimately ten times more valuable than the Gold Rush.

The American nation was the winner, because the discovery of gold reversed a recession that was emerging after the recent Mexican War. It opened up the Pacific territories – California for its gold, and Oregon and Washington for their timber. It encouraged the railroads to cross the Continent, and it shifted wealth to the west. California rightly became 'The Golden State' and the mouth of San Francisco Harbour 'The Golden Gate'.

But there was one real loser, at least in his opinion; the unfortunate John Sutter, whose commercial enterprises were so wrecked by the loss of labour and who was cheated of his gold rights.

'By this sudden discovery of the gold, all my great plans were destroyed. Had I succeeded for a few years before the gold was discovered, I would have been the richest citizen on the Pacific shore'.

Without Sutter and his mill there might never have been a Golden Gate Bridge, or the San Francisco we know today.

See: Kimberley's Big Hole, Nome, Silicon Valley

TACOMA NARROWS BRIDGE
Washington, USA

In celebration of the millennium year 2000, a new footbridge, costing £18 million, was built across the Thames between London's St Paul's Cathedral and the Tate Modern Gallery. From the very first day, it became notorious for an unsettling, swaying motion which made those crossing the construction feel sick. Within two days of its inauguration the bridge was closed, and it took many months and millions of pounds to

correct this unfortunate phenomenon.

Sixty years earlier and eight thousand miles away something similar occurred, with much more spectacular results.

The Tacoma Narrows Bridge was built in 1940 to connect Washington State in America's Pacific north west with its Olympic Peninsular. It was a prime example of the design of suspension bridges at the time; light, graceful and flexible.

The bridge twists in the wind before collapsing.

Unfortunately, even in a light wind, the bridge began to twist up and down like a roller coaster. It was soon called 'Galloping Gertie', and even became a popular tourist attraction – but it was also a major worry for the Washington Toll Bridge Authority.

On November 7th 1940, the bridge was being filmed by engineers with several 16mm cameras to study its peculiar motion, when the wind began to rise. Soon the roadway was twisting and writhing like a mad animal, with the sidewalks rising 18 feet above each other. One car was on the bridge and the driver, terrified, ran back down the roadway, as the whole span suddenly collapsed into the water. His dog, trapped inside the car, was the only sad casualty of the much sadder engineering disaster which had all been captured on film.

The world's bridge builders had just been given a dramatic lesson on the effects of 'resonance', and how a bridge's roadway can act like an aircraft wing. From then on, all new bridge designs were tested in wind tunnels. Factored in nowadays are the effects of vibration, aerodynamics, wave phenomena and harmonics.

Other bridges have fallen down mysteriously, but none have been made famous by such a spectacular filmed recording.

See: Arnhem, Fourteenth Street Bridge, Rock Island, Tay Bridge

TAJ MAHAL
India

On the banks of the Jamuna River near Agra stands perhaps the most evocative memorial to man's love for a woman.

In 1612, Mumtaz Mahal married the future Shah Jehan, soon to become the fifth Mogul Emperor. It was not only a wonderful love match from the start, but she was to be his constant companion, his inseparable friend and counsellor, even going with him on every military campaign and also influencing him in the many acts of charity that were to make a wise and popular ruler and also help him to take the Mogul Empire to the height of its powers.

His reign was also the time when the Moguls, descendants of both the Turkish Timur and the Mongul Genghis Khan, created a flowering of magnificent architecture, replacing the traditional red stone with spectacular white marble, combined with semi-precious stones like lapis lazuli, onyx, jasper, topaz and carnelian.

Mumtaz bore Jehan fourteen children, but tragically died in 1630 bearing the last, during a military expedition in the Deccan. The Emperor was absolutely overcome by grief and was determined to perpetuate his wife's memory with the finest memorial and a symbol of their love. He succeeded magnificently.

The architect Ustad Ysa, working with master craftsmen from all over India and the Middle East and directing over twenty thousand workmen, took twenty-two years to create the masterpiece, a vast complex with the Taj Mahal (Crown Palace) as its centrepiece. With its shining dome and minarets, its white marble is mirrored in four reflecting pools. Particularly at dawn and dusk in changing light, it takes on an extraordinary ethereal quality and in misty weather appears to float above the Jamuna River. Even if its romantic history were set aside, many people think that it is quite simply the most beautiful building in the world.

Centuries later another royal bride – Princess Diana – understood the power of imagery. It was no accident that, at the height of her misery over her marriage to Prince Charles, she chose to be photographed, pensive and alone, in front of the Taj Mahal. The pictorial symbolism was instantly understood by the media and then by the world, the contrast between her own life and that of the Mogul Emperor and his greatly beloved Empress.

See: Actium, Alma, Amritsar, Bhopal, Dum Dum, Jodhpur

TAMMANY HALL
New York, USA

On the corner of New York's East 17th Street and Union Square stands a fine example of American 'Colonial Revival' architecture. It is now a theatre, but its fame rests on its first purpose in 1927 as Tammany Hall, the headquarters of the Tammany Society.

Originally a social organisation when it was formed in 1786, the Tammany Society had rapidly become a powerful political organisation, controlled by wealthy men but supported by working men, especially immigrants. After the destruction caused by the New York City Draft Riots during the Civil War, Tammany actually helped the city. Under the leadership of William M. (Boss) Tweed, the city received some autonomy, and 'home rule'. Tweed pushed forward much-needed infrastructure like roads and sewers, but unfortunately, was so blatantly corrupt that any good work became steadily mired in scandal. In 1870, with the city firmly in the grip of Tammany and the Democratic Party, 'Boss' Tweed became New York's Commissioner of Public Works, resulting in even worse corruption and graft. For example, he bought park benches for $5 and sold them to the city for $600. Thermometers were costing $7,500 each and brooms $41,000. One carpenter was even paid $360,000 in a month, while not surprisingly, the cost of building City Hall Park leapt from a budgeted $350,000 to $13 million.

It was Thomas Nast, a cartoonist who worked for *Harpers Weekly*, who first and most effectively, began to expose Tweed, who furiously told *Harper's* Editor, 'I don't care a straw for your articles, my constituents don't know how to read. But they can't help seeing those damned pictures'.

Tammany pressure mounted. The Harper brothers lost their New York school book supply contract, and Nast was offered a massive bribe of $500,000 to desist. But their campaign stubbornly continued. In 1871, Samuel Tilden investigated Tweed, aided by secret evidence provided by New York's Sheriff, Jimmy O'Brien, who was annoyed that he was not getting enough of Tweed's takings. 'Boss' Tweed was finally jailed for 12 years. He had done little for the name of Tammany, the Democratic Party or the city, which had its home rule charter revoked.

But even with Tweed's removal, Tammany Hall did not lose its power over the city. Under 'Honest' John Kelly, it began to model itself on the organisation of the Catholic Church, with precinct captains, (parish priests), district leaders (bishops) and country leaders (cardinals). It also functioned as a social welfare system while never losing its power to mobilise its political muscle. From the end of the Civil War in 1865 right up to the 1930s, the

'Boss' Tweed, was constantly attacked by Thomas Nast.

Mayors of New York were nearly all put into place by the Tammany Hall 'machine'.

It is ironic that the physical move of Tammany Hall – from its East 14th street headquarters to the grand building in Union Square in 1929 – coincided with the beginning of the end of its power and influence. Fiorella La Guardia, was elected Major in 1933. A vociferous opponent of Tammany, he held power until 1945. A Tammany come-back under Carmine De Sapio was finally blocked by the event of Robert F. Wagner, Jr becoming Mayor. The extraordinary power and influence of Tammany Hall was broken forever.

See: Camp David, Chequers, Cliveden, Downing Street, Stowe

TARANTO
Italy

On the night of 11th November 1940, the Italian port of Taranto lay silent, dark, and calm, with six of Italy's finest battleships gently at anchor. For decades, battleships had been the symbol of a nation's power and prestige, and Italy had joined the race to have her share.

There had been those who had questioned the future supremacy of the naval 'Big Gun', especially aviators who were convinced that a comparatively cheap aeroplane with a bomb or torpedo could sink the largest and most expensive battleship.

The British had planned attacks by carrier-borne torpedo aircraft on both the German and Austro-Hungarian fleets back in 1918, the latter ironically, from Taranto. In 1923, the planes of 'Billy' Mitchell had sunk old German ships – including the battleship *Ostfriesland* and, during the Abyssinian crisis in 1935, the British had considered attacking the Italian Fleet in Taranto. It was bad luck for the Italians that the British Commander in Chief, Admiral Sir Andrew Cunningham, had as his Rear Admiral at the time, Lumley Lyster, a Fleet Air Arm officer who had been thinking about an air attack on Taranto for years, ever since serving there in 1918. Cunningham's planned date for the raid, 21st October, ' Trafalgar Day', had to be postponed, so he next chose 11th November – 'Armistice Day'. His weapon was to be the Fairey Swordfish, a single-engined, biplane torpedo bomber affectionately nicknamed 'The Stringbag.' It was so slow that, once, in a strong headwind, a fast Italian fleet had actually out-run the lumbering Swordfish. However, this ancient-looking aircraft had already shown its worth at Narvik, and was to do so again in 1941 when a Swordfish torpedo jammed the Bismarck's rudder, leaving her circling to her doom. Amazingly, it became the most successful Allied torpedo bomber of the war.

Just twenty one Swordfish took off for Taranto from the carrier *Illustrious*. The first twelve, their crews freezing in their open cockpits, arrived at eleven o'clock at night - some dropping flares to silhouette the Italian capital ships, some bombing to distract the gunners. The others, skimming 30 feet above the water at a stately 85 mph, avoided the nets, balloons and booms, and struck *Cavour* and the brand-new *Littorio* with torpedoes. The second wave, nine planes, also sank *Duilio*.

For the loss of two planes and just one life, enormous damage had been done. Three out of six Italian battleships had been put out of service. In their anxiety, the Italians withdrew all their heavy units away from where they were needed near Malta and the Desert War, up to Naples, La Spezia and Genoa. British ships could thus be released to

'Swordfish attack at Taranto' by Robert Taylor

THE MILITARY GALLERY, BATH

vital Atlantic duties. Italian naval aggression was replaced by caution throughout the Mediterranean, and British morale given its first fillip since the fall of France.

But Taranto's fame had another effect. Japan's Naval Attaché in Rome left for home, and joined her naval planners to muse: *'If just twenty one slow biplanes can pull that off, what could hundreds of bomber and torpedo planes, well-trained and coordinated, do to a major fleet at anchor?'*

Thus, the fate of the American Fleet at Pearl Harbor, fourteen months later, was sealed at Taranto. The age of the majestic battleship was over.

Enter the dragon – the aircraft carrier.

See: El Alamein, Midway, Pearl Harbor

TARIFA
Spain

Gibraltar is not, as so commonly thought, at the narrowest point of the legendary 'Pillars of Hercules' – the western exit of the Mediterranean. In fact, it is the nearby little town of Tarifa, taking its name from Tarif Ibn Malluq, one of the first Islamic explorers who crossed from Morocco in 709.

Tarifa was always in the front line in conflict between the Spanish and the Arabs, who, under Tarik Ibn Zayad, invaded across the straits of Gibraltar in 711, landing men and horses at nearby Guadarranque *(River of the Mares)*. After five centuries, Tarifa was recaptured from the Moslems in 1292 by Sancho IV of Castile, 'the Brave', who put the town in the hands of Alonso Perez de Guzman. Two years later, the Infante Don Juan, Sancho's brother, committed treason against the Crown of Castile, offering to help the Moslem King Mohammed to recover Tarifa. Baulked by its defence, the Infante threatened Guzman that if he did not surrender the town, his kidnapped son would be executed. Guzman's response has gone down in history, 'If you do not have a dagger with which to kill him, here, take mine'. For his stout defence of Tarifa, he was nicknamed Guzman el Bueno (The Good).

While Tarifa's strategic position made it famous in Spanish history, its topographical position made it famous as a word in many languages.

Water flows in relatively fast from the Atlantic, replacing the evaporation of the shallow waters of the Mediterranean. Sailing ships were often reduced by this current to a crawl, and it was easy for the swift galleys from Tarifa to row out and impose, officially or unofficially, a levy – which we now call a 'tariff'.

Gibraltar, (originally *Gibel Tarik*,

The Rock of Gibraltar, still in dispute

Tarik's mountain), with its fortress in the 'Rock' and its protected harbour, was bound to become more important than Tarifa. Handed to the British at the Treaty of Utrecht in 1713, it has been a constant point of friction ever since, besieged 15 times – once for three and a half years.

When Britain thought of giving it independence in the late 1950s, Foreign Secretary Selwyn Lloyd later admitted that Spain was right over many things. The Treaty stipulated that only enough civilians as were needed to service the garrison should be allowed in Gibraltar, no Arabs or Jews could live there, and above all, no smuggling was allowed. Every rule had been broken, especially the smuggling, which had become so flagrant and wide-scale that it was damaging the Spanish economy. Even more important, the Treaty stipulated that if Britain wanted to give up sovereignty, she had first to offer it to Spain.

While nobody can be sure where Gibraltar's future lies, we know where Tarifa's does. With its strong winds, it has become the kite-surfing capital of Europe.

TAY BRIDGE
Scotland

'Beautiful Railway Bridge of the Silv'ry Tay!
Alas! I am very sorry to say
That ninety lives have been taken away
On the last Sabbath day of 1879,
Which will be remember'd for a very long
time.'

This is the first verse of the laughably bad poem written by William McGonagall, a Dundee weaver, who had an amazing belief in his own genius and has been described as *'the greatest bad verse writer of his age.'* But the disaster he described was real enough and a tragedy that belied the poet's bizarre description.

The engineer Thomas Bouch had long pushed for a bridge across the estuary of the Tay River, and in 1873, the Tay Bridge Company started work following his design – on what was to be the longest railway bridge in the world. Opening in June 1878, Queen Victoria's Royal Train used it to reach Balmoral a year later and Bouch was duly knighted, becoming Sir Thomas Bouch. But engine drivers were worried, complaining that the bridge swayed as they crossed and bolts were loosening.

On the night of 28th December 1879, in a ferocious storm, the bridge fell into the river taking a complete train with it and killing 75 people. Bouch was disgraced for his poor workmanship and for choosing wrong materials, and he died within months of a broken heart. He had been dismissed from the project to build the massively strong Forth Bridge which was to use the same builder William Arrol, and designer William Barlow, for the new, lower and wider replacement bridge over the Tay. This, McGonagall again recorded in his inimitable style:

'Beautiful new railway bridge of the Silvery Tay,
With your strong brick piers and buttresses in so grand array,
And your thirteen central girders, which seem to my eye
Strong enough all windy storms to defy...
'Thy structure to my eye seems strong and grand,
And the workmanship most skillfully planned;
And I hope the designers, Messrs Barlow & Arrol, will prosper for many a day
For erecting thee across the beautiful Tay...'

Although the poet, in his enthusiasm, became rather dismissive of the efforts of other non-Scottish bridge builders:
'The New Yorkers boast about their Brooklyn Bridge,
But in comparison to thee it seems like a midge...'

The two bridges enabled the railways to open up the Highlands to tourism. Arguments have raged as to whether that was good for either the people or the wildlife.

But probably the most important long term effect of the Tay Bridge disaster was because two significant people missed the train. Booked to travel, Marx and his collaborator Friedrich Engels would have died in the accident, if they had not become so engrossed in a discussion. It was Engels who, after Marx's death in 1883, devoted himself to editing and translating his work, including the vastly influential *Das Kapital*. If these great communist figureheads had caught the train, it is just possible that the world might not have experienced the effects of Communism to the extent it has.

Karl Marx. We might never have heard of him if he had caught the train across the Tay Bridge.

See: Fourteenth Street Bridge, Rock Island, Tacoma Narrows Bridge

TEXAS SCHOOL BOOK DEPOSITORY
Texas, USA

It is likely that most people will never have heard of 411 Elm Street, Dallas, but on 22nd November 1963 the building was thrust into the limelight when a tragedy occurred which was to shock the world – the real-life 'Nightmare on Elm Street' of President John F. Kennedy's assassination. Conspiracy theories abound with 61 people currently listed as possible suspects. The official enquiry however, the much criticised Warren Commission, concluded that President Kennedy was killed and the Texas Governor John Connally seriously wounded by a lone gunman positioned in the sixth floor corner window of 411 Elm Street – The Texas School Book Depository.

Constructed in 1898 on land owned by the Southern Rock Island Plow Company who leased the then five-storey brick warehouse to sell farm implements, the building was burned to the ground when struck by lightning in 1901. It was rebuilt, with two additional storeys, and Dallas investor Harold Byrd, after his purchase of the company in 1937, named it the Carraway-Byrd building.

By 1928, repeated flooding in downtown Dallas led city engineers to construct levees to move the Trinity River a mile west, and this in turn led to the creation of a city park called Dealey Plaza. It was named after George Bannerman Dealey, a prominent local civic leader and publisher of the Dallas Morning News. 411 Elm Street, now on the edge of Dealey Plaza, was home to several companies before 1962, when the Texas School Book Depository moved in. This private firm stocked and distributed public school text books for the northern half of Texas. Four floors were leased to book publishers, while floors five, six and seven were used for storage of stock.

A year later in October 1963, Lee Harvey Oswald took a $1.25 per hour job at the Depository. Immediately prior to this he had been in Mexico, trying, unsuccessfully, to get a visa for Cuba.

A former Marine, he had lived in Moscow and married Marina, a Russian girl, before returning to America where he seemed to espouse various strange causes. Some think he was a Soviet agent, some a CIA agent, some a 'patsy', some just a nut.

The President was to arrive in Texas on Thursday afternoon, 21st November, and would visit Dallas on Friday. The route of the Presidential motorcade was published in the press days earlier and Oswald overheard fellow workers saying that Kennedy would be passing their building during the lunch hour. The motorcade would turn from Main Street into Houston Street, and then turn again on to Elm Street. The Texas School

Book Depository would be an ideal location for an assassination attempt, because the cars would have to slow right down in order to make the turns. From the depository, there was a direct view of the intersection, more than enough to take a clear shot at the President and ample time to make it.

On Thursday afternoon, Oswald travelled to nearby Irving with a fellow employee, saying that he wanted to pick up some curtain rods. He also went to visit Marina, who had recently given birth to their second daughter. Oswald almost overslept, left $170 and his wedding ring in a cup on the dresser and, with $14 in his wallet, returned to work in Dallas on Friday morning. He concealed the 'curtain rods' package in the depository. Investigators concluded that the package in fact held a 6.5 mm Mannlicher-Carcano rifle, a cheap, Italian-made weapon that Oswald had bought by mail-order.

At noon on Friday, the other workers at the Texas School Book Depository went out for lunch, or into the street, to watch the President pass by. Oswald was last seen on the sixth floor about thirty minutes before the assassination. The Hertz advertising sign on top of the building, a local landmark with its hundreds of lightbulbs and temperature and time display, read 12.30pm. Shots rang out. Terror and chaos reigned. History was created, and legend and mystery ensued.

Mystery, because we know that some shots were indeed fired from the sixth floor corner window and, since his rifle was found on the same floor, Oswald probably fired them. But were these the only three shots, or was the fatal shot fired from the much closer 'grassy knoll'

(Top) The unimposing Book Depository, with the much closer 'grassy knoll' on the left

(Bottom) The motorcade wends its way through Dallas, minutes from tragedy.
PHOTO: SIXTH FLOOR MUSEUM AT DEALEY PLAZA

in front of President Kennedy in Dealey Plaza? (Studies of Dallas Police Department radio transmissions at the time suggested four shots and not three had been fired, and the third came from the grassy knoll. Follow-up studies suggest there are either no shots on the recording, or there are four shots – and the debate about its contents continues). So was Oswald alone or not? Oswald himself never provided any answers because, almost beyond belief, he was gunned down just hours later by Jack Ruby in the Dallas Police Station, and right in front of the world's media.

If there was a conspiracy, who was responsible? Pro-Castro Cubans? Anti-

See: Ambassador Hotel, Bay of Pigs, Dallas, Lorraine Motel

Castro Cubans? The CIA? the FBI? Angry Texas oil barons? The Mafia, furious with Jack Kennedy's brother Robert for supposedly reneging on pre-election deals and hounding organised crime? Even if there was no conspiracy to assassinate, there seemed to be one to cover up certain details, which is perhaps even more sinister.

But whatever the truth (and it is unlikely ever to be conclusively revealed) the nondescript building on Dealey Plaza is worldfamous. Today it houses a permanent museum to the events of 1963 called 'The Sixth Floor museum at Dealey Plaza', and that corner window remains propped half-open forever.

ASSASSINATION COINCIDENCES

Abraham Lincoln was elected to Congress in 1846, Kennedy in 1946.
Lincoln was elected President in 1860, Kennedy in 1960.
Both were particularly concerned with civil rights.
Both Presidents were shot on a Friday.
Both Presidents were shot in the head.
Lincoln's secretary was named Kennedy.
Kennedy's Secretary was named Lincoln.
Both Presidents were assassinated by Southerners.
Both were succeeded by Southerners named Johnson.
Andrew Johnson, who succeeded Lincoln, was born in 1808.
Lyndon Johnson, who succeeded Kennedy, was born in 1908.
John Wilkes Booth, who assassinated Lincoln, was born in 1839.
Lee Harvey Oswald, who assassinated Kennedy, was born in 1939.
Both assassins were known by their three names.
Both names are composed of fifteen letters.
Lincoln was shot at the theatre named 'Ford'.
Kennedy was shot in a car called 'Lincoln' made by Ford.
Booth and Oswald were killed before their trials.

THREE MILE ISLAND
New York, USA

Meltdown *– a dangerous situation in a nuclear power station when the material becomes so hot that it melts, burns through its container, and radiation energy very harmful to living things escapes (Cambridge International Dictionary of Phrasal Verbs).* Meltdown is one of the most terrifying prospects known to mankind. The film *The China Syndrome* illustrated the potential horrors of a such a major disaster in a nuclear reactor, and the film is based on real events in America in 1979, in the nuclear power stations of Three Mile Island.

At 4.00 am on March 28, a sequence of errors began in the reactor of TMI 2;

a vital valve was stuck open, so water was not being properly fed into the reactor core. Unfortunately, the warning light was 20 feet from the controller's desk, and so remained unnoticed. Faulty instruments indicated to the staff that water levels were reasonable, while, unseen, those levels continued to fall around the core. Eventually, a water-free void began to form around the radioactive fuel itself. The temperature soared, and the fuel rods began to crack, and then even melt. And as the heat increased, so also did the levels of radioactivity. Radioactive forms of Xenon, Iodine and Krypton began to seep out into the environment. By 9.15 all non-essential personnel had been ordered to leave the plant, and a genuine disaster was in progress.

Phone calls were now pouring into Washington, warning the Government of the looming menace. In fact telephones were to form an added danger in the whole affair; the limited number of telephones in the offices of Three Mile Island had become jammed by the number of calls, which would make communications extremely difficult. To make matters worse, the local telephone system also jammed. The issue of evacuation was becoming increasingly real. However, it soon became clear that removing the inhabitants of the surrounding areas would be a huge and dangerous task. If the twenty miles surrounding TMI 2 were to be cleared, 640,000 people would need to leave home. In preparation for the worst, Jack Watson, the Presidential assistant, arranged for 240,000 vials of potassium iodide (designed to prevent radioactive iodine from entering the thyroid gland) to be sent to the area, and for blankets to be sent to evacuation centres outside the twenty mile radius.

Meanwhile, the situation inside the reactor had become even more bleak. The heat levels had continued to rise, and they had become so intense that the water had begun to split into its component molecules – oxygen and hydrogen. This had led to the formation of a huge hydrogen bubble which was potentially the largest threat so far. A Princeton scientist worked out that if it was to explode, the huge forces released could be enough to rip open the reactor dome, releasing terrifying amounts of radioactive material into the air. The plume of toxic gas would have carried a radioactive dose of around 150 rems, enough to kill children or the elderly. Meltdown was still a possibility, which would have made the area uninhabitable for over 30 years. (Incidentally, the film got it wrong. Had the reactor really melted all the way through the earth, it would have popped up in the Indian Ocean, in the Diamintina Trough, and not in China. However, this would have ruined the film's title, so the writers probably made the right decision).

By this time, between 80,000 and 200,000 people had fled their homes in

panic, but control was being reasserted by the plant's technicians. The hydrogen bubble was gradually bled off, and coolant was fed into the system. The immediate danger was over, and residents could gradually begin returning to their homes. But even then, the difficulties were not past. The plant, which had cost $700 million to construct, could never be used again. The clean-up would take over 10 years, and cost over $10 billion. The work was as perilous as it was slow. The workers, clad in radiation suits, cannot stay at the edge of the opening into the reactor for long, and cannot even look directly into it. The tools they must use are on the end of 40 ft poles, to keep them at a safe distance. Piece by piece, the radioactive materials were removed and transported to the federal nuclear reservation at Idaho falls.

In the years that followed, TMI 1 – the other Three Mile Island power station – changed almost everything about the way it operated. Whereas in 1979 there were 350 workers between the two plants, ten years later TMI 1 employed 800 itself. The attention to detail in the new regulations included repainting the control panel to make warning lights more obvious. These days, American power plants are constantly policed by NRC (Nuclear Regulatory Commission) inspectors. Extra auxiliary and safety systems such as reserve water pumps have been added in all nuclear power stations. Employees even undergo fitness for duty initiatives, to ensure that drugs or alcohol never affect performance. Hopefully, the near catastrophe of Three Mile Island has led to a greater awareness of the dangers and necessary precautions in nuclear power. However, in Chernobyl, 7 years later, it would become clear that not all of the lessons had been learned.

TIANANMEN SQUARE
China

'There can be no doubt that the authorities will crack down, and crack down hard, if stability seems to be being called into question'.

Ominous words from *The People's Daily*, the official Chinese state newspaper, in 1986. Between 1985 and 1987, a number of student protests had taken place in both Beijing and also Shanghai, with such slogans as 'Long Live Democracy'. The Communist

The world watched one Chinese with his shopping bags as he halted a column of tanks.

'Every communist must grasp the truth - political power grows out of the barrel of a gun'.

Mao Tse-Tung

Chinese government was worried, especially as Nicolai Ceaucescu, the communist leader of Romania, had recently been toppled and shot. The biggest protest of all came after the death of ex-Communist Party Secretary, Hu Yaobang on April 15th, 1989. He had been a popular figure, widely seen as tolerant of political opposition, and groups of students formed to mourn him. They created 'dazibao', large commemorative posters, with slogans such as: *The one who should not die, died. Those who should die, live'.*

The crowds grew and grew, and on April 17th, 5,000 students marched on historic Tiananmen Square, containing

both the Emperor's Palace (the Forbidden City) and now the symbolic meeting place for the Communist regime. There they stayed, and students continued to join in. By the time of Hu Yaobang's funeral 5 days later, 100,000 people filled the square. State officials at the funeral, in the adjacent Great Hall of the People, were so intimidated that they left through back exits. Chanting 'Down with dictatorship', the crowd staged daily protests, while the Government pondered how to handle the situation.

It is important to understand that this was not a riot. The protesters, who by now often totalled more than a million people, had created a festive, carnival atmosphere, and the people of Beijing lined the streets in sympathy with their cause. The students were adamant that they were not trying to overthrow the Government, merely to petition for reform, and stressed this by frequently singing *Internationale*, the Communist anthem.

The demonstration went on for weeks. On 13th May, it entered a new phase: a hunger strike. While the protests were already becoming increasingly famous throughout the country, and even abroad, this was to add a new level of publicity. The nation was forced to watch some of its most intelligent citizens begin to starve, and the sympathy which already existed for the students increased immeasurably. The visit of Mikhail Gorbachev from the Soviet Union to Beijing threw further international limelight on to the event. The protest was fuelled by the support of the local people, who gave wages, food and blankets to help the protesters maintain their stand against autocracy. The atmosphere remained upbeat, with a belief spreading that some political change could genuinely be achieved.

But, in the halls of power, a terrible decision had been reached. On the 3rd of June, the People's Liberation Army rolled into Beijing. It was the move that everyone had hoped the Government would not take. The army's approach did not go unresisted. Citizens of Beijing flooded the streets, forcing the tanks and personnel carriers to change their route continually. They even offered the soldiers cigarettes and ice-creams, epitomising the protest's spirit of gentleness. One of the most famous photographs of all time was taken at this time. An anonymous figure with a shopping bag stands alone in front of a column of Chinese tanks, defying its progress by his bravery and resolve. The photo made the cover of *Time* magazine, among others, and embodies every ounce of quiet defiance that the protesters stood for. But the army pressed on towards the square and the students demonstrating within it.

When they arrived, the soldiers, whether through direct orders or nervous panic, began gassing and firing upon the crowds. The students fought desperately to defend themselves, and even managed to destroy several of the army's APCs. But the troops were fighting with helmets and guns. Stones and bottles were all that the unfortunate student protesters had. Surrounded and overwhelmed, many of them huddled together and sang *Internationale* as they were gunned down. The protest was wiped away, and the PLA was in control of Tiananmen Square and Beijing. The government tried to filter the media coverage of the massacre by only broadcasting the pictures of the students retaliating, creating the image that the army were putting down some sort of

CLARE SUTTON

armed uprising. However, coverage was provided by the American Embassy nearby, and the whole world became aware of the tragedy unfolding. Some facts are still hard to ascertain; the Chinese media say that only a few hundred people were killed, but in the west the figure is calculated as thousands.

The international response, and particularly from America, came quickly. President Bush, on June 6th, banned sales from the US Government to China, forbade the exchange of weapons technology, and banned his military leaders from visiting the country. US feeling is still so strong that President Clinton's visit to the square during a visit to China was seen by many as controversial.

Defences for the People's Liberation Army's conduct has been offered. In 1999, Zhu Muzhi, the President of the Governmental China Society for Human Rights Studies pointed out that the troops were ill-equipped to deal with the situation. 'They had never witnessed such large-scale protests…They did not have rubber bullets then, nor gas masks … The only weapons they had were their guns'.

But no amount of retrospective writing will ever eradicate the horror that people still feel about what happened in Beijing. Nor should it.

CLARE SUTTON

See: Amritsar, Bonus City, Great Wall of China, My Lai, Sharpeville

TIMBUKTU
Mali

What chance happening made so many of us use mysterious phrases like, 'From here to Timbuktu', or, 'I'll knock you clear to Timbuktu?' Indeed, how many people know what Timbuktu is? Or where it is, if it is a place at all? Because, no doubt, some people think it is a myth or a mere symbol of great distance and remoteness.

Timbuktu is real enough – a town on the southern edge of the Sahara Desert, close to the Niger River.

In about 1100 AD, a Tuareg woman called Buktu found an oasis, decided to settle there and dug a well. The seasonal camp was soon called Timbuktu (Buktu's Well), and its location made it an ideal

stopping point for the caravan trade which had existed for hundreds of years. Soon, merchants built permanent markets and buildings. The town became the centre of the west African trade in precious salt, carried on thousands of camels from desert deposits 500 miles to the north to be shipped south on the River Niger, while gold came the other way.

Soon, the town fell under the control of Mali, Africa's first great Muslim kingdom. The result was that Timbuktu became a religious centre, with its Koranic University and three Mosques full of scholars, and attracting students from all over Africa and the Middle East. Being both a major trading hub and a religious centre, Timbuktu played a vital role in the spread of Islam.

Leo 'Africanus' was sent by the Renaissance Pope Leo X to do a detailed survey of Africa, a report that provided Europeans with most of their information about Africa for centuries. He visited Tumbuktu in 1526. *'The inhabitants are very rich, grain and animals are abundant, so that the consumption of milk and butter is considerable. Instead of coined money, pure gold nuggets are used. The people are peaceful and in the evening walk continuously about the city between 10pm and 1am, playing musical instruments and dancing'.*

The importance of what seemed an affluent and rather pleasant place declined

when Morocco captured it in 1591, reducing its religious status, but without protecting it from marauding tribes. Steam ships on Africa's west coast helped to destroy the Trans-Sahara camel trains, and when the French arrived in 1893, they never bothered to provide the town with a paved road, nor link it with a railway line.

See: Bastille, Great Hedge of India, Venice,

So what made Timbuktu, for Africans a thriving and long established trading and religious centre, such a byword for mystery and inaccessibility?

Its curious fame was probably earned in a quite short period in the early 19th century when it briefly became the last great exotic goal for intrepid European travellers seeking treasure and fame. Major Gordon Laing was killed there in 1826, but two years later, René Caillé made a safe return.

There is another curiosity that may have contributed to Timbuktu's fame. For two hundred years, on all British Admiralty naval charts, Timbuktu was the only inland town in Africa which was marked.

Timbuktu is still difficult to reach, although riverboat and camel have been joined by an airfield. Its three great Mosques have been saved from the encroaching sands of the Sahara by UNESCO funding and maintenance by the enthusiastic locals, passing the material in a human chain to the sound of drums and flutes.

It may always remain a mystery for most people, especially those used to travelling comfortably. Because it is the second hottest inhabited place on earth.

TIN PAN ALLEY
New York, USA

It is rather hard to imagine home entertainment in the US of the 1890s: no television, no radio, not even record players. And no cars, just horses on local roads.

But one thing many Americans did have was a piano, and for that you needed sheet music. As *The New York Times* put it, *'The consumption of songs in America is as constant as the consumption of shoes, and the demand is similarly met by factory output'*.

Gradually, New York City came to dominate this industry, churning out hundreds of songs which would be distributed by travelling salesmen to stores, bars, theatres and even brothels. The music had to be tried out by piano players in small, non-soundproofed rooms. Most of the time, publishers had congregated in just one street – West 28th Street between Fifth Avenue and

Broadway. In 1899, the New York Herald asked songwriter and journalist, Monroe Rosenfeld, to write some articles about the new industry. Emerging from Harry von Tilzer's offices, he was struck by the extraordinary racket of hundreds of pianos playing through the open doors and windows, reminding him of tin pans being banged together. So he coined the phrase *'Tin Pan Alley'* for West 28th Street, but later of course, it was applied to the whole popular music industry.

Several of the piano players thought they could do better than the songs they were asked to demonstrate, the most famous being George Gershwin. Another was a singing waiter called Izzy Baline whom we know as Irving Berlin.

The need to illustrate the covers of the music sheets provided another group with their first artistic opportunities.

Artists who had their start in the music business included Charles Dana Gibson (famous for his 'Gibson girl'), Norman Rockwell, Charles Schulz (Peanuts), Al Capp (L'il Abner) and a young Walt Disney.

The first really big hit was *After the Ball*, in 1892, selling five million copies – amazingly a copy for every 20 people then in America. *Till we meet Again* in 1918 sold seven million.

What is astonishing is how enduring the products of Tin Pan Alley have been. People still sing and play *She was only a bird in a gilded cage, I Can't Tell You Why I Love You But I Do* (1900), *By the Light of the Silvery Moon* (1910), *I Wonder Who's Kissing Her Now, Give my Regards to Broadway* (1904), *Shine on Harvest Moon* (1911), *T'aint nobody's business if I do* (1922), *Alexander's Ragtime Band, The Entertainer* (1902) and many more.

See: Abbey Road, Dogpatch USA, Harlem, St. Louis, Storyville, Tulsa

TITUSVILLE
Pennsylvania, USA

For Titusville and Pennsylvania it was a very good thing that the US mail service was slow. Before 1859, the oil industry was neither glamorous nor powerful. The problem was, although people had long ago realised that oil was extremely useful for both lighting and machine lubrication, and oil refineries were already in operation, no-one had yet found a way to harvest it in large quantities. Whale oil was the primary source, but the supply was dwindling along with the numbers of the whales themselves. The only other way to obtain oil was to find a place that it seeped out of the ground, and then 'skim' it off. This entailed using a wool cloth to absorb the oil, and then after that wringing it out to collect the contents. Obviously however, this was not a method that was able to produce large yields.

However, a concept was brewing in the Pennsylvania Rock Oil Company. A suggestion had been made as to whether oil could be obtained by drilling, as had been achieved for salt and water for centuries, and the idea was seen as an exciting one. But not all reactions were auspicious. One banker, when asked to lend money to the venture, scoffed

'Oil coming out of the ground, pumping oil out of the earth as you pump water? Nonsense!'

But the company was not to be deterred. It hired a railroad conductor, Edwin L. Drake, to travel to Titusville in Pennsylvania, and make a historic attempt to drill for oil.

Everything started off rather slowly. Colonel Drake (a title he had made up solely to impress the locals) spent an entire year both searching for funding and constructing his equipment, including a steam engine to power the rig. Worse still, his early attempts came to nothing as each hole that he drilled soon collapsed. Drake, in an admirable piece of lateral thinking, employed the services of William Smith (affectionately known as 'Uncle Billy'), who worked in drilling salt wells. He suggested the technique of containing the drill inside a metal pipe in order to stop the well collapsing. It was to be the basis of all modern oil drilling.

Edwin Drake (right) with his first drilling rig and engine house

But as encouraging as this was, the Pennsylvania Rock Oil Company was not happy. It was beginning to look as if the entire project was a non-starter. As unease grew, it was decided that the company should cut its losses. Accordingly, bosses sent a letter to Drake ordering him to abandon the project, and pay off his creditors. Had the postal system been quicker, Titusville would never have broken into the history books. But, against all odds, whilst the letter was en route to the drilling site, Drake was finally about to meet with spectacular success.

On August 27th, at a depth of 69 feet, the drill slipped into an underground cavern, and it then became apparent that the prospectors had finally struck oil. So by the time the letter arrived, its contents were totally irrelevant. Now nothing could keep Titusville off the map.

A town that, in 1858, housed only 250, soon bloomed into a population of 10,000. Titusville was now a 'boom town'. Well-known names also flocked to the area, such as future steel magnate Andrew Carnegie, Mark Twain and John D. Rockefeller, who was soon – by some fairly dubious methods – to create Standard Oil, and to dominate the oil industry. Soon others, searching for similar prosperity, scoured the surrounding area, and eventually, the whole of America – for 'black gold'. Improved transportation systems were constructed to move the oil, with railways being closely followed by pipelines; the first of these, 5 miles long, was built in 1865.

At the turn of the century, coinciding with the gusher at Spindletop in Texas, an innovation arrived which was make the oil industry a dominant force; the internal combustion engine. The modern oil industry had been born and would help to power America to world leadership.

Today, the USA oil industry employs 300,000 workers, and oil is a vital and powerful business on the world stage, making otherwise rather empty and unlikely countries like Saudi Arabia and Brunei fabulously wealthy. In Titusville itself, the discovery is commemorated in the 1901 Drake Memorial Pavilion - and the Drake Well Museum and Park, featuring his first well - and replicas of his original rig and engine house. And what do the people of Titusville think about their town's history? Their pride is best summed up by C.J. Tisi, the Executive Director of Titusville's Chamber of Commerce,

'Most of us have a little oil in our veins, and we thrive on it. You might say we're born to it. Our roots go very deep, and we treasure the past and the historic impact our community had on our nation and the world'.

See: Great Hedge of India

TOLPUDDLE
England

The remains of the Tolpuddle sycamore tree, under which the Martyrs swore their oaths of secrecy and brotherhood.

Colourful banners, marching bands, political speeches and street entertainment – a scene found each July in the village of Tolpuddle in England's sleepy Dorset. Welcome to the Tolpuddle Martyrs' Festival, a great celebration of a turning point in the trade union movement.

It seems incredible in these days of EU directives on everything from wages to working hours that it was not until the 1830s that such rights were acknowledged by the English 'Establishment'. Certainly, the six men who became known as 'the Tolpuddle Martyrs' paid a high price for asserting their position. Condemned to seven years transportation to Australia, a punishment second in severity only to death, they were shackled and chained like criminals of the most murderous and depraved kind.

It was a harsh and poverty-stricken existence for farm workers in nineteenth century rural England. The recent Reform Act of 1832 had made legal the first trade unions, and soon factory workers in towns and cities had joined together to secure increased wages and improved conditions. But in the country, the rigid social structure still locked the poor into subservience to wealthy landowners, and change was much harder to achieve.

George Loveless, a Tolpuddle farmhand who had taught himself to read and write, managed to persuade the village parson to approach the landowners on behalf of local farm workers. Initially successful, 'the masters promised to give the men as much for their labour as the other masters in the district', (which was 10 shillings – 50p.) The promise was broken, however, and Tolpuddle workers received only 9 shillings. If they complained, it was threatened that wages would be cut still further. This threat was carried out, so that by 1834 they were receiving just 6 shillings a week (30p.)

Hoping to seek justice through affiliation with the 500,000 strong National Consolidated Trades Union, Loveless and his brother James – together with Thomas Stanfield and his son John, James Hammett and James Brine – formed the Tolpuddle Lodge of the Agricultural Labourers' Friendly Society. They met beneath an old sycamore tree and also at Thomas Stanfield's cottage, where they swore an oath of secrecy and brotherhood. In a climate of illiteracy, downtrodden spirits and religious fear, such oaths were not uncommon in the forming of trades unions. In fact, appealing to workers' superstitions was virtually the only way to impress upon them the significance of their undertaking. However, it was this oath which was to prove the Martyrs' downfall.

When news of the Friendly Society reached the Dorset landowners, they were outraged. The whole *status quo* of the rural class system was in jeopardy. It could even lead to a revolution as in France.

Particularly incensed was James Frampton, an influential magistrate and landowner, who wrote to the Home Secretary Lord Melbourne stating that local labourers were being encouraged to *'enter into combinations of a dangerous and alarming kind, to which they are bound by oaths administered clandestinely'.* Frampton asked Melbourne how he should use the law.

The Home Secretary knew that the formation of the Friendly Society was not in itself illegal, so he advised Frampton to invoke two little-used laws. The 1799 Act *'for the more Effectual Suppression of Societies Established for Seditious and Treasonable Purposes',* and the 1797 naval Mutiny Act. One clause made it a felony to *'administer an oath binding a person not to reveal an unlawful confederacy'.* The combination of the two acts carried a sentence of seven years transportation. Notices warning that those taking 'unlawful oaths' would be prosecuted, signed by nine magistrates, were posted in Tolpuddle on 22nd February 1834. Just two days later, the six men were arrested and charged.

At Dorchester Assizes Court on 17th March, the Judge, Baron Williams, was biased and hostile, informing the carefully chosen jury of country squires and rich farmers that 'trades unions were evil' and that 'the use of secret oaths made the defendants guilty of sedition and treason'. In his summing up, he said: 'If you do not find them guilty you will forfeit the goodwill and confidence of the Grand Jury'. In his sentencing, he had the gall to say that the punishment was 'not for anything they had done, but as an example to others'.

On 11th April, five of the men were transported on the *Surrey,* bound for Port Jackson (Sydney). George Loveless had fallen ill, and sailed for Tasmania on 25th May.

Public support grew for the Martyrs' cause. Petitions pleading for their sentences to be overturned poured into Parliament from every quarter of the nation, with direct protests made to King William IV. At first, Melbourne stood his ground, hoping that the fuss would die down. A year later, however, it had not. An election and cabinet re-shuffle in 1835 saw him become Prime Minister, and his successor as Home Secretary was Lord John Russell. Russell argued that 'if being members of a secret society and administering secret oaths were a crime, the reactionary Duke of Cumberland, as head of the Orange Lodges, was equally deserving of transportation'.

On 14th March 1836, the Government finally conceded, and agreed to full pardons for all six men. Their ordeal was not yet over, because the Martyrs themselves were not informed of the pardons. The Governors of New South Wales and Tasmania made no attempt to trace them. If George Loveless had not seen the news by chance in a copy of an old London newspaper, they might have remained in Australia in ignorance.

Loveless returned to England on 13th June 1837, and the others followed in 1838 and 1839. Farms in Essex were purchased for the men, but their notoriety meant that they could not live the peaceful lives they yearned for. In 1844, all except James Hammett emigrated to Canada.

The Martyrs played a pivotal role in the history of trade unionism. In Tolpuddle, they were eventually honoured in 1934, with the building of six memorial cottages and the founding of the Tolpuddle Martyrs' Museum. The tree still stands, and a commemorative seat and shelter allow us sit and dwell on this momentous shift in history.

Five of the returned 'convicts'

Thomas Stanfield, aged 51

John Stanfield, aged 25

James Loveless, aged 29

George Loveless, aged 41

James Brine, aged 25

TOLPUDDLE MARTYR'S MUSEUM

See: Ballingarry, Botany Bay, Triangle Shirtwaist Company, River Rouge

TONKIN GULF
Vietnam

The millions of Americans and Vietnamese who suffered the consequences of the Vietnam War will draw very little comfort from the dubious evidence for America's open involvement – The 'Tonkin Gulf Incident'. In fact, not since the Germans fabricated the 'Polish attack on the Gleiwitz radio station' has there been such a feeble and flawed excuse for a war.

As far as the American media, public and Government were concerned the American destroyer USS *Maddox*, while 'innocently' eavesdropping electronically (Operation Desoto), was attacked on August 2nd 1964 by North Vietnamese patrol boats, and two days later the *Maddox* and the USS *Turner Joy* were attacked again, both outside the three mile territorial waters limit.

What nobody was told at the time was that the United States was simultaneously supporting an aggressive series of South Vietnamese bombardment attacks on the very same stretch of shoreline by torpedo boats – and appropriately named 'Nasty' boats made in Norway. These were equipped with 20mm, 40 mm and 57mm weapons and were part of operation Plan 34A, which General William Westmoreland, the Commander of Military Assistance Command, had not only approved, but said on 30th July would *'increase by 283 per cent over the July programme and 516 per cent over June'*. That night, four boats attacked Hon Me

President Johnson announces the Tonkin Gulf Resolution.

The Tonkin Gulf incident created a vast escalation of the war.

island, and the next night Hon Nieu. The North Vietnamese protested to the International Control Commission.

Understandably, the North Vietnamese thought that operations Desoto and 34A appeared to be well co-ordinated, which in fact they were not, and they moved their Swatow patrol boats south to try to counteract the American and South Vietnamese hostile activity. This led directly to the attack on the *Maddox*. The second apparent 'attack' on the *Maddox* and *Turner Joy* may never have occurred, being just a radar scare caused by nervousness and an electrical storm.

The 34A boats were quickly moved 300 miles south to Cam Ranh Bay, hiding the evidence. Defence Secretary Robert McNamara did not mention them when he told the Senate Committee that, *'The attack on the Maddox was no isolated event, part and parcel of a continuing Communist drive to conquer South Vietnam'*. President Johnson knew the truth. On 7th August, he asked CIA Director John McCane, 'Do they want a war by attacking our ships in the *middle* of the Gulf of Tonkin?' McCane replied sensibly, 'No. They are acting defensively to our attacks on their offshore islands'.

Such honesty did no good. That very day, Congress passed the Tonkin Gulf Resolution *'authorizing all necessary measures to repel attacks against US forces and all steps necessary for the defence of US allies in Southeast Asia'*.

This hastily written 'blank cheque' meant that within eight months, the United States had 200,000 troops in Vietnam, rising to 540,000 two years later.

Secret tapes now reveal that Lyndon Johnson ruefully admitted to Robert McNamara, 'when we got through with all the firing, we concluded maybe they hadn't fired at all'. The war was to kill 54,000 Americans and millions of Vietnamese. It would scar America for a generation and would break Johnson. But whatever his other achievements like civil rights, he could only blame his own dishonesty for his own greatest failure.

See: Kent State, Khe Sanh, My Lai

TOPKAPI
Turkey

The city of Istanbul, over 2,500 years old and straddling the border of Europe and Asia, holds many treasures. One of the finest is Topkapi Palace, for five centuries 'Seraglio' of the Ottoman Sultans of Turkey. Many will associate the evocative and romantic name of Topkapi with the *Topkapi* 1964 film, starring Audrey Hepburn and Peter Ustinov. In the film, a gang of ingenious jewel thieves attempts to steal a magnificent emerald-studded dagger from a secure display case in the palace. In fact, the thieves had picked just one item from a fascinating treasure-trove of beautiful and priceless objects.

Topkapi lies on high ground where the mouth of Istanbul's famous inner harbour, the Golden Horn, opens out into the Sea of Marmara. Topkapi means 'Cannon Gate' in Turkish, and commemorates one of the fortified gates in the extensive walls of the great city that the Turks eventually took by storm (by innovative use of their own massive ordnance) in 1453. The site, which covers several acres, was once the acropolis of ancient Byzantium, the Greek colony guarding the entrance to the Black Sea that was to become Constantinople in 334 AD. Its campus – like complex of palace buildings, gardens, pavilions and kiosks – with kitchens which once fed 5,000 people every day – is now a group of museums, with the infamous Harem occupying much of the western side. The museums reflect the power and world influence, through conquest and trade, of the Ottoman Empire in its heyday: weaponry, armour, jewels, porcelain and religious relics sacred to both Islam and Christianity. Exhibits are as varied as a truly wonderful collection of Chinese vases, the miniature figure of a seated potentate whose body is carved from a single huge pearl, a reliquary holding the arm of John the Baptist, and hairs from the beard of the prophet.

It is amusing that the other actress in the attempted robbery in *Topkapi* was Melina Mercouri, who later as the Greek Minister of Culture – attempted to make the British give back the Elgin Marbles 'stolen' from Greece.

Peter Ustinov and Melina Mercouri

The harem

TOUR DE FRANCE
France

While Britain has its football and America its baseball, undoubtedly the most popular sport in France is cycling. 'Le cyclisme' is a national obsession and, since 1903, the nation has hosted an annual race which lays just claim to being the toughest sporting event in the world.

The Tour is not technically a place, but a series of places and the route changes each year, so different towns and villages throughout France and even nearby countries get their yearly chance to experience fifteen minutes of fame. And fifteen minutes is literally what it is. Communities lobby for months or years to be included on the route, and the towns where a stage of the race starts or ends pay large amounts of money for the kudos of being associated with it. But, in a flash of multi-coloured jerseys, it is over as the main pack, the 'peloton', pass through at speeds of 40kph.

The Tour began by chance under a bizarre set of circumstances, originating

with a political quarrel between the industrialist Comte Dion and the newspaper owner Pierre Giffard. Dion advertised many of his cycling products in Giffard's sporting journal *Le Velo,* but then there was a bitter argument between the two over the famous trial of French army officer, Alfred Dreyfus, who had been accused of passing military secrets during the French/German dispute over the Alsace region. As a result, Dion set up a rival publication called *L'Auto Velo,* (later shortened to *L'Auto*). This was published on yellow paper in contrast to *Le Velo's* green. The editor was Henri Desgrange, former holder of the World Hour Bicycle record.

Capitalising on the growing popularity of long-distance road cycle races – as opposed to track events – the Desgrange camp wanted something to help them win the circulation war. It was to be Desgrange's twenty six year old assistant, Geo Lefevre, who came up with the idea of a cycle race around the country ('La Grande Boucle' – The Big Loop) and coined the phrase 'Tour de France'.

In January 1903, *L'Auto* announced *'A cycle race to cover 2,428 km in (six) stages between 31 May and 5 July. No trainers or physios for the first five stages so that all riders will compete on equal terms'.* But, with just a week to go before the closing date for entries, only fifteen riders had taken up the challenge. The conditions were considered too harsh. Desgrange reduced the entry fee from twenty to ten francs, offering an incentive of five francs per day expenses to be paid to the first fifty finishers. Eventually, on 1st July, 60 riders began the race which was to last until 19th July. Twenty-one of them were sponsored, some being established French cycling stars of the era, others provincial French as well as Swiss, Belgian and German riders. Maurice Garin, a 32-year old chain-smoking chimney sweep, won this first edition, also winning three of the six stages which made up the route.

The Tour was a roaring success. Thousands of spectators turned out to greet the riders, sales of L'Auto soared and interest from commercial sponsors was generated. But by the second year sabotage and dirty tricks became a feature of the race. Competitors tried everything from spiking the drinks of their rivals to putting obstacles, even including nails, in the road, and filing through a bike frame so that it collapsed and threw off its rider. Such treachery is no longer a part of the modern Tour, although in recent years professional cycling has been subjected to intense scrutiny over allegations of drug use to gain competitive advantage.

To those who like to take a leisurely cycle ride on a Sunday afternoon, the idea that such a past-time could be an almost impossibly gruelling feat of athletic performance, endurance and competition might seem hard to believe. But the distances covered and speeds maintained by the Tour de France riders mark them out as athletes of the highest calibre. Some have compared it to running a marathon every day for a month. The modern Tour, although varying in route, always includes several mountain stages taking the riders up the steep, winding roads of the French Alps where freezing fog and snow, even in July, add to the misery of the altitude and the gradient, and down again faster than most speed limits. Some riders have paid the ultimate price. In 1967, British rider Tom Simpson collapsed with heart failure whilst challenging for the leader's yellow jersey on a climb up Mont Ventoux. As he lay there, rasping for breath, his dying words were 'Put me back on my bike'.

The most prestigious and well-known prize in the Tour is the Yellow Jersey (Maillot Jaune). This is worn by the rider with the shortest accumulated time overall. There are also two other accolades. The Polka Dot Jersey denotes the rider who is 'King of the Mountains', and the Green Jersey is based on points awarded for the first finishers of each stage of the race.

The Tour de France is the largest live spectator event in the world, averaging 750,000 a day, and with daily coverage in many countries, it is second only to the Olympics as a television sport. Whereas the commentators used to crouch in cars a mile behind the field, watching the race on tiny monitors, today they sit in commentary boxes at the finish line. Constantly making the commentary interesting is an extremely skilled job in itself, and occasionally, during quieter moments of the race, commentators have been known to discuss what they had for breakfast.

Pro-cycling is very much a team sport, and a wide variety of organisations put their name and money behind the teams. Of the 198 riders who start the race, only two or three have any realistic hope of winning. Just to complete the race is a feat in itself, and for most of the junior riders, the sole object is to support the team by playing tactical games, 'slipstreaming' and 'breaking away', which will enable their leader to stay ahead.

In its centenary year, The Tour de France is now more lucrative and more international than ever. For many years it was dominated by European cyclists, some of the greats including Belgian Eddy Merckx and Frenchman Bernard Hinault. Now, not surprisingly, Americans have started to compete and to win. Greg LeMond became the first, in 1986, and the current champion, Texan Lance Armstrong, leader of the US Postal Service Team, has won every year since 1999, now joining an elite group of riders who have won the Tour five times. What makes both even more remarkable is that each have made a spectacular return to victory after serious

Lance Armstrong, wearing the leader's yellow jersey, toils up a mountain stage.

illness. LeMond suffered major back injuries after an accidental shooting incident and in 1996, at the age of just 25, Armstrong was diagnosed with testicular cancer which had spread to his abdomen and lungs. The subsequent fightback of both riders, not only to health, but to supreme fitness of a level most people could not even begin to contemplate, has made them sporting legends.

Meanwhile, reinforcing the shift away from European dominance, the Tour de France has not seen a Frenchman win since 1985, a fact which undoubtedly rankles the national pride of the passionate host nation.

See: Aintree, Brescia, Brooklands, Indianapolis, Le Mans, Wembley, Wimbledon

TRAFALGAR
Spain

Cape Trafalgar might have remained just another rocky Spanish headland, but for the fact that Admiral Villeneuve lost his confidence. In October 1805, he should have been hundreds of miles further north, joining up with Napoleon's *Grande Armée* at Boulogne which had been waiting to invade Britain.

Of all the foreign invasion threats, including the Spanish Armada's, (beaten by Drake and the weather in 1588), and Hitler's, (beaten by the Battle of Britain in 1940), Napoleon's was probably the most dangerous and likely to succeed, though Napoleon was hampered by his own lack of knowledge about the true

realities of sea power. 'The Channel is a mere ditch, and will be crossed as soon as someone has the courage to attempt it'. Moreover, he foolishly turned down the offer by the American inventor of steamboats, Robert Fulton, to use them in becalmed conditions to tow his invasion barges to England: 'What Sir, you would have my boats fight the wind and waves by lighting bonfires under their decks? Pray you, excuse me. I have no time for such nonsense!'

It is easy to feel sorry for poor Villeneuve. He had received the

Nelson looks down from his column in Trafalgar Square. Curiously, he has no eye patch.

See: Berezina, Elba, Hampton Roads, Tsushima, Waterloo

The lower gun deck of HMS Victory. From the Battle of Trafalgar attraction at The Royal Navy Museum, Portsmouth.

order *Come to the Channel. Bring our united fleet and England is ours. If you are only here for 24 hours, all will be over and six centuries of shame and insult will be avenged.* British Admiral Jervis drily commented, 'I do not say they cannot come, I only say they cannot come by sea'.

As a feint, Napoleon ordered Villeneuve to sail to the West Indies. pursued there and back by Nelson. At a skirmish with Admiral Calder off Finisterre, Villeneuve then lost his nerve and turned south, not east, failing to fulfil his Emperor's orders to join the French navy at Brest. Instead, he joined a Spanish navy even more ramshackle and ill-trained than his own. He also knew that he was about to be replaced by Admiral Rosily, and even that Napoleon had left Boulogne to begin his march across Europe to conduct the brilliant Austerlitz campaign against the Russians and Austrians. The whole logic for a battle was now removed, but Napoleon had petulantly ordered a now humiliated Villeneuve out anyway to attack Nelson. The scene was set for one of the most decisive battles in history.

Villeneuve's formidable adversary, Admiral Horatio Nelson, was already a legend. In a long and brilliant naval career, he had lost an eye before his victory at Cape St Vincent – and later his right arm. Off Copenhagen, he had ignored his vacillating superior's signals by famously holding his telescope to his missing eye. He had conducted a scandalous affair with Emma, wife of Sir William Hamilton (albeit with her husband's acquiescence) and had a daughter by her, Horatia.

The problem for Napoleon was that his 2,000 ships had been blockaded in their ports for years by the Royal Navy which constantly patrolled, with nothing to do but watch and endlessly practise seamanship and gunnery to perfection.

With British superior sailing and gunnery, the Battle of Trafalgar was nearly a foregone conclusion. 'ENGLAND EXPECTS THAT EVERY MAN WILL DO HIS DUTY' signalled Nelson as the two fleets approached each other at a majestic walking pace.

As the ships battered each other with devastating broadsides with the British gaining the advantage, something terrible and unexpected happened. A well-trained French sniper, concealed high in the rigging of *Redoubtable*, Villeneuve's flagship, hit Nelson, who was rushed below decks to the surgeon. 'Ah, Mr Beatty you can do nothing for me. I have but a short time to live; my back is shot through'. After hours of long agony, Nelson was visited by Captain Hardy, 'We have got twelve or fourteen of the enemy's ships in our possession'. 'I hope none of our ships have struck?' asked Nelson. 'No, my Lord, there is no fear of that'. Later Hardy returned to report. After his last orders, Nelson said, 'Kiss me, Hardy'. After the Captain had kissed his cheek, Nelson sighed, 'Now I am satisfied. Thank God I have done my duty'. Two hours later he was dead.

The British had not lost one ship, but 1,700 men were dead or wounded. However, the French and Spanish lost 18 ships, 6,000 men dead or wounded and 20,000 prisoners, including poor Villeneuve who was released the next year – and committed suicide rather than face his Emperor. Napoleon fought on for ten years, but without naval power he was doomed.

The results of Nelson's achievement off that rocky Spanish cape lasted much longer. Britain's navy would dominate the seas for 150 years, and help a tiny island create one of the world's greatest empires.

COURTESY OF SARNER LTD

TRANQUILLITY
The Moon

'Houston. Tranquillity base here. The Eagle has landed'.

There are thousands of famous places on earth but only one on the moon, the spot on which the lunar module of Neil Armstrong and 'Buzz' Aldrin was *meant* to land – the Sea of Tranquillity.

It all started in October 1957, when American scientists experienced the deep shock of hearing the beeping of the tiny Soviet satellite *Sputnik 1*, followed in November by the half ton *Sputnik II*, orbiting with a dog, 'Laika'.

America's mood was not improved when, a month later, an attempted launch of a three-pound satellite with a Navy rocket ended in an explosion. *'Kaputnik', 'Flopnik', 'Stayputnik'* – the embarrassing headlines, were the result of ignoring the German rocket expert Werner von Braun. He soon had successful satellites launched with Army rockets. But three years had been lost, a fact well rubbed in by Yuri Gagarin when he became the first man in space.

President John Kennedy was furious at the idea of America lagging behind the Soviets. 'If somebody can just tell me how we catch up. Let's find somebody – anybody. I don't care if it's the janitor over there'.

In fact, things were not as bleak as they seemed. America's genius for science and technology and her huge financial strength were to bear fruit. Moreover, unknown to the West, the Soviets were being dogged by accidents and poor technology. Years later, American scientists were able to examine the never-used Soviet lunar space craft and they compared its controls to the 'cab of a locomotive' – and they meant a steam locomotive.

Kennedy launched America's efforts, saying, 'I believe that this nation should commit itself to achieving the goal before this decade is out, of landing a man on the moon and returning him safely to earth'. He meant an American man, of course.

Eight years, billions of dollars and two Presidents later, the dream was fulfilled.

363 feet of Saturn V rocket lifted off with Apollo 11 – the *Columbia* command module, the *Eagle* Lunar Module and Neil Armstrong, 'Buzz' Aldrin and Michael Collins. Four days later, circling the moon, *Eagle*, with Armstrong and Aldrin, separated from *Columbia* and headed for the moon's surface.

At the last moment, Armstrong, whose heart rate had jumped from 70 to 176, decided the Sea of Tranquillity was too rocky, and guided the *Eagle* a little further before setting it down safely with only seconds of fuel left.

Six hundred million people on Earth watched Armstrong set foot on the surface, and utter the immortal line, 'That's one small step for man, one giant step for mankind'. Veteran CBS reporter Walter Cronkite babbled less historically, 'There's a foot on the moon. Wow! Oh Boy! Hot diggity dog! Yes sir!'

Armstrong and Aldrin carried out experiments, collected samples and moved about in 'kangaroo hops' made possible by the moon's low gravity. They left an American flag and a plaque which read, *'Here men from the planet Earth first set foot on the moon. July 1969 A.D. We came in peace for all mankind'.*

After taking off and reuniting with a very anxious Michael Collins, they headed for home. On the recovery ship, President Richard Nixon greeted them with the words, 'This is the greatest week in the history of the world since the creation'. A bit of an exaggeration perhaps, but Nixon, mired in the Vietnam war, needed good news.

Thanks to incredible effort by thousands, America had its three brave men on to the moon, even though not exactly on the Sea of Tranquillity.

See: Cape Canaveral, Peenemünde

TRANSYLVANIA
Romania

Dracula, like Frankenstein, Tarzan and Robin Hood, has proved a mainstay of the cinematic industry for almost a century. He comes to us from Bela Lugosi, via Lon Chaney to Christopher Lee, in the guise of a dinner-suited and fanged Count, from the 1897 book by Anglo-Irish writer Bram Stoker, but his roots lie in the western Romanian province of Transylvania. Lying within the bend of the Carpathians as they turn westwards at their southern end, this is an ancient, romantic and largely unspoiled landscape of sleepy villages, wildflower-rich meadows, thick woods that still shelter some of Europe's last wolves and bears, and historic towns with fine old buildings and churches. It is a peaceful place, but one with a most bloody past, fought over by Romans, Dacians, Cumans, Hungarians, Romanians and Austrians, Tartars and Turks, only being united with Romania in 1919.

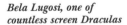
COURTESY OF HUMPHREY STONE

Unspoiled sleepy villages.

Transylvania was always a remote and mysterious country, where old stories of vampires and other monsters thrived. And one monster was all too real. Transylvania's most famous, and bloodiest, son was Vlad Tepes, 'Vlad the Impaler'. He was, in fact, a native of Wallachia, the Romanian province to the south of the Carpathians, and three times became ruler of that turbulent realm. His father, named Dracul had been exiled to Sighisoara, one of the seven cities founded in Southern Transylvania by medieval German immigrants. Here, Vlad was born in 1431, in a house that is now the 'Dracula Restaurant and Bar'. Sighisoara, a walled city with fourteen towers, had been built as a bastion against Tartar and Turk, and Vlad spent much of his life bravely engaging these feared and brutal invaders from the east. As a teenager, he had been a Turkish hostage to ensure his father's good behaviour, which seems both to have embittered him and taught him bad social attitudes and some really unpleasant habits, especially a taste for revenge and the truly horrible art of impalement.

Bela Lugosi, one of countless screen Draculas

Those were cruel times – and Vlad's father and most of his family died violently. Indeed, Vlad fought Turkish ruthlessness with even greater cruelty. When he received Turkish envoys, he accused them of lack of respect by not doffing their headgear, and when he was told that their religion would not allow removal, he nailed their turbans to their heads to show his contempt for both the Turks and their Muslim faith. Famously, too, the Sultan of Turkey once came across the remains of one of his armies – a field of 20,000 men (and women and children) – horribly impaled whilst alive. The Sultan Mehmed, himself no man of peace, apparently burst into tears at the sight. Vlad treated his own subjects with as much cruelty, executing and usually impaling – anybody who opposed him, nobles as well as common criminals, even debtors and adulterers. With 100,000 deaths to his credit, Vlad was an early exponent of what the American political classes now call 'zero-tolerance'.

Astonishingly, a century later, Transylvania threw up another mass murderer, one literally steeped in blood, and thus very much part of the Dracula legend. This time it was a woman, Countess Elizabeth Bathory, born in 1560 into one of the Hungarian families that then ruled Transylvania. Hers was a dysfunctional family of unpleasant eccentrics (such as a bisexual aunt who tortured her servants), and she herself was mentally disturbed and prone to fits. Elizabeth was beautiful, intelligent, educated and very rich. She became a good mother, but could not resist sexual depravity, involving both men and women, nobles and peasants – and violence, mostly towards girl servants or 'the lower orders'. After the death of her husband (another sadist) in 1604, Elizabeth sank deeper into depraved cruelty. With a small team of faithful female servants she used to horribly and systematically torture young women, partly to extract their blood for witchcraft rituals that were a vain attempt to preserve her fading looks. Nobody was too concerned about the death of village girls. Only when she murdered those of high birth did the authorities come to worry about her deeds. As the bodies began to clutter the castle and the estate, the peasants spoke of vampires.

Eventually, the rumours could not be kept from her family and other nobles, and even reached the ears of the Holy Roman Emperor. Her cousin Count Thurzo, Palatine Prince of Transylvania was sent to investigate Elizabeth's activities and finally raided her castle lair. He and his men found numerous corpses, and at the subsequent trial a witness revealed an inventory of 650 murders, made out, incredibly, in the countess's own careful handwriting. The court sentenced Elizabeth to be walled up in a cell in her own castle, where she died four years later.

It is not surprising that the word 'Transylvania' causes a slight chill.

> *The films of Dracula, the monster of Transylvania, outnumber that of his rival, the 'Frankenstein Monster', by 160 to 115.*

= TRIANGLE SHIRTWAIST COMPANY =
New York, USA

They called it 'the fire that changed everything', and indeed it started a worldwide movement to improve the lives of women.

In 1911, there were hundreds of thousands of women working in New York's garment industry, in workshops and factories called *'fire and death traps'* by the Factory Investigating Committee. There were just 47 inspectors to combat violations in 50,000 buildings.

Two years earlier, 200 women, mostly young Italian and Jewish emigrants at the Triangle Shirtwaist Company, tried to join the International Ladies' Garment Workers' Union. On being fired, they staged an independent strike, which others joined. At this point, the owners hired thugs to beat them up, and the police arrested the victims. This then triggered the largest strike by women, 'The Uprising of the Twenty Thousand', backed by many women's suffrage and trade union organisations. The strikers won a few concessions, but it was the fire on 25th March 1911 that really shook the world.

On the 8th floor of the Asche Building, on the corner of Green Street and Washington Place, the fire seemed to erupt from beneath the overcrowded tables. Scattered paper patterns and pieces of fabric went up in seconds. The girls rushed to the exits or the elevator, which had immediately stopped working. On the ninth floor the situation was even worse. The stairways had been purposely restricted, so the girls could be searched for stolen material each evening. The elevators never came, and the lone fire escape collapsed.

Soon, the fire department, whose ladders only reached to six floors, watched helplessly as girl after girl, clothes and hair blazing, jumped from the windows to escape from the heat, sometimes hand in hand – a horrible precursor of the World Trade Center, ninety years later.

The poor girls, some only thirteen years old, were falling right through the safety nets and then thudding on to the pavement, creating piles of bodies. 146 people died, 100 of them still in the building. After years of wrangling, the owners finally paid $75 for each life.

The appalling sight of the fire at last triggered New York's conscience. Ninety five per cent of similar buildings were found to be defective, and new laws were rushed through.

The incident also had a major effect on the protection of women. Only a week before the fire, the first International Women's Day took place in Europe, with over one million participants. The Triangle Shirtwaist fire was invoked from then on as a prime example of how women should not be abused and exploited.

Hoses play too late on to the blackened 8th and 9th floors.

See: Pudding Lane, River Rouge Overpass, Tolpuddle, World Trade Center

TROY
Turkey

'I fear the Greeks, particularly when they bear gifts'.

When they woke up to find a huge wooden horse outside their gates, apparently a gift to the gods from the departed Greek army, it must have been quite a dilemma for the Trojans. Should they burn it? Should they leave it for a few days, sitting in the hot sun of Asia Minor? If they had chosen either course of action, the small team of volunteer Greek fighters concealed inside the horse would have perished, and, Troy would have survived. A Trojan priest, Laocoon, wisely advocated the destruction of this highly suspicious gift. However, his only reward was for him and his children to be eaten by two serpents that rose from the sea. After this

grisly spectacle, even the most hardened sceptics were subdued and dragged the horse quickly into the city.

The siege of Troy took place nearly four hundred years before it was first described in 850 B.C. by the blind poet Homer, in the first substantial work of literature in the western world, his epic *The Iliad*. So, the whole story of Troy, or Ilium, is surrounded by myths, passed down verbally through the years.

We are told that Helen of Troy, 'the most beautiful woman who ever lived', born of Zeus himself, was given to a human called Paris, for judging that

Aphrodite was the fairest of the gods. Helen, unfortunately, already had a husband, Meneleus, whose brother was, regrettably, Agamemnon, king of the Greeks. Unaware of the god's divine involvement, the Greeks plainly considered Paris a mere kidnapper and pursued him back to Troy, his home city. Thus, Helen was famously said to have had *'a face that launched a thousand ships'*.

The siege lasted ten years, and destroyed many of the heroes on both sides, including Achilles – who had been dipped in the river Styx to make him invulnerable. By bad luck, his heel, by which his mother dipped him, remained untouched by the magic river, and that is where he was fatally wounded by an arrow from Paris.

King Priam of Troy's daughter, Cassandra, had been blessed by Apollo with the power to always see the future correctly, but also cursed that she should never be believed. She had foretold the sack of Troy but, as usual, nobody else believed her, leaving her raving to herself in frustration.

The concealed Greeks slipped out and opened the gates for their now returned army. The sack of the city itself was so violent that the gods themselves were said to be joining in: 'Neptune has loosened the foundations with his great trident and is shaking the walls'. – (Virgil, *Aeneid*).

The story of Troy is in every sense a tragic one. Nearly all the Trojans were killed, their aged King Priam murdered on his own altar. Even the surviving Greeks, with the gods now furiously turned against them, were scattered across the seas. Some, like poor Agamemnon, murdered by his own (adulterous) wife upon his return, met pitiable ends. Those who lived still faced years of hardship and wandering, most notably Odysseus, who only returned to his wife and son 10 years after the actual fall of Troy.

The only silver lining is the story of Aeneas, the main topic of Virgil's *Aeneid*, who escaped Troy, fled eventually to Italy, and settled his people, who were to become the ancestors of Rome.

The problem with the story of Troy is that it was so long before any sort of written record, that it is impossible to know what is true. However, a German amateur archaeologist, Heinrich Schliemann, was so fanatically dedicated to proving that the city had existed, that he conducted nine expeditions between 1870 and 1890 to do so. He discovered a mound on the probable site of Troy, consisting of the compressed remains of nine different cities, the earliest from the Bronze Age. His work was taken up by many other archaeologists after his death, and Carl W. Blegen, of Cincinnati University concluded that the layer known as Troy VIIa was the most likely to be the legendary city. Dated between 1260 and 1240, it contained extraordinary numbers of buried food jars, as might be used during a siege, and bones in the streets, as might be left by dying soldiers.

It is also possible that the war may have been less linked with a beautiful woman and more with trade, due to Troy's lucrative position guarding the Hellespont – entrance to the Dardanelles. However, whatever the conclusion, the number of stories written about the city, as well as the scientific interest in it, are unrivalled. We still use the phrases, 'Achilles Heel', 'being a Cassandra' and 'Trojan Horse'. It is one of the most significant and influential legends in the western world. As G.K. Chesterton said:

'The end of Troy will never end, the flame that consumed it will itself never be consumed'.

See: Actium, Delphi, Elba, Ibiza, Olympos, Pompeii

TRUTH OR CONSEQUENCES
New Mexico, USA

There are plenty of places, real or not, which have given their names to radio or television shows – *Dallas, Peyton Place, Sesame Street, Brookside, Knots Landing, Hollyoaks, Emmerdale*. However, there is just one city that has taken on the name of a show.

Palomas Springs in New Mexico was well known to the Native American Indians for its healing water and mud, joining such august Roman bathing centres as Bath or Spa, although they never had such a feared customer as Geronimo, the Apache leader.

In 1914, the town changed its name to Hot Springs, but with the disadvantage for the US mail that there were several such towns in America.

Thus, the town grasped at a bizarre opportunity in 1950. Ralph Edwards, the Master of Ceremonies of the radio show *Truth or Consequences,* promised that he would bring the show for an annual nationwide broadcast to any city that would change its name to 'Truth or Consequences'. On 31st March 1950, after several votes, and a protest from 295 upright (or uptight) citizens – who no doubt found the decision somewhat frivolous – the town took its new name.

Ralph Edwards kept his promise, and the first live coast-to-coast broadcast took place from the city of Truth or Consequences. The convention has never been broken, with a Ralph Edwards Park and a Ralph Edwards room in the Geronimo Museum.

Sometimes there is nothing stranger than the truth – or its consequences.

See: Bath, Spa, Leavenworth

Geronimo in later life

TSUSHIMA
Japan

The fishermen from Hull were most surprised to see the battleships appearing out of the North Sea fog. They assumed they were British, until inexplicably, they opened fire, sinking one fishing smack and damaging others.

The warships were, in fact, Russian and the 'Dogger Bank Incident' of 24th October 1904 was one of the more bizarre events in the murderous conflict between Russia and Japan, which culminated in the Battle of Tsushima in

1905. This battle would change naval warfare, and even more importantly, the relationship between east and west forever.

In the forty years since the first real contact with Europeans in 1853, Japan had transformed itself from a mediaeval state to a thoroughly modern one. Having taken Korea in a war with China, it now coveted Manchuria and especially Port Arthur, the ice-free base which sheltered the Russian Czar's 'Pacific Ocean Squadron'.

Faced by the intention of the Russians to strengthen this squadron, British trained Admiral Heihachiro Togo made the decision to act first, attacking the Russian ships, who retreated into the protected safety of Port Arthur, which the Japanese then surrounded and attacked by land.

With his Pacific fleet bottled up, Czar Nicholas II resolved to send his Baltic Fleet across the world, no less than 18,000 miles, to relieve Port Arthur. Under the taciturn and unimaginative Admiral Rozhdestvensky, the fleet set sail on 15th October. Far-fetched rumours of Japanese torpedo boats in the North Sea set off the foolish Dogger Bank fiasco, but other Russian problems were real enough, with untrained crews, bursting boilers and failing engines making the long odyssey unbearable. At Madagascar, they heard dispiriting news. The Japanese had captured a key observation hill overlooking Port Arthur, enabling them to use plunging shells from their distant massive 11 inch howitzers to batter the moored Russian

See: Corregidor, Hiroshima, Midway, Pearl Harbor

Russian battleships sinking in the Straits of Tsushima

ships to junk.

Days later, the news was even worse. In spite of brave Russian resistance, Port Arthur had succumbed in January 1905, in a savage battle involving all of the techniques soon to be horribly familiar in Europe; heavy artillery, mortars, trenches, barbed wire, grenades and machine-guns. The victorious Japanese suffered 60,000 casualties, with another 33,000 sick.

The logic for the Russians' marathon voyage was now gone. But the creaking fleet slowly carried on, waiting until 16th March for unwelcome reinforcements in the form of even more ancient ships. At Cam Ranh Bay in French Indo-China, the fleet waited again, and finally set sail on 14th May. Admiral Felkerzam, the second in command, died on 25th May – but instead of nominating his successor, the ever-taciturn Rozhdestvensky did not even tell the fleet.

Now, after seven long months, the Russian fleet opted for a route through the straits between Japan and Korea, near the island of Tsushima where Admiral Togo waited. At noon on 27th May the battle began – and soon turned into a disaster for the Russians with the better-trained Japanese out-gunning them. The Russians lost thirty-four out of thirty-seven warships, with thousands of casualties and prisoners. By contrast, the Japanese suffered negligible losses.

Technically, all navies now opted for the Dreadnought 'all-big-gun' design of battleship. But much more important was the political influence. With the Treaty of Portsmouth, brokered by US President Theodore Roosevelt, the balance of power was radically changed in the Far East. Both Russian morale and confidence in her leadership were dealt a huge blow that may have contributed to the Russian Revolution twelve years later. What is more, the defeats of Port Arthur and Tsushima demonstrated to the subjugated peoples of the East that Europeans were no longer invincible. It would take a further fifty years but whole colonial empires – British, Dutch and French – were to be doomed by two distant battles in a long-forgotten war.

TULSA
Oklahoma, USA

'Oh, I was twenty four hours from Tulsa,
Ah, only one day away from your arms…'

Popular music, led by America, has been making obscure places famous for years. Few of us outside Oklahoma would have heard of Tulsa until Gene Pitney sang about his interrupted journey, nor Wichita but for that *Wichita Lineman*. Warm feelings for the Illinois town are expressed in *I wish was in Peoria*, just as *Lubbock, Texas in our rearview mirror* reflects equal disappointment. And many of us do *Know the way to San José*, but it would be nice to know who *The Man from Laramie* was, or who inspired *The Girl from Ipanema* or who was the *Tallahassee Lassie*. Or for that matter, how many jumped from the *Tallahassee Bridge*. And where are Tina Turner's *Nutbush City Limits*? And when they are *Stompin' at the Savoy*, which Savoy is it? Certainly not the one in London, more likely the Harlem 'Lindy Hop' ballroom where Chick Webb blew Benny Goodman right off the stage.

In America, to find songs about really local places, turn first to jazz. New Orleans gave us dozens, sounding like a street directory, with *Basin Street Blues, Bourbon Street Blues, South Rampart Street Parade* and *St Phillip Street Breakdown*, You could find your loved one in the hospital, 'stretched out on the long white table, so still, so cold, so bare' in *St James' Infirmary Blues*. New Orleans's red light district, Storyville, had 292 brothels and *Mahogany Hall Stomp* celebrates the one at 235 Basin Street – probably the smartest in the country.

Memphis, always a centre of music, and later made even more famous by

Elvis Presley, gave us *Memphis Blues, Memphis, Tennessee* and *Beale Street Blues*. It was on a visit to St Louis from Memphis that W.C. Handy wrote his most famous work, *St Louis Blues*.

New York provided *42nd Street* and no less than forty songs about Broadway, together with *No Sleep till Brooklyn, New York New York, Slaughter on 10th Avenue, 59th Street Bridge Song, Harlem Twist* and *Spanish Harlem*. *I left my heart in San Francisco* echoes the romance of California, while Frank Sinatra insisted that *Chicago is my kind of town*.

The automobile centre of the world gave us the whole Motown phenomenon, plus *Panic in Detroit* and *Detroit City*.

The railroads helped to create America, and it is not surprising that their trains and stations often feature in song, sometimes extolling them with *Chattanooga Choo Choo, Wabash Cannonball* and *Rock Island Line*, some reflecting sad partings like the two *Last Trains (San Fernando* and *Clarksville), Midnight Train to Georgia* or even echoing their sad decline as in *The Train they call the Spirit of New Orleans*.

America is a big place, and its songs have often featured long journeys, first on horseback as in the cattle drives of the *Old Chisholm Trail* and then the first tarmac road running right across the continent, The Lincoln Highway or *Route 66*.

Rivers include many songs about the *Mississippi*, plus *Banks of the Ohio* and, of course, *Swannee River*. The romance of the open road, the railroad or the river does not seem to have rubbed off on to air travel – few, if any US airports have been sung about.

While whole States are usually famous already, it is interesting to see how few appear in a song. Georgia leads the way with *Marching through Georgia* from the Civil War and *Georgia on my mind* and

Left to right: Gene Pitney, New Orleans, The 59th Street Bridge in New York and Frank Sinatra's Chicago

Many American songs reflect their love of their rural past.

One night in Georgia. Others have just one: *My Old Kentucky Home, My Tennessee Mountain Home, Alabamy Bound, Maryland, My Maryland, Massachusetts, Carolina Moon, California Girls, Oklahoma!*

Britain has had its fair share of places put on the map. Few have gone quite as far as American songs, but the Beatles took London's *Abbey Road* and their hometown Liverpool's *Penny Lane* and *Strawberry Fields* to the world. Paul McCartney later did the same with his Scottish retreat The *Mull of Kintyre*, as did Roger Whittaker with *Durham Town*, although his lyricist had the river wrong.

War has influenced British songs about places with classics like *White Cliffs of Dover* and *Mademoiselle from*

Armentiers. It's a long way to Tipperary perhaps reflects the thousands of Irishmen who fought for the British.

London is a very old city and has songs from many eras, like the nursery rhyme about churches, *Bells of St Clement's*, *The Lambeth Walk* and *Burlington Bertie from Bow*, about boroughs and the bizarre *Wombles of Wimbledon* about a suburb. Britain's provinces fought back with the *Longhaired Lover from Liverpool*, no doubt familiar with *Ferry across the Mersey*, if not with the *Fog on the Tyne*, or enjoying the *Day we went to Bangor*.

Ireland's songs reflect its intimacy and the nostalgia for home: the *Mountains of Mourne, the Rose of Tralee, Fields of Athenry, Carrickfergus* and *Galway Bay*.

No doubt music in every country glorifies places we may never have been to but have heard of through song.

In 'Durham Town' Roger Whittaker erroneously sang about the River Tyne instead of the Wear.

COURTESY OF ROGER WHITTAKER

TUXEDO CLUB
New York, USA

The black-tie 'Tuxedo' became as fashionable as 'white tie and tails.'

HENRY POOLE

In 1986, the American Formalwear Association celebrated the centenary of the first wearing of a short evening jacket by Griswold Lorillard, the tobacco heir, at his club – The Tuxedo Club in Tuxedo Park, New York. While the club can justifiably claim the fame of creating the 'Tux', whether it was Lorillard as the wearer can be disputed.

The first candidate is another member of the Tuxedo Club, New York financier James Brown Potter. Then there is Evander Berry Wall, 'King of the Dudes', who was ejected from a grand Saratoga event for wearing such informal attire, instead of the normal 'white tie and tails'. Others claim that the elegant Viscount Dupplin brought it back from Germany.

The key to this mystery may be that all four gentlemen, Lorillard, Potter, Wall and Dupplin, were all customers of the Savile Row Court tailor, Henry Poole.

In 1865, another regular client, The Prince of Wales, had asked Poole to design a short smoking jacket which was to be worn 'privately at home'. The next

year, the Prince met James Potter and his lovely wife Cora, and invited them to come and stay for the weekend at Sandringham. He added that 'they always wore short coats in the evening'. So Potter asked Poole quickly to make up such a garment in time for the great weekend. On returning to New York, he proudly wore it to his club on the basis that 'If it was good enough to be worn by the Prince of Wales, it was probably good enough for the Tuxedo Club!'

In the end, the name's use in America is a toss up between Lorillard and Potter, but the Tuxedo Club's role in popularising the famous garment is not in dispute.

See: Carnaby Street, Harley Street, Savile Row, Wall Street

Lord Dupplin, one of Britain's best-dressed men, a good friend of the Prince of Wales who called him 'Duppy'

UNTER DEN LINDEN
Germany

For three centuries the people of Berlin were highly superstitious about the lime trees which had given the name to their grandest boulevard, *Unter den Linden*, meaning under the lime trees. An old song by Walter Kollo was still a favourite, and reflected a legend. *'As long as the old lime trees still bloom on Unter den Linden, nothing can defeat us. Berlin will stay Berlin'.*

In 1936, unfortunately, the lime trees *were* threatened. Adolf Hitler had inherited the Berlin Olympic Games, and quickly realised they could become a symbol of Germany's re-birth and of Nazi superiority. Berlin soon initiated a massive facelift, not least a cynical cover-up of anti-Jewish graffiti. And, as part of his grandiose plans, Hitler decided on a wider, more dramatic boulevard, which would also provide a avenue for huge military parades. As a result, many of the famous limes were cut down.

The Berliners were appalled, and the bad feeling so worried the authorities that they replanted lime saplings. But, these were so dwarfed by the new tall lanterns that the Berliners cynically called the street *'Unter die Laterne'*.

It was the Friedrich-Wilhelm, the Elector of Brandenburg, who had first planted the lime trees in 1647 to form an avenue from his castle to his hunting lodge. This soon became the most important street in Berlin, leading as it did to the monumental Brandenburg Gate, itself to become a symbol of Prussia – and then of an ever stronger united Germany. In 1806 Napoleon carried away the Quadriga of horses on top of the Brandenburg Gate, but only eight years later it became the scene of triumph over the French, and the square was named Pariser Platz. By the 1930s, the boulevard boasted some of Berlin's most famous buildings – the Café Bauer, The Adlon Hotel, the Hotel de St Petersburg, and the Café Kranzler, and boasted even grander edifices including the City Palace, the Opera House and the Zeughaus (Arsenal).

In April 1945, Adolf Hitler, who had never liked or trusted Berlin – and hardly ever stayed in a city which had never voted for him – found himself trapped there, trying to control his collapsing Reich from the confines of his bunker deep underground, below the Reich Chancellery garden.

As the Russians closed in on Berlin, its defenders wanted to cut down the lime trees to create a wide airstrip suitable for large aircraft. Hitler adamantly refused, perhaps remembering the legend of the trees. However, the decision did him no good. On 30th April, he and his new wife Eva Braun committed suicide and Berlin finally fell, then to endure months of horror and hardship.

With both Germany and Berlin divided amongst the victors, the Brandenburg Gate became the entrance to the Russian zone, and worse, when the Berlin Wall was suddenly erected to stop the exodus to the West, Unter den Linden became a dead end.

On November 10th 1989, the hated 28 mile wall at last began to be dismantled, with souvenir hunters eagerly taking chunks of history. Six weeks later, with Communist regimes collapsing all over Eastern Europe, Helmut Kohl, the West German Chancellor and Hans Modrow, the East German Prime Minister, at last walked together through the Brandenburg Gate. Soon Germany was reunited, and Berlin is now once again its capital, its principal boulevard a source of pride – and lined with lime trees.

The boulevard leading from the Brandenburg Gate fulfils its Nazi parade role

See: Berchtesgaden, Landsberg, Nuremberg, Reichstag, Wannsee

UTOPIA
Nowhere

There are few people who have never complained about any aspect of the world around them. Most of us must be dissatisfied with something about our day-to-day existence. Lamentation on such topics often contains the phrase 'in an ideal world', such as 'in an ideal world I wouldn't live next door to a practising drummer'. But what if we did live in an ideal world, a place where everything was organised in the perfect way possible? To think along such lines is known as 'Utopian thinking'. The word itself is the Greek for 'nowhere', illustrating the theoretical nature of the concept. But although the idea itself may be of nowhere, it had to come from somewhere.

Plato's *Republic* is the earliest, and one of the most famous, portrayals of a Utopian society. In the work, his mentor, Socrates, is portrayed as saying that all the inhabitants of the state are divided into three categories, including, 'auxiliaries', 'guardians' and 'producers'. The 'auxiliaries' are those who are outstandingly brave, and form the military and policing service of the Republic. The most intelligent and wisest individuals would be its 'guardians', who were the governors and administrators and the 'producers' constituted all the rest – the workers of manual labour and industry. His system was one of order; everyone had a place and a role in the state, and power was held by the 'aristoi' – the best people. Perhaps most importantly of all, the 'auxiliaries' willingly obey the 'guardians', and the 'producers' would similarly obey both levels above them. This happy acceptance of one's place was key to this Utopian state. Plato also added innumerable other stipulations for the smooth running of his Republic. He said that poetry and literature only had negative effects on people, and so he would ban them, with the only exceptions being hymns to the gods and praises of good men. Although it may not sound

See: Middle Earth, Valhalla

perfect to everyone, the *Republic* is one of the key texts illustrating the philosophical quest for an ideal world.

The other primary work on a Utopia actually has the word as its title. Sir Thomas More's *Utopia*, published in 1516, is a description of an island on which the perfect society has evolved, as recounted by the fictitious narrator, Raphael Nonsenso. This whole narrative is laced with satire about More's own times. Like that in the *Republic*, More's world is governed in a manner intended to be flawless. And in the same way, order seems to be the key. Everyone goes to bed and gets up at exactly the same time. They only have to work a 6 hour day (good), on weekends as well as weekdays (not so good), and this is enough to produce absolutely anything the community needs. There is no money; when you want something, all you need to do is ask for it. *Utopia* contains other interesting ideas, like the fact that gold and jewels contain no special significance, and in fact, the former usually denotes low status. The concepts in the book have caused huge debate, and a wide range of interpretations. For instance, William Morris believed it to be a socialist instruction manual. In fact *Utopia* had such an effect, that some people proposed sending missionaries to this new country!

The problem with such models is that they will never be universal; many would not want to live in Plato's world, devoid of poetry, books, or art – and the robotic regularity of More's island might well have driven some people insane. In fact, a very different way of looking at a perfect society exists in George Orwell's *1984*. There, though bleak and horrible, the state has been designed to be perfect. Like Plato's *Republic* everyone has a place, and the relentless efficiency of More's *Utopia* exists in abundance. So is this, or is this not, a form of Utopia?

There can never be a totally perfect world for everyone, neither in the real world, nor even in literature or theory. So in answer to the question, 'where is Utopia', its meaning of 'nowhere' could not be more appropriate.

VALHALLA
The Afterlife

One of the most desired human goals is a long, happy, peaceful life, and a death that comes quietly and painlessly in the night.

But not always. If you were an ancient Viking, this thought would have sent a shiver down your spine. For any Viking who underwent what they called 'strawdeath', (dying of old age in bed), would surely be bound for the most ignominious and terrible of afterlives, the bleak land of *Niflheim*. This was a dark and miserable place ruled over by Hel, who wielded power from her distinctly uncheery palace of *Elvidnir* – 'Misery'. Hel herself was a fairly depressing figure, half light and half dark, half alive and half dead.

Unpleasant. But if you were lucky enough to have died in battle, an entirely different fate awaited you. The 'Valkyries', divine warrior maidens whom Wagner would immortalise, would watch the battlefields of the world, looking for fighters who died heroic deaths. These would become the *Einherjar* – souls of honoured slain warriors. If you were one of them, then the Valkyries would scoop up your soul and whisk you away to the *Bifrost Bridge*. Your journey at this point would be taking a turn for the surreal, as the bridge before you took the form of an enormous rainbow. But the trip was worth it; crossing the bridge, you would have entered *Asgard*, the realm of Viking heaven, and your next stop was the hall of Valhalla. The word itself derives itself from the old Icelandic word 'Valholl', which means 'hall of the slain'.

It would have been quite something to see. The greatest edifice in all of Asgard, its walls were made of gold, and its roof coated with shields. The entrance was shaded by the *Grove of Glasir*, where the trees had golden leaves. Inside, armour and weapons hung everywhere, and giant spears held up the roof. Each of the doors, all 540 of them, were so huge that 800 heroes could pass through them at once. Welcome to Valhalla!

Ruling over the realm was the king of the gods, Odin, whose pair of ravens, *Huginn* (thought), and *Muninn* (memory) would fly around the world every day to keep their master informed about the events of the world.

An afterlife in Valhalla was very different from many other religions' idea of heaven. The *Einherjar* would spend every single day furiously fighting, only to return to Valhalla every night to feast and drink with Odin. Presumably, this was the ancient Vikings' idea of an extremely good time.

But their days in Valhalla were numbered, and they knew it. All this constant fighting was not meaningless scrapping, but training for the greatest battle of all – Ragnarok. When the time came, the giants of earth and fire threatened to take over the world, and Odin was forced to do what he had always known he would have to, lead the heroes of Valhalla out for one final fight. In all the world's mythology, they can be few battles so gory. The heroes and giants completely annihilated each other, and Odin himself was slain by the great Fenrir Wolf. But at least Valhalla had been enjoyable while it lasted.

See: Middle Earth, Utopia

VARANASI
India

Mark Twain once said of Varanasi, also known as 'Benares' or 'Kashi': 'Benares is older than history, older than tradition, older even than legend and looks twice as old as all of them put together.' The 'eternal city' is a place of extremes; poverty, riches, body and spirit, life and death.

Varanasi lies between the Varuna and Asi rivers where they meet the great Ganges. It is the most sacred of cities for the Hindu religion. While not the largest, with its 500 million followers this is the oldest religion in the world, a faith which has been developing for over 5,000 years. It has influenced, and been influenced by,

Pilgrims enter the Ganges at a 'ghat.'

See: Amritsar, Bethlehem, Bhopal, Dum Dum, Jodhpur, Mecca, Taj Mahal

other religions, Buddhism, Judaism, Islam, Sikhism and even Christianity. Involving the worship of several gods, its principal belief is one of continuous reincarnation. A good 'karma', or sum of all human actions, may ensure that you reappear in a higher form, while bad behaviour may condemn you to return either at a lower caste or even as an animal. So it is not surprising that Hindus hate to kill animals. 'Ahimsa', Sanskrit for 'non-injury', means that many Hindus are vegetarians, and it also accounts for the sacred status of the cows which wander the fields, streets and roads.

Varanasi might never have achieved its Hindu significance. It was at nearby Sarnath, twenty-five centuries ago, that Buddha, son of a local rajah, first preached his message of 'enlightenment'. Muslim invasions in the eleventh century might have meant that it would be a city of mosques. But while Varanasi is still a holy city for Buddhism, Sikhism and Jainism, its overwhelming significance remains for Hindus, for whom there are no less than 1,500 temples and shrines.

Varanasi is the city of the god Shiva, one of the Hindu trinity of Brahma,

Vishnu and Shiva who is The Creator, The Preserver and The Destroyer. He is a god so multi-faceted that he has 1,008 names in scripture, and it is said that he has walked the streets of the city itself.

As a site for pilgrimage, Varanasi is a place to die, or to be reborn. Pilgrims wash themselves in the Ganges, holiest of rivers, believing that it will cleanse them both spiritually and physically, leaving their soul a clean slate, born anew. Thousands descend the 'ghats' (sets of steps leading down to the river) to the sounds of chanted mantras, and the fragrance of incense. Four miles of ghats line the north bank, not only a practical way to enter the river, but also representing the plateaus of the Himalayas from which the Ganges descends.

And here too, in a city soaked with mysticism, a dying Hindu can achieve 'moksha', the spiritual salvation that escapes the endless cycle of reincarnation. At the 'burning ghats', shrouded bodies are cremated, and the ashes scattered by relatives in the waters of the holy river.

Despite a crumbling appearance of overpopulation and under-development, the deeply spiritual nature of Varanasi remains undimmed; a unique place where knowledge, inner peace, and even death can be sought by those who would choose to look for them.

VENICE
Italy

By the year 1500, the city-state of Venice was one of the richest and most powerful places in the world. Controlling much of northern Italy, her empire stretched into Turkey, the Dalmatian coast and many Mediterranean islands, with a population, at 3,500,000, larger than that of Great Britain. The island city was the greatest marketplace and clearing house of every type of commodity from Arabia, China and the Indies. The largest merchant fleet was protected by the world's largest navy, often hired out at immense profit to other powers. The Arsenale covered no less than

sixty acres of sheds and shipyards, capable of building and repairing 100 ships at a time, and with 15,000 workers, was the largest single industry of the age.

Nor was this city a dull and commercial place. It was a magnificent array of gleaming domes, towers, elegant bridges and piazzas and superb palaces, designed and decorated by some of the greatest architects, craftsmen and painters of all time.

'Miracle' is an overused word but Venice really was exactly that – and by chance.

It was the most terrifying of the barbarians, Attila the Hun, the 'scourge of God' who most directly created Venice. The collapse of the Roman

Empire, and the successive waves of barbarians that destroyed its towns had created temporary Roman refugees who fled to the lagoon – which had only been the home of fishermen – 'living like marsh birds.' In 1452, Attila, blocked by the Great Wall of China in the east, arrived in Italy, and boasted: 'the grass will never grow again where I have trod!' Not an idle boast, as he soon levelled Aquileia, one of the richest Roman cities, and forty other towns in the region of Venetia.

The surviving refugees became permanent. At first, they tried to settle on the rim of the lagoon, but realising they were still vulnerable, opted for the muddy, reed-covered islands of the Rivo Alto. There, they discovered that the mud covered a hard clay base into which they hammered thousands of 15 foot wooden piles, using larches from the forest of Cadore. It is on this very platform that the 'Rialto' and the whole magnificent city is supported, on 118 islands linked with 400 bridges – for most people a miracle in itself.

The Venetians had indeed created an almost invulnerable haven. Only expert navigators familiar with the tides and shallows could avoid being stranded on mudflats, or swept away by the currents. The Franks discovered this when, under the command of Charlemagne's son, their fleet was marooned, and the men

killed and drowned. There was nothing now to stop the steady increase in trade and power, especially after Venice's profitable (but hardly moral) diversion of the Fourth Crusade to sack its only rival city, Constantinople, in 1204, and to loot its priceless works of art such as the famous winged Horses of Saint Mark.

The chance landing of Roman refugees on some muddy islands in a lagoon had certainly paid off.

See: Getto, Silk Road, Topkapi

VERSAILLES
France

In fairness, the Palace of Versailles was never really an obscure or little known place. How could it be? Built for Louis XIV, a man so autocratic he once said 'L'état c'est moi' – 'I am the state', it was both huge and opulent, designed to keep the nobility closest to the king, even containing a staggering 1,400 fountains.

It would also be inaccurate to say that its history was uneventful. It had been stormed during the French Revolution and was the home of the treaty that ended the Franco-Prussian war. However, despite all this, at the end of the First World War, a well-known French landmark was about to become a cornerstone of world history.

Though the First World War came to an end on 11th November 1918, many of the issues had not been resolved and what now happened at Versailles would

'The Big Four'. Left to right: Lloyd George, Orlando, Clemenceau, Wilson.

sow the seeds of a future disaster. A complicated war would mean a complicated peace. The Paris Peace Conference, which culminated in several peace treaties (Versailles being the most important) was not to run a smooth course.

With no German delegate invited, the conference was attended by the 'Big Four'. These were the leaders of France (Georges Clemenceau), England (David Lloyd George), the United States (Woodrow Wilson) and Italy (Vittorio Emanuele Orlando). And with four individual statesman would come four very different sets of priorities and opinions.

America had not been in the conflict for long (since April 1917), not suffered much, and her views on the punishment of Germany were accordingly liberal. Woodrow Wilson presented some noble ideas at the conference, famously known as his 'Fourteen Points', including self determination for the peoples of Europe, and the prototype for the modern United Nations – called the League of Nations. He felt that heaping punitive terms on Germany would be a mistake. But Wilson's clout in the debates would be limited. America's shorter involvement in the war would give her less influence. Also, Wilson's hands were partially tied by his own Senate. The US government, a resolutely isolationist body, believed that some of the President's ideas, such as The League of Nations, would force the USA to be far more involved in world politics than was desirable.

Lloyd George realised that there was a great deal of popular anger towards Germany in England. Indeed, slogans at the time included 'Make Germany pay', and 'Squeeze them until the pips squeak'. His proposals were not as liberal as Woodrow Wilson's, but he did not believe in crippling Germany or taking too much territory. If the treaty had been between America, Britain and Italy (whose only real demand was to be given the Adriatic Coast, a term of the secret Treaty of London, 1915), then the Treaty of Versailles may have been penned very differently. That is to say, were it not for Georges Clemenceau.

For the beleaguered German people, the French Prime Minister was their worst nightmare come true. His outspoken views on punishing the Germans were so savage that he was often called 'The Tiger.' For over four years he had seen his country torn to shreds, and the youth of his nation cut down. With 1.3 million dead, every village in France has a sad monument to whole families destroyed. Revenge was the focus of all his grief and anger. For the damage done to France's people and landscape (750,000 houses and 23,000 factories), Germany was going to have to pay. He demanded that France should be awarded the territory of Alsace-Lorraine (which Germany had annexed in 1871), and the entire Rhineland. He also wanted to inflict such huge financial reparations that Germany would never again be a leading European power. Clemenceau's rage was to the be the driving force behind Germany's punishment.

In fact, some of Woodrow Wilson's 'Points' were included in the final Treaty of Versailles, signed on 28th June 1919. A League of Nations was created, and several states were granted self-determination, such as Poland, Finland and Yugoslavia (although the creation of the latter totally denied Italy her one claim of the conference, and left her furious, eventually turning, under Mussolini, from an ally to an enemy). However, the President's liberal suggestions were not all observed. Although France was not allowed to annex the Rhineland (it was merely demilitarised indefinitely), she was given Alsace-Lorraine, and allowed to mine Germany's Saarland for 15 years. This was a disastrous blow for the Germans, the Saar being a key industrial area. The Treaty of Versailles also crushed Germany's military strength, forbidding her an airforce and limiting her army to 100,000 men and her navy to an insignificant six ships. She was also to lose her colonies. Official blame for the war was heaped upon Germany in the infamous 'War Guilt Clause'. She would never be allowed to forget. But the worst was still to come.

The sum of the reparations that Germany was to pay to the Allies, predominantly to France, came to a crippling £6.6 billion, or £180 billion in modern terms. The repayments of even some of this debt would cause hardship for the country for years to come. With hindsight, it is often said that the punitive measures of the treaty were a mistake. The tottering financial state of the new German Weimar Republic left it precariously weak, and dissident movements began to spring up almost as soon as the war had ended. Returning soldiers formed into armed gangs called Freikorps, and tried to take over the Government. In 1919, there was a communist uprising, the Spartacist Revolt. Many Germans believed that their own Government had betrayed them in allowing such an 'iniquitous peace', branding those who signed the surrender 'The November Criminals'. As discontent festered, extremist parties sprang up, and one of these, the German Workers' Party, was headed by a young man called Adolf Hitler. Soon Europe would pay the price for the stringent clauses of Versailles.

Marshal Foch to The New York Times, 1919: 'Next time remember, the Germans will make no mistake. They will break through into Northern France and seize the Channel ports as a base for operations against England'.

See: Gallipoli, Landsberg, Nuremberg, Sarajevo, Somme, Vichy, Waterloo

VICHY
France

In 1940 it became starkly obvious to the French that they were in serious trouble. The German army had poured through the Ardennes, and, like an armoured tide, had rushed for the French coast – splitting the Allies, just as Foch had predicted (panel). The British Expeditionary Force had managed to escape from the beaches of Dunkirk. The Germans turned south and, on 14th June, their tanks rumbled through the boulevards of Paris. France was soon defeated.

The shattered French nation and its leaders were split into two camps. Some believed that the Government should flee to north Africa, and continue the war. However, others, including Vice-Premier Henri Philippe Pétain and Commander-in-Chief General Maxime Weygand, disagreed. They argued that the correct course of action would be to remain in France and seek peace with Germany. This conflict caused the robustly pro-British Prime Minister, Paul Renaud, to resign, and on 16th June Pétain was to succeed him. Six days later, France surrendered to Germany.

Pétain himself had been a national hero in the First World War, famous for his stalwart defence of Verdun in 1916; 'Ils ne passeront pas', (actually said by Nivelle). But when he signed away the liberty of France, he soon erased this fine reputation. France was carved into two areas. The Germans were in direct control of one half – north and western France – including the Channel and Atlantic coasts. The rest was under the control of the new French Government under Pétain.

This Government needed a new capital. Without much delay, the spa town of Vichy, famous for its 'Vichy' water, was selected. The reasons were neither strategic nor political. It was Vichy's pre-war status as a health and tourist resort that made it such a strong contender. The town had an impressive number of hotels, perfect for the new ministries. Furthermore, the local telephone system was extremely modern, and would allow the Government to co-ordinate the newly named 'Etat Français'. To cap it all, the Vichy Opera House was ideal as a parliamentary chamber. So for four years the little spa town would hold the nation's reins of power. The old French national slogan 'Liberté, égalité, fraternité' (liberty, equality, brotherhood) was replaced by the new 'Travail, famille, patrie' (work, family, country).

The armistice was not without harsh conditions. The French army was reduced to a token 100,000 men, and France was put through the indignity of having to pay occupation fees to the Germans. No French prisoners of war returned. Hitler also established a special police force, the soon-hated 'Vichy Milice', to enforce German laws and suppress the French Resistance. But there were harsher conditions to come. To assist the Nazi war machine, large

Pétain (left) with Hitler

'The Pétain cult' involved selling millions of photographs and postcards and a book of the most 'touching reasons' why children loved him.

numbers of French workers were employed to help the Germans, building roads and munitions. Then about 694,000 Frenchmen were deported to Germany (including 44,000 women), for forced manual labour. In this respect, the Vichy government was vital for Germany; France was the second highest contributor of foreign workers (after Poland), and comprised forty per cent of the total wealth that Germany extracted from its occupied territories, including the Belgian gold reserves held in France, which Vichy authorised to be handed over in 1940. Worst of all, Jews were first banned from certain professions, and later sent to the concentration camps. With the connivance of the Vichy regime, over 70,000 French Jews were deported, many to die.

Collaboration was encouraged on all levels. Magazines such as *Au Pilori* and *Je Suis Partout* urged the French people to reveal the location of underground resistance fighters – and Jews.

Meanwhile, in Britain, General Charles de Gaulle, head of the France Libre movement, was working towards the eventual resurrection of a democratic French Government. In his famous speech on 18th June, he encouraged them to resist their oppressors, and hold on to the hope that France would be liberated. But Pétain's Vichy Government remained committed to acceding to Germany's wishes. Often to make such acquiescence appear to be its own decision, Vichy anticipated Hitler's commands and carried out orders before they were even issued.

When the Allies invaded France, Pétain's cabinet fled to Sigmaringen and established a Government in exile. In 1945, many of them were arrested. Some of the leading politicians, such as Laval and Darnand, were sentenced to death and executed for what they had allowed to happen in France. Pétain himself received life imprisonment, and died at the age of 95, incarcerated on the Isle d'Yeu. The Vichy Government had come to represent misplaced collaboration and permitted atrocities. Though the town is still famous as a spa, and for its bottled water, its name will always, for the French, be touched with shame.

See: Casablanca, Dachau, Dunkirk, Great Hedge of India, Mers-el-Kebir, Oradour, Sedan, Versailles, Wannsee

VINCI
Italy

M any people can become rather irritated and jealous when faced by someone who appears to be good at just about everything. So it is a miracle that the little boy who made the little Tuscan town of Vinci famous went on to win almost universal praise and approval. Leonardo was arguably the most versatile, artistic and inventive genius who has ever lived.

Vinci itself has changed very little since Leonardo was born there in 1452. The same stone houses cluster around the castle. The tall church bell tower remains an important landmark, which can be seen for miles. And it is still surrounded by fertile farmland and hillsides planted with vines, fruit and silvery green olive trees.

The area around Vinci was a wonderful childhood home for an inquisitive boy who loved nature. Leonardo explored the woods and streams, and studied the insects, animals and especially birds in flight, sketching in great detail the anatomy that would influence his future paintings. He was soon at school in nearby Florence, receiving an education in Italy's cultural centre of the Renaissance, and was lucky enough to become an assistant to the famous painter Andrea del Verrocchio. This was to be his big break. Showing faith in his gifted understudy, Verrocchio allowed Leonardo to paint one of the angels on his *Baptism of Christ*, using oil paints instead of egg tempera. (There is a story that Leonardo's angel was so much better than any of those of his master that Verrocchio decided never to paint again).

After leaving to become a painter in his own right, Leonardo spent his life passing between a bewildering array of jobs for a large number of employers. He was the Duke of Romagna's chief architect and engineer, court painter to Louis XII of France, and sculptor and military-scientist to Duke Ludovico Sforza – ruler of Milan. It seemed that he could turn his hand to absolutely

Leonardo da Vinci

anything. But talent was not his only gift. Leonardo was also said to be a muscular and handsome man, both witty and interesting in conversation, and even a fine musician and singer. On top of all these assets, he was remarkably kind, and with such a love of animals that he would frequently buy caged ones just so that he could set them free. The only real run-in he ever had with the law was an accusation of homosexuality (a grievous crime at the time) from which he was acquitted.

Probably Leonardo da Vinci's most famous area of expertise is his prodigious artistic talent, with the fresco *The Last Supper* and, of course, the *Mona Lisa*, probably the best known work of art in the world – reproduced everywhere on postcards, posters and advertisements. The masterpiece itself is a perfect example of one of Leonardo's revolutionary techniques. A popular complaint of contemporary painters was that their subjects ended up looking more like statues than real people. Leonardo decided to surmount this problem with a method that the Italians call 'sfumato', which means blurring the edges and colours at key points of the painting to leave them slightly vague. This eliminated the stiffness of other artists by leaving part of the image to the reader's imagination. In the *Mona Lisa*, the 'sfumato' occurs around the corners of the sitter's eyes and mouth, the most expressive features of the human face. The result is a remarkably lifelike ambiguity in the *Mona Lisa's* expression, and that famously enigmatic smile. Even the background of the piece is uneven, with the horizon higher on one side. Thus, the subject seems to have a different posture depending on the side from which she is approached.

Frustratingly, Da Vinci had a tendency to leave unfinished the artistic projects he had begun, rendering his genius always slightly elusive. Moreover, so few works have survived that we must rely on copies, and documents written about them. To add yet more difficulty, all the writing that the master entered in his notebooks was scrawled down backwards.

Just as important as Leonardo's art was his extraordinary gift for science and invention. He produced designs for such modern inventions as military tanks (which the BBC built and made to work), diving suits, and unbelievably, submarines. His busy workshop also contained the blueprints for flying machines which, if not actually workable, certainly adhered to realistic aerodynamic principles. Indeed, if his plans had actually been fully developed at the time, they could have revolutionised the science of his day. As well as these concepts, he also conducted radical studies into scientific arenas ranging from the human eye to geology.

Da Vinci died in 1519 in Cloux, France. With so many of his inventions still undeveloped and his paintings and sculptures unfinished, the world had been given just a fraction of what he had to offer. Sculptor, painter, teacher, engineer, architect, inventor, Italy had lost a man and a mind the likes of which might never exist again.

Leonardo's enigmatic Mona Lisa

See: Sistine Chapel

WACO
Texas, USA

David Koresh

Until February 1993, Waco might only have been celebrated as the birthplace of the drink Dr Pepper, or where the Texas Rangers established themselves on the Brazos River, fighting the Cherokees and Comanches who had forced the gentler Huacos (Waco) Indians to move on. Or it might have been known to some as one of the rowdier towns on the old cowboy Chisholm Trail – dubbed 'Six-shooter Junction'.

It was not at first regarded as peculiar that a religious community near Waco seemed to be armed to the teeth, with assault rifles, sub-machine guns, heavy machine-guns and grenades. After all, Waco reflected the attitudes of the Lone Star State, in which more people die by guns than traffic accidents, and 16,500 residents in 1991 owned machine-guns.

The Branch Davidians were part of a religious cult who thought

387

they were chosen to be among *virtuous 144,000 souls who would be borne to Heaven.* Unluckily for them, the cult in Waco had fallen under the spell, and then the control, of a good-looking, guitar-playing young man called Vernon Howell. Changing his name to David Koresh, he had ousted all rivals and dominated his flock with apocalyptic religious speeches, sometimes lasting hours. As with many cults, his followers came from all over the world, and had turned over their money. However, unlike most cults, they had also turned over their women to Koresh, who began to run the compound as a one-man harem called the 'House of David', and fathered several children. Some of the disillusioned cultists left, and worrying stories gradually spread about under-age sex and child abuse. The sound of regular automatic gunfire was also reported to police by local farmers. Pressure built up to do something.

ATF agents, sheltering behind an armoured vehicle, watch the compound go up in flames.

The Bureau of Alcohol, Tobacco and Firearms are the direct descendants of Eliot Ness and the famous 'Untouchables', once called 'revenuers', 'prohibition agents' or 'Treasury men'. It was the ATF who decided to intervene because of the allegedly huge stockpile of weapons, and mounting public anxiety about how they might be used.

Early one Sunday morning, a convoy of ATF vehicles approached the Waco compound, the agents leaping out and heading forward in squads. Koresh peered out of the door.

'Federal Agents, with a search warrant!' A hail of gunfire burst out. Using heavy weapons, the cultists even fired through thick walls. The surprised ATF agents were dropping, some already dead. Although very heavily armed themselves, they had actually been outgunned. No less than ten thousand rounds had been fired.

A truce was called which was to last 51 days, while the whole world looked on. Four agents were dead, and sixteen wounded. Casualties among the cultists were never exactly established, although Koresh was wounded.

The siege went on for weeks with a cordon of heavily armed men and women – and plenty of tourists. Patient negotiating experts tried to reason with Koresh, who constantly broke his word and delayed. 'God told me to wait'.

Then, one morning the second half of the tragedy played itself out. With permission from President Clinton and Attorney General Janet Reno, and because of fears that Koresh was attempting to orchestrate a mass suicide, an assault was attempted using heavy armoured vehicles – which were greeted with bullets. The vehicles tried to break up the buildings and shoot tear gas into them. After 6 hours, cultists were seen setting fires. Suddenly the buildings were ablaze, with explosions of ammunition and chemicals adding to the holocaust. The world watched helplessly, and in minutes it was all over. Of 94 people, only eight survived. The cult had achieved its Apocalypse.

There are many who have since sided with the cult, feeling that it was the Government's heavy-handed tactics that were out of control. One such supporter was Timothy McVeigh who decided to wreak revenge on the second anniversary of Waco by blowing up a Federal Building in Oklahoma, killing 168 innocent workers and many children.

See: Chisholm Trail, Jonestown

WALL STREET
New York, USA

'Greed is good!', exclaimed the slick and unscrupulous Gordon Gekko, played by Michael Douglas in the film, *Wall Street.* A recent poll of revealed that sixty one per cent of Americans thought Wall Street was 'dominated by greed and selfishness', but seventy per cent thought that was good for America.

Wall Street was named after a wooden palisade that the Dutch leader Peter Stuyvesant erected across the tip of Manhattan in 1663 to keep out bears, Indians and the English (although not necessarily in that order). Sadly for the Dutch; only a year later the English came by sea, assaulted Fort Manhattan and took over 'New Amsterdam'.

Soon after, at the Treaty of Breda in 1667, the Dutch elected to give up what they saw as the rather worthless, rocky island of Manhattan, together with the other New Netherland settlements of Queens, Brooklyn, the Bronx and Staten Island, for the 'much more valuable' tiny nutmeg island of Run in the East Indies – hardly a very wise long-term decision.

Wall Street's significance as the world's greatest financial centre began in 1790, when there were only two types of securities to trade – Revolutionary War Bonds to pay off the debt incurred while removing the British, and stock in the first national bank, The Bank of the United States.

Among the places where the early stockbrokers, merchants and the auctioneers used to meet was under the shade of a large buttonwood tree outside 68 Wall Street. In May 1792, twenty-four traders agreed to trade only with each other, and what is called 'The Buttonwood Agreement' was the beginning of the New York Stock Exchange, now the world's largest. It was first housed in a rented room at 40 Wall Street and eventually, in 1903, a few yards away at 18 Broad Street in the magnificent building it still occupies.

Wall Street continued to grow, and in the booming Jazz era of the 1920s, more and more ordinary people began to trade in stocks, which always seemed to go higher and higher in value. People who could ill afford to take such risks crouched around ticker-tape machines, betting 'on margin', only needing to put down ten per cent. By 1929, the whole country was gripped by speculation and, of course, the bubble had to burst. On 'Black Tuesday' October 29th 1929, the 'Wall Street Crash' saw stocks plummet, accelerated by brokers' demands for cash from those 'on margin'. Rich and poor alike were suddenly ruined.

The economic effect of the lack of confidence was almost instant. Car sales slumped, house building stopped, thousands were thrown out of work-in some places fifty per cent of the workforce, and there were many suicides. Vagrants wandered the country, and the sad melody *'Buddy, can you spare a dime?'* became a chorus of the time. The Depression spread abroad as America repatriated money, and trade dried up all over the world. The collapse of economies ruined Governments and, most spectacularly and directly, the poverty in Germany led to the rise of Adolf Hitler.

Every few decades, similar crashes occur, nearly always starting in Wall Street. Perhaps greed is not quite so good after all.

Twenty-three Wall Street, the House of Morgan, where a group of top bankers and stock owners met to try and restore confidence in 1929

See: Mrs Astor's Ballroom, Bedloe's Island, Broadway, Empire State Building, Harlem, Madison Avenue, Manhattan, Run Island

WANNSEE
Germany

But for a careless oversight, Am Grossen Wannsee, No 56/58, might have remained a completely unknown address, a large villa in a fashionable resort looking out over the larger of the two Wannsee lakes near Berlin. But an American officer, preparing for the 1947 Nuremberg War Crimes Tribunals, was searching through some files in the old German Foreign Ministry when he came across a folder. It contained copy number 16 of the minutes of a secret meeting which had taken place five years before on 20th January 1942, and was the only one of thirty copies which had not been destroyed. The *Wannsee Protokoll,* when produced as evidence, was described 'as perhaps the most shameful document of modern history'. It was no less than the plan for the *'Final Solution of the Jewish Question',* the blueprint of the Holocaust.

A.	
Germany proper	131,800
Austria	43,700
Eastern Territories	420,000
Poland (GG)	2,284,000
Bialystok	400,000
Bohemia & Moravia	74,200
Estonia	free of Jews
Latvia	3,500
Lithuania	34,000
Belgium	43,000
Denmark	5,600
France/occupied	165,000
France/unoccupied	700,000
Greece	69,600
Netherlands	160,800
Norway	1,300
B.	
Bulgaria	48,000
England	330,000
Finland	2,300
Ireland	4,000
Italy	58,000
Albania	200
Croatia	40,000
Portugal	3,000
Romania	342,000
Sweden	8,000
Switzerland	18,000
Serbia	10,000
Slovakia	88,000
Spain	6,000
Turkey (European)	55,500
Hungary	742,800
USSR	5,000,000
Ukraine	2,994,684
White Russia	446,484
Total over	11,000,000

The horrific list of those planned to be killed.

The smiling technocrat, Adolf Eichmann

See: Anne Frank's Annexe, Berchtesgaden, Changi, Dachau, Devil's Island, Getto, Kwai, Landsberg, Lidice, Nuremberg, Oradour, Reichstag

Why did Himmler's deputy, SS-Obergruppenführer Reinhard Heydrich, convene the meeting of fifteen top civil servants, SS and police officials?

Anti-Jewish measures had been in place and enforced for years since 'Kristallnacht', the night of looting of shops and the burning of synagogues in 1938. German Jews had been removed from public life. The notorious Nuremberg Laws had made life virtually impossible. Many had been forced to, or encouraged to emigrate. Others were already in concentration camps.

With the annexation of Poland in September 1939, its 2.5 million Jews had been herded into ghettoes. After the attack on the Soviet Union with its five million Jews in 1941, killer squads from Heydrich's mobile *Einsatzgruppen* were shooting Jewish men, women and children in their thousands every day.

But from the Nazi standpoint, it was all too 'muddled and slow'. There were 27 different agencies dealing with Jewish matters. Poland, now called the *'Generalgouvernement'*, was becoming a disorganised dumping ground for Jews from elsewhere, and its Governor Hans Frank, objected violently, urgently wanting a 'Jew-free model colony'. The idea was also rapidly fading of settling the Jews in some overseas colony like Madagascar (impossible with British sea power) or in Russia (probably no longer militarily possible). Thus Heydrich and his faithful henchman, Adolf Eichmann, needed to sort everything out under SS control. This explains why the Wannsee Conference was set up, to manage the chilling concept of genocide. In the comfortable villa, 15 competent, well-educated, senior but mainly youthful men gathered, not knowing quite what to expect. Some were slightly anxious because Heydrich was ruthless, and he had all the power of Heinrich Himmler behind him. All were Nazis, however, and not one of them would be likely to lift a finger to help the Jews.

Heydrich opened the meeting, reviewing the 'struggles against the Jew'

in the immediate past, discussed the 'storage problem' and a list was given out of the European countries and their eleven million Jews, including those in Britain and Ireland, to be involved in the *Endlosung*, 'Final solution'. This proposed 'Evacuation to the East', a euphemism for mass killing. A discussion followed concerning the fate of the many half and quarter Jewish. After token resistance on legal grounds by some of the civil servants, most of these *Mischlinge* were now to be included in the tally.

The Generalgouvernement team expressed great satisfaction, and requested that activities should start there quickly 'to clear Poland of its useless Jews'. After calm and friendly discussion over food, wine, cigars and brandy, the meeting was closed and the officials drove off into the snowy evening.

The effect of Wannsee was immediate. Up to March 1942 only ten per cent of the Holocaust's victims died, but the furious activity of the next 12 months saw half of its victims perish. In February 1942, any surviving German Jews were killed and that month, the gas chambers were installed at Auschwitz. The terrible extermination camps of Belzec, Chelmno and Sobibor only added to the horrific toll. By June, the small camp at Treblinka, with its cruelly disguised railway station complete with phoney ticket office and paper shop, was gassing 7,000 Warsaw ghetto Jews a day. Some actually escaped back to Warsaw, where their warnings were at first not believed. 875,000 bodies would eventually be buried under the camp. July saw the colossal camp at Auschwitz-Birkenau reach its horrific optimum efficiency, with thousands gassed and cremated *every hour*, eventually killing the appalling total of three million in that one camp alone.

Until almost the last days of the collapsing Third Reich, Eichmann and his men were still diligently 'combing Europe from west to east' as the *Wannsee Protokoll* had directed. Six million Jews eventually perished, the greatest, most methodical and horrific mass murder in history.

It had all been decided in a couple of hours over polite cakes and cognac in that pleasant lakeside house.

WATERGATE BUILDING
Washington DC, USA

When young Bob Woodward of *The Washington Post* was woken by the telephone on 17th June 1972, he was not best pleased. To have to go in to the office on a Saturday morning to cover a routine burglary was not what he was looking for. But this was no ordinary local burglary. First, it had taken place at the Headquarters of the National Democratic Committee in the complex of offices, apartments and a hotel called the Watergate, a building otherwise full of Republican interests and tenants and partly financed by the pension fund of Britain's National Coal Board. Secondly, the five burglars were very unusual. They were all caught dressed in business suits with wallets stuffed with new bank notes. They wore surgical gloves, carried a walkie-talkie, two cameras and film, lock-picks, tear-gas guns and bugging devices. They had stayed the night at the Watergate Hotel and had eaten lobster together in the dining room. Unusual burglars indeed.

In court, Woodward jerked upright when one of the burglars, James McCord, claimed he was ex-CIA. So began one of the most epic and brilliant journalistic investigations in history. Both Woodward and Carl Bernstein, backed by *Washington Post* owner Katherine Graham and Executive Editor Ben Bradlee, would gradually peel away layer after layer of lies and subterfuge from the Nixon administration. The desperate two year cover-up would eventually bring down all Nixon's top advisers: former Attorney General, John Mitchell; White House Chief of Staff, Bob Haldeman and Presidential Assistant, John Ehrlichman (The 'Prussian Guard' or the 'German Shepherd's); Patrick Gray, Head of the FBI; Richard Kleindienst, the Attorney General, and highest law officer in the land – and dozens of smaller fry. Many went to jail. Only Henry Kissinger would emerge unscathed. Eventually it would even force Richard Nixon out of office, under threat of impeachment or worse.

It emerged that the clumsy and stupid burglary at the Watergate (which was in fact, merely a *return* visit to 'improve the sound quality' of the bugs successfully planted there twenty days earlier) was just one of many illegal and reprehensible dirty tricks of both burglary, harassment and also subterfuge carried out by Nixon's lieutenants against the Democratic Party in the run-up to the 1972 Presidential Election. The question must be: Why?

After four years in power, Nixon was a comfortable nineteen points ahead of his weak Democrat rival, Senator George McGovern, and would indeed – that very November – win every state except for Massachusetts, with more popular votes than in any election (47 million), and with a crushing victory of 521-17 in the electoral college. This triumph was to be destroyed by the apparently ridiculous and unnecessary risk of the Watergate burglary.

The answer lies in Richard Nixon's extraordinary personality. He was paranoid about his perceived enemies including political opponents, 'the bureaucracy who are here to screw us' and 'the goddamned intellectual élitists'. 'None of those Harvard bastards in my Cabinet', he had ordered Haldeman. He was obsessed with leaks, especially after *The New York Times* had published 'The Pentagon Papers', the leaked secret history of the Vietnam War. He had the suspected source, Daniel Ellsberg, bugged and he even ordered the burglary of the office of Ellsberg's psychiatrist. It emerged that Nixon was fully involved from the beginning in the programme of dirty tricks, and later the cover-up. He had even bugged his own office, and the tapes, that he was forced to hand over revealed

The Watergate complex

'There will be no whitewash at the White House', Nixon promised.

a foul-mouthed, suspicious, weird and unworthy encumbent in the White House. A vital eighteen and a half minute section of the tape 'erased by accident' was the final nail in Nixon's political coffin.

Richard Nixon finally resigned in August 1974, fully two years after the Watergate burglary. The American Constitution had rescued itself from a very ugly period, and Carl Bernstein and Bob Woodward were awarded the Pulitzer Prize. Nixon, pardoned by President Gerald Ford, miraculously turned himself into an elder statesman, a guru of the public speaking circuit. Watergate itself never returned to obscurity, because the world's media – whenever faced with suspected intrigue or subterfuge – has learned automatically to tack on the symbolic word 'gate.' So we have since had 'Irangate', and in Britain, 'Dianagate', 'Camillagate' and even 'Cheriegate'.

See: Ambassador Hotel, Bay of Pigs, Kent State, Texas School Book Depository, Tranquillity

WATERLOO
Belgium

Every day Eurostar trains leave Paris, plunge through the Channel Tunnel and arrive at a railway station called Waterloo – a constant rubbing of salt into the wound of a French defeat. It is as if the Gard du Nord or Charles de Gaulle Airport were called Hastings. But for a century after 1815, Britain was not only the leading railway and industrial nation in the world, but one of the richest and most powerful – and did not care much about French feelings until she found herself a century later fighting alongside her former Napoleonic enemy.

As with many battles, the fascination is often not the battle itself, but why it ever occurred – and why it happened at a certain place. The famous battle near an obscure Belgian village should probably never have occurred but for the foolishness of the Allies.

After eighteen years, the brilliant, ambitious, destructive Napoleon had finally been forced to abdicate. His losses in men and prestige in the 1812 Russian campaign had never allowed him to recover, although he had still, after Leipzig, been able to win a series of defensive battles on French soil. If, after his exile, the Allies and the French Government had stuck to the terms of the Treaty of Fontainebleau, he might have stayed on Elba. But his pension was unpaid, his money confiscated, his wife and son not allowed to join him and there was even talk of exile to a more distant island. Meanwhile, France seethed under Louis XVIII, with returning nobles threatening to take back their land, and above all, the veterans of the Army, both officers and men, humiliated and turned adrift. On 26th February 1815, feeling that the Treaty had been dishonoured, Napoleon suddenly left Elba with 1,100 men, landed at Antibes and began his legendary march into France. At Laffrey, he opened his overcoat to the blocking French troops. 'If there is in your ranks a single soldier who would kill his Emperor, let him fire. Here I am'. Then, at Auxerre, Marshal Ney – his 'bravest of the brave' – who had casually promised the King to bring Napoleon back *'in an iron cage'*, quickly fell under the spell of his old Commander.

By 20th March, Napoleon was back in Paris. He offered the Allies peace which was rejected, so he swiftly devoted his huge energy to rebuilding his veteran army into a formidable force, ready to strike at the foreigners invading France. When one thinks about it, it is truly extraordinary – as if Petain and de Gaulle had decided the Nazi terms in 1940 were unacceptable, and had gone back to war. Or if the Confederates had re-armed and counter-attacked after Appomattox in 1865. Or if Hitler had – re-emerged to throw the occupying Russians, British and Americans out of Germany in 1945. Soon Napoleon, in a surge of sustained energy and resourcefulness, had in eight weeks re-clothed, re-armed and re-organised his army into 360,000 experienced and eager veterans.

But his enemies were on the move – the Russians, with 200,000 men, and the

The Duke of Wellington

The heavy cavalry of The Household Brigade which charged at Waterloo, still parade in London.

HENRY DALLAL

Austrians with 210,000. Much closer were 128,000 Prussians in Belgium – under Blücher – as was a polyglot army, commanded by the Duke of Wellington of 106,000 Dutch, Belgians and Germans, including less than 33,000 British, few of whom had served under him in the Peninsula War. Napoleon had a choice: to conduct a defensive war, or to attack. He decided that if he could first destroy his most accessible enemies he could then turn on the more distant Russians and Austrians. In his campaign, above all, he must never let Blücher and Wellington combine.

Cleverly masking his intentions, Napoleon crossed the Sambre River at Charleroi on 15th June. It took some time for Wellington and Blücher to appreciate his line of advance, which was straight at the vulnerable hinge between them. Final confirmation came to Brussels during the glitter of the Duchess of Richmond's Ball. 'Humbugged, by God', admitted the Duke, sending for a map and despatching his orders – almost too late.

Only the 'intelligent disobedience' of the commanders of Dutch forces, to stay at the crossroads of Quatre Bras, ensured that the French were opposed there long enough for a tough stalemate battle to develop. Three miles away at Ligny, the Prussians were badly mauled. Wellington had promised them 20,000 men, which now he could not spare. When they failed to arrive, it deepened Prussian suspicions of Wellington which had started back at the Congress of Vienna. Blücher, aged 72, personally leading his cavalry in furious charges, was trapped under his dead horse. It was supremely lucky for the Allies that he was rescued and returned to command, because his deputy Gneisenau, burning with raw resentment against Wellington, was all for retreating north-east away from him. But Blücher insisted that he had 'given his word', and so the Prussians retreated to Wavre, parallel to Wellington. But for this, both Allied armies might have been defeated piecemeal, and we might never have heard of Waterloo.

Wellington, after years of perfecting the defensive battle in the Peninsula, had chosen the ridge of Mont St. Jean, south of Waterloo, a year before. He now arranged his forces on this ridge anchored by three farmhouses,

Hougoumont, La Haye Sainte and Papelotte. On the night of 17th June, it poured with rain. The waterlogged ground meant that the French could not deploy their heavy guns until the ground had dried, and for the Prussians – now intent on joining Wellington – it meant they would take many hours to arrive. At 11.30, Napoleon began the battle by sending Reille's Corps, spearheaded by his brother Jerome, to attack Hougoumont, manned by Foot Guards and German riflemen. It resisted all day, sucking in far more Frenchmen than Napoleon could afford. Then, at 1.30, after bombardment by his formidable 'Grand Battery', he launched d'Erlon's divisions to pierce Wellington's centre. They were beaten back by artillery, disciplined musketry, and then a memorable cavalry charge by Lord Uxbridge's Household and Union Brigades, which cut through the French infantry and then went too far; to be virtually destroyed by French lancers. Hot-headed Marshal Ney, thinking the British were retreating and perhaps when Napoleon was indisposed, led 7,000 cavalry into the attack, unsupported by infantry. On the reverse slope of the ridge, Wellington's infantry calmly formed 20 squares and resisted all efforts by the milling horsemen to break them. At 6.30, La Haye Sainte fell to the French at last, but Napoleon knew that the village of Plancenoit *to his rear* was now much more important because, after eleven hours of struggling through the mud, the Prussians had arrived. There, he was forced to throw in eight battalions of his precious Young Guard and then two veteran battalions of his Old Guard. The fighting at Plancenoit fatally weakened the strength of his final reserve.

And so it was that, when Napoleon played his final card, it was no longer an ace. His Imperial Guard marching at Wellington's centre was not fifteen battalions, but eight. As they reached the crest, already lacerated by artillery and infantry fire, Napoleon's élite met that of

'Hougoumont Farm' by Ernest Crofts. Napoleon regarded the closing of this gate as a decisive moment in his life.

The monument at Plancenoit, recording the Young Guard's bravery holding off the Prussians.

393

Wellington, Maitland's Brigade of Guards. Wellington himself shouted, 'Up Guards! Make ready! Fire!' The Imperial Guard staggered back, as did the whole French Army – as more Prussians also burst on to the battlefield. Wellington rose in the saddle, waved his hat, and his army advanced against the routed French. When he met Blücher at the farm at 'La Belle Alliance', that is what Blücher suggested they call *their* battle. But Wellington, perhaps determined that it should be regarded as a British victory, insisted on Waterloo.

The Lion Monument, erected where The Prince of Orange was wounded, used 32,000 cubic metres of earth, removing Wellington's ridge.

See: Berezina, Elba, Trafalgar

WATTS
California, USA

People get arrested all the time, and usually, the arrest of a man for drink-driving will not make headlines, let alone go down in history. In Watts, however, the situation was to be very different. On the hot summer evening of August 11, 1965, the traffic cop from the all-white Los Angeles Police Department who pulled over African-American Marquette Frye had no idea what terrible consequences his action would unleash.

Few people now remember one of the additional roots of racial tension in Los Angeles. For years, the city had been served by fast inter-urban railcars used by everyone. Just after World War Two, the network was bought out by a consortium of oil and bus interests which quickly consigned the 'Big Red Cars' to the scrapheap. For this cynical destruction they were found guilty and fined $5,000, the price of one bus. The long-term effect was to make the city dependent on the car, to build huge freeways, and to increase the separation and ghetto effect of racially divided areas, because people without cars could not travel easily.

In 1965, racial tension had reached the surface. The Watts neighbourhood was extremely overcrowded, and the summer heat-wave had made things worse. The black locals had become increasingly enraged by their unpleasant housing conditions, as well as a lack of jobs and schooling. The recent Civil Rights Act of 1964, it seemed, had not yet managed to redress racial iniquities, and the black community was close to boiling point. The seemingly insignificant arrest of Marquette Frye proved to be the last straw.

As Frye began to argue with the policeman, a crowd gathered, and when he and others were bundled into squad cars and driven away, the mood turned ugly. A bottle was broken, fights broke out and more policemen were called in. As the crowd of angry African-Americans grew, a riot rapidly escalated; here at last was a way to release the frustration and anger that had been boiling up for so long. Soon the mob turned its pent up rage on local buildings and shops, which began to be looted and burned.

With 35,000 people involved in the riot, the hopelessly outnumbered police found themselves unable to cope with the situation. In a desperate bid to achieve control, 16,000 National Guardsmen were called in. For six days, the area was ravaged by violence. Thirty four people died, over 1,000 were injured, 4,000 were arrested and the damage to property was huge – over $200 million dollars worth. Such destruction was not indiscriminate. Businesses and homes known to be owned by black residents were largely left alone, whereas those associated with white or Asian ownership were systematically ransacked. The authorities arrested 4,000 black rioters in their attempts to quell the disturbances.

When the horrors of the Watts riot had finally died town, the dazed city was left wondering exactly what had happened. Some officials tried to blame external agitators, but in fact the vast majority of the rioters were long-term Watts residents. The riot itself had been a new and frightening phenomenon. Few people had ever seen such devastation caused by racial tension. Many blamed liberal Governor 'Pat' Brown, who was later voted from office in favour of right-wing Ronald Reagan, soon to be President.

Lessons from the Watts riots were not properly learned. In 1992, the brutal beating of Rodney King was captured on video. Four white policemen were acquitted by a white jury. This time, the toll was 54 dead, thousands injured, 17,000 in jail and $1 billion of damage.

See: Cotton Club, Getto, Harlem, Lorraine Motel, Montgomery, Robben Island, Sharpeville

WEMBLEY
England

On 7th February 2003, a large German mechanical excavator called 'Goliath' began to demolish the famous twin towers at Wembley Stadium. It was the end of one era, but hopefully the beginning of another in British sporting history.

In 1889, when the idea of developing the 'Wembley Park Leisure Grounds' was conceived, the intentions were rather mundane. The Chairman of the Metropolitan Railway, Sir Edward Watkin, decided to introduce a main attraction – so that more people would be encouraged to use the railway to visit it. He planned a four-legged tower, 350m (1,150ft) high, bigger and better than the Eiffel Tower itself. It was a plan doomed to fail. In only the first stage, the foundations shifted, and the project ran out of funds. It had only reached a height of 61m (200ft) when work was abandoned. Known as 'Watkin's Folly', the half-built edifice loomed over the grounds in north-west London, a curious tourist attraction in itself until it was finally dynamited in 1907.

After the First World War, the British Government came up with a much more practical idea. They planned to construct a national stadium as a centrepiece of a British Empire Exhibition. Named the Empire Stadium, it took only 300 days to complete, despite the magnitude of the project – involving 25,000 tons of concrete, 1,000 tons of steel and half a million rivets. When the Exhibition was opened on 23rd April 1924, the ceremony was performed by King George V himself, the first occasion that a monarch was to broadcast on radio, and he even cut the first turf in the stadium.

Renamed Wembley Stadium in the '70s, the venue has earned its place in history. It hosted the first FA cup final between Bolton Wanderers and West Ham, the only occasion that the public was able to pay at the gate. So many were admitted (or climbed over the walls) that around 200,000 squashed into the stadium, even covering the pitch. Eventually, PC George Scory, on the back of a white police-horse, pushed back the crowds – and the match was able to begin. It has been known ever since as the 'White Horse' final.

One of the most significant events ever staged at Wembley was the 1948 Olympic Games, with the Olympic Way being built specially for the occasion, despite being forced to prepare with only a few months notice. Most memorable and prestigious of all, however, was the 30th of July 1966, when Bobby Moore held aloft the

Spectacular Wembley moments; above: the huge Live Aid concert of 1985 and below: England's World Cup triumph of 1966

The cranes and demolition crews move in. A few days later Wembley's famous twin towers were gone.

See: Aintree, Brooklands, Bonneville, Cowes, Indianapolis, Le Mans, Wimbledon

World Cup as victorious captain, the only time England have ever won the football tournament. Alf Ramsay, the England coach, had always been confident, being quoted as saying that his team would definitely win. He was right. England, as hosts, battled through the competition, winning the legendary final against West Germany by 4-2. The match is one of the most remarkable in British sporting history, spawning the best known and most repeated piece of sporting commentary of all time. As Geoff Hurst raced down the left of the pitch to complete his hat-trick, the commentator Kenneth Wolstenholme uttered the famous words: 'Some people are on the pitch, they think it's all over…..it *is* now!'

Prestigious events at Wembley have not

been limited to sport. It has also been host to many of music's biggest names, such as Madonna, Michael Jackson, The Rolling Stones and Elton John. Most impressive was Live Aid in 1985, when the world's leading musical acts played an all-day concert to raise money for Bob Geldof's campaign to relieve world hunger.

Until 2003, the only significant changes to the stadium were the introduction of floodlights in 1955, and the roof and electronic scoreboard in 1963. But the demolition of the old Wembley and the twin icons of its towers will make way for a completely new 90,000 seater stadium. It will feature a massive arch 133 metres tall, which while not quite matching Edward Watkin's tower in 1889, has the practical advantage of supporting the roof, much of which will slide back and forth – as will a platform which will create enough room to enable the stadium to host athletics as well as football.

Enthusiasts, planners and politicians all have their fingers crossed for Wembley. Projected costs have to date jumped from £240 million to £660 million, and supporters will be hoping that the stadium will be ready to open as planned in 2006. But since Watkin's dream became a reality 120 years ago, there's no reason why the new stadium for Wembley should not succeed.

WEST POINT
New York, USA

Contrasting human behaviour ensured the fame of a beautiful escarpment overlooking the Hudson River. Treachery is the first, because it was West Point which Benedict Arnold tried to betray to the British in the War of Independence. Arnold had been an American hero, at Fort Ticonderoga on Lake Chaplain, and as a Major-General at Saratoga. But, embittered by his treatment by Congress, he volunteered to command the river fortress at West Point, where he planned to disable the great chain across the Hudson and, for financial reward, betray the fort to the British. But his accomplice, Major John André, was caught with incriminating plans hidden in his boot. Benedict Arnold fled, to serve the British as a Brigadier-General – and to become an American byword for treachery.

'Honor and Service' are the watchwords of the other reason that West Point has become famous, as America's oldest military academy. The need for such academies is linked to the need for a professional officer corps. While the oldest recorded is, curiously, in Vietnam in the 14th century, it was the emerging technologies of engineering and artillery which created the Royal Military Academy at Woolwich in England in 1741, and the École Polytechnique in revolutionary France. For infantry and cavalry officers, it was assumed that their social position as 'gentlemen' would give them all the heroic guidance necessary to lead men into battle. However the size and the complexity of armies in the Napoleonic age meant that young officers needed to learn to command. Hence,

Sandhurst (1799), St. Cyr (1802) and the Prussian Kriegsakademie (1806).

West Point was founded by President Jefferson in 1802, once again as an engineering school – and for a special, American, reason. The new nation had an aversion to standing armies, but if its army performed public works, it would be much more acceptable. West Point graduates would map the nation, build forts, weather stations, roads, canals, telegraph systems, towns, harbours and railroads. The Panama Canal was a triumph of West Point skills.

But the Revolutionary War and the 1812 war with Britain had shown that America was in need of better officers generally. Amateurism, lack of administration and high turnover led to *'an Ægean stable of anarchy and confusion'*, as one General wrote in 1797. Moreover, there were flaws in America's love of the militia system and 'the right to bear arms'. In 1808, a Congressman prophesied, *'To talk about every soldier being a citizen and every citizen a soldier is very captivating. But it will not do at all in practice'*.

So it was West Point that had to create professional officers, and it was Colonel Sylvanus Thayer, Superintendent from 1817-33, who transformed it with the help of his Professor of Engineering, Dennis Mahan. Modelled on the École Polytechnique, each student was assessed every day – and cumulative 'demerits' ensured discipline, honesty and general deportment, in a gruelling, monastic regime. In spite of political criticism that West Point was 'Un-American and élitist', the proportion of its graduates in the army went from 15 per cent in 1817 to 76 per cent in 1860. During the Civil War, 294 Union and 151 Confederate Generals were West Point graduates, including Lee

(Superintendent in 1852), Grant, Sherman and President of the Confederacy, Jefferson Davis. The terrible sadness of fighting old friends led to poignant incidents. Confederate General George Pickett became a father during the war. Former fellow cadets fighting for the other side managed to smuggle a congratulatory silver teapot through the lines for him. At Gettysburg, Confederate General Lewis Armistead, mortally wounded, asked for his watch to be given to his old friend and classmate, Union General Winfield Hancock, for safekeeping.

In 1919, Douglas MacArthur, enhanced another West Point tradition; sporting prowess, which still continues. Of those entering West Point in 2004, 88% have played sport for their school, and half of those have captained their teams.

Discipline and order are strict. In cadets' rooms, all uniforms are hung in the closet in a certain order, with a fixed space between each. Books must be put on the shelves in a 'biggest-smallest' order. And, as if this was not enough, all socks must be rolled so that the crease looks like a smiley face!

The academy now has 4,000 cadets, and has admitted women since 1976. It is also a tourist attraction with 2.5 million visitors a year. There is a museum which celebrates the USMA itself, and also examines the history of warfare. It has a treasure-trove of historical artefacts, including the plug pulled from the Nagasaki atomic bomb, and Napoleon's sword. West Point, turning out the officers of the future, will not easily forget its past, except, perhaps, for Benedict Arnold.

See: Balaclava, Bonus City, Corregidor, Fort Sumter, Gettysburg, Little Big Horn, Panmunjom, Pearl Harbor, Sandhurst

WIMBLEDON
England

Sprawling from the counties of Kent and Essex in the east to Surrey and Berkshire in the west, London is surrounded by many suburbs, most of which have unprepossessing names that have never caught the world's attention – Pinner, Surbiton, Penge, Croydon, Chigwell. But one, perhaps a little more leafy and genteel, has achieved

worldwide fame.

The Wimbledon Lawn Tennis Tournament of today boasts Royal Patronage, showbiz glamour, phenomenal athletic achievement, and of course a global audience. But this was not always the case. Only twenty-two men took part in the very first tournament in 1877. This would have meant that there were eleven matches, but one player, C.F. Butler, failed to turn up for the first day's play, thus reducing the number to ten. There were no women at all, the first women's tournament being established in 1884. There was also seating for only thirty people, and the total attendance for the final was just two hundred, a very far cry from the packed Centre Court of today, with its capacity of 13,812.

The first Wimbledon tournament was, in fact, played at the All England Club in Worple Road, a croquet venue founded in 1868 – and was regarded as a low priority. The final had to be delayed by two days, as the Eton-Harrow cricket match was being played at Lord's, an event seen as so socially important that nothing could clash with it. The tennis final was played the following Monday, July 16th, and was won by Wimbledon's first champion, W. Spencer Gore.

However, lawn tennis soon became increasingly popular, and eclipsed sedate croquet as the preferred Wimbledon sport. The transition was marked by the creation of a proper bathroom at the club by Dr. Henry Jones, a key figure in the tournament's foundation, resulting from the need to provide for a more physically demanding sport – although traditional England probably still stuck to the Victorian adage, *'Horses sweat, gentlemen perspire, but ladies only glow!'*

Pete Sampras, Wimbledon winner for six consecutive years.

Dr Jones was also instrumental in drawing up the rules for the first Wimbledon competition, modifying the original official rules that had been written by Major Walter Wingfield in 1873. These differed in many respects from the modern system. All players were of course, amateurs. The court was not a rectangle, but resembled an hourglass, and only the server was permitted to win a point. However, the 1877 rules are almost identical to those of the present day. The one significant exception is the tie-break, introduced in the Davis Cup of 1989.

Wimbledon continues to be something special. It is not just the quintessential Britishness of it all, nor the strawberries and cream in the Members' Enclosure. Jimmy Connors, who won the tournament twice, calls it 'the Olympics of his sport'. Some players have structured most of their tennis career around it, such as the great champions, Arthur Ashe, Bjorn Borg, Chris Evert, Martina Navratilova and Boris Becker.

'Part of the reason that Wimbledon attracts such attention is that it is a bona fide, certified British tradition, and British traditions are just a bit more traditional that anyone else's'.

See: Aintree, Brooklands, Bonneville, Cowes, Indianapolis, Le Mans, Lord's, Wembley

WOODSTOCK
New York, USA

The legendary Woodstock Festival was the largest musical event of the Sixties in the United States. Confusingly, however, it did not take place at Woodstock at all.

It all started in February 1969, when four young men – John Roberts, Joel Rosenman, Artie Kornfeld and Michael Lang – decided to run some kind of concert to finance a recording studio in the countryside where Bob Dylan lived, and to where many other rock stars were moving. That town *was* indeed called Woodstock, so they called their company 'Woodstock Ventures Inc'.

Their first proposed site for the event was an industrial park at Wallkill, and the publicity soon gathered momentum – especially after they signed up groups

including Jefferson Airplane, Credence Clearwater Revival and British band The Who. But the residents of Wallkill were getting nervous, opposition grew and in July the Woodstock Festival was banned. Wallkill's decision was, in fact, a blessing in disguise, because the site had never really been right atmospherically, and the ban led to even greater publicity.

Disapproving of the 'unfair' Wallkill's decision, hotelier Elliot Tiber invited the promoters to his land in White Lake, and, when told it was not big enough, recommended his friend – dairy farmer Max Yasgur – who had 600 acres at Bethel. Michael Lang recalled, 'It was magic. Perfect with the sloping bowl, a little rise for the stage, a lake in the background'. With permission to run the festival, the news leaked, especially when the hugely popular Jimi Hendrix signed up – and the 3,900 residents of Bethel began to panic when they realised the potential numbers involved. Curiously, Bob Dylan did not sign up for the festival named after his town, although his back-up group, 'The Band', did.

Two weeks before the festival, 180,000 tickets had already been sold, and everyone knew it was going to be big. Tiber and Yasgur were receiving anonymous threats from their neighbours and the residents plotted a last ditch effort against the concert – planning to block the local Route 17B the day before the event. But, it was much too late. On the Tuesday morning, three days before the festival, five lanes of headlights stretched back to the highway. By Thursday, there were 25,000 people camped in fairly idyllic conditions with kitchens and stages. What did not arrive on time, however, were the ticket booths; everyone from now on would get in free.

Tens of thousands began to pour in, with a nine mile traffic jam on Route 17B. Even at this early stage New York State Governor Nelson Rockefeller was consulted as to whether Bethel should be declared a disaster area, but declined to do so. Food ran out and had to be airlifted in, as did the performers, who were unable to reach the venue because of the parked cars and stalled traffic blocking the area. Helicopters came to the rescue, but slowly. Ironically, in view of the festival's anti-Vietnam war stance, the concert was saved by the sterling efforts of an Army helicopter flying in the performers.

At five in the evening on Friday, 15th August, Richie Havens started singing. He had to continue for three hours before other musicians, not too stoned, could be thrust on to the stage. Light rain started to fall when Ravi Shankar was playing his sitar. It became heavier when Bert Sommer performed, and really poured as Joan Baez sang 'We shall overcome'. Five inches of rain fell in three hours, turning Yasgur's farm into a quagmire. The next day, a tractor drove over a pile of soaked garbage and sleeping bags and tragically killed sleeping 17 year old Raymond Mizak, whose father later said, 'I should have

locked him in his bedroom'. Other casualties were caused by acid trips that went wrong, and more often, from bare feet cut on broken bottles.

To keep the vast but happy crowd (probably now 450,000) under control, the music was made continuous. On Saturday night, Janis Joplin, 'The Who' and 'The Grateful Dead' refused to play without more money and the local bank manager had to be persuaded to fight his way through the traffic to go and obtain the cash.

Sunday morning was 'Breakfast in bed for 400,000', as Wavy Gravy (leading the Hog Farm food effort) put it. The next threat, heat-stroke, was removed by more rain as Joe Cocker, Crosby, Stills and Nash, 'Ten Years After', Johnny Winter, and Jimmy Hendrix played. Two young people died of drug overdoses that afternoon, making a total of three fatalities.

By Monday morning, when Jimi Hendrix played an amazing 'Star Spangled Banner', the party was over. Luckily, Michael Wadleigh had recorded it all on 16mm film with 12 cameramen. The audience began streaming out of the rain-soaked site, and it took five days work by volunteers and $100,000 to clean up the mess. The Roberts family paid off the debts of a festival that had gone way over budget. Twenty years later, thousands of unused Woodstock tickets found in long unopened safes made an unexpected fortune when they were sold for $30 each.

Over the years, two signs were put up showing where the festival had been – but both were stolen. Then, in 1984, Wayne Steward built a five and a half ton cast iron and concrete marker, which has become a counter-culture shrine.

Woodstock was unique, not only for the huge numbers but also for the spirit and the diversity of those attending, the amazing peacefulness and the rock stars and their music. Nothing had happened like it, nor will probably happen again.

Visiting Israel, Max Yasgur met David Ben-Gurion. Standing in line, he said, 'I'm Max Yasgur of Bethel'. Israel's first Prime Minister said, 'Oh yeah, that's where Woodstock was, wasn't it?'

See: Glastonbury

WORLD TRADE CENTER
New York, USA

They were always impressive of course. At 1,368 feet the Twin Towers of New York's World Trade Center had overtaken, in 1974, the Empire State Building as the tallest buildings in the world. But they were eclipsed the very next year by Chicago's Sears Tower, and in 1996 by the Petronas Towers in Malaysia. Perhaps, too, with their rather monolithic appearance, they lacked the architectural interest of older New York skyscrapers like the Woolworth, Chrysler, Empire State and Flat Iron buildings.

The World Trade Center had been built as an act of enthusiastic urban regeneration in a run-down area called 'Radio Row'. With millions of square feet, it had more office space than Liverpool, as *Readers Digest* enthused, 'the biggest building project since the Pyramids'. It was also one of the most efficient, built at the rate of six floors a month. The towers, with enough steel to build twenty Eiffel Towers, were assembled with an unique 'tube' structure which would one day prove their undoing.

For New Yorkers, the towers on their skyline soon became a source of pride, a 'must' for visitors on the tourist trail and, for their thousands of workers, an excellent environment.

It's hard to be down when you're up. Up on the Top of the World, boomed the commercials.

But they were still not really famous worldwide, in spite of Philippe Petit illegally walking on a high wire between the Towers, or the remake of the movie *King Kong*. Things changed with a first sinister warning. In 1993, a truck loaded with hydrogen and explosives was detonated in the basement below the Plaza by a then unknown group called 'Al Qaeda'. Six people died and a thousand were injured, but the massive buildings stood fast.

Then on September 11th 2001, the unimaginable occurred. After months of careful preparation, nineteen young men from the same 'Al Qaeda' group boarded, in small teams, four internal US flights, choosing aircraft heavily loaded with enough fuel to reach the West Coast. All four aircraft were hijacked and turned back towards their targets. American Airlines Flight 77 from Washington hit the Pentagon, killing 125 on the ground as well as all sixty-four passengers and terrorists on the aircraft. United Airlines Flight 93 from Newark crashed in a field in Pennsylvania with forty-four deaths, after an attempted takeover by desperate passengers who had heard on their mobiles what had already happened in New York. Meanwhile, two Boeing 767s, originally bound for Los Angeles, had been flown into each of the Twin Towers. After American Airlines Flight 11 had hit the North Tower, millions of us across the globe were watching the live pictures on our television screens, and witnessed, with mounting and incredulous horror, United Flight 175 as it banked towards the South Tower and turned it into a fireball. It was the most watched terrorist act ever and, endlessly repeated for days all over the world, became the most

While the North Tower burns, the United Airlines Boeing 767 banks towards the South Tower, creating a fireball just seconds later.

watched event in history, especially the appalling sight of people jumping to their deaths to escape the inferno. Anguished calls to loved ones came from mobiles – a modern nightmare.

Then came the ultimate horror. Fifty three minutes after it had been struck, the South Tower suddenly and without warning collapsed, apparently slowly falling in on itself, but actually with its 500,000 tons hitting the ground at 120 mph. Half an hour later the North Tower did the same. Doomed were 3,000 workers, visitors, staff and the incredibly brave firemen who had struggled half way up the towers to rescue those trapped inside.

The stories of bravery and luck do a little to offset the grief and misery of what was not just New York's and America's loss but the world's. People from twenty-six nationalities died at the Trade Center including 600 from British stockbroker Cantor Fitzgerald, whose colleagues and friends over in London were forced to listen in agony to their plight on open phones.

How all this happened is still emerging. The role of the renegade Saudi, Osama Bin Laden, in the financing and meticulous planning of the operation. The suicide pilots, trained at American flying schools, who were strangely not interested *'to learn about landing'*. The usual lack of coordination between the various intelligence agencies and the ignored warnings, which gave extra meaning to the media's 'second Pearl Harbor' allusion. The structural weakness of the buildings which nobody had envisaged being hit by large, aircraft, loaded with fuel, flying at high speed. Even the suspicion that the light truss frames, so distrusted by firefighters, were not adequately protected against the high temperatures that eventually melted them and caused the Towers to collapse.

America has since invaded Afgahanistan to destroy the Taleban, Al Qaeda's protectors, and has toppled Saddam Hussein. But with bombings and killings of innocent people from Bali to Morocco continuing, there is no doubt that the 'Pandora's Box' of international terrorism, first opened at the World Trade Center, may never be closed.

See: Empire State Building, Pearl Harbor

WOUNDED KNEE
North Dakota, USA

For the Sioux, their successful battle in 1876 against General George Custer at the battle of Little Big Horn had been the high water mark of the resistance to the destruction of their way of life and the theft of their land. Broken treaties and broken promises had marked the demise of the Sioux, just as it had all the other Indian tribes. Split up and starving, even Crazy Horse had finally led his Oglala Sioux on to the reservation, refusing an offer to go to Washington to meet the President after seeing the useless results of such visits in the past. On 5th September 1877 the Army, aided by his old friend and comrade Little Big Man, tried to arrest him and, in the scuffle, a soldier bayoneted him to death. Crazy Horse's parents took his remains to a place near *Chankpe Opi Wakpala*, a creek called Wounded Knee. Sadly it was not the last time the place would attract fame.

Sitting Bull, the other victor of the Little Big Horn, had gone to Canada for four years seeking the protection of Queen Victoria, in 'Grandmother's land.' He was forced to leave in 1881 with 186 of his followers, but was so popular that he was asked to the ceremony linking the Trans-Continental line of the Northern Pacific Railway at Bismarck, North Dakota. Only the interpreter knew what he said in Sioux; 'I hate all the white people. You are thieves and liars. You have taken away our land and made us outcasts!' This outburst met with thundering applause from the uncomprehending audience. Sitting Bull spent a popular year with *Buffalo Bill's Wild West Show* in 1885, but in 1889 was appalled as he saw the last great Sioux reservation broken up when his fellow chiefs were once again tricked before he could stop them signing. 'Indians' he shouted at a reporter 'there are no Indians left but me!' A year later Sitting Bull was also dead, killed in a bungled attempt to arrest him.

A Sioux medicine man, one of many bodies frozen stiff in the snow at Wounded Knee

See: Little Big Horn

And so it was that in the frozen December of 1890 a last pathetic little group of Sioux under Big Foot was intercepted by the 7th Cavalry, significantly the very regiment that had fallen at the Little Big Horn. Big Foot, under a white flag, and coughing up blood from pneumonia, was told to move to Wounded Knee Creek, to where he was transported in an army ambulance. 120 men and 230 women and children camped in the snow by the creek.

The next day the 500 soldiers, backed by four Hotchkiss shell-firing machine-guns, tried to disarm the Sioux. Most of the arms were safely stacked but one deaf brave, Black Coyote, tried to resist the taking of his new Winchester and, by mistake, a shot went off. The disarmed Indians were massacred in a hail of bullets and shells. Big Foot and probably 300 of his 350 followers died in the snow. Twenty five troopers died, mostly by their own crossfire. Shamefully, twenty Congressional Medals of Honor were awarded to the 7th Cavalry in what must have been the worst desecration of that honourable award.

The tragedy was not to stop there. In 1973, the village of Wounded Knee was seized at gunpoint by Sioux descendants and yet more of them died.

Dee Brown's famous book *Bury My Heart at Wounded Knee* ends with the cryptic comment by one old Indian. 'They made us many promises, more than I can remember, but they only kept but one; they promised to take our land, and they took it'.

YALTA
Russia

Only weeks remained of the Second World War. Except for Hungary and Northern Italy, the Germans were compressed back into their homeland by overwhelming Allied forces. But, for the British and Americans, Russian behaviour over Poland was now causing real alarm. On January 5th 1945, they had recognised their puppet 'Lublin Government', rather than the British-backed Polish Government in exile. Churchill, who had fought a six-year war over Poland, demanded a conference of the 'Big Three' to resolve such issues. Yalta in the Crimea was chosen. After convivial meetings on February 2nd on their warships in Malta, Churchill, his friend Roosevelt and 700 advisors set off in fleets of aircraft to Saki, and then by car for eight hours to their various villas and palaces in the old Czarist Black Sea resort.

To comprehend the momentous results of Yalta, one needs to understand the participants. Britain's Prime Minister Winston Churchill was a descendant of the Duke of Marlborough, born at Blenheim Palace, educated at Harrow and Sandhurst, and had enjoyed a tempestuous career. As a cavalry officer he charged the Dervishes at Omdurman; as a correspondent he escaped from the Boers; and fame made him a Member of Parliament and then First Lord of the Admiralty. Replaced because of the Gallipoli disaster, he fought in the infantry on the Western Front, found himself 'in the political wilderness' during the 1930s – painting, writing and warning his country of the Nazi menace until at last he fulfilled his destiny as Britain's defiant war leader.

Franklin D. Roosevelt was good-looking, rich and patrician. He became a Senator and then Assistant Secretary of the Navy, but his debonair, political career was changed suddenly by polio. Nevertheless, overcoming his disability, he, as President, with his jaunty optimism and political skills, created the 'New Deal' which rescued America from the Depression. Before being propelled into war by Pearl Harbor, he had helped Britain and Russia survive and became a steadfast ally. But, now, at Yalta, in his fourth term, he was an ill man.

Joseph Stalin, their ally and future foe, was from a very different block. A squat, pock-marked Georgian peasant, he had cunningly worked his way from the shadow of Lenin to ruthless power, soon destroying all his old Politburo comrades after show trials. He exiled and assassinated Trotsky, murdered ten million peasant *kulaks* and wiped out 35,000 of his own officer corps. He had signed the treaty with Germany that carved up Poland and started the War. He ordered the murder of the Polish officer prisoners at Katyn, and then, having been caught out by the German invasion of Russia, blamed everyone else – and thereafter pestered Churchill and Roosevelt for a 'second front'. This scheming, suspicious, half mad 'father of the Gulags' was the 'human tiger' that Churchill and Roosevelt had to deal with. At Yalta, they were to be outwitted by his dogged, secretive determination to reach his own ends.

As soon as the Yalta discussions began, it was Poland that immediately became the bone of contention, discussed at seven out of eight meetings – and with 18,000 words on this one topic. Churchill was particularly concerned, with 150,000 Poles fighting with the Western Allies and a Government in exile waiting in London. It was, after all, the country over which Britain had risked everything by declaring war (in contrast to Stalin's cynical takeover of half of Poland). Churchill saw it as something which 'could break the Grand Alliance'. Under pressure, Stalin promised 'free and unfettered elections in six months', a promise he had no intention of keeping. Roosevelt, perhaps through naiveté, or through illness, was beginning to leave Churchill out of the negotiations, saying the differences with the Russians 'were a matter of words'. The Yalta Conference broke up, with Poland and numerous other issues unresolved. Churchill suspected that he would never see his now frail comrade again.

Within weeks the fruits of Yalta turned sour. No free elections were held in Poland, no observers were allowed in to see the cruel grip the Soviets were imposing. The key Polish underground leaders went under safe conduct to Moscow, and were arrested and put on trial. Prague was handed to the Russians by the Americans. In Bucharest, King Michael of Romania was brutally ordered by Vychinsky to dismiss his all-party Government, and the next day Soviet forces took over. And this on the very day that Churchill was desperately trying to convince the House of Commons that he had succeeded at Yalta. The Russians then tried to make their 'Lublin' Poles the only delegates at the United Nations conference in San Francisco. When refused, Soviet Foreign Minister Molotov did not attend. Churchill tried to get Roosevelt to join with him in a tough new letter to Stalin, but Roosevelt was fading and died on April 12th. It was to the new President Truman that Churchill first used the phrase 'Iron Curtain'. The war ended and the Americans and British began to pull out from Europe. The Russians now controlled all Eastern Europe, 763,000 square miles and 134 million subject people. Churchill was ousted at the General Election, but as a private citizen at Fulton, Missouri, made the speech with these key words:

Churchill and Stalin flank an ailing Roosevelt.

'A shadow has fallen upon the scenes so lately lighted by the Allied victory...

From Stettin in the Baltic to Trieste in the Adriatic, an iron curtain has descended across the Continent. Behind that line lie all the capitals of the ancient states of Central and Eastern Europe. Warsaw, Berlin, Prague, Vienna, Budapest, Belgrade, Bucharest and Sofia, all these famous cities and the populations around them lie in what I must call the Soviet sphere, and all are subject in one form or another, not only to Soviet influence but to a very high and, in many cases, increasing measure of control from Moscow ....

Whatever conclusions may be drawn from these facts - and facts they are - this is certainly not the liberated Europe we fought to build up. Nor is it one which contains the essentials of a permanent peace'.

For fifty years, millions in Europe would have reason to regard the word Yalta with bitterness.

See: Andrassy, Bretton Woods, Ekaterinburg, Gulag, Katyn Wood, Ladoga, Stalingrad

ZEEBRUGGE
Belgium

Zeebrugge means 'sea bridge' in Flemish, and the thriving port continues to provide a bridge between Britain and the Continent. It was thrust into the limelight twice in the last century, once honourably and once with dishonour.

At the height of the First World War, the threat to Britain from Germany's submarines was becoming acute. If the German U-boats could achieve a target of sinking 500,000 tons of shipping each month, Britain would starve. On 9th January 1917, the Kaiser ordered 'unrestricted warfare'. The effect was immediate, and the number of British ships sunk jumped, from 37 a month, to 105 in February and 118 in April. One out of every four ships that left port did not return. A convoy system helped to reduce the sinkings, but more were needed. Their bases must be neutralised.

Most of the U-boats were based at the inland port of Bruges, whence they emerged by canal at Oostende and Zeebrugge. An ambitious operation was mounted to block these exits. A fleet of blockships arrived in April 1918, consisting of old cruisers filled with cement. At Oostende, the raid was foiled by marker buoys being moved, but at Zeebrugge, the Germans were distracted by landing parties storming ashore, and two of the blockships were successfully sunk in position – and a British submarine blown up to destroy the harbour's viaduct. HMS *Vindictive*, the headquarters ship, loaded with casualties, made her escape.

The daring raid had a tonic effect on British morale in the last difficult months of the war.

But Zeebrugge was to mean something less heroic in 1987. The roll-on, roll-off ferry *Herald of Free Enterprise* was in a hurry because she was late leaving Zeebrugge, caused by an unusual number of passengers on a cheap Channel crossing promotion. The ship reversed as usual into a side dock, and then headed out to sea. Unbelievably, the main front car deck door had been left open. (Even more unbelievable, this was common practice).

At 18 knots, a wave of water poured down the car deck. Worse, as the ship rolled, the hundreds of tons of water also rolled and, within just one minute, the ship capsized onto her port side. Inside the ship, there was chaos – men, women and children fought to escape the rising waters in the dark – with the lack of familiarity compounded by not even being upright.

The Belgian rescue teams saved 408 passengers and crew, but nearly 200 died. The Board of Inquiry found the company *'infected with the disease of sloppiness from top to bottom'*.

Ferries were now to be fitted with an indicator light to tell the captains that the doors had shut – a rather elementary example of 'too late'.

It is tragic for any town that its ill-fame should be created through the neglect of its visitors.

The stricken ferry lies on her side, her front doors still gaping open.

See: Ararat, Dieppe, Dunkirk, Maelstrom, Mers-el-Kebir, Pearl Harbor, Trafalgar, Tsushima

BIBLIOGRAPHY
&
INDEX

SELECTED BIBLIOGRAPHY

ABRAHAM, Tom — *The Cage.* London 2002
ACKROYD, Peter — *London, the Biography.* London 2000
AMBROSE, Stephen — *Crazy Horse and Custer.* New York 1975

BEEVOR, Anthony — *Stalingrad.* London 1998
BELL, Walter George — *The Great Fire of London.* London 1923
BERG, A. Scott — *Goldwyn.* New York 1989
BERG, A. Scott — *Lindberg.* New York 1998
BIERMAN, John (with Colin Smith) — *Alamein.* London 2002
BLANDFORD, Edmund — *Fatal Decisions.* Shrewsbury 1999
BOLIN, Luis — *Spain, the Vital Years.* London 1967
BODDY, William — *The History of Brooklands Motor Course.* London 1979
BOSTON, Ray — *The Essential Fleet Street.* London 1990
BREDIN, A.E.C. — *History of the Irish Soldier.* Belfast 1987
BROWN, Dee — *Hear that Lonesome Whistle Blow.* London 1977
BROWN, Dee — *Bury my Heart at Wounded Knee.* London 1971
BRYSON, Bill — *The Lost Continent.* London 1989
BRYSON, Bill — *Made in America.* New York 1989
BRYSON, Bill — *Mother Tongue.* London 1990
BUTLER, Rupert — *Gestapo.* Wisconsin 1996

CHURCHILL, Winston — *The Second World War.* London 1950
COHEN, Stan — *East Wind Rain.* Montana 2001
COLTRANE, Robbie — *Engines that Turned the World.* London 1997
CONNELY, S J — *The Oxford Companion to Irish History.* Oxford 1998
COOGAN, Tim Pat — *The Irish Civil War.* London 1999
COOGAN, Tim Pat — *Wherever Green is Worn.* London 2000
COWLEY, General Sir John — *Memoirs.* London 1998
COWLEY, Robert — *What if?* London 2000
CRONIN, Vincent — *Napoleon.* London 1994

DAMONE, Led — *Senatorial Privilege.* New York 1988
DAVID, Saul — *The Homicidal Earl.* London 1997
DEIGHTON, Len — *Blitzkrieg.* London 1979
DILLON, Richard — *North American Indian Wars.* Greenwich CT 1983
DOBROW, Larry — *When Advertising Tried Harder.* New York 1994
DUNNIGAN, James — *Dirty Little Secrets of World War II.* New York 1994
DURSCHMIED, Erik — *The Hinge Factor.* London 1999
DURNEY, James — *The Mob.* Naas 2000

EASTLAKE, Keith — *World Disasters.* Chicago 2001
ESPOSITO, Vincent — *Military History and Atlas of the Napoleonic Wars.* London 1996
EVANS, Harold — *The American Century.* London 1998
EVANS, Harold — *Pictures on a Page.* London 1978

FAGAN, Brian — *The 70 Great Mysteries of the Ancient World.* London 2000
FALK, Quentin — *The Golden Gong.* London 1987
FAULK, Odie — *Tombstone, Myth and Reality.* New York 1972
FORD, Brian — *German Secret Weapons.* London 1966
FORD, Roger — *The Grim Reaper, Machine Guns and Machine Gunners.* London 1996
FRANKEL, Philip — *An Ordinary Atrocity, Sharpeville.* Johannesburg 2001
FRASER, George McDonald — *Quartered Safe out Here.* London 1992
FROST, David — *The Rich Tide.* London 1986

GOLDHAGEN, Daniel — *Hitler's Willing Executioners.* London 1997
GREAVES, Adrian — *Rorke's Drift.* London 2002
GREHAN, Ida — *Irish Family Histories.* Dublin 1997
GUTTSTEIN, Linda — *History of the Jews in America.* Secaucus 1988

HALL, Allan — *War Crimes.* Leicester 1993
HAMMAN, Henry — *Mayday at Chernobyl.* London 1987
HANKIE, Julie — *A Passion for Egypt.* London 2001
HARCUP, Guy — *Code Name Mulberry.* London 1977

HARRISON, Salisbury   *The 900 Days.* London 1969
HARVEY, Robert   *Clive.* London 1998
HASTINS, Jim   *The Cotton Club.* New York 1977
HASTINGS, Max   *Das Reich.* London 2000
HASTINGS, Max   *The Korean War.* London 1987
HAYTHORNTHWAITE, Philip   *Die Hard.* London 1996
HEUVELMANS, Bernard   *In the wake of the Sea Serpents.* Paris 1965
HILL, Maureen   *Women in the Twentieth Century.* London 1991
HODGES, David   *Ford GT40, an Anglo American Supercar Classic.* London 1984
HOFSCHRÖER, Peter   *The Waterloo Campaign, A German Victory.* London 1999
HOGG, Ian   *Weapons of the American Civil War.* London 1987
HOLMES, Richard   *War Walks.* London 1996
HOLMES, Richard   *The Oxford Companion to Military History.* Oxford 2001
HOLMES, Richard   *The Western Front.* London 1999
HOLMES, Richard   *Redcoat.* London 2001
HOMBERGER,   *The Historical Atlas of New York City.* New York 1998
HORNE, Alistair   *How far from Austerlitz?* London 1996
HOWARTH, Stephen   *Henry Poole.* London, 2003
HUGHES-WILSON, Col. John   *Military Intelligence Blunders.* London 1999

IONS, Veronica   *The History of Mythology.* London 1997

JACKSON, Robert   *Aerial Combat.* London 1976
JACKSON, Robert   *Suez, the Forgotten Invasion.* Shrewsbury 1996
JENKINS, Roy   *Churchill.* New York 2001
JOHNSON, Paul   *Ireland Land of Troubles.* London 1980
JOHNSON, Paul   *A History of the American People.* London 1997
JONES, R.V.   *Most Secret War.* London 1978

KAHN, David   *The Codebreakers.* London 1977
KEELER, Christine   *The Truth at Last.* London 2001
KENEALLY, Thomas   *The Great Shame.* London 1998
KNIGHT, Ian and LABAND, John   *The Anglo-Zulu War.* London 1996
KOCH, H.W.   *The Age of Total Warfare.* London 1983
KOSTOF, Spiro   *America by Design.* New York 1987
KURLANSKY, Mark   *Salt, A World History.* London 2002

LAMB, Richard   *Mussolini and the British.* London 1997
LANNING, Michael   *100 Most Influential Military Leaders.* London 1997
LARGE, David   *Berlin, a Modern History.* London 2001
LAMONT-BROWN, Raymond   *Kamikaze.* London 1997
LAXTON, Edward   *The Famine Ships.* London 1996
LICHFIELD, Patrick   *The Most Beautiful Women.* London 1981
LICHFIELD, Patrick   *In Retrospect.* London 1998
LINEDECKER, Clifford   *Massacre at Waco.* London 1993
LOMAX, Eric   *The Railway Man.* London 1995
LONGFORD, Lord   *Abraham Lincoln.* London 1975
LORD, Tony   *Gardening at Sissinghurst,* London 1995
LOSSIN, Yigal   *Pillar of Fire – The Rebirth of Israel.* Jerusalem 1983

MACARTHUR, General Douglas   *Reminiscences.* London 1964
MACDONALD, John   *Great Battlefields of the World.* London 1984
MACKAY, James   *Michael Collins. A Life.* Edinburgh 1996
MACMILLAN, Harold   *War Diaries. The Mediterranean 1943-45.* London 1984
MACMILLAN, Margaret   *Paris 1919.* London 2002
MAILER, Norman   *Miami and the Siege of Chicago.* New York 1968
MAJOR, Norma   *Chequers.* London 1996
MCORMACK, Goran (& Hank Nelson)   *The Burma Thailand Railway.* Thailand 1993
MCMURTY, Larry   *Crazy Horse, London.* London 1999
MILTON, Giles   *Nathaniel's Nutmeg.* London 1999
MORGAN, Chris   *Facts and Fallacies.* Exeter 1981
MOXHAM, Ray   *The Great Hedge of India.* London 2001
MOYNAHAN, Brian   *The British Century.* London 1999
MURPHY, Emmett   *Great Bordellos of the World.* 1993
MURRAY, Williamson   *The Luftwaffe, Strategy for Defeat.* London 1986

NASH, Jay Robert   *World Encyclopaedia of Organised Crime.* London 1993

O'BRIEN, Donough   *Fringe Benefits.* London 2000

O'BRIEN, The Hon Donough	*History of the O'Briens.* London 1949
O'BRIEN, Hon Grania	*These are my Friends and Forebears.* Clare 1991
O'CONNOR, Ulick	*The Troubles.* London 1975
O'CONNOR, Ulick	*Brendan Behan.* London 1970
OGILVY, David	*Ogilvy on Advertising.* London 1993
OGILVY, David	*Confessions of an Advertising Man.* London 1993
PAKENHAM, Thomas	*Meeting with remarkable trees.* London 1996
PREBBLE, John	*Glencoe.* Aylesbury 1996
PRESTON, Anthony	*Send a Gunboat.* London 1967
PRESTON, Anthony	*Sea Combat off the Falklands.* London 1982
READ, Anthony (with David Fisher)	*The Fall of Berlin.* London 1992
READERS DIGEST	*Illustrated History of South Africa.* Cape Town 1989
READERS DIGEST	*The World at Arms.* London 1989
REES, Laurence	*Horror in the East.* London 2001
REGAN, Geoffrey	*Someone Has Blundered.* London 1987
RHODES, Anthony	*Propaganda.* New York 1976
RIDLEY, Jasper	*Mussolini.* London 1999
RIPLEY, Tim	*Bayonet Battle.* London 1999
ROSA, Joseph	*Age of the Gunfighter.* London 1993
ROSEMAN, Mark	*The Villa, the Lake, the Meeting.* London 2002
SAMPSON, Anthony	*Anatomy of Britain.* London 1962
SCHAMA, Simon	*A History of Britain.* London 2002
SCOTT-JAMES, Anne	*Sissinghurst.* London 1975
SETH-SMITH, Michael	*The Cresta Run.* Slough 1976
SHIRER, William	*The Rise and Fall of the Third Reich.*
SIFAKIS, Carl	*Encyclopaedia of Assassinations.* London 2001
SILVESTER, Christopher	*The Penguin Book of Interviews.* London 1993
SIMON, Kate	*Fifth Avenue, a Very Social History.* New York 1978
SIMPSON, Ivan	*Singapore, Too little, too late.* London 1970
SMITH, Charlene	*Robben Island.* Cape Town 1997
SPELLMOUNT	*Irish Guards, The First Hundred Years.* Staplehurst 2000
SUMMERS, Anthony	*The Secret Life of J.Edgar Hoover.* London 1993
SWINSON, Simon	*Kohima.* London 1978
TAYLOR, Colin	*The Plains Indians.* London 1997
TAYLOR, Peter	*Provos.* London 1997
TAYLOR, Rich	*Indie.* New York 1991
THATCHER, Margaret	*The Downing Street Years.* London 1993
THOMAS, Gordon	*Ruin from the Air.* London 1977
TIME LIFE	*WWII.* New York 1989
TOFFLER, Alvin	*Future Shock.* London 1970
TOFFLER, Alvin	*The Third Wave.* London 1980
TOUHILL, Blanche	*William Smith O'Brien.* Missouri 1981
TSUJI, Masanobu	*Singapore, The Japanese Version.* London 1951
TWISS, Miranda	*The Most Evil Men & Women in History.* London 2002
VARIETY EDITORS	*Variety, History of Show Business.* London 1993
VERNEY, Peter	*The Micks. The Story of the Irish Guards.* London 1970
VINCENT, Edgar	*Nelson, Love and Fame.* Yale 2003
WARD, Geoffrey	*Jazz.* New York 2001
WARD, Geoffrey	*The Civil War.* New York 1990
WARD, Geoffrey	*The West.* London 1996
WARRY, John	*Warfare in the Classical World.* London 1980
WATERHOUSE, Keith, et al	*The Book of Useless Information.* London 2002
WIER, Hugh	*Brian Boru,* Clare, Ireland 2002
WILSON, Harold	*A Prime Minister on Prime Ministers.* London 1970
WOOD, Derek	*The Narrow Margin.* London 1969
WOODMAN-SMITH, Cecil	*The Great Hunger.* London 1962
YATES, Brock	*Enzo Ferrari,* London 1991
YEAGER, Chuck	*Yeager.* London 1986

INDEX